The Retailing Reader

Most of us think we know something about retailing: we shop, we buy, we consume. But retailing, perhaps more than any other economic sector, has been transformed fundamentally over the last thirty years, both economically and culturally. Consumers are now more sophisticated, retailers are more strategic in anticipating change, and the market has become more – or in some areas arguably less – competitive.

Featuring work from seminal theorists in the area, and charting the development of retailing as an important discipline in its own right, this volume examines the key themes in contemporary retailing. Organized into five chapters, each of which includes an editorial overview, *The Retailing Reader* examines:

- Consumers and Shoppers
- Retail Branding and Marketing
- Merchandising and Buying
- Strategy, Power and Policy
- International Retailing

The book also explores current issues in retailing, from the social legitimization of retailers through the sophisticated use of branding, to the strategic planning involved in choosing store location. Extensive case studies include an analysis of the British grocery market, the strategies embodied by Nike Town stores, and the development of retail economies in China and Latin America.

The Retailing Reader presents a comprehensive overview of this important area of study, and is an ideal companion for any student of retailing, marketing or business and management.

John Dawson holds chairs at the University of Edinburgh and University of Stirling, UK. He is Visiting Professor at ESADE, Barcelona and Distinguished Professor, University of Marketing and Distribution Sciences, Kobe, Japan. He has researched and written on retailing since the 1960s.

Anne Findlay is a research fellow at the Institute for Retail Studies, University of Stirling, UK. Her main interests include retail planning and food retailing, with ongoing research funded by MRC and the National Retail Planning Forum.

Leigh Sparks is Professor of Retail Studies at the University of Stirling, UK. He has been a Visiting Professor at Florida State University and at the University of Tennessee, USA. He is co-editor of the leading European retail journal and has published widely on aspects of spatial-structural change in retailing.

The Retailing Reader

Edited by

John Dawson, Anne Findlay and Leigh Sparks

LONDON AND NEW YORK

First published 2008
by Routledge
2 Park Square, Milton Park, Abingdon, Oxon OX14 4RN

Simultaneously published in the USA and Canada
by Routledge
270 Madison Ave, New York, NY 10016

Routledge is an imprint of the Taylor & Francis Group, an informa business

Typeset in Perpetua and Bell Gothic by
RefineCatch Ltd, Bungay, Suffolk
Printed and bound in Great Britain by
The Cromwell Press, Trowbridge

British Library Cataloguing in Publication Data
A catalogue record for this book is available from the British Library

Library of Congress Cataloging in Publication Data
Dawson, John A.
The retailing reader / John Dawson, Anne Findlay, and Leigh Sparks.
    p. cm.
  Includes bibliographical references
  ISBN 978–0–415–35638–1 (hardback) – ISBN 978–0–415–35639–8 (pbk.)   1. Retail trade.
I. Findlay, A. M.   II. Sparks, Leigh.   III. Title.
  HF5429.D337 2008
  658.8′7–dc22
  2007038210

ISBN 0–415–35638–5 (hbk)
ISBN 0–415–35639–3 (pbk)

ISBN 978–0–415–35638–1 (hbk)
ISBN 978–0–415–35639–8 (pbk)

Contents

List of figures

List of tables

Acknowledgements

The authors and publishers would like to acknowledge the following for permission to reprint this material:

- The McGraw-Hill Companies for permission to reprint Sherry, J. The soul of the company store: Nike Town Chicago and the emplaced brandscape. In John Sherry (ed.) *Servicescapes: the concept of place in contemporary markets*, Lincolnwood: NTC Business Books, 1998, 109–146.
- Elsevier for permission to reprint Arnold, S., Handelman, J. and Tigert, D. The impact of a market spoiler on consumer preference structures (or, what happens when Wal-Mart comes to town), *Journal of Retailing and Consumer Services* 5(1),1998: 1–13. www.elsevier.com
- Taylor and Francis Limited for permission to reprint Betts, E. and McGoldrick, P.J. The strategy of the retail 'sale': typology, review and synthesis, *International Review of Retail, Distribution and Consumer Research* 5(3), 1995: 303–331. www.tandf.co.uk and Wrigley, N. and Currah, A. The stresses of retail internationalization: lessons from Royal Ahold's experience in Latin America, *International Review of Retail, Distribution and Consumer Research* 13(3), 2003: 221–243. www.tandf.co.uk.
- Emerald Group Publishing Limited for permission to reprint Burt, S.L. The strategic role of brands in British grocery retailing, *European Journal of Marketing* 34(8), 2000: 875–890. www.emeraldinsight.com; Dawson, J. and Shaw, S. The move to administered vertical marketing systems by British retailers, *European Journal of Marketing* 23(7), 1989: 42–52. www.emeraldinsight.com and Salmon, W.J. and Tordjman, A. The internationalisation of retailing, *International Journal of Retailing* 4(2), 1989: 3–16. www.emeraldinsight.com.

- Blackwell Publishing for permission to reprint Dobson, P. and Waterson, M. Retailer power: recent developments and policy implications, *Economic Policy* 28, 1999: 134–156, 162–164. www.blackwellpublishing.com and Burt, S. and Sparks, L. Power and competition in the UK retail grocery market, *British Journal of Management* 14, 2003: 237–254. www.blackwellsynergy.com.
- The Institute for Operations Research and Management Sciences (INFORMS), 7240 Parkway Drive, Suite 310, Hanover, MD21076 USA, for permission to reprint Dhar, S.K. and Hoch, S.J. Why store brand penetration varies by retailer, *Marketing Science* 16(3), 1997: 208–227.
- ESOMAR᪲ – The World Association of Research Professionals for permission to reprint Kapferer, J.-N. Beyond positioning: retailer's identity. In *Strategies for Retailer Growth – Retailing Mix*, ESOMAR June 1986: 167–175 © Copyright 1986 by ESOMAR᪲.
- Louis N. Stern School of Business, New York University for permission to reprint Arnold, S., Kozinets, R. and Handelman, J. Hometown ideology and retailer legitimation: the institutional semiotics of Wal-Mart flyers, *Journal of Retailing* 77(2), 2001: 243–271; Goldman, A. The transfer of retail formats into developing economies: the example of China, *Journal of Retailing* 77(2), 2001: 221–242; Parasuraman, A., Zeithaml, V.A. and Berry, L. SERVQUAL: a multiple-item scale for measuring consumer perceptions of service quality, *Journal of Retailing* 64(1), 1988: 12–37.
- Westburn Publishers Ltd for permission to reprint Dawson, J. Internationalization of retail operations, *Journal of Marketing Management* 10, 1994: 267–282. © Westburn Publishers Ltd. 1995. www.westburn.co.uk.

Introduction

VIRTUALLY EVERYONE IS EXPOSED to retailing, due both to its ubiquity and their personal activities as shoppers and consumers. We can not help but notice changes in retailing whether through new products, stores, locations, retailers or even new ways of retailing and shopping, such as the Internet. Yet, despite this sense of change and newness, and a tendency to focus on current controversies and issues, there is a permanence about the retail activity and even some retail locations and retailers. Retailing is a long-established method of product distribution that holds significance for its practitioners, consumers and increasingly media commentators and governments. As societies have evolved to become consumer cultures, so the social importance of retailing has increased. These increases in perceived importance have resulted in increasing academic study of retailing and shopping and a need for research and publications that present current understandings of retail issues and retail change to various wider audiences.

This volume is one such attempt to present an understanding of retailing and retailing research. This introduction to the book covers three main areas. First, a brief discussion of the concept of retailing and its importance is presented. Second, an attempt to frame this understanding of the subject and the current issues confronting retail management and retail research is developed. Finally, the rationale for the structure of this volume and the selection of the material included is outlined.

What Is Retailing and Why Is It Important?

It might have been thought that given the sheer numbers and presence of retail outlets and the long history of retailing, that standard definitions and understandings of what retailing is and what makes a retailer would be developed and widely accepted.

However, as Peterson and Balasubramanian (2002) show, there are many definitions of retailing and retailers, many of which appear to be mutually inconsistent. Peterson and Balasubramanian (2002) argue that the definition of retailing tends to be taken for granted, to be ambiguous and/or to cover only store-based selling activities. It is widely accepted that retailing is directed at the ultimate consumer, but what comprises this availability and selling activity remains somewhat unclear. Despite their problems with existing definitions however, Peterson and Balasubramanian (2002) shy away from presenting their own definition of retailing, calling instead for a panel of experts to consider the matter!

To some extent, definitional niceties around the subject are of little consequence in that we all know retailing when we see it and can readily identify retailers – or at least we believe that we can. But, on the other hand, accuracy in definition can be important, as for example in industrial classifications and statistics, to ensure an appropriate understanding of the dimensions and change in retailing both nationally and comparatively. For this book, such specificities may not be necessary, in that readers will in all probability hold their own definitions of retailing and retailers and use them accordingly. The working definition we adopt, however, is 'the sale of products and services, typically in small volumes, to the final consumer'. The activities that have to be brought together to achieve this outcome vary over time and place and so the comment by Peterson and Balasubramanian (2002) that retailing is time and context specific has merit.

The current context for retailing, almost worldwide, is that it has grown in importance and significance at a number of levels. The sector itself has increased in scale in many societies and plays a vital role in providing employment and economic activity and in linking production and consumption. The switch of societies towards greater marketing orientation has been reflected in the status and significance afforded by government and others to effective, efficient and modern retail distribution systems. For some this is the development of 'new commerce' (Dawson 2001). These changes are, of course, not without problems in some situations, as the transition from a production and small-scale retailing focus towards a marketing and large-scale retail sector requires substantial personal and organizational adjustments, not only for the retailers involved, but also for the consumers, and in both economic and social terms.

The economic importance of retailing has grown in parallel with an increasing social significance of shopping. Retailing and shopping have a major impact on people's lives, not only in how they access products, but also in terms of satisfaction levels and perceived quality of life. Whilst retailing has expanded economically it has also increased as a signifier in, and of, people's lives. Retailing and shopping have become more central and important in a number of ways as they have moved away from purely functional transactions to more symbolic and hedonic activities and spaces.

Retailing is also important in an academic world. The changing nature and role of retailing and its altered position economically and socially require an academic response. This has been forthcoming particularly over the last thirty or so years. Retailing is an acceptable subject and object of study, both academically in its own right and as a subject for students seeking a career in retailing or its support industries. However, there is another significance of the study of retailing, and one that perhaps unfortunately has been under-recognized. Retailing is different. The activities of retailing and the organization and management of retail businesses are not the same as traditional agriculture or manufacturing industries or even innovative creative industries. Many of the developmental and operational issues are distinct and require different conceptualizations and explanations. For example retailing differs through:

1   its relationships with final consumers and thus its need to respond to the local culture in various ways;
2   the spatial disaggregation and dispersed nature and sometimes extensive network of operations (e.g. shops);
3   the requirement to bring together a large number of items to provide an extensive range of products and services for consumers;
4   the ways in which operations are financed through working capital and the low levels of profit generated per individual activity (e.g. a transaction or other input measure).

Whilst it is possible for many sectors of the economy to claim 'difference', the implication here is that retailing poses distinct and special operational challenges and that the study of the subject has to create new ways of understanding and explaining activities. Simply 'borrowing' unchanged ideas from other spheres of operation or study is inadequate. Retailing demands especial consideration and study. This volume demonstrates and contributes to this.

Understanding Retailing and Retail Challenges

Retailing as an economic activity is, as noted above, long established. It is not a new sector or industry, though it contains within it, aspects that are clearly new, modern or changing. Understanding and conceptualizing retail change may be somewhat different to attempts to do similarly in other sectors. Therefore, the challenges facing retail management and the questions being addressed by retail research are distinct and need clear identification.

A number of authors (e.g. Dawson 2000; Peterson and Balasubramanian 2002; Levy *et al.* 2005) have recently pointed out that there is an absence of explanatory and predictive theory in, or of, retailing. Whilst there have been contributions that have descriptive power, for example the 'Wheel of Retailing' and the 'Retail Accordion' (Hollander 1960, 1966), Dawson (2000) argues that these should now be seen as 'useful historical ideas' and that new conceptualizations are required at least at the levels of the firm and the sector. Levy *et al.* (2005) offer as a starting point the concept of the 'Big Middle', though again this would seem at this stage to have stronger descriptive rather than analytical capabilities. Interestingly, however, they identify five 'levers' that they see as being utilized by firms in retailing in their search for growth and profitability. These provide some indication of current activities that are deemed significant for retail management. Their 'levers' are innovative merchandise, technology use, supply chain management, price optimization and the development of store name/image.

Being a long-established sector, it has often been claimed (e.g. Savitt 1989) that examining retail history helps in understanding the future for retailing. Dawson (2000) at the outset of his review of retail challenges at the end of the twentieth century looks back to the end of the nineteenth century and identifies significant roots for current retail developments. His analysis of retailing focuses on issues of branding, supply chain relationships and sourcing internationally, new technologies, the growth of large firms leading to large/small firm conflict potentially requiring public policy measures and the development of key retail locations and centres. These issues he claims have shaped retailing over the last century at least. It is perhaps significant that there is a similarity between this listing and the 'levers' identified by Levy *et al.* (2005) as noted earlier.

This similarity has at least two implications. First it would appear reasonable that the topics they cover in common, for example branding, supply chain, technology and product sourcing, are at the core of retail operations and at the forefront of issues that firms in retailing tackle day in and day out. It is therefore important to study and understand them. Second, the consistency of the issues suggests that, in the main, retailing changes in an evolutionary fashion through continuous adjustments, adaptations and learning, within environmental constraints on, for example, location, competition and public policy. There may therefore be scope to consider retail change through new ideas in evolutionary change (e.g. Davies 1998), which allow for both long periods of relative quiescence, but also disruptive periods as perhaps seen recently in Central Europe (e.g. Dawson 2000).

The issues identified thus far are clearly focused on retail management and retail operations and outcomes in terms of sectoral change. However, as noted before, retailing deals with consumers directly and thus has to respond to consumers and their changing demands and behaviours. This response can be seen in the changing locations, products, prices and so forth that firms in retailing offer. More directly at a tactical level, firms in retailing are keen to understand what consumers are doing and how this is changing. They therefore have a strong focus on consumer market dimensions such as demographics and spending power, and consumer attitudes such as towards convenience. Whilst it is demonstrably certain that consumer demand as a whole has altered, and will continue to change, basing an understanding or conceptualization of retailing purely on consumers is somewhat difficult given their localized and individualized unpredictability and volatility. Retail firms do focus on consumers, particularly now consumer demands and choices have expanded so considerably, but operationally they focus on the elements that allow them to supply consumers with what they believe they require. The core of retailing is thus the operational practices that allow an understanding of, and then satisfaction of, consumer retail demands.

So, as consumers and retailing have altered in developed countries over the last fifty years in particular and are altering significantly in developing areas of the world, so the agenda for retail management and for retail research has shifted focus somewhat. For Peterson and Balasubramanian (2002) the agenda currently comprises seven elements:

- the role of retailing;
- retail space;
- time;
- consumers;
- retail management;
- public policy;
- retailing as an industry itself.

For Dawson (2000) there are six major challenges for retail management:

- the limits to 'bigness';
- brands and brand extension;
- over-supply of retail floorspace;
- turbulence in the retail environment;
- externalization or internalization of functions;
- e-retail.

Whilst there are, understandably, different emphases in these two agenda, there are clear overlaps. The issues that these authors develop have informed the way in which this book has been brought together.

The Retailing Reader

Retailing is both a local and a global activity. It has greater significance now beyond anything previously seen. Retailing presents distinct and difficult challenges to operators, consumers, society, governments and academics. These challenges are of course also its fascination. This volume therefore attempts to make sense of retailing, retail change and retail research over essentially the last twenty-five years. As the significance of retailing has grown and as retailing has changed, so there has been an explosion of research interest into retailing, particularly outside the USA. Given the nature of retailing, so too different approaches to retail research have been adopted, adding layers of complexity and difference to the retail literature. This is an extraordinarily important development, but it makes producing this volume more of a challenge.

Condensing twenty-five years of retail research and retail change in less than twenty articles and associated commentaries is not a simple task. The approach taken here has three main considerations:

1   To provide a reflection of the issues and challenges for retailing, focused around key topics deriving from an understanding of retailing and retail change.

2   In any subject there are seminal articles which need to be considered. However, this volume is not simply a collection of classics (see Findlay and Sparks 2002), but is rather a current introduction and guide to the subject. As such a balance of articles from those that are widely viewed as academically seminal and those we judge as pedagogically significant is required.

3   The expansion of retailing and retail research globally demands a broad coverage of topics and debates. The selection has to be driven by a concern to present different approaches to retail research, to cover different parts of the world and to recognize significant authors. Nonetheless, it has to be noted that we are working in a British context primarily.

The volume is presented in five chapters. These will each be recognizable as deriving from the debates over retailing and retail challenges presented earlier. Within each chapter a specially written commentary to the subject is provided followed by the reproduction of the selected articles. The commentaries provide the context in retailing and retail research terms for the selected papers and outline their significance. These commentaries thus function as a guide to the academic literature for each topic. They record a view of how the subject has developed in recent decades and provide an extensive set of further reading.

The selection of the articles has involved considerable debate. Long lists of potential articles have been drawn up for each subject based on citation and bibliometric analyses. These were then reduced through debate and discussion. Copyright and reproduction issues were identified and resolved. Concern over scope, debates and authorship, as well as impact, informed the discussions. Finally, fifteen articles were chosen and the commentaries were developed around these, the long preliminary literature lists and ongoing research. A short bibliographic piece on the authors of each of the articles is also included. These locate the authors in the academy and, together with the commentaries, in the development of the literature and the subject.

Chapter 1 covers Consumers and Shoppers, naturally enough given the focus of retailing. The chapter, however, is based around how retailers understand and react to consumers rather than being a standard review of consumer behaviour. Focusing on very different research traditions, the chapter covers the measurement of service quality, experiential consumption spaces and retail positioning in the minds of consumers and shoppers.

Chapter 2 is on Retail Branding and Marketing. It begins with concepts of retail identity and ends with a discussion of the concept of retailer legitimation in society and economy. Sandwiched between these are two very different approaches to retailer brands (own label, private label, store brands) deriving from the very different traditions of practice and research in the USA and in the UK.

Merchandising and Buying are the foci of Chapter 3. Operationally these are hugely diverse areas and ones where very different outcomes can be seen according to retailers' strategies, tactics and operational disciplines. This chapter uses two papers on the topics of retail 'sales' and retailer–manufacturer supply and marketing relationships to explore the variations in retail practice and the changes that are underway in the scope of, and demands on, retailing.

Chapter 4 covers a broad area of Strategy and Power. Retailers have become more powerful in recent decades. As their scale and scope have expanded and been more clearly strategically articulated and leveraged, so public policy concerns have begun to increase. Retailers have always been subject to regulation, but the type and extent of this have changed and continue to evolve and develop. The two papers in this chapter cover the potential for scale to become an issue of dominance of single retail firms and the rise of retail power generally. The consequences of this and the changing ways in which legislation/regulation has endeavoured, not always successfully, to control retailing are covered *inter alia*.

Finally, Chapter 5 is on International Retailing. The approach here is to mirror the way in which retail research on international retailing has developed, particularly by European academics, as it in turn has reflected retail internationalization practice. The four papers comprise a 'journey' from patterns, through explanations, to specific processes and operations and then finally on to wider contexts, here represented by new work on international retail failure.

The volume is concluded by a 'look forward'. Whilst retailing may have elements of both predictability and unpredictability, and we certainly have no crystal ball, there would seem to be certain issues that we believe will focus retail management attention and retail research activity in the coming two decades. These are developed in our concluding remarks on retailing and retail research in the future.

It is recognized that many may disagree with our selection, commentaries and conclusions, but in one sense, that is the point. The commentaries show how we feel retailing and retail research has progressed. It would be disturbing if all readers had the same view of these activities. This volume is a guide to the subject to encourage further study, reflection and debate, as well as helping in the accumulation and use of knowledge. It is not an encyclopedia of retailing. The emphases in our conclusions and forward look will differ to those that others may wish to give, but time will tell. One thing is certain, we are sure: retailing, as a business sector and operation, and as an academic area of study has many more challenges to reveal.

References

Davies BK (1998) Applying evolutionary models to the retail sector. *International Review of Retail, Distribution and Consumer Research*, 8, 165–181.

Dawson JA (2000) Retailing at century end: some challenges for management and research. *International Review of Retail, Distribution and Consumer Research*, 10, 119–148.

Dawson JA (2001) Is there a new commerce in Europe? *International Review of Retail, Distribution and Consumer Research*, 11, 287–299.

Findlay A and Sparks L (2002) *Retailing: Critical Concepts*. Routledge: London. Four Volumes.

Hollander SC (1960) The wheel of retailing. *Journal of Marketing*, 24, 37–42.

Hollander SC (1966) Notes on the retail accordion. *Journal of Retailing*, 42, 29–40, 54.

Levy M, Grewal D, Peterson RA and Connolly B (2005) Editorial: the concept of the 'Big Middle'. *Journal of Retailing*, 81, 83–88.

Peterson RA and Balasubramanian S (2002) Retailing in the 21st century: reflections and prologue to research. *Journal of Retailing*, 78, 9–16.

Savitt R (1989) Looking back to see ahead: writing the history of American retailing. *Journal of Retailing*, 65, 326–355.

Chapter 1

Consumers and Shoppers

RETAILERS DEPEND ON CONSUMERS. Without people going shopping and purchasing products and services, retailers do not have a viable business. The process of understanding what consumers want and how they behave is thus fundamental to the practice of retailing. This knowledge may be obtained in a variety of ways ranging from implicit approaches of simply being aware of repeat business or consumer patronage to explicit loyalty and consumer research programmes. The complications in this are that neither retail practices, nor consumer behaviours, are static.

In historical terms, consumer choices have been constrained. Many societies were essentially self-sufficient and thus had little need or capability for shops. Whilst trade has existed for millennia, the nature of this trade was focused on essentially fixed consumers, limited production capabilities and itinerant pedlars. Markets and fairs subsequently provided one mechanism for consumers to exchange or buy products and perhaps even to compare producers and eventually retailers. But for a long time, consumers were restricted to very local search areas by constraints of mobility. The development of market towns and then urban settlements changed the nature of trade and retailing. The rise of personal mobility in the nineteenth and twentieth centuries further altered relationships, impacting not only on consumers and retailers but also the role of consumption in society.

The picture of constrained consumers is not one that we would recognize in many countries today, where personal mobility is an essential freedom. Consumers can be highly mobile and can exercise choice, selecting centres and retailers from a repertoire of potential locations and options. Whilst some ties to distance remain, particularly for some products, in many cases consumers are unconstrained. They may pass some stores to reach others selling essentially the same product and may use the Internet to purchase internationally.

Consumers choose shops on the basis of an evaluation of a mix of retail and other characteristics. Both retail stores and town centres are thus engaged in competition for this fickle but increasingly complex consumer trade. Town and city centres are amalgams of retailing and other services and facilities. These get evaluated both individually and collectively by consumers and selected or rejected as destinations for travel and then spending. This choice mechanism is perhaps more sophisticated than in the past. It is also essentially individual, though the end result of many individual choices may be collectively similar, and particular shops or locations may be more widely patronized than other, seemingly equivalent places or options. There has also in many countries been a shift in emphasis from a production-led to a consumption-led society. This is articulated through a switch from satisfaction of needs through acquisition of goods to the satisfaction of desires through the meaning and symbolism attached to goods and to the places (shops and towns) from where they are obtained.

How do we understand these choices and behaviours? What drives shoppers? How do retailers make sense of these decisions and utilize this knowledge in their approach to store operations? What can retailers and place managers do to attract consumers? How do consumers react to retail offers? How do retail, land-use and transport planners plan the retail system and network of stores? Knowledge of consumer behaviour patterns, preferences and change in these would seem to be central to answering such questions.

There are many texts and volumes on consumer behaviour. Some of these examine shopping behaviour in detail. A number of different approaches to the topic could therefore have been taken in preparing this chapter. There are limits, however, to what could be included. This is a book on retailing. The focus is thus on retail dimensions to the questions of understanding and using consumer choice and practice. Three rather different topics are considered here:

1   *Customer Perceptions and Expectations of Service Quality.* Consumers make their choices of stores based on a variety of factors. It has been argued that in a service sector such as retailing, service quality is a vital component of the choice matrix. The essential problem then is to understand how to measure service quality on an effective, consistent and managerially valuable basis. The best known of the quantitative measurement scales in this area is SERVQUAL, developed by Parasuraman, Zeithaml and Berry. Their 1988 *Journal of Retailing* paper introducing SERVQUAL is the paper included here. This paper set off a major stream of research in service quality, though it is not without its critics, and SERVQUAL details have been subject to modification.

2   *Consumer Experiences and Experiencing Consumers.* Retailers create consumer landscapes through their brands, stores and formulae. These creations in some cases go far beyond the simple idea of retailing a product. The consumer is at once part of the retail offer and part of the retail and store positioning. They react to and are watched reacting to and engaging with the offer of the retailer, and the retailer themselves. Shopping may thus be as much emotional as functional. Understanding the ways in which consumers view retail space, how they use and engage with this space (which here includes the products, staff, media,

buildings and other customers) and the impact this has on them and others requires a very different view of what retailing (and consumer research in retailing) can be about. This qualitative, more culturally oriented reading of retailing is represented here by a 1998 book chapter from Sherry on Nike Town Chicago, an iconic retail flagship store.

3   *Retail Positioning and Consumer Preferences.* Retailers obviously operate stores which they hope will satisfy consumer needs and wants. Many retailers however are 'chasing' the same consumer markets. They try therefore to differentiate themselves from the competition in the minds of the consumers. But in the same way that consumer demands can vary over time, so too retailers can position themselves differently or can present a 'new' position for consumers. This could involve an existing retailer repositioning or a new retailer entering a new market and affecting the existing consumer behaviours. Consumer reactions to a 'new' retailer are vital not only to the success or failure of the new entrant, but also to the trading fortunes of existing retailers. When a retailer has a strong offer, reinforced by a rigorous approach to putting over that position to consumers, then consumers en masse may re-evaluate what is important to them in shopping, that is, their consumer preferences. The paper included here introduced the idea of a 'market spoiler', that is, a company that by its entry forces such a re-evaluation of consumer preferences (Arnold *et al.* 1998).

Customer Perceptions and Expectations of Service Quality

One of the components of many retail patronage models is service quality. The issue of quality was one of the key components of business and management practice in the 1980s, popularized by books on excellence and excellent companies and by the introduction of Japanese management techniques. For example, the just-in-time technique and its associated emphasis on aspects such as zero defects, introduced particularly into the car manufacturing industry, focused attention on quality consistency and improvement. In order to compete successfully businesses were encouraged to achieve high quality in goods and services. This quality achievement in services of course presupposes that service quality can be identified and measured and, in turn, that these measurements have meaning, in both a business and an academic context. One of the assumptions is that higher quality produces higher profitability, through the mechanism of the generation of more satisfied and more loyal customers. Accepting this assumption and assertion leads to the research question of how best to measure, and then improve, service quality?

Parasuraman, Zeithaml and Berry produced a series of papers between 1985 and 1988 (Parasuraman, Zeithaml and Berry 1985, 1986; Zeithaml, Berry and Parasuraman 1985, 1988) which effectively culminate in a *Journal of Retailing* paper (Parasuraman, Zeithaml and Berry 1988). They argued that it was possible to measure consumers' perceptions of service quality and that the comparison of these perceptions against consumers' expectations held information and value. Their paper described the development of a twenty-two-item survey instrument, which they termed SERVQUAL. They proposed this as a tool for assessing customer perceptions and expectations of service quality in 'service and retailing organizations' (p. 12). Perceived quality was at the heart of their development of SERVQUAL. They saw this as representing the consumer's judgement about an entity's overall excellence or superiority, being derived from this comparison of expectations against perceptions of performance. Put simply, did the service you receive as a customer from that organization exceed or fail to meet the service you expected to receive and in what ways was it different?

Parasuraman, Zeithaml and Berry (1988) initially identified ten potentially overlapping dimensions of service quality resulting in a ninety-seven-item survey instrument. This was then refined through data collection. This first involved an intercept survey at a shopping mall in which respondents answered the questionnaire (ninety-seven-items for expectations and the same ninety-seven-items for perceptions) for one service category (from appliance repair and maintenance, retail banking, long-distance telephone, securities brokerage and credit cards). From these data the scale was purified and a revised thirty-four-item scale tested again in the same way and with the same service categories. Further purification of the scale after this second stage of data collection resulted in the twenty-two-item scale on five dimensions (Parasuraman, Zeithaml and Berry 1988, p. 23):

1   *Tangibles* – physical facilities, equipment and appearance of personnel;
2   *Reliability* – ability to perform the promised service dependably and accurately;
3   *Responsiveness* – willingness to help customers and provide prompt service;
4   *Assurance* – knowledge and courtesy of employees and their ability to inspire trust and confidence;
5   *Empathy* – caring, individualized attention the firm provides its customers.

SERVQUAL results are often framed in terms of 'differences' or 'gaps' between expectations and performance at item, dimension and overall levels, thus leading to the common terminology of the 'GAPS' model. Parasuraman, Zeithaml and Berry (1988) proposed that SERVQUAL had many possible applications, particularly in retailing. They noted that 'it provides a basic skeleton . . . (which) . . . can be adapted or supplemented to fit the characteristics or specific research needs of a particular organization' (pp. 30–31) and argued for its periodic use in a business and as a supplemental tool for use in association with other service quality measurements.

The development of SERVQUAL generated a 'cottage industry' of replicative studies and applications, in many situations, sectors and countries. For a paper that has become the most cited one ever published in the *Journal of Retailing*, it is interesting that the scale (SERVQUAL) did not derive from any consideration of service quality in retailing. The scale itself was not retail focused. This curiosity aside, SERVQUAL has had, and continues to have, considerable impact on issues of, and research into, service quality, including in retailing.

SERVQUAL itself came under considerable discussion almost immediately (e.g. Carman 1990; Babakus and Boller 1992; Cronin and Taylor 1992; Brown *et al.* 1993). Parasuraman, Zeithaml and Berry soon recognized that the scale needed further justification and minor refinement, and they re-assessed it in a second paper in the *Journal of Retailing* (Parasuraman, Berry and Zeithaml 1991). This re-assessment focused on testing in three other types of services (telephone repair, retail banking and insurance). Yet again, retail service quality was neglected despite the challenge laid down (and cited in Parasuraman, Berry and Zeithaml 1991) by Finn and Lamb (1991) whose evaluation of SERVQUAL in retailing had concluded that 'data gathering regarding different types of retail stores did not fit the SERVQUAL measurement model' (p. 489). Parasuraman, Berry and Zeithaml (1991) concluded that whilst minor refinements were needed to SERVQUAL, their summary of the early studies using it suggested that it did provide a sound base. They emphasized the skeleton nature of SERVQUAL and re-iterated that it could be supplemented with context-specific items or additional quantitative or qualitative research.

Additional refinements appeared in a further *Journal of Retailing* article (Parasuraman, Berry and Zeithaml 1993), which for the first time did include some testing with customers in a retail chain. This paper also reflected on published studies by others using SERVQUAL and the criticisms that had been laid against the original approach. In particular, questions had arisen over:

- the need to measure expectations (e.g. Cronin and Taylor 1992, 1994);
- the interpretation and operationalization of expectations (e.g. Teas 1993, 1994);
- the reliability and validity of SERVQUAL's difference-score formulation (e.g. Babakus and Boller 1992; Brown *et al.* 1993; Peter *et al.* 1993);
- SERVQUAL's dimensionality (e.g. Carman 1990; Finn and Lamb 1991).

Some of these criticisms led to refinements and clarifications and the occasional rebuttal (e.g. Parasuraman, Berry and Zeithaml 1991, 1993; Zeithaml, Berry and Parasuraman 1993; Parasuraman, Zeithaml and Berry 1994a, b). Buttle (1996) provides a review and critique of the issues surrounding SERVQUAL and its criticisms, refinements and usefulness, which focuses on theoretical and operational criticisms. Asubonteng *et al.* (1996) perform a similar function. Both point, however, to the widespread adoption of SERVQUAL in academia and industry. The 'independent' and anonymous executive summary appended to Asubonteng *et al.* (1996) by the publisher/editor makes the point:

> SERVQUAL is popular with managers because it combines ease of application and flexibility with a clear and uninvolved theory. Managers know that results obtained using the model are probably not objective truth, but also know that they help identify the direction in which the firm should move.
>
> (p. 80)

As noted earlier, SERVQUAL was not really designed in terms of retail service quality and Finn and Lamb's (1991) study found it wanting in the sector. Dabholkar *et al.* (1996) modified and extended SERVQUAL to produce a Retail Service Quality

Scale, deriving from a conclusion that a single measure of service quality across all industries is not feasible. Kim and Jin (2001) in turn found this scale lacking. SERVQUAL itself has continued to be used in retailing (e.g. Gagliano and Hathcote 1994; de Ruyter and Wetzels 1997; Vázquez *et al.* 2001; Zhao *et al.* 2002), sometimes with modifications and generally with mixed findings. Extensions to Internet retailing have been suggested (e.g. Barnes and Vigden 2001; Long and McMellon 2004). Debates about appropriate measurement scales for retailing and e-retailing have continued (e.g. Winsted 1997; Hussey 1999; Mehta *et al.* 2000; Parasuraman *et al.* 2005; Collier and Bienstock 2006). Finn and Kayande (2004) strike a cautionary note about scale modification when they show that modifying or adapting SERVQUAL (as many have done) have unintended consequences and effects. They conclude 'Our findings suggest serious problems in assuming multi-purpose adequacy of scale modification approaches' (p. 50).

There can be little doubt over the impact of SERVQUAL on research into service quality. It has also been applied in many business situations. The scale has had problems and the 1988 paper included here is best seen as a work-in-progress. The authors, however, from the outset did clearly see SERVQUAL as only a partial solution. This has perhaps been forgotten as SERVQUAL has taken on a life of its own. Retailers and researchers have also moved on somewhat and become more concerned about the exact nature of the relationship between service quality and profitability (e.g. Zeithaml 2000) and the hotly debated relationship between service quality and satisfaction (e.g. Brady *et al.* 2005).

The linkages of service quality with satisfaction have of course a relationship with the issue of customer loyalty. One of the beliefs is that more satisfied and more loyal consumers are more profitable (Reichheld and Sasser 1990). The construct of loyalty, however, is not straightforward. It is generally viewed as comprising two perspectives – behavioural and attitudinal (Dick and Basu 1994). Behavioural outcomes do not necessarily demonstrate affective loyalty components, whereas the reverse is more likely to be true (Oliver 1999) and there are differences in terms of the relationships with profitability (Reinartz and Kumar 2002). A full review of these issues is beyond the scope of this commentary, but a useful starting point is found in Kumar and Shah (2004).

Questions remain, however. How do we best measure service quality in retailing and what can businesses gain from this knowledge? What is meant in totality by service quality? How are service quality, satisfaction, loyalty and profitability or value related? Perhaps most fundamentally we should ask if measurement in a quantitative fashion is the best way to understand service quality in a service industry with the characteristics of retailing, where intangibles may be more influential and where mood and situation can play such a vital part in the service encounter or exchange.

Consumer Experiences and Experiencing Consumers

The questions of how consumers shop, and why they shop where they do, are multi-layered and subject to many different interpretations and answers. A caricature of the SERVQUAL scale would argue that managers sought to reduce shopping and consumer behaviour to a single element (service quality) and a set of numerical scores. But, if we consider how we shop and why we shop, then it is clear that whilst service quality is of considerable relevance, the answer to why we shop where we do and how we shop is not forty-two.

To some degree the emphasis should perhaps be less on service quality and more on experiences. Sociologists, ethnographers and culturalists perceive shopping and retailing in very different ways than would perhaps managers and certainly management academics. The 'cultural turn' in much social science in the 1980s and its reflection in post-modernism (which came late to marketing, see Brown 1995) argued for very different research approaches and tools of analysis (Sherry 1991). Put simply, to understand consumers and consumer behaviour, we have to experience and observe what consumers and retailers experience.

Even as SERVQUAL was making its mark, this very different set of ideas was beginning to emerge in retailing. There is a long history of ethnographic studies generally. Interpretivist consumer research began to develop through the 1980s (e.g. Hirschman and Wallendorf 1982; Holbrook and Hirschman 1982; Belk *et al.* 1988, 1989; Hirschman 1989). However, these did not really penetrate retailing studies until late in the decade. Two early retail-focused papers of this genre appeared in the *Journal of Retailing* in 1989 and 1990. McGrath (1989) examined the ethnography of a gift store, whilst Sherry (1990) provided an ethnography of informal retailing in a periodic (flea) market. These two papers have a number of common characteristics:

- The research extended over a long time frame (3 years for McGrath and 2.5 years for Sherry).
- Participant observation was a main part of the methodology (e.g. McGrath worked in the gift store).
- The ethnographic research approach is described as naturalistic.
- Both focus on stores and details rather than surveys and aggregation.

Sherry (1990) points to experiential aspects of dealing in the periodic (flea) market and to the notion that for consumers the experience of the market is more than the product assortment found there. For McGrath (1989) an ethnographic approach provides 'an opportunity for academics to observe and discover the wisdom and strategies of practitioners' (p. 447). The researcher is no longer the privileged studying an object, but is rather a component part of the subject under investigation.

Sherry and McGrath continued the development of this type of retail research (see also Arnould and Price 1993; Celsi *et al.* 1993; and Goss 1993 for other contemporary examples) with a number of other papers following quickly. Sherry *et al.* (1992) again examined gift retailers and gifts, this time using projective research techniques including sentence completion, picture-based thematic apperception tasks and the development of consumer fantasies and stories. McGrath *et al.* (1993) in an ethnographic study of a farmers' market used an extended case study, thick with description, in an economic anthropological approach. They note that 'shopping with customers and selling with vendors proved particularly useful methods of interviewing' (p. 285). This paper uses verbal and photographic logs, archives and field notes as research techniques, records and reporting mechanisms. They see this form of marketplace as an antidote or reaction to the depersonalization of retailing (Forman and Sriram 1991) and note it 'develops a servicescape best likened to retail theater' (p. 311).

This concept of a 'servicescape' had been promoted by Bitner (1992) who focused on the impact of the building and physical surroundings on the performance and interactions of employees and customers. Whilst atmospherics in stores had been researched, it was mainly practical work focused on generating consumer reactions and ignored employees and employee/customer interactions. She utilized the environmental psychology work of the 1980s (e.g. Donovan and Rossiter 1982) which focused on the reciprocity and interactivity of organisms and their environments, to develop a conceptual framework and servicescape typology. This terminology and approach was further used by Sherry (1998b) in a seminal edited collection of writings that explored ideas of how place impacts contemporary markets, including shops and shopping.

Sherry's chapter (1988a) in his edited volume (Sherry 1998b) and another paper by Peñaloza (1999) on the same retail site (Nike Town, Chicago), though carried out entirely separately, are together seminal in this ethnographic and cultural view of retailing and consumers. Their focus on consumption and how it is co-created by retailers, consumers and others represents a radically different approach to 'standard' retail consumer research, and certainly from the service-quality approach outlined earlier. Their 'readings' of space, behaviour and interactions, with its strong emphasis on the use of brands, icons and mythology to generate space and consumption, open up a different retail world. This has links to concepts of new forms of consumption, including experiential consumption (e.g. Gottdiener 1997, 2000; Ritzer 1999) and the need for consumers to be engaged more in their shopping experiences.

Sherry's (1998a) chapter is included in this collection. He describes his chapter as the 'lineal descendent of the wave of ethnographic investigations of periodic markets and upscale specialty stores ... that is helping consumer researchers better understand the experiential dimensions of servicescapes' (p. 113). The chapter is an account of Sherry's own engagement with Nike Town, Chicago 'hedged about' with observations and interpretations from other participants and consumers who are 'enacting the servicescape'.

Sherry's and Peñaloza's studies have generated a number of follow-up and extended studies, particularly by Sherry and his colleagues. Much of this work has focused on ESPN Zone Chicago (e.g. Kozinets et al. 2002, 2004; Sherry et al. 2004a, b), in which particular aspects such as retail theatre, gendered behaviour and spectacular consumption have been pursued. In the UK the 'cultural' turn in geography was reflected in more cultural and ethnographic retail research, including work on car-boot sales (e.g. Gregson and Crewe 1997a, b; Crewe and Gregson 1998) and farmers' markets (e.g. Holloway and Kneafsey 2000). A characteristic of this work (see Crewe 2000 for a review) is a multi-layered qualitative approach to the subject (e.g. Jackson and Holbrook 1995; Gregson et al. 2002; Jackson et al. 2006) which came from many subject backgrounds (e.g. Falk and Campbell 1997; Miller *et al.* 1998; Miller 1995, 1998, 2001; Jackson *et al.* 2000; Mansvelt 2005).

Any reading of this body of work immediately sees the relationship of places (shops) and consumers/shoppers in very different ways. Much of this may be to do with the selection of the sites and stores for research. At the outset, the approach was to look for highly interactive situations (e.g. farmers' markets, flea markets, car-boot sales, charity shops and gift shops) in the belief that situations such as these are better representations of consumer behaviour and shopping desires and retailer/consumer interactions. Certainly they are portrayed as more 'fun' and engaging than are functional cum industrial retail spaces such as discount stores and supermarkets. Many of the later papers in this research stream again focus on 'special' places, often involving manufacturer brands and brand icons, flagship stores and sport. These serv-icescapes are representative of places that have moved from 'functionality to fantasy', where people go to 'experience not only to buy' and where 'stores tell stories' and the servicescape is 'staged and a stage' (Kozinets *et al.* 2002). This of course begs the question whether these highly differentiated retail spaces and the co-created con-sumer behaviour they encourage are meaningful in a world where much retailing remains functional or even industrial and where consumer preferences often revolve around price and convenience rather than engagement and play. In the search for the 'special' has the 'normal' been forgotten?

Retail Positioning and Consumer Preferences

In many of the studies thus far discussed, it is implicit that consumers have preferences, which can be revealed through their behaviours and then perhaps acted upon by mar-keters and retailers. Consumers frequent shops for particular purposes and reasons, exhibiting repeat patronage where their 'preferences' or desires are best met. These preferences tend to be thought of as some sort of value dimension. This 'value' prefer-ence is the result of trade-offs amongst aspects or motives such as price, quality, time, convenience, location, experience, fun and service, which together in some way provide utility for the individual consumer. Tauber (1972) in attempting to answer the question 'why do people shop?' produced a typology of personal and social motives. Tauber's typology was a departure from a view of shopping as purely or mainly an economic exchange activity, though there are situations where economic considerations have preference (see also Westbrook and Black 1985 and Laaksonen 1993).

Most of the approaches to retail patronage and consumer preferences tend to assume (mainly implicitly) that consumer preferences are unchanging or at least fixed and exogenous to the influence of stores and competitors. Success in retailing would thus appear to be a function of identifying these consumer preferences and meeting them more effectively than competitors. In the case of grocery products, it is thus often assumed that the most efficient and effective retailer generates the lowest prices and thus becomes the most successful in the market, provided they continue to meet these stated consumer preferences. In short, the consumer preferences influence the marketing and retailing strategies.

Arnold *et al.* (1998) turn this proposition on its head by developing the concept of a 'market spoiler', that is, a retailer which shifts consumer preferences towards its own market position. Their view is that marketing and retailing strategies can influence consumer tastes and preferences and thus behaviour. It is therefore not only important that the retailer is good at what they do (i.e. they outperform the competition on key attributes) but that the retailer through its performance and position encourages the market itself to value more strongly the retailer's key positioning dimensions above those of the competition. The retail position is one of being both better and distinct from the competition, with that distinctiveness being focused on the key (i.e. most significant) attributes of the retailer and of the market.

The conceptual base for this was provided by Carpenter and Nakamoto (1989). They proposed that consumer preferences are endogenous to, and evolve with, the market. They and others confirmed this in experimental studies (e.g. Carpenter and Nakamoto 1990; Kardes *et al.* 1993; Carpenter *et al.* 1994). The context for their studies was that of market 'pioneering' i.e. where the market is essentially being created and first mover advantages may be important (Kalyanaram and Urban 1992). For Arnold *et al.* (1998) it was a short leap to seeing the concept as 'market spoiling', that is, a new entrant to an existing market. They focused on the world's largest and perhaps most feared retailer, Wal-Mart (for a recent collection of academic work on Wal-Mart, see Brunn 2006), and sought to test the market spoiling hypothesis by looking at markets in the USA and Canada where consumer tracking studies allowed the examination of attribute importance and stated behaviour over time. The introduction of the concept of the 'market spoiler' is the major contribution of this paper.

The key question for Arnold *et al.* (1998) to answer was whether any market share gain by Wal-Mart in these tracking studies demonstrated that the market attributes had shifted towards Wal-Mart's position or whether indeed the gain represented the better meeting of latent (but fixed) consumer needs in these markets. Three key elements thus became important:

1   Consumer ambiguity – consumers are uncertain as to the saliency of attributes in some situations and thus exhibit ambiguity over attributes, i.e. no business stands out on important attributes and the rating of attributes may itself be unclear.
2   Ambiguity resolution – marketers can help consumers resolve any ambiguity in directions that favour their company, its positioning and its branding.
3   Asymmetric advantage – dominant brands develop an asymmetric competitive advantage that inhibits weaker brands.

They summarize their argument (pp. 3–4):

> Market spoilers can shift consumer preferences in their favour . . . [as they] . . . capitalize on consumer ambiguity on attribute preferences. Such ambiguity is created by the market spoiler with the use of strong advertising of attributes that are different from those of the present market

leaders. Such strong differentiating messages alter rather than resolve the consumer's information environment, thus creating the potential for change.

In their tracking studies of Wal-Mart, Arnold *et al.* (1998) point to the scale of Wal-Mart's advertising, its message consistency (see also Arnold *et al.* 2001) and the huge media interest its market entry generates. Wal-Mart becomes the dominant presenter of market information and this information is focused unceasingly towards the attributes on which Wal-Mart performs best. These accord primarily with its 'Every Day Low Prices' (EDLP) proposition and its service delivery. Even if no ambiguity existed in the market before, this onslaught creates that attribute ambiguity in the consumers' minds. They also note that this ambiguity may be seen by an increased spread of price points in the market (e.g. Arnold *et al.* 1983, 1998). As Wal-Mart becomes more powerful in the market (household preferences change and market share rises), so the ambiguity declines as the message becomes consistent with the (changed) consumer preferences.

Arnold *et al.*'s (1998) tracking studies in Atlanta, Chicago and Kingston (Ontario) over time show the following:

1   Wal-Mart's market share rose sharply, demonstrating that Wal-Mart attracts and keeps shoppers from competitors on entry.
2   Attributes that consumers rank highly shifted over time, with these attributes being consistent with those that define Wal-Mart's EDLP positioning, i.e. 'low/best prices' becomes more important and 'sales/promotions' and 'quality' decline in importance.
3   Consumer ambiguity (as measured by store characteristic identification and recall) fell over time.

In short, they conclude that Wal-Mart had entered and destabilized these markets ('spoiled' them for existing retailers). The new stable pattern eventually generated was focused on different consumer attributes and preferences. Competitors were forced to respond to this new reality or continue to lose market share, but only the very best were able to compete on Wal-Mart's terms, which now define the market.

The 'market spoiler' impact of Wal-Mart as revealed by Arnold *et al.* (1998) was drawn from studies in two cities in the USA and one in Canada. Other similar studies have shown similar effects with supercentres (including Wal-Mart) in the USA (e.g. Seiders and Tigert 2000). They have also linked the market spoiler effect with the generation of institutional legitimacy in both economic and social terms (see Arnold *et al.* 1996; Handelman and Arnold 1999; Arnold and Luthra 2000).

For Steve Arnold, the 1990s internationalization of Wal-Mart's retail operations provided the possibility of testing the 'market spoiling' hypothesis in other countries and comparing results with his base of research on Wal-Mart and supercentres in the USA and Canada. Fernie *et al.* (2006) present early results from their studies in the United Kingdom (UK) and Germany (see Burt and Sparks 2006 for a brief discussion of some of the results they presented in preceding conference papers). Fernie *et al.* (2006) argue that the studies show that the market spoiler effect is apparent in the UK in that price has become more important as an attribute across all shopper groups and Asda has had success in overtaking a less value-oriented retailer such as Sainsbury. The results for Germany, however, show that whilst Wal-Mart performs well in the surveys on most norms/attributes, it does not do so on the key norms. They conclude (p. 262):

> (Wal-Mart) did not take into account the strong price competition in Germany where price leadership is occupied by discounters ... It had hoped to invoke the market spoiler effect through customer service initiatives but the German notion of customer service is different from that in the United States.

Fernie *et al.* (2006) also contrast the operational performance of Wal-Mart in Germany and the UK, showing Germany lacking in scale, cohesion and efficiency. The August 2006 sale of Wal-Mart Germany was thus not a surprise to many, other than in the psychological terms of Wal-Mart publicly admitting 'defeat'. The market spoiler effect thus did not work in Germany and possibly Wal-Mart never achieved institutional legitimacy (Bianchi and Arnold 2004 argue a similar point for the failure of Home Depot in Chile). Wal-Mart was neither good at retailing in Germany nor distinct and did not move customer preferences to favour its retail proposition.

The 'market spoiler' thesis has also some linkages with aspects of store loyalty. For the thesis to work, consumers have to switch stores and thus alter their behaviour. The outcome is that a new set of 'loyalties' is generated. This store-switching activity, including its effect on loyalty in terms of behaviours and probably attitudes, has been somewhat under-researched. It is unclear for example as to the balance between 'normal' store-switching and loyalty and that generated by the competitive impact of the new store entry. Research has tended to suggest that a baseline 'store-switching' level exists, probably resulting from variety seeking and locational changes (e.g. East *et al.* 1995, 2000; Sieders and Tigert 1997; Rhee and Bell 2002). The market spoiler concept may thus need to reflect more on this baseline activity and lack of loyalty as well as the attitudinal rather than the behavioural measurement of changing shopping patterns. Shopper loyalty remains an important research issue (Kumar and Shah 2004).

Is there such a thing as the 'market spoiler effect'? The evidence from Arnold *et al.* (1998) is convincing that Wal-Mart in North America affected consumer perceptions and attitudes in markets and gained from its competitors. Whether this evidence says anything beyond Wal-Mart in North America is, however, still unclear. International developments raise many questions, not least whether consumer preferences are similar or different in different countries and how this might affect the pattern and success of retail international market entry. This touches in part on debates (e.g. standardization versus adaptation) in retail internationalization which are covered in Chapter 5 of this book. Consumer preferences do vary and change and are not in reality fixed, but the degree of movement remains uncertain given that retailing is clearly a reflection of culture. If a retailer is both good at basic retail functions and demonstrates distinctiveness in consumers' minds in ways that align with their current needs, wants and shopping preferences, then success is pretty much assured. But, the margin for error is not great and consumers can change their minds, as shown by the decline of Marks & Spencer in the late 1990s (Mellahi *et al.* 2002).

So, the question remains; is the 'market spoiler' concept anything more than a description of successful market share gain on market entry? How does this relate to 'loyalty'? More longitudinal research in a variety of contexts and situations may be needed to generate a fully convincing conclusion.

Summary

'Consumers and shoppers' is a vast topic, encompassing many different areas, approaches and research questions. This chapter has selected three very different areas and approaches. We have attempted to trace the research significance within each area of each of our selected contributions. The papers collectively show the huge variation in how we think about consumers and retailers and the ways they come together in retail spaces. Understanding why, how and where consumers shop is thus a vital, but never-ending function of retailers (and retail academics). How this understanding is achieved may well depend on the particular circumstances confronting retailers and researchers at the time.

References

Arnold SJ and Luthra M (2000) Market entry effects of large format retailers: a stakeholder analysis. *International Journal of Retail and Distribution Management*, 28(4/5), 139–154.

Arnold SJ, Oum T and Tigert DJ (1983) Determinant attributes in retail patronage: seasonal, temporal, regional and international comparisons. *Journal of Marketing Research*, 20, 149–157.

Arnold SJ, Handelman J and Tigert DJ (1996) Organisational legitimacy and retail store patronage. *Journal of Business Research*, 35, 229–239.

Arnold SJ, Handelman J and Tigert DJ (1998) The impact of a market spoiler on consumer preference structures (or, what happens when Wal-Mart comes to town). *Journal of Retailing and Consumer Services*, 5, 1–13.

Arnold SJ, Kozinets R, and Handelman J (2001) Hometown ideology and retailer legitimation: the institutional semiotics of Wal-Mart flyers. *Journal of Retailing*, 77, 243–271.

Arnould E and Price L (1993) River magic: extraordinary experience and the extended service encounter. *Journal of Consumer Research*, 20, 24–45.

Asubonteng P, McCleary KJ and Swan JE (1996) SERVQUAL revisited: a critical review of service quality. *The Journal of Services Marketing*, 10(6), 62–81.

Babakus E and Boller GW (1992) An empirical assessment of the SERVQUAL scale. *Journal of Business Research*, 24, 253–268.

Barnes SJ and Vigden R (2001) An evaluation of cyber-bookshops: the WebQual method. *International Journal of Electronic Commerce*, 6, 11–30.

Belk R, Sherry JF and Wallendorf M (1988) A naturalistic enquiry into buyer and seller behavior at a swap meet. *Journal of Consumer Research*, 14, 449–470.

Belk R, Wallendorf M and Sherry JF (1989) The sacred and the profane in consumer behavior: theodicy on the odyssey. *Journal of Consumer Research*, 16, 1–38.

Bianchi CC and Arnold SJ (2004) An international perspective on retail internationalization success: Home Depot in Chile. *International Review of Retail, Distribution and Consumer Research*, 14, 149–169.

Bitner MJ (1992) Servicescapes: the impact of physical surroundings on customers and employees. *Journal of Marketing*, 56, 57–71.

Brady MK, Knight GA, Cronin JJ, Tomas G, Hult M and Keillor BD (2005) Removing the contextual lens: a multinational multi-setting comparison of service evaluation models. *Journal of Retailing*, 81, 215–230.

Brown S (1995) *Postmodern Marketing*. London: Routledge.

Brown SW, Churchill GA and Peter JP (1993) Improving the measurement of service quality. *Journal of Retailing*, 69, 127–139.

Brunn S (ed.) (2006) *Wal-Mart World*. New York: Routledge.

Burt SL and Sparks L (2001) The implications of Wal-Mart's takeover of Asda. *Environment and Planning A*, 33, 1463–1487.

Burt SL and Sparks L (2003) Power and competition in the UK retail grocery market. *British Journal of Management*, 14, 237–254.

Burt SL and Sparks L (2006) Asda: Wal-Mart in the UK. In S Brunn (ed.) *Wal-Mart World*. New York: Routledge, ch. 18.

Buttle F (1996) SERVQUAL: review, critique, research agenda. *European Journal of Marketing*, 30, 8–32.

Carman JM (1990) Consumer perceptions of service quality: an assessment of the SERVQUAL dimensions. *Journal of Retailing*, 66, 33–55.

Carpenter GS and Nakamoto K (1989) Consumer preference formation and pioneering advantage. *Journal of Marketing Research*, 26, 285–298.

Carpenter GS and Nakamoto K (1990) Competitve strategies for late entry into a market with a dominant brand. *Management Science*, 36, 1268–1278.

Carpenter GS, Glazier R and Nakamoto K (1994) Meaningful brands from meaningless differentiation: the dependence on irrelevant attributes. *Journal of Marketing Research*, 31, 339–350.

Celsi R, Rose R and Leigh T (1993) An exploration of high-risk leisure consumption through sky-diving. *Journal of Consumer Research*, 20, 1–23.

Collier JE and Bienstock CC (2006) Measuring service quality in e-retailing. *Journal of Service Research*, 8, 260–275.

Crewe L (2000) Geographies of retailing and consumption. *Progress in Human Geography*, 24, 275–290.

Crewe L and Gregson N (1998) Tales of the unexpected: exploring car boot sales as marginal spaces of contemporary consumption. *Transactions of the Institute of British Geographers*, 23, 39–53.

Cronin JJ and Taylor SA (1992) Measuring service quality: a re-examination and extension. *Journal of Marketing*, 56, 55–68.

Cronin JJ and Taylor SA (1994) SERVPERF versus SERVQUAL: reconciling performance-based and perceptions-minus-expectations measurement of service quality. *Journal of Marketing*, 58, 125–131.

Dabholker PA, Thorpe DI and Rentz JO (1996) A measure of service quality for retail stores: scale development and validation. *Journal of the Academy of Marketing Science*, 24, 3–16.

de Ruyter K and Wetzels M (1997) On the perceived dynamics of retail service quality. *Journal of Retailing and Consumer Services*, 4, 83–88.

Dick A and Basu K (1994) Customer loyalty: toward an integrated conceptual framework. *Journal of the Academy of Marketing Science*, 22, 99–113.

Donovan R and Rossiter J (1982) Store atmosphere: an environmental psychology approach. *Journal of Retailing*, 58, 34–57.

East R, Harris P, Willson G and Lomax W (1995) Loyalty to supermarkets. *International Review of Retail, Distribution and Consumer Research*, 5(1), 99–109.

East R, Hammond K, Harris P and Lomax W (2000) First store loyalty and retention. *Journal of Marketing Management*, 16, 307–325.

Falk P and Campbell C (1997) *The Shopping Experience*. London: Sage.

Fernie J, Hahn B, Gerhard U, Pioch E and Arnold SJ (2006) The impact of Wal-Mart's entry into the German and UK grocery markets. *Agribusiness*, 22, 247–266.

Finn A and Kayande U (2004) Scale modification: alternative approaches and their consequences. *Journal of Retailing*, 80, 37–52.

Finn DW and Lamb CW (1991) An evaluation of the SERVQUAL scales in a retailing setting. *Advances in Consumer Research*, 18, 483–490.

Forman A and Sriram V (1991) The depersonalization of retailing: its impact on the lonely consumer. *Journal of Retailing*, 67, 226–243.

Gagliano KB and Hathcote J (1994) Customer expectations and perceptions of service quality in retail apparel specialty stores. *Journal of Services Marketing*, 8, 60–69.

Goss J (1993) The magic of the mall: an analysis of form, function and meaning in contemporary retail built environment. *Annals of the Association of American Geographers*, 83, 18–47.

Gottdiener M (1997) *The Theming of America*. Boulder, CO: Westview.

Gottdiener M (2000) *New Forms of Consumption: Consumers, Culture and Commodification*. New York: Rowman and Littlefield.

Gregson N and Crewe L (1997a) Performance and possession: rethinking the act of purchase in the light of the car boot sale. *Journal of Material Culture*, 2, 241–263.

Gregson N and Crewe L (1997b) The bargain, the knowledge and the spectacle: making sense of consumption in the space of the car boot sale. *Environment and Planning D*, 15, 87–112.

Gregson N, Crewe L and Brooks K (2002) Shopping, space and practice. *Environment and Planning D*, 20, 597–617.

Handelman JM and Arnold SJ (1999) The role of marketing actions with a social dimension: appeals to the institutional environment. *Journal of Marketing*, 63, 33–48.

Hirschman E (ed.) (1989) *Interpretive Consumer Research*. Provo, UT: Association for Consumer Research.

Hirschman E and Wallendorf M (1982) Characteristics of the cultural continuum: implications for retailing. *Journal of Retailing*, 58, 5–21.

Holbrook M and Hirschman E (1982) The experiential aspects of consumption. *Journal of Consumer Research*, 9, 132–140.

Holloway L and Kneafsey M (2000) Reading the space of the farmers' market: a preliminary investigation from the UK. *Sociologia Ruralis*, 40, 285–299.

Hussey MK (1999) Using the concept of loss: an alternative SERVQUAL measure. *Service Industries Journal*, 19, 4, 89–101.

Jackson P and Holbrook B (1995) Multiple meanings: shopping and the cultural politics of identity. *Environment and Planning A*, 27, 1913–1930.

Jackson P, Lowe M, Miller D and Mort F (2000) *Commercial Cultures*. Oxford: Berg.

Jackson P, Perez del Aguila R, Clarke I, Hallsworth A, Kervenoael de R and Kirkup M (2006) Retail restructuring and consumer choice 2: understanding consumer choice at the household level. *Environment and Planning A*, 38, 47–67.

Kalyanaram G and Urban GL (1992) Dynamic effects of the order of entry on market share, trial penetration and repeat purchases. *Marketing Science*, 11, 235–250.

Kardes FR, Kalyanaram G, Chandrashekaran M and Dornoff R (1993) Brand retrieval, consideration set, composition, consumer choice and the pioneering advantage. *Journal of Consumer Research*, 20, 62–75.

Kim S and Jin B (2001) An evaluation of the Retail Service Quality Scale for U.S. and Korean customers of discount stores. *Advances in Consumer Research*, 28, 169–176.

Kozinets RV, Sherry JF, Deberry-Spence B, Duhachek A, Nuttavuthisit K and Storm D (2002) Themed flagship brand stores in the new millennium: theory, practice, prospects. *Journal of Retailing*, 78, 17–29.

Kozinets RV, Sherry JF, Storm D, Duhachek A, Nuttavuthisit K and Deberry-Spence B (2004) Ludic agency and retail spectacle. *Journal of Consumer Research*, 31, 658–672.

Kumar V and Shah D (2004) Building and sustaining *profitable* customer loyalty for the 21st century. *Journal of Retailing*, 80, 317–330.

Laaksonen M (1993) Retail patronage dynamics: learning about daily shopping behaviour in contexts of changing retail structures. *Journal of Business Research*, 28, 3–174.

Long M and McMellon C (2004) Exploring the determinants of retail service quality on the Internet. *Journal of Services Marketing*, 18(1), 78–90.

Mansvelt J (2005) *Geographies of Consumption*. London: Sage.

McGrath MA (1989) An ethnography of a gift store: trappings, wrappings and rapture. *Journal of Retailing*, 65, 421–449.

McGrath MA, Sherry JF and Heisley DD (1993) An ethnographic study of an urban periodic marketplace: lessons from the Midville Farmers' Market. *Journal of Retailing*, 69, 280–319.

Mehta SC, Lalwani AK and Han SL (2000) Service quality in retailing: relative efficiency of alternative measurement scales for different product-service environments. *International Journal of Retail and Distribution Management*, 28, 62–72.

Mellahi K, Jackson TP and Sparks L (2002) An exploratory study into failure in successful organizations: the case of Marks and Spencer. *British Journal of Management*, 13, 15–29.

Miller D (1995) *Acknowledging Consumption: a Review of New Studies*. London: Routledge.

Miller D (1998) *A Theory of Shopping*. Cambridge: Polity Press.

Miller D (2001) *The Dialectics of Shopping*. Chicago, IL: University of Chicago Press.

Miller D, Jackson P, Thrift N, Holbrook B and Rowlands M (1998) *Shopping, Place and Identity*. London: Routledge.

Oliver R (1999) Whence customer loyalty? *Journal of Marketing*, 63, 4, 33–44.

Parasuraman A, Zeithaml VA and Berry LL (1985) A conceptual model of service quality and its implications for future research. *Journal of Marketing*, 49, 41–50.

Parasuraman A, Zeithaml VA and Berry LL (1986) *SERVQUAL: a Multiple-item Scale for Measuring Consumer Perceptions of Service Quality*. Report No. 86–108, Cambridge, MA: Marketing Science Institute.

Parasuraman A, Zeithaml VA and Berry LL (1988) SERVQUAL: a multiple-item scale for measuring consumer perceptions of service quality. *Journal of Retailing*, 64, 12–37.

Parasuraman A, Berry LL and Zeithaml VA (1991) Refinement and reassessment of the SERVQUAL scale. *Journal of Retailing*, 67, 420–450.

Parasuraman A, Berry LL and Zeithaml VA (1993) Research note: more on improving service quality measurement. *Journal of Retailing*, 69, 140–147.

Parasuraman A, Zeithaml VA and Berry LL (1994a) Alternative scales for measuring service quality: a comparative assessment based on psychometric and diagnostic criteria. *Journal of Retailing*, 70, 201–230.

Parasuraman A, Zeithaml VA and Berry LL (1994b) Reassessment of expectations as a comparison standard in measuring service quality: implications for further research. *Journal of Marketing*, 58, 111–124.

Parasuraman A, Zeithaml VA and Malhotra A (2005) E-S-QUAL: a multiple item scale for assessing electronic service quality. *Journal of Service Research*, 7, 213–233.

Peñaloza L (1999) Just doing it: a visual ethnographic study of spectacular consumption behaviour at Nike Town. *Consumption, Markets and Culture*, 2, 337–400.

Peter JP, Churchill GA and Brown TJ (1993) Caution in the use of difference scores in consumer research. *Journal of Consumer Research*, 19, 655–662.

Reichheld F and Sasser EW (1990) Zero-defections: quality comes to service. *Harvard Business Review*, 68(5), 105–111.

Reinartz WJ and Kumar V (2002) The mismanagement of customer loyalty. *Harvard Business Review*, 80(7), 86–94.

Rhee J and Bell DR (2002) The inter-store mobility of supermarket shoppers. *Journal of Retailing*, 78, 225–237.

Ritzer G (1999) *Enchanting a Disenchanted World: Revolutionizing the Means of Consumption*. Thousand Oaks, CA: Pine Oaks/Sage.

Seiders K and Tigert DJ (1997) Impact of market entry and competitive structure on store switching/store loyalty. *International Review of Retail, Distribution and Consumer Research*, 7(3), 227–247.

Seiders K and Tigert DJ (2000) The impact of supercenters on traditional food retailers in four markets. *International Journal of Retail and Distribution Management*, 28(4/5), 181–193.

Sherry JF (1990) Dealers and dealing in a periodic market: informal retailing in ethnographic perspective. *Journal of Retailing*, 66, 174–200.

Sherry JF (1991) Postmodern alternatives: the interpretive turn in consumer research. In T Robertson and H Kassarjian (eds) *Handbook of Consumer Behavior*. Englewood Cliffs, NJ: Prentice Hall, 548–591.

Sherry JF (1998a) The soul of the company store: Nike Town Chicago and the emplaced brandscape. In JF Sherry (ed.) *Servicescapes: the Concept of Place in Contemporary Markets*. Lincolnwood, IL, NTC Business Books, 109–146.

Sherry JF (ed.) (1998b) *Servicescapes: the Concept of Place in Contemporary Markets*. Lincolnwood, IL: NTC Business Books.

Sherry JF, McGrath MA and Levy SJ (1992) The disposition of the gift and many unhappy returns. *Journal of Retailing*, 68, 40–64.

Sherry JF, Kozinets RV, Duhachek A, Deberry-Spence B, Nuttavuthisit K, and Storm D (2004a) Gendered behaviour in a male preserve: role playing at ESPN Zone Chicago. *Journal of Consumer Psychology*, 14, 151–158.

Sherry JF, Kozinets RV, Storm D, Duhachek A, Nuttavuthisit K and Deberry-Spence B (2004b) Being in the Zone: staging retail theater at ESPN Zone Chicago. *Journal of Contemporary Ethnography*, 30, 465–510.

Tauber EM (1972) Why do people shop? *Journal of Marketing*, 36(4), 46–49.

Teas KR (1993) Expectations, performance evaluation and consumer's perceptions of quality. *Journal of Marketing*, 57, 18–34.

Teas KR (1994) Expectations as a comparison standard in measuring service quality: an assessment of a re-assessment. *Journal of Marketing*, 58, 132–139.

Vázquez R, Rodriguez-del Bosque IA, Diaz AM and Ruiz AV (2001) Service quality in supermarket retailing: identifying critical service experiences. *Journal of Retailing and Consumer Services*, 8, 1–14.

Westbrook RA and Black WC (1985) A motivation-based shopper typology. *Journal of Retailing*, 61, 78–103.

Winsted KF (1997) The service experience in two cultures: a behavioural perspective. *Journal of Retailing*, 73, 337–360.

Zeithaml VA (2000) Service quality, profitability and the economic worth of customers. *Journal of the Academy of Marketing Science*, 28, 67–85.

Zeithaml VA, Berry LL and Parasuraman A (1985) Problems and strategies in services marketing. *Journal of Marketing*, 49, 33–46.

Zeithaml VA, Berry LL and Parasuraman A (1988) Communication and control processes in the delivery of service quality. *Journal of Marketing*, 52, 35–48.

Zeithaml VA, Berry LL and Parasuraman A (1993) The nature and determinants of customer expectations of service. *Journal of the Academy of Marketing Science*, 21, 1–12.

Zhao X, Bai C and Hui YV (2002) An empirical assessment and application of SERVQUAL in a Mainland Chinese department store. *Total Quality Management*, 13, 241–254.

Editors' Commentary

THIS PAPER REMAINS THE most cited ever from the *Journal of Retailing*. Its impact, however, extends well beyond that of retail interests. The measurement scale it introduces – SERVQUAL – has had significant impact in developing the field of service quality generally. Its significance can not be underplayed, though the concept at the core of the paper has received criticism and development over the years, nor can the impacts of the three authors on marketing thought, particularly in the field of service quality. 'SERVQUAL: A Multiple-Item Scale for Measuring Consumer Perceptions of Service Quality' is the seminal article in the field. At the time of publication, it received the Honorable Mention Award for the best paper that year in the *Journal of Retailing*, something which understates its subsequent impact and influence.

The trio of authors (A. Parasuraman, Valarie Ziethaml and Leonard Berry) at the time were working together at Texas A&M. They have in two cases subsequently moved away from Texas, but the three have worked together since on aspects of service quality. They have extended their early work through further research and article and book publications and have continued to win awards for their work. Together they have more than twenty joint publications. The SERVQUAL concept stimulated service quality research within retailing but each of the authors has also gone on to develop the concept in other contexts as well, including financial services, healthcare and new technology readiness.

A. Parasuraman's academic career began with a degree in mechanical engineering in Madras, India, before he took an MBA at the Indian Institute of Management in Ahmedebad, India and then a DBA in Indiana University, focusing on marketing with quantitative business analysis and statistics as minor fields. He worked at Texas A&M University from 1979 to 1994, being the Federated Professor of Marketing at the end of this period. He then moved to the University of Miami to take up the James W. McLamore Chair in Marketing. His research interest remains in the field of defining, measuring and leveraging service quality, with his interest in technology developing research into the role of technology in service delivery and in strategies for effectively marketing technology-based products and services.

Valarie Ziethaml is the Roy and Alice H. Richards Bicentennial Professor of Marketing at the Kenan-Flagler Business School at the University of North Carolina at Chapel Hill. She is an internationally recognized pioneer of services marketing and has devoted her career to issues in service quality, services management and customer equity. She holds a BA from Gettysburg College and MBA and PhD degrees from the University of Maryland. Valarie Zeithaml spent six years as an account executive in an advertising firm and in the 1990s also spent four years as the principal of a consultancy firm (Partners for Service Excellence). Her academic career began at the University of Maryland before she went to Texas A&M, moving to Duke University in 1986. Since 1996 she has been involved with the University of North Carolina at Chapel Hill, becoming the Bicentennial Professor in 2001.

Leonard Berry has had a long and distinguished career in marketing, working in Texas A&M University's Department of Marketing since 1982. He arrived at Texas A&M following positions at Virginia, Georgia State, Virginia Commonwealth and Denver universities. His initial degrees (BA and MBA) were from the University of Denver and his PhD is from the Arizona State University. Len Berry currently holds the position of Distinguished Professor of Marketing and the M. B. Zale Chair in Retailing and Marketing Leadership, having previously held the JC Penney Chair of Retailing Studies. He is also Professor of Humanities in Medicine in the College of medicine at the Texas A&M University System Health Science Centre. In 2001-2 Len Berry was a Visiting Scientist at the Mayo Clinic, studying healthcare services. He was the founder of Texas A&M's Center for Retailing Studies and served as its director from 1982 to 2000. The centre was an innovative venture which was early amongst academic institutions to recognize and concentrate upon the academic and pedagogic aspects of retailing. His academic career is stellar and Leonard Berry has been recognized as the most frequent contributor to the services marketing literature. He has won many awards for his single and co-authored work and has served on the boards of retail companies including Lowe's, CompUSA and Hastings Entertainment.

Key Publications

Kunkel JH and Berry L (1968) A behavioural conception of retail image. *Journal of Marketing*, 32(October), 21–27.

Zeithaml VA (1982) Consumer response to in-store price information environments. *Journal of Consumer Research*, 8, 357–369.

Zeithaml VA, Berry LL and Parasuraman A (1985) Problems and strategies in services marketing. *Journal of Marketing*, 49(2), 33–46.

Parasuraman A, Zeithaml VA and Berry LL (1985) A conceptual model of service quality and its implications for future research. *Journal of Marketing*, 49(4), 41–50.

Parasuraman A, Zeithaml VA and Berry LL (1988) SERVQUAL: a multiple item scale for measuring consumer perceptions of service quality. *Journal of Retailing*, 64, 12–37.

Zeithaml VA (1988) Consumer perceptions of price, quality and value: a conceptual model and synthesis of research. *Journal of Marketing*, 52, 2–22.

Zeithaml V, Parasuraman A and Berry L (1990) *Delivering Quality Service: Balancing Customer Perceptions and Expectations*. New York: Free Press.

Parasuraman A, Zeithaml V and Berry L (1991) Refinement and reassessment of the SERVQUAL scale. *Journal of Retailing*, 67, 420–450.

Zeithaml V, Berry L and Parasuraman A, (1993) The nature and determinants of customer expectations of service. *Journal of the Academy of Marketing Science*, 21, 1–12.

Parasuraman A, Berry L and Zeithaml V (1993) More on improving service quality measurement. *Journal of Retailing*, 69, 140–147.

Boulding W, Kalra A, Staelin R and Zeithaml V (1993) A dynamic process model of service quality: from expectations to behavioural intentions. *Journal of Marketing Research*, 30, 7–27.

Parasuraman A, Zeithaml V and Berry L (1994) Alternative scales for measuring service quality: a comparative assessment based on psychometric and diagnostic criteria. *Journal of Retailing*, 70, 210–230.

Parasuraman A, Zeithaml V and Berry L (1994) Reassessment of expectations as a comparison standard in measuring service quality: implications for future research. *Journal of Marketing*, 58, 111–124.

Zeithaml V, Berry L and Parasuraman A (1996) The behavioural consequences of service quality. *Journal of Marketing*, 60, 31–46.

Berry L (1999) *Discovering the Souls of Service: the Nine Drivers of Sustainable Business Success*. New York: Free Press.

Parasuraman A (2000) Technology readiness index: a multiple-item scale to measure readiness to embrace new technologies. *Journal of Service Research*, 2, 307–320.

Zeithaml VA (2000) Service quality, profitability and the economic worth of customers. *Journal of the Academy of Marketing Science*, 28, 67–85.

Parasuraman A and Colby CL (2001) *Techno-Ready Marketing: How and Why Your Customers Adopt Technology*. New York: Free Press.

Berry L and Parasuraman A (2001) *Marketing Services: Competing Through Quality*. New York: Free Press.

Parasuraman A, Zeithaml V and Malhotra A (2002) Service quality of websites: a critical review of extant knowledge. *Journal of the Academy of Marketing Science*, 30, 362–375.

Berry L, Seiders K and Grewal D (2002) Understanding service convenience. *Journal of Marketing*, 66, 1–17.

Rust R, Lemon K and Zeithaml V (2004) Return on marketing: using customer equity to focus marketing strategy. *Journal of Marketing*, 68, 109–128.

Parasuraman A, Zeithaml V and Malhotra A (2005) E-S-QUAL: a multiple-item scale for assessing electronic service quality. *Journal of Service Research*, 7, 213–233.

Zeithaml V and Bitner MJ (2006) *Services Marketing*, 4th edn. London: McGraw-Hill.

Berry L and Seltman KD (2007) Building a strong services brand: lessons from the Mayo Clinic. *Business Horizons*, 50, 199–209.

Websites

http://www.bus.miami.edu/index.php?option=com_content&task=view&id=
    538&Itemid=685
http://www.kenan-flagler.unc.edu/Faculty/search/detail.cfm?person_id=143
http://wehner.tamu.edu/mktg/faculty/berry/

SERVQUAL: A MULTIPLE-ITEM SCALE FOR MEASURING CONSUMER PERCEPTIONS OF SERVICE QUALITY

A. Parasuraman, Valarie A. Zeithaml and Leonard L. Berry

This paper describes the development of a 22-item instrument (called SERV-QUAL) for assessing customer perceptions of service quality in service and retailing organizations. After a discussion of the conceptualization and operationalization of the service quality construct, the procedures used in constructing and refining a multiple-item scale to measure the construct are described. Evidence of the scale's reliability, factor structure, and validity on the basis of analyzing data from four independent samples is presented next. The paper concludes with a discussion of potential applications of the scale.

INTENSIFYING COMPETITION AND RAPID deregulation have led many service and retail businesses to seek profitable ways to differentiate themselves. One strategy that has been related to success in these businesses is the delivery of high service quality (Rudie and Wansley 1985; Thompson, DeSouza, and Gale 1985). Delivering superior service quality appears to be a prerequisite for success, if not survival, of such businesses in the 1980s and beyond.

Unlike goods quality, which can be measured objectively by such indicators as durability and number of defects (Crosby 1979; Garvin 1983), service quality is an abstract and elusive construct because of three features unique to services: intangibility, heterogeneity, and inseparability of production and consumption (Parasuraman, Zeithaml, and Berry 1985). In the absence of objective measures, and appropriate approach for assessing the quality of a firm's service is to measure consumers' perceptions of quality. As yet, however, no quantitative yardstick is available for gauging these perceptions.

The purpose of this article is twofold: (1) to describe the development

---

Journal of Retailing, Vol. 16, No. 1 (1988), pp. 12–37.
The research reported in this article was made possible by a grant from the Marketing Science Institute, Cambridge, MA.
A. Parasuraman is a Foley's/Federated Professor of Retailing and Marketing Studies, Texas A & M University, College Station, Texas. Valarie A. Zeithaml is Associate Professor of Marketing, Duke University, Raleigh-Durham, N. Carolina. Leonard L. Berry is a Foley's/Federated Professor of Retailing and Marketing Studies, Texas A & M University, College Station, Texas.

of a multiple-item scale for measuring service quality (called SERVQUAL) and (2) to discuss the scale's properties and potential applications. The basic steps employed in constructing the scale closely parallel procedures recommended in Churchill's (1979) paradigm for developing better measures of marketing constructs. Figure 1 provides an overview of the steps.

This article is divided into five sections. The first section delimits the domain of the service-quality construct and describes the generation of scale items (Steps 1, 2, and 3 in Figure 1). The second section presents the data-collection and scale-purification procedures (Steps 4 through 9), while the third section provides an evaluation of the scale's reliability and factor structures (Step 10). The next section deals with assessment of the scale's validity (Step 11). The final section discusses potential applications of the scale.

Domain of the Service-Quality Construct

In deploring the inadequacy of measurement procedures used in the marketing discipline Jacoby (1978) wrote:

> Many of our measures are developed at the whim of a researcher with nary a thought given to whether or not it is meaningfully related to an explicit conceptual statement of the phenomena or variable in question. In most instances, our concepts have no identity apart from the instrument or procedures used to measure them.
>
> (p. 92)

The need for scale development to be preceded by, and rooted in, a sound conceptual specification of the construct being scaled has been emphasized by other scholars as well (e.g., Churchill 1979; Peter 1981). The conceptual foundation for the SERVQUAL scale was derived from the works of a handful of researchers who have examined the meaning of service quality (Sasser, Oisen, and Wyckoff 1978; Gronroos 1982; Lehtinen and Lehtinen 1982) and from a comprehensive qualitative research study that defined service quality and illuminated the dimensions along which consumers perceive and evaluate service quality (Parasuraman, Zeithaml, and Berry 1985).

Conceptualization of service quality

The construct of quality as conceptualized in the services literature and as measured by SERVQUAL, the scale that is the focus of this article, involves perceived quality. Perceived quality is the consumer's judgment about an entity's overall excellence or superiority (Zeithaml 1987). It differs from objective quality (as defined by, for example, Garvin 1983 and Hjorth-Anderson 1984); it is a form of attitude, related but not equivalent to satisfaction, and results from a comparison of expectations with perceptions of performance.

Perceived quality versus objective quality. Researchers (Garvin 1983; Dodds and

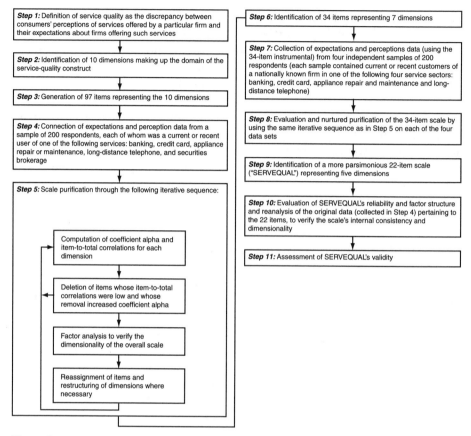

Figure 1 Summary of steps employed in developing the service-quality scale

Monroe 1984; Holbrook and Corfman 1985; Jacoby and Olson 1985; Zeithaml 1987) have emphasized the difference between objective and perceived quality. Holbrook and Corfman (1985), for example, note that consumers do not use the term quality in the same way as researchers and marketers, who define it conceptually. The conceptual meaning distinguishes between mechanistic and humanistic quality: "mechanistic (quality) involves an objective aspect or feature of a thing or event; humanistic (quality) involves the subjective response of people to objects and is therefore a highly relativistic phenomenon that differs between judges" (Holbrook and Corfman 1985, p. 33). Garvin (1983) discusses five approaches to defining quality, including two (product-based and manufacturing-based) that refer to objective quality and one (user-based) that parallels perceived quality.

Quality as attitude. Olshavsky (1985) views quality as a form of overall evaluation of a product, similar in many ways to attitude. Holbrook concurs, suggesting that quality acts as a relatively global value judgment. Exploratory research conducted by Parasuraman, Zeithaml, and Berry (1985) supports the notion that service quality is an overall evaluation similar to attitude. The researchers conducted a total of twelve focus group interviews with current or recent consumers of four different services—retail banking, credit card,

securities brokerage, and product repair and maintenance. The discussions centered on issues such as the meaning of quality in the context of the service in
question, the characteristics the service and its provider should possess in order
to project a high-quality image, and the criteria customers use in evaluating
service quality. Comparison of the findings from the focus groups revealed that,
regardless of the type of service, customers used basically the same general
criteria in arriving at an evaluative judgment about service quality.

Quality versus satisfaction. Oliver (1981) summarizes current thinking on satisfaction in the following definition: "[satisfaction is a] summary psychological state
resulting when the emotion surrounding disconfirmed expectations is coupled
with the consumer's prior feelings about the consumption experience" (p. 27).
This and other definitions (e.g., Howard and Sheth 1969; Hunt 1979) and most
all measures of satisfaction relate to a specific transaction. Oliver (1981) summarizes the transaction-specific nature of satisfaction, and differentiates it from
attitude, as follows:

> Attitude is the consumer's relatively enduring affective orientation
> for a product, store, or process (e.g., customer service) while satisfac-
> tion is the emotional reaction following a disconformation experience
> which acts on the base attitude level and is consumption-specific.
> Attitude is therefore measured in terms more general to product or
> store and is less situationally oriented.
>
> (p. 42)

Consistent with the distinction between attitude and satisfaction, is a distinction between service quality and satisfaction: perceived service quality is a global
judgment, or attitude, relating to the superiority of the service, whereas satisfaction is related to a specific transaction. Indeed, in the twelve focus group interviews included in the exploratory research conducted by Parasuraman, Zeithaml,
and Berry (1985), respondents gave several illustrations of instances when they
were satisfied with a specific service but did not feel the service firm was of high
quality. In this way, the two constructs are related, in that incidents of satisfaction over time result in perceptions of service quality. In Oliver's (1981) words,
"satisfaction soon decays into one's overall attitude toward purchasing products."

Expectations compared to perceptions. The writings of Sasser, Olsen, and Wyckoff
(1978); Gronroos (1982); and Lehtinen and Lehtinen (1982), and the extensive
focus group interviews conducted by Parasuraman, Zeithaml, and Berry (1985),
unambiguously support the notion that service quality, as perceived by consumers, stems from a comparison of what they feel service firms should offer
(i.e., from their expectations) with their perceptions of the performance of firms
providing the services. Perceived service quality is therefore viewed as the degree
and direction of discrepancy between consumers' perceptions and expectations.

The term "expectations" as used in the service quality literature differs from
the way it is used in the consumer satisfaction literature. Specifically, in the
satisfaction literature, expectations are viewed as *predictions* made by consumers
about what is likely to happen during an impending transaction or exchange. For
instance, according to Oliver (1981), "It is generally agreed that expectations are

consumer-defined probabilities of the occurrence of positive and negative events if the consumer engages in some behavior" (p. 33). In contrast, in the service quality literature, expectations are viewed as desires or wants of consumers, i.e., what they feel a service provider *should* offer rather than *would* offer.

Dimensions of service quality. Exploratory research of Parasuraman, Zeithaml, and Berry (1985) revealed that the criteria used by consumers in assessing service quality fit 10 potentially overlapping dimensions. These dimensions were tangibles, reliability, responsiveness, communication, credibility, security, competence, courtesy, understanding/knowing the customer, and access (a description of the dimensions can be found in Parasuraman, Zeithaml, and Berry 1985, p. 47). These 10 dimensions and their descriptions served as the basic structure of the service-quality domain from which items were derived for the SERVQUAL scale.

Generation of scale items

Items representing various facets of the 10 service-quality dimensions were generated to form the initial item pool for the SERVQUAL instrument. This process resulted in the generation of 97 items (approximately 10 items per dimension). Each item was recast into two statements—one to measure expectations about firms in general within the service category being investigated and the other to measure perceptions about the particular firm whose service quality was being assessed. Roughly half of the statement pairs were worded positively and the rest were worded negatively, in accordance with recommended procedures for scale development (Churchill 1979). A seven-point scale ranging from "Strongly Agree" (7) to "Strongly Disagree" (1), with no verbal labels for scale points 2 through 6, accompanied each statement (scale values were reversed for negatively worded statements prior to data analysis). The expectation statements were grouped together and formed the first half of the instrument. The corresponding perception statements formed the second half. An abbreviated version of the instrument, containing a set of expectation statements (labeled as E's) and a corresponding set of perception statements (labeled as P's), along with directions for responding to them, is included in the appendix. Negatively worded statements are identified by a minus sign within parentheses in the appendix.

Data Collection and Scale Purification

The 97-item instrument was subjected to two stages of data collection and refinement. The first stage focused on: (1) condensing the instrument by retaining only those items capable of discriminating well across respondents having differing quality perceptions about firms in several categories, and (2) examining the dimensionality of the scale and establishing the reliabilities of its components. The second stage was primarily confirmatory in nature and involved re-evaluating the condensed scale's dimensionality and reliability by analyzing fresh data from four independent samples. Some further refinements to the scale occurred in this stage.

Data collection, first stage

Data for initial refinement of the 97-item instrument were gathered from a quota sample of 200 adult respondents (25 years-of-age or older) recruited by a marketing research firm in a shopping mall in a large metropolitan area in the Southwest. The sample size of 200 was chosen because other scale developers in the marketing area had used similar sample sizes to purify initial instruments containing about the same number of items as the 97-item instrument (e.g., Churchill, Ford, and Walker 1974; Saxe and Weitz 1982). The sample was about equally divided between males and females. Furthermore, the respondents were spread across five different service categories—appliance repair and maintenance, retail banking, long-distance telephone, securities brokerage, and credit cards. These categories were chosen to represent a broad cross-section of services that varied along key dimensions used by Lovelock (1980, 1983) to classify services. For each service category, a quota of 40 recent users of the service was established. To qualify for the study, respondents had to have used the service in question during the past three months.

Screened and qualified respondents self administered a two-part questionnaire consisting of a 97-statement expectations part followed by a 97-statement perceptions part. For the first part, respondents were instructed to indicate the level of service that should be offered by firms within the service category in question. For the second part, respondents were first asked to name a firm (within the service category) that they had used and with which they were most familiar. Respondents were then instructed to express their perceptions about the firm.

Scale purification, first stage

The 97-item instrument was refined by analyzing pooled data (i.e., data from all five service categories considered together). The pooling of data was deliberate and appropriate because the basic purpose of this research stage was to develop a concise instrument that would be reliable and meaningful in assessing quality in a variety of service sectors. In other words, the purpose was to produce a scale that would have general applicability.

Purification of the instrument began with the computation of coefficient alpha (Cronbach 1951), in accordance with Churchill's (1979) recommendation. Because of the multidimensionality of the service-quality construct, coefficient alpha was computed separately for the 10 dimensions to ascertain the extent to which items making up each dimension shared a common core.

The raw data used in computing coefficient alpha (and in subsequent analyses) were in the form of difference scores. Specifically, for each item a difference score Q (representing perceived quality along that item) was defined as $Q = P - E$, where P and E are the ratings on the corresponding perception and expectation statements, respectively. The idea of using difference scores in purifying a multiple-item scale is not new. This approach has been used in developing scales for measuring constructs such as role conflict (Ford, Walker, and Churchill 1975).

The values of coefficient alpha ranged from .55 to .78 across the 10 dimensions and suggested that deletion of certain items from each dimension would improve the alpha values. The criterion used in deciding whether to delete an item was the item's corrected item-to-total correlation (i.e., correlation between the score on the item and the sum of scores on *all other* items making up the dimensions to which the item was assigned). The corrected item-to-total correlations were plotted in descending order for each dimension. Items with very low correlations and/or those whose correlations produced a sharp drop in the plotted pattern were discarded. Recomputation of alpha values for the reduced sets of statements and examination of the new corrected item-to-total correlations led to further deletion of items whose elimination improved the corresponding alpha values. The iterative sequence of computing alphas and item-to-total correlations, followed by deletion of items, was repeated several times and resulted in a set of 54 items, with alpha values ranging from .72 to .83 across the 10 dimensions.

Examining the dimensionality of the 54-item scale was the next task in this stage of scale purification and was accomplished by factor analyzing the difference scores on the 54 items. The principal axis factoring procedure (Harman 1967) was used and the analysis was constrained *a priori* to 10 factors. When the 10-factor solution was rotated orthogonally, no clear factor pattern emerged. Many of the items had high loadings on several factors, thereby implying that the factors may not be independent of one another. Moreover, some degree of overlap among the 10 conceptual dismensions was anticipated by the researchers who initially identified and labeled the dimensions (Parasuraman, Zeithaml, and Berry 1985). Therefore the 10-factor solution was subjected to oblique rotation (using the OBLIMIN procedure in SPSS-X) to allow for intercorrelations among the dimensions and to facilitate easy interpretation.

The oblique rotation produced a factor-loading matrix that was by and large easy to interpret. However, several items still had high loadings on more than one factor. When such items were removed from the factor-loading matrix, several factors themselves became meaningless because they had near-zero correlations with the remaining items, thereby suggesting a reduction in the presumed dimensionality of the service-quality domain. Furthermore, the highest loadings of a few of the remaining items were on factors to which they were not originally assigned. In other words, the factor loadings suggested reassignment of some items.

The deletion of certain items (and the resultant reduction in the total number of factors or clusters of items) and the reassignment of certain others necessitated the recomputation of alphas and item-to-total correlations and the reexamination of the factor structure of the reduced item pool. This iterative sequence of analyses (Step 5 in Figure 1) was repeated a few times and resulted in a final pool of 34 items representing seven distinct dimensions. The alpha values and factor loadings pertaining to the 34-item instrument are summarized in Table 1.

As shown in Table 1, five of the original 10 dimensions—tangibles, reliability, responsiveness, understanding/knowing customers, and access—remained distinct. The remaining five dimensions—communication, credibility, security, competence, and courtesy—collapsed into two distinct dimensions (D4 and

Table 1 Summary of results from first stage of scale purification

Dimension	Label	Reliability coefficients (alphas)	Number of items	Factor loadings of items on dimensions to which they belong[a]
Tangibles	D1	.72	4	63
				75
				62
				47
Reliability	D2	.83	5	74
				56
				73
				71
				47
Responsiveness	D3	.84	5	60
				73
				59
				76
				66
Communication	D4	.79	4	35
Credibility				53
Security				66
Competence				56
Courtesy	D5	.85	7	41
				62
				47
				50
				75
				52
				54
Understanding/	D6	.85	4	80
Knowing				76
customers				62
				77
Access	D7	.78	5	57
				50
				75
				52
				71
Reliability of linear combination (Total-scale reliability)		.94		

[a] Numbers are the magnitudes of the factor loadings multiplied by 100. The loadings of items on dimensions to which they did not belong were all less than .3. The percentage of variance extracted by the seven factors was 61.7%.

D5), each consisting of items from several of the original five dimensions. The average pairwise correlation among the seven factors following oblique rotation was .27. This relatively low correlation, along with the relatively high factor loadings shown in Table 1, suggested that service quality might have seven fairly unique facets.

The high alpha values indicated good internal consistency among items within each dimension. Moreover, the combined reliability for the 34-item scale, computed by using the formula for the reliability of linear combinations (Nunnally 1978), was quite high (.94). Therefore, the 34-item instrument was considered to be ready for further testing with data from new samples.

Data collection, second stage

To further evaluate the 34-item scale and its psychometric properties, data were collected pertaining to the service quality of four nationally-known firms: a bank, a credit-card company, a firm offering appliance repair and maintenance services, and a long-distance telephone company. For each firm, an independent shopping-mall sample of 200 customers 25 years-of-age or older were recruited by a marketing research firm in a major metropolitan area in the East. To qualify for the study, respondents had to have used the services of the firm in question within the past three months. Each sample was divided about equally between males and females. As in the first stage of data collection, questionnaires were self-administered by qualified respondents.

Scale purification, second stage

A major objective of this stage was to evaluate the robustness of the 34-item scale when used to measure the service quality of the four firms. Therefore the data from each of the four samples were analyzed separately to obtain alpha values (along with corrected item-to-total correlations) and a factor-loading matrix following oblique rotation of a seven-factor solution. The results from each sample facilitated cross-validation of the results from the other samples.

The results of the four sets of analyses were quite consistent, but differed somewhat from the first-stage findings summarized in Table 1. Specifically, two differences emerged. First, the corrected item-to-total correlations for several items (particularly among items making up the dimensions labeled D4 and D7 in Table 1) and the alphas for the corresponding dimensions were lower than those obtained from the first stage. Second, the factor-loading matrices obtained from all four analyses showed much greater overlap between dimensions D4 and D5, and between dimensions D6 and D7. Because these differences occurred consistently across four independent samples and data sets, further purification of the 34-item scale was deemed necessary.

A few items with relatively low item-to-total correlations were deleted. Furthermore, as suggested by the factor analyses, the items remaining in D4 and D5, as well as those in D6 and D7, were combined to form two separate dimensions. For each sample, alpha values were recomputed for the reduced set of five dimensions and a factor analysis (involving extraction of five factors followed by oblique rotation) was performed. In examining the results of these analyses, an iterative sequence similar to the one shown in Step 5 in Figure 1 was followed. This procedure resulted in a refined scale ("SERVQUAL") with 22 items spread among five dimensions (D1, D2, D3, a combination of D4 and D5, and a combination of D6 and D7). The expectation and perception statements in the final SERVQUAL instrument are shown in the appendix.

An examination of the content of the final items making up each of SERVQUAL's five dimensions (three original and two combined dimensions) suggested the following labels and concise definitions for the dimensions:

Tangibles: Physical facilities, equipment, and appearance of personnel
Reliability: Ability to perform the promised service dependably and accurately
Responsiveness: Willingness to help customers and provide prompt service
Assurance: Knowledge and courtesy of employees and their ability to inspire trust and confidence
Empathy: Caring, individualized attention the firm provides its customers

The last two dimensions (assurance and empathy) contain items representing seven original dimensions—communication, credibility, security, competence, courtesy, understanding/knowing customers, and access—that did not remain distinct after the two stages of scale purification. Therefore, while SERV-QUAL has only five distinct dimensions, they capture facets of all 10 originally conceptualized dimensions.

SERVQUAL's Reliability and Factor Structure

Table 2 shows the component and total reliabilities of SERVQUAL for each of the four samples. The reliabilities are consistently high across all four samples, with the possible exception of a couple of values pertaining to the tangible dimension. The total-scale reliability (i.e., reliability of linear combination) is close to .9 in each of the four instances.

Results of the factor analyses of data from the four samples are summarized in Table 3. The overall patterns of factor loadings are remarkably similar across the four independent sets of results. With few exceptions, items assigned to each dimension consistently have high loadings on only one of the five factors extracted. The distinctiveness of SERVQUAL's five dimensions implied by the results in Table 3 was further supported by relatively low intercorrelations among the five factors—the average pairwise correlations between factors following oblique rotation were .21, .24, .26, and .23 for the bank, credit card, repair and maintenance, and long-distance telephone samples, respectively.[1]

As an additional verification of the reliabilities and factor structure of SERVQUAL, the first-stage data set that resulted in the 34-item instrument with seven dimensions was reanalyzed after deleting the 12 items that dropped out during the second stage of scale purification. The results of this reanalysis are summarized in Table 4 and reconfirm the high reliabilities and dimensional distinctiveness of the scale. The average pairwise correlation among the five factors following oblique rotation was .35.

Table 2 Internal consistencies of the five service-quality dimensions following second stage of scale purification

Dimension	Label	Number of items	Samples[a]				Items[b]
			B	CC	R&M	LDT	
Tangibles	F1	4	.52	.62	.64	.64	
Reliability	F2	5	.80	.78	.84	.74	Q5
							Q6
							Q7
							Q8
							Q9
Responsiveness	F3	4	.72	.69	.76	.70	Q10
							Q11
							Q12
							Q13
Assurance	F4	4	.84	.80	.87	.84	Q14
							Q15
							Q16
							Q17
Empathy	F5	5	.71	.80	.72	.76	Q18
							Q19
							Q20
							Q21
							Q22
Reliability of linear combination (Total-scale reliability)			.87	.89	.90	.88	

[a] B = Bank; CC = Credit card company; R&M = Repair and maintenance company; LDT = Long-distance telephone company

[b] The item numbers correspond to those of the expectation and perception statements in the appendix.

It is worth nothing that the interative procedure used to refine the initial instrument was guided by empirical criteria and by the goal of obtaining a concise scale whose items would be meaningful to a variety of service firms. The reliabilities and factor structures indicate that the final 22-item scale and its five dimensions have sound and stable psychometric properties. Moreover, by design, the iterative procedure retained only those items that are common and relevant to all service firms included in the study. However, by the same token, this procedure may have deleted certain "good" items relevant to some but not all firms. Therefore, while SERVQUAL can be used in its present form to assess and compare service quality across a wide variety of firms or units within a firm, appropriate adaptation of the instrument may be desirable when only a single service is investigated. Specifically, items under each of the five dimensions can be suitably reworded and/or augmented to make them more germane to the context in which the instrument is to be used.

Table 3 Factor loading matrices following oblique rotation of five-factor solutions[a]

Factor loadings

	Bank					Credit card company					Repair and maintenance company					L-D telephone company				
Items	F1	F2	F3	F4	F5	F1	F2	F3	F4	F5	F1	F2	F3	F4	F5	F1	F2	F3	F4	F5
Q1	34	28		—	—	36		35			34					42				
Q2	64			—	—	70					70					72				
Q3	39			28	—	52					53	—	—	—	—	51				
Q4	28			28		52					65	—	—	—	—	59			30	
Q5		72					54					73					52			
Q6		63	—				43	27				51					40			
Q7		71	—	—			87					84					79		—	—
Q8		80	—	—	—		83					88					59		—	—
Q9		39	—	—	—		49					29		30			54			
Q10	—	—	37	—	—	—	—	43	—	26	—	—	56	—	—	—	—	39	—	—
Q11	—	—	55	—	—	—	—	48	—	—	—	—	52	—	—	—	—	43	—	—
Q12	—	—	62	—	—	—	—	54	—	—	—	—	74	—	—	—	—	92	—	—
Q13	—	—	69	—	—	—	—	33	—	—	—	—	71	—	—	—	—	53	—	—
Q14	—	—	—	68	—	—	—	—	65	—	—	—	—	86	—	—	—	—	69	—
Q15	—	—	—	84	—	—	—	—	76	—	—	—	—	89	—	—	—	—	81	—
Q16	—	—	—	72	—	—	—	—	73	—	—	—	—	65	—	—	—	—	61	—
Q17	—	—	—	64	—	—	—	—	61	—	—	—	—	64	—	—	—	—	66	—
Q18	—	—	—	—	37	—	—	—	—	64	—	—	—	—	42	—	—	—	—	59
Q19	—	—	—	—	48	—	—	—	—	72	—	—	—	—	61	—	—	—	—	79
Q20	—	—	—	—	41	—	—	—	—	63	—	28	34	—	46	—	—	—	—	55
Q21	—	—	—	—	33	—	—	—	—	59	—	—	—	—	32	—	—	—	—	36
Q22	—	—	—	—	68	—	—	—	—	64	—	—	—	—	61	—	—	—	—	59

[a] All numbers in the table are magnitudes of the factor loadings multiplied by 100. Loadings that are .25 or less are not shown. The percentage of variance extracted by the five factors in the bank, credit card, repair and maintenance, and long-distance telephone samples were 56.0%, 57.5%, 61.6%, and 56.2%, respectively.

Table 4 Reanalysis of first-stage data for the five-dimensional scale

Dimension	Label	Number of items	Reliability coefficients (alphas)	Items	Factor loadings of items on dimensions to which they belong[a]
Tangibles	F1	4	.72	Q1	69
				Q2	68
				Q3	64
				Q4	51
Reliability	F2	5	.83	Q5	75
				Q6	63
				Q7	71
				Q8	75
				Q9	50
Responsiveness	F3		.82	Q10	51
				Q11	77
				Q12	66
				Q13	86
Assurance	F4	4	.81	Q14	38
				Q15	72
				Q16	80
				Q17	45
Empathy	F5		.86	Q18	78
				Q19	81
				Q20	59
				Q21	71
				Q22	68
Reliability of linear combination (Total-scale reliability)			.92		

[a] Numbers are magnitudes of the factor loadings multiplied by 100. The loadings of items on dimensions to which they did not belong were all less than .3. The percentage of variance extracted by the five factors was 63.2%.

Assessment of SERVQUAL's Validity

SERVQUAL's high reliabilities and consistent factor structures across several independent samples provide support for its trait validity (Campbell 1960; Peter 1981). However, while high reliabilities and internal consistencies are necessary conditions for a scale's construct validity—the extent to which a scale fully and unambiguously captures the underlying, unobservable, construct it is intended to measure—they are not sufficient (Churchill 1979). The scale must satisfy certain other conceptual and empirical criteria to be considered as having good construct validity.

The basic conceptual criterion pertaining to construct validity is face or content validity. (Does the scale appear to measure what it is supposed to? Do the scale items capture key facets of the unobservable construct being measured?) Assessing a scale's content validity is necessarily qualitative rather than quantitative. It involves examining two aspects: (1) the thoroughness with which the construct to be scaled and its domain were explicated and (2) the extent to which the scale items represent the construct's domain. As discussed in earlier sections, the procedures used in developing SERVQUAL satisfied both these evaluative requirements. Therefore the scale can be considered to possess content validity.

The scale's validity was also assessed empirically by examining its convergent validity—i.e., the association between SERVQUAL scores and responses to a question that asked customers to provide an overall quality rating of the firm they were evaluating. Respondents in the second stage of data collection rated the service firm's overall quality (referred to hereafter as "Overall Q") by checking one of four categories—excellent, good, fair, poor. The correspondence between the Overall Q ratings and the SERVQUAL scores was examined using one-way ANOVA. The treatment variable in the ANOVA's was Overall Q—with three categories instead of four because very few respondents checked "poor," thereby necessitating creation of a combined "fair/poor" category. The dependent variable was the average difference score (i.e., perception-minus-expectation score) on each SERVQUAL dimension as well as on the total SERVQUAL scale (separate ANOVA's were conducted for each dimension and for the total scale). Significant ANOVA results were investigated further using Duncan's multiple range test to identify significant differences across the Overall Q categories. The results of these analyses for each of the four samples are summarized in Table 5 under the heading "Overall Q".

The numbers reported in Table 5 are average SERVQUAL scores within each Overall Q category, measured on a −6 to +6 scale on which the higher (less negative) the score, the higher is the level of perceived service quality. In each of the four samples, the combined SERVQUAL score for those in the "excellent" category is significantly higher (less negative) than for those in the "good" category. Furthermore, respondents in the "good" category have a significantly higher combined SERVQUAL score than those in the "fair/poor" category. A similar pattern of findings is evident for the scores on the individual SERVQUAL dimensions as well. The strength and persistence of the linkage between the Overall Q categories and the SERVQUAL scores across four independent samples offer strong support for SERVQUAL's convergent validity.

SERVQUAL's validity was further assessed by examining whether the construct measured by it was empirically associated with measures of other conceptually related variables. Respondents in each sample answered two general questions that provided measures of variables (labeled 'Recommend" and "Problem" in Table 5) which one could expect to be related conceptually to perceived service quality: (1) whether the respondents would recommend the service firm to a friend and (2) whether they had ever reported a problem with the services they received from the firm. Respondents answering yes to the first (Recommend) question and no to the second (Problem) question could be hypothesized to perceive higher service quality than other respondents. As Table 5 shows, the results are consistent with this hypothesis. These findings provide additional support for SERVQUAL's validity.

Table 5 Significant differences in mean scale values for respondents – segmented according to the variables overall Q, recommend, and problem[a]

Bank

Individual scale dimensions	Overall Q			Recommend		Problem	
	Excellent	Good	Fair/Poor	Yes	No	Yes	No
Tangibles	−0.04[b]	−0.52[c]	−1.08[d]	−0.41[b]	−0.98[c]	−0.75[b]	−0.45[b]
Reliability	−0.25[b]	−0.96[c]	−2.30[d]	−0.82[b]	−2.21[c]	−1.55[b]	−0.92[c]
Responsiveness	−0.32[b]	−0.97[c]	−1.54[c]	−0.74[b]	−1.81[c]	−1.22[b]	−0.84[b]
Assurance	−0.49[b]	−1.03[c]	−1.98[d]	−0.88[b]	−2.12[c]	−1.52[b]	−0.96[c]
Empathy	−0.30[b]	−1.02[c]	−1.52[c]	−0.76[b]	−1.88[c]	−1.07[b]	−0.91[b]
Combined scale	−0.22[b]	−0.92[c]	−1.61[d]	−0.72[b]	−1.77[c]	−1.22[b]	−0.80[c]
Sample size	46	112	40	164	33	47	151

Credit card company

Individual scale dimensions	Overall Q			Recommend		Problem	
	Excellent	Good	Fair/Poor	Yes	No	Yes	No
Tangibles		−0.61[c]	−0.79[c]	−0.39[b]	−0.80[b]	−0.76[b]	−0.29[c]
Reliability		−0.94[c]	−2.32[d]	−0.82[b]	−2.50[c]	−1.42[b]	−0.82[c]
Responsiveness		−1.13[c]	−1.71[c]	−0.75[b]	−2.59[c]	−1.31[b]	−0.77[c]
Assurance		−1.31[c]	−2.29[d]	−1.08[b]	−2.83[c]	−1.49[b]	−1.15[b]
Empathy		−1.38[c]	−1.94[c]	−1.03[b]	−2.77[c]	−1.62[b]	−1.01[b]
Combined scale		−1.10[c]	−1.79[d]	−0.83[b]	−2.27[c]	−1.29[b]	−0.83[c]
Sample size		112	28	183	17	50	149

Repair and maintenance company

Individual scale dimensions	Overall Q			Recommend		Problem	
	Excellent	Good	Fair/Poor	Yes	No	Yes	No
Tangibles		−0.40[b,c]	−0.86[c]	−0.36[b]	−0.85[b]	−0.58[b]	−0.34[b]
Reliability		−1.30[c]	−3.20[d]	−1.14[b]	−3.48[c]	−2.14[b]	−1.18[c]
Responsiveness		−1.08[c]	−2.41[d]	−0.83[b]	−2.54[c]	−1.71[b]	−0.80[c]
Assurance		−1.35[c]	−2.84[d]	−1.16[b]	−2.91[c]	−2.04[b]	−1.13[c]
Empathy		−1.11[c]	−2.17[d]	−0.85[b]	−2.19[c]	−1.67[b]	−0.74[c]
Combined scale		−1.07[c]	−2.30[d]	−0.88[b]	−2.40[c]	−1.65[b]	−0.85[c]
Sample size		114	40	168	30	65	132

Long-distance telephone company

Individual scale dimensions	Overall Q			Recommend		Problem	
	Excellent		Fair/Poor	Yes	No	Yes	No
Tangibles	−0.08[b]	−0.44[c]	−0.50[c]	−0.26[b]	−0.95[c]	−0.42[b]	−0.26[b]

Reliability	-0.45^b	-1.42^c	-2.53^d	-1.05^b	-2.71^c	-1.54^b	-1.03^c
Responsiveness	-0.30^b	-1.43^c	-1.90^c	-1.00^b	-2.03^c	-1.46^b	-0.86^c
Assurance	-0.39^b	-1.45^c	-2.10^d	-1.00^b	-2.64^c	-1.62^b	-0.87^c
Empathy	-0.33^b	-1.19^c	-2.10^d	-0.86^b	-2.34^c	-1.16^b	-0.90^b
Combined Scale	-0.30^b	-1.15^c	-1.83^d	-0.83^b	-2.13^c	-1.24^b	-0.76^c
Sample Size	69	104	25	178	19	78	120

[a] Numbers are *mean values* on a scale ranging from −6 to +6, on which zero implies that consumer perceptions and expectations coincide, negative values imply that perceptions fall short of expectations, and positive values imply that perceptions exceed expectations.
[b,c,d] Means with the *same* superscripts are not significantly different. Means with *different* superscripts are significantly different.

Applications of SERVQUAL

It is difficult to identify any retailer that offers no services whatsoever. Some retailers offer facilitating services, such as sales assistance and delivery, to help sell goods. Some retailers sell services directly, in addition to offering facilitating services. Some retailers sell only services. Quality of service is an important issue for all of these retailers. Competing goods retailers (department stores, supermarkets) may sell many identical products and quality of service is a primary means of competitive differentiation. Retailers that sell only services (telephone companies, airlines) have little to offer if their service is poor (Berry 1986).

SERVQUAL is a concise multiple-item scale with good reliability and validity that retailers can use to better understand the service expectations and perceptions of consumers and, as a result, improve service. The instrument has been designed to be applicable across a broad spectrum of services. As such, it provides a basic skeleton through its expectations/perceptions format encompassing statements for each of the five service-quality dimensions. The skeleton, when necessary, can be adapted or supplemented to fit the characteristics or specific research needs of a particular organization.

SERVQUAL is most valuable when it is used periodically to track service quality trends, and when it is used in conjunction with other forms of service quality measurement. A retailer, for example, would learn a great deal about its service quality and what needs to be done to improve it by administering both SERVQUAL and an employee survey three or four times a year, plus systematically soliciting and analyzing customer suggestions and complaints. The employee survey should include questions concerning perceived impediments to better service, e.g., what is the biggest problem you face trying to deliver high-quality service to your customers? If you could be president for a day, what one change would you make in the company to improve quality of service?

SERVQUAL can be used to assess a given firm's quality along each of the five service dimensions by averaging the difference scores on items making up the dimension. It can also provide an overall measure of service quality in the form of an average score across all five dimensions. Because meaningful responses to the perception statements require respondents to have some knowledge of or experience with the firm being researched, SERVQUAL is limited to current or past customers of that firm. Within this constraint, a variety of potential applications are available.

One potential application of SERVQUAL is to determine the *relative importance* of the five dimensions in influencing customers' overall quality perceptions. An approach for doing this is to regress the overall quality perception scores on the SERVQUAL scores for the individual dimensions. The results of such a regression analysis for the four companies in the present study are shown in Table 6 (the dependent variable was Overall Q, coded as excellent = 4, good = 3, fair = 2, and poor = 1).

The adjusted R^2 values are statistically significant in all four cases and are also quite respectable, particularly in view of the fact that the dependent variable had only four categories, and the first three accounted for most of the responses. A striking result in terms of the relative importance of the five dimensions in predicting overall quality is that reliability is consistently the most critical dimension. Assurance is the second most important dimension in all four cases. Tangibles is more important in the case of the bank than in the other three firms, while the reverse is true for responsiveness. Empathy is the least important dimension in all

Table 6   Relative importance of the five dimensions in predicting overall quality

Dimension	Standardized slope coefficient	Significance level of slope[a]	Adjusted R^2
Bank			
Tangibles	.13	.07	.28 ($p < .00$)
Reliability	.39	.00	
Responsiveness	.07	.35	
Assurance	.13	.09	
Empathy	.01	.89	
Credit card company			
Tangibles	.07	.26	.27 ($p < .00$)
Reliability	.33	.00	
Responsiveness	.12		
Assurance	.17	.02	
Empathy	.04	.58	
Repair & maintenance company			
Tangibles	.04	.48	.52 ($p < .00$)
Reliability	.54	.00	
Responsiveness	.11	.09	
Assurance	.16	.02	
Empathy	.01	.81	
L-D telephone company			
Tangibles	.08	.17	.37 ($p < .00$)
Reliability	.45	.00	
Responsiveness	.12	.09	
Assurance	.15	.03	
Empathy	.02	.78	

[a] Significance levels are for two-tailed tests.

four cases. However, the relatively small magnitudes of the regression coefficients for empathy and their lack of statistical significance should be interpreted with caution because empathy did have a statistically significant simple correlation with overall quality, ranging from .20 in the case of the bank to .40 in the case of the repair and maintenance company. Empathy also had significant correlations of the same order of magnitude with reliability and assurance (the two most important dimensions), thereby implying that its importance in the regression analyses may have been masked somewhat by possible multicollinearity. Therefore, while empathy is apparently the least important of the five SERVQUAL dimensions, it is by no means *un*important.

Another application of the instrument is its use in categorizing a firm's customers into several perceived-quality segments (e.g., high, medium, and low) on the basis of their individual SERVQUAL scores. These segments then can be analyzed on the basis of (1) demographic, psychographic and/or other profiles; (2) the relative importance of the five dimensions in influencing service quality perceptions; and (3) the reasons behind the perceptions reported. For example, suppose a department store found that a large number of SERVQUAL respondents falling in the "medium" perceived-quality group fit its prime target market based on demographic and psychographic criteria. Suppose further that reliability and assurance were found to be the most important quality dimensions and, based on perception-exception gap scores for items concerning these dimensions, the items relating to record-keeping accuracy and behavior of contact personnel revealed the biggest gaps. With these data, the department store's management would understand better what needs to be done to improve its image in the eyes of a very important group—customers within the firm's prime target market who give the firm "medium" service quality scores and who are in position to either respond to improved service from the firm or defect to the competition.

SERVQUAL can also be used by multi-unit retail companies to track the level of service provided by each store in the chain. By asking respondents to indicate the particular store in the chain with which they are most familiar, and to provide perception responses for that unit, the researcher can compare each store's average SERVQUAL score with the scores from other stores. Service quality scores can then be a factor in store manager performance appraisals and compensation, among other uses. Also, SERVQUAL scores for the individual stores can be used to group outlets into several clusters with varying quality images. A careful examination of the characteristics of the stores in the different clusters may reveal key attributes that facilitate—or hinder—the delivery of high quality service.

A retailer can also use SERVQUAL to assess its service performance relative to its principal competitors. The two-section format of the instrument, with separate expectation and perception sections, makes it convenient to measure the quality of several firms simply by including a set of perception statements for each firm. The expectations section does not have to be repeated for each firm. For example, a supermarket chain could include its two principal competitors in a total market survey, asking respondents to provide perception ratings for each of the companies with which they have shopping experience. A retailer that uses

SERVQUAL to identify the most salient service quality dimensions for its target markets, and to compare itself to the competition in terms of strengths and weaknesses on these particular dimensions, will certainly have a sense of what its priorities should be with regard to service quality.

In summary, SERVQUAL has a variety of potential applications. It can help a wide range of service and retailing organizations in assessing consumer expectations about and perceptions of service quality. It can also help in pinpointing areas requiring managerial attention and action to improve service quality. In addition, we hope the availability of this instrument will stimulate much-needed empirical research focusing on service quality and its antecedents and consequences.

Note

1   Complete matrices of the interfactor correlations can be obtained from the first author.

References

Berry, Leonard L. (1986), "Retail Businesses Are Service Businesses," *Journal of Retailing*, **62** (Spring), 3–6.

Campbell, Donald T. (1960), "Recommendations for APA Test Standards Regarding Construct, Trait, or Discriminant Validity," *American Psychologist*, **15** (August), 546–553.

Churchill, Gilbert A., Jr. (1979), "A Paradigm for Developing Better Measures of Marketing Constructs," *Journal of Marketing Research*, **16** (February), 64–73.

Churchill, Gilbert A., Jr., Neil M. Ford, and Orville C. Walker, Jr. (1974), "Measuring the Job Satisfaction of Industrial Salesmen," *Journal of Marketing Research*, **11** (August), 254–260.

Cronbach, Lee J. (1951), "Coefficient Alpha and the Internal Structure of Tests," *Psychometrika*, **16** (October), 297–334.

Crosby, Philip B. (1979), *Quality is Free: The Art of Making Quality Certain*, New York: New American Library.

Dodds, William B. and Kent B. Monroe (1984), "The Effect of Brand and Price Information on Subjective Product Evaluations," *Advances in Consumer Research XII*.

Ford, Neil M., Orville C. Walker, Jr., and Gilbert A. Churchill, Jr. (1975), "Expectation-Specific Measures of the Intersender Conflict and Role Ambiguity Experienced by Industrial Salesmen," *Journal of Business Research*, **3** (April), 95–112.

Garvin, David A. (1983), "Quality on the Line," *Harvard Business Review*, **61** (September-October), 65–73.

Gronroos, Christian (1982), *Strategic Management and Marketing in the Service Sector*, Helsingfors: Swedish School of Economics and Business Administration.

Harman, Harry H. (1967), *Modern Factor Analysis*, 2nd ed., Chicago, IL: The University of Chicago Press.

Hjorth-Anderson, Chr. (1984), "The Concept of Quality and the Efficiency of Markets for Consumer Products," *Journal of Consumer Research*, **11** (September), 708–718.

Holbrook, Morris B. and Kim P. Corfman (1985), "Quality and Value in the Consumption Experience: Phaldrus Rides Again," in *Perceived Quality*, J. Jacoby and J. Olson (eds.), Lexington, MA: Lexington Books, 31–57.

Howard, John and Jagdish Sheth (1969), *The Theory of Buyer Behavior*, New York: John Wiley and Sons.

Hunt, Keith (1979), *Conceptualization and Measurement of Consumer Satisfaction and Dissatisfaction*, Cambridge, MA: Marketing Science Institute.

Jacoby, Jacob (1978), "Consumer Research: A State of the Art Review," *Journal of Marketing*, **42** (April), 87–96.

Jacoby, J. and J. Olson, eds. (1985), *Perceived Quality*, Lexington, MA: Lexington Books.

Lehtinen, Uolevi and Jarmo R. Lehtinen (1982), "Service Quality: A Study of Quality Dimensions," unpublished working paper, Helsinki: Service Management Institute, Finland OY.

Lovelock, Christopher H. (1980), 'Towards a Classification of Services," in *Emerging Perspectives on Services Marketing*, L. L. Berry, G. L. Shostack, and G. Upah (eds.), Chicago: American Marketing Association, 72–76.

——— (1983), "Classifying Services to Gain Strategic Marketing Insights," *Journal of Marketing*, 47 (Summer), 9–20.

Nunnally, Jum C. (1978), *Psychometric Theory*, 2nd ed., New York: McGraw-Hill Book Company.

Oliver, Richard (1981), "Measurement and Evaluation of Satisfaction Process in Retail Settings," *Journal of Retailing*, **57** (Fall), 25–48.

Olshavsky, Richard W. (1985), "Perceived Quality in Consumer Decision Making: An Integrated Theoretical Perspective," in *Perceived Quality*, J. Jacoby and J. Olson (eds.), Lexington, MA: Lexington Books.

Parasuraman, A., Valarie Zeithaml, and Leonard Berry (1985), "A Conceptual Model of Service Quality and Its Implications for Future Research," *Journal of Marketing* (Fall), 41–50.

Peter, J. Paul (1981), "Construct Validity: A Review of Basic Issues and Marketing Practices," *Journal of Marketing Research*, **18** (May), 133–145.

Rudie, Mary, J. and H. Brant Wansley (1985), "The Merrill Lynch Quality Program," in *Services Marketing in a Changing Environment*, Thomas Bloch, Gregory Upah, and Valarie A. Zeithaml (eds.), Chicago, IL: American Marketing Association.

Sasser, W. Earl, Jr., R. Paul Olsen, and D. Daryl Wyckoff (1978), *Management of Service Operations: Text and Cases*, Boston, MA: Allyn & Bacon.

Saxe, Robert and Barton A. Weitz (1982), "The SOCO Scale: A Measure of the Customer Orientation of Salespeople," *Journal of Marketing*, **19** (August), 343–351.

Thompson, Phillip, Glenn DeSouza, and Bradley T. Gale (1985), *The Strategic Management of Service Quality*, Cambridge, MA: The Strategic Planning Institute, PIMSLETTER No. 33.

Zeithaml, Valarie (1987), *Defining and Relating Price, Perceived Quality, and Perceived Value*, Report No. 87–101, Cambridge, MA: Marketing Science Institute.

Editor's Commentary

JOHN F. SHERRY IS the Raymond W. and Kenneth G. Herrick Professor of Marketing at the Mendoza College of Business, University of Notre Dame, a post he took up in 2005, returning to his alma mater, from where he had obtained his undergraduate degree in English and anthropology in 1974. He was formerly Professor of Marketing in the Kellogg Graduate School of Management at Northwestern University, a university he joined in 1984 after being at the University of Florida. He has also spent time as a Visiting Professor at the Katholieke Universiteit Leuven and Chulalongkorn University in Bangkok. Using his anthropological training (he has a PhD in this field from the University of Illinois at Urbana-Champaign) John Sherry has focused on understanding culture, consumption and marketing. His writing is mainly in the consumer research field and journals but he has published widely in the *Journal of Retailing*. Both his consumption and anthropology interests are reflected in his positions as President of the Association for Consumer Research in 1998 and as a Fellow of the American Anthropological Association.

John Sherry has made a significant mark on the field of retailing and consumption. His work has been on the proximate and familiar, western shopping malls and spaces, but also includes a wide range of spaces of consumption, including swap meets, farmers' markets, flea markets and periodic markets. He makes the usual unusual as he explores unseen dimensions of retail spaces and their meanings through a post-modernist cultural lens.

The chapter 'The Soul of the Company Store: Nike Town Chicago and the Emplaced Brandscape' appeared in a book that John Sherry edited, entitled *Servicescapes: The Concept of Place in Contemporary Markets*. The book reflects Sherry's long time interest in markets and sites of consumption. The chapter comes in the first section of the volume, which is concerned with the cognitive, cultural and experiential aspects of the built environment. It tries to understand the experience of being in the marketplace through the ways in which the Nike brand is used to create a place, captured in the introduced concept of 'brandscape'. This qualitative, more culturally oriented reading of retailing and retailing space has generated a considerable body of similarly oriented work in a variety of retail situations.

Key Publications

Belk R, Sherry JF and Wallendorf M (1988) A naturalistic enquiry into buyer and seller behavior at a swap meet. *Journal of Consumer Research*, 14, 449–470.

Belk R, Wallendorf M and Sherry J (1989) The sacred and the profane in consumer behaviour – theodicy on the odyssey. *Journal of Consumer Research*, 16, 1–38.

Sherry JF (1990) A sociocultural analysis of a Midwestern American flea market. *Journal of Consumer Research*, 17, 13–30.

Sherry JF (1990) Dealers and dealing in a periodic market – informal retailing in ethnographic perspective. *Journal of Retailing*, 66, 174–200.

Sherry JF (1991) Postmodern alternatives: the interpretive turn in consumer research. In T Robertson and H Kassarjian (eds) *Handbook of Consumer Behavior*. Englewood Cliffs, NJ: Prentice Hall, 548–591.

Sherry JF, McGrath M and Levy S (1992) The disposition of the gift and many unhappy returns. *Journal of Retailing*, 68, 40–65.

McGrath MA, Sherry JF and Heisley DD (1993) An ethnographic study of an urban periodic marketplace: lessons from the Midville Farmers' Market. *Journal of Retailing,* 69, 280–319.

Sherry JF (ed) (1998) *Servicescapes: the Concept of Place in Contemporary Markets.* Lincolnwood, IL: NTC Business Books.

Kozinets R, Sherry JF, DeBerry-Spence B, Duhachek A, Nuttavuthisit K and Storm D (2002) Themed flagship brand stores in the new millennium. *Journal of Retailing,* 78, 17–29.

Sherry JF (2003) Teaching old brands new tricks: retro branding and the revival of brand meaning. *Journal of Marketing,* 67, 3, 19–33.

Brown S and Sherry JF (2003) *Time, Space and the Market: Retroscapes Rising.* New York: M.E. Sharpe.

Kozinets J, Sherry JF, Storm D, Duhachek A, Nuttavuthisit K and DeBerry-Spence B (2004) Ludic agency and retail spectacle. *Journal of Consumer Research,* 31, 658–672.

Sherry JF, Kozinets J, Duhachek A, DeBerry-Spence, Nuttavuthisit K and Storm D, (2004) Gendered behaviour in a male preserve: role playing at ESPN Zone Chicago. *Journal of Consumer Psychology,* 14, 151–158.

Belk R and Sherry JF (2007) *Consumer Culture Theory.* Greenwich, CT: Jai Press.

Website

http://www.nd.edu/~jsherry/

THE SOUL OF THE COMPANY STORE: NIKE TOWN CHICAGO AND THE EMPLACED BRANDSCAPE

John F. Sherry, Jr.

But before there could be wonder (or theory, or philosophy, or architectral treatises), there had to be the well-made thing.

—McEwen (1993)

[Nike Town Chicago is] built as a theater, where our consumers are the audience participating in the production. Nike Town gives us the opportunity to explore and experiment with innovative ways to connect with our consumers.

NTC (1992a)

From John F. Sherry (ed.) (1988) *Servicescapes: the Concept of Place in Contemporary Markets.* Lincolnwood, IL: NTC Business Books, 109–146. Copyright © 1998 by NTC/Contemporary Publishing Company. All rights reserved.

John F. Sherry, Jr., is Professor of Marketing at the J. L. Kellogg Graduate School of Management, Northwestern University, Evanston, Illinois. The author would like to thank Jennifer Chang, Morris Holbrook, Sidney Levy, and Victor Margolin for their helpful comments on earlier versions of this manuscript.

Fuck the world. Fuck the numbers. Air feels right. Air feels like Nike.
—Strasser and Becklund (1993)

IF WE ACKNOWLEDGE THE existence of an "ancestral blood tie between architecture and philosophy" (McEwen 1993, 2), then Nike Town Chicago (NTC) is surely the embodiment of the corporate dictum "Just Do It." As this tagline—part New Age mantra, part secular ejaculation—has been embroidered into the fabric of adcult (Twitchell 1996), so also has the building expanded our notion of alternative translations of retail space. With the exception of pricing strategy, every designed element of the servicescape encourages impulsive behavior and invites instant gratification.[1] NTC is perhaps the most current incarnation of a retail theater alive to the liturgical roots of drama. A paean to design, NTC crosscuts genres of experience to evoke in consumers a range of synergistic thoughts, emotions, and behaviors that encourages active engagement with its servicescape. NTC is not merely the site of "commercial athleticism" (Agnew 1986), nor is it solely a "spiritual gymnasium" (Mandel 1967, 16) or "cathedral of consumption" (O'Guinn and Belk 1989). Neither is it primarily an amusement-centered themed environment (Gottdiener 1996) nor a megaboutique. While this chapter explores the polysemous possibilities the site affords, I begin, as is my custom, with a vignette drawn from my field notes, which I regard as a revelatory incident (Fernandez 1986) opening a window onto the phenomenology of this marketplace:

> Even in the company of key informants, I find myself shifting from the role of social scientist to flaneur [perhaps tending toward *dériveur?*] and back again, as I watch consumers watch me watch them watch their surroundings [note: revisit Benjamin's optical unconscious], trying all the while to attend to the observations of my interviewees without allowing my own engagement with the place to mute their comments.
>
> Don and Larry, two entrepreneurs in their mid-thirties, have invited me to accompany them on their visit to Nike Town Chicago, even though we have just met here on the spot. Each is an industrial designer, and together they create, restore, and market religious goods. As we wander, Larry speaks of the "mystical" quality of the setting, and compares NTC to a "basilica." Don compares his experience of NTC to being in a "museum," observing that "when you 'do' Chicago, you go to the Museum of Science and Industry, the Art Institute, and Nike Town." [Many of my informants are quick to proclaim the "accepted fact" that Nike Town is the "biggest tourist attraction" in the city.] Building on this remark, Larry allows that the building is more than a museum: "It's a museum of the future. You never have to remodel. George Jetson could pull up outside and never tell the difference!" Don supports his contention with an expansive arm gesture: "Look at all these parents showing their kids around; they're *teaching*. Just like a museum."
>
> The two have come to NTC today not to shop, but to study the

store, in particular its products and their merchandising. They are keenly aware of the synergies between their own enterprise and Nike's. They've come for "inspiration" and "ideas." Beyond their reverence for the sacral tones of the ambience lies an even more intriguing respect for the products on display. In Don's estimation, "This all speaks to the integrity of their products. If you spend so much effort to showcase your product, it must be really good. They've paid attention to every detail—from door handles and railings to sound effects. They try to reach all your senses. Even the salespeople are low-key. There's no sales pressure." As if to sum up his evaluation of the NTC servicescape, Larry concludes. "There's a carryover effect. Next time I see Nike products in a regular store, I'll recall this good experience." As our conversation unfolds, I notice each of them actively engage the environment, handling products, touching fixtures, closing eyes, and cocking heads to discriminate background sounds, and scanning constantly. They are curiously hypervigilant and yet relaxed, as they absorb the grand design.

I have selected this introductory vignette because it resonates with my own experience of the store and intuitions about the affecting nature of servicescapes. The field note addresses the influence of the designed environment on brand equity in general and on the more numinous dimensions of brand identity in particular. Elsewhere (Sherry 1995a, 36), I have called attention to an obverse strategy of the one McCracken (1988, 105–106) has called "meaning displacement." I think of this strategy as one of *emplacement*, whereby culture instantiates the mundane "by encoding its folk-ways in holographic fashion into the material vehicles of social life, to be recovered discontinuously, and often outside conscious awareness" (Sherry 1995a, 36). Emplacement is at work on a molecular level as well, when a corporation embodies its vision not only in the product it makes, but also in the other elements of its marketing mix. Integrated marketing communication (Schultz, Tanneubaum, and Lauterborn 1994), for example, is a manifestation of the emplacement process writ small.

The delight inspired in consumers by their discovery of the larger significance of a corporation's attention to detail—the "aha" experience or epiphany that occurs in the unwrapping of unanticipated added value—shapes relationships developed with a brand. Emplacement is especially intriguing in an era of eroding brand loyalty and "cereal monogamy" (Sherry 1985), when place increasingly becomes (de facto if not de jure) the brand (Sherry 1995b). So it is with NTC, where brand is both a noun and a verb. Consumers are invited to enhance their brandscape through engagement with this polysemous environment.

A brandscape is a "material and symbolic environment that consumers build with marketplace products, images and messages, that they invest with local meaning, and whose totemic significance largely shapes the adaptation consumers make to the modern world" (Sherry 1985). Brandscaping is one of the ways in which consumption is actively produced by consumers. Emplacement and brandscaping act in tandem to ground or root a consumer's experience in the artifact, while at the same time allowing the artifact to become a projectible field or projective vehicle for culturally mediated idiosyncratic meaning. The cocreation of experience by marketers and consumers—the performance of negotiated meanings—is engendered in NTC by design.[2] Whether or not they are shoppers, once inside the doors of NTC, consumers become flaneurs and *bricaleurs*.

In this chapter, I explore the interaction of emplacement and brandscaping by focusing on the experience that design conspires to elicit from visitors to NTC. By attending to design cues and affordances provided by the marketer, and observing the effects their reception exerts upon consumers, I highlight aspects of the NTC servicescape that are illustrative of the affecting presence (Armstrong 1974) that all marketplaces become when extraeconomic issues are considered.

Methodology

This account is a lineal descendant of the wave of ethnographic investigations of periodic markets and upscale specialty stores (McGrath 1989; McGrath, Sherry, and Heisley 1993; Sherry 1990a, 1990b; Sherry and McGrath 1989) that has contributed to the rejuvenation of retailing studies in recent years. It is a collateral relative of the renewed exploration of museums and galleries (Duhaime, Joy, and Ross 1995; McCracken 1990) that is helping consumer researchers better understand the experiential dimensions of servicescapes. After Buttimer (1993, 202), I attempt to "read" vernacular architecture "as text to be decoded in terms of the values of its human inhabitants." In temperament, this account is a hybrid effort that seeks to combine something of the studied alienation of ethnographic inquiry (Sherry 1995) with something of the disciplined reflexiveness of introspection (Gould 1991; Holbrook 1988a, 1988b; Rose 1995; Sherry 1996). I intend the result to be somewhere between the unreflectively critical, idiosyncratic tradition of cultural studies and the conventionally dispassionate stakeholder-focus of ethnographic consumer research. What I strive to produce in this chapter is a phenomenological account of my own engagement with a particular marketplace hedged about with observations and interpretations drawn from other participants in process of enacting the services cape. In tacking between self and other. I construct an account that is at once "producerly" (Sherry 1990b) and grounded in "reader-response" (Scott 1994). In conveying my own experience of "being-in-the-marketplace" (Richardson 1987; Sherry and McGrath 1989) in tandem with that of fellow consumers, I offer a perspective that is comparative rather than privileged, and probative rather than definitive.

I began this investigation in the summer of 1992 and have continued to visit the site through the autumn of 1996, the time this chapter was written.[3] During this prolonged engagement. I immersed myself in the round of life at the marketplace, gaining an appreciation for the seasonal flux of activity and variety of stakeholder perspectives (Sherry 1990). I employed participant observation extensively throughout the study. I conducted intercept interviews with fifty consumers and observed hundreds of others in their encounter with the servicescape. Interviews ranged from ten minutes to an hour, and from highly unstructured to structured. I shopped with consumers (Otnes, McGrath, and Lowrey 1995) and loitered with intent among clerks and cashiers, interviewing in context. Structured interviews were conducted with the store manager, marketing manager, and various staff members. I photographed dimensions of the servicescape and conducted autodriving interviews (Heisley and Levy 1991; Rook 1989) with some consumers.

Concurrently with the ethnography, and cognizant both of the risks (Wallendorf and Brucks 1993) and rewards of intraceptive intuition (Murray 1943; Sherry 1991). I practiced what Holbrook has called "subjective personal introspection" (Holbrook 1988a, 1988b), in an effort to capture my own experience of NTC. Thus, what follows is a composite account, and an inevitable confounding of emic and etic perspectives, of the NTC servicescape. While it may well be that the lawyer who defends himself has a fool for a client, I suspect that many social scientists resonate with poet Gary Snyder's (Tarn 1972) discovery that he'd rather be an informant than an anthropologist. In this essay, I attempt just such a shift in perspective.

Managerial Précis

NTC, the second in a series of seven company stores launched to date, opened in Chicago in the summer of 1992. Designed in-house by Gordon Thompson, the 68,000-square-foot store boasts three selling floors and eighty feet of frontage on the "Magnificent Mile" of Michigan Avenue. The store is designed to deliver a "landmark experience," comparable to "enter[ing] Wrigley Field or hop[ping] on a ride at Disneyland" (NTC 1992a). The NTC "retail theater" concept is intended to combine "the fun of Disneyland and FAO Schwarz, the museum quality of the Smithsonian Institution and the merchandising of Ralph Lauren with the sights and sounds associated with MTV" (NTC 1992b). The store comprises eighteen pavilions that display products related to twenty different sports. Before I present an ethnographic overview of the built environment and experiential dimensions of NTC, it may be instructive to provide an account of the store from the perspective of its principal managers.

Marketing managers envision NTC as a "showcase" for the range of Nike products local dealers are not able to stock as comprehensively or merchandise as effectively. NTC dramatizes the breadth and depth of the Nike product mix. This presentation is expected to benefit dealers. NTC observes a policy of "non-competition" with dealers, in an effort to be "sensitive" to their livelihoods. NTC does not run sales, does not have exclusive or advance availability of product, and offers training in merchandising to dealers in an effort to export the essence of Nikeworld. NTC exists strategically to enhance the brand without alienating dealers.

Consumers appear to respond to this strategy. Among the most common unelicited product-related consumer comments in my field notes reflect amazement both at the range of products and the premium pricing at NTC. Variations of "I didn't know Nike made this much stuff or was into this many sports!" compete with "Do you believe this [price]? I can get this much cheaper at home!" in my record of emic evaluations. Customers and staff readily acknowledge that "new" products encountered in NTC are eventually ordered through local dealers.

Marketing managers describe their concession to dealers—the emphasis on equity building over sales—as a "museum" (versus a "warehouse") strategy.

While headquarters ultimately dictates objectives and evaluates end results, the regional Nike Town marketing managers are encouraged to innovate within a standardized pattern. Designers of these servicescapes eschew a cookie-cutter approach to design, and are invited to combine common elements and modules with local touches to "fit the space" the stores must occupy. At NTC, marketing managers have "wide parameters" for meeting "budget constraints" and revel in the "individual initiative" that the "loose organization" of their "creative company" permits. "Just Do It" is treated as a mandate for "entrepreneurial initiative." Managers and clerks alike speak of "shooting from the hip" in pursuit of servicescape refinement.

A Note on Brand Equity: Mythology and Soul

At the time of this writing, the Nike "swoosh" logo has become so thoroughly identified with the brand that it is iconic. The company name no longer must accompany the mark to achieve recognition among consumers. The symbol and the brand are one. Serendipity and heroic marketing have conspired to produce this iconicity.

The "swoosh" name is derived from the Japanese nylon fabric that gave the company its original distinctive edge. The swoosh symbol—commissioned for thirty-five dollars from a young artist—was designed to combine structural functionality with visibility. Initial corporate reception of the logo was lukewarm. The Nike name was adopted after the logo was designed, as an expedient compromise in the face of deadline pressure. The name was inspired by an awakening dream of a company saleman—an anthropology graduate student turned social worker—and again received a lukewarm initial response (Strasser and Becklund 1993). The correspondence of name and symbol with mythology—the wings of Victory, the talaria (winged sandal) of Hermes—and of mythopoeia with onomatopoeia, has been achieved through marketing.

Over time, the logo has been refreshed to emphasize the company's commitment to quality and innovation in design. The company's "discovery" of marketing, and its pursuit of integrated marketing communication (of the "There Is No Finish Line" kind) dates from the historic brand-from-a-brand launch of the Air Jordan line – complete with the Jump Man trademark, which itself has achieved global iconicity – that was commemorated by the launch director (and author of this chapter's third epigraph) in these prescient words: "On this rock . . . we will build a church" (Strasser and Becklund 1993, 455). While the marketing director was eventually exorcised from the firm before the building of NTC, his New Testament diction was strategically prophetic. Principal among the many meanings of NTC is that of sacred space. NTC is not merely emblematic of the sacralization of sport in America, nor of our recently recovered awareness of its eroticization (Guttmann 1996). It is a basilica of basketball, complete with reliquaries, and monumental witness to the apotheosis of Michael Jordan.[4]

Ethnographic Overview

In the following pages. I provide an ethnographic overview of NTC phenomenology. I begin with a description of the larger retail environment of the store and devote attention to the building's exterior. I then undertake a sort of "walking tour" of the interior of the store, discussing the ambient surroundings and exploring reactions to them. I employ the pontifical *we* and address the reader rhetorically, as a fellow traveler. Finally, I offer an interpretive summary of the NTC experience.

Let me begin this section with another field note excerpt, to remind the reader of the emic input that has shaped my own perceptions:

> So many informants profess to have come to NTC "not to buy something," but to "see" it, whether on their own, with family and friends, or with out-of-town guests, because it is "more than just a store." A teenage boy describes the "peaceful feeling" elicited by the "music and colors" of the surroundings and likens his experience to being in an "amusement park" or "museum." He tells me he "sees things [products] here [he] doesn't see in other stores." "Maybe I'll buy something, but I came here because Dad wanted to see it." Consumers seem not to search or browse so much as inspect the store. [Note: explore the commercio-aesthetic dynamic of the visual at NTC. Revisit Urry on the tourist gaze.]
>
> Marie and Anna, two "out-of-town" women in their early twenties, have come to NTC specifically to buy sports shoes in their "hard to find" sizes, and graciously allow me to shop with them. "I come right to the source," proclaims Marie, a former basketball player, in describing her decision to shop NTC. "It's amazing how they draw you up four stories," Anna offers. "The open heights, the use of space . . . You're *up* here, on the same level . . . It's like a fantasy. There's the player, there's the player's shoe, there's the shoe for sale—it's all together. It's like a shrine." The immediacy produced by such vertically integrated merchandising is palpable for these two shoppers. Notes Marie, "The store changes with the sports. If there's a development in the sport, it shows up in the store. They constantly change the pictures and exhibits." As we continue to examine shoes, Anna concludes, "It's amazing. It's hard to verbalize. It makes you feel like you can 'do it.' " "Yeah," agrees Marie. "I was a player. I like the court. You can pretend to dunk." Even though physically present with me and their purchases, the women each wander a field of dreams, dwelling in an Erehwon of athletic accomplishment not bounded by the walls of NTC.

Cultural Geography of NTC: Location, Location, Location

A significant measure of the experience NTC affords consumers derives from its prestigious location on "the Boule Mich," a celebrated stretch of North Michigan

Avenue also known as "the Magnificent Mile." NTC is flanked by a range of upscale retail outlets and galleries. The art-and-commerce ambience of this setting is not reflected solely in discrete and distinctive offerings by specialized shops. Rather, the effect is heightened by the kind of hybridized merchandising that gives NTC its own particular appeal, and the architectural diversity for which Chicago is renowned.

Facing north from the NTC entrance, the consumer's gaze takes in the Water Tower district of fine shops (including the vertical mall Water Tower Place) and assorted architectural wonders (the Old Water Tower, the Hancock Building, and the like). Directly across from the entrance, facing west, consumers encounter an architectural pastiche: the majestic Chicago Place, an enormous vertical mall designed in an agglomeration of styles and reminiscent of a European arcade. The Terra Museum of American Art also is prominently visible from the entrance. As if to challenge the primacy of the gaze, the visually unobtrusive Garrett Popcorn Shop, whose door is always open to accommodate the long line of consumers snaking into the extremely narrow shop, emits a pleasingly intense aroma of popcorn, caramel corn, and cheese corn onto the boulevard and into the surrounding stores. Passersby slowing to negotiate the queue or savor the scent often create something of a bottleneck on the sidewalk, giving pedestrians occasion to notice itinerant vendors and street musicians in their wandering orbit.

Facing south, and immediately next door to NTC, consumers are greeted by the Sony store. Sony has also affected a museum-cum-gallery servicescape, which allows consumers to admire state-of-the-art electronics while field-testing them in the store. On the corner southwest of the NTC entrance, Crate and Barrel has a flag-ship store, conveying, in its cylindrical glass facing, the essence of many of the wares it offers for sale.

Thus, as one looks up and down the boulevard, this urban marketplace resembles nothing so much as a canyon of consumption, its glass and concrete walls reigning over a river of pedestrian and vehicular traffic. As a transparently designed canyon, its cultural ecology is characterized by spectacle and desire. The energy and pace of this urban setting contribute to the immediacy of NTC's external presence and mirror the phenomenal realms contained within the building.

The exterior of the NTC building is fairly unremarkable, concealing its internal wonders in a fashion reminiscent of the way the outers of Nike footwear conceal their own internal engineering marvels. A landscaped parkway—whose concrete abutments invite consumers to sit and rest, observe and ruminate— gives the store an initial curb appeal. The facade is strongly reminiscent of an old gymnasium. Banners hang between the windows in columns on the middle stories. Two entranceways flank a bank of windows at street level. In those windows, consumers see not only product offerings and vestibule merchandising, but also reflections of their own images and the surrounding streetscape. Reflection is an activity greatly encouraged by the NTC servicescape. Above this central glassworks, the corporate name and logo are centered on a filigree grillwork. On the four structural columns bracketing the entranceways, bas-relief sculptures executed in material resembling aluminum are framed above eye level. These sculptures depict the body parts of athletes engaged in sport—a cyclist's torso, a runner's trunk and limbs, basketball players' arms, torso, and head, the profile of a female enacting aerobics. These sculptures appear to be emerging from the building (or merging with it), and the functions they embody make them suitable genius loci for this marketplace. If we allow the temple or shrine conceit to shape our interpretation, the fixity of these cult statues is not simply appropriate, it is also essential to the shaping of experience the consumer will undergo upon crossing the threshold. (Indeed, the *nikai*, or victories [McEwen 1993, 104] themselves, embodied in all the offerings of the corporation, from whence its name was derived, alight in this building.) That threshold crossing marks the entrance of the consumer into an alternative phenomenal realm, an existential condition of being-in-the-marketplace, a participation in a lifeworld just shy of a total institution.

Inside the Building: a Walking Tour

Because space limitations make it impossible to describe all the pavilions in sufficient detail. I limit my discussion to those interior structures that both give the reader an overall sense of the enterprise and reflect the degree of consumer interest that promoted my own initial introspection. That is, I confine my treatment more to the remarkable than the mundane as communicated to me by intuition and the enthusiasm of informants. I employ a bottom-up approach describing phenomena encountered in ascending the building.

Vestibule

The vestibule has undergone considerable change since I began this investigation. The original window display consisted of a large rimless paddle wheel whose spokes terminate in athletic shoes, giving the impression of perpetual motion sustained by the product. Over this display, a banner proclaims, "There Is No Finish Line," reminding exiting visitors that true athletes remain suspended in an existential present of achieving, and that Nike will support them in their Sisyphean pursuit. Mounted on a side wall are framed covers of *Sports Illustrated*— each bearing the picture of a Nike celebrity endorser—that look like pictures in an exhibition.[5] An accompanying plaque pays tribute to the performance of "great athletes," the accomplishments of which confraternity the cobranding sponsors enable the customer to experience vicariously.

The performance motif conjoined with the opportunities for touching greatness (O'Guinn 1989) are impressed upon the consumer at the very outset of the visit. Consumers walk across a set of inlaid embossed concentric circles, at the center of which is the globe (North America featured prominently), ringed about with the Nike Town trademark. This same design, adorned with cardinal compass points, is also reproduced on what appear to stimulate manhole covers on street level floors inside the building. Crossing these globes gives us the impression that we are standing at the epicenter of athletics. As if to confirm this impression, a statue of Michael Jordan stands[6] at the center wall of the vestibule. Accompanying signage identifies him as "The Man," and as a "good guy" who plays "great ball." Consumers read of Jordan's accomplishments while they touch the exhibit. In the background, the sounds of ringing mauls and hammers and the noises associated with the basketball court merge with ethereally atonal New Age music, as we ponder the relationship between effort and reward, and marvel at the retailer's attempt to forge an identity between them.

First Floor

Crossing the threshold of the vestibule, we enter NTC proper and step directly into a spectacular illusion. Walking through NTC's "Town Square" simulates the feel of strolling outdoors through a small-town shopping district. The open-air feel is enhanced by the vaulted ceiling, the brick-faced and window-studded exteriors of the pavilions, the street-paved flooring complete with sewer grates, the birdsong soundscape, and booths that simulate vendor carts. This feeling is further enhanced later on during consumers' meanderings to other floors, where you can look out of pavilion windows, over balconies, and down to the "street" below.

The initial sensory rush consumers experience is delightfully overwhelming. "Oh my God!" "Pretty cool!" "Gorgeous colors!" "Boy I like this!" These and other spontaneous exclamations in many languages other than English can be captured by the casual auditor standing in Town Square. Hushed voices are audible as well. Postersize photographs of athletes of varying renown—local, national, international—adorn some walls, where their accomplishments are documented. Exhibit cases containing products and memorabilia proliferate, confounding the boundary between the categories and reinvigorating the notion of commodity aesthetics.

The sheer verticality of the Town Center brick facade reinforces the "Flight" motif signage at its pinnacle. The consumer's gaze is drawn upward to encounter the suspended white plaster statues of athletes in motion—some recognizable as basketball players Scottie Pippen and David Robinson; others, like the nameless cyclists, as anonymous as ghost riders in the sky—and the Nike footgear they wear. Where Sergey Bubka's vaulting effigy once soared at the beginning of my field study, now stands the soccer pavilion sign, a merchandising tribute to the waxing and waning of celebrity.

At ground level, the open sight lines reinforce feelings of expansiveness and connectivity. Visible everywhere are colorful escalators, catwalks, transparent delivery tubes, and hordes of roaming consumers. People and goods move in concert, passing each other numerous times in transit. These delivery tubes in particular (as well as their associated terminals) fascinate consumers, as shoe boxes whiz along, almost pneumatically, from stockroom to sales floor, visible to all throughout the journey. "Can you ride in them?" children wonder, as their parents reminisce to them about "The Jetsons." It is a sanitized scene from *Blade Runner*, a transmogrified *Our Town*. Black-and-white murals of athletes, executed in the socialist realism style of wood engravings of the kind sponsored during the

Depression by the WPA and FAP, and made commercially viable by artists such as Rockwell Kent, adorn some walls, giving sport the heroically populist cast the corporation seeks to foster. The waffle-patterned sole—the firm's original innovation, showcased in floor exhibits[7]—is prominently featured in these murals. Macro-photographs of Nike endorsers mounted on a wall are shielded by vertical blinds painted in neo-impressionist style to resemble athletes, creating an optical illusion that weds present with past, technology with art, and fantasy with reality, again in the service of corporate vision. All art at NTC is performance art.

A curious effect is achieved by signage mounted over the ground floor elevator. A directory for the three showroom floors of NTC gives specific pavilion information. The sign calls attention to the uninterestingness of the fourth-floor "Command Center" of the building in a way that intrigues consumers. Consumers are prohibited from visiting this floor. The attractiveness of a backstage area in what is apparently a completely transparent frontstage is almost irresistible to consumers, and the corporation piques this interest strategically. Images of an inner sanctum—part holy of holies, part behind the curtain of Oz—pepper consumers' commentaries as they ride the elevator. We are in a high-tech tabernacle.

Perhaps the most compelling consumer experience on the ground floor of NTC is achieved on water. Two liquid media engage our attention here. The more apparent of the two is the large aquarium that provides the backdrop for shelving units full of sandals and Aquasocks. A tankful of exotic fish, color-coordinated to products (Katz 1994), draws consumers toward the outdoor-gear boutique. Adults rush children to "see the pretty fish," lifting the children for a better view and a chance to touch the glass. "Are they real fish?" is a frequent question, as children try to discriminate the fantasy-reality boundaries of the NTC environment.

Even more alluring is the video pond set off in a grotto flanked by lava lamp lighting and wave-contoured shelving, hard by a set of wave-contoured benches with acrylic swoosh inlays. The pond is a bank of nine video screens set in the floor, which projects the illusion of water and underwater scenes. Children flirt with its visual cliff appeal, while adults joke about "walking on water." Kids, often lost to the biblical subtext but not the fantasy feeling of such walking, are as apt to respond that they've never "walked on TV before." Consumers often gather around the pond, either standing or sitting, and gaze deeply into the video screens. Cast by design as Christ and Narcissus, we imagine perhaps that the brand will work miracles for us, and mask our self-absorption as reflection. Now literally bathed in the glow of the electronic hearth, perhaps we feel that Nike Town is Our Town. This transformation is especially relevant in our postmodern era, where "third places" (Oldenburg 1989) are as likely as not to be retail "drop-in centers" (Katz 1994, 271).

Second Floor

Riding the escalator to the second floor, consumers continue to cock and swivel their heads to absorb the sights and sounds of NTC, pointing out discoveries, calling out observations, and anticipating what they are likely to encounter next. Their curiosity whetted by having seen display cases of heroes' relics, corporate sacra, public-service projects, and products themselves, consumers take direction from the engaging signage—sometimes neon, sometimes contoured to follow the building's angles, sometimes varied typographically to suit the pavilion —as they debark.[8] Indeed, the escalators have something of the feel of an amusement park ride or monorail shuttle, and encourage a festive attitude among riders. Their fluorescent lights and transparency intensify this feeling.

Roaming the floor, we soon encounter benches built to resemble the air-support technology that has given Nike one of its distinctive competitive advantages. The bench is in effect a deliciously visual oxymoron that renders the corporation's distinctive technology transparent: we experience visible air. By encouraging consumers to see and feel on a grander scale what benefits design delivers to them, NTC facilitates a *being-in-the-shoe* experience. Consumers are quick to seize on the cue, and they grow increasingly alert to the affordances designers have built into merchandising fixtures. They are pleased to discover shelving that consists of basketball goals and backboards, or to recognize and learn from the head-to-toe merchandising strategy that dictates sartorial propriety from sport to sport. Squeals of delight and a summoning of witnesses accompanies the discovery by children and adults alike of door handles and railing support struts cast in the shape of the distinctive swoosh. Almost universally, this visual detection prompts a fondling of these fixtures, as if a palpable grasping of brand essence were to make the experience of NTC tangible. Design promotes the hands-on philosophy that corporate vision seeks to instill in consumers. Such tangibility is self-consciously showcased at the pinnacle of the consumer's journey, as I describe in the upcoming section.

While other sports such as aerobics, tennis, and golf are featured here (captured often enough in the soundscape itself), and while the memorabilia of Nike celebrities from sports such as baseball are on display, the focus of the second floor, and arguably of NTC at large, is the half-court basketball unit that serves a number of functions. As a sales floor, it periodically houses temporary shelving for shoe displays. It provides a realistic opportunity for customers to field-test footwear under consideration for purchase. It is the site of the occasional pep rally to celebrate the victories of the Chicago Bulls basketball team. Indeed, the team introduction music is audible in the background. Perhaps most importantly, its scale and soundscape encourage the mystical participation of visitors in the lifeworld of Michael Jordan.

As consumers wander the court, or sit on benches whose seat pads bear the jersey numbers of Nike endorsers, or jump, feint, and pivot, they are dwarfed by a multistory fantasy photograph of His Airness soaring through the clouds behind the net, in his iconic Jump Man pose. A caption appended to the photo is an epigraph taken from William Blake:

> No bird soars too high.
> If he soars with his own wings

The epigraph ceremonializes Jordan's near-mythic abilities and legendary work ethic while at the same time encouraging the projective fantasy in individual consumers of infinite perfectibility, of effort rewarded by success.[9] The words are a denial of hubris, the image one of a divine messenger, if not an avenging angel.

More than one young consumer advised me, as we gazed at this picture, that "Michael Jordan is God." Adults would often murmur, "Amazing!" in response to both the built environment and Jordan's presence. That Jordan embodies "flight" is ironically, and perhaps even mechanically, undeniable. That he embodies the virtuous face of "pride" is also apparent. Consumers' behaviors in this half-court room range from hushed reverence as they regard the wall display, to noisy exuberance as they squeak soles on the hard court and leap for the rim. The disinhibiting effect of the servicescape extends to adults as well as children. Sometimes it's irresistible to laugh in church. Especially, in the reflexively self-referential adcult (Goldman and Papson 1995; Twitchell 1996) instant where we try to "be like Mike."

The second-floor experience is encapsulated for consumers in their being surrounded by the memorabilia displays and their attaining the same physical heights as the suspended statues of the superstar endorsers. We are literally immersed in a milieu of accomplishment, whether we make eye contact with the soaring likenesses of Scottie Pippen and David Robinson or place our own hands and feet into the casts of those of Charles Barkley and Penny Hardaway. Consumers tell me that NTC is the best place to "learn" about NBA superstars, that "the history is important," and that here "it feels like you get to know them [the players] personality." A momentary merging of consumer with consumed is achieved. Looking back into the half-court room, where other consumers become a tableau for us, allowing us to enjoy a bit of the improvisational theater that we had only moments before provided for others, we are reminded by design of the interactive nature of the products the corporation desires us to desire. We are literally the stuff of which dreams are made.

Third Floor

The pinnacle of the building is notable for the aerial views of the store it affords its birdsong soundscape, and its diorama-like sign fixtures. The Air Jordan Pavilion—a shrine to the Jump Man—is here. The kids' pavilions are here. Consumers can prowl the cat-walks, gaining a perspective of all they have seen, or contemplate a ceiling display of our solar system, composed of orbiting planets tricked out as sports balls. Sports become the fabric of the universe. On this floor, exhibits of sports memorabilia and cinema paraphernalia confound the distinction between athletics and movies, work and leisure, and artifact and experience.[10] T-shirts and posters, framed like prints and displayed as if in a gallery, give some pavilions the feel of a museum gift shop. In these pavilions reside the most affordable of NTC artifacts, to which consumers are drawn in search of a souvenir to commemorate their pilgrimage. It is in these pavilions that products are perhaps most dramatically aestheticized. But the most public proclamation and visible enactment of commodity aesthetics at NTC takes place at two third-floor sites in particular: the design exhibit and the video theater.

In a cased exhibit resting atop a large cut-block-letter acronym N.T.C., "The Dimension of Nike Design" is displayed in elaborate fashion. The case holds three-dimensional architectural models, artists' renderings and blueprints, early merchandising concepts, and other assorted artifacts that illustrate the corporation's commitment to an integrated design philosophy. Graphics inform the viewer that every element of Nike Town is consciously *designed*. Everything the corporation produces—products, fixtures, displays, buildings, and all—springs "from the Mind of Nike Design"[11] and is intended to embody a corporate vision. Nike artifacts are described as "tangible examples of innovation" and a "testament to team thinking," resulting from the teamwork that is the collective "effort of every Nike employee." The exhibit is an explicit recognition and promotion of the role of design to the distinctiveness of the corporation. It is also an affirmation of the heroism of production reflected in wall murals viewed earlier by consumers. It is ultimately a dramatic staging of the "Just Do It" attitude that drives heroic performance to great achievement.

The exhibit both reminds and reveals. Consumers (re-)discover what NTC is designed to produce in them: a confluence of cosmology and technology that inspires faith in the brand and enflames desire in the direction of purchase, no matter how delayed. Insightful design captures the ways in which artifacts mediate between mythological and material worlds (Krippendorf 1989).

Adjacent to the design exhibit is the video theater, built to simulate an open-air structure more like a drive-in or living room than a conventional cinema. The video screen curves to follow the contour of the wall in which it is embedded. Advertising for Nike products plays almost continuously across the screen, as some consumers linger to watch and listen, while others amble through en route to the next pavilion. Signage notifies us that the commercials portray products "in their natural habitat," working for and through athletes who pulse with a "primitive rhythm" that the corporation has sought to embed in its offerings. A rock video format is used to help capture this pulse. "Products in action" are enfolded over time into the "performance" motif that the theater's signage now proclaims. Once again, as in any museum or gallery, visitors are reminded in text of what they've (not) experienced in person. Further, the setting produces discussion among viewers. At any given moment, parents classify images for children, as do children for parents. Presentation sets didacticism in motion, here just as at the display cases.

As consumers move across the catwalks and wander through the setlike pavilions, the frontstage/backstage contrast of wandering through a dramatic production is reinforced. The music, the visuals, the soundscape, the vantage points, and the constant parade of other consumers taking in these same servicescape elements makes the third-floor experience both a summary or closure occasion and an opportunity to make further discoveries upon descent. By the time we have attained the third floor, we are used to seeing sales personnel interact with consumers, joking with them, providing tourist as well as product information, allowing children to push delivery tube buttons, and in general contributing to the built environment of the store.

Interpretive Summary

The Nike Town concept has been described as a "brand-building, 3-D commercial" whose theatrical embrace is reminiscent of a "1939 World's Fair" and whose inspiration stems to part from "The Jetsons" and *Back to the Future* (Katz 1994, 95, 272). It is, however, much more than just a curious hybrid of infomercial and edutainment, jointly produced by marketers and consumers. In Table 1, I characterize the mythopoeic merchandising that makes the NTC servicescape so engaging. In Table 2, I unpack some of the design features that contribute to this engagement. The intent of these efforts is to reveal the world as a company store (Idris-Soven, Idris-Soven, and Vaughn 1978), that is, to describe a phenomenological lifeworld contained in microcosm by a local marketplace, and to explore the mechanisms that animate that microcosm.

Table 1 Mythopoeic merchandising at NTC: experience by design

Phenomenal realm	Experiental dimension*	Servicescape venue	Analogies and variants	Cues and affordances
"Supernatural"			Pantheon	Nike Spirit
			Cathedral	Invisible fourth floor
			Basilica	Windows/lighting
			Church	Suspended statues
			Shrine	Vestibule
			Reliquary	Lamps/altars
			Grotto	Memorabilia/sacra
	Sacred	Museum		Interactive exhibits
				Bas-relief sculptures
				Display cases
design				Diagrams
				Statues
				Extramural banners
		Gallery		T-shirt displays
				Poster displays
				Banner/blind paintings
				Geographic location
		Theater		Frontstage-sets
		Cinema		Backstage—catwalks/ lights
		(TV/living room)		Improvisation
				Living tableaux
				Video screen
				Commercials
"Cultural"		Playground	Stadium/arena	Hardwood court
			Ball court	Basketball goal
				Jordan photo
				Soundscape arena
			Theme park	Cross-promotion
			Mall	(Warner Bros.)
			Category killer	Spot merchandising

Continued overleaf

Table 1 Continued

Phenomenal realm	Experiential dimension*	Servicescape venue	Analogies and variants	Cues and affordances
design		Marketplace	Boutique Gift shop Open-air market	Booths Kiosks Displays Design exhibit Socialist realism murals
			Factory of the future	Ethereal music Transparent escalators Computer terminals Soundscape: hammers
		Street	United Airlines terminal	
			Our Town	Pneumatic tubes
			"Sesame Street"	Neon lighting
			"Mr. Rogers" Neighborhood" "Toon Town" "Wacky Warehouse"	Escalators
	Profane		Epcot Center Gotham City *Blade Runner*	Rough brick facades Windows Balconies
		Outside	Town square	Sewer covers
"Natural"			Water Aerie Heights Promontory	Pond Aquarium Vertical space Open sight lines Clouds Natural light Soundscape: birdsong

* This is less a continuum than a dialectic, since all dimensions may be sacralized. It resembles more a Möbius strip, where the "natural" may be either base or exalted.

NTC, like the ancient city, is a symbol of the cosmos (Tuan 1974, 247). Perhaps more vividly than many buildings, it "condenses culture in one place" (Casey 1992, 32). Its theatrical underpinnings draw from ancient and contemporary dramaturgy (Fletcher 1991). Its architecture is a merger of Hestian and hermetic traditions—centered, self-enclosed curvilinear space abuts rectilinear, decentered, outward-reaching space, inviting simultaneous experience of the stationary and the mobile—that foster empathic connection (Casey 1993, 132–142). NTC is an interesting example of "design that begins and ends with the lived-experience of the users for whom the place is being transformed" (Dovey

Table 2 Discovering delight

Servicescape artifact	Design feature	Sensory engagement	Experiential impact
Doorknobs	Swoosh logo		Threshold fantasies; tangibility of brand essence
Railing supports	Swoosh logo	Visual/tactile	Brand stability and integrity
Bench cushions	Air support; shoe skeuomorph; endorser numbers	Visual/tactile	Transparent tool; *being-in-the-shoe*
Signage	Sport-specific	Visual	Draw flaneur through pavilions; naturalism
Artwork	Socialist realism; macro-photography	Visual	Labor-value musings; WPA-esque inherent dignity of work and effort
Sewer covers	Nike logo	Visual/tactile/aural	Groundedness; permanence
Aquarium fish	Color-coordinated with products	Visual/tactile	Aesthetic engagement; wonderment, speculation
Video theater	Nike commercials	Visual/aural	Edutainment
Merchandising fixtures	Pavilion-specific decor (shelves, sport benches, etc.)	Visual	Organic unity; muted didactics
Statuary	Celebrity sculptures; body parts	Visual	Veneration; cathexis
Soundscapes	Birdsong; music; street noise; court noise	Aural	Immediacy
Exhibit displays	Museum cases; local material	Visual/tactile	Historical grounding; sacral-aesthetic engagement
Sales personnel	Youthful; knowledgeable; athletic attire	Visual/aural/tactile/olfactory	Humanity; relationship
Video pond	CRT hard water	Visual/tactile	Awe; Christ/Narcissus
Catwalks/lights	Interrupted sight lines; inaccessible scaffolding; spot-/klieg-light effect	Visual/tactile	Theatricality (director/performer/audience)
Ball court	"Jordan"	Visual/tactile/aural	Physicality; biblicality
Sports Illustrated covers	Celebrity endorser champions	Visual/tactile	Historicity; veneration
Blinds/banners	Optical illusion	Visual	Stability/change dialectic
Delivery tubes	Transparency; velocity	Visual/tactile	Atemporality

1993, 260). More often than immediate sales, its ambience promotes alternation between a hypervigilant mode of exploration and a species of meditative bliss that has been christened "commodity Zen" (Fjellman 1992, 310, 401).

If we understand marketing to mean primarily the shaping of consumer experience, and consumption to mean the creative interpolation of marketing mix variables with extraeconomic concerns, then NTC is kind of a commercial Biosphere II of cosmological significance. NTC is a world where children hop-scotch on water and ride or resist stairways to heaven, while products emerge from some invisible source of plenty and fly through inside/outside space in transparent arteries, in sync with the music of the spheres. It reminds children of their favorite television haunts: "Toon Town," the "Wacky Warehouse," "Mr. Rogers' Neighborhood," "Sesame Street." It is a world where adults worship athletic idols, pontificating and proselytizing as they wander about, fondling fixtures, brailling product, vetoing extravagant economic demands, and occasionally feeling sheepish about living in a culture that appears to have too much time on its hands. It reminds adults of Gotham City and Epcot Center. NTC is ultimately an unfolding experience, where regression and exaltation work in tandem in the service of brand equity. NTC is both surreal and hyperreal. NTC is "awesome," "amazing," "fantastic," "futuristic," "incredible," "unbelievable," and positively "cool," but most especially, it is *here*. It is Nike Town *Chicago*, where the word is made flesh and dwells among *us*.

Given his belief that "being number one is not very cool" because it breeds risk aversion. Gordon Thompson, the force behind Nike design (and the author of this chapter's second epigraph), has become "obsessed with going beyond Nike Town" and intends to explore the "new frontier of retailing" by creating such outlets as "hands-on sports environments," "sports bars inside digitized environments," and "interactive TV technologies" that would permit customers to measure their feet on a home screen and place orders for digitally customized shoes (Katz 1994, 273–274). Nike is in the process of building a global "event marketing" division charged with the task of "possessing control of how its brand is presented and perceived," and intends to explore opportunities "from the sublime to the ridiculous" for "creating experiences that will tangibly communicate the brand's values and U.S. mystique" (Jensen 1996a, 2). As the corporation seeks increasingly relevant vehicles for tangibilizing the brand's essence—emplacing it in vessels consumers will in turn decant—the strategy of building local showcases remains firmly entrenched.

Nike Towns have recently arisen at the intersection of Rodeo Drive and Wilshire Boulevard (the "spiritual center" of Beverly Hills) and in the Union Square area of San Francisco, as the "entertainment retail" trend spreads to more traditionally "chic" shopping districts (Pacelle 1996, B1). The newest Nike Town at the time of this writing has been installed in New York (Lefton 1996). As history attests (Leach 1993; Monod 1966), such retail spectacle is linked as inextricably to the growth of consumer culture in the United States as it has been in Europe (Sack 1992). We can imagine exporting Nike Towns to other international centers of commerce, as we have witnessed the cross-cultural diffusion of McDonald's, Disney World and the Hard Rock Cafe.[12] It seems quite likely that Nike Towns will be the outposts from which the frontiers of retailing will be exploited. In that sense, NTC is both a site magnet and a beacon product (Sherry 1996, 359), drawing consumers to the source of the brand's production.

Let me conclude this section with a final field note excerpt that returns the reader to informants' perspectives:

> I have encountered relatively few skeptics or ardent critics over the course of these interviews. Most of these seem to be young women or mothers acting as family financial officers. [Note: Is the masculine feel of NTC as gendered space my own idiosyncratic reaction, or does it reflect a corporate reading of U.S. cultural sportways?] And still, even criticism is muted, or framed in terms of the sunk cost of delight. "They spent a lot of money on this place—I wonder if it was worth it," speculates one young woman on a sight-seeing stroll. "Do you think they spent too much money on all this?" a teenage boy wonders aloud to his mates, as they take a break from Rollerblading down the boulevard to explore the building. "Can this spectacle be profitable?" is the unspoken subtext of these queries.
>
> Prices for most items—T-shirts excepted, given their unique designs and parity prices—are contrasted with those found in less opulent settings, and suffer in comparison. "Get your ideas here but buy stuff at Sportmart" is a common observation. One mother advises, "It's like FAO Schwarz. You go there to look, but you buy at Toys 'Я' Us."
>
> Metacriticism—of capitalism, commercialism, materialism— seems similarly restrained, transmitted perhaps through the aura of Michael Jordan. Again, it is young women who have told me things like, "It [NTC] doesn't impress me too much, but I like the Jordan posters," and "It's strange . . . I don't see why people get so excited about a brand name. But I do like Michael Jordan, and I like to see the exhibits."

Conclusion

Let me return finally to the notion of emplacement to summarize my experience of the NTC servicescape. Nike brand essence is both embodied in the built environment and realized in apprehension, in an act of cocreation transacted by the firm's stakeholders. Consider some of the root meanings of *technology*: to build, to give birth, to allow to appear (McEwen 1993). Consider as well how meanings are gathered to an artifact. In Heideggerian perspective, a thing "things" in a provisive carrying out of itself; it is a genuine happening. When we dwell in the world, we experience the "living out of openness specifically in relation to things" (Lovitt and Lovitt 1995, 173, 187). The design of NTC conspires to imbue artifacts with the "particulate sensuosity" that gives goods their "fetish quality" in consumer culture (Taussig 1993, 23).

Like drama, sport has its roots in religious ritual, but sport has long been suffused with a sense of erotic pleasure (Guttmann 1996, 172), which arguably makes athletics and its requisite equipment the most eminently suited vehicles of sublimation that retail theater/therapy could imagine. Consumption at NTC is ultimately about "tactile knowing" and "proprioception"; the servicescape engages what Benjamin called our "optical unconscious" (Taussig 1993, 25, 97). Our imaginative fondling of the sacra/erotica that these props of retail theater have become—branded products, exhibits, fixtures, and the like—impels their literal handling. NTC evokes the kind of "simultaneous perception"—utter watchfulness, split-second attention to innumerable variables, fluid body boundary—that disrupts and alters our everyday consumer experience by encoding in its servicescape such dimensions as legibility and mystery, refuge and prospect (Hiss 1990). Not only is the superfluous stuff of consumer culture fetishized at NTC (Debord 1983), the retail inscape of NTC works to invest all objects housed there with enduring cultural values. Not only has Nike harnessed air, it has transmuted this base element into gold by designing its quintessence into every aspect of the servicescape.

The conflation of commerce with other domains of cultural experience—the transformation of commodities or brands into increasingly complex polyvocal artifacts and back again by filtering them through novel cultural institutions—is at the heart of the NTC servicescape. Our experience of consumption is recodified in ways that ramify beyond exchange but bear ultimately upon exchange. The aura of the outlet (like the spirit of the gift) drives future sales at other outlets; a species of immersion advertising works to recontextualize, validate, and sacralize products at a distance. NTC becomes a numinous link in the distribution chain, part of the totemic circuitry that makes the brand iconic. The sensory rhetoric of the place, and its confounding of categories, keeps stuff interesting.

At the time of this writing, the architecture critic of the *Chicago Tribune* is lamenting the fall from grace of the Magnificent Mile to the "Mediocre Mile," as designers seek ineffectually to transcend the "mold of the sterile urban mall" by razing hallowed older structures and replacing them with "mixed use behemoths" that repeat the "overdesigned" and "garish" mistakes of trendy redevelopment without capturing any of its "extraordinary" triumphs (Kamin 1996, 12). The 600 block in particular is the site of contested meanings, as the forces of historic preservation clash with the demands of marketplace immediacy. In the critic's estimation, the "showroom approach" to retail design is destroying the aesthetic appeal of the Nike Town neighborhood.

During the course of my fieldwork, companies such as Eddie Bauer and Levi Strauss have established flagship brand sites on this block, providing consumers with the spectacle so central to the being-in-the-marketplace experience that entertainment retail engenders (Debord 1983). An inversion of guerilla theater, retail theater becomes a public enactment of retail therapy (Cushman 1990). Where mise-en-scène is merchandising, search is sensually choreographed. Consumers are encouraged to cathect commodities, infusing them with a kinetic libidinal energy summoned from energy's dormant potential as much by the built environment as by desire itself. If the external edifice of the Michigan

Avenue marketplace is in decline, its internal artifice is in ascendancy.[13] Being-with-brands in situations simulating the natural through the supernatural, under cultural conditions from low – through highbrow, is the experience this artifice invokes, in the service of secular prayer. Like a latter-day Euhemerus, we realize at some deep level that toys *are* us. I have titled this chapter (with apologies to Tennessee Ernie Ford) in ironic and allusive recognition of the reciprocal relationship of commodity fetishism to self-actualization.

Economists have estimated that Michael Jordan's presence annually generates in excess of $600 million for Chicago's economy (McCarthy 1993). One-third of these dollars is linked to tourism. I have described NTC as a site magnet for secular pilgrims. Among the retail trends afoot in Chicago that have drawn popular attention—destination merchandising, service-with-a-smile, clutter busting, designer private label, next-generation shopping, novel promotions, and surprising product placement (Spethman 1995)—each is in evidence at NTC. Just as revealing, a recent *Brandweek* survey of 12 influential young (under 40) marketers identifies Nike as the "favorite marketer" of 5 of these managers, who cite such factors as iconic equity, risk taking, authenticity, attention to details, execution, and consumer identification in their admiration of the brand (Khermouch 1996). Each of these factors is also in evidence at NTC. Where an entire line can be merchandised in ways that designers intend (Kuntz 1995), marketers can influence the shape of consumer brandscapes more precisely than in the past. Further, sheer abundance, if not cornucopian display (Sherry and McGrath 1989) of products, contributes to the immediacy of the marketplace. As a stage for such merchandising, NTC is unparalleled. The company itself has been honored as the 1996 Marketer of the Year by *Advertising Age*, which claims the brand to be a "cultural icon" more "recognized and covered" than "arguably any brand" (Jensen 1996b, 16).

Nike. Mikey. Mike. Here prosody prevails. By aural rhyme and by sight rhyme, the words and their adcult essences (Twitchell 1996) converge upon one another at NTC. The site is, after all, Mike Town.[14] He is the soul of the company store. Let me conclude by returning to the emplacement conceit with which I began this chapter. Once meanings are emplaced in artifacts, these artifacts in turn contribute "to our definition of the spatial situation, and the reciprocal amplifying effects that occur when artifacts resonate with space" (Sherry 1995, 360). As work in environmental and architectural phenomenology suggests (Seamon 1993; Walter 1988), our relationship to objects is often geomantic. Artifacts situate us in a "moral geography of culturally significant quality space" and help foster among visitors—in this case, liminoid pilgrims sharing a communitas of psychophysical, commercio-aesthetic origin—a groundedness rooted in air. While the essence of Nike Town is ineluctably local, the experience of *Nike World* travels as far as the products and images of the firm diffuse.[15]

As marketers attempt to forge a retailing agenda for the twenty-first century (Peterson 1992), it is painfully apparent that we lack both a theory that comprehends the obvious world and a chorography that accounts for and taps the spirit of the place (Walter 1988). In our era of hyperconsumption and image-driven search, where the boundaries between marketplaces and other public forums blur, we are beginning to understand "cognitive acquisition," but we have no true feel for its ethos, which may simultaneously stimulate and sedate (Crawford 1992, 13–14). Venues such as NTC are especially fertile field sites for the kinds of discovery that humane social scientific inquiry can facilitate. Perhaps this chapter will provide encouragement for just such discovery.

Notes

1   And yet, when your sales receipt is presented to you in a small logo-emblazoned upscale envelope, ennobled by its package and giftlike in greeting card-esque aspect (the slip may even approximate a stock certificate or deed of ownership), the premium you've paid feels less like self-indulgence and more like wise investment. Ironically, the most elemental form of everyday retail theater—haggling—is absent from NTC (Sennett 1976).

2   The "performance" motif emphasized in current NTC merchandising, emblazoned on signage and free-floating in air via optical illusion in the video theater, is both an ironic and reflexive reminder to consumers that their in-store behavior whether scripted or improvisational, is ultimately theatrical.

3   Thus, while I employ the ethnographic present tense, my account is actually diachronic, which produces some distortion in synchronic accuracy. For example, exhibits and merchandising displays change over time, rendering some descriptions and photographs anachronistic. Yesterday's *Batman* exhibit becomes today's *Jurassic Park* exhibit. Wherever significant, I note such change in the text.

4   Upon returning to his career as hard-court demigod shortly before Easter at the United Center (the House that Jordan built, and site of his statue), after having undertaken the archetypal heroic journey involving great challenges, personal sacrifice, and wondrous encounters—enduring the murder of his father and a sojourn as a baseball player—Jordan was greeted by a multistory banner hung from NTC, proclaiming "He's back!!". Part Christ, part poltergeist (like Muhammad Ali before him), Jordan is revered by Chicago as its current patron saint.

5   This concept has recently been reinterpreted in an upstairs wall-of-fame gallery that features photographs of area amateur athletes and accounts of their achievements, while the original vestibule exhibit has been retired Whether the removal of these covers coincides with the end of history, or the corporation's transcendence of the historic into the realm of the fantastic, if not mythic, is interesting to consider. It may enable viewers to enter more easily into a culture-bound delusional system if they are not reminded so graphically of the firm's historical situatedness. Perhaps history has been "captured totally by the spin-doctors of market forces" (Fjellman 1992, 308).

6   Once suspended like other NTC statues, now encased in a tubular transparent time capsule not unlike a vertical analogue of the resident of Lenin's tomb, this white plaster sculpture —part museum specimen, part gallery exhibit—invites veneration. A charitable reading of the "whiteness" of the bleached black statues throughout NTC marks this homogenization as an homage to classical antiquity in the service of projection and visibility. Though these be giants, they are self-made Everymen whose greatness we all can emulate, if not appropriate, through purchase.

7   These exhibits and others displaying the evolution of footgear through time, however simulated, give viewers the feeling of being in the presence of the original, perhaps even the Ur-shoe, thus facilitating reflection upon the ownership of one's own shoes and resonance of "original" with "own." Sensory rhetoric helps link primal and unique aura to ownership.

8   Those riding the elevator—itself summoned by logo-emblazoned buttons—encounter display cases within as they shuttle betwen floors. Even the bathrooms contain exhibits, such as Hollywood-style shoes made by Nike for Elton John.

9   "God bless the child that's got his own," goes one song. "Angels in the architecture," goes another. The allusions to this wall display are dizzying in their multistrandedness. The

biblicality of Blake's poetry and the woodcuts gives the display a cosmological significance. Jordan's ethnicity gives the display a sociopolitical presence. Jordan as bird. Jordan as angel. Michael the Archangel Blackbird. Jim Crow. Stealth bomber. Basketball as a black man's game. Mobility tied to athletics. Even the dangling statues commingle in this cosmology. Alabaster African-Americans homogenized in obverse minstrelsy and hanged in effigy in parodic lynching, hover as so many marionettes on the strings of the felt yet unseen presence of the corporations. And still, recall that binding animated cult statues of the archaic world, the bonds making manifest the divine life in the images (McEwen 1993, 5). Jordan sacra—golf clubs, clothing worn in commercials, images, etc.—are everywhere on display, Jordan products are NTC's bestsellers. At the time of this writing, the athlete has breached the boundaries of the cosmetics industry to launch a fragrance labeled—what else?—"Michael Jordan," to remind us of the revival of interest in the synergy between sexuality and athletics (Guttmann 1996) Chrism? Holy water? Aqua vitae? Ergodisiac? Whether we invoke P. T. Barnum or David Copperfield to account for brand extension, we can only marvel at the oxymoron that is Jordan's bottled essence liquid air.

10   It will come as no surprise that *Space Jam*, the first genre-bending movie-made-from-a-commercial starred Michael Jordan and Bugs Bunny

11   Not like Athena, full-blown from the head of Zeus, but rather painstakingly and incrementally evolving through the "ambition" of architects and the integrity of the "design process."

12   Whether Michael Jordan's persona would prove crucial to international success, it appears not to have driven domestic diffusion of Nike Towns. Local heroes are featured locally, as emplacement might dictate, and as quick-turnover merchandising might demand. While Jordanworld may be rooted in Chicago, its essence may travel well to emerging sports markets outside the United States, as basketball, entertainment genres, and fashion diffuse globally. Where Al Capone's persona all too recently caricatured the city for its foreign visitors. Michael Jordan's now promises a semiotic urban renewal (Gallagher 1993). Worldwide, Nike strives to "make the brand part of the cultural fabric" (Jensen 1996b, 16).

13   A young female informant provides the following anecdote:

> The essence of Nike Town definitely follows you out the door. I bought my brother's fiancee a Michael Jordan T-shirt at NTC. The salesperson wrapped it in nice Nike Town-emblazoned tissue and put it in a shopping bag. Feeling completely accomplished, I strolled down Michigan Avenue carrying the Nike Town shopping bag on my wrist as if it were a Louis Vuitton handbag. Anyhow, when I got home, I had to pack the T-shirt in my suitcase for San Francisco. I pretty much refused to take the shirt out of the bag for fear that some of the essence would escape. Somehow I packed it in my suitcase completely intact.
>
> When I got to San Francisco. I gave the intact gift to my brother, who was packing his own suitcase to visit his fiancée. Then he did the unfathomable. He proceeded to pull the T-shirt *out* of the bag and *out of* its nice Nike tissue paper and put it in his suitcase. Not only had he unwrapped the gift for her, but he had stripped her of the Nike Townness of the gift. Of course, I told my brother he was completely wrong and that it must be rewrapped (a minor consolation). Unfortunately, you see, my brother is an engineer. It was a question of utility (a lighter suitcase—by a whole two ounces), and I was irrational. I think we ended up settling on putting the tissue around the shirt.

14   Again, allusions are alluvial. Boys Town. Boyz'N the Hood. The Island of Wayward Boys. Boys will be boys. Boy toys. Here in this commodity kiddie land, play is the thing.

Regression in the service of fantasy enables us to be like Mike. For the brief, shining moment, life is nothing but net.

15   Like seeds, spores, starter dough, or the theft of fire (Sherry, McGrath, and Levy 1995), Nike will be everywhere you want to be. Whether its brand equity—in this case, the authenticity of any particular Nike *Town* as a pilgrimage site—is diluted in extension remains to be seen.

Bibliography

Agnew, Jean-Christophe. 1986. *Worlds Apart: The Market and the Theatre in Anglo-American Thought*. New York: Cambridge University Press.

Armstrong, Robert. 1974. *The Affecting Presence*. Urbana, IL: University of Illinois Press.

Buttimer, Anne. 1993. *Geography and the Human Spirit*. Baltimore, MD: Johns Hopkins University Press.

Casey, Edward. 1993. *Getting Back into Places Toward a Renewed Understanding of the Place-World*. Bloomington, IN: Indiana University Press.

Crawround, Margarit. 1992. "The World in a Shopping Mall." In *Variations on a Theme Park*, edited by Michael Sorkin. New York: Noonday Press, 3–30.

Cushman, Peter. 1990. "Why the Self Is Empty: Toward a Historically Situated Psychology." *American Psychologist* (May): 599–611.

Debord, Guy. 1983. *Society of the Spectacle*. Detroit: Black and Red.

Dovey, Kimberly. 1993. "Putting Geometry in Its Place: Toward a Phenomenology of the Design Process." In *Dwelling, Seeing and Designing: Toward a Phenomenological Ecology*, edited by David Seamon. Albany, NY: SUNY Press, 247–269.

Duhaime, Carole; Annamma Joy; and Ginus Ross. 1995. "Learning to 'See': A Folk Phenomenology of the Consumption of Contemporary Canadian Art." In *Contemporary Marketing and Consumer Behavior: An Anthropological Source-book*, edited by John F. Sherry, Jr. Thousand Oaks, CA: Sage, 351–398.

Fjellman, Stephen. 1992. *Vinyl Leaves: Walt Disney World and America*. Boulder, CO: Westview Press.

Fletcher, Rachel. 1991. "Ancient Theatres as Sacred Spaces." In *The Power of Place and Human Environments*, edited by James Swan, Wheaton, IL.: Quest, 88–106.

Gallagher, Winifred. 1993. *The Power of Place: How Surroundings Shape Our Thoughts, Emotions and Actions*. New York: Praeger.

Goldman, Robert, and Stephen Papson. 1996. *Sign Wars: The Cluttered Landscape of Advertising*, New York: Guilford.

Gottdiener, Mark. 1996. *The Theming of America: Dreams, Visions and Commercial Space*, Boulder, CO: Westview Press.

Gould, Stephen. 1991. "The Self-Manipulation of My Pervasive, Vital Energy Through Product Use: An Introspective—Praxis Approach." *Journal of Consumer Research* 18(a): 194–207.

Guttmann, Allen. 1996. *The Erotic in Sports*. New York: Columbia University Press.

Heisley, Deborah, and Sidney Levy. 1991. "Autodriving: A Photoelicitation Technique." *Journal of Consumer Research* 18(2): 257–272.

Hiss, Tony. 1990. *The Experience of Place*. New York: Knopf.

Holbrook, Morris. 1988a. "The Psychoanalytic Interpretation of Consumer Behavior: I Am an Animal." *Research in Consumer Behavior* 3: 149–178.

———. 1988b. "Steps Toward a Psychoanalytic Interpretation of Consumption: A Meta-Meta-Meta-Analysis of Some Issues Raised by the Consumer Behavior Odyssey."

In *Advances in Consumer Research* 15, edited by Michael Houston. Provo, UT: Association for Consumer Research, 537–542.

Idris-Soven, A.; E. Idris-Soven; and M. K. Vaughn, eds. 1978. *The World as a Company Town: Multinational Corporations and Social Change.* The Hague: Mouton.

Jensen, Jeff, 1996a. "Nike Creates New Division to Stage Global Events." *Advertising Age* (September 30): 2, 62.

———. 1996b. "Marketing of the Year." *Advertising Age* (December 16): 1, 16.

Kamin, Blair. 1996. "Mediocre Mile." *Chicago Tribune* (November 10): sec. 7, p. 12.

Katz, Donald. 1994. *Just Do It: The Nike Spirit in the Corporate World.* New York: Random House.

Khermouch, Gerry. 1996. "Marketing's Most Wanted: 1997's Hot Marketers." *Brandweek* (November 4): 35–76.

Krippendorf, Klaus. 1989. "On the Essential Context of Artifacts, or On the Proposition that 'Design is Making Sense (of Things)." *Design Issues* 5(2): 9–38.

Kuntz, Mary. 1995. "These Ads Have Windows and Walls." *Business Week* (February 27): 74.

Leach, William. 1993. *Land of Desire: Merchants, Power and the Rise of a New American Culture.* New York: Pantheon.

Lefton, Terry. 1996. "Nike uber Alles." *Brandweek* (December 9): 25–36.

Lovitt, William, and Harriet Lovitt. 1995. *Modern Technology in the Heideggerian Perspective*, vol. 1. Lewiston, NY: Edwin Mellen Press.

Mandel, David. 1967. *Changing Art, Changing Man.* New York: Horizon Press.

McCarthy, Michael. 1993. "Jordan's Retirement Will Make No Cents to Chicago Economy." *The Wall Street Journal* (October 7): B12.

McCracken, Grant. 1988, *Culture and Consumption: New Approaches to the Symbolic Character of Consumer Goods and Activities.* Bloomington, IN: Indiana University Press.

———. 1990. "Marketing Material Cultures: Person-Object Relations Inside and Outside the Ethnographic Museum." In *Advances in Nonprofit Marketing* 3. edited by Russell Belk. Greenwich, CT: JAI Press, 27–49.

———. 1996. "Culture and culture at the Royal Ontario Museum: A Ghost Story." Working paper, Department of Ethnology. Royal Ontario Museum, Toronto, Ontario, Canada.

McEwen, Indra. 1993. *Socrates' Ancestor: An Essay on Architectural Beginnings.* Cambridge, MA: MIT Press.

McGrath, Mary Ann. 1989. "An Ethnography of a Gift Store: Trappings, Wrappings and Rapture." *Journal of Retailing* 65(4): 421–449.

McGrath, Mary Ann; John Sherry; and Deborah Heisley. 1993. "An Ethnographic Study of an Urban Periodic Market Place: Lessons from the Midville Market." *Journal of Retailing* 69(3): 280–319.

Monod, David. 1996. *Store Wars: Shopkeepers and the Culture of Mass Marketing,* 1890–1939. Toronto: University of Toronto Press.

Murray, Henry. 1943. *Thematic Apperception Test Manual.* Cambridge, MA: Harvard University Press.

Nike Town Chicago. 1992a. "Nike Town Comes to Chicago." Press release, Nike Town Chicago, Chicago, July 2.

———. 1992b. "Nike Town Chicago Fact Sheet." Press release, Nike Town Chicago, Chicago, July 2.

O'Guinn, Thomas. 1989. "Touching Greatness: The Central Midwest Barry Manilow Fan Club." In *Highways and Buyways: Naturalistic Research from the Consumer Behavior*

Odyssey, edited by Russell Belk. Provo, UT: Association for Consumer Research, 102–111.

O'Guinn, Thomas, and Russell Belk. 1989. "Heaven on Earth: Consumption at Heritage Village." *Journal of Consumer Research* 16(1): 147–157.

Oldenburg, Ray. 1989. *The Great Good Place*. New York: Paragon House.

Otnes, Cele; Mary Ann McGrath; and Tina Lowrey. 1995. "Shopping with Consumers: Usage as Past, Present and Future Research Technique." *Journal of Retailing and Consumer Services* 2(2): 97–110.

Pacelle, Mitchell. 1996. "Razzmatazz Retailers Jolt Chic Shopping Streets." *The Wall Street Journal* (October 4): B1, B10.

Peterson, Robert, ed. 1992. *The Future of U.S. Retailing: An Agenda for the 21st Century*. New York: Quorum.

Richardson, Miles. 1987. "A Social (Ideational-Behavioral) Interpretation of Material Culture and Its Application to Archaeology." In *Mirror and Metaphor*, edited by Donald Ingersoll and Gordon Bronitsky. Lanham, MD: University Press of America, 381–403.

Rook, Dennis. 1989. "I Was Observed (*In Absentia*) and Autodriven by the Consumer Behavior Odyssey." In *Highways and Buyways: Naturalistic Research from the Consumer Behavior Odyssey*, edited by Russell Belk. Provo, UT: Association for Consumer Research, 48–58.

Rose, Dan. 1995. "Active Ingredients." In *Contemporary Marketing and Consumer Behavior: An Anthropological Sourcebook*, edited by John F. Sherry, Jr. Thousand Oaks, CA: Sage, 51–58.

Sack, Robert. 1992. *Place, Modernity and the Consumer's World*. Baltimore, MD: Johns Hopkins University Press.

Schultz, Don; Stanley Tannenbaum; and Robert Lauterborn. 1994. *The New Marketing Paradigm: Integrated Marketing Communications*. Chicago: NTC Business Books.

Scott, Linda. 1994. "The Bridge From Text to Mind: Adapting Reader-Response Theory to Consumer Research." *Journal of Consumer Research* 21(3): 461–480.

Seamon, David. 1993. *Dwelling, Seeing and Designing: Toward a Phenomenological Ecology*. Albany, NY: SUNY Press.

Sennett, Richard. 1976. *The Fall of Public Man*. New York: Vintage.

Sherry, John F., Jr. 1985. "Cereal Monogamy: Brand Loyalty as Secular Ritual in Consumer Culture." Paper presented at the 17th annual conference of the Association for Consumer Research. Toronto, Ontario, Canada.

——. 1990a. "A Sociocultural Analysis of a Midwestern American Flea Market." *Journal of Consumer Research* 17(1): 13–30.

——. 1990b. "Dealers and Dealing in a Periodic Market: Informal Retailing in Ethnographic Perspective." *Journal of Retailing* 66(2): 174–200.

——. 1991. "Postmodern Alternatives: The Interpretive Turn in Consumer Research." In *Handbook of Consumer Behavior*, edited by Thomas Robertson and Harold Kassarjian. Englewood Cliffs, NJ: Prentice Hall, 548–591.

——. 1995a. "Bottomless Cup, Plug-In Drug: A Telethnography of Coffee." *Visual Anthropology* 7(4): 351–370.

——. 1995b. *Contemporary Marketing and Consumer Behavior: An Anthropological Sourcebook*. Thousand Oaks, CA: Sage.

——. 1996. "Reflections on Giftware and Giftcare: Whither Consumer Research?" In *Gift Giving: A Research Anthology*, edited by Cele Otnes and Richard Beltramini. Bowling Green. OH: Bowling Green State University Popular Press, 217–227.

Sherry, John F., Jr.; and Mary Ann McGrath. 1989. "Unpacking the Holiday Presence: A Comparative Ethnography of Two Midwestern American Gift Stores." In *Interpretive Consumer Research*, edited by Elizabeth Hirschman. Provo, UT: Association for Consumer Research, 148–167.

Sherry, John F., Jr.; Mary Ann McGrath; and Sidney Levy. 1995. "Monadic Giving: Anatomy of Gifts Given to the Self." In *Contemporary Marketing and Consumer Behavior: An Anthropological Sourcebook*, edited by John F. Sherry, Jr. Thousand Oaks, CA: Sage, 399–432.

Spethman, Betsy. 1995. "Shopping for Answers." *Brandweek* (February 27): 30–32.

Strasser, J. B., and Laurie Becklund. 1993. *Swoosh: The Unauthorized Story of Nike and the Men Who Played There*. New York: Harper Business.

Tarn, Nathaniel. 1972. "From Anthropologist to Informant: A Field Record of Gary Snyder." *Alcheringa* 4 (Fall): 392–401.

Taussig, Michael. 1993. *Mimesis and Alterity: A Particular History of the Senses*. New York: Routledge.

Tuan, Yi-Fu. 1974. *Topophilia: A Study of Environmental Perception, Attitudes and Values*. New York: Columbia University Press.

Twitchell, James. 1996. *Adcult U.S.A.: The Triumph of Advertising in American Culture*. New York: Columbia University Press.

Wallendorf, Melanie, and Merrie Brucks. 1993. "Introspection in Consumer Research: Implementation and Implications." *Journal of Consumer Research* 20(3): 339–359.

Walter, Eugene. 1988. *Placeways: A Theory of the Human Environment*. Chapel Hill, NC: University of North Carolina Press.

Editors' Commentary

WAL-MART IS THE WORLD'S largest retailer and its expansion has often created controversy. This volume contains two readings that focus on Wal-Mart. Wal-Mart has held a particular fascination for Stephen Arnold and Jay Handelman who are authors of both these papers (joined in the other paper by Robert Kozinets, see pp. 179–180). In this paper they are joined by co-author Douglas Tigert, whose interest, for many years, has been in big retail spaces and retail company strategy and operations.

Stephen Arnold has spent his academic career in the School of Business at Queen's University, Kingston, Ontario where he is currently Emeritus Professor. He obtained a BSc in Applied Science from the Royal Military College and began a career in the Canadian Armed Forces. By 1974 he had obtained a PhD in Marketing from the University of Toronto and soon after joined the staff at Queen's University.

Stephen has an extensive research record and has been a Visiting Professor in a number of European universities including, Stirling, Eindhoven, Laval and Surrey. His early research was in a variety of fields of marketing, but from the mid-1980s retail patronage issues began to feature more prominently. This area has been focused in recent years around the impact of Wal-Mart on consumers and retailers, and it is perhaps for this work that Stephen Arnold is best known (see also his paper in Chapter 2 of this volume).

Jay Handelman works with Stephen Arnold at Queen's University, having studied there as a PhD student and returning to a post there in 2003 from Lethbridge University. He is Associate Professor of Marketing and Director of the Centre for Corporate Social Responsibility. His research centres on ways in which marketers integrate emotional, social and cultural dimensions into their product, service and corporate marketing strategy and operations. He has collaborated with Arnold and Tigert on a number of projects, and has been published in many of the leading journals.

Doug Tigert retired from his position as Charles Clarke Reynolds Professor of Retail Marketing at Babson College, MA in 2001 after a long and distinguished retail academic career. Retirement has not meant that he has been inactive and Doug has continued to comment and teach on retail trends, notably with respect to big box retailers such as Wal-Mart. Doug Tigert received a B. Commerce degree from Queen's University, Kingston, Ontario in 1961, an MBA degree from Northwestern University in 1962 and his PhD Marketing from Purdue University in 1966. He joined Babson after working at the University of Toronto. Tigert began to work with Stephen Arnold over thirty years ago with a joint research report in 1976 on consumer attitudes in Toronto. Since then they have collaborated extensively on research projects on a range of topics including warehouse clubs, supercentres and consumer attitudes to different shopping environments. Some of this work has also involved Jay Handelman.

'The Impact of a Market Spoiler on Consumer Preference Structures (or, What Happens When Wal-Mart Comes to Town)' challenges conventional marketing theory which suggests that consumer preferences are independent of stores. It is based on extensive work over a number of studies, focusing particularly on the impact of Wal-Mart on consumer preferences once they enter a market. The paper's significance is primarily theoretical, although the survey results incorporated in the paper are of course significant in terms of appreciating the challenge to the market that Wal-Mart poses. The Wal-Mart example shows that when a new store opens, the expressed preferences of those surveyed switch from relatively ambiguous positions to become aligned with what Wal-Mart was offering. This suggests that a store can change and shape consumer preferences.

Key Publications

Arnold SJ and Tigert DJ (1974) Market monitoring through attitude research. *Journal of Retailing.* 49, 3–22.

Arnold SJ, Oum T H and Tigert DJ (1983) Determinant attributes in retail patronage: seasonal, temporal, regional and international comparisons. *Journal of Marketing Research*, 20, 149–157.

Arnold SJ, Handelman J and Tigert DJ (1996) Organisational legitimacy and retail store patronage. *Journal of Business Research*, 35, 229–239.

Handelman J and Arnold SJ (1999) Marketing actions with a social dimension: appeals to the institutional environment, *Journal of Marketing*, 63 (3), 33–48.

Arnold SJ and Luthra M (2000) Market entry effects of large format retailers: a stakeholder analysis. *International Journal of Retail and Distribution Management*, 28(4/5), 139–154.

Arnold SJ and Fernie J (2000) Wal-Mart in Europe: prospects for the UK. *International Marketing Review*, 17, 416–432.

Seiders K, Simonides C and Tigert DJ (2000) The impact of supercenters on traditional food retailers in four markets. *International Journal of Retail & Distribution Management*, 28, 181–193.

Arnold SJ, Kozinets R and Handelman J (2001) Hometown ideology and retailer legitimation: the institutional semiotics of Wal-Mart flyers. *Journal of Retailing*, 77(2), 243–271.

Fernie J and Arnold SJ (2002) Wal-Mart in Europe: Prospects for Germany, the UK and France. *International Journal of Retail and Distribution Management*, 30, 92–102.

Bianchi CC and Arnold SJ (2004) An institutional perspective on retail internationalization success: Home Depot in Chile. *The International Review of Retail, Distribution and Consumer Research*, 14, 149–169.

Tigert DJ and Serpkenci RR (2006) Wal-Mart's new normal is here: is everyone ready to accept the future? *International Journal of Retail and Distribution Management*, 34, 85–100.

Fernie J, Hahn B, Gerhard U, Pioch E and Arnold SJ (2006) The impact of Wal-Mart's entry into the German and UK grocery markets. *Agribusiness*, 22, 247–266.

Websites

http://business.queensu.ca/faculty_and_research/faculty_list/sarnold.php
http://business.queensu.ca/faculty_and_research/faculty_list/jhandelman.php

---

THE IMPACT OF A MARKET SPOILER ON CONSUMER PREFERENCE STRUCTURES (OR, WHAT HAPPENS WHEN WAL-MART COMES TO TOWN)

Stephen J. Arnold, Jay Handelman and Douglas J. Tigert

Traditional market structure theories assume that consumer preferences are fixed and exogenous to the influence of market competitors. An alternative

---

Journal of Retailing and Consumer Services, Vol. 5, No. 1 (1998), pp. 1–13. © 1998 Elsevier Science Ltd. All rights reserved.

The authors appreciate the comments of David Dunne, Ida Berger and two anonymous reviewers on an earlier version of this paper. (revision of).

theory from the pioneering advantage literature suggests that a competitor can actually alter preference structures by shifting attribute saliencies in its own favour. The 'market spoiler' achieves this result by capitalizing on consumer preference ambiguity. Support for this alternative theory is found in a series of surveys tracking Wal-Mart's entry into three North American markets. The results show that the importance attached to different retail store choice attributes change to become more consistent with Wal-Mart's particular strengths.

SINCE THE FIRST 'WAL-MART Discount City' opened July 2, 1962 (Vance and Scott, 1994), Wal-Mart has grown to become the largest retailer in the world. Net sales of Wal-Mart Stores, Inc. and its subsidiaries were $82.5 billion in 1995 (Wal-Mart Stores, Inc. Annual Report 1995). Wal-Mart focused on small US towns and cities in its early years and then, in the 1980s, began entering the large urban markets. Growth in recent years has been exponential (Figure 1) and Wal-Mart might expect to exceed $100 billion in sales by 1997.

As a major retailer, Wal-Mart affects competitor retailing practices. For example, Wal-Mart has lead many retailers away from a regimem of sales and promotions, and towards the practice of 'everyday low prices' (Hoch et al., 1994). Other Wal-Mart practices have also been influential, including its logistics and distribution system (Stalk et al., 1992).

Wal-Mart has certainly had an impact on retailing practice. But what about Wal-Mart's impact on consumer preferences for different retail attributes? The traditional view of consumer preferences (eg Stigler and Becker, 1977) states that the saliencies consumers attach to attribute offerings are fixed and exogenous. These preferences exist to be measured and used as input in the development of a marketing strategy. From this perspective, it might seem that Wal-Mart has simply out performed its competitors in identifying and winning on attributes that consumers find most salient.

In contrast to the traditional view, Carpenter and Nakamoto (1989) raised the intriguing possibility that rather than consumer preferences influencing marketing strategy, marketing strategy may actually influence consumer preferences. Carpenter and Nakamoto (1989) proposed that consumer preferences are endogenous to, and evolve with, the market, a premise that has been supported in experimental studies conducted in a market pioneering context (Carpenter et al., 1994; Carpenter and Nakamoto, 1989; Kardes et al., 1993). Findings from these studies show that a 'market pioneer' assumes the ideal position because it is able to develop consumer tastes which favour its own position. In an analogous manner, a 'market spoiler' shifts consumer tastes towards its own position except that the effect occurs in existing as opposed to new markets.

The entry of Wal-Mart into three existing retail markets and tracking data from these markets provided the occasion to explore Carpenter and Nakamoto's (Carpenter and Nakamoto, 1989) argument. The results of five independent consumer surveys conducted over the course of twelve years all showed considerable shifts in consumer preferences. However, the question that remains unanswered is whether these shifts represent the impact of a market spoiler,

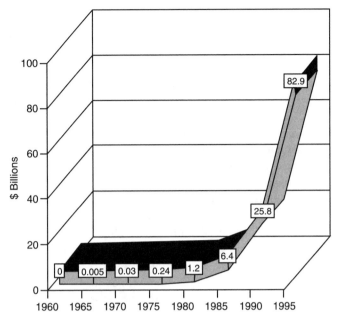

Figure 1 Sales of Wal-Mart Stores, Inc. 1962–95
Source: Vance and Scott (1994) and Wal*Mart Annual Report 1995

ie changes in attribute saliency in Wal-Mart's favour, or whether the shifts simply indicate that there is now a competitor who can satisfy latent (but fixed) consumer needs? The answer to this question is tied to showing changes in 'consumer ambiguity'. The concept of consumer ambiguity is explained in the next section where comparisons are made between two competing theories for explaining changes in consumer preference structures.

Theories on Changes in Consumer Preference Structures

Changes in the attribute saliency can be accounted for by at least two different and competing explanations: a market competitor is better able to respond to an underlying, fixed consumer preference structure, or, a market competitor fundamentally alters the consumer preference structure.

The traditional view – fixed consumer preference structures

The first explanation for an increase in saliency attached, for example, to the low everyday price attribute, would go like this:

> An efficient market competitor is better able to satisfy an underlying, latent desire for low prices. More consumers overtly mention low price as being the most important reason for choosing the store where they shop most often because there is now a store that

> convincingly demonstrates a superior low price position. Such a
> desire or preference has always been present but it is only the entry of
> the market spoiler that permits it to be expressed.

This first explanation is consistent with neo-classical economic theory. Consumer preferences are assumed to be fixed and exogenous – existing outside of the influence of competitors. For instance, Stigler and Becker (1977) stated that individuals consume commodities and each consumer possesses a given utility function for a given commodity. Some may argue that consumer fashions or fads provide evidence that consumer preferences are not fixed but subject to shifts due to influences from other sources. Stigler and Becker (1977) refuted this argument by observing that the commodity consumed with the latest fashion is 'social distinction.' The utility of social distinction does not change from one situation to another for a given consumer. Therefore, a consumer who derives great utility from social distinction will always seek to consume the commodity of the latest fashion. In this sense, consumer preferences, whether social distinction or 'everyday low prices,' are stable and exogenous.

The assumption of fixed and exogenous consumer preferences is also consistent with contemporary expressions of the marketing concept (cf. Houston, 1986; Kohli and Jaworski, 1990; Narver and Slater, 1990; Webster, 1988). With the emergence of a demanding 'consumer society,' the ideals of achieving long term customer satisfaction become paramount (Webster, 1988). This goal can be achieved by a greater understanding of the demands of customers (Houston, 1986). Such demands are measured and the findings shared with all parts of the organization (Kohli and Jaworski, 1990; Narver and Slater, 1990). In this way, products and services are developed which meet consumer needs and the firm is able to maximize long run profits (Narver and Slater, 1990; Slater and Narver, 1994). Clearly, in this statement of the marketing concept, consumer preferences are fixed and exogenous, waiting to be discovered, understood, and acted upon (ie satisfied) by the marketer.

Porter's competitive market analysis also assumes a fixed preference structure. For Porter (1985), a key element that determines industry structure is the buyer. The buyer comes with a set of preferences (ie price sensitivity, quality expectations, etc.). These preferences then determine the structure of the industry since the competitive advantage will accrue to the firm that best creates value for these buyers. Therefore, industry structure is built around firms trying to best satisfy these fixed and exogenous customer preferences. Through superior strategy, firms may be able to change their relative competitive position, but Porter's model does not include the possibility of firms changing consumer preferences.

Retail patronage models also assume exogenous consumer preference structures. For instance, in Darden's (Darden, 1979) patronage model, an individual consumer's 'shopping orientation' is seen to determine the salience of attributes offered by a store. This shopping orientation is made up of one's values, social class, stage in family life cycle, and life style. Therefore, parallel to the neo-classical view of consumer preferences, one's shopping orientation exists prior and exogenous to the attributes offered by a retailer. Given one's shopping orientation, the consumer will then decide whether or not a store attribute will be determinant in the patronage decision. The retailer must determine which store attributes consumers will find salient, and then implement a retailing mix that satisfies these consumer preferences.

Mason *et al.* (1983) suggested that the best predictors of store attribute saliency are consumer values. Values, being stable and enduring, predict which attributes retailers should offer in order to best meet the needs of their consumers. Dawson *et al.* (1990a) posited that it is the shopping motives of the consumer which will determine the saliency of store attributes. Other predictors of store attribute saliency include: social isolation and need for community contact (Forman and Sriram, 1991); social class (Dawson *et al.*, 1990b); and mode of transportation, and time available (Bucklin and Gautschi, 1983).

In the traditional view expressed in each of the preceding behavioural models, consumers are seen to come to the market with a given, fixed preference structure. It is this set of preferences that will determine whether or not the attributes offered by retailers are determinant in store choice.

A market spoiler can change consumer preference structures

The assumption of fixed and exogenous consumer preferences is consistent with the theory underlying traditional investigations of the pioneering advantage (Kalyanaram and Urban, 1992). The argument here is that pioneers benefit from an order of entry effect (Kalyanaram and Urban, 1992; Urban *et al.*, 1986) in which they are first to satisfy existing consumer needs. Being the first also allows the pioneer to gain other economic advantages over later entrants by accruing lower production costs, pricing advantages, better distribution, a broader product line, and higher levels of advertising (Fershtman *et al.*, 1990). All of these factors act as barriers to entry for later entrants.

There has also emerged out of the pioneering advantage literature, however, a 'behavioural basis' that directly contrasts the assumption of fixed and exogenous consumer preferences (Kalyanaram and Urban, 1992). Carpenter and Nakamoto (1989) observed that in the early stages of a market, consumers know very little about the importance of attributes or their ideal combinations. The research evidence is that consumers are uncertain as to what attributes should be salient. With this 'ambiguity' over the saliency of attributes, market pioneers have the opportunity to shift preferences to favour the pioneer's attributes over those of later entrants (Carpenter and Nakamoto, 1989).

Hoch and Deighton (1989) suggested that consumer preference ambiguity, which they defined as the potential for multiple interpretations of attribute importance, is a critical factor in enabling the management of experiential learning. This perspective states that marketers can 'help' the consumer to resolve the ambiguity in directions that favour that marketer's brand (Hoch and Deighton, 1989). In this context, consumer ambiguity is an important antecedent to the formation of consumer preference structures. Consumer ambiguity exists as an opportunity for the marketer to shift consumer preferences in a desired direction.

Another concept that allows for the possibility of a market pioneer defining consumer preference structures is the idea of asymmetry. Dominant brands can have a powerful, asymmetric competitive advantage (Carpenter and Nakamoto, 1990) in that their presence inhibits the recall of other, less dominant brands (Alba and Chattopadhyay, 1986). The result is that the attributes salient in consumer choice will be consistent with those offered by the existing dominant market competitor and less consistent with those offered by the lesser known, weaker brands.

It appears that later entrants, also known as a market spoilers, can also shift consumer preferences in their favour. They can do this because they are able to capitalize on consumer ambiguity on attribute preferences. Such ambiguity is created by the market spoiler with the use of strong advertising of attributes that are different from those of the present market leaders (Carpenter and Nakamoto, 1990). Such strong differentiating messages alter rather than resolve the consumer's information environment, thus creating the potential for change (Hoch and Deighton, 1989).

This possibility appears quite feasible when Wal-Mart's role as a market spoiler is considered. Not only does Wal-Mart's size allow for competitive levels of advertising of its unique attributes (eg EDLP versus sales and promotions), but Wal-Mart's entry into any market typically attracts considerable media attention. For instance, when Wal-Mart announced its acquisition of 122 Canadian Woolco outlets, many stories were written and commentaries made by questioning the impact that the American retailing giant would have on Canadian retailers and consumers. This tremendous media attention and a different advertising emphasis puts the retail market into a state of flux by altering the 'information environment' (Hoch and Deighton, 1989). This information bombardment challenges the retail status quo and creates consumer uncertainty with respect to preferences for various retailers and their attribute offerings. During this stage of consumer preference ambiguity, no one market player is likely to possess an asymmetric competitive advantage with respect to consumer preferences.

With a state of consumer preference ambiguity greeting the actual market arrival of Wal-Mart, the stage is set for this retailer to assume the role of market spoiler. It is able to shift consumer preferences in its own favour because it is the dominant presenter of market information (Hoch and Wa, 1986). If the market spoiler has the power to create consumer preference ambiguity where it did not exist before, then it is also in the position to create an asymmetric competitive advantage for itself out of this market ambiguity. As the asymmetric consumer preference structure favouring the market spoiler gels (ie consumers become more certain of the store attributes they prefer), it follows that consumer ambiguity will decrease.

In sum, if the proposition holds that a market spoiler shifts consumer preferences, a specific pattern of results is expected. Specifically, three conditions must be observed:

1   The entry of the market spoiler into a given market is immediately preceded by, and runs concurrent to, a state of consumer preference ambiguity.

2   After the entry of the market spoiler, consumer preferences will shift asymmetrically in favour of the market spoiler.
3   This asymmetric shift in consumer preferences will be accompanied by a resolution in consumer preference ambiguity.

One final point has to do with the sustainability of the market advantage for the market spoiler over time. Carpenter and Nakamoto (1990) stated that asymmetries in consumer preferences can be a source of persistent competitive advantage. Fershtman *et al.* (1990) acknowledged that a market share advantage accrued to the market pioneer, but questioned whether or not this advantage is sustainable in the long run. Proponents of the behavioural stream have tested their hypotheses primarily in experimental settings and have been unable to determine whether the pioneering advantage, underpinned by shifting consumer preferences, is sustainable over the long run (Carpenter *et al.*, 1994). With the survey data being investigated here, the Kingston and Atlanta markets are examined over time. An examination of the long-term Atlanta results (over eight years) in conjunction with the shorter term Kingston results (which are taken over one year) allows for a look into the long term sustainability of the market advantage accrued to the market spoiler.

Wal-Mart Defined

Wal-Mart emphasizes a very clear and unique set of attributes. The most predominant attribute is 'everyday low prices' (EDLP).

> [D]iscounters like Wal-Mart have led the EDLP wave and successfully encroached on the turf of supermarkets and department and drug stores by advertising that their everyday prices are *always* the lowest to be found (Hoch *et al.*, 1994, p. 16).

Actual price baskets consistently show Wal-Mart underprices its major competitors (Tigert *et al.*, 1995). Further, this EDLP strategy is seen in Wal-Mart's motto ("Always Low Prices. Always Wal-Mart") and in its current advertising ("Watch for falling prices").

This emphasis on EDLP is in contrast to the retail norm of 'Hi-low' pricing or temporary promotional discounts (Hoch *et al.*, 1994). Hoch *et al.* (1994) pointed out that according to a survey conducted in 1992 of the top 50 US retail markets, only 26%, of supermarket retailers were employing some form of EDLP, and the remaining 74% were Hi-Lo promotion-oriented operators. Wal-Mart runs a flyer only once a month while all other direct competitors (Target, Zellers, Kmart, Target) run a flyer every week and commit perhaps 75% of their advertising dollars to promotions.

Another distinguishing attribute for Wal-Mart is friendly, courteous service. Roach (1993) noted that by inculcating a sense of ownership with their associates (employees), the stage is set for the employees to treat customers with the utmost courtesy. Timm (1992) notes that the use of store greeters allows

Wal-Mart to exceed the expectations of its customers when it comes to friendly service.

Another attribute of interest is store layout. In a national survey of American retail consumers, Rinne and Swinyard (1992) showed that Wal-Mart stands out from its competitors when it comes to having the best store layout. This finding underlies a purposeful strategy on Wal-Mart's part. For instance, when Wal-Mart took over 122 Woolco stores in Canada in 1994, it spent millions in store renovations.

A final attribute by which Wal-Mart distinguishes itself is active involvement in the community (Arnold *et al.*, 1996). In its instore displays and advertising, Wal-Mart records their donations to local charities, support of local and national suppliers, and contributions to community causes such as youth education.

While Wal-Mart has a strong reputation for everyday low prices, it is not distinguished on the quality of its merchandise (Miller, 1993). Jacob (1993) pointed out that, at best, Wal-Mart is at parity with other retailers when it comes to issues of product quality. On measures of product quality, Wal-Mart has consistently fewer product quality mentions, particularly in apparel (Tigert *et al.*, 1993, 1994, 1995).

Wal-Mart differs from its competitors with respect to offering customer credit. Where other chains offer customer credit (ie store credit cards), Wal-Mart has no similar credit card system.[1]

In sum, Wal-Mart can be described as a mass merchandiser which offers products of acceptable quality at everyday low prices. It aims to offer friendly, courteous service, but no store credit, in stores that are well laid out. Further, Wal-Mart is seen to be actively involved in contributing to the communities in which its located.

Atlanta, Chicago, and Kingston Surveys

The opportunity to examine the effects upon consumer preference structures of Wal-Mart's entry came about as a result of telephone surveys conducted over time and in three different markets. Interviews were conducted with randomly-selected female heads of households in the Atlanta, Chicago and Kingston markets. In each market, a series of diallings were made using random telephone numbers drawn from the corresponding metropolitan area. Numbers that were 'not in service,' 'non-residence,' or 'no female head of household' were eliminated from each sample. Therefore, only residences in which there was a female head of household met the initial qualification. Respondents in this group who agreed to be interviewed were then further qualified by stating they had shopped at a low-priced department store (eg Wal-Mart, Kmart, Target, Zellers) at least once within the previous eight weeks.

Table 1 lists the survey dates, response rates and samples sizes. The first of the two Atlanta surveys was conducted in 1985, about two years after Wal-Mart's entry into that market. The second was completed eight years later in 1993 with the same marketing research firm and identical procedures.

Survey results from a Chicago survey are separated out depending upon

Table 1 Dates, response rate and sample sizes of Atlanta, Chicago and Kingston surveys

Market	Date survey conducted	Survey response rate among contacted households (%)	Sample size among qualified shoppers	Total observations for logit analyses
Atlanta	April 1985	*N.A.	750	2626
Atlanta	February 1993	36	550	2533
Chicago	March 1994	25		
City			177	813
Suburbs			212	1029
Outer			256	1278
Kingston	March 1994	47	417	1437
Kingston	October 1995	47	400	1613

* N.A. Not available

whether the respondent lived in the City of Chicago, the suburbs immediately surrounding the City, or the outer Chicago suburbs (Figure 2). The significance of comparing survey results across these three concentric rings is that Wal-Mart had no stores in the inner circle at the time of the survey, some presence in the middle circle and was readily accessible in the outer circle.

The first of the two Kingston surveys was conducted in March 1994, six weeks after Wal-Mart announced its acquisition of the Woolco chain of Canadian discount department stores but well before their actual entry into the market. Conversion of the Kingston store to Wal-Mart occurred in October 1994. The second Kingston survey was done one year later in October 1995. Sample comparisons indicated similar profiles on nearly one dozen demographic and socio-economic measures.

Survey results

In order to support the concept that Wal-Mart (the market spoiler) has shifted consumer preferences in its own favour, the survey results must concur with the pattern identified in the three points listed above in the theory section. It is necessary to establish that the consumer preference structure has shifted and that this shift has occurred in favour of the market spoiler. Also to be ascertained are changes in consumer ambiguity.

Share of shoppers

Wal-Mart's share of shoppers ('Which store do you shop at most often?') among Atlanta female heads of households expanded from 8 percent in 1985 to 53% in 1993 (Table 2). The market shares of Kmart, JC Penney and Sears shrunk correspondingly. Even another new entrant, Target, could not prevent a loss of share from its 1985 position when the stores were then known as Richway.

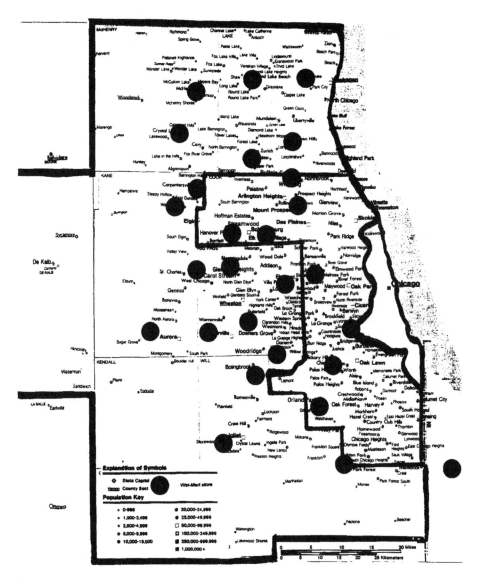

Figure 2 Wal-Mart stores in the three concentric rings of the Chicago market

Each of the changes in proportions associated with each of the stores listed in Table 2 are statistically significant. That is, it is possible to reject the null hypotheses that there were no changes in the shares of shoppers in the Atlanta population from which the samples were drawn.

Similar results were observed in the Kingston and Chicago markets (Table 2). Over an 18-month period, Wal-Mart more than doubled its share of shoppers for the single Kingston store, from 7% when it was a Woolco, to 22% as a Wal-Mart. In Chicago, only 11% of City respondents reported they shopped most often at Wal-Mart. In the outer ring, it was 41%. This first set of results

Table 2 Share of shoppers

Store	Atlanta*		Chicago 1994			Kingston*	
	1985 (%)	1993 (%)	City (%)	Inner (%)	Outer (%)	1994 (%)	1995 (%)
Wal-Mart	8[b]	53[a]	11	21	41[a]	7	22[a]
Target	2	12[a]	8	10	12	—	—
Kmart	30	19[a]	20	11	14	9	7
JC Penney	13	5[a]	11	9	9	—	—
Sears	13	3[a]	7	6	3	19	10[a]
Zellers	—	—	—	—	—	40	39
Other	7	8	43	43	21[a]	25	22
Totals	100	100	100	100	100	100	100
(Sample size)	749	531	177	212	256	413	394

[a] Change in proportions significant at $p<0.05$, two-tailed, for Atlanta 1985 vs 1993, Chicago City vs Outer, Kingston 1994 vs 1995.

[b] In the 1985 Atlanta survey, 8% said they shopped most often at Wal-Mart.

* The Wal-Mart store in the 1995 Kingston survey was known as Woolco in the 1994 survey. The Target stores in the 1993 Atlanta survey were known as Richway in the 1985 survey.

establishes that Wal-Mart attracts shoppers from other chains whenever it enters a market.

Reasons for store selection

Reasons given for store selection also shifted in Wal-Mart's direction. We show this shift with two different kinds of data and supporting analyses. In the first set of data, respondents were asked to name the single and second most important reasons for shopping at the store where they shop most often. Between 1985 and 1993, the proportion of Atlanta respondents mentioning 'low/best prices' rose from 34 to 50% (Table 3). A similar result (30–47%) occurred in Kingston over a much shorter period of time. Low/best price mentions also increased from 39% in the City of Chicago to 49% in the outer suburbs. Again, each of these changes in proportions are statistically significant.

Consistent changes were also observed on some of the other reasons for shopping. The second reason which showed a consistent increase in all three markets is 'helpful/friendly' employees. Here, the increases are in the range of 2–3 percentage points although none are statistically significant.

The consistent increases in importance being attached to the low/best prices and helpful/friendly reasons were offset by consistent decreases in importance associated with the 'sales/promotions/ads,' 'quality' and 'credit card' reasons. The decreases in the Atlanta and Chicago markets on sales/promotions/ads, in particular, are proportionately large and statistically significant. The role of quality declined across the three cities, by a significant amount in Atlanta, but by

Table 3 Most important reasons for shopping at store shopped most often

Reason	Atlanta		Chicago 1994			Kingston	
	1985 (%)	1993 (%)	City (%)	Inner (%)	Outer (%)	1994 (%)	1995 (%)
Low/best prices	34[b]	50[a]	39	36	49[a]	30	47[a]
Helpful/friendly	5	7	7	7	10	5	8
Sales/promotions/ads.	16	10[a]	27	17	14[a]	18	15
Quality	13	5[a]	12	12	8	13	12
Credit card	4	2[a]	3	2	1	10	4[a]
Find what I want	10	16[a]	5	10	9	6	7
Convenient location	58	58	46	40	50	52	45[a]
Variety/assortment	19	33[a]	38	48	31	35	35
Know layout	2	5[a]	4	3	8	10	7
Value for the money	4	4	1	5	5[a]	3	3
Other	27	8[a]	13	14	10	12	15
Totals	192	198	195	194	195	194	198
(Sample size)	741	502	153	194	239	412	394

[a] Change in proportions significant at $p<0.05$, two-tailed, for Atlanta 1985 vs 1993, Chicago City vs Outer, Kingston 1994 vs 1995.
[b] In the 1985 Atlanta survey, 34% mentioned 'low/lowest/best prices' as the 'single' or 'second most important' reason for shopping at the store where they shop most often.

smaller amounts in Kingston and Chicago. Finally, there was a consistent decline in importance across all three cities for having store credit cards. These increases and decreases in importance are consistent with Wal-Mart's profile established in the previous section.

Comparison of Wal-Mart shoppers with 'other' shoppers

While Table 3 shows that changes in consumers' reasons for shopping in the three markets are consistent with the attributes that Wal-Mart identifies itself on, Table 4 provides evidence that Wal-Mart is the source of these changing consumer preferences. Table 4 compares the attributes that Wal-Mart shoppers and shoppers of other mass merchandisers find most important when considering store choice. As the results show, Wal-Mart shoppers consistently attach significantly greater importance to the low/best prices and helpful/friendly attributes and less to the sales/promotions/ads, quality, and credit card attributes. For instance, in all three markets, those who identified Wal-Mart as the store they shopped at most often also identified low prices as an important attribute significantly more than shoppers who identified another retailer as the store they shop at most often. This same pattern holds for the attribute of helpful/friendly staff. The pattern is reversed for the attributes of sales/promotions/ads, quality, and credit card. These attributes were significantly more important for shoppers of other stores than for shoppers of Wal-Mart in all three markets.

Table 4 Most important reasons for shopping at store shopped most often: other shoppers and Wal-Mart shoppers

Reason	Atlanta 1993		Chicago 1994		Kingston 1995	
	Other (%)	Wal-Mart (%)	Other (%)	Wal-Mart (%)	Other (%)	Wal-Mart (%)
Low/best prices	41[a]	57[b]	32[a]	64	41[a]	69
Helpful/friendly	5	8	7[a]	15	6[a]	16
Sales/promotions/ ads.	17[a]	4	24[a]	4	17[a]	6
Quality	9[a]	2	12	8	14[a]	6
Credit card	4[a]	0	3[a]	0	5[a]	0
Convenient location	60	57	46	46	49[a]	33
Variety / assortment	32	33	38	39	34	39
Know layout	7	4	5	3	8	7
Find what I want	12[a]	19	8	8	8	7
Value for the money	4	4	5[a]	2	3	2
Other	8	8	14[a]	7	14	15
Totals	199	196	194	196	199	200
(Sample size)	220	282	477	172	306	88

[a] Differences in proportions significant at $p<0.05$, two-tailed.
[b] In the 1993 Atlanta survey, 57% of those who shopped most often at Wal-Mart mentioned 'low/lowest/best prices' as the 'single' or 'second most important' reason for shopping at this store.

Store best characteristic

In the second data set, respondents were asked a series of questions in which they had to mention the 'one chain' they felt performed best on a store characteristic. The questions related to locational convenience, price, sales/promotions, value, assortment, layout, community concern, advertising, service, store environment, quality and being in stock. For each question, respondents chose the one chain from a specified list of low-priced department store/chains.

The shares of mentions for each chain in response to the question "Which store has the lowest everyday prices?" are found in Table 5. In every market, Wal-Mart's share of mentions increased significantly, either over time (Atlanta and Kingston) or across concentric circles (Chicago). Thus, Wal-Mart was found to be capturing more share of mentions on a reason for shopping which was shown in Table 3 to have grown significantly in importance, ie low/best prices.

These store best data were then transformed into vectors of store observations, where a vector was created for each store mentioned by each respondent. An element in an observation vector corresponding to a store characteristic was either a 0 or 1 depending upon whether for that store, the respondent identified it as being best on that characteristic. The final element in each vector was another 0/1 dichotomous measure dependent upon whether for the store

Table 5 Share of low price mentions

Store	Atlanta[b]		Chicago 1994			Kingston[b]	
	1985 (%)	1993 (%)	City (%)	Inner (%)	Outer (%)	1994 (%)	1995 (%)
Wal-Mart	13[a]	74	24	37	62	8	44
Target	25	9	13	16	16	—	—
Kmart	48	14	26	17	11	15	6
JC Penney	2	1	1	I	0	—	—
Sears	1	1	2	2	0	2	1
Zellers	—	—	—	—	—	55	37
Other	11	1	34	27	11	20	12
Totals	100	100	100	100	100	100	100
(Sample size)	668	514	177	210	237	311	323

[a] In the 1985 Atlanta survey, 13% said that Wal-Mart had the 'lowest everyday prices.'
[b] The Wal-Mart store in the 1995 Kingston survey was known as Woolco in the 1994 survey. The Target stores in the 1993 Atlanta survey were known as Richway in the 1985 survey.
Change in proportions significant at $p<0.05$, two-tailed, for Atlanta 1985 vs 1993, Chicago City vs Outer, Kingston 1994 vs 1995.

represented by the observation vector, the respondent also said they shopped most often at that store.

The store best data permitted another way of examining the Wal-Mart shopper, parallel to the Table 4 comparison of the Wal-Mart shopper with other shoppers. The 1993 Atlanta store best data were split into groups corresponding to those who shopped most often at Wal-Mart, those who shopped most often at Kmart and those who shopped at another store. Conditional logit models of choice behaviour (TSP International, 1995, pp. 136–139) were estimated for each of the three shopper groups. The conditional logit model allows for identification of the attributes that are salient in store choice. In effect, store choice was regressed on a subset of the store best characteristics.

The results of the logit regressions are found in Table 6. The largest and most significant coefficient for the Wal-Mart shopper is 'lowest everyday prices.' Location, value, assortment and community concern are also salient in store choice. In contrast, location is the dominant variable for Kmart shoppers while other shoppers evidence the more traditional influences of location, prices and advertising.

Thus, Tables 3–6 show that the attributes that consumers prefer have shifted and this shift is consistent with the attributes that define Wal-Mart. This provides evidence of the impact that Wal-Mart has had as it enters these various markets. The attributes that best define Wal-Mart are everyday low prices, helpful/friendly service, stores that are well laid out, and active involvement in the community. On the other hand, Wal-Mart is not noted to stand out on the attributes of quality, offering customer credit, and sales and promotions.

Table 6 Conditional logit coefficients of store shopped most often with store best characteristics of Wal-Mart, Kmart and other shoppers

Reason	Atlanta 1993		
	Wal-Mart	Kmart	Other
Lowest everyday prices	5.3[a]	0.6	−0.8[a]
Best concerned about and involved in the community	3.8[a]	−0.7	−0.6
Best at being in-stock with advertised or special items	3.4[a]	0.8[a]	0.2
Largest overall selection or assortment of merchandise	3.4[a]	0.1	0.1
Easy to get to from your home	3.2[a]	3.0[a]	1.2[a]
Best overall value for the money	3.0[a]	0.5	0.4
Lowest prices for promotions and sales	1.5	0.5	0.5[a]
Most informative, helpful advertising on television	−2.4	0.5	1.2[a]
Best at easy to return or exchange merchandise	−2.2	0.7	0.7[a]
Best layout for ease shopping, finding what you want	1.4	0.2	0.4
Most fun place to shop	0.9	−0.5	0.8[a]
Best at being in-stock with regular merchandise	−0.0	0.1	0.7[a]
Sample size	282	99	150
Total observations	1341	482	710

[a] Significant at the $p<0.05$ level (t-statistic > 1.96 or <-1.96, two-tailed test).

The pattern of results show that the consumer preference structure in the three markets has shifted and this shift has been in the direction consistent with the definition of Wal-Mart's attributes.

These results show the impact that Wal-Mart has on the markets that it enters. They establish the first condition for Wal-Mart being a market spoiler because of its ability to instigate changes in the consumer preference structure. The question left to be examined, however, is the mechanism by which these consumer preferences have shifted. Does the shift simply represent Wal-Mart's ability to satisfy existing consumer preferences that competitors did not adequately satisfy before Wal-Mart's entry? Or has Wal-Mart been able to change attribute saliency? This question is answered by considering consumer ambiguity.

Consumer preference ambiguity

Hoch and Deighton (1989) defined ambiguity as the potential for multiple interpretations. If, for instance, when responding to the question "Which store has the lowest everyday prices," the respondent mentioned more than one store, then this result would be an indication of ambiguity on the respondent's part. The respondent is unable to pinpoint one store that is the best on that characteristic.

Taking Hoch and Deighton's (1989) definition to the more general case, we defined consumer ambiguity as the inability of the respondent to pinpoint one specific store as being best on the given characteristic being asked. Therefore, multiple mentions is only one measure of this ambiguity, If the respondent states that s/he does not know which store is the best on a given characteristic and is unable to identify any store, then this too represents consumer ambiguity. Therefore, consumer ambiguity was measured by the inability of the consumer to confidently identify any one store as being best on a certain characteristic. The sum of the proportions of 'multiple mentions', 'don't knows', and 'no answers' serves as a measure of consumer ambiguity.

The results of the consumer ambiguity are shown in Table 7. In the two markets in which surveys were conducted over time (Atlanta and Kingston) the proportions of ambiguity clearly follow the proposed trend. When Wal-Mart entered the Kingston market in 1994, it faced a market with quite a high level of

Table 7 Proportions of none, multiple mentions, don't know or refused on store best characteristics

Store best	Atlanta		Chicago 1994			Kingston	
	1985 (%)	1993 (%)	City (%)	Inner (%)	Outer (%)	1994 (%)	1995 (%)
Lowest everyday prices	11	7	8	11	16	25	20
Value for the money	7	5	7	9	6	18	14
Easiest to get to	5	8	14	14	19	23	17
Best concern community	—	19	27	29	26	60	48
Most helpful clerks, cashiers	23	11	14	14	17	39	25
Best easy return merchandise	—	16	22	25	24	51	41
Most fun place to shop	—	7	11	11	11	31	23
Lowest prices specials	7	7	6	9	10	18	21
Best assortment	—	5	10	8	10	21	14
Best clothing assortment	10	5	10	7	7	20	14
Best selection children wear	22	13	15	9	14	35	26
Best HBA assortment	7	9	10	16	12	28	23
Best selection housewares	—	6	8	9	11	24	14
Best overall layout	—	7	8	7	7	22	16
Best advertising	12	10	14	28	26	26	22
Most helpful TV ad	—	11	11	15	19	49	45
Fastest checkout	14	8	13	14	14	34	18
Most exciting environment	17	10	12	17	14	37	30
Best store interiors	—	11	13	16	11	28	28
Best lighting level	—	16	16	19	20	38	35
Best overall displays	—	6	10	10	9	20	14
Best in store signs, aids	—	12	14	15	14	35	28
Highest quality products	8	7	9	7	9	24	16
Highest quality clothing	—	6	9	7	5	30	12
Best casual clothing women	11	6	11	9	12	21	17
Best casual clothing men	14	8	11	11	13	30	25
Best new items, trends	—	10	14	13	13	34	31
Best in stock regular merchandise	15	9	13	13	15	41	28
Best in stock adv items	13	10	10	14	17	29	28

ambiguity. In 1994, at least one third of the respondents were unable to clearly identify one store as being best at 11 different characteristics. Only one year after Wal-Mart's entry into the Kingston market, there were only four character-istics that one third or more respondents were unable to identify one store as being best. Also, ambiguity fell in 27 of the 29 characteristics between 1994 and 1995.

A similar pattern of results can be found with the Atlanta market. Between 1985 and 1993, ambiguity fell in 13 out of 16 characteristics.

The Chicago survey presents a different situation from the Atlanta and Kingston surveys. Rather than time being the differentiating factor, distance is the factor in the Chicago survey. The first surveys in each of the Atlanta and Kingston markets coincided with the entry of Wal-Mart. As discussed above, Wal-Mart's entry into a market can prompt a number of events (ie extensive media coverage) that may drastically change that market's information environ-ment, and thus create consumer preference ambiguity. The Chicago survey was taken at one point in time and broken down into three concentric rings. Unlike the instability in the Atlanta and Kingston markets at the time of the first surveys, the Chicago survey was taken a time when Wal-Mart has already been well established in the outer area of Chicago. In other words, unlike the Atlanta and Kingston markets, the Chicago market is really not in the same state of 'information flux' at the time of the 1994 survey. Therefore, evidence of any differences in levels of ambiguity between the three Chicago areas was neither expected nor found.

One final empirical issue to discuss is the sustainability of market asym-metry. In the Atlanta market, after eight years Wal-Mart holds over half of the market share (see Table 2) and the level of ambiguity in the Atlanta market is, on average, the lowest of all three markets. It seems that in the Atlanta market, Wal-Mart capitalized on the initial ambiguity present in 1985. Since then, Wal-Mart has solidified its hold on the market. As a result, consumer preference ambiguity has dropped while consumer preferences have remained asymmetric in Wal-Mart's favour (see Tables 3 and 4). The evidence seems to suggest that the key to sustaining asymmetric consumer preferences in the long run is a low level of consumer ambiguity. As long as ambiguity remains low, there is no reason to believe that consumer preferences, which are in Wal-Mart's favour, will shift. Therefore, in the Atlanta market, Wal-Mart's dominant market pos-ition has been sustained for eight years which has been accompanied by a low level of consumer preference ambiguity.

Discussion and Conclusions

Wal-Mart has been a major force in North American retailing. In each market that it enters, this retailer has the ability to substantially affect many aspects of that market. The research presented in this paper has tracked Wal-Mart in three different markets. In each of these markets, there was evidence that with Wal-Mart, consumer preferences shift asymmetrically in favour of the attributes that characterize Wal-Mart. Moreover, examination of these shifting consumer preferences has provided the occasion to investigate the possibility that a retailer, through its marketing strategy, is actually the cause of the shifting consumer preference structure. This notion, introduced by Carpenter and Nakamoto (1989) within the market pioneering context, is supported by the results in this study. By capitalizing on consumer preference ambiguity, Wal-Mart has been able to shift consumer preferences in its favour. As this shift occurs, the level of consumer ambiguity falls. This solidifies consumer preferences and since these preferences have been in Wal-Mart's favour, Wal-Mart's market share also solidifies. It can be predicted that this market advantage will hold for Wal-Mart at least until some new force again creates consumer preference ambiguity.

It is interesting to project this pattern of results on the Kingston market. The second survey was conducted only one year after Wal-Mart's entry where the second Atlanta survey was eight years later. The implication is that assuming no other force recreates consumer preference ambiguity, it can be predicted that Wal-Mart's market share in the Kingston market will continue to climb while consumer preference ambiguity will continue to fall. The reason is that after only one year, consumer preferences have already moved asymmetrically in Wal-Mart's favour. It is this asymmetry in consumer preferences that is the source of competitive advantage (Carpenter and Nakamoto, 1990). This advantage will persist at least as long as consumer preference ambiguity continues to fall in the Kingston market.

Results from the Chicago survey at least partially support the proposition that a market spoiler can change consumer preferences in its own favour. While consumer preferences are different in the outer Chicago area where Wal-Mart is present as compared to Chicago city, consumer preference ambiguity really does not differ between the areas for reasons discussed in the previous section. However, this lack of difference in preference ambiguity between the three areas of Chicago does not necessarily run counter to the propositions. It may well happen that if Wal-Mart moves into the core city area of Chicago, and therefore is present in all of the metropolitan Chicago area, not only may consumer preferences shift in Wal-Mart's favour in the city area, but ambiguity may drop in all three areas. With all three areas of Chicago providing similar retail offerings, consumer preference ambiguity may drop uniformly across all three areas.

Managerial implications

This research presents some interesting managerial implications. While managers are typically interested in research that defines consumer preferences, having a sense of the degree of consumer preference ambiguity in a given market may also provide important strategic information. A market that has a high degree of consumer preference ambiguity may represent a market that is most 'ripe' for implementation of new marketing strategies. However, in a market in which consumer preference ambiguity is low, it may not be very productive to try and implement strategies that attempt to move consumer preferences. A maintenance strategy may be best in such a situation.

The other issue has to do with the ability of a marketer to create consumer preference ambiguity in the first place. As discussed above, Wal-Mart's entry into a given market is often met with heavy media attention. This is often enough to create great ambiguity in the market. But the creation of this ambiguity cannot be attributed directly to Wal-Mart's marketing strategy. It may be that such environmental forces beyond the direct control of the marketer are the most important factors at creating consumer preference ambiguity. If this is the case, then the implication for management, as alluded to above, is to be aware of such forces and the degree of ambiguity created. Such awareness then puts the marketer in the position to capitalize on the ambiguity.

Limitations

The results in this study were gathered by way of market surveys. The underlying assumption is that the noted changes in each market structure arose as a result of Wal-Mart's impact on each of the markets. It must be acknowledged, however, that other factors or market forces besides Wal-Mart's entry could also have accounted for the changes observed over time in Atlanta and Kingston or across regions in Chicago. For instance, the populations of each of the Chicago regions are different. Also, all three markets have been effected by recessionary cycles at one time or another over the past decade, eg Atlanta in 1991–92. Such extraneous market forces could also influence market preference structures through the emergence, for instance, of more value-oriented consumers.

Another extraneous influence would be the entry of other chains. One example would be the purchase by Target of the Richway stores between the 1985 and 1993 surveys and the conversion of the Woolco store to a Wal-Mart store between the 1994 and 1995 Kingston surveys. Whereas Wal-Mart ownership more than tripled the share of shoppers from 7 to 22% in Kingston, Target was not able to halt a decline from 29% in Atlanta in 1985 for the stores known as Richway to 12% in 1993 when the same stores were now known as Target. In contrast, Wal-Mart's share in the Atlanta market rose from 8 to 53%.

Still another extraneous variable would be an increase in advertising effort or a change in advertising strategy by the other competitors. In Kingston, Zellers appeared to dramatically increase its advertising spending in response to the Wal-Mart threat, with respect to both hi-lo promotional and its 'Where the lowest price is the law' campaign. The latter campaign could have contributed to a shift towards low price and away from promotions/sales.

It would have been ideal to have surveyed a market where Wal-Mart did not enter and where there were no other extraneous activities. We were not able to identify such a 'control' market. At least as far as North America is concerned, Wal-Mart entry into new markets is leveling off as there are few markets left where it does not have a presence. Similarly, tracking studies in additional markets beyond the three here would also be helpful in assessing the pervasiveness of the market spoiler effect. Nonetheless, surveys from three markets was a step beyond the typical one market project.

As noted earlier in the paper, the concept of marketers changing consumer preferences has been studied by way of experimental design. While experiments provide a controlled environment in which to test a particular theory, they cannot capture all the dynamics of the actual market place. By using market surveys over time, as was done in this paper, actual changes in market structure can be tracked. However, the tradeoff is that one cannot control for all of the market forces present in any given market. Therefore, the market survey results here should be considered in the context of the experimental results that have preceded this paper, as well as in the context of future studies on this topic. The results in this paper offer another dimension of support for the proposition that market spoilers can change consumer preferences.

Future research

One way to account for the potential of other market forces explaining the changes in consumer preferences is to conduct market surveys in 'control markets.' As Wal-Mart expands into new markets outside North America, the opportunity arises again to trace Wal-Mart's entry into these new markets, while simultaneously conducting these same tracking studies in markets in which Wal-Mart is not present. If the results of these continued studies show that consumer preferences are changing in the markets in which Wal-Mart enters then this would provide further support for the findings presented in this paper. Meanwhile, if these same changes are not occurring in the markets in which Wal-Mart is not present, then there is more confidence in discounting the extraneous market forces as an explanation.

Note

1   As of December 1996, Chase Manhatten operates a co-branded Master Card/Wal-Mart credit card.

References

Alba, J. W. and Chattopadhyay, A. (1986) Salience effects in brand recall. *Journal of Marketing Research* **23**(November), 363–369.
Arnold, S. J., Handelman, J. and Tigert, D. J. (1996) Organizational legitimacy and retail store patronage. *Journal of Business Research* **35**(3), 229–240.
Bucklin, L. P. and Gautschi, D. A. (1983) The importance of travel mode factors in the patronage of retail centers. In *Patronage Behaviour And Retail Management*, eds W. Darden and R. Lusche, pp. 45–55. North Holland, New York.
Carpenter, G. S., Glazier, R. and Nakamoto, K. (1994) Meaningful brands from meaningless differentiation: the dependence on irrelevant attributes. *Journal of Marketing Research* **31**(August), 339–550.
Carpenter, G. S. and Nakamoto, K. (1989) Consumer preference formation and pioneering advantage. *Journal of Marketing Research* **26**(August), 285–298.
Carpenter, G. S. and Nakamoto, K. (1990) Competitive strategies for late entry into a market with a dominant brand. *Management Science* **36**(10), 1268–1278.

Darden, W. R. (1979) A patronage model of consumer behaviour. In *Competitive Structures In Retail Markets: The Department Store Perspective*, eds R. Stempfl and E. Hirschman, pp. 43–52. American Marketing Association Proceedings Series, Chicago.

Dawson, S., Bloch, P. H. and Ridway, N. M. (1990a) Shopping motives, emotional states and retail outcomes. *Journal of Marketing* **66**(4), 408–427.

Dawson, S., Stern, B. and Gillpatrick, T. (1990b) An empirical update and extension of patronage behaviour across the social class hierarchy. In *Advances in Consumer Research*, 17, eds M. E. Goldberg, G. Gorn and R. W. Pollay, pp. 833–838. Association for Consumer Research, Provo, UT.

Forman, A. W. and Sriram, V. (1991) The depersonalization of retailing: its impact on the lonely consumer. *Journal of Retailing* **67**(2), 226–243.

Fershtman, C., Mahajan, V. and Mullar, E. (1990) Market share pioneering advantage: a theoretical approach. *Management Science* **36**(8), 900–918.

Hoch, S. J. and Deighton, J. (1989) Managing what consumers learn from experience. *Journal of Marketing* **53**(April), 1–20.

Hoch, S. J., Drèze, X. and Purk, M. E. (1994) EDLP hi-lo, and margin arithmetic. *Journal of Marketing* **58**(October), 16–27.

Hoch, S. J. and Wa, Y.-W. (1986) Consumer learning: advertising and the ambiguity of product experience. *Journal of Consumer Research* **13**(2), 221–233.

Houston, F. S. (1986) The marketing concept: what it is and what it is not. *Journal of Marketing* **50**(April), 81–87.

Jacob, R. (1993) Beyond quality and value. *Fortune* **128**(13), 8–11.

Kalyanaram, G. and Urban, G. L. (1992) Dynamic effects of the order of entry on market share, trial penetration, and repeat purchases. *Marketing Science* **11**(3), 235–250.

Kardes, F. R., Kalyanaram, G., Chandrashekaran, M. and Dornoff, R. J. (1993) Brand retrieval, consideration set, composition, consumer choice, and the pioneering advantage. *Journal of Consumer Research* **20**(June), 62–75.

Kohli, A. K. and Jaworski, B. J. (1990) Market orientation: the construct, research propositions, and managerial implications. *Journal of Marketing* **54**(April), 1–18.

Mason, J. B., Durand, R. M. and Taylor, J. L. (1983) Retail patronage: a causal analysis of antecedent factors. In *Patronage Behaviour And Retail Management*, eds W. Darden and R. Lusche. North Holland, New York.

Miller, C. (1993) Nordstrom is tops in survey. *Marketing News* **27**(4), 12–13.

Narver, J. C. and Slater, S. F. (1990) The effect of a market orientation on business profitability. *Journal of Marketing* **54**(October), 20–35.

Porter, M. E. (1985), *Competitive Advantage. Creating And Sustaining Superior Performance*. The Free Press, New York.

Rinne, H. and Swinyard, B. (1992) Christmas customers at discount department stores: a national survey. *Retail Business Review* **60**(8), 16–21.

Roach, L. (1993) Wal-Mart's top ten. *Discount Merchandiser* **33**(8), 76–77.

Slater, S. F. and Narver, J. C. (1994) Does competitive environment moderate the market orientation-performance relationship? *Journal of Marketing* **58**(1), 46–55.

Stalk, G., Evans, P. and Shulman, L. E. (1992) Competing on capabilities: the new rules of corporate strategy. *Harvard Business Review* (March-April), pp. 57–69.

Stigler, G. J. and Becker, G. S. (1977) De gustibus non est disputandum. *American Economic Review* **67**(March), 76–90.

Tigert, D. J., Cotter, T. and Arnold S. J. (1993) The low priced department stores in

Atlanta, Indianapolis and Dallas/Ft. Worth — Vols I, II and III. Boston: Babson College Retailing Research Reports, Report No. 7, April. (Summarized in Winning on price, location, assortment. *Chain Store Age Executive*, Special issue, mid-July 1993, pp. 11–78.)

Tigert, D. J., Cotter, T. and Arnold S. J. (1994) The mass merchandisers in Chicago: consumer attitudes towards and buying habits at the major chains. Babson College Retailing Research Reports, Report No. 8, May. (Summarized in Chicago poses tests for new and old retailers. *Chain Store Age Executive*, Section 3, August, pp. 3B–30B.)

Tigert, D. J., Cotter, T. and Arnold, S. J. (1995) Supercenters: can they build market share against the supermarkets – Vol. I: Victoria, Texas and II: Gainesville, Georgia. Babson College Retailing Research Reports, Report No. 10, April and May. (Summarized in The squeeze is on: Wal-Mart and Kmart supercenters put the squeeze on supermarkets. *Chain Store Age*, Section Three, August 1995, pp. 4B–31B.)

Timm, P. R. (1992) Retaining customers, *Executive Excellence* 9(11), 20 TSP International, (1995) *Time Series Processor Reference Manual Version 4.3* TSP International, Palo Alto, CA.

Urban, G., Carter, T., Gaskin, S. and Mucha, Z. (1986) Market share rewards to pioneering brands: an empirical analysis and strategic implications. *Management Science* 32(June), 645–659.

Vance, S. S. and Scott, R. V. (1994) *Wal-Mart: A History of Sam Walton's Retail Phenomenon.* Twayne Publishers, New York.

Webster Jr, F. E. (1988) Rediscovering the marketing concept. Working paper, Marketing Science Institute.

Chapter 2

Retail Branding and Marketing

RETAILERS ARE IN A constant battle for consumer attention and spending. Whilst some retailers may have a captive market for a variety of reasons, most actively have to attract consumers to shop at them. In some countries there could be thousands of different shops potentially available to a consumer. For the retailer, however, whether there are many competitors, or only one, the problem is essentially the same: how do I get the consumer to notice and to patronize my business?

A starting point for this is the external identification of the shop for consumers; in historical times this was the sign of the trade or of the products carried, and nowadays the 'name' or fascia of the retailer. As consumers use stores, they become aware of differences or distinctions amongst them. Some of these may be perceptual or psychological in terms of meeting consumers' preferences and tastes, whilst others may be more economically or 'factually' based, as in product availability, price levels or services offered. Over time, retailers become 'known' for particular things and gain a reputation.

A second process is also at work here, however. In addition to consumer evaluations of retailers and the development of a retailer's reputation through consumer inter-actions, retailers can be more proactive. In seeking to attract consumers, retailers aim to differentiate themselves from their competitors. Some retailers may be able to differentiate themselves in terms of the supply of exclusive products or services. Other retailers begin to recognize where they are 'better' than the competition and thus have an advantage. This advantage or difference can be built upon, marketed and used to attract consumers. Retailers thus gain a reputation for their operations and how well or not these meet either general or particular consumer needs. They actively promote this reputation or image to attract more consumers and spending and thus to become more profitable and expand.

When retailers were essentially the passive recipients of products from manufacturers, the ability to differentiate was somewhat constrained and was related mainly
to advantages of location and the personality of the independent shopkeeper. With the
development of chain-based retailing, so efficiencies in operations and supply could
be developed and marketed to the consumer. In modern-day retailing, the retailer has
the potential to position themselves away from the competition and to 'stand' for
something in the consumers' minds. They thus promote, market and operationalize
this image or position in their retail and support activities. Tesco's 'Every Little Helps'
or Wal-Mart's 'Lowest Prices – Always' are convenient shorthand for the positions
these retailers want consumers to believe. Simply mentioning IKEA, Aldi, Zara, Next,
Primark or Dollar General to consumers conjures up an image or position in their
minds.

As retailers have gained power in their channel relationships, so their scope to promote themselves over competitors and manufacturers has increased. The development
of common retailer fascias and brands has allowed centralized promotion and advertising by the retailer. Retailers have seen the potential within this for the development
of their own retail brands, which have taken an increasing share of spending. Retailer
brands are not new, but the modern conceptualization amongst some retailers is far
removed from the original 'name on a product' trademark or indeed from the 'private
label' approach, where the true potential of retailer branding has perhaps been less
well developed and understood. Retailer brands can go beyond a 'product label' by
making a statement and positioning the retailer in consumers' minds. This is perhaps
most obvious in high-fashion brands such as Louis Vuitton, Dolce & Gabbana or
Alexander McQueen, but is equally apparent in mass-market retailers such as Tesco,
where arguably the conceptualization and operationalization of the retailer brand
power is even stronger, as a broader brand architecture has been developed.

A visit to a shopping centre or a high street for a consumer now confronts them
with a variety of retailer images and positions and a range of branding strategies. The
most famous UK retail brand name was arguably 'St Michael' from Marks & Spencer,
but this has been quietly dropped in recent years, in favour of a different branding strategy and to separate the business from a recent difficult period. Some retailers (e.g.
Debenhams) are essentially a 'house of brands' with many manufacturer or designer
brands represented. Even here though there may be Debenhams retail brands which
are controlled, organized or owned by the retailer. Some of these retailer brand names
may be known as Debenhams brands by consumers; others may not. Some products
may carry the Debenhams name, whilst others will not. Similarly, in Asda, there will
be various price and segmented brands under the Asda name, as well as other brands
(e.g. George) that are well known as being exclusive to, and owned by, Asda. These are
in addition to a range of manufacturer brands. For a retailer, identifying the right brand
strategy and mix to produce a clear and coherent image is thus a major task.

This section of the book considers these aspects of branding and marketing. It does
this not from the viewpoint of the consumer but from the standpoint of the retailer.
How can a retailer develop a coherent image? Where does product branding fit into
store image? Can retailers become corporate brands? What do retailers 'stand for'
and how do they convey this to consumers?

There are many ways in which these questions could be tackled. One of the fundamental distinctions in this area is the role of the retailer brand (or store brand, own label/own brand, or private label as they are mainly called in the USA). There appears to be a fundamental difference between the USA and Europe (UK) in the business practice and academic conceptualization in this area. In the USA most concern is with low-quality, low-price private labels. In Europe (and particularly the UK) the concern is more with the totality of the retail brand offering. This difference is central to the discussion of the research and papers that follows. Here, however, it is also placed in the wider context of store image and image presentation. This chapter thus comprises four papers:

1   *The Retailer's Identity.* The idea that retailers have an image or a reputation that they portray and uphold is not a new one. However, for a long time the way that image was advertised was perhaps somewhat mechanical and focused on items that could be readily copied, such as price. By considering the concept of identity rather than image, it becomes possible to create a broader position from which to promote the retailer. Rather than focusing on product attributes, retailers can focus on the corporate attributes that come together as the retailer's product. This 'identity' is multifaceted, needs to be coherent, but involves both physical and perceptual components. Kapferer's (1986) identity prism is used here as one approach to such identity generation and differentiation of retailers.

2   *Store Brands.* The North American business practice and academic tradition in this area is exemplified in the terminology used. The focus is mainly on store brands or private labels and the concern tends to be on the 'battle' such products have with manufacturer brands. Much of this may be because the context in the USA is different from that in Europe. Product branding by retailers in the USA has tended not to go beyond lower-quality 'generic'-style products and cheap manufacturer-brand copies. This is a result of consumers' preferences for manufacturer brands, the supply system and power of the manufacturers, retailers' reluctance to challenge the status quo and other contextual factors. Private labels tend to be viewed as cheap, being bought by lower-income families, often in times of recession. The paper included here by Dhar and Hoch (1997) is representative of this genre of store-brand research in the USA. However, it also has hints of the differences found elsewhere and the potential that retail branding has to promote the retailer's desired image.

3   *Retailer Brand Strategy.* By contrast, the development of retailer branding in Europe (and particularly, but not solely, the UK) rapidly moved through the phases of generics and low-value imitations of manufacturer brands. Retailers began to realize that the focus on product branding was only part of the processes of retailer branding. By developing further generations of higher quality products under a retail-brand umbrella, retailers began both to challenge manufacturers across the board but also to drive innovation in products. They also began to see retailer branding as encompassing *all* operations of the business, including store formats, employees and even in some senses customers. By bringing these elements together in a true brand strategy, retailers positioned

the retailer as the brand and portrayed a particular image and set of expectations for consumers in every activity they carried out. They developed the brand as corporate identity. Burt's (2000) paper is a discussion of the strategic nature of retail branding in grocery retailing in the UK and demonstrates the breadth and the coherence of the approach.

4   *Retailer Legitimation.* Retailers have often been portrayed as simple sellers of items. But, when retailer branding is developed strategically it becomes clear that the retailer is selling far more than the physical products carried in the stores. They are positioning the company as a worthy place for a consumer to spend money, time and effort. Retailers are selling a product (their store), products (items and services) and an image (what the store says about the retailer and the consumer). The 'selling' of the image needs to be congruent with the requirements and the desires/dreams of the consumers and the local/national economy and society. In short, everything a retailer does 'says something' about them and to consumers. Arnold *et al.* (2001) use institutional semiotics to discuss how Wal-Mart utilizes 'a rich blend of family, community and national norms' to portray (legitimate) its operations. There are clear links here to the 'market spoiler' concept that concluded Chaper 1. The retailer brand and identity is shown to be so much more than the 'label on the can'.

The Retailer's Identity

The idea that retailers seek competitive differentiation is of course not a new one. Martineau (1958) suggested that competitive differentiation derived from the store image, which was defined as the 'personality' a store possesses in consumers' minds (see also Myers 1960 and Kunkel and Berry 1968). Subsequent research has varied in whether this personality or store image is the sum of a set of distinctive parts or components (e.g. Lindquist 1974; Oxenfeldt 1974) or the overall perception that consumers hold of the store (Doyle and Fenwick 1974; Dichter 1985).

At the same time effort has been spent on trying to identify what the components of store image might be and how this might be used (Marks 1976). Lindquist (1974) identified a set of tangible and intangible factors which contributed to store image. Others have amended that list (e.g. Hansen and Deutscher 1977; Zimmer and Golden 1988). One of the problems with this approach is that consumer perceptions of stores vary over place and time and relative to the existing competition in the market (McGoldrick 1998). Whilst of interest and use, not least to retailers, store image may be better considered from different starting perspectives.

It is generally held that a positive store image is one of the important determinants in success in retailing (Jacoby and Mazursky 1984) being linked to store choice, store loyalty and store positioning (e.g. Davies and Brooks 1989; Walters and Knee 1989). However, the complexity of defining and measuring store image leads to inconsistencies in conceptualization and operationalization (Keaveney and Hunt 1992). What is clear is that retailers themselves consider the positioning of their stores in competitive markets and use their brands and corporate activities to differentiate themselves and to produce an image in consumers' minds. The question may not be what is a retailer's store image? Rather it may be better posed as what is a retailer's identity?

This is the starting point for Kapferer (1986). The overall approach in the paper begins with the view that retailers' advertising is generally very 'mechanical'. Here, advertising is used as a proxy for the generation of a retailers' image. The mechanical nature of the approach is in Kapferer's view due to a focus on the behavioural components of consumers rather than on their attitudinal components. Thus, advertising focuses on price, service, own brands which are readily copyable, functional parts of the retail offer. Consumers 'buy' these attributes and so marketers use them. Kapferer's point is that consumers have reasons for their actions, some of which are perceptual and attitudinal. It is this 'engagement' with the retailer that is the true mark of differentiation and identity. In essence, Kapferer condemns retailers for not advertising their product (i.e. the store) in a coherent, consistent and total manner.

The product of the retailer is the store and its attributes. What tends to be advertised, he argues, are products with their prices, some store brands to compete on price against manufacturer brands and perhaps some functional services. The real 'product' is never advertised: what is the store or company personality and how will this help consumers do their shopping and live their lives? As a result, many retailers are engaged in an advertising battle focused on the latest price cuts, never-ending sales and the drive to be the cheapest. What does this tell you about the retailer and what does it teach consumers to do? Where does loyalty fit into this?

Kapferer (1986) develops the idea that retailers need to differentiate or to produce a 'singularity' in terms of their positioning. This differentiation allows consumers to see them as different to (better than) competitors and thus to offer some reason for long-term patronage. This belief in difference combines behavioural and attitudinal aspects of behaviour (and foreshadows similar approaches to consumer loyalty, e.g. Dick and Basu 1994). By focusing on attitudes, Kapferer moves from what should be 'said' to consumers, to how to say it. He thus introduces semiotics to the retailers' approach to the consumer arguing that the repertoire of words, visuals, symbols, colours and so forth that they use are important in achieving the objective of differentiation. Branding clearly fits this approach.

Kapferer produces an 'identity prism' to focus retailers' attention on the communication with consumers. This identity prism has six facets:

1   *Physical:* the functional attributes of the store and of the offer, e.g. opening hours, price position.
2   *Personality:* often composed of symbols or personalities used in promotion, e.g. Toys 'R' Us uses a giraffe.
3   *Relational:* essentially conveyed by sales staff and the support they give and are given (or not).
4   *Cultural:* retailers relate to the culture from which they originate, e.g. IKEA has a strong culture deriving from Sweden.
5   *Customers' Reflection:* the image of the customers that the retailer portrays, e.g. aspirational imagery.

6   *Customers' Self-Concept:* the image of the customer that is portrayed by the customer patronizing the store, e.g. astute, price-conscious shopper signified by using Aldi.

The importance of the identity prism is that it forces retailers to look beyond the main functional attributes of the retail offer. These are of course necessary for retail operations, but in meeting consumer needs, other attributes or facets also come into play. A store can have good products and sell them at a 'good' price, but if the image is not meeting current consumer needs and perceptions and is seen to be outdated or out of step, then the retailer will struggle. One could argue that this is what occurred to C&A in the UK, where the image remained stuck in the 1960s as consumers moved on, and C&A's focus on functional attributes, such as price, proved insufficient to meet changed perceptions.

The six facets of the identity prism also stress the importance of symbolic actions and approaches. Beyond functionality, Kapferer points to the way in which signs, symbols, colour and so on can be used to match the needs of consumers. Words and text in stores, on leaflets, on advertisements are understood and decoded by consumers. Colours for keen pricing mainly focus on harsh reds and yellows, whereas high quality is often seen through silver and black. Retailer brands and branding obviously contributes to the symbolism and image. Aldi's branding change in the early 2000s in the UK involves in part a move to silver packaging in recognition of UK consumer expectations from retailer brands.

Kapferer's overall message is that retailers are in control of their broad environments and need to construct these as a whole to focus on consumers. Retail stores are artificial, controlled environments, but they need to 'speak to' the consumers the retailer is targeting (Floch 1988). But this goes beyond the product and the store. All the actions and statements of a retailer are subject to interpretation by consumers. Thus retailers need to manage not only in-store actions but all communications, whether verbal or not (Arnold *et al.* 2001; Christensen and Askegaard 2001). This approach suggests that retailers are not engaged so much in store image generation or brand presentation but rather in the development of retailer corporate branding (Burt and Sparks 2002).

Perhaps because Kapferer's (1986) paper was presented at a conference and published in proceedings, or perhaps because some of his work has been first published in French the direct take-up of the identity prism in retailing has been perhaps limited. It does appear, however, in his major books on general branding (Kapferer 1998, 2001, 2004) and has been taken up in general branding work. The underlying ideas have pervaded much research, as will be seen later, and it is clear that retailers think about attitudes and functions in creating their image and position in consumers' minds.

Store Brands

The idea of retailers or distributors putting their name on products (branding them) is not new. However, when power and advertising are concentrated at the manufacturer level, consumers get used to the idea of manufacturer brands and seek them out. In such circumstances retailers, the recipients of manufacturer products, primarily become shelf-space providers for the various manufacturers, with pricing guided by the manufacturers.

This positioning of retailers and manufacturers has altered in many countries over time. Retailers have become larger and more powerful and less inclined to accept the dictates and whims of manufacturers and distributors. This battleground was fought out initially over price and the ability or not for retailers to price away from, usually below, the recommended re-sale price. If most retailers have the same products at the same price then competition is difficult, particularly in price-sensitive times or locations. By reducing price and discounting, retailers could target consumers with the lowest price. But such operations required a source of supply of non-price-controlled manufacturer products which could be price positioned below the prices of main manufacturer products. Retailers obtained some of these products via non-traditional sources or markets (e.g. the grey market) or else contracted with lesser known manufacturers to produce directly for them. Such products might carry names unknown to the consumer, not carry any branding at all, or be sold under a brand name related in some way to the store or retailer. Such products undercut the manufacturer products on price, also often on quality, but allowed price competition to attract consumers. For smaller manufacturers producing private label may be sensible and profitable as they seek to compete with leading brands and use their own (sometime spare) production capacity.

The description above suggests in brief the origins of generics (no-name products), private labels (a label controlled by the retailer) and store brands (a label controlled by, and possibly named for the retailer). Initially, such products were positioned to compete with the manufacturer brands and to attract the price-conscious and price-concerned consumer. There are also other reasons why retailers might want to introduce such products. They could for example provide a higher margin to the retailer and be used in supply and price negotiations with main manufacturers. For manufacturers, as such products grew in popularity, the inevitable question was whether or not to get involved in the production and distribution of such products. For the manufacturer, their customer has become a competitor, which raises a number of questions (Cotterill *et al.* 2000).

In the USA, in the main this has remained the position for private labels. As Dhar and Hoch (1997) point out, 'US store brands usually are not quite up to the quality standards of the top national brands and always are priced at a discount' (p. 209). The context in which research into store brands and retail branding takes place is important. The view of retail branding in the US tradition has tended to focus over-whelmingly on the role of private labels/store brands (these terms tend to be used interchangeably) and not on Kapferer's (1986) wider conceptualization or the prac-tices of European grocery retailers (as we will see later in Burt 2000). The approach is thus to European eyes somewhat narrow, but does fit the cultural position and current practice of the USA (Bhasin *et al.* 1995; Quelch and Harding 1996). The question it begs is whether retailers in the USA are missing a trick by being too functionally oriented in their brand and brand promotion?

The North American approach to retailer branding has been summarized in the review article by Ailawadi and Keller (2004). They begin by considering the attributes of store image (as we have done in this chapter). They build on the work by Lindquist (1974) and Mazursky and Jacoby (1986) to produce five attributes which are fundamental to store image (and thus in their conceptualization in turn to retailer brand equity):

- access (store location and distance) and its importance to store-choice decisions;
- store atmosphere;
- price and promotion, focusing on store price perception, retailer pricing format and price-promotion store switching;
- cross-category assortment, i.e. the breadth of assortment;
- within-category assortment, i.e. the depth of assortment.

In at least three of these attributes, the presence or not and the positioning of 'private labels' (to use the terminology used by Ailawadi and Keller 2004) have had a direct effect on the store image. The role of the 'private label' is thus seen to be an important research area. In common with others, Ailawadi and Keller (2004) provide three reasons for the retailers' development of 'private labels'. These are the opportunity to enhance margin (Hoch and Banerji 1993), the possibility of gaining negotiating leverage with manufacturers (Narishiman and Wilcox 1998) and the 'implicit assumption' that private labels foster enhanced retailer loyalty by consumers (Steenkamp and Dekimpe 1997).

The North American literature has tended to focus on a specific series of questions when considering the position of store brands or 'private labels'. These questions tend to be based around the following issues.

- Who buys private labels? e.g. Richardson *et al.* 1994, 1996a, 1996b; Ailawadi *et al.* 2001; Sprott and Shimp 2004.
- Do retailers gain leverage over manufacturers? e.g. Mills 1995; Narashiman and Wilcox 1998; Ailawadi and Harlam 2004; Morton and Zettelmeyer 2004; Pauwels and Srinivasan 2004.
- What categories best suit private labels? e.g. Sethuraman 1992; Hoch and Banerji 1993; Raju *et al.* 1995; Sayman *et al.* 2002; Dhar and Hoch 1997; Sayman and Raju 2004; Choi and Coughlan 2006.
- What are the pricing issues for private labels? e.g. Connor and Peterson 1992; Chintagunta *et al.* 2002.
- When should manufacturers produce private labels? e.g. Hoch 1996; Dunne and Narishiman 1999.
- How should manufacturers react to private label development? e.g. Hoch 1996; Mills 1999; Karray and Zaccour 2006.

The context of this work is important. It is based on data from within the USA and is focused in particular on the store-brand level of development and mostly on 'private label'. However, as Dhar and Hoch (1997) indicate, this form of retailer branding is not universal and the low-price, low-quality branding, mainly represented by 'private label', may not be the best formulation of retailer branding to adopt. Nonetheless, this is the form prevalent in the USA and is the focus of the paper selected for inclusion here (Dhar and Hoch 1997).

The Dhar and Hoch (1997) paper considers the performance of private labels amongst retailers. It is based on the largest retail markets in the USA and focuses on thirty-four food categories for 106 major retail supermarkets. A mathematical modelling approach to these data is taken and systematic results are identified. These show that whilst national brand performance is important, as are the tactics and promotions of leading manufacturers, a substantial part of the variation in market share for private labels comes about as a result of the actions (or not) of the retailer. Where retailers have a strong promotional support and a commitment to private labels, then performance is enhanced. Likewise, where private labels have a quality reputation but also have a good price, performance is better. For manufacturers, one defensive mechanism is to encourage retailers to have deeper assortments as this mitigates against retailer-brand power. Dhar and Hoch (1997) conclude that store-brand share could increase dramatically in the USA if the stronger retailers more intensively promote their store brands and if the weaker retailers begin to imitate best practice. Manufacturers, they conclude, have much to be worried about.

The Dhar and Hoch (1997) paper is important for a number of reasons. It is clearly focused on and situated in the North American context. Its methodological approach and indeed its questions are typical of the way in which 'private labels' have been approached in this research tradition. However, this paper, unlike some of the other research cited, is not unaware of either different contexts or the possibilities of broader conceptualizations. Early in the paper the authors make the point that elsewhere retailer brands are not low-price, low-quality private labels and they return to this in their conclusions. They also pick up on the idea of quality of retailer product branding and the potential this might have to provide different models, results and outcomes in stores.

This beginning of an emergence of a broader sense of retailer branding is perhaps reflected in one of their concluding remarks 'As European retailers with high-powered *corporate branding programs* continue to acquire regional chains in the US, the threat to national brands becomes more immediate' (Dhar and Hoch, 1997, p. 224, emphasis added). This threat comes not only directly from the takeover and altered practices, but also from the learning that American retailers are beginning to implement after seeing such programs in, for example, Wal-Mart, CVS and Kroger.

This wider view of retailer branding is also reflected in part by some of the points made by Ailawadi and Keller's (2004) review article. They raise the question as to whether retailer private labels are related to store loyalty. They are somewhat ambivalent in their answer pointing to Steenkamp and Dekimpe (1997), Corstjens and Lal (2000), Ailawadi *et al.* (2001) and Ailawadi and Harlam (2004) as having mixed results and unclear on causality. The conflation of US and European research here may not help clarity. More interestingly perhaps, in their research questions for the future they ask about the potential for retailer branding to fit with experiential marketing and brand architecture (Ailawadi and Keller 2004). In both cases, Europeans would argue that such questions point to the futility of considering private labels *per se*. By linking experiential marketing and concepts of brand architecture, the retailer is clearly presenting its total offering as a brand and engaging in corporate retailer branding (Burt and Sparks 2002).

However, the research in the USA overall appears not to have fully picked up on these issues and the changing practices in some of the US retail sectors. Sprott and Shimp (2004, p. 313) maintain: 'Most retailers do not actively promote their own brands but rather make them passively available in expectation that price conscious shoppers will select these value items over more expensive NB (national brand) alternatives.' Leaving aside why retailers would act so passively, if private labels provide higher margins and other benefits, such behaviour is patently not the case in much of the world, where retailer branding is more developed. It may even be becoming less true in the USA. As Choi and Coughlan (2006) argue, for a 'strategic' retailer enhancing product quality for private label is a positive move. Similarly, Woodside and Walser (2006) in a paper on building strong brands in retailing, conceptualize the brand as 'an encompassing concept that includes retail firms as well as physical products and services'.

Retailer Branding

The European perspective on retail branding, as has been noted above, is somewhat different to that of the work in North America. Some of this is due to the methodological and philosophical differences between retail research generally in the two traditions, but part of this is also due in this area to fundamental differences in practices. As has been noted in the discussion of 'retailer branding' in the USA (Ailawadi and Keller 2004), most of the research has focused on private labels. In contrast the work in Europe has been focused more on retail brands (e.g. Burt 2000) and their development from earlier generations of 'own-labels' (e.g. Morris 1979; Simmons and Meredith 1984; Davies *et al.* 1986; Martell 1986). There are a number of implications of this (which are not always recognized in the literature):

> This apparent divergence of opinion across the Atlantic raises a fundamental issue in the study of retail brands, namely a clear understanding of the object of study. The assumption is often made that the term 'retail brand' in one country or context is the same as 'retail brand' in another. In reality the composition of retail brand ranges, the market positioning of these products and the origin and development of these differences is important when assessing academic work or trade press commentaries.
>
> (Burt 2000, p. 876)

The most widely used description of the development of retailer brands in Europe (and particularly appropriate to the UK) is that proposed by Laaksonen and Reynolds (1994). They proposed four generations of retailer brand, each with important differences in product characteristics, production technology input, market position and customer motivation. They were clear as well that these generations of categories or countries do not 'progress' though the same sequence. The value of the schema is thus in illustrating and/or describing the different forms of retail brand that can exist or have existed. The four generations are generally described as:

1   *First Generation* – generics or 'non-name' products focusing on basic products with lower quality and inferior image compared to manufacturers' brands. Price is the key reason for purchase.

2   *Second Generation* – own label products often under retailer name but again medium to low quality and portioned as a cheap secondary brand. Price is important with the product used to increase margins and reduce manufacturers' power.

3   *Third Generation* – own brand products which are essentially 'me-too' copies of leading manufacturers' brands. These products are close to the leading brand in position but slightly undercut them on price. These products are sold mainly under the retailers' name and aim to position the retailer in consumer minds and to build the retailers' image.

4   *Fourth Generation* – Extended retail brand which focuses on adding value for consumers, sometimes by narrow specialized segmentation. Such products are focused on differentiating the retailer and providing a strong positive image. These products, e.g. ready meals, could be technologically advanced and priced above any manufacturer competition.

Any visit to a UK superstore would show that the retailer focus has been mainly on the latter generations of this sequence. Retailers such as Tesco have developed a tri-brand positioning strategy in terms of price points (e.g. Tesco Value, Tesco and Tesco Finest) supplemented with a large selection of segmented retail brand products (e.g. vegetarian meals, low-carb. diets and organic). The contrast with a much more manufacturer-brand-led US supermarket is quite considerable. In the USA the retail (store) brand products found would mainly tend to be from the second and third generations. This focus on private labels, to reiterate, is very different to the focus on the retailer brand and image in the UK (Hughes 1996). Two further quotations reinforce the point:

> Simple improvements in the extrinsic cues associated with store brands may go a long way towards increasing consumer acceptance of private label brands. European retailers understand this and have been successful in increasing store brand market share though dramatic improvements in package design, labeling, advertising and branding strategies.
>
> (Richardson *et al.* 1996a, p. 178)

> The European experience shows that store brands, if properly marketed, can create the competitive advantage that most retailers in the USA have yet to achieve.
>
> (Dick *et al.* 1995, p. 201)

If one accepts the four generation model of Laaksonen and Reynolds (1994) it becomes interesting to surmise what is, or will be, the fifth generation, as retail branding will not stop with the fourth generation (e.g. Burt and Sparks 2002).

It is therefore not surprising that in the title to the paper included here, Burt (2000) refers to the 'strategic role' of retail brands in the UK grocery retailing. His thesis is that there is a fundamental difference in approach in the UK, where the retail brand is treated as a 'true brand'. This distinguishes British retail branding and marketing from many other countries, particularly in grocery retailing (see the Tesco 'journey' in Leahy 1994; Mason 1998; and Kelly 2000). He accounts for this difference in three main ways:

- The basis and use of retail power in the distribution channel. As retailers have gained power in the UK so they have restructured relationships with manufacturers, including those of product supply.
- The centralization of management activities. UK retailing is highly centralized and exerts a considerable degree of control over the production, promotion, stocking, supply and characteristics of products.
- The recognition of the source of retail image. UK retailers have been clearer than perhaps many of the value their name possesses. The development of conforming stores and added services as non-price competition exploded (Burt and Sparks 1994; Wileman and Jary 1997; Seth and Randall 1999) focused attention on image promotion at many levels, including product, brand and store.

At the start of this process, research tended to focus on the development of generic and low-value retail brands (generations one and two) and to ask questions similar to those posed subsequently in the USA. Work by McGoldrick (1984) and de Chernatony (1988, 1989) is typical of the issues under investigation as own-label developed (Davies *et al.* 1986).

As the sophistication of retailer branding grew (e.g. Davies 1992), so conflicts between manufacturer and retailer emerged. The main area of concern here was the way in which retailer branding was seen to 'copy' manufacturer brands in terms of colour, packaging, style and terminology (e.g. Rafiq and Collins 1996; Balabanis and Craven 1997; Sparks 1997). High-profile court cases and media attention ensued, with retailers being forced to ensure some difference between their brands and manufacturer brands in terms of how they looked and thus would be seen and perceived by consumers. For some this issue was a 'theft of identity' by retailers and showed a lack of innovation at the retail level (Davies 1998). This was not a phenomenon restricted to the UK (Kapferer 1995). Evidence seemed to show consumer confusion amongst retailer product brands as well (Burt and Davis 1999) particularly as most UK retailers sought to mimic Marks & Spencer's colouration and packaging in food products in the 1990s.

As foreshadowed in Burt (2000) retailers have subsequently begun to see how far they can 'push' their branding. There has been a major extension of, for example, Tesco product branding into services such as finance, banking, computing, opticians, pharmacy, will preparations and mortgages, diet advice and Internet providing. For some

(Burt and Sparks 2002), the strategic approach that retailers are adopting goes beyond product or service extensions and approaches true corporate branding (Ind 1997; Balmer 2001). As a consequence, they propose that we are now, for some retailers, seeing a fifth-generation additional to the Laaksonen and Reynolds (1994) sequence. This further generation positions all actions that the retailer undertakes as supportive of their branding and image position. It also sees the brand proposition as encompassing not just product branding but store format branding (e.g. Tesco Express, Tesco Extra, Tesco.com) and indeed all corporate activities. In essence a broadbrand architecture is developed. Whilst only a few retailers might be considered to have gone this far, this does open up possibilities for the future for others, though there are dangers in brand architecture design and brand extensions if not fully thought through (Alexander and Colgate 2005; Grunert *et al.* 2006).

A further potential problem is raised by Burt and Sparks (2002) and has also been considered in other work by Burt (e.g. Burt and Carralero-Encinas 2000; Burt and Mavrommatis 2006). If retailers develop a strong position in a national context, then what components of this brand proposition have meaning in other, e.g. international, contexts? How can retailers transfer brand propositions across cultures and how does this relate to core internal and competitive positioning? This is also raised in Chapter 5 of this reader.

These two aspects come together to some extent in fashion branding and fashion brand internationalization. Fashion branding is somewhat different from the grocery branding which has been the main sector considered in the literature. There are commonalities with aspects of store image development (e.g. Birtwistle and Freathy 1998; Birtwistle *et al.* 1999). The development of retail brands/store brands has also been a concern for some fashion businesses (e.g. Moore 1995). Indeed retailers such as Zara, Gap and H&M are dependent on retailer brands and are, in effect, examples of retailer corporate branding. Fashion branding internationalization in retailing does differ, however, in the process involved and its speed (e.g. Moore *et al.* 2000; Wigley *et al.* 2005). The brand position projected remains fundamentally important, however.

North Americans might at this point begin to ask 'show me the evidence'? Much of the approach in Europe and the UK has focused on descriptions and conceptualizations of practical behaviour. The success of leading retailers such as Tesco and Zara is assumed to be due in part to enhanced loyalty through corporate branding. But, do we know this for certain?

Retailer Legitimation

The last two sections have counter-pointed two approaches to retailer branding and caricatured them as being typical of the USA (private labels) and the UK (corporate branding) respectively. This is, of course, a pedagogical tool and the situation is more complex than has been presented. European researchers have been concerned with the economics of private label (e.g. Bergès-Sennou *et al.* 2004; Soberman and Parker 2004) and American researchers have become concerned with strong retail branding (e.g. Woodside and Walser 2006). The core point, however, is consistent: retailers that are concerned with more than product functionality in branding appear more likely to have success. The question that arises from this is how best to achieve this 'corporate' approach to branding? It is clear that retailers that simply try to dictate their view of the world to consumers are likely to have a hard time. Instead, retailers have to be embedded in the social and cultural norms of the country in which they are operating. In the terminology they need to seek, or even create, 'legitimation' (e.g. Arnold *et al.* 1996; Handelman and Arnold 1999).

There are situations when consumers are looking for something 'different'. For retailers, focusing too much on embeddedness or sameness may then be a problem. For internationalizing retailers for example the point of difference may be important; IKEA brings Swedish design and style to the world. But it can not be too distinct or retailers simply will not convince consumers to 'get it'. Marks & Spencer spent twenty-five years in Canada without much success, being seen as too peculiar for the market. On the other hand, if retailers copy the local market too much, then consumers question the point; some would argue that Carrefour failed in Japan by being too Japanese and insufficiently French.

The key point is that retailers need to be aware of the social and cultural environments as well as the economic ones. They then need to think how this knowledge can be used to further their position, image and reputation. This of course was the message from Kapferer (1986). Being socially and culturally embedded will mean that a retailer must be closely aligned with the values, ethos and position of the group they most want to target. The wider that target spectrum of society the greater the challenge to be able to bridge social, cultural and value differences. There is an important choice as to whether these differences can be bridged within a single format or as a series of niche stores. In the process of internationalization retailers have on occasion failed to adapt to different cultural norms or to the way that society groups itself in the consumer market. Of course, this is an ever-changing process with new societal groupings emerging and the privileging of different aspects of the sociocultural and value nexus.

The social and cultural world is inhabited not only by prices and opening hours and other economic facets, but by symbols, signs, beliefs, attitudes, perceptions, brands and other appeals. Decoding such intangible (and tangible) attributes is the function of semiotics. Lawes (2002) defines semiotics as 'the ways people communicate with each other, consciously and unconsciously, through things such as language, visual images and music' (p. 253). Semiotics examines the generation of meaning from communication signs. The use of semiotics is an established tool in consumer research (e.g. Gottdiener 1985; Mick 1986, 1997) but has perhaps had less consideration in retailing. The main exception is the work of Floch (1988) who used a semiotic approach to identify the values underpinning store layout and hypermarket shopping.

This absence of semiotic study in retailing is a little curious given the presence of so many signs and symbols in retailing (including brands) and the concern that retailers (and researchers) have had for atmospherics at the store level (e.g. Baker *et al.* 1993; Chebat and Dube 2000; Summers and Hebert 2001), including the impact on private label purchase (e.g. Richardson *et al.* 1996b), links to brand perceptions (e.g. Beverland *et al.* 2006) and in merchandising (see Chapter 3). Perhaps this is a further example of where the functions of retailing have been the focus and obscured some of the wider issues?

This is the context for the paper by Arnold *et al.* (2001). Their paper looks at the institutional semiotics of Wal-Mart flyers (i.e. the advertising leaflets provided in newspapers or in-store). This subject is chosen in part because Wal-Mart is a fascination for retail researchers and because as Arnold *et al.* (2001) note, Wal-Mart flyers are 'distinctive'. This distinctiveness causes them to seek to 'unravel the symbolic puzzle . . . of Wal-Mart flyers . . . and draws attention to the importance of retail image and retail symbolism' (p. 243). The tool they use to do this is what they term 'institutional semiotics'. The introduction of this approach is a major contribution of this paper.

Institutional semiotics is the combination of a semiotic analysis (Lawes 2002) driven by institutional theory (Meyer and Rowan 1977). The semiotic framework used by Arnold *et al.* (2001) involves asking three questions: Who is being addressed? Who is the sender? What are the mythologies (or 'stories' being told)? Institutional theory can then be used to interpret the answers by identifying the underlying economic and sociocultural norms. The investigation thus looks at characteristics, tone, emotion and stories/norms revealed by the communication, particularly in terms of family, community and national institutions.

The best summary of the findings of Arnold *et al.*'s (2001) investigation of Wal-Mart flyers is provided by his later broader work on Wal-Mart flyers in a number of countries (Arnold *et al.* 2006). Their conclusion is worth providing at length to illustrate the approach and its potential (p. 145):

> The reader was determined to be a working- or middle-class American female between the ages of 25 and 55 whose main concern was her family and especially her children. In turn, the Wal-Mart speaker was revealed to be an ordinary, plain spoken person who might also be a friendly neighbour or even a trusted friend. The interpretation further identified the mythology of *Homo economicus* – adherence to the Puritan/Calvinist virtue of thrift through paying low prices and being a smart shopper.
>
> The analysis also identified the mythology of family, emphasizing the institutional norms of caring, loyalty and commitment. Furthermore, it revealed the mythology of America, which is characterized by the norms of anti-statism, populism, egalitarianism and especially patriotism. Finally, the mythologies of community and hometown pointed to an idealized small-town America where friends, family and neighbours meet and socialize while shopping at their local, friendly, Wal-Mart store.

Their analysis points to the ways in which Wal-Mart and its customers experience each other through communication media and through their interactions (tangible or intangible) reinforce common beliefs about economics, society and culture. Some of the symbolism is implicit and understated whereas other components are explicit and up-front. The key message however for this book is that none of this happens by accident, but is generated by a sophisticated understanding of consumer desires and beliefs as well as their hopes and often unstated ambitions. Unreal and almost unbelievable it may seem – after all Wal-Mart is the world's biggest company not a 'neighbourly, small-town shop-keeper' – the synergy between the company and its consumers appears to hold and to be part of its success. Wal-Mart has portrayed an image rather than a product position and is essentially a brand with tangible and intangible attributes that 'chime' with consumers (cf. the concluding paper in Chapter 1). In a different context Christensen and Askegaard (2001) use a semiotic analysis in a consideration of corporate identity and corporate image; an approach which could be useful to consideration of retail corporate branding.

As has been noted before, this congruence between a retailer, its market and the image it wishes to portray raises a number of research questions. Directly following from the work in Arnold *et al.* (2001), a similar exercise using Wal-Mart flyers in the USA, UK, Germany and China has been conducted (Arnold *et al.* 2006). Posing the same questions and using the same tools of institutional semiotics they again reveal the mythologies to be based around *homo economicus*, credibility (price legitimacy), family, community, patriotism and racial tolerance. Arnold *et al.* (2006) note variations in the ways community and nation are represented in different countries, but argue this is Wal-Mart adopting their approach to local norms and seeking local legitimacy. They question the approach to multicultural societies in the flyers, and wonder about the racial composition of images in the non-USA locations. They also conclude that the flyers in Germany appear 'less thoughtful' than those in other countries.

The importance of the Arnold *et al.* (2001) conceptualization is in its clear identification of economic and sociocultural attributes on which retailers can target consumers and base their images, branding and marketing. The significance of legitimation is considerable. Indeed this example illustrates the ways that retailers actually begin to construct identities which match their offer and which build on their understandings of the sociocultural situation. Some have argued that a failure to adhere to sociocultural norms can be more damaging to a retailer than failure to adhere to economic norms (Bianchi and Arnold 2004). In one sense we have come full circle from Kapferer.

Summary

Over a decade ago, Richardson *et al.* (1994) wrote that:

> Retailers have a choice. They can view themselves either as passive distributors of manufacturers' brands or as active marketers of their own proprietary store brands. The former strategy has been the prevalent one adopted by American retailers . . . The problem with this strategy is obvious: chains become little more than warehouses for manufacturers' products.
>
> (p. 35)

This chapter of the book is based implicitly on the belief that retailers know their position with respect to consumers more clearly than do many manufacturers. By portraying a clear image based not only on economic considerations but on socio-cultural ones and by turning all activities into support activities for the retailer brand, retailers can become clear leaders in branding and marketing. Failure to do this on the other hand leads to a subservient position compared to manufacturers. Consumers want both manufacturer and retailer brands, but they need to be persuaded about the benefits from both, time and again. This requires careful consideration of how the image and brand are developed, how they relate to consumer needs, demands and perceptions and an understanding of the importance of economic and symbolic dimensions of activities. Images and positions are hard earned, but easily lost, and retailers need to ensure that their organization as a whole is supporting the image and the brand in its entirety.

References

Ailawadi KL and Harlam B (2004) An empirical analysis of the determinants of retail margins: the role of store brand share. *Journal of Marketing*, 68, 147–166.

Ailawadi KL and Keller KL (2004) Understanding retail branding: conceptual insights and research priorities. *Journal of Retailing*, 80, 331–342.

Ailawadi KL, Gedenk K and Neslin S (2001) Pursuing the value conscious consumer: private labels versus national brand promotions. *Journal of Marketing*, 65, 71–89.

Alexander N and Colgate M (2005) Consumer responses to retail brand extension. *Journal of Marketing Management*, 21, 393–419.

Arnold SJ, Handelman J and Tigert DJ (1996) Organisational legitimacy and retail store patronage. *Journal of Business Research*, 35, 229–239.

Arnold SJ, Kozinets R, and Handelman J (2001) Hometown ideology and retailer legitimation: the institutional semiotics of Wal-Mart flyers. *Journal of Retailing*, 77, 243–271.

Arnold SJ, Bu N, Gerhard U, Pioch E and Sun Z (2006) The institutional semiotics of Wal-Mart flyers and signage in the United States, United Kingdom, Germany and China. In S Brunn (ed.) *Wal-Mart World: The World's Biggest Corporation in the Global Economy*. Routledge: New York, 143–162.

Baker J, Levy M and Grewal D (1993) An experimental approach to making retail store environmental decisions. *Journal of Retailing*, 68, 445–460.

Balabanis G and Craven S (1997) Consumer confusion from own brand look-alikes: an exploratory investigation. *Journal of Marketing Management*, 13, 299–313.

Balmer JMT (2001) Corporate identity, corporate branding and corporate marketing – seeing through the fog. *European Journal of Marketing*, 35(3/4), 248–291.

Bergès-Sennou F, Bontems P and Réquillart V (2004) Economics of private labels: a survey of literature. *Journal of Agricultural and Food Industrial Organization*, 2, Article 3, p. 23. Retrieved from http://www.bepress.com/jafio on 23 October 2006.

Beverland M, Lim EAC, Morrison M and Terziovski M (2006) In-store music and consumer-brand relationships: relational transformation following experiences of (mis)fit. *Journal of Business Research*, 59, 982–989.

Bhasin A, Dickenson R and Nandan S (1995) Retail brands – a channel perspective: the United States. *Journal of Marketing Channels*, 4(4), 17–36.

Bianchi CC and Arnold SJ (2004) An institutional perspective on retail internationalization success: Home Depot in Chile. *International Review of Retail, Distribution and Consumer Research*, 14, 149–169.

Birtwistle G and Freathy P (1998) More than just a name above the shop: a comparison of the branding strategies of two UK fashion retailers. *International Journal of Retail and Distribution Management*, 26, 318–323.

Birtwistle G, Clarke I and Freathy P (1999) Store image in the UK fashion sector: consumer versus retailer perceptions. *International Review of Retail, Distribution and Consumer Research*, 9, 1–16.

Burt SL (2000) The strategic role of retail brands in British grocery retailing. *European Journal of Marketing*, 34(8), 875–890.

Burt SL and Sparks L (1994) Structural change in grocery retailing in Great Britain: a discount re-orientation? *International Review of Retail, Distribution and Consumer Research*, 4, 195–217.

Burt SL and Davis S (1999) Follow my leader? Lookalike retailer brands in non-manufacturer-dominated product markets in the UK. *International Review of Retail, Distribution and Consumer Research*, 9, 163–185.

Burt SL and Carralero-Encinas J (2000) The role of store image in retail internationalisation. *International Marketing Review*, 17, 433–453.

Burt SL and Sparks L (2002) Corporate branding, retailing and retail internationalisation. *Corporate Reputation Review*, 5, 194–212.

Burt SL and Mavrommatis A (2006) The internationalization of store brand image. *International Review of Retail, Distribution and Consumer Research*, 16, 395–413.

Chebat JC and Dube L (2000) Introduction to the Special Issue: Evolution and challenges facing retail atmospherics: the apprentice sorcerer is dying. *Journal of Business Research*, 49, 89–90.

Chintagunta PK, Bonfrer A and Song I (2002) Investigating the effects of store brand introduction on retailer demand and pricing behaviour. *Management Science*, 48, 1242–1267.

Choi SC and Coughlan AT (2006) Private label positioning: quality versus feature differentiation from the national brand. *Journal of Retailing*, 82, 79–93.

Christensen LT and Askegaard S (2001) Corporate identity and corporate image revisited – a semiotic perspective. *European Journal of Marketing*, 35(3/4), 292–315.

Connor JM and Peterson EB (1992) Market-structure determinants of national brand-private label price differences of manufactured food products. *Journal of Industrial Economics*, 40, 157–171.

Corstjens M and Lal R (2000) Building store loyalty through store brands. *Journal of Marketing Research*, 37, 281–291.

Cotterill RW, Putsis WP and Dhar R (2000) Assessing the competitive interaction between private labels and national brands. *Journal of Business*, 73, 109–137.

Davies BK, Gilligan C and Sutton CJ (1986) The development of own label product strategies in grocery and DIY retailing in the United Kingdom. *International Journal of Retailing*, 1, 6–19.

Davies G (1992) The two ways in which retailers can be brands. *International Journal of Retail and Distribution Management*, 20, 24–34.

Davies G (1998) Retail brands and the theft of identity. *International Journal of Retail and Distribution Management*, 26, 140–146.

Davies G and Brooks J (1989) *Positioning Strategy in Retailing*. London: Paul Chapman.

De Chernatony L (1988) The fallacy of generics in the UK. *Marketing Intelligence and Planning*, 6(2), 36–8.

De Chernatony L (1989) Branding in an era of retailer dominance. *International Journal of Advertising*, 8, 245–60.

Dhar SK and Hoch SJ (1997) Why store brand penetration varies by retailer. *Marketing Science*, 16, 208–227.

Dichter E (1985) What's in an image. *Journal of Consumer Marketing*, 20, 85–98.

Dick A and Basu K (1994) Customer loyalty: toward an integrated conceptual framework. *Journal of the Academy of Marketing Science*, 22, 99–113.

Dick A, Jain A, and Richardson P (1995) Correlates of store brand proneness: some empirical observations. *Journal of Product and Brand Management*, 4(4), 15–22.

Doyle P and Fenwick I (1974) How store image affects shopping habits in grocery chains. *Journal of Retailing*, 50(4), 39–52.

Dunne D and Narishiman C (1999) The new appeal of private labels. *Harvard Business Review*, 77(3), 41–48.

Floch J-M (1988) The contribution of structural semiotics to the design of a hypermarket. *International Journal of Research in Marketing*, 4, 233–252.

Gottdiener M (1985) Hegemony and mass culture: a semiotic approach. *American Journal of Sociology*, 5, 979–1002.

Grunert KG, Esbjerg L, Bech-Larsen T, Brunsø and Juhl HJ (2006) Consumer preferences for retailer brand architectures: results from a conjoint study. *International Journal of Retail and Distribution Management*, 34, 597–608.

Handelman J and Arnold SJ (1999) The role of marketing actions with a social dimension: appeals to the institutional environment. *Journal of Marketing*, 63, 33–48.

Hansen RA and Deutscher T (1977) An empirical investigation of attribute importance in retail store selection. *Journal of Retailing*, 53(4), 59–72.

Hoch SJ (1996) How should national brands think about private labels? *Sloan Management Review*, 37, 89–102.

Hoch SJ and Banerji S (1993) When do private labels succeed? *Sloan Management Review*, 34, 57–68.

Hughes A (1996) Retail restructuring and the strategic significance of food retailers' own labels: a UK–USA comparison. *Environment and Planning A*, 28, 2201–2226.

Ind N (1997) *The Corporate Brand*. Basingstoke: Macmillan.

Jacoby J and Mazursky D (1984) Linking brand and retailer images – do the potential risks outweigh the potential benefits? *Journal of Retailing*, 60, 105–122.

Kapferer J-N (1986) Beyond positioning: retailer's identity. In *ESOMAR seminar on Strategies for Retail Growth – Retailing Mix*. Amsterdam: ESOMAR, 167–175.

Kapferer J-N (1995) Brand confusion: empirical study of a legal concept. *Psychology & Marketing*, 12, 551–568.

Kapferer J-N (1998) *Strategic Brand Management*. London: Kogan Page.

Kapferer J-N (2001) *Re-inventing the Brand*. London: Kogan Page.

Kapferer J-N (2004) *The New Strategic Brand Management*. London: Kogan Page.

Karray S and Zaccour G (2006) Could co-op advertising be a manufacturer's counterstrategy to store brands? *Journal of Business Research*, 59, 1008–1015.

Keaveney SM and Hunt KA (1992) Conceptualization and operationalization of retail store image: a case of rival middle-level theories. *Journal of the Academy of Marketing Science*, 20(20), 165–172.

Kelly J (2000) Every little helps: an interview with Terry Leahy, CEO, Tesco. *Long Range Planning*, 33, 430–439.

Kunkel JH and Berry L (1968) A behavioural conception of retail image. *Journal of Marketing*, 32 (October), 21–27.

Laaksonen H and Reynolds J (1994) Own brands in food retailing across Europe. *Journal of Brand Management*, 2(1), 37–46.

Lawes E (2002) Demystifying semiotics: some key questions answered. *International Journal of Market Research*, 44, 251–264.

Leahy T (1994) The emergence of retail brand power. In Stodart P (ed.) *Brand Power*. Basingstoke: Macmillan, 121–136.

Lindquist JD (1974) Meaning of image: a survey of empirical and hypothetical evidence. *Journal of Retailing*, 50(4), 29–38, 116.

Marks RD (1976) Operationalising the concept of store image. *Journal of Retailing*, 52(3), 37–46.

Martell D (1986) Own labels: problem child or infant prodigy. *Quarterly Review of Marketing*, 11, 4, 7–12.

Martineau P (1958) The personality of the retail store. *Harvard Business Review*, 36, 47–55.

Mason T (1998) The best shopping trip? How Tesco keeps the customer satisfied. *Journal of the Market Research Society*, 40(1), 5–12.

Mazursky D and Jacoby J (1986) Exploring the development of store images. *Journal of Retailing*, 62, 145–165.

McGoldrick P (1984) Grocery generics – an extension of the private label concept. *European Journal of Marketing*, 18, 5–24.

McGoldrick PJ (1998) Spatial and temporal shifts in the development of retail images. *Journal of Business Research*, 42(2), 189–196.

Meyer JW and Rowan B (1977) Institutionalized organizations: formal structure as myth and ceremony. *American Journal of Sociology*, 83, 340–363.

Mick DG (1986) Consumer research and semiotics: exploring the morphology of signs, symbols and significance. *Journal of Consumer Research*, 13, 196–213.

Mick DG (1997) Semiotics in marketing and consumer research: balderdash, verity, pleas. In S Brown and D Turley (eds) *Consumer Research: Postcards from the Edge*. London: Routledge, 249–262.

Mills DE (1995) Why retailers sell private labels. *Journal of Economics and Management Strategy*, 4, 509–528.

Mills DE (1999) Private labels and manufacturer counterstrategies. *European Review of Agricultural Economics*, 26, 125–145.

Moore CM (1995) From rags to riches: creating and benefiting from the fashion own brand. *International Journal of Retail and Distribution Management*, 23(9), 19–28.

Moore CM, Fernie J and Burt SL (2000) Brands without boundaries: the internationalization of the designer retailer's brand. *European Journal of Marketing*, 34, 919–937.

Morris D (1979) The strategy of own brands. *European Journal of Marketing*, 13, 59–78.

Morton FS and Zettelmeyer F (2004) The strategic positioning of store brands in retailer–manufacturer negotiations. *Review of Industrial Organization*, 24, 161–194.

Myers R (1960) Sharpening your store image. *Journal of Retailing*, 36(3), 124–137.

Narashiman C and Wilcox R (1998) Private labels and the channel relationship. *Journal of Business*, 71, 573–600.

Oxenfeldt AR (1974) Developing a favourable price–quality image. *Journal of Retailing*, 50(4), 8–14, 115.

Pauwels K and Srinivasan S (2004) Who benefits from store brand entry? *Marketing Science*, 23, 364–390.

Quelch JA and Harding D (1996) Brand versus private labels. *Harvard Business Review*, 74, 99–109.

Rafiq M and Collins R (1996) Lookalikes and customer confusion in the grocery sector: an exploratory study. *International Review of Retail, Distribution and Consumer Research*, 6, 329–350.

Raju JS, Sethuraman R and Dhar S (1995) The introduction and performance of store brands. *Management Science*, 41, 957–978.

Richardson PS, Dick A and Jain AK (1994) Extrinsic and intrinsic cue effects on perceptions of store brand quality. *Journal of Marketing*, 58, 28–36.

Richardson PS, Jain AK and Dick A (1996a) Household store brand proneness: a framework. *Journal of Retailing*, 72, 159–185.

Richardson PS, Jain AK and Dick A (1996b) The influence of store aesthetics on evaluation of private label brands. *Journal of Product and Brand Management*, 5, 19–27.

Sayman S and Raju JS (2004) How category characteristics affect the number of store brands offered by the retailer: a model and empirical analysis. *Journal of Retailing*, 80, 279–287.

Sayman S, Hoch SJ and Raju JS (2002) Positioning of store brands. *Marketing Science*, 21, 378–397.

Seth A and Randall G (1999) *The Grocers: the Rise and Rise of the Supermarket Chains*. London: Kogan Page.

Sethuraman R (1992) Understanding cross-category differences in private label shares of grocery products. *MSI Working Paper, Report No. 92–128*.

Simmons M and Meredith B (1984) Own label profile and purpose. *Journal of the Market Research Society*, 26(1), 3–27.

Soberman DA and Parker PM (2004) Private labels: psychological versioning of typical consumer products. *International Journal of Industrial Organization*, 22, 849–861.

Sparks L (1997) From Coca-Colonization to Copy-Cotting : The Cott Corporation and retailer brand soft drinks in the UK and the US. *Agribusiness*, 13, 153–167.

Sprott DE and Shimp TA (2004) Using product sampling to augment the perceived quality of store brands. *Journal of Retailing*, 80, 305–315.

Steenkamp J-B EM and Dekimpe MG (1997) The power of store brands: intrinsic loyalty and conquesting power. *Long Range Planning*, 30, 917–930.

Summers TA and Hebert PR (2001) Shedding some light on store atmospherics – influences of illumination on consumer behaviour. *Journal of Business Research*, 54, 145–150.

Walters DW and Knee D (1989) Competitive strategies in retailing. *Long Range Planning*, 22(6), 74–84.

Wileman A and Jary M (1997) *Retail Power Plays: From Trading to Brand Leadership*. Basingstoke: Macmillan.

Wigley SM, Moore CM and Birtwistle G (2005) Product and brand: critical success factors in the internationalization of a fashion retailer. *International Journal of Retail and Distribution Management*, 33, 531–544.

Woodside AG and Walser MG (2006) Building strong brands in retailing. *Journal of Business Research*, 60, 1–10.

Zimmer MR and Golden LL (1988) Impressions of retail stores: a content analysis of consumer images. *Journal of Retailing*, 64, 265–294.

Editors' Commentary

JEAN-NOËL KAPFERER IS PROFESSOR in the Department of Marketing and Doctoral Thesis Director at HEC School of Management in Paris. His first degree was obtained at the Université de Paris 1 – Sorbonne and his PhD at Northwestern University in Chicago. He has, however, been based throughout his academic career at HEC Paris, although much of his work is also organized through his consultancy company (run with Patricia Kapferer), which specializes in communication and brand expertise (www.kapferer.com). He is one of the most internationally recognized experts on aspects of branding.

His volume *Rumors* gained him a reputation for his expertise on communication in companies but Jean-Noël Kapferer is best known for his expertise on branding. His academic interests have consistently featured brand strategy, both in terms of retailing and more widely as a marketing concept. He is on the editorial board of the *Journal of Brand Marketing*. His publications are in both French and English. Jean-Noël Kapferer is probably best known, at least by marketing students, for his key textbook on strategic brand management. Now in its third edition the volume has a new title: *The New Strategic Brand Management: Creating and Sustaining Brand Equity Long Term*. The first two editions were very highly praised. Anglophone audiences are less well acquainted with his publications in French but these too focus on brand strategies. His key publications read like a journey on the development of brand strategy literature, as he has been at the forefront of research and teaching on the subject for some thirty years.

'Beyond Positioning: Retailer's Identity' sets out the basic premises of the ways in which retailers differentiate themselves. It shows that retail branding and positioning differ in many important ways from other product branding and develops the 'identity prism' for retail positioning and branding which has become Kapferer's trademark. By considering the concept of identity rather than image, it suggests it becomes possible to create a broader position from which to promote the retailer. Rather than focusing on product attributes, retailers can focus on the corporate attributes that come together as the retailer's product. This 'identity' is multifaceted, needs to be coherent, but involves both physical and perceptual components. This emphasis on identity has become ever more significant in understanding how retailers interact with consumers.

Key Publications

Kapferer J-N and Thoenig J-C (1989) *La Marque: facteur de croissance*. New York: McGraw-Hill.

Kapferer J-N (1990) *Rumors: Interpretations and Images*. Piscataway, NJ: Transaction Books.

Kapferer J-N and Thoenig J-C (1992) Les consummateurs face à la copie – étude sur la confusion des marques crée par l'imitation. *Revue Française du Marketing*, 136, 53–69.

Laurent G, Kapferer J-N and Roussel F (1995) The underlying structure of brand awareness scores. *Marketing Science*, 14(3), G170–179.

Kapferer J-N (1995) Brand confusion – empirical study of a legal concept. *Psychology and Marketing*, 12, 551–568.

Kapferer J-N (2001) *Reinventing the Brand*. London: Kogan Page.

Kapferer J-N (2001) Marques: Nike ne fabrique rien, Nike vend Nike. *Temps Stratégique*, Autumn 2001.

Azoulay A and Kapferer J-N (2003) Do brand personality scales really measure brand personality? *Journal of Brand Management*, 11, 143–155.

Kapferer J-N (2004) *The New Strategic Brand Management: Creating and Sustaining Brand Equity Long Term*, London: Kogan Page. (Earlier versions: Kapferer J-N

(1992) *Strategic Brand Management*, London: Kogan-Page and Kapferer J-N (1998) *Strategic Brand Management: New Approaches to Creating and Sustaining Brand Equity*. London: Kogan-Page).

Kapferer J-N (2004) Les Marques face au hard discount. Quelles strategies? *Revue Francaise du Gestion*, 30(15), 203–210.

Schuiling I and Kapferer J-N (2004) Real differences between local and international brands. *Journal of International Marketing*, 12(4), 97–112.

Kapferer J-N (2005) The post-global brand. *Journal of Brand Management*, 12, 319–324.

Websites

http://www.kapferer.com/english/
http://www.hec.fr/hec/eng/professeurs_recherche/p_liste/p_fiche.php?num=60

BEYOND POSITIONING: RETAILER'S IDENTITY

Jean-Noël Kapferer

Advertisers working with retailers often find it difficult to differentiate them from competitors. The retailing mixes are so close that the bases of differences shrink. Advertising and communication now receives the task of creating this difference, a singularity, an identity. But what is an identity? How can it be analyzed? What are the possible sources of communication differentiation?

A model of identity analysis is presented: a retailer's identity has six distinct but inter-related facets, which can be used to differentiate it from its close competitors. This model, called identity prism, is used as a guide for maintaining singularity and coherence across all retailer's communication outputs. Today the message style has become the message itself: the identity prism is an attempt to control what was so far abandoned to the hazards of mere creativity.

Introduction

VERY FEW SECTORS exhibit as much fierce competition as the distribution sector. The necessity of permanently regaining and holding clients leads the major companies to watch each other and never let one of them run ahead of the ruck. As soon as a distributor brings in an innovation, the other distributors adopt it not to be outdistanced. For instance, in the French grocery market, this me-too process concerned the introduction of store brands, of generics, of services, of cafeterias, of rebates on gas, . . .

Strategies for Retailer Growth-Retailing Mix, ESOMAR (June 1986), pp. 167–175.

This situation creates a major difficulty for advertisers in search for a lasting difference. Normally, as textbooks prescribe, each distributor should have a specific image, motivating and grounded. But what are the possible sources of differentiation if, by commercial necessity, all competitors are prompt to imitate each other in terms of products, services, price, days and hours of opening, . . .

This paper aims at presenting a new conceptual scheme to analyse and guide the distributors' images. Called the "identity prism", this scheme is a scanner: it decomposes distributors' image in six facets. Each of them is a basis for image differentiation and a source of value for the distributor. Before detailing the identity prism, we shall first point out why the role of advertising for distributors is necessarily different of that of manufacturers and brands. The limits of the positioning concept will also be underlined.

How Distributors Perceive the Role of Advertising

Most distributors now have an advertising agency. They use such terms as image, positioning, identity. The rules guiding distributors' communication decisions seem now to draw nearer to those of manufacturers. This is true only on the surface. Actually, the formers' logic is fundamentally different to that of the latter.

Any form of distribution is fully defined by its structural parameters: location (inner-city or suburbs), surface, price level, price competitiveness, width and depth of the product range, amount of advice and services, shelves used as locomotives or grabbers. These parameters define the basic store equation, its structural capacities. But they also delineate its limits, its degrees of freedom. These parameters create objective boundaries inside which each store will try to maximize its consumer franchise.

Distributors consider that the role of advertising is strictly mechanic and behavioral. It aims at drawing as much as possible out of the potential market delineated by the basic structural equation of the store. Then, in a second step, advertising aims at extending this potential beyond what the basic structure had set. The chain tries to divert to its own profit customer purchases that could as well be done elsewhere, in some other chain or store. Advertising tries to stretch the limits inherited from the retailing mix basic parameters and to intercept volatile purchasers.

As a consequence, distribution advertising is necessarily mechanic:

- In the primary zone around the store, advertising objectives are to maximize the number of customers, to encourage store loyalty and to maximize the average value of customer purchases.
- In the secondary zone, it provides a rhythm for visiting the store, by means of a sequential and turning presentation of some focal departments of the store, highlighting its product mix.
- In the tertiary zone, advertising creates occasions to pay a visit to the store.

Thus advertising objectives are essentially behavioral and merchant. The problem is that this advertising has fostered an endless escalade and created much confusion: consumers have difficulty to recognize who said what? Each store sings the same song "here tomatoes are cheaper!". The result is a poor attribution of advertising claims and some lack of credibility of all this advertising.

To avoid this, the first endeavor consisted in finding some advertising slogan. As soon as a distributor got a nice one, advertising agencies were summoned at competitors' headquarters and urged to find some slogan "as good". This endeavor had three objectives: (i) to emerge out of the concert of advertising noise (ii) to wrap up the basic commercial claims in some nice ribbon, thus creating some imaginary added value (iii) to capitalize on the many successive advertising campaigns: at least, from an offer to another, this would leave some memorable track.

Thus distributors entered backwards in the logic of identity. The main focus still was mechanic and sales oriented. However, since heavy budgets had to be spent in advertising, one had to put an identity dress on this huge machinery. Since some identity had to be created, one might as well do it properly. Far beyond the slogan, this raised the question of the facets of this identity.

The Limits of Advertising Positioning

Brand advertising has created the concept of positioning: advertising should state the difference between the brand and the competitor it chose as source of business. Positioning basic motto says: "be different". The problem is that distributors' advertising positioning is not as free as that of brands. Each store has a basic structural positioning in terms of pricing, product mix, location, level of services . . . Advertisers call for a selection of one of these facets: distributors stress the need to promote equally all these facets: they constitute altogether the equation of success.

Furthermore distributors are permanently keeping an eye on their competitors: should a distance appear for instance in price image or in service image, they will react in trying to eliminate this difference if it is at their disadvantage.

Thus advertising positioning is of little help for differentiating competitors sharing the same strategy. How should one differentiate two inner city department stores such as "Les Galeries Lafayette" and "Le Printemps", in Paris, or the hypermarket chains of the grocery trade?

The positioning concept has another limitation: it leaves totally free advertising creativity. Focusing on such attributes as products, price, location, service etc . . . it is not really concerned with the language, the signs that will be used in the communication, as long as they are understandable. This position is no longer tenable: today everything communicates. At an age where the basic messages are more and more alike, we have to rely on signs and symbols to create and maintain an identity.

Traditionally, strategic communication platforms were only concerned by the "what to say". Nowadays the "how to say it" is as important. It just cannot be abandoned to the hazards of mere creativity. There has to be some guidelines to monitor creativity and to codify what the language of the distributor will be (its repertoire of words and visuals).

A first move consisted in borrowing the concept of brand "personality". After all, if two salesmen propose the same products and services, the prospects determine themselves on the basis of "source effects": who speaks? Therefore advertising should aim at creating a personality to the brands, and why not to the distributors.

This empirical step towards a search for differences is partial and constitutes only one of the many facets making up the distributors identity. We now turn to a conceptual model whereby store's unicity of image is decomposed in six facets. This model is called the identity prism.

The Six Facets of Retailer's Identity

The uniqueness of a distributor can be analysed along six facets: the physical, personality, relational, cultural, reflection and self-concept facets. Although each of them is specific, these facets are inter-related. If two facets happened to be dissonant, one meaning the opposite of the other, there would be no coherent identity.

The structure of the identity prism is threefold (Figure 1). At the top, two facets describe the "constructed sender": who speaks, what are its character-istics and its character? At the bottom, two facets describe the "constructed

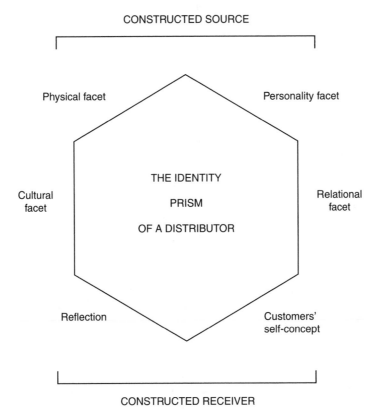

Figure 1 The facets of identity

receiver": to whom is the distributor addressing? The two remaining facets are links or bridges between the sender and the receiver. One is a cultural link, the other describes what type of relation should exist between both parties. In speaking of "constructed sender or receiver", the word constructed is essential. It underscores the fact that communication creates a reality: it is not a mere description of what is, but a purposive construction of what we would like people to believe about the sender (the distributor) or the clients of this distributor.

What is the meaning of each facet making up store's identity? Any person may be described by this or her physical appearance and characteristics, and by his or her personality traits. The same is true for the first and the second facets of distributors' identity.

The physical facet refers to the savoir-faire. It is the traditional repertoire of distributors' communication. Positioning is here: I know how to be the cheapest, how to select the best products, how to be open when the others are closed, I can propose many services. It is an essential facet which can be compared to the stalk of a flower. The stalk is the functional support of all flowers: a necessity. However, most of the appeal and of the differences between flowers lie elsewhere, in the petals. This is why there is a need to codify the other facets of the identity, beyond the physical facet.

The personality facet has been acknowledged for long by distributors. To convey their specific personality compared to their immediate competitors, they have often chosen animals as totems. For instance among major French chains one finds a beaver (Castorama), a sea-gull (Carrefour), a mammoth (Mammouth).

Distributors like also to borrow the personality traits of some well known star. For instance the popular singer Pierre Perret is optimistic, relaxed and astute. He is the spokesman of Castorama, the leading chain in the do-it-yourself market. The entertainer Jacques Martin is typically French and resourceful: he conveys the personality traits sought by Mr Meuble, a leader in home furniture distribution. Henri Salvador is tender, romantic and smiling: he gives these traits to the multi-specialist chain "Conforama" in order to differentiate it from the competitor "But", whose personality is more masculine and aggressive, in a market dominated by price sensitivity.

Actually, among projective interviewing techniques, the Chinese Portrait captures what consumers think the distributors' personality to be. They express their image through symbolic figures such as animals, flowers, movie actors . . . The making up of a distributor's personality uses the reverse way.

The relational facet highly concerns all service activities. Throughout its communication, its way of being, the attitudes of its salespeople, any distributor proposes some kind of relationship to the clients. There are many ways of analyzing these relationships: for instance transactional analysis would use a parent-child classification. There are other schemes. For instance Castorama proposes a pedagogical relationship: it literally takes by the hand the novice in the do-it-yourself market. No other chain has as much developed a library of leaflets, notes, guides to be able to succeed. It is also the first to introduce videotex data bases in store in order to pursue this shouldering the consumers. In the grocery market, Leclerc and Intermarché propose a *protection relationship*: they fight against the producers to make them bend and lower their prices. The FNAC chain, in the hifi, video, and personal computer markets, proposes a *guidance relationship*, as a scout would do in the ambushes of the innumerable innovations. Some distributors want to appear as a friend, as a father, as a brother, as someone on whom consumers may rely.

Naturally this facet is essentially conveyed by the sales-force itself, the people in contact with the customers, before or after the sale. But it can also be decoded "between the lines", in the product leaflets, in the vocabulary, the tone, the photographs.

The cultural facet concerns mostly the specialized trade. Such points of purchase have deep cultural roots: to be one of their clients is to share their values, their underlying philosophy, or myth. For instance IKEA and Habitat do not belong nor convey the same culture, although both cater to the young-couple market. When Carrefour launched its own brand, the cultural facet was prominent. By calling these unbranded products "produits libres" (freedom products), Carrefour injected a strong cultural myth where competitors only mentioned price and quality. Thus behind most well built identities, it is possible to identify some prominent figures of mythology: the myth of nature, of handicrafts, of humanism, of Ali Baba's cavern, etc . . .

The fifth facet concerns *customers' reflection*. What image of his customers does the distributor want to convey? The reflection is not the description of the target. A comparison will make this crucial point clear. Most Pierre Cardin handkerchiefs are bought by secretaries or middle class women: this is the target market. However in his advertising P. Cardin presents always upper class people: this is the customers' reflection. Thus it is a construction, a model worthy of imitation, of identification.

Generally distributors get concerned by this facet when marketing research tells them that people have a poor image of their customers. Then they buy large pages in magazines and dailies to foster a new image of their attributed clientele. Actually, this facet needs permanent monitoring: the choice of talents in the casting of pictures and movies is highly relevant for this facet. Little by little, small impressionistic touches delineate a precise figure of what the consumers look like, even if the reality is at odds.

The sixth facet refers to the instrumental role of the store for customers' self-concept. The reflection facet was consumers external mirror. This latter facet is consumers internal mirror: In fact consumers get or entertain an image of themselves in patronizing such or such store. Although the two latter facets may be similar, they may also differ. The chains which fostered generics and their own brands built their identity around this mentalization facet: in France; Ed sells only one brand per product category: the store brand. It's identity is not based on the classical self-concept of being astute and able to make a good bargain. It develops consumer's self-concept of being able to control oneself, to free oneself from the sirens of marketing.

These six facets define the full singularity of distributors following close paths. For instance Table 1 presents to the identity prism of three leading distributors in the TV, hi-fi; video and personal computer markets: FNAC, DARTY and NASA.

Table 1 Comparing three competitors' identities

Facets	FNAC	DARTY	NASA
Physical	All brands, competent salesmen, average price	All brands, low price, after sales service	Specialization, electronics, low price
Personality	Elitist, snob, content	Popular	Pioneer, enthusiastic
Relation	Full taking in charge Pedagogy	Defend and democratize	Sharing same passion
Culture	Gutenberg The humanities Tradition	Republican (Liberty, Equality, Fraternity)	The future Video culture The hero
Reflection	Highly educated persons well-to-do	The average French family	Young, curious, technology oriented
Self-concept	To belong to a restricted circle	To make the best bargain	To prove he is in

A Guideline for Communication Decisions

The identity prism is a tool for both diagnosis and control. It is used to summarize the results of communication audits and image studies: here the objective is to describe a current identity in order to diagnose its coherence or its pertinence. It is also used as a platform to guide all communication decisions and to enforce coherence between medias and across time periods. It is especially useful to evaluate the pertinence of creative proposals. Positioning was mostly concerned with what communication said. The identity concept recognizes that store's identity encompasses all signs and symbols. Since the style of a communication is often more important than the basic message, there had to be a conceptual scheme permitting some guidance and some control on the outputs of creativity. This recent attempt is already used by distributors and advertising agencies in France.

Editors' Commentary

SANJAY DHAR IS CURRENTLY James H. Lorie Professor of Marketing and Neubauer Family Faculty Member at Chicago University, having worked there since gaining his PhD from the University of California at Los Angeles in 1992. His background is in management. He has been particularly recognized for his enthusiasm and professionalism in teaching marketing, winning the 1994 Emory Williams Award for Excellence in Teaching and the 2000 McKinsey Award for Excellence in Teaching. The research areas which interest him include category management, assortment, brands, merchandising, pricing, shelf management, price elasticity. His interests are in pricing strategies, price sensitivities, advertising, promotions, category management and brands as well as non-retail topics.

Stephen Hoch became the Patty and Jay H. Baker Professor of Marketing at the Wharton School, University of Pennsylvania in 2005, having previously held the post of John H. Pomerantz Professor there since 1995. He is the Director of the Jay H. Baker Retail Initiative. Prior to this he was at the University of Chicago, having moved there after gaining his PhD from Northwestern University in 1983. His research interests range from retail strategy to consumer behaviour and the psychology of forecasting. He has an interest in how experts interact with new technologies and has been involved with retailers in the process of using scanner data for pricing, assortment and loyalty programmes. Store brands have always been a key interest and he has a long-standing interest in how to use visual design to solve marketing problems. He is (or has been) a member of a number of editorial boards including the *Journal of Retailing, Journal of Marketing* and the *Journal of Marketing Research* and is the Associate Editor for *Management Science* and the *Journal of Consumer Research*.

Stephen Hoch and Sanjay Dhar have collaborated on several projects and have a number of joint publications. Their joint focus has been on in-store product management – breadth of assortment, private labels, pricing and advertising role of specific products within overall assortment. 'Why Store Brand Penetration Varies by Retailer' brings together this joint expertise of these two USA-based researchers. The article investigates the ways in which private labels interact within the assortment mix in order to understand why performance of private labels varies across retailers. It does this through the use of four data sources, most notably AC Nielsen SCANTRAK data and a survey of private label strategies by retailers.

Product branding by retailers in the USA has tended not to go beyond lower-quality 'generic'-style products and cheap copies of manufacturer brands. This is due to consumers' preferences for manufacturer brands, the supply system and power of the manufacturers, retailers' reluctance to challenge the status quo and other contextual factors. Private labels have tended to be viewed as cheap, bought by lower income families, often in times of recession. This has conditioned the research approach used. This paper is representative of this genre of store-brand research in the USA. However, it also has hints of the differences found elsewhere and the potential that retail branding has to promote the retailer's desired image and as such hints at a more general significance. The work carried out in this paper has been extended subsequently by these authors and others.

Key Publications

Hoch SJ and Deighton J (1989) Managing what consumers learn from experience. *Journal of Marketing,* 53(2), 1–20.

Hoch SJ and Banerji S (1993) When do private labels succeed? *Sloan Management Review,* 34(4), 57–67.

Hoch SJ, Dreze X and Purk, M. (1994) EDLP, Hi-Lo and margin arithmetic. *Journal of Marketing,* 58(4), 16–29.

Dreze X, Hoch SJ and Purk M. (1994) Shelf management and space elasticity. *Journal of Retailing,* 70, 301–326.

Raju JS, Sethuraman R and Dhar SK (1995) The introduction and performance of store brands. *Management Science,* 41(6), 957–978.

Hoch SJ (1996) How should national brands think about private labels? *Sloan Management Review,* 37(2), 89–102.

Dhar SK and Hoch SJ (1996) Price discrimination using in-store merchandising. *Journal of Marketing,* 60(1), 17–30.

Hoch SJ, Bradlow E and Wansink B (1999) The variety of assortment. *Marketing Science,* 18, 527–546.

Dhar SK, Hoch SJ, Kumar N (2001) Effective category management depends on the role of the category. *Journal of Retailing,* 77, 165–184.

Sayman S, Hoch SJ and Raju J (2002) Positioning of store brands. *Marketing Science,* 21, 378–397.

Fox EJ and Hoch SJ (2005) Cherry picking. *Journal of Marketing,* 69(1), 46–62.

Bronnenberg BJ, Dhar SK, Dub J-P (2007) Consumer packaged goods in the United States: national brands, local branding. *Journal of Marketing Research,* 44(1), 4–13.

Websites

http://www.wharton.upenn.edu/faculty/hoch.html
http://faculty.chicagogsb.edu/sanjay.dhar/

WHY STORE BRAND PENETRATION VARIES BY RETAILER

Sanjay K. Dhar and Stephen J. Hoch

Our objective in this paper is to explain across-retailer variation in private label performance. Although retailers have lots to gain by better understanding the determinants of successful store brand programs, this knowledge also is very valuable to manufacturers. Lessons learned from competing with other national brands may not transfer one-to-one to the store brand case because, quite simply, a popular private label program changes the status of the retailer from being solely a customer to also a competitor. When customers are competitors, standard predatory tactics may not be appropriate; instead there is a premium on creating a successful basis for coexistence. Our findings from this study are therefore expected to have a broad based appeal both to practitioners and academics working in the evolving area of store brands.

Marketing Science, Vol. 16, No. 3 (1997), pp. 208–227. Copyright © 2001. All rights reserved.

Store brands are the only brand for which the retailer must take on all responsibility—from development, sourcing, and warehousing to merchandising and marketing. Unlike decisions retailers take about national brands, which in large measure are driven by the manufacturer's actions, the retailer plays a more determinant role in the success or failure of its own label. Based on data from 34 food categories for 106 major supermarket chains operating in the largest 50 retail markets in the U.S., we use regression-based analyses to show that variation in store brand performance across retailers is systematically related to underlying consumer, retailer, and manufacturer factors.

The key insights provided by our analysis are as follows:

1   Overall chain strategy in terms of commitment to quality, breadth of private label offerings, use of own name for private label, a premium brand offering, and number of stores consistently enhance the retailer's store brand performance in all categories. Also, the extent to which the retailer serves a customer base containing less wealthy and more elderly households and operates in less competitive markets improves the performance of the store brand.

2   The everyday low price (EDLP) positioning benefits the store brand but only in lower quality categories where the value positioning of the store may be better aligned with the price advantage of the store brand.

3   Supporting recent statements in the popular press, our analysis suggests that retailer promotional support can significantly enhance private label performance.

4   Retailers often use national brands to draw customers to their stores. Retailers who pursue this traffic building strategy usually carry more national brands, deeper assortments, and offer better everyday (lower price gap) and promotional prices on national brands. Each of these actions works against the retailer's own brands, highlighting the important balancing act the retailer must perform to profitably manage the sales revenue and margin mix in each of their categories. At the same time, adding a higher quality premium store brand program may mitigate this tradeoff.

5   Unlike cross-category studies, our within-category across-retailer analysis shows that the national brand-private label price differential exerts an important positive influence on store brand performance.

6   When retailers obtain more than their fair share of a category (high category development index), they also do much better with private labels.

7   From the national brand's perspective, encouraging the retailer to carry more brands and deeper assortments may be the most effective way to keep store brands in check. The importance of these variables, however, may depend on the national brand's market position. For example, a category leader may be glad to see a rise in store brand share if it comes at the expense of one of its secondary national brand competitors.

8   The exact impact of most of the variables depends on the underlying quality of store brands in a category. When store brand quality is high, competition at the retail and brand level is more important, as are variables

capturing economies of scale and scope enjoyed by the retailer. In contrast, demographics associated with consumer price sensitivity and EDLP pricing matter more in low quality categories.

9   Finally, premium store brands offer the retailer an avenue for responding to the national brand's ability to cater to heterogeneous preferences. This appears more likely in categories where store brands already offer high quality comparable to the national brands.

We argue that private labels threaten national brands most in categories when there is high variance in share across categories (as opposed to high average share per se). In high variance categories, store brand share could increase dramatically if the poor performing retailers imitate best practices. Future research can extend this work in several ways both on the substantive and methodological fronts.

Why Store Brand Varies by Retailer

IN THE PACKAGED GOODS world, store brands (or private labels) behave much the same as any other brand. They face downward sloping demand with respect to price and upward sloping demand with respect to quality. Promotional price elasticities are greater than everyday price elasticities. And display and feature activity magnify the effects of temporary price reductions. But store brands also are different (Hoch 1996). They are the only brand for which the retailer takes on all responsibility—from development, sourcing, and warehousing to merchandising and marketing. Unlike decisions retailers take about national brands or regional players, which in large measure are determined by the actions of the manufacturer, the retailer plays a bigger role in the success or failure of its own label.

Although retailers have lots to gain by better understanding the determinants of successful store brand programs, this knowledge may be more valuable to manufacturers. Lessons learned from competing with other national brands may not transfer one-to-one to the store brand case because, quite simply, a popular private label program changes the status of the retailer from being solely a customer to also a competitor. When customers are competitors, standard predatory tactics may not be appropriate; instead there is a premium on creating a successful basis for coexistence.

This paper explains the across-retailer variation in store brand performance for the U.S. food retailing industry as shown in Table 1. We utilize sales data from 50 U.S. markets to identify key determinants of retailer performance and draw implications for channel interactions.[1] Previous research has focused on explaining across-category variation, illustrated in the table by the differences between edible grocery and dairy (Hoch and Banerji 1993; Sethuraman 1992; Raju et al. 1995a, 1995b). We have a good understanding, for example, of why store brands constitute 65% of sales of canned green beans but only 1% of deodorants. But no research has considered across-retailer variation in private label sales within a category, a more relevant issue to national manufacturers interested in their own brands.

Table 1 Variation in store brand share across markets, retailers, and category groups

Market	Share	Retailer	Share	Category group	Share
Atlanta	23.74%	A & P	11.15%	Dairy	15.78%
				Edible Grocery	9.32
		Kroger	21.41	Dairy	29.47
				Edible Grocery	20.23
		Publix	18.45	Dairy	24.67
				Edible Grocery	11.93
		Winn-Dixie	29.03	Dairy	35.16
				Edible Grocery	22.36
Chicago	15.29	Dominick's	20.58	Dairy	32.84
				Edible Grocery	9.81
		Eagle	10.49	Dairy	16.10
				Edible Grocery	7.50
		Jewel	16.32	Dairy	18.79
				Edible Grocery	11.45
		Omni	5.30	Dairy	8.35
				Edible Grocery	4.29
Los Angeles	16.31	Albertson's	20.41	Dairy	32.64
				Edible Grocery	11.45
		Alpha-Beta	7.36	Dairy	7.90
				Edible Grocery	8.06
		Boys/Viva	9.64	Dairy	8.75
				Edible Grocery	13.32
		Hughes	9.08	Dairy	19.05
				Edible Grocery	1.24
		Lucky	17.79	Dairy	26.50
				Edible Grocery	11.45
		Ralphs	16.77	Dairy	28.38
				Edible Grocery	7.68
		Vons	14.48	Dairy	24.77
				Edible Grocery	7.09
New York	17.06	A & P	13.98	Dairy	17.36
				Edible Grocery	10.73
		Grand Union	11.07	Dairy	13.46
				Edible Grocery	8.76
		Pathmark	17.36	Dairy	24.88
				Edible Grocery	12.37
		Shoprite	20.52	Dairy	26.54
				Edible Grocery	15.37
		Waldbaum's	17.05	Dairy	23.27
				Edible Grocery	10.53
Portland	32.28	Albertson's	32.29	Dairy	49.42
				Edible Grocery	14.21
		Fred Meyer	29.28	Dairy	40.62
				Edible Grocery	15.17
		Safeway	33.60	Dairy	50.84
				Edible Grocery	13.69

Based on data from 34 food categories for 106 major supermarket chains operating in the largest 50 retail markets in the U.S., Table 1 shows private label performance in five key markets broken down by three potential sources of variance—geographic market, retail chain within a market, and broad category groups within a chain within a market. We see substantial variation in aggregate performance across major metropolitan markets. For example, looking across the entire data set (not just that portion shown in Table 1), we find that private label share ranges from a low of 15% in Chicago to a high of 32% in Portland. Similarly, there are large differences between retailers; the average difference in private label performance between the best and worst retailer within a market is 11%, the narrowest range is 1% in Baltimore, and the widest range 36% in New Orleans. Finally, although there are stable differences at the retailer-market level, some retailers achieve quite different levels of store brand performance depending on commodity type. For instance, Omni has a weak program across the board, whereas Winn-Dixie has a strong program. On the other hand, Dominick's is very strong in dairy but weak in edible grocery.

We carried out a more formal analysis of the complete data underlying Table 1: private label market shares for each of three years broken down by the top 106 retailer/market combinations in 34 food categories (3 × 34 × 106 = 10,812 observations). We estimated a series of hierarchical models by regressing store brand market share onto subsets of intercept terms representing categories, markets, retailers, and retailer × market interactions. The results appear in Table 2.

Not surprisingly, most of the explainable variance is due to differences between categories. Differences between markets explain an additional 4% of the variance. Differences between retailers account for almost 17% of the variance and in fact subsume local market effects because most retailers operate in single regions. Our empirical work focuses on this 17% variance. We ask the following question, "After controlling for category differences, what are the key determinants of store brand market share for a specific retailer?" We also show that coefficients differ depending on whether the average quality of store brand alternatives in a category is high or low relative to the national brands.

The rest of the paper is organized as follows. The next section lays out a conceptual scheme that attributes the factors that might influence store brand performance to one of three parties—consumers, retailers, and national manufacturers (Hoch and Banerji 1993). We then describe the dataset, the predictor

Table 2 Hierarchical analysis of category, market and retailer determinants of store brand penetration

Intercepts	Variance explained (R^2)
Category	40.2%
Category + Market	44.3
Category + Retailer	56.7
Category + Market + Retailer	57.1
Category + Market + Retailer + M*R Interactions	57.2

variables, and the results. We report directional results and then average coefficients across all 34 categories. To recognize the heterogeneity that exists across categories, we utilize a random coefficient approach and pool the categories into high and low quality types. Fortunately, the analyses offer a clean picture of the major issues. The concluding section draws implications for both retailers and manufacturers.

Background

We would prefer that a parsimonious theory could explain the across-retailer variation in Table 1, but previous cross-category research suggests that this is unlikely (Hoch and Banerji 1993; Raju *et al.* 1995a). The story is more complicated because store brands sit right in the middle of the manufacturer–retailer–consumer vertical relationship. Unlike the typical national brand, where consumer demand results from response to the pull tactics of the manufacturer, U.S. store brands are the prototypical push product. If the retailer decides to push the product, consumers will be exposed and respond accordingly depending on underlying quality and other retailer actions, as well as whatever actions national manufacturers coincidentally pursue.

Following Hoch and Banerji (1993), we localize the drivers of store brand performance with the three parties that make up the retail channel: consumers, retailers, and manufacturers. In a cross-sectional analysis of 185 grocery categories, they found that six variables could explain 70% of the variance in market shares. Store brands obtained higher market share when:

- quality relative to the national brands was high;
- quality variability of store brands was low;
- the product category was large in absolute terms ($ sales);
- percent gross margins were high;
- there were fewer national manufacturers operating in the category;
- national advertising expenditures were low.

The first two variables show that, all else equal, consumers are more likely to buy private labels that provide parity quality. The middle two factors reflect the retailer's scarce resource allocation problem. Because retailers must draw on internal funds for the branding, packaging, production, and advertising of their store brands, they invest more heavily in large categories offering high profit margins so as to maximize their return. The last two variables demonstrate the influence of manufacturers and show that private labels can be crowded out of the market when national brand competition is high and when those brands invest advertising resources into the consumer franchise. The differences between dairy and edible grocery in Table 1 are consistent with this story—dairy has high quality store brands (regulated by the USDA), huge sales volume and big margins, and few national brands who spend little on advertising.

Determinants of performance in a cross-category analysis, however, are not necessarily the ones that explain performance across retailers within a category.

For example, quality, size of the market, and gross margins vary more across categories than across retailers within a category. Alternatively, demographic characteristics, level of promotion, and pricing policy vary more across retailers than across categories. Conceptually, however, it is possible to localize the responsibility with the consumer, the retailer, or the manufacturer, and so we will organize our discussion of the drivers of store brand penetration in this manner.

Consumer factors

For consumers to influence retailer-specific store brand performance, not only must demographics matter but also differ by retailer. For economists, the typical store brand sold in the U.S. is an inferior good and as such should be purchased more frequently by price sensitive shoppers. Becker (1965) argues that systematic differences in price sensitivity should emerge due to differences in opportunity costs of time associated with demographic characteristics (Blattberg et al. 1978). Starzynski (1993) found that heavy private label users had lower incomes and larger blue collar households with part-time female heads of household. In a study of micromarket differences in demand for private labels, Hoch (1996) found that stores with larger category price elasticities had higher private label share; moreover, there were systematic differences due to the demographic characteristics of a store's trading area. Store brands obtained higher share when the trading area contained more elderly people, lower housing values and lower incomes, more large families, more working women, and higher education levels. Each of these demographic relations is consistent with Becker's opportunity cost story except education.

Even though store-level sales of private label can be linked to consumer characteristics, it is an empirical question whether these distinctions emerge when aggregating up to the chain level. Do supermarket chains serve and attract sufficiently distinct clienteles? Demographics could vary across retailers because of differences in targeting, positioning, and real estate. Our data reveal wide disparities in demography by geographic region. Compared to Los Angeles, Philadelphia has a larger elderly population (23% vs. 17%) and significantly lower housing values (19% vs. 41% of homes > $250,000). Demographic profiles also vary by retailer within a market. In New Orleans, A&P serves a better educated clientele than Winn-Dixie (21% vs. 16% college educated), while Schwegmann's trading area contains more blacks and hispanics (37%) than Delchamps (23%).

Retailer factors

There are a large number of retailer characteristics that position some supermarket chains to better develop and exploit a store brand program than others. First, we discuss those factors largely fixed across categories and then address those that vary from category to category.

Retail competition. Retailers face different levels of competition depending on: (a) the number of retail competitors, and (b) the heterogeneity in their market shares. More competitors and a uniform distribution of shares lead to greater competition (Waterson 1984). Facing a large set of competitors increases uncertainty; witness Los Angeles retailers who must think about the potential actions of 10 other major players versus Chicago where Jewel (35% share) is the long-term price setter and Dominick's (21%) the price follower. Retailers operating in markets with lots of competitors have smaller market shares on average and must focus on stealing customers and defending their own turf. Retailers could use their store brand program to help in this effort, but more likely will leverage national brand resources to build store traffic. In contrast, with few competitors retailers have larger shares on average and plenty to gain by exploiting existing store traffic, an objective that private label is particularly well suited to achieve because of higher margins. Heterogeneity in market shares moderates the effect of a fixed number of competitors: When a few chains dominate a market, the retailer can safely focus attention on the major players and not worry about the minor competitors. In the highly concentrated European food retailing scene, some retailers appear to use store brands to differentiate themselves from the few big competitors they face.

Economies of scale and scope. Large retailers are better positioned to build scale economies than smaller chains. Higher sales volumes bring down unit costs through: (a) lower printing and holding costs for package labels, (b) better prices from suppliers due to longer production runs and negotiating clout, and (c) lower inventory holding costs through more continuous supply. These scale economies allow the retailer to provide better value for the money.

Retailers achieve economies of scope when corporate brand programs extend across a larger percentage of the 350 categories that full-service supermarkets typically carry. Presence in more categories increases salience of the store brand concept and justifies investment in resources dedicated to private label, such as in-house quality assurance, unique promotion events, and a premium store brand program (e.g., Safeway Select). Retailers also signal commitment through naming of the store brand—placing the chain name prominently on 1,000 + items makes the relation to the parent firm transparent. This reduces consumer risk in trying products with unknown manufacturing origins and increases the motivation of employees responsible for merchandising the product. These scope factors serve as surrogates for retailer effort and commitment to a store brand program.

EDLP and depth of assortment. Consider the effect of EDLP versus Hi-Lo pricing on store brand performance (Hoch *et al.* 1994). With less promotion activity and simpler merchandising tactics, EDLP makes the normal price difference between the national brands and private label more apparent and facilitates parity comparisons. EDLP's value orientation also is consistent with typical store brand positioning. Depth of assortment also influences private label performance. Retailers committed to a full service look offer more variety and deeper assortments, including more slow moving items as they sacrifice efficiency for satisfying customer needs. Narrow assortments favor the store brand; specialty items are more likely to be eliminated, not private labels positioned against the leading national brands, sizes, and flavors.

Category expertise. Retailers may develop special expertise in particular categories. Some retailers excel in their presentation of meat and produce, while others have expertise in better serving the eating needs of particular ethnic groups. Category expertise develops in response to the demand side, but once developed it becomes part of the organization's intellectual capital. The expert retail buyer is less dependent on national brands to provide category knowledge and may use private labels to enhance the margin mix for an already high performance (in unit sales) category.

Price gaps and promotion. Category level pricing and promotion strategies could influence store brand performance. The bigger the price gap between national brands and private labels, the bigger is the incentive for the consumer to trade down to the private label. Despite obvious economic arguments, evidence is mixed as to the importance of relative price. In the cross-category work of Raju *et al.* (1995b; Mills 1995; Sethuraman 1992), price differential actually is negatively related to private label performance: Categories with big gaps have lower private label penetration than those with smaller gaps. Raju *et al.* (1995b) argue that this result is due to cross-sectional aggregation. In equilibrium, differences in price sensitivity across categories lead to bigger gaps in price-insensitive categories (analgesics) and smaller gaps in price-sensitive categories (canned vegetables) where demand for private label is high. Hoch (1996) conducted single retailer pricing experiments where the price gap varied from 10–35%. Private labels were twice as sensitive to the gap as national brands, but price elasticities generally were low, and so a profit maximizing retailer was better off with larger than smaller gaps. If category price elasticities vary across retailers, however, different optimal price gaps may emerge and within-category differences in price differentials may prove an important predictor of store brand performance.

Just as the everyday pricing tactics of the retailer can influence private label performance, so can the manner in which they promote products. Some markets and retailers engage in aggressive week to week promotion battles; retailers use national brands as loss leaders to build store traffic (Drèze 1995). Store brands lose their comparative advantage when national brands are heavily promoted, especially among more price-sensitive buyers and heavy users who stockpile promoted products. Other retailers could elect to aggressively promote private label—using shallow deals to help maintain a good margin mix across products. But research on asymmetric cross-price elasticities between high and low quality brands suggests that such tactics will be less effective for store brands (Allenby and Rossi 1991) because they are more vulnerable to national brand promotion and their own promotional efforts have less clout (Kamakura and Russell 1989).

Retailer summary. All retailer factors are to some degree endogenous, even retail competition and chain size. For econometric purposes, however, we assume that only price gap, promotion, and assortment decisions are short term and endogenous enough to require special treatment. Retailers can change chain-wide policies (e.g., quality level) but only in the long run.

Manufacturer factors

Brand competition. National brands influence store brand performance directly with various consumer pull tactics and indirectly through push tactics offered to the retail channel. Probably the biggest influence on store brands is competition in the category. As with retail competition, we follow the IO literature that characterizes brand competition as higher when: (a) there are a large number of national brands, and (b) market shares are evenly distributed among the different brands (Waterson 1984). When retailers carry many brands, there is a pure crowding out effect; on average, each brand (including the store brand) will command a smaller share of a fixed pie (Raju *et al.* 1995a). Further, for a fixed number of national brands, higher concentration in market shares among a few brands indicates less heterogeneity in tastes and possibly a price umbrella, both conditions that are attractive to the store brand. When competing against a couple of large share brands that may benefit from a price umbrella, store brands can pursue a focused positioning strategy and offer an attractive alternative at a lower, but still quite profitable, price. Alternatively, a store brand facing numerous same size competitive national brands requires diffuse marketing effort in response to multiple fronts. Greater brand competition hurts the store brand. Clearly the retailer has the final say over how many brands they carry; we deal with this endogeneity in our econometrics.

Pull promotion. A highly fragmented category is more sustainable for a national brand than a private label because national brands benefit from the substantial economies of scale in production and advertising that accrue through national distribution (Schmalensee 1978). Consider the RTE cereal category, where about 200 brands are alive at any point in time and 120 of them are actively marketed. Only a handful of brands obtain more than 1% of the market and a majority have less than 1/2%. But 1/2% of an $8 billion market is still an economically viable $40 million brand. The problem for the store brand in a differentiated category is that the only way for the retailer to grab significant share is to enter with multiple brands in disparate locations in the product space, a practice that is self-limited by insufficient scale economies. In the long run most manufacturer pull tactics serve to increase differentiation, reduce price sensitivity, and increase top-of-mind awareness, each of which increases demand for national brands and hurt store brands. To the extent that advertising (TV, newsprint, and magazine) and consumer promotion (coupons, sweepstakes, etc.) differ by markets, pull promotion spending should limit store brand penetration.

Push promotion. Trade promotion activity varies dramatically by geographic market. Although manufacturers legally must offer identical terms of trade to resellers competing in the same market, national brands can and do allocate trade dollars disproportionately across markets depending on: category development (consumption rate), brand development (market share), and presence or absence of regional competition. Trade promotion dollars take many forms but eventually are expressed at retail as reductions in everyday prices, temporary price reductions, or feature advertising and display. Because manufacturers cannot directly set prices, these decisions are partly endogenous to the retailer. At the same time, higher levels of trade spending do result in lower prices and manufacturers can contractually mandate performance requirements for feature advertising and display. Greater levels of national brand promotion should limit private label performance (Lal 1990).

Summary

Table 3 shows the predicted impact of each variable on store brand performance. Understanding the determinants of store brand performance requires a recognition that consumers, retailers, and manufacturers all influence the process. We localized the source of influence at one level of the distribution channel, but clearly interdependencies between the supply side and demand side make some of these distinctions fuzzy. For example, manufacturers and retailers jointly determine retail pricing and promotion. The next section describes the empirical work.

The Study

We utilized four different data sources. A large packaged goods firm provided us with the main database—syndicated sales data from A.C. Nielsen for all of their major product categories and key retail accounts. Before reporting the results we present a detailed description of the data sources and measures developed. We

Table 3 Predicted impact of key determinants of store brand share

Key determinants	Expected sign
Consumer factors	
Wealthy people in customer base	−
Elderly people in customer base	+
Higher education level in customer base	+
Ethnic composition of customer base	+
Retailer factors	
Retail competition	
−Number of retailers	−
−Heterogeneity in market shares	+
Economies of scale (chain size)	+
Economies of scope	
−Private label SKU's as fraction of total	+
−Quality commitment (in-house quality assurance)	+
−Chain name for private label	+
−Premium store brand program	+
EDLP strategy	+
Depth of assortment	−
Category expertise	+
National brand—private label price gap	+
Promotion intensity for private label	+
Manufacturer factors	
Brand competition	
−Number of brands	−
−Heterogeneity in market shares	+
Pull promotion	−
Push promotion	−

estimate individual category regressions and then use a random coefficient approach to pool categories into two quality types. Both analyses produce convergent findings about what drives variation in store brand performance across retailers.

Data sources

(1) We use account data for 106 major U.S. grocery retail chains in the 50 Nielsen SCANTRACK markets.[2] This includes all retailers with average annual store sales of $2 million +. These retail chains account for 60% of total supermarket sales in the markets they serve. For each retail account, the data set includes monthly brand level information for 34 categories over three calendar years. The categories represent a wide range of both edible grocery and dairy products including major categories such as RTE cereal, coffee, cheese, and more minor ones like rice, marshmallows, and mustard. Nielsen brand totals are used, aggregating all sizes and forms of each brand name. Separate brand totals are reported for each distinct variant; for example, in cereal Kellogg's Corn Flakes and Kellogg's Raisin Bran are reported as separate brands. Due to confidentiality agreements all private label variants are aggregated into one brand total even in cases where the retailer carries more than one label (e.g., President's Choice).

The data provide detailed brand level information on both total equivalent unit sales and dollar sales, which is further subdivided into different components. Separate subtotals are reported for sales accompanied with different forms of retail promotion including the use of feature advertising, display, and temporary price reductions. Print media expenditures (newspapers and magazines) are reported for all 50 markets but TV advertising for only 23 major metropolitan markets. The database also includes information on brand level consumer promotion offers.

(2) We obtained detailed annual demographic data for each retailer from a syndicated data service that overlay the trading area of each store onto the underlying census tracts. This provided distributional information on age, income, ethnicity, education, and home value.

(3) Two published secondary data sources provide additional information on characteristics of the retail chains and the markets served. For each SCANTRACK market, *Market Scope* and *Marketing Guidebook* report each retailer's (chains and independents) overall market share, the number of stores operated, the average floor area, and the names of the store brand lines carried to determine whether the chain uses its own name or carries a premium store brand line. Both publications are well-known sources published annually by Trade Dimensions, a unit of the Progressive Grocer Data Center.

(4) We also surveyed each of the retail accounts in the database. Retailers were asked for information on their private label strategy, specifically for each of the three years: (a) an estimate of the total number of private label stock-keeping units (SKUs) and the number of categories where they carried a private label, (b) whether or not they had a quality assurance program for their private labels, and (c) names of key private label lines they carried. Retailers also provided us

with information on whether they followed an EDLP or Hi-Lo pricing strategy. Multiple calls were made to the retail accounts leading to 93 of the 106 retailers completing the questionnaire.

Measures used in the analysis

We developed all measures at the retailer-market level. This means that Winn-Dixie in Tampa is treated as a separate entity from Winn-Dixie in Dallas. We created yearly aggregates for each measure resulting in three data points per retailer per category. We do so for purposes of stability and the fact that about half of our measures are only available at the annual level. This allows us to use the time series nature of our data to address certain endogeneity issues.

Private label share (PLSHARE). To normalize for differences in package size and facilitate comparisons across categories, the dependent measure is the equivalent unit (lbs) share of private labels (normal and premium variants) in a category for a retail-market account. Share is calculated as the ratio of total pound sales for the private label to total pound sales for the whole category. For exposition, share is expressed in percentage terms. Using dollar sales instead of equivalent unit sales or a logit transformation of these market shares led to similar insights.

Home value (HOMEVAL). This variable measures the extent to which the customer base for a retail account comprises wealthier individuals. HOMEVAL measures the fraction of total number of households for a retail account owning homes with value higher than $250,000; it is highly correlated ($r = 0.79$) with income (% > $50K). We expect a negative coefficient because wealthier consumers are less price sensitive due to higher opportunity costs.

Elderly (ELDERLY). This variable is operationalized as the fraction of a retailer's customer base that is older than 55 years. Because the elderly have lower opportunity costs and more severe budget constraints, the coefficient should be positive.

Education (EDUC). This variable is given by the fraction of households in a retail account's customer base with a four-year college degree. Despite obvious income effects, we predict a positive coefficient (Hoch 1996). If educated consumers have greater shopping expertise, they may rely less on brand name as an indicator of product performance.

Ethnic (ETHNIC). The extent to which a retail account serves minority groups is measured by the fraction of black and hispanic households. Although conventional industry wisdom suggests that blacks and hispanics are more likely to buy well-known brand names, we predict a positive coefficient as found by Hoch (1996).

Retail competition (#RETAIL, RETVAR). Two measures capture the extent of retail competition in a local market: the number of retail competitors (#RETAIL); and the heterogeneity in shares across these retailers (RETVAR). #RETAIL is directly measured from *Market Scope.* Heterogeneity is captured as the variance (σ^2) in market shares. Retail competition is higher with lots of competitors and is lower when heterogeneity in shares is greater, implying a negative coefficient for #RETAIL and a positive one for RETVAR.

Chain size (SIZE). Size of the chain is captured by the number of stores each retailer operates in a particular market. Conceptually, it represents the potential for a retailer to benefit from economies of scale and should be positively related to private label share. Using total square footage of the chain (# of stores × average square footage) produced similar results.

Private label SKUs (PLSKU). This variable is the total number of private label SKUs expressed as a fraction of the total number of SKUs across all categories in the store and represents the potential for economies of scope. As with SIZE, the coefficient should be positive.

Quality assurance for private labels (QUAL). This is an indicator variable, where QUAL = 1 if the retail account has a quality program and QUAL = 0 otherwise. This variable represents a signal about the retailer's commitment to private label quality and to some extent may capture actual quality differences across retailers. The coefficient should be positive.

Own name label (PLNAME). Using information on private label names provided in the *Marketing Guidebook* and cross verifying through the survey, we create an indicator variable PLNAME = 1 when the chain uses its own label and 0 otherwise. It should have a positive sign.

EDLP/Hi-Lo pricing strategy (EDLP). EDLP = 1 when chains use an everyday low pricing strategy and 0 when they go Hi-Lo. Retailers initially were classified based on their answers to the survey and corroborated through a search of trade press. The regular price gap between national and store brands was 36% in EDLP chains versus 44% in Hi-Lo chains. EDLP chains also sold less product on deal, 20% of private label, and 25% of national brands compared to 24% and 30%, respectively, in Hi-Lo chains. We expect EDLP to have a positive sign.

Premium label (PREMIUM). Using information from the manufacturer's salesforce, the retailer survey, and published secondary sources, PREMIUM = 1 when a retailer stocks a higher quality and price premium label (e.g., President's Choice) in addition to their normal store brands. We would prefer to examine premium private labels separately, but confidentiality agreements require Nielsen to aggregate across store brand types when providing syndicated data to manufacturers. The premium variable probably captures both the effect of a larger number and likely greater differentiation of store brands in any one category (normal plus premium) and may serve as a surrogate for retailer commitment to the whole idea of a store brand program. The expected sign is positive.

Depth of assortment (AVGSKU). The extent of category specific item proliferation is measured by the average number of SKUs carried in that category averaged across stores in a particular retail chain. This measure was created from another database providing more detailed item level information. By accounting for the number of national brands separately, this variable measures the level of variety that the retailer offers for the average national brand. We endogenize this variable because the retailer has final say. AVGSKU should have a negative sign.

Category development index (CDI). The CDI for a retail account is an index measuring the account's category share of total equivalent unit sales volume in a market relative to its total size (measured by All Commodity Volume—ACV $) in the market. By normalizing for the relative size of the retail account, the measure captures the extent to which the retailer does well in a specific category relative to performance across all categories. This is given by,

$$\text{CDI} = \frac{\text{Account Eqvt. Unit Volume for Category}}{\text{Market Eqvt. Unit Volume for Category}}$$

$$\times \frac{\text{Market ACV\$}}{\text{Account ACV\$}}.$$

Normalizing retailer volume by the Total U.S. leads to the same results. Categories with a high CDI are relatively more important to that retailer and therefore likely to draw more attention. We view CDI as a long-run surrogate for category expertise, though we recognize the likely recursive relationship between expertise and the demand side. Although we are unaware of any studies showing that heavy category users buy a disproportionate amount of private label, this could lead to a contemporaneous correlation between CDI and private label share and so we endogenize the variable. The CDI coefficient should be positive.

National brand-private label price differential (PRDIFF). The price gap is measured as the price difference per equivalent unit between the average national brand and the private label divided by the average national brand price. We compute both the shelf price differential and the regular price differential using information on total and nonpromoted sales, respectively. Sales (in equivalent units) weighted as well as unweighted average brand prices were computed. Since alternate measures—weighted or unweighted, shelf or regular price differentials— led to the same insights, we report results only for the unweighted regular price differential measure. Larger price gaps should lead to better store brand performance. Since national brand and private label cross-price effects can influence the setting of the price differential and store brand share, we endogenize this variable.

Percentage private label volume sold on deal (PLPROMO). This variable measures the average retail promotion intensity for the store brand and is given by the fraction of total equivalent unit volume sold when accompanied by any kind of retail promotion including temporary price reductions, feature advertising, and display. Collinearity precluded use of more detailed breakups. The coefficient should be positive.

Percentage national brand volume sold on deal (NBPROMO). Promotion intensity of national brands is measured by the fraction of its total equivalent unit sales volume sold with any kind of retail promotion. The coefficient should be negative. Conceptually both PLPROMO and NBPROMO are equivalent to promotion elasticity times frequency of promotion. For reasons cited for PRDIFF, we endogenize both PLPROMO and NBPROMO.

Brand competition (#BRANDS, BRNDVAR). As with retailer competition, we measure brand competition using two variables: the number of brands carried by the retailer (#BRANDS) and heterogeneity in brand market shares (BRNDVAR) as captured by the variance (σ^2) in shares. Since we are interested in the degree of national brand competition, we compute the variance in shares after dropping the store brand and renormalizing the remaining brand shares to sum to 1. Because retailers ultimately control the number of brands they let on their shelves, we endogenize both #BRANDS and BRNDVAR. #BRANDS should have a negative coefficient because of crowding out. BRNDVAR should dampen the number of brands effect (+ sign); a lumpy distribution of shares means that store brands can concentrate their efforts on the big players, ignore the minor brands, and still appeal to a large percentage of the market.

Consumer advertising (ADVPROMO). Print and magazine advertising and consumer promotion information is available for all 50 markets. TV advertising, however, is available for only 23 of the major metropolitan markets but is highly correlated (0.88) with print media spending in those markets. Because consumer promotions typically focus on price whereas advertising focuses on attributes, we initially separated these two promotions. Unfortunately because of multi-collinearity ($r = 0.92$) and the fact that consumer promotions make up only 14% of spending, we could not estimate separate effects. Consequently, we combined advertising and promotion into a common ADVPROMO measure equal to the sum of number of all newsprint and magazine impressions and consumer promotion offers. This measure is computed for each national brand, averaged across them, and then normalized by the number of households in the market. ADVPROMO should have a negative sign.

Model estimation

We postulate a regression relationship between private label share and these measures. Individual category level regressions were estimated across the 93 retail-market accounts for which we had information on all measures. Retailers are included only if they stock a store brand in that category. We use the time series nature of the data to address possible endogeneity problems. Specifically, underlying retailer specific characteristics may simultaneously determine private label share and the setting of NB-PL price gaps, promotional intensity of both national and store brands, CDI, assortment size, number of brands, and heterogeneity in shares. Since this results in a contemporaneous correlation of the endogenous explanatory variables with the error term, we endogenize PRDIFF, NBPROMO, PLPROMO, CDI, AVGSKU, #BRANDS, and BRNDVAR and replace them with instruments. We created instruments using the standard two-stage least squares approach, first regressing the current values of the endogenous variables versus the one-year lags and then using the predicted values.[3] The instrumented variables do not remain constant from year to year. We also checked for a first order autoregressive process by assuming the same serial coefficient across retailers. We estimated the serial correlation using the data for all retailers by regressing the estimated error for a year against the preceding year's estimated error. We lost one year of data due to the instrumented variables. Our analysis indicated no serial correlation in the data.[4]

For each category, we regress account level private label share against the corresponding explanatory variables for a two-year period since we lose the first year of data when computing the instruments. Pooling tests show no differences in the value of the estimated coefficients across the two years in any of the category regressions. Therefore, we run individual category level regressions by pooling the data across the two years.

To avoid overwhelming the reader with all the minutiae inherent in considering the influence of 20 predictor variables in 34 product categories, we adopt an analysis plan that goes from more general to more specific. First, we estimate a separate regression relationship for each of the 34 categories and examine whether the coefficients generally are of the same predicted sign across categories. The third column of Table 4 shows the number of positive/negative coefficients out of 34 total that are statistically significant ($p < 0.05$). To get a handle on the overall pattern of results, we average the coefficients from the individual category regressions, test whether they are statistically significant from zero, and compute a measure of substantive importance by determining the impact of each variable on store brand share (columns 4–7). Finally, although considerable commonality in coefficients exists across categories, we consider various pooling methods to deal with category heterogeneity. Specifically, we find systematic differences in slope coefficients for categories that ex ante are known to contain higher quality store brand alternatives (Table 5).

Category level results

The predictor variables explained a substantial amount of the variability in private label share across retail accounts in all 34 categories. The regressions have an average adjusted R^2 of 0.69 (median $= 0.75$) ranging from a low of 0.39 to a high of 0.90. Variance inflation factors (VIF) for each independent variable, ranging from 1.6 to 2.8, indicated no serious multicollinearity. Since cross-sectional analysis is used, errors could be heteroskedastic over retail accounts in the same category. Examination of the errors (White's test 1980) revealed no heteroskedasticity.

Table 4 provides several different measures of the impact of the independent variables on store brand share. Before discussing the table in detail, we offer the following stylized facts as summary. Clearly the main take-away should be that the retailer has a big impact on the penetration level of their own store brands. When categories are uncrowded, both in terms of number of brands and assortment, and to a lesser extent when heterogeneity in brand shares is high, store brands can do very well. They also do well when attractively priced and promoted compared to the national brand. And although each of these variables is influenced by national brand policies, the final decision rests with the retailer. The only variable totally controlled by the manufacturer is local advertising and consumer promotion, and, although statistically significant, it does not have as much impact. The retailer also controls its own destiny through a variety of chainwide policies, including quality control, store brand naming, and a premium line. Although greater retail competition does reduce store brand penetration, it is much less important than brand competition. Finally, most consumer characteristics, except wealth, do not have much impact at all. We are not arguing that the demand side is unimportant but the direct impact is small. Possibly retailers have already adjusted their policies to consumer behavior and so the effect of demographics is

Table 4 Substantive impact of predictor variables (34 categories)

Variable	Predicted sign	Significant coefficients #+/#−	Average coefficient	Average category std deviation	Market share effect 1 S.D. around mean	Standardized coefficient
			Consumer factors			
HOMEVAL	−	3/11	−5.62ᵃ	14.83	−1.67%	−0.071
ELDERLY	+	7/0	4.50	3.72	0.33	0.023
EDUC	+	5/5	−4.90	4.67	−0.45	−0.023
ETHNIC	+	2/6	0.21	8.83	0.04	0.011
			Retailer factors			
#RETAIL	−	3/7	−0.05ᵃ	16.24	−1.62	−0.042
RETVAR	+	8/1	9.10ᵃ	0.04	0.73	0.051
SIZE	+	8/2	0.01ᵇ	40.25	0.81	0.007
PLSKU	+	10/2	6.10ᵇ	7.71	0.94	0.042
QUAL (0–1)	+	11/1	2.31ᵃ	na	2.31	0.061
PLNAME (0–1)	+	12/2	2.10ᵃ	na	2.10	0.082
EDLP (0–1)	+	8/3	1.40ᵇ	na	1.40	0.041
PREMIUM (0–1)	+	13/2	2.51ᵃ	na	2.51	0.096
AVGSKU	−	5/12	−0.20ᵃ	10.36	−4.14	−0.043
CDI	+	12/4	3.23ᵃ	0.22	1.42	0.063
PRDIFF	+	14/2	8.21ᵃ	14.12	2.32	0.082
NBPROMO	−	1/12	−9.40ᵃ	8.74	−1.64	−0.064
PLPROMO	+	9/1	9.48ᵃ	16.98	3.22	0.128
			Manufacturer factors			
#BRANDS	−	0/31	−0.72ᵃ	10.26	−14.77	−0.387
BRNDVAR	+	21/5	51.30ᵃ	0.06	6.16	0.270
ADVPROMO	−	2/9	−0.20ᵃ	0.58	−0.23	−0.012

ᵃ $p < 0.01$, ᵇ $p < 0.05$, ᶜ $p < 0.10$.

partially subsumed in other variables. The remainder of this section describes the more detailed results.

Column 3 reports the number of statistically significant ($p < 0.05$) positive and negative coefficients. In the average category 8.0 out of 20 coefficients were statistically significant, 6.5 with "right" sign and 1.5 with the "wrong" sign. The maximum number of statistically significant wrong signs in an individual category was 3, indicating deviations from theoretical expectations were not systematic or isolated to a few outlying categories.

To get a better idea about the substantive impact of each variable, column 4 shows the value of each coefficient averaged across the individual category regressions along with t-test significance levels.[5] For example, looking at the average coefficients for the four dichotomous variables indicates that store brands gain 2.3 share points when the retailer has a quality assurance program, 2.1 points when the private label carries the retailer's own name, 1.4 points when the retailer follows an EDLP strategy, and 2.5 points when they merchandise a premium store brand in addition to their regular private label. Adding all of these effects together implies a 8.3% difference in share points. It is more difficult to interpret the other variables, either because the scale is unfamiliar (BRNDVAR) or the likely extent of variation in the variable is unknown. Therefore, we calculated the average standard deviation of each variable in each category across categories (column 5), and for each of the nondichotomous variables, we report the market share difference for a variation of one standard deviation on both sides of the variable's mean (column 6). This is like comparing retailers in the bottom third to the top third on that variable. In column 7, we report standardized beta coefficients (averaged across categories) for each of the variables. In summary:

(1) Brand competition, represented by #BRANDS and BRNDVAR, has the highest substantive impact among all the predictor variables, in fact more than the combined impact of PRDIFF, NBPROMO, and ADVPROMO. Both PRDIFF and NBPROMO are in the top half in terms of impact and more important than ADVPROMO. Combined, factors over which manufacturers have partial or complete control have about the same impact as the retailer factors.

(2) AVGSKU, PLPROMO, QUAL, PLNAME, and PREMIUM are the most important retailer factors closely followed by CDI and EDLP. A more detailed comparison of the different factors reveals that PLPROMO has a higher substantive impact than NBPROMO, suggesting that private label promotions are quite effective in leading to higher market share for private labels. Also, the extent of competition among national brands and private label is a much more important determinant of private label share than the extent of retail competition, #RETAIL and RETVAR.

(3) Finally, consumer factors have a much lower impact on private label share performance than either the manufacturer or retailer factors; HOMEVAL is the only demographic variable having a substantial impact.

Pooled analysis across categories

It is unrealistic to expect that the slope coefficients are homogeneous across all 34 categories and so in this section we consider methods of pooling information across categories. This will help not only in getting precise estimates of the common pattern but also better summarize central tendencies in the data. We specify the system of category regressions as part of a multivariate regression system making the following error assumptions and using the following notation:

$$ms_c = X\beta_c + \varepsilon_c; \quad c = 1, 2, \ldots . 34.$$

We assume that,

$$\varepsilon' = (\varepsilon'_1, \varepsilon'_2, \ldots, \varepsilon'_c) \sim MVN(0, \Lambda \otimes I_n);$$

$$\Lambda = \text{Diag}(\sigma^2_1, \ldots . ., \sigma^2_c).$$

ms_c is the vector of private label shares for the cth category expressed in terms of deviations from the mean category share across the retail accounts. X is the $N \times k$ matrix of values for the k independent variables, each variable being expressed in terms of deviations from the within-category mean across retailer accounts. N is the number of retail accounts. β_c is the cth category slope coefficient vector and ε_c is the $N \times 1$ vector of error terms for the cth category. Mean centering by category of both the dependent and independent variables is equivalent to removing the main effect (category intercepts) of category. Consequently, our pooled analysis seeks to explain the variation in private label share across retail accounts as opposed to identifying factors that might explain differences in mean private label share across categories.

We also assume that (a) the error terms are independent across retail accounts within a given category, i.e., $\varepsilon_c \sim MVN(0, \sigma^2_{cl}I_n)$, and (b) that the errors across categories for the same retail account are independent. Our careful selection of the relevant independent variables justifies the first assumption. The second assumption is justified by an analysis of the correlation matrix of the errors across individual category level regressions.

Formal testing of the pooling restriction assuming that the slope coefficients are the same across the category regressions is rejected. This is not surprising given large differences in within-category variance in private label share across the categories. Therefore, we searched for a partitioning variable that satisfied two criteria: (a) it led to a substantial reduction in within-group heterogeneity, and (b) it was theoretically justified so as to facilitate interpretation of any differences in slope coefficients that might emerge. Past research suggests that actual quality of the store brand is an important determinant of store brand performance (Hoch and Banerji 1993). In categories offering lower quality store brands, the price gap and demographic factors influencing consumer price sensitivity may be more influential in explaining retailer performance. In contrast, factors related to the retailer's reputation and ability to differentiate itself from competition may be more important in categories with higher quality store brand. To complete this analysis, we took recent category quality estimates from Hoch and Banerji (1993). They elicited category level estimates of store brand quality from 25 quality assurance managers at leading U.S. supermarket chains and wholesalers. We utilized their ratings, rank ordered the 34 categories, and performed a median split into higher and lower quality types. Although this ex ante quality measure is not perfect, it was the best available to us.

We use a random coefficient regression procedure to estimate the mean coefficients for the two quality groups. Our procedure is similar to that used in the pooling literature (Bass and Wittink 1975, 1978; Hoch et al. 1995). We assume that the category coefficient vectors for the high quality categories are draws from a super-population distribution with mean β^h and variance $V_{\beta h}$. Similarly, the coefficient vectors for the low categories are draws from a super-population distribution with mean β^l and variance $V_{\beta l}$. That is, within the high and low quality category groups, the category coefficient vectors are distributed i.i.d. with means β^h and β^l and corresponding variances of $V_{\beta h}$ and $V_{\beta l}$. To characterize the central tendency or commonality among the categories within each quality type, we would like to infer the means for each of the quality types. Using the procedure in Hoch et al. (1995), we use the entire data set to obtain consistent estimates of the mean slope coefficient vector for the low quality categories and the differences in the mean slope coefficients between the two quality types. This is used to compute the mean slope coefficient vector for the high quality categories. Asymptotically justified estimates of the variance-covariance matrix are used to determine the significance level of the two mean slope coefficient vectors.

Table 5 presents the mean slope coefficient vectors for the two quality types. We also report the interaction terms testing the differences in the mean slope coefficients between the high and low quality categories. The pooled analysis presents quite a clean picture, one that generally reinforces the conclusions from the individual category regressions. Only the EDUC variable is not statistically significant for either the high or low quality groups or both. The 3.16 intercept difference between the two quality types indicates that even after controlling for all the other variables, higher quality categories have higher store brand penetration than lower quality categories. For 4 of the 20 predictor variables, the slope coefficients do not differ by quality level: PRDIFF, NBPROMO, PLPROMO, and ADVPROMO. Several of the variables have more impact (i.e., absolute value) in the low quality categories. For example, the fact that low quality categories have larger coefficients (in absolute value) for HOMEVAL, ELDERLY, and EDLP suggests that price and consumers' reaction to it are more important when store brand quality is not up to the standards of the national brands, that is when the store brand truly is an inferior good in the economic sense. CDI also is more important in lower quality categories, a finding that might indicate that category expertise is more important when it is difficult to offer a top-quality store brand.

The remaining coefficients have larger slopes in the high quality categories. Degree of competition, at both the brand and retail level (#RETAIL, RETVAR, #BRANDS, BRNDVAR), and economies of scale and scope (SIZE, QUAL, PLSKU, PLNAME, PREMIUM) are more important when category quality is higher. The larger coefficients for the scale and scope variables may indicate the greater importance of retailer reputation in categories where the consumer does

Table 5 Pooled analysis across categories

Variable	Average coefficient low quality categories	Average coefficient high quality categories	Difference between low and high quality categories
Consumer factors			
HOMEVAL	−8.08[a]	−3.29[b]	4.79[b]
ELDERLY	8.21[a]	3.37[c]	−4.84[c]
EDUC	−6.25	8.45	14.70[b]
ETHNIC	+7.25[a]	−6.34	−13.99[a]
Retailer factors			
#RETAIL	−0.03[a]	−0.08[a]	−0.05[a]
RETVAR	5.03[b]	9.99[b]	4.96[c]
SIZE	0.007	0.023[c]	0.016[b]
PLSKU	5.00[b]	7.00[b]	2.00[c]
QUAL(0–1)	0.30	2.14[a]	1.84[a]
PLNAME (0–1)	1.34[a]	3.01[a]	1.67[c]
EDLP (0–1)	5.43[b]	0.21	−5.22[c]
PREMIUM (0–1)	2.39[a]	3.71[a]	1.32[a]
AVGSKU	−0.21[a]	−0.14[b]	0.07[b]
CDI	6.99[a]	0.80	−6.19[a]
PRDIFF	8.96[a]	6.25[b]	−2.71
NBPROMO	−6.58[a]	−11.55[a]	−4.97
PLPROMO	9.28[a]	11.67[a]	2.39
Manufacturer factors			
#BRANDS	−0.29[a]	−0.95[a]	−0.66[a]
BRNDVAR	13.51[b]	87.22[a]	73.71[a]
ADVPROMO	−0.21[b]	−0.13	0.08

[a] $p < 0.01$, [b] $p < 0.05$, [c] $p < 0.10$.

not have to make a price-quality tradeoff when buying the store brand. Finally, the coefficient for ETHNIC flips signs and the difference is statistically significant; we have no ready explanation for this.

Conclusions

This study shows how and why the performance of private label programs systematically varies across retailers. Although our analysis shows that the pull and push tactics of the national brands exert an important influence on store brand performance, we find that a substantial part of the variation in market share comes about from actions taken by the retailer, either independently as part of its overall marketing strategy or in response to manufacturer actions. Key insights are as follows:

(1) Overall chain strategy in the use of EDLP pricing, commitment to quality, breadth of private label offerings, use of own name for private label, a premium store brand offering, and number of stores consistently enhance the retailer's private label share performance in all categories. Also, the extent to

which the retailer serves a customer base containing less wealthy and more elderly households and operates in less competitive markets improves the performance of the store brand.

(2) Although an EDLP positioning (and the concomitant lower level of national brand promotion and reduced assortment) helps the store brand, there are countervailing effects. A lower price gap and less private label promotion accompanying EDLP work in the opposite direction. Furthermore, the EDLP positioning benefits the store brand only in lower quality categories where the value positioning of the store may be better aligned with the price advantage of the store brand. Our regression models suggest, however, that the net result is quite positive for the average EDLP store. By plugging in the average values for all the other variables into the equations, we find that the average predicted EDLP store captures 3.8 more store brand share points when compared to the average Hi-Lo competitor.

(3) Recent statements in the popular press document an increased use of merchandising activities by retailers. Our analysis suggests that retailer promotional support can significantly enhance private label share performance.

(4) Retailers often use national brands to draw customers to their stores. Retailers that pursue this traffic building strategy usually carry more national brands, broader assortments, and offer better everyday (lower price gap) and promotional prices on national brands. Each of these actions work against the retailer's own store brands, highlighting the important balancing act the retailer must perform to profitably manage the sales revenue and margin mix in each of their categories. At the same time, adding a higher quality premium store brand program may mitigate this tradeoff.

(5) Unlike cross-category studies, our within-category across-retailer analysis shows that the national brand-private label price differential exerts an important positive influence on store brand performance. Across all categories, the average gap is about 40% (range 20–60%). Our data show that a 10% change in the price gap fraction results in a 0.8% change in store brand share (average $\beta = 8.2$). This supports the contention that the negative sign for price gap observed in previous research probably results from cross-category aggregation problems (Raju *et al.* 1995b).[6]

(6) When retailers obtain more than their fair share of a category (high CDI), they also do much better with private label. On average a retailer performing 10% better than the norm (CDI = 110 vs. 100) will have a store brand with 3% higher market share.

(7) From the national brand's perspective, encouraging the retailer to carry more brands (#BRANDS) and deeper assortments (AVGSKU) may be the most effective ways to keep store brands in check. And although an even distribution of brands also works against the store brand, it is unclear how manufacturers can influence BRNDVAR. The importance of these variables, however, may depend on the national brand's market position. For example, a category leader may be glad to see a rise in store brand share if it comes at the expense of one of its secondary national brand competitors. For instance, although P&G's efforts to streamline assortment appear aimed at creating marketing and operating efficiencies, the end result may be an increase in store brand sales at the expense

of minor brands. Low share underdogs are extremely vulnerable to assortment reductions.

(8) The exact impact of most of the variables depends on the underlying quality of store brands in a category. When store brand quality is high, competition at the retail and brand level is more important, as are variables capturing economies of scale and scope enjoyed by the retailer. In contrast, demographics associated with consumer price sensitivity and EDLP pricing matter more in low quality categories.

(9) Finally, premium store brands may offer the retailer an avenue for responding to the national brand's ability to cater to heterogeneous preferences. This appears more likely in categories where store brands already offer high quality comparable to the national brands.

Appreciating what separates the best from the worst retailers is important for both retailers and manufacturers. Although understanding "best practices" is generically important no matter the industry, we would argue that it is even more important in retailing. The reason is that retailers can easily observe each other's actions, assess the impact of those actions, and quickly imitate successful strategies. For retailers, arguably the most important practices are those that successfully build store traffic (e.g., new store formats, store appearance, perimeter departments, advertising) and produce significant shifts in market share.[7] Leading manufacturers must be alert to these changing practices, but in general will get their fair share of category sales irrespective of which retailer makes the sale. On the other hand, retailer imitation of successful store brand programs is more threatening to national manufacturers because within-store loss of share to the retailer's store brand (or for that matter another national brand) is not likely to be made up with a sale at a different retailer. As European retailers with high powered corporate branding programs (e.g., Sainsbury) continue to acquire regional chains in the U.S., the threat to national brands becomes more immediate.

The foregoing implies that national manufacturers need to: (a) identify which categories in their product portfolio are most vulnerable to retailer investments in private label, and (b) understand what actions they can take to limit store brand encroachment in key retail accounts. The usual starting point for answering the first question is to focus on categories where store brands already have achieved high share. This type of analysis, however, only identifies categories that are already a problem. It does not distinguish problem categories that national brands can do nothing about (e.g., salt and other commodities) from those problems that could get worse, nor does it suggest which categories could turn into bigger problems in the future.

Consider the 2 × 2 matrix in Figure 1 where we classify the 34 categories into one of four cells formed by jointly considering "average private label share across retailers" and "variance in private label share across retailers." Each cell can be labeled as categories in which private labels pose: (A) *no problem*—low average share and low variation; (B) *possible future threat*—low average share and higher variation; (C) *little hope* without a major product innovation—high average share and low variation; and (D) *biggest threat*—high average share and high variation. Due to confidentiality restrictions, we report the names of only a couple of categories for each cell.

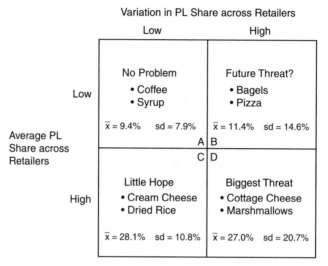

Figure 1 Classification of categories: average and variation in store brand performance across retailers

National brands are most vulnerable in high variance categories (cells B and D)—it is here that imitation of best practices could result in substantial increases in store brand share. When average private label share also is high, these categories pose big current threats if low share retailers start doing as well as the best performers. When average private label share is low, categories pose a future threat, mainly because poor performers are starting from scratch and will imitate in the high threat categories before allocating resources here. National brands should spend less time worrying about how retailers manage their store brands in categories where there is little variation across retailers (cells A and C). In cell A, manufacturers can take comfort in knowing that no retailer has figured out how to sell store brands in these categories and therefore allocate resources against their national competitors. Cell C represents categories where private label share growth probably has peaked, having reached a natural asymptote. And instead of overspending on push promotions that the retailer can arbitrage through forward buying and diversion or pull tactics that do not work anymore, manufacturers (at least the leading brands) may get higher returns by investing in the type of product innovations that got them where they were in the first place. Although the above analysis may serve as a useful decision support tool for national brand manufacturers, it is important to note that our analysis assumes that private label quality will remain comparable to that in the existing market. However, discontinuous increases in store brand quality can occur. Witness the successful introduction of quality Cola to the soft drink market by COTT, which posed an immediate threat to national brands in an otherwise low share, low variation no problem category.

Table 6 contrasts the substantive impact of each of the independent variables for the following three category groups: all categories (same as in Table 4); biggest threat (cell D); and little hope (cell C). Store brands have an important position in both the big threat and little hope categories; the difference is that

Table 6 Comparison of market share difference one standard deviation around mean

Variable	All categories	Biggest threat categories	Little hope categories
Consumer factors			
HOMEVAL	−1.67%	−3.02%	−1.52%
ELDERLY	0.33	1.21	0.18
EDUC	−0.45	−2.10	−1.74
ETHNIC	0.04	−0.97	1.30
Retailer factors			
#RETAIL	−1.62	−2.59	−3.25
RETVAR	0.73	0.70	1.91
SIZE	0.81	2.69	0.53
PLSKU	0.94	2.32	1.68
QUAL (0–1)	2.31	4.14	2.30
PLNAME (0–1)	2.10	3.80	2.01
EDLP (0–1)	1.40	1.92	0.30
PREMIUM (0–1)	2.51	4.10	1.50
AVGSKU	−4.14	−7.14	−3.29
CDI	1.42	2.48	0.73
PRDIFF	2.32	3.57	1.08
NBPROMO	−1.64	−1.87	−1.17
PLPROMO	3.22	1.64	3.17
Manufacturer factors			
#BRANDS	−14.77	−24.37	−6.37
BRNDVAR	6.16	19.27	4.49
ADVPROMO	−0.23	−0.14	−1.22

variation in performance across retailers is about four times greater in the big threat categories (average σ^2 of .047 vs. .012). Because of greater variation in the dependent variable, it is not surprising that most of the independent variables have a greater impact on performance in the high variance categories. Table 6 shows that brand competition (#BRANDS, BRNDVAR, AVGSKU) variables have about two times the impact in the high threat categories, suggesting that reductions in assortment could lead to big increases in store brand share. Most of the retailer variables (SIZE, PLSKU, QUAL, PLNAME, EDLP, PREMIUM, PRDIFF) also have substantially more impact in the big threat categories compared to either the all category or little hope averages. In contrast, manufacturer pull tactics (ADVPROMO) make more of a difference in the little hope categories, a finding for which we do not have a ready explanation.

Although our study provides a number of interesting insights, its limitations suggest several issues for future research. First, we could not obtain a direct measure of the quality of each retailer's store brands, a variable previous research has shown is very important. Our two quality type random coefficient pooling approach provides us with an overall picture of how a large set of characteristics influences store brand performance; but we have not systematically modeled how these underlying relationships (represented by the slope coefficients) might vary with other category distinctions. However, given the large number of characteristics we consider (many of which are themselves category descriptors) and lack of a theoretical framework for how the slopes might vary by category, we feel that more could be gained by supplanting our rich but admittedly descriptive approach with a more elemental structural model (e.g., Allenby and Rossi 1991). Finally, although we have adjusted our econometrics to deal with endogeneity whenever we could clearly identify it, data on about half of our variables were available on an annual level for three years. Consequently, this limited our ability to fully utilize the procedures recommended by Boulding and Staelin (1995).

There also are substantive findings worth pursuing. We found that private label promotions had more impact on private label share than opposing national brand promotions. This could be due to recent improvements in quality that place private labels in the same tier as some national brands or an increase in the intensity of private label merchandising activities by retailers. Separating premium from standard private labels may be a potentially fruitful topic to pursue, something that we could not completely address with the current data.[8] The positive impact of using the chain name for private labels across categories warrants further investigation into the individual cross-category purchasing behavior of consumers and the impact on retailer's image. The importance of the #BRANDS and the AVGSKU variable suggests that national manufacturers could benefit from a more detailed examination of the economics of using brand-extension and flanker strategies versus line-extension strategies. Future research at an individual store and category level needs to investigate the impact of changing the price gap between national brands and the private label.

Finally, our results are decidedly bound to the U.S. grocery market. It is well known that store brands play a more dominant role in several European markets and Canada. For example, store brands have 45% share in Switzerland, 37% in the UK, and 22% in Canada. Moreover, store brands in many European markets are reputed to be of much higher quality than in the U.S. and so some might argue that the regularities we find in the U.S. are less relevant to other markets. We have no problem accepting the fact that the rules are not exactly the same as in the U.S. For example, retail concentration is much higher in Europe (three-firm concentration ratio ranging from 45–80% vs. 17% in the U.S.). At the same time, however, the extent of variation in store brand performance across countries is not that different in magnitude from what we observe within the U.S. We look forward to examining these issues in other markets as data become available.

Our research shows that the substantial differences that exist across retailers systematically affect the success of a chain's private label program. Not controlling for this in empirical studies can lead to biased conclusions (e.g., effect of national brand-private label price differential on private label share). The study also identifies a set of basic factors describing the retailer's strategy that account for the differential success of their private label programs. Our research serves as the starting point for future inquiry that formally recognizes the leading role of the retailer in the store brand equation.[9]

Notes

1   U.S. store brands usually are not quite up to the quality standards of the top national brands and always are priced at a discount; and so our findings may be less applicable to countries where these same conditions do not hold.

2   Each SCANTRACK area covers a designated number of counties, with an average of 30 and a range from 1 to 68. All markets include central city, suburban, and rural areas.

3   Hausmann's (1978, Johnston 1984) test procedure was used to show that we need to endogenize these variables. Furthermore, to show that appropriate instruments were chosen, we selected alternate instruments for the endogenous variables. Since the planning horizon for promotions (PLPROMO and NBPROMO), price differential (PRDIFF), and product stocking (#BRANDS, AVGSKU, BRNDVAR) are likely to be well within a year, the further we go back in time to select alternate instruments, the less likely they are to be contemporaneously related with the current error term. Since two years is the maximum our data-set allows us to go back to, we use two-stage least squares to create alternate instruments using two-year lagged values. Two-year lag instruments are not significant in a regression containing one-year lags (Spencer and Berk 1981), and so we feel comfortable using one-year lagged instruments.

4   In addition, we also estimate the serial correlation coefficient using the three full years of data. This analysis also supports our earlier findings.

5   This also provides an alternative estimator for pooling coefficients across categories when the random coefficient approach cannot be used, either due to violation of underlying assumptions or data limitations (Bass and Wittink 1978).

6   A cross-category analysis for the current data set also leads to a similar result for the price gap.

7   We do not mean to downplay the importance of practices that increase operational efficiency, such as improved logistics, but for present purposes we contend that these practices are less observable and therefore more difficult to imitate (witness Kmart vis a vis Wal-Mart).

8   We did run separate regressions after dividing the sample of retailers into two groups, those with and without a premium store brand line. We found no differences in the signs of the coefficients across the two groups. The pattern of differences in magnitudes between coefficients for premium and nonpremium retailers was similar to what we found in our high versus low quality category analysis.

9   We acknowledge the help of the packaged goods firm that wishes to remain anonymous in providing us with access to the data. We also thank A. C. Nielsen Company, Spectra Marketing, and participating retailers for their contributions in assembling the database. Invaluable research assistance was provided by Nanda Kumar, Dilip Soman, Liyun Wang, John Wright, Xavier Drèze, Subranshu Mukherjee, and P.B. Seetharaman. We also acknowledge helpful comments from Jagmohan Raju, Peter Rossi, and participants at a Wharton Marketing Workshop. Partial funding came from the firm providing us with the data, the Bozell, Jacobs, Kenyon and Eckhardt Fund at the Graduate School of Business, University of Chicago, and the Wharton School Faculty Research Fund at the University of Pennsylvania.

References

Allenby, Greg M. and Peter E. Rossi (1991), "Quality Perceptions and Asymmetric Switching Between Brands," *Marketing Science*, 10, 3, 185–204.

Bass, Frank M. and Dick R. Wittink (1975), "Pooling Issues and Methods in Regression Analysis with Examples in Marketing Research," *Journal of Marketing Research*, 12, 4, 414–425.

—— and —— (1978), "Pooling Issues and Methods in Regression Analysis with

Examples in Marketing Research: Some Further Reflections," *Journal of Marketing Research*, 15, 2, 277–279.

Becker, Gary (1965), "A Theory of the Allocation of Time," *Economic Journal*, 75, 493–517.

Blattberg, Robert C, Gary D. Eppen, and Joshua Lieberman (1978), "A Theoretical and Empirical Evaluation of Price Deals for Consumer Nondurables," *Journal of Marketing*, 45, 1, 116–129.

Boulding, William and Richard Staelin (1995), "Identifying Generalizable Effects of Strategic Actions on Firm Performance: The Case of Demand-Side Returns to R&D Spending," *Marketing Science*, 14, 3, G222–G236.

Drèze, Xavier (1995), "Loss Leaders and Cherry Picking: A Theoretical and Empirical Analysis," Unpublished Dissertation, University of Chicago, Graduate School of Business, Chicago, IL.

Hausmann, J. A. (1978), "Specification Tests in Econometrics," *Econometrica*, 46, 6, 1251–1271.

Hoch, Stephen J. (1996), "How Should National Brands Think About Private Labels?" *Sloan Management Review*, 37, Winter, 89–102.

—— and Shumeet Banerji (1993), "When Do Private Labels Succeed?" *Sloan Management Review*, 34, Summer, 57–68.

—— , Xavier Drèze, and Mary E. Purk (1994), "EDLP, Hi-Lo, and Margin Arithmetic," *Journal of Marketing*, 58, 4, 16–29.

—— , Byung-Do Kim, Alan L. Montgomery, and Peter E. Rossi (1995), "Determinants of Store-Level Price Elasticity," *Journal of Marketing Research*, 32, 1, 17–29.

Johnston, Jack (1984), *Econometric Methods*, New York: McGraw-Hill.

Kamakura, Wagner A. and Gary J. Russell (1989), "A Probabilistic Choice Model for Market Segmentation and Elasticity Structure," *Journal of Marketing Research*, 26, November, 379–390.

Lal, Rajiv (1990), "Manufacturer Trade Deals and Retail Price Promotions," *Journal of Marketing Research*, 27, 4, 428–444.

Mills, David E. (1995), "Why Do Retailers Sell Private Label?" *Journal of Economics and Management Strategy*, 4, 3, 509–528.

Raju, Jagmohan S., Raj K. Sethuraman, and Sanjay K. Dhar (1995a), "The Introduction and Performance of Store Brands," *Management Science*, 41, June, 957–978.

—— , —— and —— (1995b), "National-Store Brand Price Differential and Store Brand Market Share," *Pricing Theory & Practice*, 3, 2, 17–24.

Schmalensee, Richard (1978), "Entry-Deterrence in the Ready to Eat Breakfast Cereals Industry," *Bell Journal of Economics*, 9, 305–327.

Sethuraman, Raj (1992), "The Effect of Marketplace Factors on Private Label Penetration in Grocery Products," *Marketing Science Institute*, Report #92–128.

Spencer, David E., and Kenneth N. Berk (1981), "A Limited Information Specification Test," *Econometrica*, 49, 4, 1079–1086.

Starzynski, Greg (1993), *The Private Label Consumer: Is There One?* Northbrook, IL: A. C. Nielsen.

Waterson, Michael (1984), *Economic Theory of the Industry*, Cambridge: Cambride University Press.

White, Hal (1980), "A Heteroskedasticity-Consistent Covariance Matrix Estimator and a Direct Test for Heteroskedasticity," *Econometrica*, 50, 483–499.

Editors' Commentary

STEVE BURT HAS BEEN on the staff of the Institute for Retail Studies at the University of Stirling since 1984, becoming Professor of Retail Marketing in 1998. His PhD from the University of Stirling was on the impact of the Loi Royer on French hypermarket retailing and followed on from a geography degree at the University of Oxford. His research interests have had a particularly European orientation. Steve Burt is currently Visiting Professor in the Institute of Economic Research in the Department of Business Administration at Lund University and also a Visiting Professor at IGR/IAE at the Université de Rennes I. He has been president of the European Association for Education and Research in Commercial Distribution since 1990.

Steve Burt's main areas of interest are comparative retailing, retail internationalization, structural change in UK retailing and retail branding. He has received funding from a range of public agencies including the UK's Department of Trade and Industry, the European Commission and the Economic and Social Research Council, as well as significant funding from commercial organizations.

'The Strategic Role of Brands in British Grocery Retailing' is one of two articles by Steve Burt in this volume. It brings together his research on structural change and retail branding. He focuses on the ways in which brands are instrumental in retailer strategies with reference to the supply chain, management issues and retailer image. This paper introduces the literature on brands and develops various conceptual and operational ideas on brands, deriving mainly from the very innovative and extensive developments in retail grocery branding in the UK. This paper began as a series of seminars over a number of years presented at Lund University and represents the synthesis of thinking about retail grocery brands in the 1990s in the UK. It is in stark counter point to the work emanating from the USA on retail brands at this time.

Since this paper, Steve Burt's work on branding has focused primarily on branding operations and impacts in an international context, linking to aspects of corporate branding, store image, brand transferability and meaning and internationalization generally. This area remains a strong feature of European retail research.

Key Publications

Burt SL (1989) Trends and management issues in European retailing. *International Journal of Retailing*, 4(4), 1–97.

Burt SL (1991) Trends in the internationalisation of grocery retailing: the European experience. *International Review of Retail, Distribution and Consumer Research*, 1, 487–515.

Burt SL (1993) Temporal trends in the internationalisation of British retailing. *International Review of Retail, Distribution and Consumer Research*, 3, 391–410.

Burt SL (1995) Retail internationalisation: evolution of theory and practice. In PJ

McGoldrick and G Davies (eds) *International Retailing: Trends and Strategies*. Pitman: London, 51–73.

Burt SL and Sparks L (1997) Performance in food retailing: a cross national consideration and comparison of retail margins. *British Journal of Management*, 8, 13–150.

Burt SL and Davis S (1999) Follow my leader? Lookalike retailer brands in non-manufacturer-dominated product markets in the UK. *International Review of Retail, Distribution and Consumer Research*, 9, 163–185.

Moore CM, Fernie J and Burt S (2000) Brands without boundaries: the internationalization of the designer retailer's brand. *European Journal of Marketing*, 34, 919–937.

Burt SL and Carralero-Encinas J (2000) The role of store image in retail internationalisation. *International Marketing Review*, 17, 433–453.

Burt SL and Sparks L (2002) Corporate branding, internationalisation and the retailer as a brand. *Corporate Reputation Review*, 5, 194–212.

Burt SL, Mellahi K, Jackson TP and Sparks L (2002) Retail internationalisation and retail failure: issues from the case of Marks and Spencer. *International Review of Retail Distribution and Consumer Research*, 12, 191–219.

Collins A and Burt SL (2003) Market sanctions, monitoring and vertical coordination within retailer-manufacturer relationships: the case of retail brand suppliers. *European Journal of Marketing*, 37, 668–689.

Burt SL, Dawson JA and Sparks L (2003) Failure in international retailing: research propositions. *International Review of Retail Distribution and Consumer Research*, 13, 355–373.

Burt SL and Sparks L (2003) Power and competition in the UK retail grocery market. *British Journal of Management*, 14, 237–254.

Johansson U and Burt SL (2004) The buying of private brands in grocery retailing: a comparative study of buying processes in the UK, Sweden and Italy. *Journal of Marketing Management*, 20(7/8), 799–824.

Burt SL and Mavrommatis A (2006) The international transfer of store brand image. *International Review of Retail Distribution and Consumer Research*, 16, 395–413.

Website

http://www.marketing.stir.ac.uk/STFPAGES/burt/page.htm

THE STRATEGIC ROLE OF RETAIL BRANDS IN BRITISH GROCERY RETAILING

Steve L. Burt

Assesses the evolution of retail brands within British grocery retailing over the past 25 years. Highlights key issues in defining retail brands which contribute to our understanding of their role and impact upon company strategy, and then explores how British retailers have managed the evolution of these product ranges. Identifies key factors as the changing basis and use of retail power in the distribution channel, the centralisation of management activities, and the appreciation of what constitutes retail image. Argues that British grocery retailers have successfully managed these factors to create a retail brand which is now regarded by customers as being at least equal to, if not better than, the established manufacturer brands.

Introduction

ONE OF THE MOST distinctive features of the British grocery market as we approach the new century, is the extent and commercial success of retail brand ranges which are now present in virtually every product class. The evolution of these product ranges over the past 25 years, from private labels offering the consumer a lower quality product alternative for a lower price, into retail brands offering a true quality brand alternative, reflects the application of a clear marketing approach in the retail environment. Recent developments, which have seen the major grocery chains extend their brand names into product and service markets beyond the core product offer, provide further confirmation of the central role that retail brands now play within corporate strategy *per se*.

One theme in many of the early studies on retail brands is a search for a common definition (e.g. Schutte, 1969; Morris, 1979; Martell, 1986; de Chernatony and McWilliam, 1988). As a base definition, that provided by Morris (1979) is often cited:

> . . . consumer products produced by or on behalf of, distributors and sold under the distributor's own name or trademark through the distributor's own outlet.

This simple quote encapsulates many of the key factors in retail brand development: the process of retail brand production; the labelling of the product range; and the unique availability of the product. This paper will review how these factors have been managed in the British grocery market, as the retail brand has

European Journal of Marketing, Vol. 34, No. 8 (2000), pp. 875–890. © MCB University Press, 0309–0566.

evolved from the status of a poor relation to challenge established manufacturer brands as an equal. First, the paper highlights important issues in retail brand definition which contribute to our understanding of previous studies. The paper then illustrates how British retailers have managed this transformation through a clear understanding of: the basis and use of retail power in the distribution channel; the implications for branding of the centralisation of management activities; and an appreciation of the source of retail image and the attributes and cues which contribute to image. Finally, the paper will suggest issues for the future extension of the retail brand concept.

Retail Grocery Brands: Interpreting Past Studies

The growth of retail brands *per se* has been a regular topic of academic study. Reviews of developments in the British grocery market have been provided by authors such as Simmons and Meredith (1984), Baden-Fuller (1984), Davies *et al.* (1986) and Burt (1992), while the US perspective is typified by the work of Hoch and Banerji (1993), Bhasin *et al.* (1995), Mills (1995), Hoch (1996) and Quelch and Harding (1996). Until relatively recently, much of the US work questioned the impact of retail brands on manufacturer brands, and suggested that penetration levels would remain lower in the USA. This apparent divergence of opinion across the Atlantic raises a fundamental issue in the study of retail brands, namely a clear understanding of the object of study. The assumption is often made that the term "retail brand" in one country or context is the same as "retail brand" in another. In reality, the composition of retail brand ranges, the market positioning of these products and the origin and development of these ranges may differ markedly. Acknowledgement of these differences is important when assessing academic work or trade press commentaries.

Although statistics on the market penetration of retail brands illustrate that these product ranges form a fundamental part of the grocery offer in the UK (see Tables 1 and 2), these figures can be misleading, owing to changes in definitions and the composition of "baskets" over time (Burt, 1992). Penetration levels, however defined, vary by company and by product sector. These headline figures also disguise important features such as the type and role of the retail brand in the overall market proposition. For example, in some product categories both high quality retail brands and price fighting "generics" are combined under a single definition, and some retailers in the UK have used the retail brand strategically to launch initiatives championing "new" consumer values such as healthy eating, animal welfare or environmental issues. General statistics also disguise the extent of change in retail brand ranges. As innovation and quality have become major positioning elements in these ranges it is not unusual for the leading grocery retailers to introduce between 800–1,000 new versions of retail brands in a year. The outcome is that the retail brands recorded in Table 1 for 1977 will be very different in nature to those recorded in 1995.

It is now accepted that an evolutionary sequence of retail brand development may exist. For example, Laaksonen and Reynolds (1994) suggest four generations of retail brand (see Table 3) each with important differences in product

Table 1 Retailer brand share of packaged grocery turnover by operator[a]

Operator	Percentage of packaged grocery turnover									Percentage of packaged grocery/toiletries turnover			
	1977	1980	1983	1985	1986	1987	1988	1989	1990	1992	1993	1994	1995
All outlets	23.1	22.2	26.2	28.0	28.9	29.1	29.6	29.4	30.5	32.3	33.3	35.3	37.6
Multiple chains	n/a	n/a	n/a	29.0	30.4	31.2	32.0	32.3	33.0	n/a	n/a	n/a	n/a
J. Sainsbury	63.0	54.2	53.3	56.0	55.8	55.4	55.1	54.8	53.4	54.0	53.8	54.0	53.4
Tesco	23.3	20.8	30.3	36.2	36.7	34.0	36.4	38.0	39.4	42.8	44.1	46.2	45.2
Waitrose	40.9	42.4	47.7	38.3	39.2	41.0	40.0	40.4	38.3	37.8	38.7	38.5	37.4
Safeway (Argyll)	31.8	27.6	33.8	35.7	34.7	36.0	35.8	33.5	33.1	36.4	36.5	38.4	41.2
Presto (Argyll)	–	–	–	26.3	29.2	30.1	26.5	24.6	25.9	25.5	25.7	30.4	34.3
Allied Suppliers	12.8	15.4	20.7	–	–	–	–	–	–	–	–	–	–
ASDA	7.6	6.4	6.5	7.6	18.2	28.1	30.0	29.8	30.6	34.5	30.0	32.9	38.6
Gateway/Somerfield	–	–	–	16.7	14.1	17.5	20.0	22.7	24.4	31.3	31.3	34.0	38.5
Fine Fare	24.1	16.8	24.3	–	–	–	–	–	–	–	–	–	–
International	12.7	19.2	21.4	–	–	–	–	–	–	–	–	–	–
Morrisons	–	–	–	–	–	–	–	–	–	27.0	29.2	30.8	32.0
Kwik Save	–	–	–	–	–	–	–	–	–	1.5	5.8	9.4	11.4
Co-operatives	n/a	n/a	n/a	33.9	31.3	29.9	29.8	29.7	29.4	22.6	22.0	23.0	21.3
CRS	–	–	–	31.1	27.1	24.8	23.8	23.8	24.4	–	–	–	–
Groups	n/a	n/a	n/a	n/a	n/a	n/a	n/a	n/a	n/a	n/a	n/a	n/a	n/a
Spar	21.9	20.1	22.4	19.9	19.2	18.2	17.0	13.4	13.1	21.9	24.4	23.6	23.8
Mace	15.4	13.5	14.3	–	–	–	–	–	–	9.2	8.4	6.6	6.8
VG	20.6	16.3	11.1	–	–	–	–	–	–	–	–	–	–
Londis	–	–	–	–	–	–	–	–	–	11.6	15.1	15.6	12.4

Note: [a] 1977–1983 data and 1985–1990 data from AGB/TCA 73 Fields Packaged Grocery; 1992–1995 data from AGB Superpanel

Source: Various sources

Table 2 Retail brand value shares by category, 1997

Operator	Dry grocery	Dairy	Delicatessen	Frozen	Bakery	Confectionery	Liquids	Petfood and care	Household	Toiletries
All stores	36.0	65.9	85.5	47.9	64.0	15.9	37.2	18.7	38.6	19.6
Sainsbury	47.5	65.9	91.0	57.9	70.2	20.2	51.8	27.4	46.0	21.9
Tesco	39.3	63.4	88.1	52.1	75.1	16.2	44.9	17.4	44.2	21.1
Safeway	36.0	61.5	84.6	45.5	67.5	13.2	41.6	19.8	38.3	17.6
ASDA	41.9	60.0	88.0	55.8	64.2	19.5	40.6	32.7	44.0	24.5
Somerfield	26.4	60.3	83.8	40.2	51.2	11.5	33.8	10.5	28.7	13.2
Kwik Save	17.1	9.6	52.2	15.3	23.8	8.1	8.9	9.1	24.3	10.1
Co-op	24.1	53.3	75.6	24.1	40.8	4.1	29.6	5.3	25.6	11.3
Morrisons	27.7	58.1	85.7	22.7	77.3	1.0	19.1	20.2	31.0	11.5
Iceland	26.7	42.1	68.1	61.3	20.8	39.7	–	–	40.9	0.8
Waitrose	35.4	61.5	82.1	40.5	64.6	23.9	32.0	14.1	35.7	10.6

Source: AC Nielsen Homescan

Table 3 A typology of retail brands

	1st generation	2nd generation	3rd generation	4th generation
Type of brand	Generic No name Brand free Unbranded	"Quasi-brand" Own label	Own brand	Extended own brand, i.e. segmented own brands
Strategy	Generics	Cheapest price	Me-too	Value-added
Objective	Increase margins Provide choice in pricing	Increase margins Reduce manufacturers' power by setting the entry price Provide better-value product (quality/price)	Enhance category margins Expand product assortment, i.e. customer choice Build retailer's image among consumers	Increase and retain the client base Enhance category margins Improve image further Differentiation
Product	Basic and functional products	One-off staple lines with a large volume	Big category products	Image-forming product groups Large number of products with small volume (niche)
Technology	Simple production process and basic technology lagging behind market leader	Technology still lagging behind market leaders	Close to the brand leader	Innovative technology
Quality/image	Lower quality and inferior image compared to the manufacturers' brands	Medium quality but still perceived as lower than leading manufacturers' brands Secondary brand alongside the leading manufacturer's brand	Comparable to the brand leaders	Same or better than brand leader Innovative and different products from brand leaders
Approximate pricing	20 per cent or more below the brand leader	10–20 per cent below	5–10 per cent below	Equal or higher than known brand
Consumers' motivation to buy	Price is the main criterion for buying	Price is still important	Both quality and price, i.e. value for money	Better and unique products
Supplier	National, not specialised	National, partly specialising to own label manufacturing	National, mostly specialising for own brand manufacturing	International, manufacturing mostly own brands

Source: Laaksonen and Reynolds (1994)

characteristics, production technology input, market position and consumer motivation. They also argue that these categories overlap and not all countries or companies progress through the same sequence. Similarly, Wileman and Jary (1997) suggest five stages of retail brands – generics; cheap; re-engineered low-cost; par quality; and leadership – which roughly correspond to the maturity of the brand concept. While the stages in these two schemes differ slightly, and one could question whether a progression from one stage to another is inevitable, their value is in illustrating that different forms of retail brand exist (or have existed) in the marketplace. It is now universally recognised that retail grocery brands in the UK have developed to the more sophisticated levels in any schema.

Similar issues of context and timing arise when interpreting studies which have attempted to profile the retail brand shopper. As the majority of these originate from the USA, the object of these studies is usually the mid-quality/mid-price retail brand, typical of the second generation in Table 3, not the high added value/high price retail brands that the British customer is familiar with today. Early work such as that of Frank and Boyd (1965), Myers (1967), Rao (1969) and Burger and Schott (1972) failed to discover any consistent distinguishing psychological or socio-economic differences between retail and manufacturer brand consumers. Similarly, in the case of generic products, American studies have again struggled to develop a consistent picture of the generic consumer (e.g. Granzin, 1981; McEnally and Hawes, 1984; Rosen, 1984; Wilkes and Valencia, 1985; Szymanski and Busch, 1987).

Whether in British or US studies, one common theme emerging from the literature is the role of perceived risk in relation to quality and value for money. In the UK, Livesey and Lennon (1978) concluded that the highest purchasers of retail brand products were the younger and more affluent consumers. They argued that these groups were more willing to take risks in purchasing new "unknown" products, whilst the income constrained preferred to buy tried and trusted brands. Bellizzi et al. (1981) and Cunningham et al. (1982) suggested that generally consumers perceive retail brands as of lower quality than national brands, particularly those groups who purchase manufacturer brands. In more recent work, Richardson et al. (1994, 1996) and Dick et al. (1995) recognise that product quality, the extrinsic cues of product quality ranging from attractive packaging, labelling and brand image, and the overall image of the store itself are crucial factors in retail brand success. They comment:

> . . . simple improvements in the extrinsic cues associated with store labels may go a long way towards increasing consumer acceptance of private label brands. European retailers understand this and have been successful in increasing store brand market share through dramatic improvements in package design, labeling, advertising, and branding strategies.
>
> (Richardson et al., 1996)

and:

> . . . The European experience shows that store brands, if properly

marketed, can create the competitive advantage that most retailers in
the USA have yet to achieve.

(Dick *et al.*, 1995)

It is this fundamental difference in approach, treating the retail brand as a true
brand with all the marketing issues this entails, which distinguishes the development of the retail brand in the British grocery market from that which persists in
many other countries.

Key Factors in Retail Brand Development

The differences between retail brand development in the UK and in other
markets can be explained by a number of inter-related factors. All of these stem
from the application of a marketing approach to the retail business.

The basis and use of retail power in the distribution channel

Often the key factor in retail brand production is regarded as the shift in channel power from the manufacturer to the retailer. Charts are produced which
measure retail concentration ratios against retail brand market share to confirm this relationship. However, more important to the strategic move from own
label to retail brand is a clear understanding on the part of the retailer of the
changing basis of power in the channel and the subsequent use that is made of
that power.

Commonly retail power is equated solely with buying power and economies
of scale. The simple argument is that as retailers have grown in size and control
an increasing proportion of floor-space, shelf space and ultimately sales they have
used their scale to exert coercive or reward power to take advantage of excess
capacity in the manufacturing sector. As retailers have searched for production
capacity they have found suppliers, typically outside the leading brand manufacturers, who are willing to produce product under the retailer name to a certain
specification at a set price. The willingness of manufacturers to comply with
retailer demands is justified in most textbooks (e.g. McGoldrick, 1990) by
reference to the need to maintain manufacturing scale economies, cover fixed
costs and to utilise full production capacity. Although this approach may have
stimulated the initial moves into retail brand, which primarily involved "me too"
product ranges consisting of technologically simple, quasi-commodity grocery
products (positioned as acceptable quality for a lower price), the innovative,
technologically complex, high price/high quality retail brand of today (positioned as at least equal to if not better than the leading manufacturer brand)
requires a more complex use of market power.

Crucial to the change in emphasis in retail brand development in the UK has
been the role of information power alongside pure scale expressed in traditional
buying power terms. The increased availability of information on both consumer
purchases and product movement within the supply chain, and the ownership of

this information by larger, more powerful retailers, has provided the impetus to reconfigure roles, functions and tasks within the traditional supply chain. Recognition of this basis of channel power has coincided with a desire on the part of the retailer to create differentiation in the marketplace through image development and products only available in their stores.

Increased scale and information power can be used in two ways to manage the distribution channel. First, simply to reinforce existing trading relationships with a focus on price. This may involve driving down manufacturer prices to the retailer, increasing manufacturer support for promotion activities for branded products, or to source low cost production of retail brands. Alternatively, the ownership of information may be used proactively to amend traditional channel relationships and roles, so that the unique skills and competencies of the retail and manufacturer base can be brought to bear for the mutual benefit of those involved. This switch in emphasis requires a rethinking of traditional channel approaches to the use of market power. In the UK grocery sector we have seen a move to this latter approach as the management of relationships has evolved from traditional trading based relationships, characterised by conflict and negotiation (primarily over price, promotional support, payment and delivery terms) to the more integrative, constructive and co-operative relationships associated with a vertical marketing systems approach to channel management (Dawson and Shaw, 1989, 1990). This switch in emphasis has been an important contributor to the development of retail grocery brands in the UK (Hughes, 1996).

Doel (1996) illustrates this subtle shift in approach. With regards to the process of initiating retail brand production, she contrasts two approaches. First, the traditional method of utilising excess capacity among existing manufacturers, and second direct (proactive) intervention on the part of retailers to develop capacity to supply them. This more proactive approach was also noted by Shaw *et al.* (1992) who argue that the retail brand buyer typically searches for a supplier who will meet pre-determined quality and positioning requirements, rather than selecting existing or new products from the supplier's portfolio. Ultimately the choice of option will depend upon the maturity of different sub-sectors, the strategic significance of certain products, and the characteristics of individual retailers.

From these two different starting points, two types of relationship evolve. Traditional arms-length governance, based upon the threat of switching to an alternative supplier, is seen as only sustainable in established, low margin markets with standardised products – for which production specifications can be easily transferred between suppliers. In contrast, when mutual product innovation and development are present, usually in higher margin and strategically more important markets, the alternatives and associated possibility of switching supplier are much less. Despite the common practice in the latter situation of working without written contracts, relationships are continuous and intense in nature, often involving open book modes of operation. Finally, these contrasting approaches are reflected in evolving organisational forms, with the latter pro-active mutual benefit approach placing a greater emphasis upon the vertical marketing systems approach to channels, characterised by intensive interaction, mutual interest and proactive retailer involvement.

The centralisation of management activities

The use of both buying and information power to reconfigure channel relationships is itself linked to the high degree of management centralisation within UK
grocery retailing. This has a number of implications for retail brand development,
particularly in respect to developing and maintaining a quality image across a
national retail chain.

The transfer of most of the operational decisions relating to product assortments, merchandising, store layout, pricing and promotion, from the store or
region to the corporate centre allowed retailers to develop a clear, consistent
image and market position to the customer. The uniformity in store operation
that such a management system provides enabled a coherent set of core values to
be built up through the retail offer, and ensured that these values were consistently
delivered. These values were further reinforced in customers' minds through an
increased above-the-line advertising spend, which emphasised quality and value
rather than a pure price message. According to MEAL, Tesco was the leading
brand advertiser between 1990–1994. A final factor in developing and maintaining a clear image was the strategic choice of most grocery retailers during the late
1980s and early 1990s to trade through a single trading format, the superstore
(Burt and Sparks, 1995). Smaller stores on high streets or in smaller connurba-
tions were closed, whilst attempts to develop alternative trading formats for
these smaller outlets, e.g. Victor Value, and Lo-Cost, were disposed of in favour
of the superstore concept. All of these moves provided the customer with a
consistent perception of the retail offer from company store to company store.

Similarly, the increased management control exercised by retailers over the
logistics chain during the 1980s and early 1990s allowed them to establish and
monitor the quality control measures necessary for supporting an added value
retail image and high quality brand range. Changes in logistics practice such as
the move to centralised distribution and composite deliveries (McKinnon, 1986;
Smith and Sparks, 1993; Fernie, 1997) also potentially extended the supply base
for retail brands. By reducing the number of delivery points this move allowed
smaller suppliers and new entrants without established distribution capabilities
to supply retail brand ranges.

The recognition of the source of retail image

The significance of wielding improved buying and information power in a more
proactive way, and the benefits of centralisation in creating a uniform retail offer,
culminated in a clear recognition by UK grocery retailers of the importance and
potential of their tradename in developing image.

It is, however, important to appreciate the context within which these
developments were taking place, as positioning is ultimately relative to others in
the marketplace. In general terms, the basic shake-out in the UK grocery sector
occurred in the late 1970s to mid-1980s following a period of price competition
initiated by Tesco's "Operation Checkout" campaign (Akehurst, 1984), and a
series of acquisitions and mergers as the Argyll Group (now Safeway) and Dee

Corporation (now Somerfield) were formed. From the mid-1980s the generic market positioning of the leading grocery retailers was to focus attention upon non-price competition, whilst maintaining price competitiveness on key lines. This generic position was further encouraged or enabled through local market monopolies reinforced by the planning process and, unlike on the Continent, the absence of any significant competitive threat from the discount segment of the market (Burt and Sparks, 1994).

The credit-driven retail boom and generally high levels of customer confidence during the early to mid-1980s also supported a move to non-price competition. This emphasis has been maintained in the 1990s with the addition of both income-generating services such as dry cleaning, coffee shops and photo-processing, and customer-service initiatives such as crèches, baby-changing facilities, dedicated car parking facilities, bag packing, one-in-front schemes and customer-service desks. In such a business environment, investment in high quality, standardised or conforming stores represented an investment in image. The realignment of retail brands during this period reflects this strategy and the release of the "value added" built up in retail stores (Wileman and Jary, 1997). A further factor during this period of reassessment was the benchmark provided by Marks and Spencer, which operated a 100 per cent retail brand policy, but one based upon high added value, innovative food products.

The crucial factor in the realignment of retail brand ranges in the UK has been a clear appreciation of what the retail tradename means to the customer. After all, it is the retail tradename which is placed on the product and the "values" that customers attribute to that tradename which are transferred to the product. If the retailer wishes its retail brand product range to be perceived as a high quality alternative, comparable to the leading manufacturer brands, it must ensure that its tradename carries the appropriate "values" and that this image has been established coherently in the minds of the consumer via its stores. Very simplistically, the consumers will transfer brand connotations to the product range from their experiences of the retail store. If the chain has a poor image, for example its stores are perceived as low quality with disinterested staff, low levels of customer service and failing to deliver a pleasant shopping experience, these "values" will be transferred to the product. It is worth noting that Aldi, despite a nearly 100 per cent retail brand strategy, does not put its own tradename on its retail brand products. The values associated with the Aldi shopping environment and service levels might not be those that one wishes to transfer directly to the product. The trials and tribulations of Gateway in its attempt to develop a strong retail brand during the late 1980s also illustrates this point. The chain grew through a series of acquisitions (e.g. Key Markets, International Stores, Lennons, Fine Fare) which hindered attempts to develop a coherent image and transfer values to a product range.

The attributes associated with a brand name are also influenced by in-store reference points. Another feature of British grocery retailing during the 1980s was the reduction of brand choice to a two or three brand alternative in most product groups. Of particular importance to the development of the quality retail brand in the UK was the relative position of these product ranges to the "generic" range (de Chernatony, 1988, 1989a, 1989b). The typical brand product range of the late 1970s/early 1980s comprised a three-tier structure of leading manufacturer brand, seen as the high-quality/high-price alternative; the retailer brand, generally positioned as a mid-quality/mid-price alternative; and a "generic" range offering acceptable quality for a low price. These three clearly positioned brand alternatives concurred with basic market segmentation principles by covering the upper, middle and low end of the market. However, as the "generic" range at this time was in effect branded by the retailer (McGoldrick, 1984) consumers tended to compare the retail brand offer with the retail generic offer. Price and quality perceptions tended to link these two brands together, in effect lowering the quality perceptions of the retail brand. Rather than the three-tier branded offer made available by the retail company, the consumer perceived a two-tier offer of manufacturer brand and retail/generic brand.

The presence in the store of this low quality/low price reference point, which was clearly linked to the retailer, proved to be a major barrier to improving consumer perceptions of the true retail brand. Hence these product ranges were removed during the mid-1980s, as grocery retailers sought to reposition their retail brands. Although these generic ranges have reappeared from 1993, as fighting brands to match the potential threat of the expanding limited line discount sector, by this time consumer perceptions of the retail brand as a high quality brand alternative had been established, and the product selection for the new generation of generics was more carefully managed by the retail chains.

The repositioning of retail brand product ranges as high quality brand alternatives to leading manufacturer brands, as opposed to a product alternative as previously offered by the lower quality/priced versions required not only changes in product quality, but in other visible clues from which consumers build their perceptions. First the nature of the product range changed, with a move away from the retail brand merely offering "me too" copies of existing products to the development of new, innovative products in high value markets. In order to develop such technologically complex products and to ensure constant quality of product, retailers were required to pursue the more proactive, partnership type relationships with suppliers that were discussed earlier. In addition, this change in product emphasis required a reconfiguration of existing buying teams whose core skills were no longer simply negotiation, but needed to encompass a range of marketing and merchandising skills, technical support and quality control.

Just as important in signalling the position of retailer brands is the packaging of these products. It has been established by a number of authors that packaging provides consumers with intrinsic clues (e.g. Louviere *et al.*, 1987; Costley and Brucks, 1992; Sirdeshmukh and Unnava, 1992). The original packaging for the mid-quality/mid-price, "me too", retail brand followed the usual formula of presenting these ranges in the corporate colour with a clear emphasis on the company tradename or logo. Thus on entering an aisle one was confronted with blocks of clearly identified corporate coded retail brand, a position still found in many retail stores on the Continent. This type of packaging draws attention to the company, not the product *per se*. With the repositioned high quality/high price retail brand, characterised by innovative products, a change in packaging occurred. As the intention was now to compete directly with established leading manufacturer brands packaging was reformulated. The uniform corporate colour, and in some cases even logo, and corporate style was abandoned in favour of packaging which emphasised the product itself. This entailed a range of colour packs, different graphics, and usually a reduction in font size and prominence of the retail brand name. The packaging mimicked more closely the conventions followed by manufacturer brand products.

In a number of cases this re-packaging has aroused accusations of copycatting from manufacturer brands. Manufacturers argue that association with their brands through packaging clues imply that the retail brand has the same product qualities or even originate from the same manufacturer. In response retailers claim that certain colour coding and packaging conventions are synonymous with particular product groups so some similarity is necessary to aid product and brand comparison. Despite a number of studies attempting to measure consumer confusion covering a range of products, methodologies and implemented in different countries, there is no clear consensus over the degree of confusion and mistaken purchase (see for example Loken *et al.*, 1986; Kapferer 1995a, 1995b; Rafiq and Collins, 1996; Balabanis and Craven, 1997).

The Strategic Role of Retailer Brands: Future Issues

This paper has reviewed the role and contribution of retailer brands in the British grocery market. The argument has been that, within a specific market context, British grocery retailers have taken an approach to retail brands which has led to a particular form of retail brand, namely a product range which is now universally accepted by consumers as a clear brand alternative offering the same quality assurance and product innovation as leading brand manufacturers. Attitudinal and behavioural changes in the use of market power, the management of image and a greater understanding of the core tenets of brand management have all contributed to the development of the retailer as a brand. As far as the future is concerned, this approach raises a number of potential implications.

The core question is how far the retail brand and the attributes attached to the brand name can be pushed. Sainsbury's announcement of a trial linked to its customer loyalty scheme whereby local village shopkeepers can obtain Sainsbury's brand products on a wholesale basis (Hollinger, 1998) provides further evidence of the acceptance of retailers as brand alternatives. Providing quality control can be maintained to protect the brand image, this move has taken the grocery brand in the UK to a new stage. There are precedents elsewhere, notably in North America where Loblaw's Presidents Choice brand has been sold in stores belonging to other companies for some time.

Recent events in the UK have seen the major grocery retailers pursuing a policy of brand extension into non-traditional product and service areas. Non-food ranges have increased, most clearly in clothing, which tended to be removed from stores during the 1980s (with the exception of ASDA). However, in most cases this move is not under the company brandname – for example ASDA's "George" range, Tesco's "Items" brand and the Safeway "Kids Own" brand. Of more significance is the move into service markets, particularly financial services. Through tie ups with a range of financial institutions an array of financial services are now on offer or promised. Interest paying debit cards, credit cards, personal loans, life insurance, travel insurance, foreign currency services and even mortgages can now be obtained under a retail brand. Strong rumours persist of further brand extension into the power supply market. It is not inconceivable that by early next century one could purchase ones home via a mortgage/loan from a retailer, insure, heat and light it from a retail account and consume retail brand products within it.

The longer term issue here, as with all attempts at brand extension, is how elastic the brand and its associated values are. There are several examples from the 1980s of failed retail brand extension, most notably the ill fated attempt by Next to develop cafes, florists and hairdressers under the single life style brand, and Marks and Spencer's struggle to develop stand-alone furniture stores. The grocery retailers undoubtedly have powerful brands and the income, profit and information potential of extending into these service markets is attractive. The core question is how do these service markets differ from the core business? When a grocery retailer has to turn down a credit card or loan application or pursue a customer for default on a loan or an unpaid power bill, the carefully nurtured retailer–customer relationship may find itself placed under new strains.

The issue of brand extension also reaches into the international arena. Despite their acknowledged expertise in a number of areas of retail operations, the leading British grocery retailers – unlike some of their Continental counterparts – have yet to make a major and sustained impact on the international stage. Sainsbury's interest in the US chain Shaw's, dating from 1983, has not led to the expected major move on the American market. The acquisition of a 50 per cent stake in Giant Food Stores in 1994 suggested a new scale dimension was imminent (Wrigley, 1997b) but this interest was sold to Ahold in 1998. Since the mid-1990s Tesco has shown commitment to more distant and less developed retail markets such as Hungary, Poland, the Czech Republic and Thailand, as well as recently re-entering the Republic of Ireland, but its first move into Ireland ended in withdrawal in 1986 after ten years, as did the brief (1993–1997) foray into France through Catteau. Finally, apart from membership of various buying and marketing alliances the other mainstream grocery multiples have stayed away from internationalisation. While a myriad of explanations may be found for avoiding such a risky diversification, the importance of retail brand to the core market proposition may in fact be a barrier to retail internationalisation. Despite attempts to replicate "British models" of food retailing, the differences in retail–supplier relationships and perceptions of the market proposition of retail brand products discussed earlier may provide a larger hurdle than anticipated (Hughes, 1996; Wrigley, 1997a). Stepping back to the level of the corporate brand and overall positioning, if a key element in competitive advantage in the domestic market is image based upon the less tangible, service-related elements of the retail offer, which are built up over time with exposure to the company, the ability to transfer this image instantly into foreign markets may be questioned (Burt and Carrelero-Encinas, 1997). It may be ironic that a major strength of British grocery retailers over the past two decades may now inhibit their moves onto an international stage.

References

Akehurst, G. (1984), "Check-out: the analysis of oligopolistic behaviour in the UK retail grocery market", *Service Industries Journal*, Vol. 4 No. 2, pp. 189–242.

Baden-Fuller, C.W.F. (1984), "The changing market share of retail brands in the UK grocery trade 1960–1980", in CESCOM-IRM, *The Economics of Distribution*, Ch. 9, Franco Angeli, Milan, pp. 513–526.

Balabanis, G. and Craven, S. (1997), "Consumer confusion from own brand lookalikes: an exploratory investigation", *Journal of Marketing Management*, Vol. 13 No. 4, pp. 299–313.

Bellizzi, J.A., Krueckeberg, H.F., Hamilton, J.R. and Martin, W.S. (1981), "Consumer perceptions of national, private, and generic brands", *Journal of Retailing*, Vol. 57 No. 4, pp. 56–70.

Bhasin, A., Dickinson, R. and Nandan, S. (1995), "Retailer brands: a channel perspective – the United States", *Journal of Marketing Channels*, Vol. 4 No. 4, pp. 17–37.

Burger, P.C. and Schott, B. (1972), "Can private brand buyers be identified?", *Journal of Marketing Research*, Vol. IX, May, pp. 219–222.

Burt, S. (1992), "Retail brands in British grocery retailing: a review", *Working Paper 9204*, Institute for Retail Studies, University of Stirling, Stirling.

Burt, S. and Carrelero-Encinas, J. (1997), "Retail internationalisation: managing store image", *Proceedings of the 9th International Conference on Research in the Distributive Trades*, Department of Applied Economics, Katholieke Universiteit Leuven, pp. B511–B518.

Burt, S. and Sparks, L. (1994), "Structural change in grocery retailing in Great Britain: a discount reorientation?", *International Review of Retail Distribution and Consumer Research*, Vol. 4 No. 2, pp. 195–217.

Burt, S. and Sparks, L. (1995), "Understanding the arrival of limited line discount stores in Britain", *European Management Journal*, Vol. 13 No. 1, pp. 110–119.

Costley, C.L. and Brucks, M. (1992), "Selective recall and information use in consumer preferences", *Journal of Consumer Research*, Vol. 18, pp. 464–474.

Cunningham, I.C.M., Hardy, A.P. and Imperia, G. (1982), "Generic brands versus national brands and store brands: a comparison of consumers' preferences and perceptions", *Journal of Advertising Research*, Vol. 22 No. 5, pp. 25–32.

Davies, K., Gilligan, C.T. and Sutton, C.J. (1986), "The development of own label product strategies in grocery and DIY retailing in the United Kingdom", *International Journal of Retailing*, Vol. 1 No. 1, pp. 6–19.

Dawson, J.A. and Shaw, S.A. (1989), "The move to administered vertical marketing systems by British retailers", *European Journal of Marketing*, Vol. 23 No. 7, pp. 42–51.

Dawson, J.A. and Shaw, S.A. (1990), "The changing character of retailer-supplier relationships", in Fernie, J. (Ed.), *Retail Distribution Management*, Ch. 1, Kogan Page, London, pp. 19–39.

De Chernatony, L. (1988), "The fallacy of generics in the UK", *Market Intelligence and Planning*, Vol. 6 No. 2, pp. 36–38.

De Chernatony, L. (1989a), "Marketers' and consumers' concurring perceptions of market structure", *European Journal of Marketing*, Vol. 25 No. 1, pp. 7–16.

De Chernatony, L. (1989b), "Branding in an era of retailer dominance", *International Journal of Advertising*, Vol. 8, pp. 245–260.

De Chernatony, L. and McWilliam, G. (1988), "Clarifying the difference between manufacturers' brands and distributors' brands", *Quarterly Review of Marketing*, Summer, pp. 1–5.

Dick, A., Jain, A. and Richardson, P. (1995), "Correlates of store brand proneness: some empirical observations", *Journal of Product & Brand Management*, Vol. 4 No. 4, pp. 15–22.

Doel, C. (1996), "Market development and organisational change: the case of the food industry", in Wrigley, N. and Lowe, M. (Eds), *Retailing, Consumption and Capital*, Ch. 3, Longman, London, pp. 48–67.

Fernie, J. (1997), "Retail change and retail logistics in the United Kingdom: past trends and future prospects", *Service Industries Journal*, Vol. 17 No. 3, pp. 383–396.

Frank, R.E. and Boyd, H.W. (1965), "Are private brand prone grocery consumers really different?", *Journal of Advertising Research*, Vol. 5, December, pp. 27–35.

Granzin, K.L. (1981), "An investigation of the market for generic products", *Journal of Retailing*, Vol. 57 No. 4, pp. 39–55.

Hoch, S.J. (1996), "How should national brands think about private label", *Sloan Management Review*, Winter, pp. 89–102.

Hoch, S.J. and Banerji, S. (1993), "When do private labels succeed?", *Sloan Management Review*, Summer, pp. 57–67.

Hollinger, P. (1998), "Village shopkeepers to sell Sainsbury brand products", *Financial Times*, 10 August, p. 1.

Hughes, A. (1996), "Retail restructuring and the strategic significance of food retailers' own labels: a UK-USA comparison", *Environment & Planning A*, Vol. 28, pp. 2201–2226.

Hughes, A. (1996), "Forging new cultures of food retailer-manufacturer relations?", in Wrigley, N. and Lowe, M. (Eds), *Retailing, Consumption and Capital*, Ch. 5, Longman, London, pp. 90–115.

Kapferer, J.N. (1995a), "Stealing brand equity: measuring perceptual confusion between national brands and 'copycat' own label products", *Marketing and Research Today*, May, pp. 96–103.

Kapferer, J.N. (1995b), "Brand confusion: empirical study of a legal concept", *Psychology & Marketing*, Vol. 12 No. 6, September, pp. 551–568.

Laaksonen, H. and Reynolds, J. (1994), "Own brands in food retailing across Europe", *Journal of Brand Management*, Vol. 2 No. 1, pp. 37–46.

Livesey, F. and Lennon, P. (1978), "Factors affecting consumers' choice between manufacturer brands and retailer own labels", *European Journal of Marketing*, Vol. 12 No. 2, pp. 158–170.

Loken, B., Ross, I. and Hinkle, R.L. (1986), "Consumer confusion of origin and brand similarity perceptions", *Journal of Public Policy and Marketing*, Vol. 5, pp. 195–211.

Louviere, J.J., Schroeder, H., Louviere, C.H. and Woodworth, G.G. (1987), "Do the parameters of choice models depend on differences in stimulus-presentation – visual versus verbal presentation", *Advances in Consumer Research*, Vol. 14, pp. 79–82.

Martell, D. (1986), "Own labels: problem child or infant prodigy?", *Quarterly Review of Marketing*, Summer, pp. 7–12.

McEnally, M.R. and Hawes, J.M. (1984), "The market for generic brand grocery products: a review and extension", *Journal of Marketing*, Vol. 48, Winter, pp. 75–83.

McGoldrick, P. (1984), "Grocery generics – an extension of the private label concept", *European Journal of Marketing*, Vol. 18 No. 1, pp. 5–24.

McGoldrick, P. (1990), *Retail Marketing*, McGraw-Hill, London.

McKinnon, A.C. (1986), "The physical distribution strategies of multiple retailers", *International Journal of Retailing*, Vol. 1 No. 2, pp. 49–63.

Mills, D.E. (1995), "Why retailers sell private labels", *Journal of Economics and Management Strategy*, Vol. 4 No. 3, pp. 509–528.

Morris, D. (1979), "The strategy of own brands", *European Journal of Marketing*, Vol. 13 No. 2, pp. 59–78.

Myers, J.G. (1967), "Determinants of private brand attitude", *Journal of Marketing Research*, Vol. IV, February, pp. 73–81.

Quelch, J.A. and Harding, D. (1996), "Brands versus private labels", *Harvard Business Review*, January-February, pp. 99–109.

Rafiq, M. and Collins, R. (1996), "Lookalikes and customer confusion in the grocery sector: an exploratory survey", *International Journal of Retail Distribution and Consumer Research*, Vol. 6 No. 4, pp. 329–350.

Rao, T. (1969), "Are some consumers more prone to purchase private brands?", *Journal of Marketing Research*, Vol. 57, November, pp. 56–70.

Richardson, P.S., Dick, A.S. and Jain, A.K. (1994), "Extrinsic and intrinsic cue effects on perceptions of store brand quality", *Journal of Marketing*, Vol. 58, October, pp. 28–36.

Richardson, P.S., Jain, A.K. and Dick, A. (1996), "Household store brand proneness: a framework", *Journal of Retailing*, Vol. 72 No. 2, pp. 159–185.

Rosen, D.L. (1984), "Consumer perceptions of quality for generic grocery products: a comparison across product categories", *Journal of Retailing*, Vol. 60, Winter, pp. 64–80.

Schutte, J.F. (1969), "The semantics of branding", *Journal of Marketing*, Vol. 33 No. 2, pp. 5–11.

Shaw, S.A., Dawson, J.A. and Blair, L.M.A. (1992), "The sourcing of retailer brand food products", *Journal of Marketing Management*, Vol. 8 No. 2, pp. 127–146.

Simmons, M. and Meredith, B. (1984), "Own label profile and purpose", *Journal of the Marketing Research Society*, Vol. 26 No. 1, pp. 3–27.

Sirdeshmukh, D. and Unnava, H.R. (1992), "The effects of missing information on consumer product evaluation", *Advances in Consumer Research*, Vol. 19, pp. 284–9.

Smith, D.L.G. and Sparks, L. (1993), "The transformation of physical distribution in retailing", *International Review of Retail Distribution and Consumer Research*, Vol. 3 No. 1, pp. 35–64.

Szymanski, D.M. and Busch, P.S. (1987), "Identifying the generics-prone consumer: a meta-analysis", *Journal of Marketing Research*, Vol. XXXIV, November, pp. 425–431.

Wileman, A. and Jary, M. (1997), *Retail Power Plays: From Trading to Brand Leadership*, Macmillan, Basingstoke.

Wilkes, R.E. and Valencia, H. (1985), "A note on generic purchase generalizations and subcultural variations", *Journal of Marketing*, Vol. 49, Summer, pp. 114–120.

Wrigley, N. (1997a), "British food retail capital in the USA – Part 1: Sainsbury and the Shaw's experience", *International Journal of Retail & Distribution Management*, Vol. 25 No. 1, pp. 7–21.

Wrigley, N. (1997b), "British food retail capital in the USA – Part 2: Giant prospects?", *International Journal of Retail & Distribution Management*, Vol. 25 No. 2, pp. 48–58.

Editors' Commentary

ALREADY IN THIS VOLUME the significance of Wal-Mart has been discussed and a paper on the impact of Wal-Mart on consumer preference structures has been included. Two of the authors of that paper (Stephen Arnold and Jay Handelman) have also combined in this paper, which explores some different, though related, themes around the impact and success of Wal-Mart. Author profiles of Steve Arnold and Jay Handelman can therefore be found on pages 77–79. In this paper they are joined by Robert Kozinets.

Robert Kozinets is currently Associate Professor of Marketing at the Schulich School of Business at York University. An anthropologist, he was formerly part of Northwestern University Kellogg School of Management where John Sherry was his mentor and an inspiration to him. Robert's first degrees are from York University, but his PhD is from Queen's University. Robert Kozinets is interested in consumption and technoculture by which is meant the interaction between technology, post-modern culture and marketing. His research has been published in a variety of leading journals and includes material on the use of the Internet (netnography) and video (videography) in consumer research.

'Hometown Ideology and Retailer Legitimation: The Institutional Semiotics of Wal-Mart Flyers' develops an application of semiotics to a retail field and was funded by the Social Sciences and Humanities Research Council of Canada. Semiotics in retailing is in itself a novel approach but links together the authors' interests through progressing an understanding of how Wal-Mart links to its consumer base and how its uses emotional, social and cultural attributes in constructing its distinctive marketing. It explores the way that Wal-Mart attempts to align itself with ideals that it believes will appeal to the prospective customer, including ideals that are deeply embedded in society, such as patriotism.

In this paper Wal-Mart flyers are used as the subject and object of study. This work has been subsequently expanded into a comparative study in other countries including Germany, China and the UK. Aspects of internationalization clearly have an impact on this subject area and as retailing increases internationalization activity, so too such work becomes more important.

Key Publications

Arnold SJ and Tigert DJ (1974) Market monitoring through attitude research. *Journal of Retailing*, 49, 3–22.

Arnold SJ, Oum TH and Tigert DJ (1983) Determinant attributes in retail patronage: seasonal, temporal, regional and international comparisons. *Journal of Marketing Research*, 20, 149–157.

Fischer E and Arnold SJ (1990) More than a labor of love – gender roles and Christmas gift shopping. *Journal of Consumer Research*, 17, 333–345.

Arnold SJ, Handelman J and Tigert DJ (1996) Organisational legitimacy and retail store patronage. *Journal of Business Research*, 35, 229–239.

Seiders K and Tigert DJ (1997) Impact of market entry and competitive structure on store switching/store loyalty. *International Review of Retail, Distribution and Consumer Research*, 7(3), 227–247.

Arnold SJ, Handelman J and Tigert DJ (1998) The impact of a market spoiler on consumer preference structures. *Journal of Retailing and Consumer Sciences*, 5, 1–13.

Handelman J and Arnold SJ (1999) Marketing actions with a social dimension: appeals to the institutional environment. *Journal of Marketing*, 63, (3), 33–48.

Arnold SJ and Fernie J (2000) Wal-Mart in Europe: prospects for the UK. *International Marketing Review*, 17, 416–432.

Kozinets RV, Sherry JF, Deberry-Spence B, Duhachek A, Nuttavuthisit K, and Storm D (2002) Themed flagship brand stores in the new millennium: theory, practice, prospects. *Journal of Retailing*, 78, 17–29.

Fernie J and Arnold SJ (2002) Wal-Mart in Europe: prospects for Germany, the UK and France. *International Journal of Retail and Distribution Management*, 30, 92–102.

Kozinets R, Sherry JF, Storm D, Duhachek A, Nuttavuthisit K and DeBerry-Spence B (2004) Ludic agency and retail spectacle. *Journal of Consumer Research*, 31, 658–672.

Sherry JF, Kozinets R, Duhachek A, DeBerry-Spence, Nuttavuthisit K and Storm D, (2004) Gendered behaviour in a male preserve: role playing at ESPN Zone Chicago. *Journal of Consumer Psychology*, 14, 151–158.

Kozinets R and Handelman J (2004) Adversaries of consumption: consumer movements, activism, ideology. *Journal of Consumer Research*, 31, 691–704.

Bianchi CC and Arnold SJ (2004) An institutional perspective on retail internationalization success: Home Depot in Chile. *The International Review of Retail, Distribution and Consumer Research*, 14, 149–169.

Fernie J, Hahn B, Gerhard U, Pioch E and Arnold SJ (2006) The impact of Wal-Mart's entry into the German and UK grocery markets. *Agribusiness*, 22, 247–266.

Arnold SJ, Bu N, Gerhard U, Pioch E and Sun Z (2006) The institutional semiotics of Wal-Mart flyers and signage in the United States, United Kingdom, Germany and China. In S Brunn (ed.) *Wal-Mart World: The World's Biggest Corporation in the Global Economy*. Routledge: New York, 143–162.

Websites

http://business.queensu.ca/faculty_and_research/faculty_list/sarnold.php
http://business.queensu.ca/faculty_and_research/faculty_list/jhandelman.php
http://schulich.yorku.ca/ssb-extra/ssb.nsf?open

HOMETOWN IDEOLOGY AND RETAILER LEGITIMATION: THE INSTITUTIONAL SEMIOTICS OF WAL-MART FLYERS

Stephen J. Arnold, Robert V. Kozinets and Jay M. Handelman

Institutional semiotics revealed a myriad of meanings in a Wal-Mart advertising flyer. Beyond a promise of deep savings on a wide assortment of merchandise, the text and illustrations in the flyer reflect a rich blend of family, community and national norms. This environmental isomorphism simulates a subtly utopian, nostalgic hometown, a place rich in American mythology where citizens achieve a balance between economic and moral pursuits. In this context, the world's largest retailer is experienced as the neighborly, small town shopkeeper, thereby legitimating itself among its consumer constituency.

Introduction

WAL-MART ADVERTISING FLYERS ARE distinctive. They emphasize low prices, not sales. Unlike competitive flyers, which use professional models, they present "plain folks," apparently ordinary people including Wal-Mart "associates," spouses, children, parents, pets, suppliers and customers. The flyers also devote an inordinate amount of space to community-oriented and patriotic topics, delving in places into philosophical monologues about American enterprise, friendly customer service and other topics. Unraveling the symbolic puzzle presented by the distinctive elements of Wal-Mart flyers draws our attention to the importance of retail image and retail symbolism.

Anything that Wal-Mart does differently from other retailers merits scholarly as well as practitioner attention. From the beginning, this retail firm and its founder, Sam Walton, have been enormously successful. For instance, the sixteen Walton Five and Dime stores held the distinction of being the largest independent variety store chain in the United States only twelve years after the first store was opened in 1950 (Vance & Scott, 1994). Wal-Mart Discount City opened in 1962 and today, Wal-Mart Stores, Inc. is the largest retailer in the world (*Chain Store Age,* 2000; Wrigley, 2000). At $191 billion in annual sales for the fiscal year ending January 31, 2001 (Wal-Mart, 2001), it is more than twice the size of the second largest competitor in the world, Carrefour of France. Threatened retailers, potential suppliers, institutional investors, retail analysts and students of retailing can learn much by studying Wal-Mart's winning ways.

Wal-Mart is the world's largest retailer but international sales account for

Journal of Retailing, Vol. 77 (2001), pp. 243–271. © 2001 by New York University. All rights reserved.
The authors wish to thank Terri L. Rittenburg, University of Wyoming, and Leigh Sparks, University of Stirling, for their contributions to this paper. The authors also acknowledge the support of a research grant from the Social Sciences and Humanities Research Council of Canada. The constructive comments of the editor and three anonymous reviewers resulted in a better paper.

only 14% of total sales (Wal-Mart Stores Inc., 2000). Furthermore, Wal-Mart is a relative newcomer to the international arena having left the U.S. for Mexico in 1991 and Canada in 1994 (Beard, Walton & Webb, 1999). Thus, a focus upon Wal-Mart's activities in its domestic marketplace, the United States of America, should be instructive.

Published research offers many reasons for Wal-Mart's success in the U.S. market. Its exemplary growth has been attributed to the large size of the U.S. market, founder Sam Walton's inspirational leadership, an associate-focused organizational culture, a capacity for innovation and reinvention, low cost operations, vendor partnering, an efficient logistics system, extensive internal communications, store focused and store-within-a-store operations, continuous merchandising, heavy television advertising, customer service orientation and competitor inattention (Arnold, Handelman & Tigert, 1996, 1998; Beard, Walton & Webb, 1999; Boyd, 1997; Davidson & Rummel, 2000; Finn & Timmermans, 1996; Graff & Ashton, 1993; McCune, 1994; McGee, 1995; McGee & Rubach, 1996; Ozment & Martin, 1990; Peterson & McGee, 2000; Seiders & Tigert, 2000; Stone, 1995; Vance & Scott, 1994).

The objective of this research is to offer still another explanation for Wal-Mart's success. Wal-Mart has grown in the US market because it connects itself symbolically to the dominant ideologies of American life. Through the imagery of frugality, family, religion, neighborhood, community and patriotism, Wal-Mart locates itself centrally on Main Street of a nostalgic hometown. These symbolic connections not only positively dispose shoppers to Wal-Mart but also "decouple" (Meyer & Rowan, 1977) Wal-Mart from unfavorable outcomes of its success. These consequences include local retailers being forced out of business, small town "STOP Wal-Mart" campaigns, accusations of predatory pricing and allegations about products being sourced from overseas sweatshop suppliers.

We explore here another explanation for Wal-Mart's success by revealing how the mythical hometown is constructed in an ordinary advertising flyer. A flyer was chosen because this form of marketing communication is nearly unique to retailers. It is especially relevant to a retailer that operates simultaneously in many different local markets, and therefore would likely contain richer examples of local symbolism and the signaling of adherence to environmental norms. Flyers are nearly unique to retailers, as opposed to the other forms of advertising, and especially relevant to a retailer that operates in the large and diverse US market. Flyers are temporally situated and geographically flexible, offering a wealth of detailed and timely, culturally-constituted information to be propitiously targeted at community microsegments (McCracken, 1986; Otnes & Scott, 1996). Furthermore, flyers, the workhorses of the retail realm, the disposable and all-too-forgettable art forms of industry, are a ubiquitous and rarely researched form of retailing.

The task of semiotics is to identify the meaning of the images in a Wal-Mart flyer. Semiotics "analyzes the structures of meaning-producing events both verbal and nonverbal" (Mick, 1986, p. 197). It is focused on signs, sign systems and codes—the "latent rules that facilitate sign production and interpretive response" (ibid.). It is a familiar tool in advertising, services marketing and consumer research (Clarke & Schmidt, 1995; Clarke et al., 1998; Gottdiener,

1985; Hirschman, 1988; Holbrook & Grayson, 1986; Langrehr & Caywood, 1995; Levy, 1981; McQuarrie, 1989; McQuarrie & Mick, 1992; Mick, 1997; Mick & Buhl, 1992; Nöth, 1988; Sherry & Camargo, 1987). Retailing applications of semiotics, however, are less apparent. A notable exception is Floch (1988) who used a semiotic square approach to identify the values operative in hypermarket shopping. On the basis of this analysis, Floch (1988) was able to identify store layout features that reflected these values.

The theoretical framework driving the semiotic analysis is institutional theory (Meyer & Rowan, 1977). This theory suggests that because consumers respond positively to family, community and national institutions, retailers can reflect the corresponding norms in functional and symbolic acts. Furthermore, institutional theory also recognizes other retailer constituencies whose meaning systems must also be understood and taken into account. Thus, in the next section, *institutional semiotics* is described whereby the constructs of institutional theory are integrated into a Jakobsonian account of semiotics (Jakobson, 1985). Jakobson's framework serves to pose a series of questions about the linguistic elements of a stimulus object as well as any photographic, pictorial or graphical images. Institutional theory suggests how these elements and images might be interpreted as revelatory of the values expressed by retailing organizations.

The brief account of institutional semiotics in the next section is followed by comparisons with traditional retail image research. Both similarities and differences are apparent. Next is the heart of the paper—a semiotic analysis of the Wal-Mart flyer. This analysis is put into context by summarizing the results of similar analyses made of eighteen flyers from three competitive retailers. The paper concludes with reflections about what was learned and what could be done next.

Institutional Semiotics

Institutional theory

Institutional theory (DiMaggio & Powell, 1983; Handelman & Arnold, 1999; Meyer & Rowan, 1977) posits that the organization is an organic part of its environment (Perrow, 1986). From this perspective (Fig. 1), a retail firm and its environment are seen to interpenetrate each other to the extent that a retailer's actions reflect the economic and cultural-moral norms of the environment in which it is immersed (Meyer, 1994). "Norms are cognitive guidance systems, rules of procedures that actors employ flexibly and reflexively to assure themselves and those around them that their behavior is reasonable" (DiMaggio & Powell, 1991, p. 20).

These environmental norms are of two forms: task and institutional. Task norms reflect the organization's economic environment to which it responds with functionally related *performative* action. In a retail context, these norms would be reflected in the shopper's expectations of a convenient location, competitive prices and appropriate assortment.

Retailers are not only integrated into environmental systems comprised of

Environment

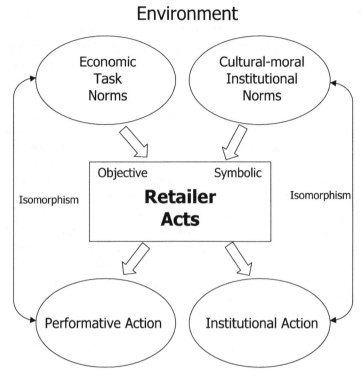

Figure 1 Institutional semiotics

"hard-wired economics." Institutional theory also recognizes that retailers are immersed in an institutional environment in which constituents make cultural and moral demands (Scott, 1987). The institutions of family, community, religion and nation are complex cultural systems that contain taken-for-granted norms of appropriate social conduct. As with the economics-driven task environment, retail firms must engage in institutional action that reflects adherence to these norms (DiMaggio & Powell, 1983; Meyer & Rowan, 1977). A retailer involved in community charities and using local workers and national suppliers demonstrates an attempt to adhere to these kinds of norms.

Norm adherence is symbolic as well as objective (Meyer & Rowan, 1977) although this distinction is more a matter of degree as every object is itself a sign. Thus, symbolic acts—such as the use of metaphors, icons, slogans and signs— have as much a role in legitimating (Suchman, 1995) an organization among its relevant constituents, as do the more tangible, specific acts. Symbolic *performative* action might include the slogan "Never knowingly undersold" as contrasted to the objective action of having the lowest priced shopping basket among a group of competing retailers. Similarly, symbolic institutional action would be the promotion of a "Buy American" policy as contrasted to the objective action of purchasing only American manufactured products. Similarly, the Body Shop states that it is "Against Animal Testing" on its packaging and promotion but can't guarantee that none of its suppliers have used animal testing. A retailer that mirrors environmental norms is defined as being isomorphic with its environment, and it is this state of isomorphism that signals the retailer's legitimacy to its relevant constituents (Meyer & Rowan, 1977).

Jakobsonian semiotics

Jakobson's (1985) framework is appropriate for unpacking the hidden meanings of symbolic performative and institutional actions. It poses three *grand tour* (McCracken, 1988) guiding analytical questions to interrogate particular communication events structurally—one dealing with the receiver of a message, one with the sender and one with the content.

To investigate the receiver of the message, the analyst must identify who is being addressed, for example, gender, age, stage of family life cycle, socio-economic status. What they are being told to do must also be determined in addition to identifying who might be excluded and who might be hidden (Stern, 1996a, 1996b).

To investigate the sender of the message, the analyst must characterize the speaker. What emotions does the speaker wish to convey about the subject matter? To investigate the content of the message, the analyst must infer its abstract and connotative meanings. What *consumer mythology* (Levy, 1981), that is, narratives, stories or parables, are suggested by the metaphors, symbols, esthetic appeals and other literary and visual devices? What contextual (across different situations) and intertextual (across different texts) points of reference are given and reinforced (Scott, 1994b)? How are the images "coded" and what norms and values do they portray? From what "myths" of ideology and contemporary life are they drawn? What are the cultural structures of difference?

Institutional semiotics and image research

Institutional semiotics provides a method whereby the meaning of retail artifacts is discerned. However, the idea that a retail store evokes a certain meaning, personality or image is not novel and there exists a rich heritage of imagery techniques employed in retailing (Arons, 1961; Birtwistle, Clarke & Freathy, 1999; Keaveney & Hunt, 1992; Kunkel & Berry, 1968; Lindquist, 1974/75; Martineau, 1958; Peterson & Kerin, 1983; Rich & Portis, 1964). Institutional semiotics is different from and similar to image research on several dimensions.

First, institutional semiotics differs from traditional image research in terms of the subject matter of the analysis. Retailer artifacts, for example, advertising, signage, store layout, merchandise presentation, tend more to be the basis of the interpretation as opposed to consumer protocols or executive transcripts.

Institutional semiotics is similar to traditional methods when the analysis of protocols and transcripts employs content analysis, for example, Zimmer and Golden (1988), projective techniques, for example, Myers (1960) and open-ended questioning, for example, Jain and Etgar (1976), McDougall and Fry (1974), that is, methods which emphasize an inductive or grounded theory methodology.

A third dimension involves the identification of meaning or image that may not have been intended by the retailer. Image research reveals that consumers don't necessarily perceive the same image as store management (Birtwistle, Clarke & Freathy, 1999; Rosenbloom, 1983). Similarly, institutional semiotics can identify unintended meanings but it may also be able to determine the reasons for such differences. The environmental norms component of institutional theory provides a basis for attributing meaning to retail artifacts as opposed to the atheortical, trait-based nature of image research.

A fourth dimension concerns the content of the meaning or image. Institutional semiotics emphasizes symbolic, institutional acts occurring in response to moral and cultural norms. In contrast, traditional techniques tend more to emphasize objective, performative acts or what Martineau (1958) referred to as the functional qualities related to the retailer's activities, for example, location, price, merchandise, and so forth. Institutional semiotics does not preclude identification of functional qualities. The emphasis, however, on the symbolic, institutional acts opens up opportunities to capture more of the retailer's character.

Fifth, the persuasiveness of an interpretation derived from institutional semiotics relies upon rhetorical as well as statistical criteria. In addition to requiring multiple examples to support an observation, the interpretation requires clear language, direct prose and a compelling turn of phrase. More generally, it is part of the "interpretive turn" in consumer research (Sherry, 1991) and invokes different criteria than research premised on scientific realism or logical positivism (Arnold & Fischer, 1994; Spiggle, 1994; Thompson & Haytko, 1997).

Finally, both approaches recognize that any analysis is incomplete and partial. As pointed out by Peterson and Kerin (1983), the image discerned by the traditional survey procedure is a function of the characteristics of the retail store, respondent, measurement instrument, mode of data collection, data collection environment and extraneous error. In institutional semiotics, it is recognized that the interpretation is socially constructed and a function of the hermeneutic, [pre-]understanding of the researchers (Arnold & Fischer, 1994). The biases of gender, demographic, socio-economic and cultural backgrounds may emphasize particular narratives of power and ideology and exclude certain questions of gender and race (see also Stern, 1996a; Thompson, Stern & Arnould, 1998).

Institutional Semiotics of a Wal-Mart Flyer

The Wal-Mart flyer that is the subject for this analysis was selected from a two-year collection of U.S. flyers issued by this retailer and contained, more than any other flyer, the icons and elements shared among all of the Wal-Mart flyers. The flyer was issued during the first week of March 1997, a retail slow time positioned between Christmas and Easter. It is period noteworthy only for its ordinariness—no holiday emphasis, no large-scale associated events and four months away from Independence Day. Although the return address for the flyer is Wal-Mart's Bentonville, Arkansas head office, the flyer was printed in Stillwater, Oklahoma.

Detailed descriptions of approximately one quarter of the images in the 32-page flyer are found in Appendix A. A wide range of products are featured including soft drinks, snacks, candies, juices, health and beauty aids, bathroom supplies, OTC (over the counter) products, baby supplies, toys, cleaning supplies, laundry equipment, home improvement products, floor coverings, lawn & garden supplies, craft supplies, sewing supplies, automotive supplies and accessories, home entertainment equipment and supplies, small appliances, furniture, household goods, computers, software, shoes, clothing apparel and towels and bedding. Many of the products are shown being used by Wal-Mart associates and their families. The flyer also contains sidebars featuring "Wal-Mart's Guiding Principles." A US flag billows at the bottom of each page.

Given the preceding section's description of institutional semiotics, the analysis of the Wal-Mart flyer in this section attempts to answer the following questions: Who is being addressed and what are they being told to do? Who is the speaker and what emotions do they wish to convey about their subject matter? What are the mythologies?

Who is being addressed?

When this semiotically derived question is posed, the Wal-Mart flyer reveals a considerable amount about the audience in terms of its nationality, age, social class and stage of the family life cycle. Clearly, the implied, intended reader of the advertising (Scott, 1994a, 1994b) is an American citizen, someone whose patriotism would lead them to be favorably predisposed to pictures of the 'Stars and Stripes' on each page (Appendices A.1, A.2, A.3, A.12). This consumer would also favor soft drinks and juice named "Sam's *American* Choice" (Appendices A.4, A.8) and many other products emphasizing their special quality of "Made in the U.S.A."ness (Appendices A.2, A.3, A.12, A.17, A.21, A.22, A.23, A.27). This 'Buy American' emphasis would have greater appeal among working class, rural and small town people (Coleman, 1983).

This demographically situated imagery must use the appropriate reference groups (Englis & Solomon, 1995). The numerous photographs and accompanying text portray parents—mainly mothers in the 25–45 age group (Appendix A.9)—and their babies (Appendix A.10) and young children (Appendices A.2, A.11, A.16, A.24, A.25). The flyer portrays slippers sitting on a mat (Appendix A.12), popped popcorn and fresh fruit (Appendix A.27) and brewed coffee, toasted bagel and waffles ready to be consumed (Appendix A.13). The home's backyard, displaying the *Better Homes and Gardens* cart (Appendix A.14) implies pride in the household and middle class status aspirations. The language used in the flyer is simple and drawls languorously off the page: "Come on up here girl, don't be embarrassed. We're all family here," says Sam to Nancy (Appendix A.7). The flyer, it seems, is speaking to someone who is working or middle class, who is raising a family, who seeks comfort and bargains. These people likely see their residence as having a "homey" feel (McCracken, 1989).

Who is the speaker?

The voice used to address the flyer's reader is plain-speaking and friendly. It is a voice with no room for pretensions or glamour. The language is simple to understand, busy, talkative, and direct. The pictures repeatedly show ordinary, plain-looking people (and not professional models) engaged in everyday situations: a man and his wife fishing (Appendix A.15), a boy playing baseball (Appendix A.16), a kid riding a bicycle (Appendix A.17). The focus is on children and their activities (Appendices A.2, A.10, A.11, A.16, A.17, A.24, A.25), and the voice says "We understand you and how may we help?"

The sender of this message is a collective *we* and *us*: "[W]e share [Sam Walton's] ideals and values and how they help us serve you better" (Appendix A.8), "Our Pledge . . . To Save you More" (Appendix A.2), "Our Commitment . . . To Satisfy All Your Shopping Needs" (Appendix A.3). These folks are obviously trusted friends and friendly neighbors who have the concerns of others at heart. "Rosie," a St. Bernard dog, is "best friend of Deni, Toy Dept." (Appendix A.2) and Sam Walton reminds us that he and his associates believe the customers to be "our guests" (Appendix A.7). Brenda understands his directives, echoing, "we should look at all our customers . . . like a neighbor down the street" (Appendix A.7).

This flyer is supposed to be the unified, chant-singing voice of the associates, the homogenized retail face of courteous counter help and smiling shelf-stockers. Yet behind the chorus facade is a single voice leading, that of "Mr. Sam" (Appendices A.7, A.8, A.21). Wal-Mart's deceased leader is featured as a spectral presence throughout the flyer, the wise old man's guiding "philosophy" in the sidebars features quotations from and stories about him: his ghostly and fatherly voice permeates the flyer.

What are the mythologies?

The mythology of homoeconomicus. In myriad ways, the Wal-Mart flyer demonstrates its link to the norms of the task environment. A family in the full-nest stage of the family life cycle, faced with rent, loans and many food, clothing and living expenses, has an urgent need to watch every penny (Schaninger & Danko, 1993). These families demand everyday food and nonfood merchandise at the lowest possible cost.

To advertise examples of low prices on frequently purchased items is a response to these norms. The Wal-Mart flyer emphasizes low prices: they pledge "To Save You More," offer "4 Great Ways to Save," promise "Savings In Store for You" and "[S]avings [which] keep getting better and better." Everything is "Low Prices," "Value-Price[s]," "[A]ffordable prices," "Better [prices]," or "fabulous prices" (Appendices A.2, A.6, A.18).

Beyond the "Every Day Low Price" (Appendix A.18), the numerous ways to save are spelled out in a systematized pattern of font sizes and styles, colors and symbols. Black is the everyday low price (Appendices A.22, A.23) and blue means an unusual sale (Appendices A.2, A.5, A.9, A.10, A.11, A.12, A.26). An inverted green triangle shouts "Special Buy" (Appendices A.2, A.12, A.18) and signifies a limited supply. A large, red price in a cartoon-like font and outlined in yellow and black represents a "price rollback" (Appendices A.13, A.18, A.20, A.27). A yellow "smiley face" that optimistically chimes "Better Every Day" accompanies it. Interpreting these images reveals a mantra of cutting costs, less spending, low prices, budget prices and value prices. Ever-increasing savings can be attained through clever spending. The Wal-Mart flyer encourages the Puritan/Calvinist virtues of thrift and maximizing one's resources—for example, "a penny saved is a penny earned." The smart shopper, the purest derivation of homoeconomicus, is promised the special reward of scarce goods at wondrously low prices. It is foolish to overpay for items that can be acquired at Wal-Mart for less.

The Wal-Mart flyer also demonstrates adherence to the social-cultural norms of the institutional environment. These norms include symbols and ideologies privileging the institutions of family, community and nation. The flyer evokes each of these constituencies.

The mythology of family. Another important feature of the flyer is its family appeal. Women, for example, Appendices A.5, A.7, A.9, A.15, A.21, A.26, children, for example, Appendices A.2, A.10, A.11, A.16, A.17, A.24, A.25, and pets, for example, Appendix A.2, populate the pictures. The Wal-Mart flyer's many pictures of infants, toddlers, young children and teenagers caught in a variety of action poses, elicit family activities and concerns. Products are pictured in a homey context, in use, in interaction with ordinary family activity.

Interrelated in webs of meaning with these concrete images are more abstract elements of caring, loyalty and commitment. Loyalty is connoted by the image of a boy and his pet (Appendix A.2), a sturdy and steadfast St. Bernard, a salvific rescue dog. The words "Pledge" (Appendix A.2) and "Commitment" (Appendix A.3) suggest trustworthiness. Family is commonplace and everyday, yet a sanctuary, a place of unequivocal acceptance. The permanence of this relationship is reflected in the motto: "*Always* Low Prices. *Always* Wal-Mart. *Always*" (Appendix A.3). "Every Day Low Price" and "Better Every Day" (Appendix A.18) evokes a family's consistency, constancy, confidence, permanence, predictability and reassurance.

At Wal-Mart, they care just as a family would. In a sidebar, the words of Sam Walton ring out "We're all family here" (Appendix A.7). Nancy obligingly responds, "we can help pick each other up just like a family member would do." The crochet thread is "Aunt Lydia's" (Appendix A.4) suggesting the extended family. The associates are also members of this extended family of caring, devotion, and compassion. Judy, a hard-working associate opines in another sidebar "taking care of customers is so important" (Appendix A.7). Dianne adds that she has the "will to always show our customers I care about their needs. . . . If you just let them know you care, they'll come back" (Appendix A.7). At Wal-Mart, they care for each other and they care for the customer, and the customer is expected to care for (and shop at) them.

Evident here are some of those excluded from the Wal-Mart family. It is not those people characterized as divorced, single-parents or those with latchkey kids. Instead, it speaks to the 1950s family of Beaver Cleaver, a small-town

America, white picket whitewash where mom does the housework and shopping and dad minds the barbecue and lawn. There is a sly promise hidden behind the gleaming allure: *Partake*, it incites of the reader. Become one of us, become cared for, become loved, become *family*!

With the exception of Walton's omnipresence, adult males tend to be absent from the Wal-Mart extended family. In the entire flyer there are only four men pictured, versus 26 adult women, 16 girls and 12 boys. Perhaps this gender imbalance reflects the family member most likely to read the flyer because they are the home's purchasing agent. However, traditional male products such as lawnmowers (Appendix A.22) and barbecues (Appendix A.23) sit at the ready and unattended by male hands. Can this instead be family without a father? Where is the excluded male, the hidden king-of-the-castle presence, the sitcom-familiar words of wisdom-spouting dad? Who, in the flyer's paternalistic monomyth, can join the obedient, happy family together?

Who else but the true voice of the flyer: not just dad, but wise old dad, the archetypal image. Mr. Sam has become elevated to universal father and tribal patriarch. Echoing the resurrection and rise of Osiris in death (and perhaps the Star of Bethlehem), Sam Walton's death in 1992 was soon followed by the stellar replacement of Wal-Mart's hyphen with a Wal*Mart star (Appendices A.2, A.3). "Sam's American Choice" becomes "Sam*s American Choice" (Appendix A.4). The rise of this star evokes the divine wisdom of holy wise men and the acquisition and giving of gifts. No mere father figure, Mr. Sam has been transfigured by time and mortality into a ritualistically guiding wise Moses or Abraham as well as a beardless Santa riding his otherworldly pickup truck and bringing the daily gift of low prices and bonded families. These images draw deeply from the paternalistic imagery and lore of Judaeo-Christian tradition.

The mythology of America. According to Lipset (1989, p. 26), the ideological consensus that defines America emphasizes four norms. *Antistatism* reflects the American preference for minimum government. *Populism* reflects the democratic belief that the will of the people should dominate over that of the elite. *Egalitarianism* favors equal social and economic opportunity for all. *Patriotism* is loyalty and devotion to one's country.

Wal-Mart's reflection of America's antistatist ideology is found in the flyer's competitive prices, the celebration of business as a way to a better future (Appendix A.8) and the empowering of ordinary citizens through flyer portrayal. The 'Buy American' policy (Appendix A.21) implies business supporting other businesses rather than businesses being aided by the government.

Populism is reflected by the use of ordinary "associates" rather than professional models to illustrate the products. With their imperfect bodies, simple and full-size "Just My Size" clothes (Appendix A.26), unglamorous hair and lack of makeup (Appendices A.7, A.9), they are just like us.

The Wal-Mart flyer indicates support of egalitarianism in its "Competitive Edge Scholarship Fund" which funds "America's future education" (Appendix A.8). It is also reflected in the nonelite schools of the scholarship recipients (Appendix A.8), the flyer's use of first names, the naming of employees as "associates" and the establishment of "partnerships" with employees and suppliers (Appendix A.7). A *melting pot* integration runs throughout with many retail categories themed and linked. For instance, scattered tree leaves integrate several different lawn and garden products (Appendices A.22, A.23), pastel dots and cartoons unify infant items spread over two pages (Appendix A.10) and the 'Stars and Stripes' at the bottom of each page (Appendices A.2, A.3) joins together all of the featured products. Every page becomes part of a seamless whole. Geography and ethnic heritage connect individual people into communities and the United States of America unites these diverse groups into a single (albeit multicultural) nation (Cohen, 1987).

A predominant feature of the chosen flyer is American patriotism. A billowing American flag waves along each page bottom of the 10½ by 12-inch flyer, for example, Appendices A.2, A.3, and A.10. A stripe underscores the "a" and a star replaces the dot in the exclamation mark in each "Sale!" sign, for example, Appendices A.2, A.5, A.9, A.10, A.11, A.12, A.24, A.26. Patriotic red, white and blue colors abound.

"Our Pledge . . . To Save You More" (Appendix A.2) invokes the pledge of allegiance to the U.S. flag. Brands possess names such as "Sam's American Choice" (Appendix A.4). "Mr. Sam" (Appendix A.7) connotes 'Uncle Sam.' The "Made in the U.S.A." label accompanying many of the advertised products (Appendices A.2, A.12, A.17, A.22, A.23, A.27) is anchored by a single star, single stripe, red and white flag. The white and blue "Wal-Mart" (Appendices A.2, A.3) header evokes the stars portion of the American flag. The "Faded Glory" brand name for boy's and men's casual clothes (Appendix A.24) evokes 'Old Glory,' an affectionate term for the flag reminiscent of the country's military heritage. The upside down green triangle unit-like badge (Appendices A.2, A.4, A.12, and A.18) and the boys "Cadet Club" (Appendix A.25) clothing name brand also reference this heritage.

The guiding principles described in six different sidebars in the Wal-Mart flyer (Appendices A.7, A.8, A.21) parallel the statement of American ideology and norms in the Declaration of Independence, Articles of Confederation, Constitution of the United States and the various Amendments. Among the "Guiding Principles" enumerated in the Wal-Mart flyer is the desire to support U.S. workers (Appendix A.21). Whenever possible, products are "Made in the U.S.A.".

Perhaps the flyer's greatest and purest expression of patriotism is its endless, literal draping of featured products in the flag. Thirteen different products featured at various flyer locations are wrapped in a ribbon displaying white stars on a blue background, for example, Appendices A.4, A.8, and A.12. The ribbons portray the stripes in the American flag, (Appendices A.4, A.10, and A.12) embracing soft drinks, juice, snacks, infant car seats and crochet thread. They envelop panties, socks, shoes and watering cans; encompass videotapes, photo albums, pillows and paint. Through contact with the ribbon, ostensibly ordinary products are sanctified with American values. They are celebrated and ritually energized by the embrace of the gift-oriented ribbon. It is clearly "sacralization through contamination" (Belk, Wallendorf & Sherry, 1989).

The mythology of community. In order to survive, any retailer must be perceived to be satisfying the many community stakeholders and constituencies it serves. Beyond the obvious customer base, retailers must gain the support of employees, suppliers, banks, municipal planners and local politicians. In order to achieve this support, institutional semiotics informs us that retailers must link to norms found in the task and institutional environments of all of these stake-holders, even if only in symbolic form (DiMaggio & Powell, 1983; Meyer & Rowan, 1977). Employees want respect as well as good jobs, suppliers rapid payment, banks security, planners stability and politicians communities where families thrive. Using flyers and other advertising to achieve this linkage may be one of Wal-Mart's most important, yet under-recognized, effects (Scott, 1987). In this manner, any conflict is excluded and only Wal-Mart's hometown marching band is privileged with presence.

Wal-Mart's advertising appeals transcend family and neighborhood and reach to the idealized American community (O'Guinn & Belk, 1989). This community—"your community"—is repeatedly elicited (Appendices A.7, A.21). Sidebars feature a line-drawn spectral image of Sam Walton in a baseball cap, beneath which are the founder's "Guiding Principles" (Appendices A.7, A.8, A.21). According to Sam Walton, "We go out of our way to instill a strong sense of community involvement in our store management and associates so they'll be even better citizens" (Appendix A.7). He also states that "I am very certain that U.S. workers . . . can produce merchandise that will be as good a value, or bet-ter, than anything we can buy offshore" (Appendix A.21). The Good Samaritan is a myth invoked by Judy, the "Health and Beauty Aids Department Manager" when she relates a tale in which she personally came to the aid of "an elderly lady" apparently in desperate need of "a specific item." "It made me feel good," Judy gushes, "I'm an emotional type person anyway" (Appendix A.7). In another tale related in a flyer sidebar, Tracey expressed her concern about "the morale in our community" (Appendix A.21). In still another, Judy was so grateful that she thanked Wal-Mart for "helping [the North Carolina town of] Asheboro" (Appendix A.21).

The mythology of hometown. Bellah *et al.* (1986) observed that during the twentieth century in North America, the single-minded pursuit of economic success resulted in businesses adhering to the task norms but not the institutional norms. The reason is that the "emphasis on self-reliance . . . led to the notion of pure, undetermined choice, free of tradition, obligation, or commitment" (Bellah *et al.*, 1986, p. 152). The resultant individuation was widely interpreted as being at odds with communitarian actions, which were held to be in the realm of government, religion, neighborhood and family. This purely economic pursuit led to what Bellah *et al.* (1986) termed the "emptiness of an unencumbered self."

While adherence to economic norms leads to self-reliance, and thus eco-nomic success, as noted above, such profit-motivated actions have been theorized not to contribute substantially to the happiness of individuals' everyday lives (Bellah *et al.*, 1986). To regain the moral balance and legitimacy people lose in pursuit of economic goals, they must increasingly seek fulfillment in social-collective-moral activities (Bellah *et al.*, 1986). The result has been an increased importance placed on retailers to demonstrate their integration of institutional norms with task norms.

The significance of this integration is that it—perhaps involuntarily—reflects a recapture of moral balance between economic and moral pursuits. Any organization that symbolically integrates or reconnects the task and institutional spheres evokes the presence of a "constituted self"—a much-needed and potent self-identity that integrates economic success with moral virtue (Bellah *et al.*, 1986; Meyer & Rowan, 1977). There may be a deeply felt need in modern American society to reconnect with others by pretending "to live in a kind of community that no longer exists" (Bellah *et al.*, 1986, p. 175). This occurs in the mythical "hometown" where friends, family and neighbors are always close at hand, where happiness is achieved through guiltless money-saving consumption, where the clerks at the idyllic store are happy to work there and happy to serve you.

The Wal-Mart that is advertised in the flyer is not simply "Wal-Mart"—it is your "Hometown Wal-Mart" (Appendix A.6). In the flyer, competitive prices commingle with community, moral family activities and good citizenship. Wrapping Wal-Mart products and Wal-Mart itself in the American flag reflects much more than mere patriotism—it demonstrates the semiotic integration of task and institutional norms. Their slogans provide other examples of this subtle integration: In Appendix A.2, "Our Pledge . . . To Save You More" invokes the institution of nation and the task environment of low prices. "Our Commitment . . . To Satisfy All Your Shopping Needs" (Appendix A.3) invokes the institutions of community/family and the task environment of wide assortment. Similarly, in Appendix A.6, "Low Prices at Your Hometown Wal-Mart" responds to the task norms of value and the institutional norm of community. Mention of smaller centers in the flyer return addresses helps it to retain a small-town emphasis. Wal-Mart advertises itself as your hometown store, as a utopian world where economic and moral lives are interconnected and virtuous. The indication in the flyer of both performative and institutional action signals to consumers and other constituents that the retailer is legitimate and therefore deserves their support.

Comparisons with flyers from Wal-Mart competitors

As part of this investigation, separate analyses were made of flyers from Kmart, Target and Sears. Eighteen flyers from a major Midwestern metropolitan area were collected during 1999 and 2000 and examined in order to compare and contrast other retailers with Wal-Mart. Institutional semiotics revealed distinctive speaker voices, specific addressees and some mythologies (Table 1). Furthermore, it was apparent that Wal-Mart did not have a monopoly on institutional appeals although it dominated the others. In one 1999 flyer, for example, Sears featured General Colin Powell on its cover and described in detail (within a full-page journalistic "cover story") Sears' "Good Life Alliance" with America's Promise. "Together, we can do more," the flyer asserted as it attempted to convince customers and other members of "our Sears family" to get involved volunteering for organizations that assist "our kids and our communities." In a weaker, yet still indicative example, a Sears's flyer in election year 2000 blended branding with (possibly satirical) nationalist civic involvement with its (Lee jeans icon) "Buddy Lee for President" campaign and contest for "a trip for 2 to Washington, D.C."

The other two retailers evidenced little institutional activity in their flyers. Kmart focused almost exclusively on the performative activities of particular brands at affordable prices. It spoke to members of its low to middle socio-economic status (SES) target segment in an imperative and advisory voice, for example, "Look your best." The one apparent mythology beyond homoeconomicus was that of family.

Target was also price-focused, but used an informative, obliging and almost sisterly speaker voice with images based on a more upscale and active lifestyle to reach its middle SES segment. Again, the only mythology portrayed beyond homoeconomicus was that of family involved in an active lifestyle. The absence of any response in the Target flyers to the other institutions is surprising in that it contrasts with the parent Target Corporation's communally-oriented and charitably-focused in-store advertising (both at Target and at the more upscale and sister chain Marshall Fields).

There are two implications of these additional analyses of Kmart, Target and Sears flyers. The first implication is that they reinforce the utility of institutional semiotics. These analyses reveal distinctive speaker voices and specific audiences in what may at first appear to be undifferentiated retail flyers. The second implication is that while flyer institutional activity is well developed at Wal-Mart, it is not the only retailer to do so. These two implications suggest the capacity to generalize institutional semiotics technique and the Wal-Mart results.

In sum, this analysis of retail flyers finds that Wal-Mart uses images and symbols to align the company with economic task and cultural-moral institutional norms, and thus legitimates itself in the retail environment. Wal-Mart's

Table 1 Analysis of Kmart, Target and Sears flyers

	Kmart	Sears	Target
Number of flyers analyzed	Seven	Five	Six
Dates of flyers	November 1999–September 2000	December 1999–August 2000	December 1999–September 2000
Who is being addressed?	Family, female, low-mid socio-economic strata	Family, youth, low-mid socio-economic strata	Family, female, mid socio-economic strata
Who is the speaker?	Advisory-imperative ("Look your best . . ." "Save all month . . .")	Communal-committed ("Together, we can do more." "The good life at a great price. Guaranteed.")	Informative-obliging-caring ("Made just for you." "So you stay warmer, drier, and more comfortable.")
What are the mythologies?	Homoeconomicus, Family (additional themes of style and hominess)	Homoeconomicus, Family, America, Community	Homoeconomicus, Family (additional lifestyle themes of outdoors, activity, self-expression)
Main performative and/or institutional action	Performative-Price	Performative-Price/brand	Performative-Price/Lifestyle

flyer images borrow from family, religious, community and national institutions in order to sell itself and to promote a subtly utopian, nostalgic "hometown" image. The findings suggest that Wal-Mart is successful not simply because it promises consumers better prices and a more enjoyable shopping experience, but because it subtly and symbolically promises them a better life and a better world.

Discussion

Support for the interpretation

Sam Walton's autobiography (Walton with Huey, 1993) and the Wal-Mart U.S. Internet sites are consistent with the conclusions drawn in the interpretation. For instance, "we've created Support American Made . . . a program to help smaller American manufacturers better produce and market their products, as well as find more efficient and more profitable ways of doing business" (http://www.wal-mart.com/sam/index.html). Similarly, "In Lewistown, Pennsylvania, a little girl needed expensive medical treatment to help her walk. The Wal-Mart associates there couldn't wait to pitch in and raise money for the Children's Miracle Network" (http://www.walmartfoundation.org/children.html).

The precedent for the conduct of semiotic analyses of consumer data without triangulation is well-established (Scott, 1994a, 1994b; Stern, 1992, 1996a, 1996b). However, the results of three consumer studies conducted in the Atlanta, Dallas/Fort Worth and Indianapolis markets are available publicly (*Chain Store Age Executive*, 1993) and support the Wal-Mart characterization drawn here. Randomly selected female heads of households were telephoned and then qualified as having shopped at Kmart, Target or Wal-Mart in the past two months. They were asked (among other questions), "Which store is best at being concerned about and actively involved in the community at large?" "Which store has the lowest everyday prices?" and "Which of these eight stores do you shop at most often?" The results (Table 2) indicated that approximately two out of three respondents in each market identified Wal-Mart as being best on community involvement and having the lowest everyday prices. The other respondents divided their answers among Kmart, Target and other department stores such as Sears and JC Penney. Furthermore, one out of two respondents are shopping most often at Wal-Mart.

The flyer comparisons revealed Wal-Mart to be clearly distinguishing itself from the other three major retailers in appeals to community norms. Wal-Mart was creating a basis for trust and acceptance. Because competitors were not identifying with these themes, they were likely seen as largely functional and impersonal entities. Furthermore, the *Chain Store Age Executive* results suggest that consumers were buying into the nonprice as well as price components of Wal-Mart's strategy. While it is not possible to link Wal-Mart's strength on the community dimension to its dominant share of shoppers against these three major competitors, the flyer comparisons connected to the survey results present tantalizing evidence to believe that played a significant role.

Table 2 Percent identifying store chain best on community involvement, lowest everyday prices and store shopped most often Atlanta, Dallas/Ft. Worth and Indianapolis 1993

Store chain *Percent identifying store chain*

Store chain	Atlanta			Dallas/Fort Worth			Indianapolis		
	Community	*Lowest prices*	*Shop at most*	*Community*	*Lowest prices*	*Shop at most*	*Community*	*Lowest prices*	*Shop at most*
Wal-Mart	67%	74%	53%	59%	65%	49%	57%	63%	48%
Kmart	13	14	19	10	11	12	12	12	13
Target	11	9	12	15	13	20	21	18	24
Other	9	3	16	26	11	19	10	7	15
Total	100%	100%	100%	100%	100%	100%	100%	100%	100%
Sample size	531			575			524		

Questions:
"Which store is best at being concerned about and actively involved in the community at large?" "Which store has the lowest everyday prices?" and "Which of these eight stores do you shop at most often?"

Source: Chain Store Age Executive, Mid July 1993, pp. 30, 32, 34, 35, 50, 51, 52, 53, 56, 66, 68, 69.

The flyer comparisons and *Chain Store Age Executive* results may also suggest traditional image research is too functionally oriented to capture the full character of a retail store. The one question on community involvement and concern was the only one that measured institutional activity in the *Chain Store Age Executive* article. The remaining thirty or so items asked respondents to identify the stores best on convenience, price, value, selection, service, quality and layout and were completely performative in their nature. It is possible to envisage additional items that ask about the retailer perceived to best support local suppliers, charities, sports teams, families and national institutions. Alternatively, institutional semiotics has demonstrated it can reveal this dimension and thereby provides a useful method for exploring the ground of retailer character and trust.

Alternative interpretations

Not all images and texts within the Wal-Mart flyer are consistent with the interpretations presented in this research. For instance, although the St. Bernard may have a reputation as being steadfast, it is also a foreign and costly breed. The "Sale!" items are inconsistent with the "Every Day Low Price" claim. Not one of the "Faded Glory" store brand apparel items has the familiar "Made in the U.S.A." tag. Instead of Sam Walton substituting as the wise father figure, another interpretation of the few men in the flyer is that their absence reflects the realities of American family life—the rise of single mother families. It might also be an intentional marketing strategy to target, through representation, the gender of the primary Wal-Mart shopper. Other exceptions may be apparent to the reader. These ironies attest to the complex cultural environment in which Wal-Mart operates, one in which consumers must negotiate between countervailing discourses to actively create their own unique consumption stories and meanings (Thompson & Haytko, 1997).

The signifiers of "hometown" identified here may not resonate with the experience of recent emigrants or urbanites who must go back generations to find the hometown evoked in the flyer. Some doubt that such a community even ever existed. A simulacrum refers to an idealized, and often entertainment-oriented and mass-mediated, construction of a time, place, or object that is preferable to its original (Baudrillard, 1983). It is possible to view the hometown depicted in the Wal-Mart flyers as a simulacrum, not unlike the idyllic village portrayed in the 1998 American movie, *The Truman Show*. The likely response then of at least some readers (maybe most) is not one based on a direct, personal experience of this idyllic hometown but instead a mass-mediated experience. Nonetheless, the pleasure derived from a Knott's Berry Farm, Disneyland's Main Street U.S.A. or any historical theme park is just as intense and likely more so than if the potentially harsh realities of the 'real' hometown could ever actually be experienced (see, for example, the discussion of Disneyland in Baudrillard, 1983).

Arnold, Handelman & Tigert (1996) observed that the symbolic presentation of Wal-Mart might be different from the objective reality. Wal-Mart projects an innocent, homespun image of a happy community involving vendor "partners," associates and customers. The extremely rich weave of cultural-moral symbols upon which this interpretation is based, however, may have as much to do with Wal-Mart's alleged illegitimacy (Ortega, 1998) as it does with its community spirit. In lieu of the "vendor-partner" persona, aspiring Wal-Mart suppliers wait long periods before meeting a buyer and are then squeezed aggressively for the lowest prices.

Many goods, apparel in particular, do not display a "Made in the U.S.A." label and 'Buy American' signs are found situated embarrassingly on racks of imported products. Furthermore, some allege the goods are sourced at overseas sweatshops and that the low prices are a consequence of child labor. Some local communities rally to block the opening of a new store because they feel Wal-Mart will shut down local merchants with predatory pricing and divert shoppers away from the community core. Newsgroups and websites have sprung up for disgruntled former Wal-Mart associates to vent their unhappiness, for example, http://walmartworkerslv.com, http://www.walmaryrs.com, http://www.walmartsucks.com. Wal-Mart is regarded by some as a wolf in sheep's clothing and the mundane flyer may serve as a propaganda instrument to construct the sheep's costume.

The relegitimizing denial of its illegitimacy through Wal-Mart's institutional activity is complete and instantaneous: Wal-Mart is "us," it says. Wal-Mart is part of our neighborhood. It is people like you and me. It is not *other*, not *they*, but *we*. Draping itself in the flag and community ideology, the Wal-Mart flyer powerfully lets loose a symbolic barrage that decouples the "hometown" store and its "folks" from any controversy that might penetrate the shopping experience.

The interesting question that remains concerns the 'reality' at Wal-Mart. Does the symbolic representation reflect the firm's position or what Wal-Mart wants consumers to believe? Wal-Mart's pricing policy is instructive in this regard. According to a former VP of Wal-Mart Store Operations, Senior VP Wal-Mart Store Planning and Development and President of the Wal-Mart Canada Transition Team, the margin schedule in the U.S. averages a competitive 27½ percent (Redman, 1998). However, 27½ percent is the average margin and there are a number of different levels for different product categories. Certain frequently purchased items, for example, toothpaste, soap, shampoo, are priced at cost or less. Wal-Mart associates monitor nearby stores to ensure these items are always the lowest priced in the local market. The price rollbacks and other devices described earlier are additional elements for projecting a low price image. Redman (1998) emphasized that the key to profitability was managing the low price *perception* to attract consumers into the store. One-stop shoppers would then "bleed" over to the less frequently purchased items on the high margin side of the average.

Is Wal-Mart successful in managing their low price image? In the *Chain Store Age Executive* results summarized in Table 2, an average of two out of three shoppers across the three markets identified Wal-Mart as best on "everyday low prices," the same number that identified this chain as best on community involvement. There is no reason to believe that the price and community personas aren't both carefully "managed."

Conclusion

The objective of research is to offer a partial explanation for Wal-Mart's growth in its domestic marketplace, the United States of America. The semiotic analysis of a Wal-Mart flyer in particular provided glimpses into the ways in which this particular retail giant achieves isomorphism, promises a more unencumbered, morally balanced self to consumers and legitimates itself among its relevant constituents. It also suggests multiple ways in which Wal-Mart's marketing strategy is symbolically attuned to the dominant ideologies of American life. The analysis yielded a series of examples in which a nostalgic "hometown" is evoked by the imagery of frugality, family, religion, neighborhood, community and American national patriotism. Wal-Mart in turn is associated with this mythical hometown.

This paper also advanced *institutional semiotics* as a theoretical tool for analyzing the meanings of retail phenomena. This objective was achieved by informing Jakobson's semiotic framework with institutional theory. The institutional semiotics analyses of the Wal-Mart and Sears flyers then suggested that retail organizations respond to important cultural-moral forces in their institutional environment. They do this by taking environmentally isomorphic action—action that helps organizations legitimate themselves by adopting institutional symbols and ideology.

Managerial implications

If Wal-Mart and Sears are isomorphic with institutional norms, does it make any difference? After the all-important economic task norms of convenience, price, assortment and service are taken into account, do the institutional norms have any role left to play in store choice? Other research demonstrates that they make a difference. In a between subjects field experiment, shopping mall subjects were presented with different video versions of a fictitious retailer, *RetailWorld* (Handelman & Arnold, 1999). The versions differed on two levels of performative action and three levels of institutional action. Institutional action was found to have a main effect on support for the retailer as well as an interaction effect. It was determined that there is a minimum acceptable level of response to the moral-cultural norms below which the effectiveness of the retailer's economic-oriented action is significantly hindered.

Elsbach (1994) found that appeals to institutional norms reflected in government regulations detract community concerns away from the technical details of the core activities of a particular production process and thus ensure that the organization is seen as legitimate. Similarly, Kozinets (forthcoming) used ethnographic evidence to argue that the legitimizing utopian discourse of entertainment programs can influence fan perceptions of the intrinsic morality of related product consumption.

Advertising flyers are but one-way organizations symbolically demonstrate environmental isomorphism. For instance, Floch (1988) showed how store architecture influenced shoppers. Besides the functionality of pertinent location, attractive prices and wide assortment, retailers can employ store layout, store format, store appearance, store brands, signage, employee deportment, visual merchandising, advertising and promotion. All signal meaning that can portray family values, community values, patriotic values and even values of excitement, subculture, sexuality and spirituality (see, e.g., Sherry, 1998). However, for success, these symbols must be culturally meaningful to consumer constituents and resonant with their norms.

Future research

The two main schools of semiotics derive from Saussure and Peirce (Mick, 1986). Institutional semiotics is a particular Saussurian form of analysis and other Saussurian forms may provide analytical prescriptions. For instance, the Barthesian technique of spectral analysis (Barthes, 1972) derives the connotative meanings of photographic, pictorial and other graphical images. Peircian semiotics is the other main structuralist approach beyond which lies poststructuralist techniques including deconstruction (e.g., Stern, 1996a, 1996b).

In consumer research, there is much current work to supplement and extend the semiotic approach taken in the current paper. The work on myth by Stern (1995) and on allegory by Stern (1990) and Otnes and Scott (1996) relate closely to the mythologies. Scott's papers on images and rhetoric, for example, Scott (1991, 1994a, 1994b) influenced the analysis reported here but deserve more explicit consideration. In addition, institutional theory covers a vast literature that is constantly evolving. There is much to draw upon and develop further in a retailing context. For instance, economic task norms can be extended to include functional and utilitarian values. Similarly, the institutional cultural-moral norms can also factor in the utopian (see Kozinets forthcoming) and the esthetic.

A single Wal-Mart flyer was the *primary* source of the interpretive conjecture presented herein and in itself points to several future research possibilities. One project might extend this investigation through the addition of data from consumers concerning their responses to flyer advertising. Such data might verify, enhance or modify the conclusions reached here.

The discussion above, however, has revealed that consumer perceptions in the form of traditional image research do not necessarily reveal the reality of retailer practice. A limitation of institutional semiotics is that it too would not penetrate careful image management. What could be done for identifying the reality of institutional activity would be similar to the construction of price baskets for identifying the objective side of performative pricing activity. Retailers could be compared at the store and corporate level on support of local charities and causes, participation in community and family support activities, employee satisfaction and purchases from local and national suppliers. Furthermore, studies of (il)legitimate(d) organizations might see if similar appeals to institutional norms were used to (re)legitimate themselves (e.g., Elsbach, 1994).

There also remains the possibility of examining Wal-Mart flyers from other regions. Of particular interest would be comparative examinations of Wal-Mart flyers from countries other than the United States. Does Wal-Mart seek to transplant its *hometown* approach holus bolus into Canada, Mexico and the other world markets to accomplish the institutional isomorphism that it expertly achieves in the U.S.A.? A diachronic analysis of the evolution and ramifications of its approaches in these countries, as well as in the United States, would be informative.

The flyers that arrive every week from other retailers also hold much interest. In addition to comparing present day Wal-Mart flyers with those of Kmart, Target, and Sears as done here, historical comparisons could be made with Woolworth's and old Sears catalogues. Differences in style would emerge in the comparisons of multiple texts. Descriptions and conceptualizations of the relative influences of the task (economic) and institutional (moral-cultural) environments on effective retailing under different relevant contexts would be theoretically and pragmatically useful. How much relative attention is accorded to price and economics and how much relative weight is given to the representations of hometown and utopian ideals of community?

A popular culture approach would seek to explore the source of these collective and cultural images. For instance, artists like Norman Rockwell and James Montgomery Flagg did much to invent American patriotic—'down home'—populist imagery, often situating it in a commercial setting. No longer mere 'junk mail,' these flyers in their myriad forms present a rich, untapped source of data in portraying everyday consumer society. With an increased consciousness of the possibilities, the authors have been accumulating the flyers of other retailers, in other retail sectors, and in other countries. This opportunity is open to all.

Appendix A. Descriptions of Wal-Mart Flyer[1]

A.1. U.S. flag

Billowing U.S. Stars and Stripes flag.

A.2. Flyer first page

First page of flyer headlined at top with "WAL★MART" in white letters on blue background. At the bottom of the page is the statement "Our Pledge . . . To Save You More" superimposed on a swirling U.S. Stars and Stripes flag. Featured between is a pair of $5.94 ("Sale! Reg. 6.94") Cadet Club® boys tops or shorts worn by "Brendon, son of Theresa, Cashier." "Rosie, best friend of Deni, Toy Dept.," is a St. Bernard dog and accompanies Brendon. Also featured are $5 Zest® 12-pack bath soaps, 2 for $3 "Special Buy" Glade® aerosol value packs, $7.50 36-roll Charmin® bath tissues and a $149.96 "Every Day" 19-inch television with remote. The aerosol and bath tissue products are "Made in the U.S.A."

A.3. Flyer last page

Last page of flyer (p. 32) with a headline at top stating "Our Commitment . . . To Satisfy All Your Shopping Needs." At the bottom of the page is a swirling U.S. stars and stripes flag, the slogan "**WAL★MART**® ALWAYS LOW PRICES. ALWAYS WAL-MART. ALWAYS," the address for Wal-Mart Stores, Inc., an illustration of the four accepted credit cards, an 88-word statement of Wal-Mart's advertising merchandise policy and the statement that the flyer is "PRINTED IN THE U.S.A. ON RECYCLED PAPER Containing 20% Post Consumer Fiber" in Stillwater, OK. In between are illustrations and prices for laundry detergent, Pampers® disposable diapers, Windex® spray, Excedrin®, Advil® or Pepcid AC® tablets, Gillette® saving gel and disposable razors, Arid® deodorant and Benadryl® tablets.

A.4. Merchandise wrapped in flag stripes

On page 31, each of the following, illustrated products are draped in a blue ribbon on which are superimposed large, white stars: Sam★s American Choice™ 6-pack soft drinks (p. 2), Sam★s American Choice™ cranberry cocktail or grape juice (p. 2), Frito-Lay® snacks (p. 3), child car seats (p. 4), Aunt Lydia's® crochet thread (p. 7), men's Fruit of the Loom® 3-pack boxer shorts (p. 10), ladies' Hanes Her Way® canvas or leather oxfords (p. 14), ladies' Hanes Her Way® 6-pack panties (p. 15), ladies', girls' and infants' shoes, pumps, oxfords, slings and sandals (p. 17), tin watering cans (p. 22), Wal-Mart® 120 T-120 3-pack video tapes (p. 24), photo albums (p. 24), pillows (p. 29), and Wal-Mart® interior wall paint.

A.5. Laura and Jessica T-shirts

On page 12, the $6.84 "Sale! Each Reg. 8.94" ladies' ribbed White Stag® T-shirts are worn by "Laura, Shoe Department Associate" and "Jessica, daughter of Marilyn, Pharmacist".

A.6. Savings claims

Low price and value-oriented headlines from the flyer including: "Your Wal-Mart Snack Bar has delicious food at affordable prices!" (p. 3), "Name Brands That Fit Your Budget" (p. 10), "Ladies' Casuals Spend Less & Still Look Great!" (p. 12), "We're Sporting Low Prices at Your Hometown Wal-Mart" (p. 18), "Cutting Costs with Value-Priced Lawn & Garden Supplies" (p. 20), "Sterilite Savings In Store For You" (p. 23), "Look To Wal-Mart for fabulous prices" (p. 24), "The Savings keep getting better and better" (p. 26), "Wow! Check Out All the Great Items $5 Can Buy" (pp. 28–29), and "Ride In For low prices on great bikes" (p. 30).

A.7. Wal-Mart "Guiding Principles"

Four of "Wal-Mart's Guiding Principles" including: "The greatest measure of our success is how well we serve the customer" (p. 5), "We go out of our way to instill a strong sense of community involvement in our store management and associates so they'll be even better citizens" (p. 11), "Our total objective should be to serve our customers every time they are in our store and make their shopping experience enjoyable. Remember, they are our guests." (p. 25) and "Our relationship (among Associates) is a partnership in the truest sense" (p. 29). Each principle is attributed to "Sam Walton Wal-Mart Founder," is accompanied by a head and shoulders, black & white sketch of Walton, a head and shoulders photograph of a female Wal-Mart associate (Brenda, Nancy, Judy and Dianne) and a quotation from the associate that illustrates the principle.

A.8. Sam's American Choice® and scholarship fund

The top half of p. 2 of the flyer contains the "Wal-Mart Guiding Principle" "[P]roviding customers what they expect and deserve . . . better quality and value." A 50-word text below it describes "The Competitive Edge Scholarship Fund" that is "Honing America's Skills." Featured are $1.18 "Your Choice Every Day" Sam★s American Choice® 6-pack soft drinks.

A.9. Mother Adena

On page 14, a $6.88 ("Sale! Your Choice Reg. 8.93") Ladies' Hanes Her Way® tunic top is worn by "Adena, mother of Adena, Pharmacy Associate."

A.10. Babies

Page 4 of the flyer carries the headline "Bringing Up Baby" and a bottom illustration of a swirling U.S. Stars and Stripes flag. In between are illustrations, prices and descriptions of car seats and clothing for infants and toddlers. Wearing the clothing are nine named children. All of the items are on "Sale!"

A.11. Young children

On page 7, eight named young female Caucasian and African American children are wearing Easter dresses, short sets and outerwear. All items are on "Sale!" and the regular prices are given.

A.12. Rugs, slippers and pillows

On page 29, the $5 ("Sale! Reg. 5.66") "Country Braided" area rugs and $5 "Special Buy" 2-pack standard size pillows are "Made in the U.S.A." On one rug is a pair of slippers. One pair of pillows is draped in a blue ribbon on which are superimposed white stars. Another photograph of the pillow set shows its cover that features the U.S. Stars and Stripes flag.

A.13. Coffee, toast and waffles

On page 27, a West Bend® coffeemaker, Proctor-Silex® toaster, Hamilton-Beach® hand mixer and Cool-Touch waffle maker each sell for $14.96. The coffeemaker, toaster and mixer have a superimposed "Better Every Day" logo accompanied by a yellow smiling happy face symbol. The waffle maker is a "Special Buy".

A.14. Better Homes and Gardens cart

On page 22, there is an illustration that shows a Better Homes and Gardens™ Floral & Nature Crafts™ artificial floral cart.

A.15. Gone fishing

On page 19, "Tammy, PMDC Associate" and "Loyd, spouse of Tammy" are shown walking hand-in-hand along a beach each wearing a $22.96 ("Every Day") Stearns sportsman's vest and carrying a fishing rod and tackle box.

A.16. Joshua's bat and baseball

On page 8, "Joshua, son of Kim, Directs," is shown holding a bat and baseball while wearing a $7.94 ("Sale! Reg. 11.48") boys' top and shorts.

A.17. Blake's bicycle

On page 30, "Blake, son of Kathy, UPC Clerk," is shown holding a "Your Choice, Every Day $88.96 Girls' or Boys' 24-inch 10-Speed" mountain climber bicycle. The bicycle is "Made in the U.S.A.".

A.18. Four ways to save

On page 27, an illustration is headlined "4 Great Ways to Save" and explains the meanings of the "Every Day Low Price" slogan and the "Bonus Buy" and "Special Buy" symbols. Also explained is the meaning of the "Better Every Day" logo accompanied by a yellow, smiling, happy face.

A.19. *Food at affordable prices*

On page 3, a headline states, "Your Wal-Mart Snack Bar has delicious food at affordable prices!"

A.20. *Happy face*

The "Better Every Day" logo/yellow, smiling, happy face symbol accompanies "9.94 Your Choice Sizes M-XL Was 11.94–13.94" men's Faded Glory® shirts.

A.21. *U.S. workers*

On page 31, a "Wal-Mart's Guiding Principle" states, "I am very certain that U.S. workers . . . can produce merchandise that will be as good a value, or better, than anything we can buy offshore." The accompanying story describes the Black & Decker Asheboro, NC plant that went from one to three shifts because of Wal-Mart's success in selling the Snake Lights manufactured by the plant. An accompanying photograph shows four smiling female plant workers, including Tracey who says, "The partnership between Wal-Mart and Black & Decker really boosted the morale in our community".

A.22. *Lawn mower*

On page 20 the illustrated $229 "Every Day" MTD® 21-inch self-propelled bagger/mulcher lawn mower is "Made in the U.S.A.".

A.23. *Gas grill*

On page 21, the illustrated $189.94 "Every Day" Sunbeam® cart gas grill is "Made in the U.S.A.".

A.24. *Levin's shirt and shorts*

On page 8, "Levin, son of Mallory, Department Manager" is shown wearing $8.94 ("Sale! Reg. 9.94") Faded Glory® shirt and shorts.

A.25. *Jared's shirt*

On page 8, "Jared, son of Mary, Electronics Department Associate" is shown wearing a boys Cadet Club® short-sleeved knit shirt.

A.26. Just my size

On page 15, generously proportioned "Sheryl, Customer Service Manager," is shown wearing a $8.88 "Sale Each Reg. 10.94," Ladies Just My Size® tunic top and $10.88, "Sale Each Reg. 12.94" Ladies Just My Size® pocket pants.

A.27. Microwave and blender

A Magic Chef® microwave oven was $124 and now has the "Better Everyday" price of $119. A bonus 7-speed blender, a $15.96 value, accompanies it. Sitting on the oven is a bowl of fresh popcorn and in the blender are pieces of fresh fruit. The two products are "Made in the U.S.A.".

Note

1   For a copy of any of the images described in Appendix A, please contact the first author.

References

Arnold, Stephen J. and Eileen Fischer (1994). "Hermeneutics and Consumer Research," *Journal of Consumer Research, 21*(June), 55–70.

Arnold, Stephen J., Jay Handelman and Douglas J. Tigert (1996). "Organizational legitimacy and retail store patronage," *Journal of Business Research, 35*, 229–239.

Arnold, Stephen J., Jay Handelman and Douglas J. Tigert (1998). "The impact of a market spoiler on consumer preference structures (or, what happens when Wal-Mart comes to town)," *Journal of Retailing and Consumer Services, 5*(1), 1–13.

Arons, Leon (1961). "Does TV viewing influence store image and shopping frequency?" *Journal of Retailing, 37*(3), 1–13.

Barthes, Roland (1972). *Mythologies*, trans. Annette Lovers. New York: Hill and Wang.

Baudrillard, Jean (1983). *Simulacra and Simulations*, trans. Paul Foss, Paul Patron and Philip Bewitchment. New York: Semiotext(e).

Beard, J., J. Walton and S. Webb (1999). *Wal*Mart in the UK*, Letchmore Heath, UK: Institute of Grocery Distribution, August.

Belk, Russell W., Melanie Wallendorf and John F. Sherry, Jr. (1989). "The sacred and the profane in consumer behavior: theodicy on the odyssey," *Journal of Consumer Research, 16*(June), 1–38.

Bellah, Robert N., Richard Madsen, William M. Sullivan, Ann Swidler and Steven M. Tipton (1986). *Habits of the Heart: Individualism and Commitment in American Life*. New York: Harper and Row Publishers.

Birtwistle, Grete, Ian Clarke and Paul Freathy (1999). "Store image in the UK fashion sector: consumer versus retailer perceptions," *The International Review of Retail, Distribution and Consumer Research, 9*(January), 1–16.

Boyd, D. (1997). "From 'Mom and Pop' to Wal-Mart: the impact of the consumer goods pricing act of 1975 on the retail sector in the United States," *Journal of Economic Issues, 31*(1), 223–232.

Chain Store Age Executive (1993). Mid July.

Chain Store Age (2000). "World's 100 largest retailers," p. 121.

Clarke, Ian and Ruth Schmidt (1995). "Beyond the servicescape: the experience of place," *Journal of Retailing and Consumer Services, 2*(3), 149–162.

Clarke, Ian, Ian Kell, Ruth Schmidt and Claudio Vignali (1998). "Thinking the thoughts they do: symbolism and meaning in the consumer experience of the 'British Pub'," *Qualitative Market Research: An International Journal, 1*(3), 132–144.

Cohen, Anthony P. (1987). *The Symbolic Construction of Community*. Chichester, England: Ellis Horwood Ltd. & London: Tavistock Publications Ltd.

Coleman, Richard P. (1983). "The continuing significance of social class to marketing," *Journal of Consumer Research, 10*(December), 265–80.

Davidson, Sharon M. and Amy Rummel (2000). "Retail changes associated with Wal-Mart's entry into Maine," *International Journal of Retail & Distribution Management, 28*(4/5), 161–169.

DiMaggio, Paul J. and Walter W. Powell (1983). "The iron cage revisited: institutionalized isomorphism and collective rationality in organizational fields," *American Sociological Review, 48*(2), 147–160.

DiMaggio, Paul J. and Walter W. Powell (1991). "Introduction," in *The New Institutionalism in Organizational Analysis*. Walter W. Powell and Paul J. DiMaggio (eds.). Chicago, IL: University of Chicago Press, pp. 30–87.

Elsbach, Kimberly D. (1994). "Managing organizational legitimacy in the California cattle industry: the construction and effectiveness of verbal accounts," *Administrative Science Quarterly, 39*(March), 57–88.

Englis, Basil G. and Michael R. Solomon (1995). "To be *and* not to be: lifestyle imagery, reference groups and *The Clustering of America*," *Journal of Advertising, 24*(Spring), 13–28.

Finn, Adam and Harry Timmermans (1996). "A Wal-Mart anchor as a repositioning strategy for suburban malls: cross-shopping and impact on image, consideration and choice," *Journal of Shopping Center Research, 3,* 7–27.

Floch, Jean-Marie (1988). "The contribution of structural semiotics to the design of a hypermarket," *International Journal of Research in Marketing, 4,* 233–252.

Gottdiener, M. (1985). "Hegemony and mass culture: a semiotic approach," *American Journal of Sociology, 5*(March), 979–1001.

Graff, Tom and D. Ashton (1993). "Spatial diffusion of Wal-Mart: Contagious and reverse hierarchical elements," *Professional Geographer, 46,* 19–29.

Handelman, Jay M. and Stephen J. Arnold (1999). "The role of marketing actions with a social dimension: appeals to the institutional environment," *Journal of Marketing, 63*(July), 33–48.

Hirschman, Elizabeth C. (1988). "The ideology of consumption: a structural-syntactical analysis of 'Dallas' and 'Dynasty'," *Journal of Consumer Research, 15*(December), 344–359.

Holbrook, Morris B. and Mark W. Grayson (1986). "The semiology of cinematic consumption: symbolic consumer behavior in *Out of Africa*," *Journal of Consumer Research, 3*(December): 374–381.

Jain, Arun and Michael Etgar (1976). "Measuring store image through multidimensional scaling of free response data," *Journal of Retailing, 52*(Winter), 61–70.

Jakobson, Roman (1985). "Linguistics and poetics," in *Semiotics: An Introductory Anthology*. Robert E. Innis (ed.). Bloomington, IN: Indiana University Press, pp. 147–175.

Keaveney, Susan M. and Keith A. Hunt (1992). "Conceptualization and operationalization of retail store image: a case of rival middle-level theories," *Journal of the Academy of Marketing Science, 20*(20), 165–172.

Kozinets, Robert V. (forthcoming). "Utopian enterprise: articulating the meanings of Star Trek's culture of consumption," *Journal of Consumer Research*.

Kunkel, J. and Berry, L. (1968). "A behavioral conception of retail image," *Journal of Marketing, 32*(October), 21–27.

Langrehr, Frederick W. and Clark L. Caywood (1995). "A semiotic approach to determining the sins and virtues portrayed in advertising," *Journal of Current Issues and Research in Advertising, 17*(Spring), 33–48.

Levy, Sidney J. (1981). "Interpreting consumer mythology: a structural approach to consumer behavior," *Journal of Marketing, 45*(Summer), 49–62.

Lindquist, Jay D. (1974/75). "Meaning of image: a survey of empirical and hypothetical evidence," *Journal of Retailing, 50*(4), 29–38, 116.

Lipset, Seymour Martin (1989). *Continental Divide: The Values and Institutions of the United States and Canada.* Toronto: C.D. Howe Institute and Washington, D.C.: National Planning Association.

Martineau, Pierre (1958). "The personality of the retail store," *Harvard Business Review, 36*(Jan.–Feb.), 47–55.

McCracken, Grant (1986). "Culture and consumption: a theoretical account of the structure and movement of the cultural meaning of consumer Goods," *Journal of Consumer Research, 13*(June), 71–84.

McCracken, Grant (1988). *The Long Interview.* Beverly Hills, CA: Sage.

McCracken, Grant (1989). "Homeyness," in *Interpretive Consumer Research*. Elizabeth Hirschman (ed.). Provo, UT: Association for Consumer Research, pp. 168–183.

McCune, J. (1994). "In the shadow of Wal-Mart," *Management Review, 83*(12), 10–16.

McDougall, Gordon H.G. and J. Nick Fry (1974). "Combining two methods of image measurement," *Journal of Retailing, 50*(4), 47–55.

McGee, Jeffrey E. (1995). "When Wal-mart comes to town: a look at how local merchants respond to the retailing giant's arrival," *Journal of Business and Entrepreneurship, 8*(1), 43–52.

McGee, Jeffrey E. and M.J. Rubach (1996). "Responding to increased environmental hostility: a study of the competitive behavior of small retailers," *Journal of Applied Business Research, 13*(1), 83–94.

McQuarrie, Edward F. (1989). "Advertising resonance: a semiological perspective," in *Interpretive Consumer Research*, C. Hirschman (ed.). Provo, UT: Association for Consumer Research, pp. 97–114.

McQuarrie, Edward F. and David Glen Mick (1992). "On resonance: a critical pluralistic inquiry into advertising rhetoric," *Journal of Consumer Research, 19*(September), 180–197.

Meyer, John W. (1994). "Rationalized Environments" in *Institutional Environments and Organizations.* Richard Scott and John W. Meyer (eds.), Thousand Oaks, CA: Sage Publications, pp. 28–54.

Meyer, John W. and Brian Rowan (1977). "Institutionalized organizations: formal structure as myth and ceremony," *American Journal of Sociology, 83*(2), 340–363.

Mick, David Glen (1986). "Consumer research and semiotics: exploring the morphology of signs, symbols, and significance," *Journal of Consumer Research, 13*(September), 196–213.

Mick, David Glen (1997). "Semiotics in marketing and consumer research: balderdash, verity, pleas," in *Consumer Research: Postcards from the Edge*. Stephen Brown and Darach Turley (eds.). London: Routledge, pp. 249–262.

Mick, David Glen and Claus Buhl (1992). "A meaning-based model of advertising experiences," *Journal of Consumer Research, 19*(3), 317–338.

Myers, Robert H. (1960). "Sharpening your store image," *Journal of Retailing,* 36 (Fall), 124–137.

Nöth, Winfried (1988). "The language of commodities: groundwork for a semiotics of consumer goods," *International Journal of Research in Marketing, 4*, 173–186.

O'Guinn, Thomas C. and Russell W. Belk (1989). "Heaven on earth: consumption at Heritage Village, USA," *Journal of Consumer Research, 15*(September), 227–238.

Ortega, B. (1998). *In Sam We Trust: The Untold Story of Sam Walton and How Wal-Mart is Devouring America*. New York: Random House, Inc.

Otnes, Cele and Linda M. Scott (1996). "Something old, something new: exploring the interaction between ritual and advertising," *Journal of Advertising, 25*(Spring), 33–50.

Ozment, J. and G. Martin (1990). "Changes in the competitive environment of rural retail trade areas," *Journal of Business Research, 21*, 277–287.

Perrow, Charles (1986). *Complex Organizations: A Critical Essay*. New York: McGraw-Hill Inc.

Peterson, Mark and Jeffrey E. McGee (2000). "Survivors of 'W-day': An assessment of the impact of Wal-Mart's invasion of small town retailed communities," *International Journal of Retail & Distribution Management, 28*(4/5), 170–180.

Peterson, Robert A. and Roger A. Kerin (1983). "Store image measurement in patronage research," in *Patronage Behavior and Retail Management*, William R. Darden and Robert F. Lusch (eds.). New York: Elsevier Science, pp. 293–306.

Redman, Mel (1998). Presentation to the "Wal-Mart in Europe" Conference, QEII Conference Centre, London, 8 October 1998.

Rich, Stuart U. and Bernard D. Portis (1964). "The 'imageries' of department stores," *Journal of Marketing, 28*(April), 10–15.

Rosenbloom, Bert (1983). "Store image development and the question of congruency," in *Patronage Behavior and Retail Management*, William R. Darden and Robert F. Lusch (eds.). New York: Elsevier Science, pp. 141–149.

Schaninger, Charles M. and William D. Danko (1993). "A conceptual and empirical comparison of alternative household life cycle models," *Journal of Consumer Research, 19*(4), 580–594.

Scott, Linda M. (1991). "The troupe: celebrities as *dramatis personae* in advertisements," *Advances in Consumer Research, Volume XVIII*. Provo, UT: Association for Consumer Research, pp. 355–363.

Scott, Linda (1994a). "Images in advertising: the need for a theory of visual rhetoric," *Journal of Consumer Research, 21*(September), 252–273.

Scott, Linda (1994b). "The bridge from text to mind: adapting reader-response theory to consumer research," *Journal of Consumer Research, 21*(December), 461–480.

Scott, W. Richard (1987). "The adolescence of institutional theory," *Administrative Sciences Quarterly, 32*(4), 493–511.

Seiders, Kathleen and Douglas J. Tigert (2000). "The impact of supercenters on traditional food retailers in four markets," *International Journal of Retail & Distribution Management, 28*(4/5), 181–193.

Sherry Jr., John F. (1991). "Postmodern alternatives: the interpretive turn in consumer research," in *Handbook of Consumer Behavior*, Thomas S. Robertson and Harold H. Kassarjian (eds.). Englewood Cliffs, NJ: Prentice-Hall, pp. 548–591.

Sherry Jr., John F. (Ed.) (1998). *ServiceScapes: The Concept of Place in Contemporary Markets*, Lincolnwood, IL: NTC Business Books.

Sherry Jr., John F., and Eduardo G. Camargo (1987). " 'May your life be marvelous:' English language labeling and the semiotics of Japanese promotion," *Journal of Consumer Research, 14*(September), 174–188.

Spiggle, Susan (1994). "Analysis and interpretation of qualitative data in consumer research," *Journal of Consumer Research, 21*(December), 491–503.

Stern, Barbara B. (1990). "*Other-speak*: classical allegory and contemporary advertising," *Journal of Advertising, 19*(3), 14–26.

Stern, Barbara B. (1992). "Feminist literary theory and advertising research: a new 'reading' of the text and the consumer," *Journal of Current Issues and Research in Advertising, 14*(Spring), 72–81.

Stern, Barbara B. (1995). "Consumer myths: Frye's taxonomy and the structural analysis of consumption text," *Journal of Consumer Research, 22*(September), 165–185.

Stern, Barbara B. (1996a). "Deconstructive strategy and consumer research: concepts and illustrative exemplar," *Journal of Consumer Research, 23*(September), 136–47.

Stern, Barbara B. (1996b). "Textual analysis in advertising research: construction and deconstruction of meanings," *Journal of Advertising, 25*(Fall), 61–73.

Stone, Kenneth E. (1995). *Competing with the Retail Giants: How to Survive in the New Retail Landscape*. New York: John Wiley and Sons.

Suchman, Mark C. (1995). "Managing legitimacy: strategic and institutional approaches," *Academy of Management Review, 20*(July), 571–610.

Thompson, Craig J. and Diana L. Haytko (1997). "Speaking of fashion: consumers' uses of fashion discourses and the appropriation of countervailing cultural meanings," *Journal of Consumer Research, 24*(June), 15–42.

Thompson, Craig J., Barbara B. Stern and Eric J. Arnould (1998). "Writing the differences: poststructuralist pluralism, retextualization and the construction of reflexive ethnographic narratives in consumption and market research," *Cultures, Markets and Consumption, 2*(June), 105–160.

Vance, Sandra S. and Roy V. Scott (1994). *Wal-Mart: A History of Sam Walton's Retail Phenomenon*. New York: Twayne Publishers.

Wal-Mart Stores, Inc. (2000). *Wal*Mart Annual Report*. Bentonville, Arkansas.

Wal-Mart Stores, Inc. (2001). "Wal-Mart reports record sales and earnings for quarter and year," Feb. 2001, http://www.walmartstores.com/newsstand/archive/prf_010220_4thqtrsales.shtml.

Walton, Sam with John Huey (1993). *Sam Walton: Made in America—My Story*. New York: Bantam Books.

Wrigley, Neil (2000). "The globalization of retail capital: themes for economic geography," in *Handbook of Economic Geography*. Gordon Clark, Meric Gertler and Maryann Feldman (eds.). Oxford: Oxford University Press, Figure 1.

Zimmer, Mary R. and Linda L. Golden (1988). "Impressions of retail stores: a content analysis of consumer images," *Journal of Retailing, 64*(Fall), 265–294.

Chapter 3

Merchandising and Buying

THE RETAIL STORE, OR indeed any other of the possible sales vehicles including catalogues and websites, is the creation of the retailer. Sales situations are complex amalgams of a variety of outcomes from different retailer processes. Consumers see these outcomes and their presentation and evaluate the retailer accordingly. Whilst consumers have their own demands and behaviours, as explored in Chapter 1 of this volume, the retail outlet interacts with these and to some extent reacts to, and leads, consumers.

Retailers have to make many decisions, both small and large, in putting together the retail offer. They have to decide the extent of the store range and the products that are included within this range, as well as the overall and detailed price positions that will be created and at which products will be sold. Decisions about promotions and displays need to be made to create the desired 'feel' to the store. Such decisions may be made effectively for the chain of stores as a whole in some cases where the chain is highly standardized. For other retailers, perhaps operating a mixture of very different forms and sizes of stores, different decisions may be necessary over merchandising at almost every level. Nor are these decisions static. Retailers have to constantly monitor the performance of products, promotions, displays and stores and refresh or amend decisions based on performance, arising from customers' reactions and behaviours, both in their own and in their competitors' stores. New products and new ways (or fashions) of selling products, developments in technologies and issues of security can all have an effect on how the store looks and feels and how products are merchandised.

That the outcomes of these decisions can lead to very different shops is obvious in any shopping trip. Retailers look and feel different and attempt to attract consumers to patronize them by aligning their offers with the presumed demands and expectations. The range in an Aldi discount store and the style of its merchandising and promotion, let alone its price positioning and its support, is radically different to, for example, a Waitrose supermarket, with its greater emphasis on a broader product range, quality, luxury and ambience. Both sell food, in some cases from store sizes that are very similar, but the decisions over range, pricing, promotion, display and ambience render them completely different retail environments and experiences. There would be no mistaking that they are different.

Whilst decisions about the range and its 'look' are important, retailers have to ensure that they are able to buy and source the products that they wish to include within their ranges. Retailers through this buying activity create the assortments that consumers see in the stores. These assortments allow the retailers to adjust the emphasis in broad ranges through more detailed decisions about the products and their pricing, packaging and so forth. If the products desired are not available, then the retailer may be in a position to create them, as for example through retailer brand development or their linkages with selected manufacturers. In other cases, the retailers are reliant on producers making the 'right' products available to them. In either case though, retailers actively have to buy products and ensure sufficient and appropriate levels of supply of these products over their lifetime. For some products, demand may be fairly smooth and constant and thus the decisions over buying are based around standard contract issues, such as price and efficiency of logistics. Other products, however, are clearly more fashion oriented and have very peaked demand that requires management to ensure that both under-supply and over-supply does not occur. There is considerable management skill required in these areas.

The buying process is fundamental to retailing in that having products available for consumers to buy would appear to be at the heart of retailing. How retailers buy, however, has not been that important to most consumers. This may be changing to some degree as consumers become more concerned about issues such as traceability and social responsibility. There is thus some pressure on retailers to be more transparent about their buying practices and policies and to ensure that they perform 'fairly'. As retailers have changed their buying locations and approaches (e.g. sourcing products from countries such as Bangladesh and Sri Lanka), so some consumer groups have begun to question ethical standards, wage rates, sustainability and so on. In other cases, labels such as Fairtrade have been developed to guarantee quality and fairness in buying and sourcing.

Retailers have seen their buying transform in scale and scope, enabled to some degree by changes in technology. Whilst retailing has internationalized its store operations increasingly in recent years, it is also the case that buying and sourcing for many products has become increasingly global, driven by desires to ensure a constant year-round supply of product, opportunities to reduce the cost of buying and supplying and by consumer demands for difference and newness in products. At the same time, there would now seem to be some reaction to this, leading to a rising concern for local and small-scale supply systems so as to reduce environmental impact.

Merchandising and buying is clearly a complex area of retail operations and one that contains a myriad of different approaches and possible outcomes. Merchandising and buying is at the heart of retail operations and in many ways is a distinctive competency of retailing. It is, therefore, different in many ways to the other areas covered in this volume. As such, a different approach is taken in this chapter. The other chapters of this volume are developed around the selected literature and its impact on our understanding of the issues and the ongoing development of the academic approach to the topic. This chapter, however, uses the selected literature as examples of the retail issues. The discussion is based much more around the processes of merchandising and buying than around a coherent unified academic approach to the area. This reflects both the practical complexity of the merchandising and buying area, the range of retail outcomes that can be generated from similar operational practices and the nature of the academic publications in the area.

In this chapter, there is first consideration of the type of activity on the shop floor, in respect of how items are presented for consideration by the customer – usually termed *merchandising*. This aspect of retailing involves a juxtaposition of art and science. The second aspect of retailer operations to be considered in this chapter is *sourcing* of the products for resale. This aspect of operations has changed massively in recent years, both in the structure of the functions and processes undertaken and also in respect of the volume and direction of spatial flows of products. Two rather different papers are included here, focusing on specific aspects within these broad areas:

1   *The Strategy of the Retail 'Sale'*. One of the key strategies for many retailers is the use of the concept of the retail 'sale'. For consumers the sense that they are somehow getting a bargain, or a product at a reduced price, is attractive. Retailers would believe that 'sales' provide a range of opportunities for them to interact with consumers and to attract them to the store and the merchandise, not only for the sale, but also for standard merchandise. The 'sale' is thus somewhat more than a pricing tactic, involving the intertwining of price and promotional concepts. Often pricing is considered to be a science and promotion an art, but it is equally possible to see these roles as reversed. The selected paper (Betts and McGoldrick 1995) provides a review of the concept and strategy of the retail 'sale' and shows how there are many different forms of sale, with different aims and objectives as well as outcomes in the minds of retailers and consumers.

2   *Vertical Marketing Systems by Retailers*. The sourcing of products by retailers has changed fundamentally in recent decades both in the structure of the functions and processes undertaken and also in respect of the volume and direction of spatial flows of products. The paper by Dawson and Shaw (1989) is concerned with the ways in which relationships between retailers and their suppliers have evolved and in particular with the ways in which retailers have taken more functions and processes and more of a coordinating and administering role in distribution and marketing channels. There is a clear link here with the issues of retail power discussed in Chapter 4, and the paper forms an example of both a genre of work in terms of distribution and marketing channels but also a bridge to concepts of power relationships in these channels. The changes the paper documents and foreshadows illustrate both the significance of the buying and supplying components of retail operations and the way in

which the nature and scope of retailing operations and management has altered.

Merchandising

Merchandising involves all the activities necessary to present the product to the customer in the sales place, sometimes termed 'sales-scape'. This includes management of the items for sale and the methods of selling. Merchandising is a core activity in retailing, whether the sales method used involves some form of shop, vending machine, web page, or any other retail technique. Whilst specific activities (e.g. store atmospherics, promotion, shelf layout and payment systems) interact with each other there is, nonetheless, a sequence of activity that may be generalized to four broad phases of merchandising: planning and range building, pricing, promotion and display, and monitoring. The sequence is not linear and contains many feedbacks.

Planning and range building

The planning and range building phase of merchandising involves responding to and delivering the marketing strategy that the retailer has decided upon. This strategy will define the parameters of width and depth of ranges and the number and uses of categories of items that make the total offer of the retailer (Cadeaux 1999). Thus in H&M, for example, the range strategy is very different from that of Primark, and different, but by not so much, from Zara. The development of sales forecasts is an integral part of the planning exercise and the models of sales then are extended to generate models of profitability (Alon *et al.* 2001). The merchandising planning and range building has close links to the buying functions where buyers source the items in the assortment (see below). The merchandising planning is at a general level and involves the macro-level modelling of categories and ranges. The links with buying involve a two-way flow of knowledge and experience. Whilst an optimal model may be developed as part of planning the merchandising, it may not be possible to implement this plan because supply is unavailable, for reasons of price, season and so on. The planning and range building is not always undertaken with deterministic models, and softer modelling can be involved.

An important aspect of the planning and range building is gaining understanding of the dynamics of the market. Moves in retail marketing towards meeting the greater variety of demand of consumers means that spatial and temporal dimensions of range planning are of increasing influence. This is evident in both Europe and the USA (Grewal *et al.* 1999) where retailers are attempting to shape merchandising more accurately to the needs of consumers as individuals in time and space. This involves the frequent introduction of new products and the provision of ranges that are specifically targeted to consumers in a local market.

The planning and range building activities are highly interactive with other aspects of merchandising and with buying. The planning involves an interaction between strategic requirements of the firm and the operations of sales outlets. The ranges change and evolve with input from all aspects of the retailer, including monitoring activities and feedback from buyers.

Pricing

Pricing is often considered to be one of the most complex areas of retailing. It is, however, a critical one because much of the success or failure of the retailer depends on getting the pricing correct from the perspectives of the consumer and of the retailer. Optimizing pricing is complex. A medium-sized supermarket may have 10,000 different items each having its own price, at any one time. Prices change over time, often in the short term, so increasing the complexity. To add even more complexity, price is a major promotional tool. Whilst this is a large and complex issue for a supermarket, for a department store with ten, or even 100, times as many items of stock, attempts at optimization are likely to fail, given current levels of knowledge of retail merchandising and of expertise in optimization procedures.

The traditional models of pricing from economics assume away much of this complexity, often limiting the number of products that require pricing decisions and viewing pricing from either manufacturer or consumer perspective. In this way, it is possible to reduce the problems to a manageable level. But the solutions are not always useful to retail managers. Betts and McGoldrick (1995) point out, 'economic models have served to help identify forces relevant to retailers' "sale" pricing decisions, although "real world violations" do preclude their use by price setters looking for prescriptive solutions'. Thus pricing in a retail managerial context becomes more of an art and has to accommodate many objectives other than those of long- and short-term profit maximization resulting from sales to rational consumers. Some of these objectives may be associated in the long term with confirming the positioning of the retailer within the market, for example in building an image of price integrity, discounting or quality exclusiveness. In other cases, the approach to pricing may be short-term tactical, for example market penetration, market defence, price matching a key competitor, or disposal of surplus stock. Pricing, therefore, in the context of merchandising is concerned with sending a message to consumers about the strategy and tactics of the retailer. This varies by firm and sector (Voss and Seiders 2003). The prices of items in a product range have to fit with this message and items will have been bought from suppliers with the selling price position firmly in the mind of the buyer. This equation of price as a mark-up over cost is important and it must be remembered that both the cost and the mark-up are variables in this equation. This approach was central to the pricing model of McGoldrick (1987) which suggested that the two variables were influenced by decisions in a geographical dimension (e.g. area and local pricing), comparative dimension (e.g. price matching of competitors), time dimension (e.g. seasonal pricing) and assortment dimension (e.g. pricing of known value items and pricing through a range). There is an extensive literature, on many aspects of retail pricing, that is reviewed in the major texts, for example Simon (1989), McGoldrick (2002), Levy and Weitz (2004).

The time dimension in the McGoldrick model underpins the paper selected in this chapter (Betts and McGoldrick 1995), entitled 'The Strategy of the Retail "Sale"'. The paper explores the history of the seasonal sale that was introduced as a way of clearing stock that had been over bought and so making space available for new products. The idea of the sale, however, was extended considerably, from this initial stock clearance objective, to cover sales undertaken specifically to generate store image and to boost sales volumes at slack times. Betts and McGoldrick (1995) point to the duration of the sale, from 'happy hours' to 'perpetual sales' and the percentage of lines involved, from single item 'loss leaders' to total range 'closing down clearance', as the two dimensions that enable a classification of sales to be established. Given the widespread use of this merchandising method it is not surprising that it has been the subject of abuse to the extent that there is a body of public policy (Fulop 1988) in most countries to control the misleading use of the merchandising method.

Promotion and display

Whilst the sale can be seen as a price-related aspect of merchandising, it is also a potent aspect of the promotional function of merchandising (Hardesty and Bearden 2003). Price is, however, only one of many promotional merchandising tools that include in-store communication tools (e.g. free standing, shelf related, point-of-sale related), product displays, store atmospherics and store design. The different promotional tools are used to engender different effects on consumers and, as such, the tools have different uses within the total merchandising activity.

Underhill (1999) and Kahn and McAlister (1997) in their reviews of how consumers use stores also provide insights into the wide range of merchandising tools used by retailers. The different tools are integrated in a variety of ways (Allway, et al. 1987) to achieve the various potential objectives of merchandising, which often are quite different in different retail sectors (Abratt et al. 1995; Fam and Merrilees 1996). Thus, for example, the promotional policy in a grocery-based convenience store will use different promotional tools to those used in a specialized delicatessen or a limited-range discount supermarket.

The research on promotional tools in merchandising generally explore issues of the effect of the various merchandising tools on consumers rather than the managerial decisions and design of the merchandising mix. Nonetheless, it is worthwhile to consider the types of study that have been undertaken in respect of promotional tools in merchandising. Each of the promotional tools has a specific use. It is not possible here to consider all the variety of tools available. The different tools have generated different studies and one, music within atmospherics, can be used to illustrate the nature of scholarship in this area.

Promotion within merchandising uses the full range of sensory tools, including colour, smell and sound (Baker et al. 2002). Within the use of sound, music is widely used to communicate the merchandising messages to customers. Garlin and Owen (2006) provide an extensive review of the use of background music. The effects of different music genres on purchase patterns and dwell time vary with the type of shop

(Yalch and Spangenberg 2000; Chebat *et al.*). The volume, key, pitch, speed and style of the music all have the potential to be varied and so be used in different ways to stimulate consumer senses. For example the volume and style of music in a fashion clothing store targeting teenage consumers will not be the same as that in a museum shop. Research generally concentrates on the impact on consumers of these promotional tools. Areni (2003) considers the impacts of music on the firm and how consumer perceptions influence retailer performance.

Whilst there are many studies of the impact of individual promotional tools, there are few studies that consider how the tools, together, can have multiple congruent or discordant effects. Mattila and Wirtz (2001) provide one example of music and scent working together but in a wider context there are relatively few studies that link together the effects of different tools. Furthermore, most of the studies are cross-sectional, yet clearly merchandising, and the promotional aspects of it, are processes. With the exception of pricing studies, the lack of research into the dynamics of promotional aspects of merchandising is notable.

Monitoring

Monitoring is a vital part of the merchandising process. Monitoring establishes the effectiveness of the process and if, as frequently happens, it is not meeting objectives, the monitoring process generates analyses of what has gone wrong.

A common problem in merchandising is that some items are not available in the retail outlet when the customer wishes to buy – the item is 'out of stock'. Under these situations the potential customer may buy a substitute product (item, brand, size), so increasing apparent demand for the substitute item. Alternatively, the consumer may move to another store to purchase the desired item. Some consumers may decide not to purchase the item or a substitute. Some will complain. The variety of responses to this failure in the merchandising process have been analysed by Campo *et al.* (2000, 2003) and Corstjens and Corstjens (1999).

An important aspect of the monitoring of merchandising is the analysis of the performance of shelf space in supermarket type stores or display space in the fashion sector. Sales space in store is limited and as such is a resource that has to be used efficiently. The determinants of 'efficiency' in this context include considerations of replenishment rates, visual impact, adjacencies of other items, and promotional possibilities. Thus end-of-shelf-aisle displays in supermarkets have different efficiency criteria than mid-aisle shelving. Monitoring the performance of the merchandising is therefore important in providing feedback to the planning phase. In general, more space generates more sales (Desmet and Renaudin 1998; Yang and Chen 1999) but this results in the exclusion of other items (Borin and Farris 1995). The profitability of individual items affect these decisions with retailer brand items usually having higher item-level profitability than manufacturer brands (Nogales and Suarez 2005).

The importance of monitoring has increased as retailers have moved increasingly to automated-sales-based ordering, such that stock is replenished as sales are monitored at the checkout (Myers *et al.* 2000). Events, such as items being out-of-stock, that result in substitute items being purchased, distort these systems and potentially reduce the stock of items that are most demanded, unless the models and systems are 'knowledgeable' in some way (Achabal *et al.* 2000).

The total merchandising process is central to the profitability of the retailer. It is at the heart of the creation of the offer to the customer. The studies of merchandising have tended to explore individual aspects of the process, partly because of its complexity and the difficulty of visualizing the totality of the process. A major challenge in understanding and modelling the retail firm as an enterprise is developing accurate, non-positivistic models of the merchandising process with its network of situation influenced cause-and-effect relationships and complex feedback mechanisms.

Buying and Sourcing

The cost of items purchased by the retailer is generally the largest expense within operational budgets. The selection of the right products, on the one hand, to meet the expectations of customers, and thus be sold to customers, and, on the other hand, to reflect the positioning strategy of the retailer, and thus deliver the business model for the firm, is a fundamental factor in influencing the success, or otherwise of the retailer. It is perhaps for this reason that undertaking research in buying is one of the most difficult areas of academic study in retailing. Not only is the process complex and dynamic but also is subject to high levels of confidentiality, not least in the nature of the relationships between retailers and their suppliers. Retailers have many suppliers and each relationship is to some extent different. Developing general conclusions across potentially many hundred relationships that are complex, dynamic and confidential is fraught with difficulties. Nonetheless, it is an area of retailing where there are a number of significant studies, but also an area where there are studies that only scratch at the surface.

There are many aspects to this component of retailing. The overall buying and sourcing process involves identification of the items that are required to satisfy the needs of target consumers, creating the assortments of these items so that they provide a coherent series of ranges of items. These activities are closely linked to merchandising as explained above. The process also includes the procurement of these items from suppliers of different types. In a similar way to most aspects of retailing, the buying and sourcing activities are not successful if undertaken in isolation from other aspects of retailing, notably consideration of demand and consumer behaviour, of overall strategy and format strategy, of merchandising as discussed above, and of financial considerations. It is difficult therefore to see the research on buying and sourcing out of the context of the total retail system. Nonetheless, we can divide, for convenience if somewhat arbitrarily, the publications in the area into four main themes:

1   creating the assortment of items that will need to be sourced;
2   the nature of the transactions, i.e. the processes, involved in obtaining the items;

3   the techniques and systems required in order to implement the sourcing processes;

4   the role of external factors that influence the way the processes operate.

Creating assortments

Creating the assortment involves decisions on what to buy and how much. The 'how much' is a direct influence on stockholdings and stock-outs as discussed above. The 'what to buy' involves resolution of the conflicts between depth and width of the range of items in the various categories that comprise the offer of the retailer. The result is a balance between depth and range that reflects the requirements of the targeted consumer. This assortment changes frequently with new item introductions and deletions of items that fail to achieve adequate sale. A seminal study of these issues of what to buy, from the buying rather than the merchandising viewpoint, was that of Nilsson and Høst (1987) which, although twenty years old, is still relevant in the way it structures the criteria that underpin decisions on what to buy. These criteria include quantitative financial and performance measures linked to items, more qualitative criteria of the nature of the marketing undertaken by the supplier and the supplier's fit with the retailer, and also consumer evaluations of the items. The links between assortment creation and consumer behaviour and consumer perceptions have been explored in several studies, for example in papers by Lee and Steckel (1999), Huffman and Kahn (1998), Cadeaux (1999) and Simonson (1999). Particular formats, for example supermarkets or department stores (Hirschman 1983; Thomas and Marr 1993; Hansen 2001), and different operational environments, for example airports (Freathy and O'Connell 1998), generate different assortment building requirements.

It is the buyers in the firm that make the decisions on assortments and so the knowledge, abilities, competences (Banting and Blenkhorn 1988), and even gender (Neu *et al.* 1988), of the buyers are an important influence. Fairhurst and Fiorito (1990) show this to be the case in the fashion area. Marr and Thomas (1999) and Ettenson and Wagner (1986) also show the individualistic nature of assortment building and how the organizational environment of the buyer affects their personal judgements. As with merchandising, positivistic models are of limited value with critical realism a more useful research philosophy under these circumstances.

Buying transactions and processes

There is a considerable body of material on the buying processes and the relationships between retailers and suppliers (Holm Hansen and Skytte 1998). Relationships in this area are extremely dynamic and at times volatile, reflecting the temporal aspect of the needs of consumers and retailers alike, although with the steady shift in power towards the retailer in the distribution channel the balance of channel control has moved in favour of the retailer. Any retailer in effect has a portfolio of relationships with their body of suppliers. Some relationships are short term, maybe one-off, transactions in which a single variable, for example price or availability, is the determining factor defining the relationship. Some relationships are likely to be long term, involving multiple transactions and contract extensions with a complex mix of many variables shaping the nature of the relationship (Davies 1994; Hughes 1999). Between these extremes there are a range of relationships. The nature of the relationships reflect the extent to which retailer and supplier are willing to make investments in the relationship.

The selected paper by Dawson and Shaw (1989) examines the shifting pattern of control in buying relationships in the UK. From the paper it is clear that the nature of relationships varies by retailer, by supplier and by sector (see also Shaw *et al*. 1992). The consistent trend identified, however, was one of retailers seeking to manage, or administer, relationships without taking ownership of the function of production. This involves investment in human and, is some cases, physical assets, in a relationship by supplier and retailer and this in turn encourages longer term and repeated purchasing relationships.

Other empirical work has generally supported these conclusions for example in the studies of Hogarth-Scott and Parkinson (1993), Biong (1993), Bowlby and Foord (1995), Foord *et al*. (1996) and Davies and Treadgold (1999). Other studies have emphasized the variations by product type (Wagner *et al*. 1989; Knox and White 1991) including retailer brands (Oubiña *et al*. 2006) and clothing (Crewe and Davenport 1992; Wall *et al*. 1994), the dynamic nature of the relationship (Collins and Burt 1999, Bengtsson *et al*. 2000), the situation when new products are involved (Pellegrini and Zanderighi 1991) and the nature of the power relationship between retailer and supplier (Brown *et al*. 1983; Gaski 1984; Knox and White 1991; Kumar 1996; Ogbonna and Wilkinson 1996a, 1998). (See also Chapter 4 of this reader for more detailed discussion in a strategic context.)

A major dimension present in considering the relationship between retailers and supplier is the organizational structure of the purchasing function. In many of the large retailers this function is undertaken, usually centrally, as part of their overall management. When large volumes of products are sourced internationally from countries in a region then often a buying office is established. This has been the case with sourcing activity from East Asia for many European firms. This situation contrasts strongly with retailers who are part of purchasing organizations in which, in effect, they out-source many aspects of their relationship with suppliers to a cooperative organization (Täger and Weitzel 1991, Shaw and Dawson 1995, Stoel 2002). In such cases the retailer often sources from a catalogue provided by the central cooperative purchasing organization. More usually this approach is one used by medium-sized retailers (Shooshtari 1988), but there are some comparable groups in which large retailers are members (Robinson and Clarke-Hill 1995), including Internet-facilitated groups, such as Agentrics, which was established with the merger of World Wide Retail Exchange (WWRE) and GlobalNetExchange (GNX) (IGD 2001). This dichotomy, between direct sourcing and use of an intermediary, results in substantially different buying processes in the two cases.

The nature of the contract that exists in the retailer–supplier relationship has generated a limited amount of research. Although this is crucial aspect of the relationship, it is an area for which it is difficult to obtain accurate data (Collins and Burt 2003). Even competition authorities that undertake inquiries have difficulty obtaining information. The Competition Commission (2000) inquiry into supermarkets in the UK provides a long list of arrangements that may be present in contracts and takes a view on the legality of the different arrangements. Nonetheless, it was not able to access substantial data on what arrangements were actually used and with what effect. The extent to which cooperative relationships infringe competition rules remains a matter of debate (Ingene and Parry 1995). This is subject to further discussion in Chapter 4 of this book.

It is over two decades since Cravens and Finn (1983) provided an inventory and prospect paper on processes in supplier–retailer relationships. Many of the suggestions of research gaps that were highlighted at that time remain areas where knowledge is still inadequate. The paper by Dawson and Shaw (1989) in this collection concludes by pointing to the changing nature of the relationship that is becoming not only more complex as a process but at the same time is less structurally complex with concentration resulting in fewer large retail firms as potential customers for suppliers.

Techniques and system supports

A third major identifiable corpus of studies is focused on the systems and methods by which the processes of retailer–supplier interactions are implemented. There are numerous studies of Category Management (CM), Quick Response (QR) and Efficient Consumer Response (ECR) that explore these managerial methods in a general way and also point to implications for the overall retailer–supplier relationship for example, Dussart (1998), Fiorito et al. (1995), Giunipero et al. (2001), and Dewsnap and Jobber (1999). These studies generally start from a presumption that longer-term cooperative relationships (Kurt Salmon Associates 1993; GEA 1994; IGD 1999) should be favoured over competitive relationships and that the programmes, that encourage longer-term relationships, generate very large financial benefits to retail and supplier (Zenor 1994; Basuroy et al. 2001). The reality is often less dramatic with certainly some benefits gained in some cases (Dhar et al. 2001), but often not on the scale that consultants' reports suggest (Dettman 1999; Kotzab and Teller 2003). Many of the studies focus on the presumed benefits of ECR and cooperative relationships without much consideration of additional costs (Freedman et al. 1997), including often an increase in transaction costs associated with the cooperative decision making implied in ECR (Dupuis and Tissier-Desbordes 1996; Whipple et al. 1999; Skjoett-Larsen et al. 2003). Whilst these techniques have been introduced most widely in the grocery sector (e.g. O'Keeffe and Fearne 2002), there are studies of their use in fashion retailing (Dewsnap and Hart 2004).

Reverse auctions, in which sellers respond, in effect compete, to a call from a retailer for the supply of a specified item, have emerged in recent years as an electronic form of relationship between retailers and suppliers (Jap 2002; Martinelli and Marchi 2007). This approach requires the initial detailed specification of all aspects (composition, quality, timescale, delivery, etc.) of the item required by the retailer. Suppliers then enter into an auction with successively reduced price bids, usually against a deadline, with the retailer contracting with the final bidder.

These various managerial approaches all require support and facilitation from technological developments that allow convergence of information and communication technologies. Various technologies for item identification, for example bar code scanning and radio frequency monitoring, are integrated with data manipulation and communication technologies to enable electronic data interchange (EDI) (Riddle *et al.* 1999) that underpins all the managerial methods of CM, QR and ECR (Bamfield 1994; Ogbonna and Wilkinson 1996b; Vijayyasarathy and Tyler 1997). Johansson (2001) and Maltz and Srivastava (1997) provide reviews that link the technological developments with the managerial approaches in this area. Kotzab (2005) reviews the link between these approaches and the logistical implementation of channel relationships.

External influences and factors in buying

The sourcing activity of retailers does not exist in isolation of the economy and society in which it operates. It is not a context-free positivistic process of cause and effect. The interplay between the external influences and the internal decisions provides a fourth stream of research on buying and sourcing and one that is relatively new in comparison with the other streams. The recent nature of the research is partly a reflection of the rejection of positivistic paradigms as the basis for theory and models in this area.

A number of studies have explored the nature of cultural influences on buyers' decisions and the extent to which national patterns can be seen. Studies have been carried out in Korea (Yu and Pysarchik 2002), Taiwan (Chang and Sternquist 1994) and comparatively (Sternquist 1994). In a similar vein there are studies of the cultural effects of the introduction of CM and QR (Lohtia and Murakoshi 1999).

In contrast to the micro-level studies of cultural influences there are a growing number of studies that relate macro-level sourcing issues to the globalization discourse. Some of these are referred to in Chapter 5 of this book dealing with internationalization. The majority of the studies have a focus on exploring issues associated with sourcing by international retailers of products from developing economies (Gereffi 1994, 2001; Schmitz and Knorringa 2001; Altenburg 2006; Ruben *et al.* 2006). Several consider sourcing of fruit and vegetable products, for example Barrett *et al.* (2004), Barrett *et al.* (1999), Neven and Reardon (2004), Burch and Goss (1999) and Dolan and Humphrey (2000, 2004).

The relationships between the international retailers and suppliers in developing economies often generate calls for public policy intervention to provide more balance in the power of the relationship (Reimer and Leslie 2004; Humphrey 2006). One of the areas where specific conflicts have occurred is in the application of quality standards within the food sector and the extent to which these are externally imposed by the retailer or part of a wider system of national standards (Berdegué et al. 2005; Fulponi 2006).

The governance through public policy of the relationship between retailer and supplier is a significant external factor in this relationship. This is explored in terms of strategy in Chapter 4 of this reader. The same issue has implications for buying. The Robinson-Patman Act in the USA has been the basis of many studies (Borghesani et al. 1997, 1998) but the issues are not limited to the USA, with major reports and papers from the OECD (OECD 1999; Boylaud and Nicoletti 2001). It is an issue that is also now starting to appear in developing economies as discussed by Reardon and Hopkins (2006). The work of Dobson and Waterson (1999) discussed in Chapter 4 relates directly to the nature of the relationship between retailer and supplier.

The research on buying and sourcing by retailers extends across a wide range of areas. The processes involve micro- and macro-level competitive relationships that are implemented in many different ways. The activities of retailers in this area have been studied and copied by manufacturers (Abernathy et al. 1999). The extent to which governments should intervene in these relationships is hotly debated, with views on one side arguing that there are imbalances in the relationships that can only be resolved through governmental action, and on the other side arguments that the efficiency of the distribution channel is best served by allowing the relationships to be resolved in a market context. An issue that is sometimes forgotten in this debate is the very considerable variety of situations that are present in buying and sourcing processes. A medium-sized retailer, in order to buy the products needed for the firm, may have many thousands of specific relationships with suppliers over a year and no two sourcing events are identical. In such a system, attempts to regulate, in a general way, will almost inevitably lead to the creation of as many problems as are solved.

Summary

This chapter has considered two major areas of retailing, namely the merchandising of products for sale and the obtaining of these products from various sources of supply. These are very broad topics with a disparate range of studies that include micro- and macro-level studies. Micro-level studies include behavioural studies of responses to, and the effectiveness of, specific merchandising actions, quantitative studies of the optimization of merchandising processes and analyses of relationships between retailers and suppliers. Macro-level studies include broad-scale changes in channel relationships, sectoral-level impacts of technologies on the buying function and shifts in global patterns of sourcing. The papers selected for reproduction are illustrative of this eclectic body of studies. Because of the broad range of studies it is not possible to identify general conclusions but from the two papers and the body of published material a number of more directed conclusions can be drawn:

- Merchandising is a complex process in which there is a high degree of connectivity within its elements and with other aspects of marketing, consumer behaviour and buying.
- Merchandising is extremely dynamic with constant adjustments being necessary and thus the temporal dimension is particularly important, although not the subject of large amounts of research.
- Merchandising uses complex models for forecasting and monitoring activities but the results of these have to be seen in the context of qualitative factors associated with consumer responses and the situational environment.
- The volume of products that are sourced by retailers, and the number of transactions, increases year on year so that buying systems have to accommodate these increased volumes.
- The role of individual buyers remains important despite applications of information and communication technologies.
- A retailer has many different types of relationship, and degrees of investment, with its body of suppliers with some relationships being longer term and cooperative in nature and others being simple transactions governed by price.
- Shifts in the relative power of retailer and supplier, notably with a shift in favour of the retailer, have repercussions for the economy generally and are the subject of public policy scrutiny and potential intervention.
- The shift in sourcing patterns towards production in East and South Asia for consumption in Europe and the USA has resulted in changes in the organization, volumes and flows of sourcing.
- Technological and managerial developments are enabling reductions in the volume of products held in the supply chain despite the increases in total volumes.
- Globalization is having substantial impacts on the nature of merchandising and buying by retailers and on the supply chains linking suppliers with retailers.

References

Abernathy F H, Dunlop J T, Hammond J H and Weil D (1999) *A Stitch in Time: Lean Retailing and the Transformation of Manufacturing – Lessons from the Apparel and Textile Industries.* New York: Oxford University Press.

Abratt R, Bendixen M and du Plessis A (1995) Manufacturer and retailer perceptions of in-store promotions in South Africa. *Journal of Marketing Management,* 11, 443–468.

Achabal DD, McIntyre SH, Smith SA and Kalyanam K (2000) A decision support system for vendor managed inventory. *Journal of Retailing,* 76, 430–454.

Allway A, Mason JB and Brown G (1987) An optimal decision support model for department-led promotion mix planning. *Journal of Retailing,* 63, 215–242.

Alon I, Qi M and Sadowski RJ (2001) Forecasting aggregate retail sales: a comparison of artificial neural networks and traditional methods. *Journal of Retailing and Consumer Services,* 8, 147–156.

Altenburg T (2006) Governance patterns in value chains and their development impact. *European Journal of Development Research*, 18, 498–521.

Areni CS (2003) Examining managers' theories of how atmospheric music affects perceptions, behavior and financial performance. *Journal of Retailing and Consumer Services*, 10, 263–274.

Baker J, Parasurman A, Dhruv G and Voss G (2002) The influence of multiple store environment cues on perceived merchandise value and patronage intentions. *Journal of Marketing*, 66(2), 120–141.

Bamfield J (1994) Technology management learning: the adoption of EDI by retailers. *International Journal of Retail and Distribution Management*, 22(2), 3–9.

Banting PM and Blenkhorn DL (1988) The mind of the retail buyer. *Management Decision*, 26(6), 29–36.

Barrett HR, Browne AW and Ilbery BW (2004) From farm to supermarket: the trade in fresh horticultural produce from sub-Saharan Africa to the United Kingdom. In A Hughes and S Reimer (eds) *Geographies of Commodity Chains*, London: Routledge, 19–38.

Barrett HR, Ilbery BW, Browne AW, and Binns T (1999) Globalization and the changing networks of food supply: the importation of fresh horticultural produce from Kenya into the UK. *Transactions of the Institute of British Geographers*, 24, 159–174.

Basuroy S, Mantrala MK and Walters RG (2001) The impact of category management on retailer prices and performance: theory and evidence. *Journal of Marketing*, 65(4), 16–32.

Bengtsson A, Elg U and Johansson U (2000) The process of internationalization: how Swedish food retailers perceive their domestic supplier relationships. *International Review of Retail, Distribution and Consumer Research*, 10, 321–334.

Berdegué JA, Balsevich F, Flores L and Reardon T (2005) Central American supermarkets' private standards of quality and safety in procurement of fresh fruits and vegetables. *Food Policy*, 30, 254–269.

Betts E and McGoldrick PJ (1995) The strategy of the retail 'sale': typology, review and synthesis. *International Review of Retail, Distribution and Consumer Research*, 5, 303–331.

Biong H (1993) Satisfaction and loyalty to suppliers within the grocery trade. *European Journal of Marketing*, 27(7), 21–38.

Borghesani WH, Jr., de la Cruz PL and Berry DB (1997) Controlling the chain: buyer power, distributive control, and new dynamics in retailing. *Business Horizons*, 40(4), 17–24.

Borghesani WH, Jr., de la Cruz PL and Berry DB (1998) Food for thought: the emergence of power buyers and its challenge to competition analysis. *Stanford Journal of Law Business and Finance*, 4(1), 39–82 .

Borin N and Farris P (1995) A sensitivity analysis of retailer shelf management models. *Journal of Retailing*, 71, 153–171.

Bowlby S and Foord J (1995) Relational contracting between UK retailers and manufacturers. *International Review of Retail, Distribution and Consumer Research*, 5, 333–360.

Boylaud O and Nicolette G (2001) Regulatory reform in retail distribution. *OECD Economic Studies*, 32, 99–142

Brown JR, Lusch R and Muehling D (1983) Conflict and power dependence relations in retail–supplier channels. *Journal of Retailing*, 59, 53–80.

Burch D and Goss J (1999) Global sourcing and retail chains: shifting relationships of production in Australian agri-foods. *Rural Sociology*, 64, 334–350.

Cadeaux JM (1999) Category size and assortment in U. S. macro supermarkets. *International Review of Retail, Distribution and Consumer Research*, 9, 367–377.

Campo K, Gijsbrechts E and Nisol P (2000) Towards understanding consumer response to stockouts. *Journal of Retailing*, 76, 219–242.

Campo K, Gijsbrechts E and Nisol P (2003) The impact of retailer stockouts on whether, how much, and what to buy. *International Journal of Research in Marketing*, 20, 273–286.

Chang L and Sternquist B (1994) Product procurement: comparison of Taiwanese and US retail companies. *International Review of Retail, Distribution and Consumer Research*, 4, 61–82.

Chebat J-C, Gelinas-Chebat CG and Vaillant D (2001) Environmental backgound music and in-store-selling. *Journal of Business Research*, 54(2), 115–123.

Collins A and Burt S (1999) Dependency in manufacturer–retailer relationships: the potential implications of retail internationalisation for indigenous food manufacturers. *Journal of Marketing Management*, 15, 673–693.

Collins A and Burt S (2003) Market sanctions, monitoring and vertical coordination within retailer–manufacturer relationships: the case of retail brand suppliers. *European Journal of Marketing*, 37, 668–689.

Competition Commission (2000) *Supermarkets: a Report on the Supply of Groceries from Multiple Stores in the United Kingdom*. Norwich: The Stationery Office.

Corstjens J and Corstjens M (1999) *Store Wars: the Battle for Mindspace and Shelf-space*. New York: Wiley.

Cravens DW and Finn DW (1983) Supplier selection by retailers: research progress and needs. In WR Darden and RF Lusch (eds) *Retail Patronage Theory*. New York: Elsevier-North Holland, 225–244.

Crewe L and Davenport E (1992) The puppet show: changing buyer–supplier relationships within clothing retailing. *Transactions of the Institute of British Geographers*, 23, 39–53.

Davies G (1994) Maintaining relationships with suppliers. *Journal of Strategic Marketing*, 2, 189–210.

Davies G and Treadgold A (1999) Buyer attitudes and the continuity of manufacturer/retailer relationships. *Journal of Marketing Channels*, 7(1/2), 79–94.

Dawson JA and Shaw SA (1989) The move to administered vertical marketing systems by British retailers. *European Journal of Marketing*, 23(7), 42–52.

Desmet P and Renaudin V (1998) Estimation of product category sales responsiveness to allocated shelf space. *International Journal of Research in Marketing*, 15, 445–457.

Dettman P (1999) Reflections on category management and ECR at ICA. *European Retail Digest,* 23, 15–17.

Dewsnap B and Hart C (2004) Category management: a new approach for fashion marketing? *European Journal of Marketing,* 38, 809–834.

Dewsnap B and Jobber D (1999) Category management: a vehicle for integration between sales and marketing. *Journal of Brand Management,* 6, 380–392.

Dhar, SK, Hoch SJ and Kumar N (2001) Effective category management depends on the role of the category. *Journal of Retailing,* 77, 165–184.

Dobson P and Waterson M (1999) Retailer power: how regulators should respond to greater concentration in retailing. *Economic Policy,* 28, 134–156.

Dolan C and Humphrey J (2000) Governance and trade in fresh vegetables: the impact of UK supermarkets on the African horticulture industry. *Journal of Development Studies,* 37, 147–176.

Dolan C and Humphrey J (2004) Changing governance patterns in the trade in fresh vegetables between Africa and the United Kingdom. *Environment and Planning A,* 36, 491–509.

Dupuis M and Tissier-Desbordes E (1996) Trade marketing and retailing: a European perspective. *Journal of Retailing and Consumer Services,* 3(1), 43–51.

Dussart C (1998) Category management: strengths, limits and developments. *European Management Journal,* 16(1), 50–62.

Ettenson R and Wagner J (1986) Retail buyers' saleability judgements: a comparison of information use across three levels of experience. *Journal of Retailing,* 62, 41–63.

Fairhurst AE and Fiorito SS (1990) Retail buyers decision making process. *International Review of Retail, Distribution and Consumer Research,* 1, 87–100

Fam KS and Merrilees B (1996) Determinents of shoe retailers' perceptions of promotion tools. *Journal of Retailing and Consumer Services,* 3(3), 155–162.

Fiorito SS, May EG and Straughn K (1995) Quick response in retailing: components and implementation. *International Journal of Retail and Distribution Management,* 23(5), 12–21.

Foord J, Bowlby RR and Tillsley C (1996) The changing place of retailer–supplier relations in British retailing. In N Wrigley and MS Lowe (eds) *Retailing, consumption and Capital: Towards the New Retail Geography.* Harlow: Addison Wesley Longman, 178–185.

Freathy P and O'Connell F (1998) The role of the buying function in airport retailing. *International Journal of Retail and Distribution Management,* 26, 247–256.

Freedman PM, Reyner M and Tachterman T (1997) European category management: look before you leap. *The McKinsey Quarterly,* 1, 156–164.

Fulop C (1988) Public policy and a marketing technique 1969–1985: comparative pricing and bargain offer prices. In E Kaynak (ed.) *Transnational Retailing.* Berlin: De Gruyter, 197–207.

Fulponi, L (2006) Private voluntary standards in the food system: the perspective of major food retailers in OECD countries. *Food Policy,* 31, 1–13.

Garlin FV and Owen K (2006) Setting the tone with the tune: a meta-analytic review of the effects of background music in retail settings. *Journal of Business Research*, 59, 755–764.

Gaski JF (1984) The theory of power and conflict in channels of distribution. *Journal of Marketing*, 48, 9–29.

GEA (1994) *Supplier–Retailer Collaboration in Supply Chain Management*. London: Coca-Cola Retailing Research Group – Europe.

Gereffi G (1994) The organization of buyer-driven global commodity chains: how US retailers shape overseas production networks. In G Gereffi and M Korzeniewicz (eds) *Commodity Chains and Global Capitalism*. Westport, CT: Greenwood Press, 95–122.

Gereffi G (2001) Beyond the producer-driven/buyer-driven dichotomy: the evolution of global value chains in the internet era. *International Development Studies Bulletin*, 32(3), 30–40.

Giunipero LC, Fiorito SS, Pearcy DH and Dandeo L (2001) The impact of vendor incentives on quick response. *International Review of Retail, Distribution and Consumer Research*, 11, 359–376.

Grewal D, Levy M, Mehrota A and Sharma A (1999) Planning merchandising decisions to account for regional and product assortment differences. *Journal of Retailing*, 75, 405–424.

Hansen K (2001) Purchase decision behaviour by Chinese supermarkets. *International Review of Consumer, Retail and Distribution Research*, 11, 159–175.

Hardesty DM and Bearden WO (2003) Consumer evaluations of different promotion types and price presentations. *Journal of Retailing*, 79, 17–25.

Hirschman E (1983) An exploration comparison of decision criteria used by retail buyers. In WR Darden and RF Lusch (eds) *Retail Patronage Theory*. New York: Elsevier-North Holland.

Hogarth-Scott S and Parkinson ST (1993) Retailer–supplier relationships in the food channel. *International Journal of Retail and Distribution Management*, 21(8), 11–18.

Holm Hansen T and Skytte H (1998) Retailer buying behaviour: a review. *International Review of Retail, Distribution and Consumer Research*, 8, 277–301.

Huffman C and Kahn BE (1998) Variety for sale: mass customization or mass confusion. *Journal of Retailing*, 74, 491–515.

Hughes AL (1999) Constructing competitive spaces: the corporate practice of British retailer–supplier relationships. *Environment and planning A*, 31, 819–839.

Humphrey J (2006) Policy implications of trends in agribusiness value chains. *European Journal of Development Research*, 18, 572–592.

IGD (1999) *Category Management in Action*. Letchmore Heath: Institute of Grocery Distribution.

IGD (2001) *A Guide of B2B Exchanges*. Letchmore Heath: Institute of Grocery Distribution.

Ingene CA and Parry ME (1995) Channel coordination when retailers compete. *Marketing Science*, 14, 360–377.

Jap SD (2002) Online reverse auctions: issues, themes, and prospects for the future. *Journal of the Academy of Marketing Science*, 30, 506–525.

Johansson U (2001) Retail buying: process, information and IT use: a conceptual framework. *International Review of Retail, Distribution and Consumer Research,* 11, 439–467.

Kahn BE and McAlister LM (1997) *Grocery Revolution: the New Focus on the Consumer.* Reading, MA: Addison Wesley.

Knox SD and White HFM (1991) Retail buyers and their fresh produce suppliers: a power dependency scenarios in the UK? *European Journal of Marketing,* 25, 40–52.

Kotzab H (2005) The automation of retail logistics. In H Kotzab and M Bjerre (eds) *Retailing in an SCP perspective.* Copenhagen: Copenhagen Business School Press, 114–159.

Kotzab H and Teller C (2003) Value adding partnerships and competition models in the grocery industry. *International Journal of Physical Distribution and Logistics Management,* 33, 268–281.

Kumar V (1996) The power of trust in manufacturer–retailer relationships. *Harvard Business Review,* 74(November–December), 92–106.

Kurt Salmon Associates (1993) *Efficient Consumer Response: Enhancing Consumer Value in the Grocery Industry.* Washington, DC: Food Marketing Institute.

Lee JKH and Steckel JH (1999) Consumer strategies for purchasing assortments within a single product class. *Journal of Retailing,* 75, 387–403.

Levy M and Weitz BA (2004) *Retailing Management,* 5th edn. New York: McGraw-Hill.

Lohtia R and Murakoshi T (1999) The adoption of efficient consumer response in Japan. *Journal of Marketing Channels,* 7, 1–28.

McGoldrick PJ (1987) A multidimensional framework for retail pricing. *International Journal of Retailing,* 2(2), 3–26.

McGoldrick PJ (2002) *Retail Marketing,* 2nd edn London: McGraw Hill.

Maltz E and Srivastava RK (1997) Managing retailer–supplier partnerships with EDI: evaluation and implementation. *Long Range Planning,* 30, 862–876.

Marr NE and Thomas WA (1999) The acceptance/rejection of new products in the retail grocery industry: the influence of background elements. *International Review of Retail, Distribution and Consumer Research,* 9, 187–202.

Martinelli E and Marchi G (2007) Enabling and inhibiting factors in adoption of electronic-reverse auctions: a longitudinal case study in grocery retailing. *International Review of Retail, Distribution and Consumer Research,* 17, 203–218.

Mattila AS and Wirtz J (2001) Congruency of scent and music as a driver of in-store evaluations and behaviour. *Journal of Retailing,* 77, 273–289.

Myers MB, Daugherty PJ and Autry CW (2000) The effectiveness of automatic inventory replenishment in supply chain operations: antecedents and outcomes. *Journal of Retailing,* 76, 455–481.

Neu J, Graham JL and Gilly MC (1988) The influence of gender on behaviours and outcomes in a retail–seller negotiation simulation. *Journal of Retailing,* 64, 427–450.

Neven D and Reardon T (2004) The rise of Kenyan supermarkets and evolution of their horticulture product procurement systems. *Development Policy Review*, 22, 669–699.

Nilsson J and Høst V (1987) *Reseller Assortment Decision Criteria*. Århus: Århus University Press.

Nogales AF and Suarez MG (2005) Shelf space management of private labels: a case study in Spanish retailing. *Journal of Retailing and Consumer Services*, 12, 205–216.

OECD (1999) *Buying Power of Multiproduct Retailers*. DAFFE/CLP(99)21 Paris: OECD.

Ogbonna E and Wilkinson B (1996a) Inter-organizational power relations in the UK grocery industry: contradictions and developments. *International Review of Retail, Distribution and Consumer Research*, 6, 395–414.

Ogbonna E and Wilkinson B (1996b) Information technology and power in the UK grocery distribution chain. *Journal of General Management*, 22(2), 30–35.

Ogbonna E and Wilkinson B (1998) Power relations in the UK grocery supply chain: developments in the 1990s. *Journal of Retailing and Consumer Services*, 5, 77–86.

O'Keeffe M and Fearne A (2002) From commodity marketing to category management: insights from the Waitrose category leadership program in fresh produce. *Supply Chain Management*, 7, 296–301.

Oubiña J, Rubio N and Yagüe MJ (2006) Relationships of retail brand manufacturers with retailers. *International Review of Retail, Distribution and Consumer Research*, 16, 257–275.

Pellegrini L and Zanderighi L (1991) New products: manufacturers' versus retailers' decision criteria. *International Review of Retail, Distribution and Consumer Research*, 1, 149–174.

Reardon T and Hopkins R (2006) The supermarket revolution in developing countries: policies to address emerging tensions among supermarkets, suppliers, and traditional retailers. *European Journal of Development Research*, 18, 522–545.

Reimer S and Leslie D (2004) Knowledge, ethics and power in the home furnishings commodity chain. In A Hughes and S Reimer (eds) *Geographies of Commodity Chains*. London: Routledge, 250–269.

Riddle EJ, Bradbard DA, Thomas JB and Kincade DH (1999) The role of electronic data interchange in quick response. *Journal of Fashion Marketing and Management*, 3, 167–184.

Robinson T and Clarke-Hill CM (1995) International alliances in European retailing. *International Review of Retail, Distribution and Consumer Research*, 5, 167–184.

Ruben R, Slingerland M and Nijhoff N (eds) (2006) *Agro-food Chains and Networks for Development*. Dordrecht: Springer (Kluwer).

Schmitz H and Knorringa P (2001) Learning from global buyers. *Journal of Development Studies*, 37, 177–205.

Shaw SA and Dawson J (1995) Organisation and control in retail buying groups. *Journal of Marketing Channels*, 4(4), 89–103.

Shaw SA, Dawson J and Blair L (1992) Imported foods in a British supermarket chain: buyer decisions in Safeway. *International Review of Retail, Distribution and Consumer Research*, 2, 35–57.

Shooshtari NH (1988) Retail trade associations: enhancing members power in relationships with suppliers. *Journal of Retailing*, 64, 199–214.

Simon H (1989) *Price Management*. Amsterdam: Elsevier.

Simonson I (1999) The effect of product assortment on buyer preferences. *Journal of Retailing*, 75, 371–386.

Skjoett-Larsen T, Thernoe C and Andresen C (2003) Supply chain collaboration: theoretical perspectives and empirical evidence. *International Journal of Physical Distribution and Logistics Management*, 33, 531–549.

Sternquist B (1994) Gatekeepers of consumer choice: a four country comparison of retail buyers. *International Review of Retail, Distribution and Consumer Research*, 4, 159–176.

Stoel LM (2002) Retail co-operatives: group size, group identification, communication frequency and relationship effectiveness. *International Journal of Retail and Distribution Management*, 30, 51–60.

Täger U Chr and Weitzel G (1991) *Purchasing Organisations*. CEC, DGxxiii, Series Studies, Commerce and Distribution, 19.

Thomas WA and Marr NE (1993) Evaluation of new products by New Zealand supermarket retail grocery buyers. *International Journal of Retail and Distribution Management*, 21, 19–28.

Underhill P (1999) *Why We Buy: the Science of Shopping*. New York: Simon and Schuster.

Vijayyasarathy LR and Tyler ML (1997) Adoption factors and electronic data exchange use: a survey of retail companies. *International Journal of Retail and Distribution Management*, 25, 286–292.

Voss GB and Seiders K (2003) Exploring the effect of retail sector and firm characteristics on retail price promotion strategy. *Journal of Retailing*, 79, 37–52.

Wall M, Sommers M and Wilcock A (1994)The retail buying of fashion goods: underlying themes of the sourcing process. *International Review of Retail, Distribution and Consumer Research*, 4, 177–179.

Wagner J, Ettenson R and Parrish J (1989) Vendor selection among retail buyers: an analysis by merchandise division. *Journal of Retailing*, 65, 58–79.

Whipple J S, Frankel R and Anselmi K (1999) The effect of governance structure on performance: a case study of efficient consumer response. *Journal of Business Logistics*, 20(2), 43–62.

Yalch RF and Spangenberg ER (2000) The effects of music in a retail setting on real and perceived shopping times. *Journal of Business Research*, 49, 139–147.

Yang M and Chen W (1999) A study on shelf space allocation and management. *International Journal of Production Economics*, 60–61, 309–317.

Yu JP and Pysarchik DT (2002) Economic and non-economic factors of Korean manufacturer–retailer relations. *International Review of Retail, Distribution and Consumer Research*, 12, 297–318.

Zenor MJ (1994) The profit benefits of category management. *Journal of Marketing Research*, 31, 202–213.

Editors' Commentary

PETER McGOLDRICK HAS SPENT his academic career of over thirty-five years pursuing retail research in the Manchester School of Management, UMIST and the Manchester Business School. He has been a significant contributor to the establishment of the academic discipline of retailing within the UK, publishing over 150 books and articles on retail topics. For many students he is perhaps best known for his major textbook *Retail Marketing*, the second edition of which appeared in 2002, some twelve years after the ground-breaking first edition. It remains one of the most thorough and detailed textbooks on the subject.

Peter McGoldrick's interests in retail research are eclectic, covering a wide range of topics including aspects of internationalization, pricing, technology use and retail design. He has always had close links with the retail industry and his research has been funded by major retailers as well as by research councils and governments. It is perhaps appropriate that his current professorial position is sponsored by Tesco. At Manchester he has been the founder and the Director of the Manchester Retail Research Forum, which involves several major retailers in the UK, and Co-Director of the International Centre for Retail Studies.

One of his main areas of research interest has been in pricing. Peter McGoldrick has done more work on this topic than any other British based retail researcher. One aspect of pricing is represented in the paper selected here – namely the retail 'sale'. His co-author Erica Betts worked with him on this project and a variety of others at UMIST as a visiting lecturer. Their joint work includes several papers on topics relating to pricing issues including work for the Office of Fair Trading and the Economic and Social Research Council (ESRC). The paper is drawn from a larger project funded by these bodies, that also included the doctoral dissertation of Erica Betts.

The paper provides a review of the concept and strategy of the retail 'sale' and shows how there are many different forms of sale, with different aims and objectives as well as outcomes in the minds of retailers and consumers.

Key Publications

McGoldrick PJ and Douglas RA (1983) Factors influencing the choice of supplier by grocery distributors. *European Journal of Marketing*, 17(5), 13–27.

McGoldrick PJ (1984) Grocery generics – an extension of the private label concept. *European Journal of Marketing*, 18, 5–24.

McGoldrick PJ (1987) A multidimensional framework for retail pricing. *International Journal of Retailing*, 2(2), 3–26.

McGoldrick PJ and Marks HJ (1987) Shoppers awareness of retail grocery prices. *European Journal of Marketing*, 21, 63–76.

McGoldrick PJ and Thompson MG (1992) *Regional Shopping Centres*. Aldershot: Avebury.

McGoldrick PJ (1994) *Cases on Retail Management*. London: Pitman.

McGoldrick PJ and Davies G (eds) (1995) *International Retailing: Trends and Strategies*. London: Pitman.

Liu H and McGoldrick PJ (1996) International retail sourcing: trend, nature and process. *Journal of International Marketing,* 4, 9–33.

Betts E and McGoldrick PJ (1996) Consumer behaviour and the retail 'sales': modelling the development of an attitude problem. *European Journal of Marketing,* 30, 40–58.

McGoldrick PJ (1998) Spatial and temporal shifts in the development of international retail images. *Journal of Business Research,* 42, 189–196.

McGoldrick PJ, Betts E and Wilson A (1999) Modelling consumer price cognition: evidence from discount and superstore sectors. *Service Industries Journal,* 19(1), 171–193.

McGoldrick PJ, Betts E and Keeling K (2000) High-low pricing: audit evidence and consumer preferences. *Journal of Product and Brand Management,* 9: 316–324.

McGoldrick PJ (2002) *Retail Marketing,* 2nd edn. London: McGraw Hill.

Mitchell V-W and McGoldrick PJ (2003) Consumer awareness, understanding and usage of unit pricing. *British Journal of Management,* 14: 173–187.

Newholm T, Keeling K and McGoldrick PJ (2004) Multi-story trust and online retailer strategies. *International Review of Retail, Distribution and Consumer Research,* 14: 437–456.

McGoldrick PJ and Collins N (2007) Multichannel retailing: profiling the multichannel shopper. *International Review of Retail, Distribution and Consumer Research,* 17: 139–158.

Website

http://www.mbs.ac.uk/research/academicdirectory/index.aspx?id=2100&action=ShowProfile

---

THE STRATEGY OF THE RETAIL 'SALE': TYPOLOGY, REVIEW AND SYNTHESIS

Erica Betts and Peter J. McGoldrick

With a history spanning over one hundred years, the seasonal 'sales' have been curiously neglected within the retailing and marketing literature. This major

From *The International Review of Retail, Distribution and Consumer Research,* Vol. 5, No. 3 (July 1995) © Routledge 1995.

element of retail pricing and promotion has received rather more attention within the cognate disciplines of psychology, economics and law. Only now are retail strategists giving the 'sales' a higher profile. A multidisciplinary review of salient contributions from within these disciplines is presented.

In order to address the problem of variable interpretation of a 'sale', a typology is developed, placing 'sales' within the wider context of promotional pricing. Price-reduction activities are positioned according to their duration and the proportion of the retail assortment involved. The paper concludes with an assessment of research priorities, including a thorough examination of the benefits, both 'hard' and 'soft', of retail 'sales' strategies.

Introduction

DURING THE 1980s, SHOPPING became a national sport, a hobby based upon collecting designer labels, electronic gadgetry and an endless stream of home improvements. Much of this was financed by consumer debt, under its new more socially acceptable name of credit, and paper gains in real estate. As consumer confidence approached consumer certainty, retailers contentedly traded-up in their over-designed stores, apparently oblivious to the accusations of 'forgetting' who their customers were.

By the end of the decade the picture had changed. The threat of unemployment moved up-market, mortgage arrears spiralled and the notion of negative equity became a widespread reality. With mounting concern over indebtedness and financial security, consumer attitudes towards spending altered accordingly. Continental discounters were quick to capitalize on this change of heart, leaving many domestic operators stranded with high-price merchandise ill-suited to the new mood of austerity. The scale and depth of mark-downs in the seasonal 'sales' reached epidemic proportions and, with no further improvement in the trading climate, the era of the perpetual 'sale' had arrived. Amid mounting consumer scepticism and cheapened store images, Armstrong (1992) reflected that:

> permanent mark-downs and frayed tags with meaningless reductions compounded by grubby, neglected displays have long extinguished the thrill (of the sales). . . . Prices have been slashed to such an extent – 50, 60 and even 70 per cent – that profits are minuscule. Look beyond the cheery 'Dress for less' and the desperate 'Dress for even less' signs and it's not hard to see undiluted panic.

For some years the term 'seasonal sale' became a misnomer, although a semblance of meaning has since been regained. However, it should not be assumed that this turnaround signifies an especially significant milestone in the long history of the 'sales'. According to the sociologist Prus (1986), the level and popularity of 'sale' activity has always been irregular and subject to wide variations. Hence, rather than the absolute level of 'sale' activity, it is the particular character, causes and antecedents of the variations which are of greater interest.

Researching the Retail 'Sale': a Multidisciplinary Framework

Although the era of the perpetual 'sale' may be coming to an end, it has high-lighted how little academic thought they have attracted from retail marketers. Despite being a major component of store pricing strategies, 'sales' have rarely received more than a cursory mention in most retailing texts, usually in the contexts of generating store traffic, clearing stock or simply demonstrating margin arithmetic. Instead, most research into the 'time dimension' of retail pricing (McGoldrick 1987) has been at the individual product level (e.g. Krishna *et al.* 1991), with a striking emphasis on grocery special offers. This situation has now started to change, with the rise of Everyday Low Pricing (EDLP) strategies prompting greater recognition of their antithesis: the 'high-low' pricing patterns typical of heavy 'sale' users. Fundamental issues, such as addressing what actually constitutes a 'sale', have still not been a great concern.

Some aspects of the 'sales' have, however, received rather more attention from other cognate disciplines. This paper reviews contributions from diverse areas of literature, identifying many varied influences on the level and character of 'sale' activity. These have been drawn together and contribute the majority of factors shown in Figure 1; the remaining elements are new propositions which have been established from the preliminary phases of this research programme. These phases have included discussions with retailers, interviews with Trading Standards Officers, examining relevant law case material and group discussions. The focus group discussions, held within Manchester's main shopping centre, were conducted with consumers shopping during the 1993 summer 'sales'.

Each factor in the framework is categorized as belonging to one of four levels: external environment, retailer, consumer psychology or consumer behaviour. The character of a 'sale' is influenced by interactions between factors, which may occur within the same level or between different levels. The opening paragraphs suggested some elementary interactions widely thought to have characterized the early 1990s: a recession (level 1) contributed to feelings of financial insecurity (level 3) and consumer spending fell (level 4). This provoked heavy markdowns from retailers (level 2), but consumers failed to respond and ultimately became tired and highly sceptical of 'never to be repeated' reductions which 'must end soon' but rarely did (level 3).

Obviously, this is a simplistic interpretation of recent events and one which scarcely warrants critical appraisal: it serves only to illustrate the process. Containing contributions from economics, psychology and the law, a management perspective and historical insights, the framework urges consideration of a much wider range of factors working in concert.

Historical Insights: the Evolution of the 'Sale'

The modern-day 'sale' has been evolving for over a century under various social, economic and legal forces. By the 1870s some retailers had begun to display fixed 'store prices' openly such that merchandise could be visibly marked-down. This, taken together with early forms of selfservice, meant that shoppers could

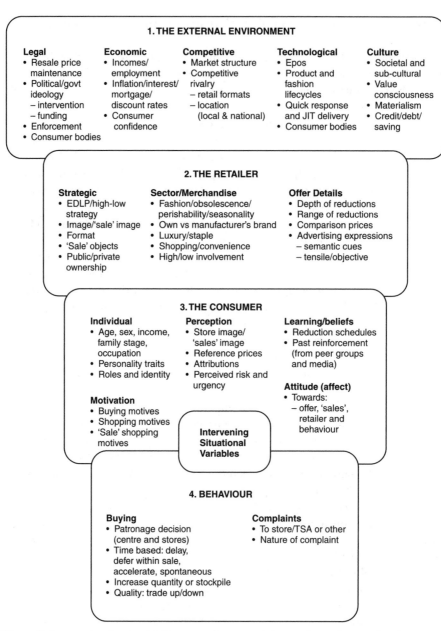

Figure 1 Interacting levels of influence: a framework for studying the retail 'sale'

actually look for bargains for the first time. Early department stores also helped develop the notion of fashion and obsolescence, moulding the tastes of the rising middle classes so that clothes, furniture and other goods were replaced when they were out-dated, not only when worn out (Davis 1966). Hence, shortening fashion cycles were already adding urgency to clearing out slower selling lines, while the expanding range of styles simultaneously increased the number of buying errors consigned to the reduced racks.

More recently, the abolition of resale price maintenance (RPM) in the UK in 1964 meant that retailers could no longer be penalized for contravening manufacturers' stipulated minimum resale prices in their 'sales'. Although RPM had not precluded 'sales', the Resale Prices Act 1964 succeeded in its intention to increase retail price competition, precipitating a vast amount of 'price comparison' advertising. Another era of the 'sale' had arrived:

> It is part of human nature that everyone likes to think they are getting a bargain. Thus the advertising is created to give the impression that what are in reality fairly normal prices are very low indeed. . . . If it can be shown that goods are offered at a price lower than something, then consumers will feel that they have got a good buy.
>
> (Bragg 1991)

The Management of Retail 'Sales'

The competitive environment

The change in 'sales' tempo described in the introductory paragraphs suggested more than the routine clearance of a few stubborn, slow-selling lines. Retailers spoke generally of anti-recessionary measures and stiff price competition became a norm in which 'sales' were an integral part. 'Sale' activity was far from uniform across retail sectors though. Retailers in the fiercely competitive DIY sector, for example, had been particularly badly afflicted by the crash in house prices. Adding over-capacity to high retail concentration, highly seasonal sales patterns and largely undifferentiated products, the 'sales' became a central part of the so-called 'price war'. In other sectors, such as grocery and clothing, price competition was provoked by an influx of Continental discounters. Their lower, more stable prices and 'bare bones' trading formats were well positioned to capitalize on the mood of austerity and rising value consciousness.

Retail image and positioning

While some prestige stores have long shunned the concept of 'sales', claiming that reduced prices would damage their credibility (James, Walker and Etzel 1975), such reservations should not be the sole preserve of prestige stores. Low prices, frequently associated with low quality (Gabor and Granger 1966), can be generalized across the store (Nystrom 1970) and customers become sceptical of the value of non-'sale' merchandise.

Although it is often intimated that a perpetual spotlight on prices can cheapen store image (Berry 1986; Buskirk and Buskirk 1979), few studies have actually mentioned the influence of 'sales' (Lindquist 1974). The failure to note that stores undergo a temporary change of image during a 'sale' is perhaps even more surprising. Shoppers in the discussion groups remarked upon stores possessing a completely different 'feel' during 'sales', not only with respect to the psychological aura of excitement, but also functional and tangible changes, such as lower levels of service, over-crowded aisles and displays, different customer profiles, bold price-led advertisements and old-fashioned or imperfect merchandise.

According to the behavioural perspective of store image (Kunkel and Berry 1968), these 'sale' characteristics lend a new identity by temporarily changing the customer's *'total conceptualised or expected reinforcement'* associated with a particular store. While retailers should be wary of assuming a full, automatic recovery of their former non-'sale' market position, the changes need be neither unfavourable nor permanent. As the Harrods' 'sale' demonstrates, when shoppers are able to discriminate between 'sale' and non-'sale' periods, the non-'sale' image is left relatively untarnished.

Retail strategies

Pre-'sale' prices were coming to be viewed as 'penalty' prices, paid only by those who were unwilling or too impatient to wait (Kaufmann *et al.* 1994). With consumers apparently tired of short-term price promotions and the necessity to shop around, discount and stable EDLP (Everyday Low Prices) strategies have become more prevalent. Recent years have also seen less extreme 'high-low' price fluctuations from retailers such as Next, which stockbrokers have praised as showing a discernibly more scientific and prudent approach to mark-downs. Even the Burton Group, whose improving fortunes were attributed in part to a co-ordinated strategy of '12 Hour Spectaculars', 'Blue Cross Sales' and other special price events (Skeel 1993), now aspire to a 'first price, right price' ideal, aided by Epos information technology and closer relationships with fewer, more responsive suppliers (Hoerner 1994).

Nevertheless, it would appear that mark-downs are still an inescapable facet of retail management. Many factors, other than the obvious fashion and product life cycles, impinge upon the retailers' ability to operate a pure EDLP strategy; these include product perishability, merchandise comparability, ticket size, consumer involvement, purchase frequency and customer boredom (Ortmeyer *et al.* 1991). 'Everyday Low Profits' can be a consequence too, when low price elasticities take their toll on margin arithmetic (Hoch *et al.* 1994).

Defining the retail 'sale'

The terminology used to depict these retail price events is far from satisfactory. As the extensive use of inverted commas suggests, referring to a 'sale' as such is inherently confusing in that all transactions are sales. Possibly in pursuit of clarification, although failing in this respect, the generic term has variously been pre-fixed by 'seasonal', 'special' and 'mark-down'. Given the duration and frequency of the events, few retailers can now lay claim to holding *seasonal* 'sales', whereas both a *special* and a *mark-down* 'sale' can refer to a price reduction on a single item, as well as departmental or store-wide reductions. The profusion of promotional titles used by retailers, such as 'closing-down sales', 'bank holiday sales', 'mid-season sales', etc., only compound the confusion.

In addition, where do 'sales' stop and 'price wars' begin? At the other end of the continuum, at what point could a collection of price promotions become a 'sale'? These ambiguities lead us to propose that two dimensions are central to discriminating between various types of 'sale' and other price promotions.

1   Store coverage (number of lines, departments, etc.). A minimum coverage is necessary to prevent promotions such as 'multibuys' and permanent reduced rails from qualifying as a 'sale'.
2   A temporal dimension. If, for example, reductions throughout the store become a requisite through definition, without a temporal dimension the daily peak load pricing tactics such as Debenhams' 'Early Bird' morning discounts and Littlewoods' 'Happy Hours', would become daily 'sales'.

Promotional objectives

Naturally, the process of designing appropriate price promotion objectives, strategic approaches and tactical manoeuvres should entail a rigorous examination of the competitive environment and the retailer's position within it. Yet, both the decision to hold a 'sale' and reduction schedules are frequently driven by competitors or habit, with no proactive content or objectives. These are unlikely to maximize the benefits of holding a 'sale' or minimize the costs incurred. Objective setting should acknowledge this and other considerations:

1   'sales' must have objectives consistent with the retailer's strategic objectives;
2   objectives are a prerequisite for evaluating success;
3   systematic evaluation would facilitate greater use of 'scientific' decision rules (e.g., timing, depth of reductions, assortment);
4   'sales' should be planned as one element of an integrated promotion, or communication, mix. Other promotion activities may achieve objectives more effectively than 'sales' (e.g., a loyalty programme, late night opening).

In this vein, James, Walker and Etzel (1975) proposed a framework (Figure 2) for judging the suitability of various 'special sales' (which can range from one to any number of items on offer) for attaining specific promotion objectives.

The model does not however rise to the challenge of classifying 'sales' or sales promotions. It does not contain a temporal dimension and, of course, retailers' motives are neither mutually exclusive nor easily identified; only a few 'sales', such as *closing-down 'sales'*, suggest clearly defined reasons. Others, such as *bank holiday 'sales'*, *clothing down 'sales'* (sic) and unadorned generic 'sales', give no indication of the retailer's motives.

Purposes of promotion	Type of special sales				
	Single item→	Limited number→ of items	Depart-mental→	Store-wide→	Joint/ mall wide
Sell specific offerings	XX	XXX	XXX	XX	X
Contribute to desired image	X	XX	X	XXX	XX
Generate shopper traffic	XXX	XXX	XX	X	XXX

Key

X   Not frequently associated
XX   Sometimes associated
XXX   Frequently associated

Figure 2 'Special sales' related to promotion purposes

Source: Adapted from James, Walker and Etzel (1975: 332)

The Economics of the Retail 'Sale'

Pricing, like most business decisions, is an art. But, continues Nagle (1984), neither art nor pricing are beyond critical judgement or scientific analysis. This section reviews a number of econometric models and empirical studies which suggest and test retailers' motives for holding 'sales'.

Intertemporal price discrimination

In economic terms, '*price discrimination is present when two or more similar goods are sold at prices that are in different ratios to marginal costs*' (Stigler 1987). More conventional definitions of price discrimination fail to recognize that different prices may simply reflect differing marginal costs (Varian 1989): additional transport costs, for example, must be passed on if the firm does not wish to discriminate against local customers. Since 'sales' involve price reductions over time, while marginal costs such as stockholding are rising simultaneously, they are a case of *intertemporal price discrimination*. The practice of using time as a medium for discrimination has been addressed only quite recently and, even then, prices are more frequently examined within Stokey's (1979) 'continuous time' framework (i.e., the adoption and diffusion paradigm). This is inappropriate for examining the 'jumpwise', rather than gradual, price changes character-izing retail 'sales' (van Praag and Bode 1992).

'Sales' are a form of second-degree price discrimination operationalized through a process of self-selection (e.g., Phlips 1988). This contrasts with the more familiar third-degree price discrimination, which addresses individual sub-market demand curves, such as old age pensioners and students. The rationale for price discrimination is to prevent individuals from acquiring goods or

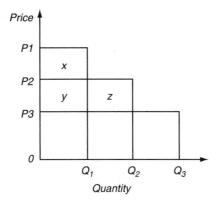

Figure 3 The diminishing consumer surplus

services for less than the highest price they are willing to pay (their reservation price). By avoiding average pricing, price discrimination decreases the consumer surplus which arises due to differences in reservation prices.

Figure 3 shows how charging an initial price of P_1 as opposed to P_2 will capture more of the consumer surplus for the quantity Q_1 (area x). The price can then be lowered to P_2, before lowering it to those marginal consumers willing to pay no more than P_3. The total consumer surplus captured by the retailer as a result of this sequence equals the area x + y + z.

The conditions necessary for price discrimination are widely discussed in many marketing and economics texts, e.g., customers must exhibit different intensities of demand (downward-sloping demand curve), the cost of administering the discriminatory pricing should not outweigh the extra revenue gained, etc., and will not be reiterated here. It is, however, necessary to note an additional condition unique to intertemporal price discrimination: retailers must have a lower discount rate, or be more patient, than consumers (Stokey 1979). The deregulation of financial markets in the 1980s allowed consumers to take on unprecedented levels of debt, while cultural values changed to embrace credit as a means to instant gratification. Patience was no longer a virtue, nor was credit seen socially as an admission of weakness or a lack of self-restraint. Retailers profited from 'sale' activity for some years, until levels of consumer debt and depreciating housing assets revived consumer hostility towards credit. The true cost of buying on the 'never never' became apparent (e.g., the APRs on store credit cards) and the appeal of paying back in 'tomorrow's devalued money' vanished with high interest rates: 'those who could afford to pay off debt found it a more attractive bargain than anything on offer in the shops' (Fildes 1993). As these changes simultaneously increased retailers' stockholding costs, the balance of patience shifted in the consumers' favour, violating the requirement for effective intertemporal price discrimination.

Econometric models

Price discrimination is addressed in a number of econometric models. Price promotions, Blattberg *et al.* (1981) suggest, discriminate against shoppers with high inventory costs. According to Varian, his 'Model of Sales' (1980) was the first work in economic theory to examine the retail 'sale'. Utilizing principles from spatial price dispersion and the economics of information (Salop and Stiglitz 1977; Shilony 1977), 'sales' effect arbitrary price changes to ensure that there will always be a pool of uninformed shoppers to discriminate against. Randomizing prices over time and space increases consumer search costs, preventing them from learning the whereabouts of the lowest prices. Hence, generating and sustaining price confusion allows retailers to retain a degree of monopoly power.

Van Praag and Bode (1992) assume that 'sales' are a standard marketing policy used to skim the consumer surplus. Their model explicitly considers three costs of holding a 'sale', promotion, repricing and service costs, i.e., staff having to attend to browsers with no intention of purchasing. It also considers the implications for price-reduction schedules, including the optimal number of reductions, the optimum price schedule and the length of different periods. They advocate extending the line of analysis to cover other types of cost, such as storage (discount rates) and purchase costs.

Lazear (1986) addressed the clearance motive, suggesting that retailers set new product prices in an arbitrary fashion on the basis of very little information. The level of sales provides feedback on how well the retailer gauged the nature of demand, and they employ Bayesian criteria to adjust prices accordingly. Knowing that it is a multi-period game creates a situation in which retailers need not risk underestimating reservation prices. This process, he alleges, results in predictable patterns of pricing and selling behaviour: the major theme being that prices start high and fall as a function of time on the shelf. Many extensions affect optimum price schedules, including market characteristics (e.g., the number of customers in a market, the proportion of genuine buyers versus window shoppers, prevailing discount rates) and product characteristics (e.g., perishability, fashionability, the threat of obsolescence, product heterogeneity and prior uncertainty about the product).

Explaining pricing practices: empirical studies

In addition to these econometric contributions, a number of empirical studies have addressed the 'sales'. According to Pashigian (1988), 'sales' can be conveniently classified as pre-season, within season or clearance. Of the three, he believes that 'clearance sales', disposing of last season's unpopular colours and styles, are the 'more familiar and somewhat easier to understand'. His empirical study credited fashion with being behind the dramatic increase in the frequency of 'sales' and the magnitude of percentage mark-ups. The growing importance of fashion and fewer well-accepted dress codes result in stores facing greater buying uncertainty and making more pricing mistakes. For example, men's clothes have historically cost less and been subject to fewer fashion fads than women's, but are simultaneously becoming more fashionable, more expensive and more likely to be substantially reduced. Although Pashigian conceded that mid-season 'sales' could not be explained by the 'clearance sale' theory, clearances do not have to be seasonally driven: retailers must constantly introduce new stock if they wish to encourage customers to make regular return visits.

Pashigian subsequently conducted an empirical examination of the relative importance of retailers' motives for putting shirts on 'sale' (Pashigian and Bowen 1991). Disregarding the rather weak regression results, 'price uncertainty' (Lazear) and 'price discrimination' (van Praag and Bode) proved the more useful of three explanations, but distinguishing between the two was problematic: some of the observed pricing practices could be explained by either and others by neither (such as large reductions at the beginning of the season). The 'peak load pricing' hypothesis proved least useful. 'Sales' were historically charged with the task of stimulating store traffic during slack periods, particularly during January, when poor weather and post-Christmas finances subdued spending. But such has been their success in this respect that January 'sale' shopping is now an institution in many countries. However, retailers have essentially only deferred the seasonal slumps, which they now seek to redress with other forms of 'dressed-up mark-downs'.

These economic models have served to help identify forces relevant to retailers' 'sale' pricing decisions, although 'real world violations' do preclude their use by price setters looking for prescriptive solutions. In particular, their rather simplistic vision of consumers as economic agents, assumptions of clear underlying economic motives behind 'sales' and the inability to contemplate less quantifiable 'soft' costs (e.g., overstretched staff, damage to image, etc.) must be questioned. However, being abstractions, economic models do hold constant variables which are not central to theoretical objectives and 'if one approaches economics expecting too much, one may well come away with too little' (Nagle 1984).

Economic psychology in the 'sales'

Economic psychology acknowledges that bounded rationality and utility optimization, rather than maximization, will introduce systematic behaviour disturbances into rigid 'laws' of economics (van Raaij 1981). For example, the supposition that all buying behaviour, from what to buy, when to buy it and in what quantity, somehow stems from the downward sloping demand curve is a highly spurious assumption (e.g. Scitovsky 1944). As demonstrated by the 'backward bending' demand curve (Monroe 1971), price is often used as an indication of quality in addition to cost. That consumers are aware of retail price schedules and learn to anticipate them is another limitation (e.g. Lazear 1986). Some shoppers in the discussion groups not only waited for the 'sales' but also tactically postponed purchases within them. How much these consumers were prepared to pay (the reservation price) was not so much the issue as how little they could manage to pay.

Equally, expected utility models are unable to take into account a host of context effects. Non-price and non-product variables which influence demand include mood states, time pressures, risk assessments and the framing of decisions (Schoemaker 1982; Thaler 1985; Tversky and Kahneman 1988; Urbany and

Dickson 1990). The influence of consumers' cognitive processes and context effects on behaviour are described below.

Psychology and the Retail 'Sales': Consumer Behaviour

Price perceptions

All forms of demand stimulation depend upon perception for their success (Kollat *et al.* 1970); as Jacoby and Olsen (1977) remark, 'external stimuli do not exert direct effects upon behaviour . . . [prices] must first be perceived and interpreted before they can affect decision processes and overt behaviour'.

Price threshold levels, or 'just noticeable differences' (JNDs), are typically the starting point for reviews of price perception. Based upon the Weber-Fechner Law, this proposes that the detectability of any change in a stimulus is a simple logarithmic function, or directly proportionate, to its initial magnitude. For a stimulus of low intensity or small size I (dim light, quiet sound, low price) a relatively small change would be noticeable, but a larger or stronger stimulus (high price) would need a larger change to be perceptible. However, if these 'psychophysics' of pricing (Kamen and Toman 1970) were accepted, retailers doing their utmost to draw attention to the most paltry of 'sale' reductions would disturb the natural detection thresholds. Hence, 'sale' reductions are more likely to pass through the perceptual filter, providing a partial explanation of why promotional elasticities are considerably higher than price elasticities (Blattberg and Neslin 1990).

Absolute price thresholds, referring to the relationship between price and response, are depicted in Gabor and Granger's (1966) 'buy response' curve and Monroe's (1971) 'price limit hypothesis'. They reveal both upper and *lower* price thresholds to show that products can be too cheap as well as too expensive to buy, due to the inferences of low quality which accompany low prices. In a retail 'sale', however, the same inferences may not apply. Consumers may infer higher quality from the previous higher price or, alternatively, they may adjust their perceptions of value in line with the lower price, using object attributions such as 'there must be something wrong with it' (attribution theories are generally concerned with how individuals look for reasons to explain events and behaviour). Lichtenstein *et al.* (1989) found the cynical product attributions to be more typical and Prus (1986) would appear to agree: 'Attempting to achieve cheapness and quality in a pile of leftovers, (shoppers) are inclined to be sceptical.' Attributions about the store, the person attributions studied by Lichtenstein *et al.* (1989), were less negative with regard to general discount claims. Shoppers were inclined to ascribe their behaviour to having to 'meet the competition' or wanting to generate more sales.

Reference prices

Little is actually known about how consumers encode (meaningfully perceive and retain) price information in the memory. However, it is widely maintained that past prices serve as cognitive reference points for future judgements and choice decisions (e.g. Jacoby and Olsen 1977). Applications of Helson's (1964) Adaptation Level (AL) theory suggest that this reference price will be a subjective average of previous price observations. Reference prices are dynamic, with each new price stimulus being averaged into the computation of a new AL (reference price). Thus, if the new stimulus (e.g. a 'sale' price) is lower than the prevailing AL, a lower reference price (AL) would be formed. Hence, regular pre-'sale' prices are left looking too high after repeated price promotions: the 'sale' price becomes the 'regular' price. Not all external reference prices are assimilated to influence price-based cognitions, implausible price claims will be contrasted or rejected (Urbany et al. 1988).

The notion of a reference price becomes notably more ambiguous on recognizing the variety of bases for comparison: some of the most common are prices last paid, prices of similar products, recommended prices and the comparison prices used by retailers in their 'sales' (Winer 1988). As consumers can use any of these price-based cognitions as reference points, they have been referred to as 'internal price standards' (Lichtenstein and Bearden 1989). Future expected prices also influence judgements of price acceptability (Jacobson and Obermiller 1990), highlighting the importance of consumers learning and anticipating reduction schedules (Groom 1994).

Retailers' comparison prices have been the subject of much controversy. Critics argue that manufacturers and retailers inflate 'regular' prices in order to exaggerate the perceived value of a price promotion. This, they allege, distorts the general level of market prices, damages the meaning of regular prices, destroys consumer trust and invites government interference (Berry 1986; Bragg 1991; Blair and Landon 1981; Fulop 1988; Liefield and Heslop 1985). Others maintain that comparison prices can be a valuable source of information, which consumers treat with due scepticism (e.g., Fry and McDougall 1974; Blair and Landon 1981) by 'discounting discounts' (sic) (Gupta and Cooper 1992). Such is their suspicion, according to Prus (1986), that shoppers are apt to exhibit signs of paranoia. The level of scepticism can be influenced by many factors, including:

(i)   contextual effects (e.g., prestige stores' claims are more credible than discounters': Barnes 1975; Biswas and Blair 1991);

(ii)   product characteristics (e.g., larger discounts needed on ownbrands than manufacturer's brands: Gupta and Cooper 1992);

(iii) the semantic cue, i.e., the phrase used in the comparison, such as 'as £x . . . now only £y' or 'seen elsewhere for £z' (Lichtenstein et al. 1991);

(iv)   vague or 'tensile' price advertising (e.g., 'save up to 50 per cent on selected lines') provides less useful information, leading to greater scepticism (Mobley et al. 1988); discounting of tensile price claims is also affected by the width of the discount bands used (e.g., '25 per cent to 50 per cent off') (Biswas and Burton 1993, 1994).

Scepticism is also a personality trait and, as Inman et al. (1990) determined, an individual's 'need for cognition' (to understand the causes of behaviour and events) does influence the extent to which special offer cues are processed.

Motivation: 'why do people shop' in the 'sales'?

> At this time of year the entire nation is on a buying frenzy, rooting out bargains, rummaging for discounts and pouncing on anything marked '50 per cent off' even if the item is not needed.
>
> (Lonsdale 1995)

Despite tales of cynical consumers and depressed retail spending, every year newspapers carry similar stories of shoppers' exploits in the January 'sales'. This enthusiasm for the 'sales' is not a peculiarly modern phenomenon either. Speaking of the turn of the century, Adburgharm (1964) noted that:

> Sales were an excitement that even wealthy women could not resist
> . . . 'the carriages which fill up the streets during the sales are a serious impediment to locomotion', wrote one spoil-sport contemporary.

Contemplating 'Why do people shop?', Tauber (1972) recognized that buying motives are 'but a partial and insufficient basis' for shopping behaviour. Many other researchers have since addressed the issue (e.g. Westbrook and Black 1985; Buttle 1992) and modified Tauber's typology of social and personal shopping motives. However, it was not their intention to capture the unusual spirit of the 'sales' or the driving forces behind the 'bargain mentality'. The group discusssions, mentioned briefly above, addressed these specific issues.

Recruited while shopping in the 'sales' and with full knowledge of the topic for discussion, shoppers agreeing to participate were generally interested and involved in the agenda. Given the exploratory nature of this phase, a degree of 'special interest' bias was, if anything, considered preferable. Shoppers were recruited immediately prior to the discussions to facilitate more accurate recall of their thoughts and emotions. The groups comprised both men and women, from adolescents to pensioners, and since participants had been approached in up-, mid- and down-market shopping districts, the cross-section of socio-economic profiles encouraged a range of contrasting perspectives.

Transaction and acquisition utility

One shopper declared that the bargain was in itself reason enough to shop in the 'sales':

> We shop in the 'sales' because we want the bargains, that's why! You're getting the thing cheaper than the normal price, it gives you a lift. . . . Why? Why does anything give you a lift? – I'm not a psychologist!

Writers have long acknowledged that consumers may pride themselves on buying bargains, regardless of quality (e.g. Sampson 1964). Thaler (1985) termed this type of psychological satisfaction 'transaction utility', which depends 'purely on the perceived merits of the "deal" ' (Thaler 1985). Hence it will be satisfaction related to the difference between the internal reference price and the price paid. The accompanying 'acquisition utility' bears more resemblance to value consciousness, being concerned with acquiring the product's need-satisfying attributes; it is 'the value of the good received compared to the outlay' (Thaler 1985).

Price reductions affect both types of utility, but not all consumers equally. However, determining to what extent a 'sale' shopper is motivated by each of the two utility components is not an easy distinction to make (e.g. Lichtenstein *et al.* 1990). Price reductions appeal to value-conscious shoppers as well as those who attach a higher subjective weight to the merit of the deal. Both are looking for bargains, but what constitutes a good buy will be interpreted quite differently, even if they have the same functional needs.

Transaction and acquisition utility serve a largely descriptive function; they do not amount to a full explanation of why bargains, or the 'sale' shopping activity, can be so appealing. A range of explanations were forthcoming from the discussion groups:

1   Excitement: 'I would love to go to the one in Harrods, it's not a matter of spending, it's just the madness of it, it's a dream.'
2   Fear of missing out: 'I'm going to make sure I get my fair share of whatever it is. Presuming I want it.' Shorter time limits within which to respond and the apparent excess of shoppers over desirable items intensify the perceived urgency to act (Prus 1986).
3   Camaraderie: sharing a common purpose and interest: 'You're with people like you, who are hunting for bargains, you can have a good laugh together.'
4   Competition: 'If someone finds something which someone else wants too, they'll tear it apart . . . It's dog eat dog.' 'My husband says he has never seen women so violent in all his life. He said it was worse than a football match!' A competitive element arises between friends and family too: 'We all boast about our bargains, to your family, friends, anyone.' Some shoppers also enjoy 'Getting one up on the shop-keeper.'
5   Guilt relief: 'When I spend money I feel guilty, but when I get a bargain I don't.' Another group member suggested parallels with the competitive element: 'If friends spend a fortune on a dress, they wouldn't tell you. But if it was a bargain, they would tell everyone.' Shoppers also felt less guilty if they bought for others too.
6   Transaction and acquisition utility: economy and self-satisfaction with getting a 'bargain'. Most respondents touched upon the recurrent theme of 'feeling clever.'

Even the well-seasoned shoppers, fully aware that the 'bargain' which hangs in the wardrobe unworn is no bargain at all, still made some mistakes. These apparently became fewer with age, as shoppers learn that buying things to slim into, or which they plan to wear when they come back into fashion, rarely proves to be good value for money. Respondents believed that with age they had become less impulsive and generally less influenced by fashion.

The ability to 'save' money, even while spending it, gives some shoppers a sense of freedom from their usual inhibitions about spending. Respondents 'saving' on one item felt more entitled to purchase others, and with the first bargain in the bag, shoppers' minds are open to the idea of buying (i.e., they 'drift'). Self-perception (Bem 1967), another attribution theory, could help to explain the comparative ease with which people spend money in 'sales'. Ill-considered purchases can be attributed to, or justified by, the 'sale', which is an external factor which does not reflect on the individual. For example, frivolous or unaffordable purchases may be justified by: 'I had to buy it, they were practically giving it away in the "sale" ', rather than accepting an internal lack of judgement or control. This theory, Bem proposes, is an 'alternative interpretation of cognitive dissonance phenomena', lessening the discomfort associated with incongruent attitudes and behaviour.

Money burnt a proverbial hole in the pockets of a small number of shoppers, adhering to 'the more you spend the more you save' philosophy. It could be suggested that these 'shopaholic', or 'compulsive consumption', tendencies are a social problem exposed if not actually exacerbated by the 'sales'. The most diligent 'bargain hunters' guarded themselves against ever having to pay more than the absolute minimum by saving receipts and obtaining refunds on merchandise subject to further reductions. Neither were such practices confined to the self-labelled 'professional sale shoppers'; the underhand behaviour was justified by the extortionate initial mark-ups which still enabled retailers to 'make a profit after slashing prices by 50 per cent'. The value these shoppers place on their time would appear to be exceptionally low, but search 'costs' are often part of the fun (e.g. Mamorstein et al. 1992).

Clothes were generally perceived to be the most satisfying 'sale' shop, but few missed out on the opportunity to anticipate or accelerate the purchase of next year's Christmas decorations, cards, presents or birthday gifts. Deferring purchasing was an equally popular strategy.

Is 'A Bargain *Always* A Bargain?': Consumer Protection

That 'bare words make no bargain' could have been written for the 'sales'. Inflated 'high-low' prices are just one of many well-practised deceptions. At the turn of the century, retailers were already buying-in consignments of cheap goods specifically for the 'sales' and advertising bankrupt or fire-damaged stock at 'Sacrificial Reductions' (Adburgham 1964). With respect to prices, the trading principle of 'caveat emptor' ('let the buyer beware') has now been succeeded by the 'truth in price claims' doctrine in all EC countries. However, their legislation remains disparate. Variations have been described in terms of direction (Reich and Micklitz 1980): the UK's 'informed market approach' (OFT 1992) being relatively *positive* in its approach, advocating that consumers be provided with information to allow informed assessment. In contrast, German legislation illustrates the *negative* direction, restricting reduction activities to certain dates at the end of each season.

While measures akin to those in Germany would be welcomed by independent retailers in the UK, feeling pressurized by multiples to commence their 'sales' too early (*Drapers' Review* 1992), the UK government would not contemplate this degree of anti-competitive interference. It unduly burdens wealth creators (OFT 1992) and, as the 1962 Molony Report argued, the taxpayer too, who ultimately pays for the enforcement bureaucracies established to protect them (Harvey and Parry 1992). Furthermore, the Government remains particularly unconvinced that detailed legislation will solve problems in the area of price comparisons (OFT 1992).

The UK legal framework

Traders who deceive the public by giving false or misleading price indications, or indulge in dubious price comparisons, have been the target of legislation since the 1968 Trade Descriptions Act. This was needed in part to redress the torrent of deceptive, if not totally dishonest, comparison prices following the abolition of RPM, but the 1959 Molony Committee on Consumer Protection had already heard evidence of 'widespread misrepresentation . . . especially at times of the seasonal or special sales'. The Molony Report expressed particular exception to the practice of quoting comparative prices for goods not previously stocked, and to the use of 'worth £x' or 'value £x' used in conjunction with 'our price only £y' (O'Keefe 1993). Section 11 of the 1968 Act endeavoured to deal with the mischief by creating two comparison price offences.

1   False comparisons with a recommended price: the only valid comparisons were to be with those suggested by manufacturers and suppliers. However, this probably served to escalate rather than deter the practice of manufacturers setting unrealistically high recommended prices (Lowe and Woodroffe 1991). Such deceptions, perpetrated at the time of setting the original price, are particularly difficult to legislate against.
2   False comparisons with the trader's own previous prices: these could be made only if the higher price had been charged for 28 consecutive days in the previous six months. Such rules, including the former US requirement that a certain percentage of sales had occurred at the previous price, are designed to simplify the prosecution procedure (Kaufmann *et al.* 1994).

However, some of the 1962 Molony Report's recommendations went unheeded and numerous loopholes and the enthusiastic use of disclaimers meant that 'the 1968 Act was limited in its scope and easily avoided. The attempt made to bolster it by the Price Marking (Bargain Offers) Orders 1979, was little better' (Bragg 1991). Both were subsequently repealed by the Consumer Protection Act 1987, within which the current law is embodied. Part III of the Act broke with tradition and introduced a general offence of giving a misleading price indication, hoping that a more flexible approach would be able to cope with constantly changing commercial practices and 'marketing' techniques (Lowe and Woodroffe 1991).

Still, the Office of Fair Trading (OFT), the National Consumer Council

(NCC) and local Trading Standards Officers (TSOs) have all voiced disquiet with the 1987 provisions. The NCC (1990) is pressing for a number of reforms, concerning issues such as 'closing down sales' when retailers immediately 're-open' in another name, in either the same or different premises. The abundance of cheap, short leases encouraged this practice, as bankruptcies and new retail property developments flooded the market with excess retail space.

Law enforcement and the Trading Standards Authorities

The principal source of controversy, however, appears to be the difficulty of enforcement (e.g. OFT 1992; Bragg 1991). The burden of proof is placed squarely on the local Trading Standards Authorities (TSAs), which require 'reasonable grounds' for suspicion in order to detain goods and request access to retailers' records. As retailers are unsurprisingly reticent about co-operating, TSAs may have to monitor traders' prices for up to six months (OFT 1992). The odds against this process uncovering untoward practices are extremely high, and the method is prohibitively expensive for some authorities.

Interviews with Trading Standards Officers (TSOs) verified that most pricing work is indeed reactive, although there was a marked lack of uniformity concerning enforcement between authorities (e.g. Circus 1988). One TSA had not secured any pricing convictions since the Code of Practice on Price Indications came into effect in 1989, while another, characterized by more generous financial backing and, possibly as a consequence, a less defeatist outlook, had obtained over twenty. The two examples below typify the reactive nature of their successful prosecutions and the importance of public support:[1]

(a)   Halfords' 'clearance' prices were unchanged from earlier prices. 'Clearance', the chain claimed, referred to the end of a line. The company pleaded guilty to having used words which, in their normal, everyday use, are likely to give the impression that a comparison is being made. A prospective buyer noticed the claim after having studied prices for some time.

(b)   A local resident, always making a note of petrol prices when buying from his local garage, was able to give a TSO 'reasonable grounds' for suspicion that the station had falsely claimed reduced petrol prices.

Enforcement is further hampered by the *Code of Practice for Traders on Price Indications* (DTI 1988), which contains no criminal or civil liability. Sanctioned by the 1987 Act to give practical guidance to promote desirable practice, it is widely perceived by TSOs as being 'poorly drafted and having no "teeth" ' (TSO).

Legal definition of a 'sale'

Central to UK retail 'sale' legislation is the 'price comparison', or 'any indication . . . that the price at which something is offered to consumers is less than or equal to some other price' (DTI 1988). Under the 1987 Consumer Protection Act, an item of *merchandise* in a 'sale' exhibiting a comparison price is subject to the 28-day/six-month rule. However, far less clear is what constitutes a *store* in 'sale'. A representative of the Consumers' Association declared that: 'There is no legal definition of the word "sale". There is nothing to stop shops from having all year round "sales" and "closing down sales" which last for several years' (Richards 1995). However, it can be inferred from the Code of Practice that, because traders 'should not use general notices, e.g., "up to 50% off" unless they apply to at least 10% (by quantity) of the merchandise on offer', a store claiming to hold a 'sale' must feature reductions on 10 per cent of its merchandise.

Given this complexity, it is unsurprising to find that shoppers in the discussion groups had little knowledge of either the rules or their rights in the 'sales', a finding which concurs with expert opinion on the issue (Combe 1994; Consumers' Association 1994; Lonsdale 1995). Most of the shoppers did not hold their beliefs with conviction, amassing a fragmented picture from friends, newspapers and problem pages in magazines. Others were more assertive, if not actually better informed: 'You get to know these things when you're a serious shopper.'

Unsure of what constitutes an offence or to whom to report it (only one respondent was able to identify a relevant complaint authority) consumers rarely lodge the complaints that TSAs need to establish a breach of law. Often grievances are directed to the retailer concerned for immediate settlement (preferably financial); many are reluctant to admit their gullibility and few expected the outcome to justify the effort. One participant believed that the public should not have to complain and would 'not do the law's job for them'; another expected honesty in price claims from well-known stores. Some shoppers believed that they could protect themselves by recognizing quality, rather than being guided by pre-sale prices.

The lack of complaints is perceived to be a serious problem for legislators too, who need them to generate more effective legislation (Lowe and Woodroffe 1991). Legislation has indeed failed to address the inferences consumers may make from price comparison information (e.g., a competitive price, a 'fair' price or a penalty price paid only by those unwilling or unable to wait), which essentially determines whether or not a price indication has been misleading (Kaufmann *et al.* 1994). Clearly, individuals are not as 'informed' as the positive approach may require to provide a satisfactory level of protection. For the foreseeable future at least, 'sale' shoppers would appear well advised by the proverb: 'at a great bargain, pause.'

Towards a Definition and Classification of Retail 'Sales'

In economics, 'sales' saw prices starting high and falling as a function of time on the shelf. As such, buying in specials, promoting 'seconds' and ex-bankrupt stock do not qualify. The law appears inclined to agree. Comparison prices, intrinsic to legal 'sale' activity, must be the trader's own previous price. Although the law does not explicitly state what constitutes a 'sale', it does contain the six-month/28-day temporal qualification for items of merchandise and a 10 per cent store coverage (by quantity) recommendation. By inference, below this 10 per cent level, the 'sale' would be a line of price promotions. Thus, both disciplines appear to be describing the clearance 'sale', rather than competitive discounting or other special price promotions. Shoppers too still describe 'real sales' as being the 'summer' and 'winter' events, in line with clearance theory.

Positioning of price promotions

However, to construct a too narrow definition of the retail 'sale' would be to ignore the rich diversity of pricing practices which have evolved under this title. It would also fail to recognize that temporary price reduction activities are often distinguishable only by degree along common continua. A more constructive approach is therefore to conceptualize the range of price promotion activities in a positioning chart, using the temporal and store coverage dimensions. Figure 4 portrays these as areas instead of points, although these positions are still highly subjective and will clearly vary according to the product, retail sector and company policy.

The broken line cutting across the '% of lines' axis represents the minimum legal condition. Temporary special price promotions on selected lines, such as multibuys and longer-term loss leaders, are both placed below this 10 per cent threshold level. 'Happy Hours', used to boost trade during non-peak periods, are the shortest of the price promotions. The proportion of the store's merchandise included does tend to be reasonably high, although variable, both in Happy Hours and in 'Special Events'. Special Events differ in that they tend to be measured in days rather than hours; '12 Hour Spectaculars', 'Blue Cross Events' (Burton Group) and '3 Day Spectaculars' (House of Fraser) are among them. The 'Traditional Seasonal Sale' is of a somewhat longer duration, often because a series of reductions is required to achieve the clearance of old stock. The proportion of merchandise covered will be dependent on many factors, such as the trading climate, the level of initial prices and the success of the store buyers in anticipating popular lines and styles. The position of the 'Closing-Down Sale' is largely self-explanatory: 'All Stocks Must Go' and reasonably quickly.

'Discounters' have been positioned in the bottom right quadrant to put their price positioning into perspective, rather than to suggest that these are temporary price promotions. It serves to distinguish these retailers from 'Perpetual Sales', which appear to be of endless duration and can include a large proportion of the retailer's stock.

Sector differences

There are of course variations in the types of retail 'sale' prevailing across different retail sectors, which would be observable on the positioning maps. The concept of obsolescence inherent in many of the econometric models is clearly

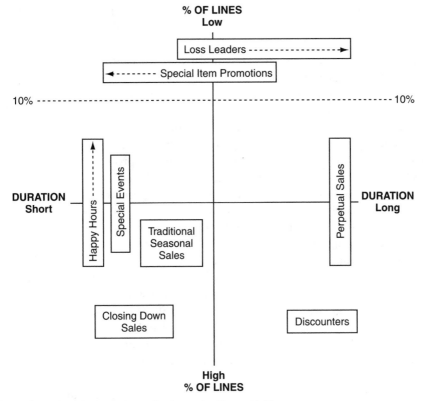

Figure 4 Authors' perceptions of price reduction activities

of relevance in fashion sectors, bringing about a large number of clearance 'sales'. It may also be applicable to electrical appliance retailing, where even very minor technological advances result in manufacturers bringing out new lines.

The risk of obsolescence can scarcely explain the profuse 'sale' activity in the DIY sector, especially in the 'heavy side' chains. As suggested earlier, their 'sales' roots are probably more firmly in the fiercely competitive environment. That grocery supermarkets utilize loss leaders and an array of short-term price promotions is possibly a consequence of the perishability of the goods, less enthusiasm for the shopping occasion on the part of the consumer and relatively low-margin/low-ticket items which provide little scope for 'bargains' (low transaction utility). Thus, the characteristics of the merchandise and the marketing environment tend to influence the nature of the price promotions used.

Summary and Research Directions

From this interdisciplinary review and the preliminary research undertaken, it has been possible to draw certain conclusions as to the major research priorities in this area. Some progress has been made towards establishing a framework for examining the determinants of the level and character of 'sale' activity. Events of the more recent past in the UK have been used to support major propositions within this framework. While these developments are noteworthy, they should not be viewed as unique or as a norm for judging other phases of 'sale' activity. Much work remains to be done on the framework; in particular, there is a need to recognize events of the early and mid-twentieth century and more of the causes of international differences.

Progress has also been made towards a framework able to withstand retailers' variable interpretation of what constitutes a 'sale', at least in the UK. The 'sale' has been placed into context within a framework of retail price promotions, and an initial attempt made to apply it to exploring the patterns of 'sales' across industry sectors, market positioning and promotion objectives.

Objectives are central to judgements of the efficiency of 'sales'. This was approached from a multidisciplinary angle, requiring scrutiny of the 'soft' costs and benefits in addition to the 'hard' quantifiable areas discussed by economists. Retailers should consider the costs and benefits of each type, such as those shown in the matrix of Figure 5.

From the consumer behaviour angle, some early steps towards a classification of 'sale' shopping motivations have been made. These are currently being expanded upon and a programme of empirical testing is being proposed. A further research priority is to develop the typology of behavioural responses to 'sales'; our preliminary qualitative research has indicated a wide range of responses, involving the time-based buying adjustments, and changes in both quality and quantity. A major challenge will be to model the determinants of these response patterns.

Opportunities clearly exist to evaluate contrasting legal frameworks with regard to retail 'sales'. Even within the countries of the EU, contrasts exist between the 'negative approach', which tries to forbid false and misleading price claims, and the 'positive approach', which aims to ensure that the consumer has

	COSTS	BENEFITS

HARD	Repricing
	Service costs
	Display materials
	Advertising
	Opportunity costs
		Clears old stock
		Increases market share
		Increases visits to store,
		    transactions, sales volume
		    and/or profits
		Contributions from
		    manufacturers

SOFT	Overstretched staff
	Cheapens store image
	Cheapens own brand
	    image (if applicable)
	Customer disappointment
	Encourages price sensitivity
	Discourages loyalty
	Damage to supplier
	    relationships possible
		Gives competitive image
		Publicity and word-of-
		    mouth recommendations
		Customer satisfaction

Figure 5 'Cost benefit analysis'

all the information necessary. Such an evaluation would necessarily require four perspectives, namely, those of consumers, policy creators, legislation enforcers and retailers. Opportunities also exist to re-examine the American work on 'semantic cues' and 'tensile price claims' within alternative legal frameworks.

While the opportunities for research in this field are clearly numerous, it is hoped that this review will have achieved at least three objectives. Firstly, the intention has been to highlight a serious gap within the retailing and marketing literature. Secondly, we have drawn the attention of researchers and practitioners to the contributions made within the cognate disciplines of economics, law and cognitive psychology. Thirdly, an attempt has been made to present a typology of price reduction activities, capable of withstanding the variable definitions of 'sales'.

Note

1   These prosecutions provide a flavour of more 'everyday' law enforcement; for details of the relevant case law see O'Keefe's, a rigorous and regularly updated directory used by professionals involved with the legalities of consumer protection, or, more generally, recent trade descriptions texts such as Bragg (1991).

References

Adburgham, A. (1964) *Shops and Shopping, 1800–1914*, London: Allen & Unwin, pp. 232–43.

Alderson, W. (1963) 'Administered prices and retail grocery advertising', *Journal of Advertising Research*, 3(1): 2–6.

Armstrong, L. (1992) 'When the shopping had to stop', *The Independent on Sunday*, 19 January: 36–7.

Barnes, J.G. (1975) 'Factors influencing consumer reaction to retail newspaper "sale" advertising', in E. Maze (ed.) *1975 Combined Proceedings*, Chicago: American Marketing Association, pp. 471–7.

Bem, D.J. (1967) 'Self-perception: an alternative interpretation of cognitive dissonance phenomena', *Psychological Review*, 74(3): 183–200.

Berry, L. (1986) 'Multidimensional strategies can combat price wars', *Marketing News*, 31: 10.

Biswas, A. and Blair, E.A. (1991) 'Contextual effects of reference prices in retail advertisements', *Journal of Marketing*, 55(3): 1–12.

Biswas, A. and Burton, S. (1993) 'Consumer perceptions of tensile price claims in advertisements: an assessment of claim types across different discount levels', *Journal of the Academy of Marketing Science*, 21(3): 217–29.

Biswas, A. and Burton, S. (1994) 'An experimental assessment of effects associated with alternative tensile price claims', *Journal of Business Research*, 29(1): 65–73.

Blair, E.A. and Landon Jr., E.L. (1981) 'The effects of reference prices in retail advertisements', *Journal of Marketing*, 45(2): 61–9.

Blattberg, R.C. and Neslin, S.A. (1990) *Sales Promotion: Concepts, Methods, and Strategies*, Englewood Cliffs, NJ: Prentice-Hall.

Blattberg, R.C., Eppen, G.D. and Lieberman, J. (1981) 'A theoretical and empirical evaluation of price deals for consumer nondurables', *Journal of Marketing*, 45(1): 116–29.

Bragg, R.G. (1991) *Trade Descriptions*, Oxford: Clarendon Press, pp. 111–48.

Buskirk, R.H. and Buskirk, B.D. (1979) *Retailing*, New York: McGraw-Hill, p. 340.

Buttle, F. (1992) 'Shopping motives: a constructionist perspective', *Service Industries Journal*, 12(3): 349–67.

Circus, P. (1988) 'Consumer law enforcement: a national trading standards service?', *Business Law Review*, 9(1): 20–1.

Combe, V. (1994) 'New trading Act to solve sale worries', *Daily Telegraph*, 31 December: 8.

Consumers' Association (1994) 'Bogus bargains', *Which?*, May: 20–3.

Davis, D. (1966) *A History of Shopping*, London: Routledge & Kegan Paul, pp. 256–9, 288–97.

Department of Trade and Industry (1988), *Code of Practice for Traders on Price Indications*, DTI/Pub 266/10K12/92/R.

Drapers' Review (1992) 'Retailers call for sale rules', *Drapers' Review*, 1 January.

Eiser, J.R. (1980) *Cognitive Social Psychology*, London: McGraw-Hill.

Fildes, C. (1993) 'Wars in the stores are no flash in the pan', *Daily Telegraph*, 5 November: 22.

Fry, J.N. and McDougall, G.H. (1974) 'Consumer appraisal of retail price advertisements', *Journal of Marketing*, 38(3): 64–74.

Fulop, C. (1988) 'Public policy and a marketing technique 1969–1985: comparative pricing and bargain offer claims' in E. Kaynak (ed.) *Transnational Retailing*, Berlin: De Gruyter, pp. 197–207.

Gabor, A. and Granger, C.W.J. (1966) 'Price as an indicator of quality', *Economica*, 33: 43–70.

Gupta, S. and Cooper, L.G. (1992) 'The discounting of discounts and promotion thresholds', *Journal of Consumer Research*, 19(3): 401–11.

Groom, A. (1994) 'Watch, wait, pounce', *The Financial Times Weekend*, 8/9 January: ix.

Harvey, B.W. and Parry, D.L. (1992) *The Law of Consumer Protection and Fair Trading*, London: Butterworths.

Helson, H. (1964) *Adaptation Level Theory*, New York: Harper & Row.

Henley Centre/Chartered Institute of Marketing (1993) *Metamorphosis in Marketing*, London.

Hoch, S.J., Dreze, X. and Purk, M.E. (1994) 'EDLP, hi-lo, and margin arithmetic', *Journal of Marketing*, 58(4): 16–27.

Hoerner, J. (1994) *The Burton Group plc: Report and Accounts 1994*, The Burton Group plc, pp. 6–7.

Inman, J.J., McAlister, L. and Hoyer, W.D. (1990) 'Promotional signal: proxy for a price cut?', *Journal of Consumer Research*, 17(1): 74–81.

Jacobson, R. and Obermiller, C. (1990) 'The formation of expected future price: a reference price for forward looking consumers', *Journal of Consumer Research*, 16(4): 420–32.

Jacoby, J. and Olsen, J.C. (1977) 'Consumer response to price: an attitudinal, information processing perspective', in Y. Wind and M.G. Greenberg (eds) *Moving Ahead with Attitude Research (Proceedings of 7th Annual AMA Conference)*, Chicago: American Marketing Association, pp. 73–86.

James, D.L., Walker, B.J. and Etzel, M.J. (1975) *Retailing Today*, New York: Harcourt Brace Jovanovich, pp. 59–60, 317–18, 332.

Kamen, J.M. and Toman, R.J. (1970) 'Psychophysics of prices', *Journal of Marketing Research*, 7(1): 27–35.

Kaufmann, P.J., Smith, N.C. and Ortmeyer, G.K. (1994) 'Deception in retailer high-low pricing: a "rule of reason" approach', *Journal of Retailing*, 70(2): 115–38.

Kollat, D.T., Blackwell, R.D. and Engel, J.F. (1970) *Research in Consumer Behaviour*, New York: Holt, Rinehart & Winston, p. 48.

Krishna, A., Currim, I.S. and Shoemaker, R.W. (1991) 'Consumer perceptions of promotional activity', *Journal of Marketing*, 55(2): 4–16.

Kunkel, J.H. and Berry, L.L. (1968) 'A behavioural concept of retail images', *Journal of Marketing*, 32(4): 21–7.

Lazear, E.P. (1986) 'Retail pricing and clearance sales', *American Economic Review*, 76(1): 14–32.

Lichtenstein, D.R. and Bearden, W.O. (1989) 'Contextual influences on perceptions of merchant-supplied reference prices', *Journal of Consumer Research*, 16(1): 55–66.

Lichtenstein, D.R., Bloch, D.R. and Black, W.C. (1988) 'Correlates of price acceptability', *Journal of Consumer Research*, 15(2): 243–52.

Lichtenstein, D.R., Burton, S. and O'Hara, B.S. (1989) 'Marketplace attributions and consumer evaluations of discount claims', *Psychology and Marketing*, 6(3): 163–80.

Lichtenstein, D.R., Netemeyer, R.G. and Burton, S. (1990) 'Distinguishing coupon proneness from value conciousness: an acquisition-transaction utility theory perspective', *Journal of Marketing*, 54(3): 54–67.

Lichtenstein, D.R., Burton, S. and Karson, E.J. (1991) 'The effect of semantic cues on consumer perceptions of reference price ads', *Journal of Consumer Research*, 18(3): 380–91.

Liefield, J. and Heslop, L. (1985) 'Reference prices and deception in consumer advertising', *Journal of Consumer Research*, 11(4): 868–76.

Lindquist, J.D. (1974) 'Meaning of image: a survey of empirical and hypothetical evidence', *Journal of Retailing*, 50(4): 29–38, 116.

Lonsdale, S. (1995) 'Buyers all beware', *Daily Telegraph*, 9 January: 14.

Lowe, R. and Woodroffe, G.F. (1991) *Consumer Law and Practice*, 3rd edition, London: Sweet & Maxwell, pp. 229–42.

McGoldrick, P.J. (1987) 'A multidimensional framework for retail pricing', *International Journal of Retailing*, 2(2): 3–26.

Mamorstein, H., Grewal, D. and Fishe, R.P.H. (1992) 'The value of time spent in price-comparison shopping: survey and experimental evidence', *Journal of Consumer Research*, 19(1): 52–61.

Mobley, M.F., Bearden, W.O. and Teel, J.E. (1988) 'An investigation of individual responses to tensile price claims', *Journal of Consumer Research*, 15(2): 273–9.

Monroe, K.B. (1971) 'Measuring price thresholds by psychophysics and latitudes of acceptance', *Journal of Marketing Research*, 8(4): 460–4.

Monroe, K.B. (1979) *Pricing: Making Profitable Decisions*, New York: McGraw-Hill, pp. 37–46.

Nagle, T. (1984) 'Economic foundations for pricing', *The Journal of Business*, 57(1, part 2): S3–S26.

National Consumer Council (1990) *The Trade Descriptions Act: Review*, Policy Document 34/90/D4, London: National Consumer Council.

Nystrom, H. (1970) *Retail Pricing: An Integrated Economic and Psychological Approach*, Economic Research Unit, Stockholm School of Economics.

Office of Fair Trading (1992) 'Better deal for consumers', *BeeLine*, Office of Fair Trading, London, 92(1): 6–8.

O'Keefe (1993) *The Law Relating to Trade Descriptions*, Sevenoaks, Butterworths, Chapter 43, Issue 40, 2/605–2/609.

Ortmeyer, G., Quelch, J.A. and Salmon, W. (1991) 'Restoring credibility to retail pricing', *Sloan Management Review*, Fall: 55–66.

Pashigian, B.P. (1988) 'Demand uncertainty and sales: a study of fashion and markdown pricing', *The American Economic Review*, 78(5): 936–53.

Pashigian, B.P. and Bowen, B. (1991) 'Why are products sold on sale?: explanations of pricing regularities', *The Quarterly Journal of Economics*, 106(4): 1013–38.

Phlips, L. (1988) 'Price discrimination: a survey of the theory', *Journal of Economic Surveys*, 2(2): 135–67.

Prus, R. (1986) 'It's on "sale": an examination of vendor perspectives, activities, and dilemmas', *Canadian Review of Sociology and Anthropology*, 23(1): 72–96.

Reich, N. and Micklitz, H.-W. (1980) *Consumer Legislation in the EC Countries: A Comparative Analysis*, Berkshire: Van Nostrand Reinhold, pp. 51–3, 65, 72–3.

Richards, K. (1995) cited in S. Lonsdale, 'Buyers all beware', *Daily Telegraph*, 9 January: 14.

Salop, S. and Stiglitz, J. (1977) 'Bargains and ripoffs: a model of monopolistically competitive price dispersion', *Review of Economic Studies*, 44: 493–510.

Sampson, R.T. (1964) 'Sense and sensitivity in pricing', *Harvard Business Review*, November/December: 99–105.

Schoemaker, P.H. (1982) 'The expected utility model: its variants, purposes, evidence and limitations', *Journal of Economic Literature*, 20: 529–63.

Scitovsky, T. (1944–5) 'Some consequences of the habit of judging quality by price', *Review of Economic Studies*, 12: 100–5.

Shilony, Y. (1977) 'Mixed pricing in oligopoly', *Journal of Economic Theory*, 14(2): 373–88.

Skeel, S. (1993) 'Burton profits rocket after January sales', *Daily Telegraph*, 14 May.

Stigler, G. (1987) *Theory of Price*, New York: Macmillan.

Stokey, N. (1979) 'Intertemporal price discrimination', *The Quarterly Journal of Economics*, 93(3): 355–71.

Tauber, E.M. (1972) 'Why do people shop?', *Journal of Marketing*, 36(4): 46–9.

Thaler, R. (1985) 'Mental accounting and consumer choice', *Marketing Science*, 4(3): 199–214.

Tversky, A. and Kahneman, D. (1988) 'Rational choice and the framing of decisions', in D.E. Bell, H.Raiffa and A. Tversky (eds) *Decision Making*, New York: Cambridge University Press, pp. 167–92.

Urbany, J.E. and Dickson, P.R. (1990) 'Prospect theory and pricing decisions', *Journal of Behavioural Economics*, 19(1): 69–80.

Urbany, J.E., Bearden, W.O. and Weilbaker, D.C. (1988) 'The effect of plausible and exaggerated reference prices on consumer perceptions and price search', *Journal of Consumer Research*, 15(1): 95–110.

Van Praag, B. and Bode, B. (1992) 'Retail pricing and the costs of clearance sales: the formalisation of a rule of thumb', *European Economic Review*, 36(4): 945–62.

Van Raaij, W.F. (1981) 'Economic psychology', *Journal of Economic Psychology*, 1(1): 1–24.

Varian, H.R. (1980) 'A model of sales', *American Economic Review*, 70(4): 651–9.

Varian, H.R. (1989) 'Price discrimination', in R. Schmalensee and R.D. Willig (eds) *Handbook of Industrial Organisation*, Vol. 1, Amsterdam: North Holland, pp. 598–654.

Westbrook, R.A. and Black, W.C. (1985) 'A motivation based shopper typology', *Journal of Retailing*, 61(1): 78–103.

Winer, R. (1988) 'Behavioural perspectives on pricing: buyers' subjective perceptions of price revisited', in Divinney, T.M. (ed.) *Issues in Pricing: Theory and Research*, Lexington, MA: Lexington Books, pp. 35–57.

Editors' Commentary

JOHN DAWSON HAS A long and distinguished career as a research leader in retail research and education in the UK. His international reputation is such that having retired in 2006 from the University of Edinburgh, he has been re-employed by them on a part-time basis, has rejoined the University of Stirling on a research professorial appointment and is currently a Visiting Professor in ESADE, Barcelona (since 1987) and Distinguished Professor at UMDS, Kobe, Japan (since 2003).

John Dawson graduated in geography from University College London in 1965 with an interest in urban geography. In 1970 he completed a PhD at Nottingham University with a thesis on the postwar changes in retailing in selected European regions. John Dawson moved to St David's University College, Lampeter in the University of Wales in the mid-1970s and collected a group of retail researchers pursuing a variety of retail topics under the broad heading of retail geography processes and changes in retail systems. In 1983 he was appointed to the first professorial post in retail studies at a UK university, the Fraser of Allander Chair of Distributive Studies, at the University of Stirling. Using this position, John Dawson established and directed until 1990 the Institute for Retail Studies, the specialist research and teaching group at Stirling. In 1990 he joined the University of Edinburgh as Professor of Marketing.

Dawson's research has mainly been on themes of the nature of change and innovation in European retailing, international activity of retailers, e-retailing and information management in retailing, the measurement of performance in retailing and distribution and inter-relationships between European and Asian approaches to retail management. In developing this work he has become more and more aware of the powerful influence of individual retail managers in generating innovative change not only in their own firm but also across the sector. The openness of retailing makes it particularly susceptible to knowledge transfer whether or not firms are within network relationships.

Involvement in practical commercial management has been gained as Chairman of a retail company operating museum shops and as a Board member of Cumbernauld New Town Development Corporation until its privatization. Opportunities have also been pursued to work in universities in other countries with visiting positions in University of Western Australia (1973), Australian National University (1978), Florida State University (1982), Chuo University (1986), University of South Africa

(1999), European University Institute (1999), University of Marketing and Distribution Sciences, Kobe (2000), Bocconi University (2000) and Saitama University (2002). He is the founding co-editor of *The International Review of Retail, Distribution and Consumer Research*.

John Dawson has two articles in the present volume, the first of which is from 1989 and represents his interests in the way that retailers become involved in the supply chain. 'The Move to Administered Vertical Marketing Systems by British Retailers' is co-authored with Susan Shaw. The second paper included here is on retail internationalization and details of Dawson's publications in this area are included in a later author profile (see pp. 385–386).

Susan Shaw is Emeritus Professor of Marketing at the University of Strathclyde. At Strathclyde she was Professor of Marketing from 1990 but also pursued a successful career in university management, being Deputy Principal and Vice Principal between 1995 and 2004. Prior to moving Strathclyde University she worked in the University of Stirling and this paper dates from that time. Her expertise and interest lies in marketing with her research focusing on the food industry. Her interest in this sector began with an interest in the marketing of fish and fish products. She and John Dawson brought their joint interests and expertise together to study relationships between the food industry and retailers by looking at the ways that supply chains operated and needed to change to meet the demands of the retail sector.

The paper was one of the results of a programme of work supported by a government development department and a major retailer. Both organizations wished to find ways to encourage more domestically sourced products. A programme of structured and unstructured interviews were undertaken to attempt to gain specific, detailed and true data on the nature of relationships in an area notorious for company secrecy and for research with less than adequate research designs. The paper is concerned with the ways in which relationships between retailers and their suppliers have evolved and in particular with the ways in which retailers have taken more functions and processes and more of a coordinating and administering role in distribution and marketing channels. The paper forms an example of both a genre of work in terms of distribution and marketing channels but also a bridge to concepts of power relationships in these channels. The changes the paper documents and foreshadows illustrate both the significance of the buying and supplying components of retail operations and the way in which the nature and scope of retailing operations and management has altered. Such concerns remain important in retail research.

Key Publications

Dawson JA (1979) *The Marketing Environment*. London: Croom Helm.
Dawson JA (ed.) (1980) *Retail Geography*. London: Croom Helm.
Dawson JA (1982) *Commercial Distribution in Europe*. London: Croom Helm.
Dawson JA and Lord JD (1985) *Shopping Centre Development: Policies and Prospects*. London: Croom Helm.

Shaw SA and Muir JF (1987) *Salmon Economics and Marketing*. London: Croom Helm.

Shaw SA, Nisbet D and Dawson JA (1989) Economies of scale in UK supermarkets: some preliminary findings. *International Journal of Retailing*, 4(5), 12–26.

Moir C and Dawson JA (1990) *Competition and Markets*. London: Macmillan.

Shaw SA, Dawson JA and Blair LMA (1992) Imported foods in a British supermarket chain: buyer decisions in Safeway. *International Review of Retail, Distribution and Consumer Research*, 2, 35–57.

Dawson JA, Harris N and Shaw SA (1994) The characteristics and functions of buying groups in the United Kingdom: results of a survey. *International Review of Retail, Distribution and Consumer Research*, 4, 83–105.

Dawson JA and Shaw SA (1995) Organisation and control of buying groups. *Journal of Marketing Channels*, 4(4), 89–103.

Shaw SA and Gibbs J (1996) The role of marketing channels in the determination of horizontal market structure: the case of fruit and vegetable marketing by British growers. *International Review of Retail, Distribution and Consumer Research*, 6, 281–300.

Dawson JA (2000) Viewpoint: retailer power, manufacturer power, competition and some questions of economic analysis. *International Journal of Retail and Distribution Management*, 28, 1, 1–4.

Dawson JA and Shaw SA (1996) The evolution of distribution channels for consumer goods. In SA Shaw and N Hood (eds) *Marketing in Evolution*. London: Macmillan, 55–78.

Dawson JA (2000) Retailing at century end: some challenges for management and research. *International Review of Retail, Distribution and Consumer Research*, 10, 119–148.

Dawson JA (2001) Is there a new commerce in Europe? *International Review of Retail, Distribution and Consumer Research*, 11(3), 287–299.

Dawson JA (2007) Wholesale distribution: the chimera in the channel. *International Review of Retail, Distribution and Consumer Research*, 17, 313–326.

Websites

http://www.retaildawson.com/
http://www.strath.ac.uk/marketing/academicstaff/shawsusanprof/

THE MOVE TO ADMINISTERED VERTICAL MARKETING SYSTEMS BY BRITISH RETAILERS

John A. Dawson and Susan A. Shaw

Retailing in Britain has undergone major structural change over the last 30 years, change which has primarily been associated with the growth in market shares of large multi-outlet retailers (see Table 1). This article is concerned with the effects of this change on the structure of distribution channels and on the implications for relationships between retailers and manufacturers. Empirical findings are based on interviews with a sample of 42 large British multiple retailers and 60 of their suppliers in four product areas – meat processing, fish processing, sports and leisure clothing and house furnishings, in autumn 1986. Additional in-depth interviews were carried out with a further 12 major British retailers, 11 manufacturers, and with 10 trade associations and sector analysts. The survey work on the 102 companies comprised structured questionnaire-based interviews on attitudes to channel relationships and views about changes in channel relationships and structures. The 33 in-depth interviews were unstructured, since the purpose was to obtain descriptions of processes rather than to collect quantitative data.

Table 1 The growth in market shares of large multi-outlet retailers

Multiple retailers in the UK	1950	1961	1971	1980	1984	1986
Number of businesses with 50 shops and over	362	430	330	300	284	910
10–49 shops	1,407	1,470	940	960	666	
Number of establishments (000s) in businesses with 50 shops and over	53	66	60	55	54	61
10–49 shops	28	30	19	19	14	
Percentage of sales in business with 50 shops and over	24	31	36	45	50	59
10–49 shops	12	9	8	8	8	

Note: Precise comparisons over the various years are not possible due to differences in coverage and methods of the surveys. The figures are indicative of a trend rather than precisely comparable.

Source: Based on Censuses of Distribution. Retail Inquiry with attempts made to improve comparability.

European Journal of Marketing, Vol. 23, No. 7 (1989), pp. 42–52.

Retail Change and its Implications for Retail Procurement Needs

THE SUCCESS OF MULTIPLE retailers has been based on particular management systems and philosophies. First, retail marketing has received increased emphasis as a weapon in competitive strategy[1]. This has led increasingly to a marketing orientation with market-led decisions on product ranges and brands. Price competitiveness within a target market remains a dominant aim, but distinctive products and product assortments are sought both as a means of achieving short-term sales and of building longer-term buyer loyalty. Secondly, multiple retailers have sought corporate size and large numbers of retailing units as a base to achieve the cost economies obtained through large-scale retailing operations and in order to improve competitive strength[2, 3]. Thirdly, a mechanism, both for implementing strategies and achieving economies associated with size, has been a strong central control of operations covering, with a few exceptions, central buying operations, central labour policies, central advertising, centralised administration and centralised distribution.

These changes have considerable significance for manufacturers, since multiple retailers seek to manage their relationships with suppliers in a way that will support and enhance these sources of competitive advantage. The accompanying rise in retail power[4] gives retailers the ability to do this. The need for distinctive product assortments has led to greater involvement in product decisions, in particular, through the development of retail brands. While retailers, in general, undertake little fundamental research, they are more proactive in product development through the initiation of new product concepts and design. For own-label lines, they provide product specifications, quality control and delivery conditions. They require suppliers to work more closely with them in product development, rather than taking a fully specified marketing package from the supplier. Central ordering and distribution also have implications for manufacturers. Out-of-stock situations become more serious, since, in order to achieve economies of scale, the burden of retail overheads is increased, so that profitability is quickly depressed if sales fall below planned levels. To maintain competitiveness, costs must also be minimised[5]. The survey evidence suggests that retailer response to this risk includes rigorous definitions of delivery conditions, moves to retailer depot operations, tight in-store energy management, reduced labour costs through more part-time workers, growing application of sophisticated shelf-space allocations systems and moves towards just-in-time distribution.

The Effect of Procurement Needs on Relationships Between Multiple Retailers and Their Suppliers

Changing procurement needs in turn have implications for retailer–supplier relationships. The traditional implicit assumption about the nature of vertical relationships between buyers and their suppliers in marketing channels is that the market mechanism provides the linking and resource allocation mechanism between stages[6]. When there are disparate activities involved at each stage, when the structure of scale economies is different and where differing economies of scope exist at different levels, the market mechanism will allocate suppliers to customers. The assumption is that there is optimisation at each level in the channel and inter-level relationships are optimised by the market mechanism which allocates different suppliers for each buyer and different buyers for each supplier on a discreet basis for each purchasing decision. Whether this meaningfully describes relationships between buyers and suppliers has been challenged in the context of industrial markets by Hakansson[7], and more broadly by Anderson and Wietz[8] and Brown[9]. There must also be doubts about whether it adequately models relationships between large retailers and their suppliers. An alternative view is that relationships between individual buyers and suppliers may be much more stable[10], involving longer-term continuing relationships over time and on-going processes of joint problem solving. Arndt[11] termed this the "domestication of markets" in which "institutional and inter-organisational structures (are) created by moving exchanges and transactions inside the boundaries of firms committed to long-term co-operation" (p. 55). Underpinning this view are the hypotheses that:

1   There are transaction cost savings resulting from stable relationships. "The relationships between organizations in the network take time and effort to create, maintain, and develop; organizations 'invest' in relation to other organizations"[12].
2   When there is non-price competition at retail level, short-term use of the market mechanism fails to optimise transactional behaviour between retailer and supplier.
3   Horizontal competitive performance can be improved by managing vertical relationships.
4   The use of negotiated power is favoured in vertical relationships in order to support market power in horizontal competition.

Within industrial purchasing, a number of arguments have been suggested to support the growth of more stable relationships. Williamson[10] has stressed the presence of personal obligations between parties and the concept of *quid pro quo* relationships. This has been further explored by Dixon and Wilkinson[13] in their suggestion of the presence of a "channel culture". Macmillan and Farmer[14] suggest a learning cost factor: "Time taken up in source search, appraisal and selection, in negotiations and in many aspects of schedule co-ordination could be substantially reduced" by stable relationships (p. 283). Blois[15] has suggested that stable relationships are favoured because they can allow renegotiation of contracts during the life of a contract.

These are not issues, however, which have received much specific attention in the distribution literature. There are some theoretical studies, notably Steiner[16] and Jeuland and Shugan[17], but few specific empirical studies. Previous work has focused on the power dimensions of relationships[18]. McCammon[19] identifies the conditions under which procedures, wholesalers and retailers act as a unified vertical marketing system through the power dominance of one channel member. Causes of conflict between channel members have been examined by Gaski[20] and others, and Porter[21] has defined the general conditions in any supplier/buyer relationship which raise the costs of switching trading partners. At the empirical level, Robinson[22] and Wright[23] have conducted studies of the buying requirements of retailers in the UK clothing industry and in Australia respectively.

Vertical Relationship Stability

The findings from the interviews conducted with UK retailers and manufacturers indicate that there is considerable stability within relationships between UK retailers and their suppliers. In vertical relationships, there are many examples of retailers and suppliers entering into long-term arrangements to do business with each other and both parties investing heavily in the development of the relationship. This is illustrated by the example from one retailer: "We are not looking for new suppliers in any of our existing product areas. We have the suppliers we want and unless something goes wrong with the relationship we will not search for new suppliers."

A retailer embarking on extension of some retail brand ranges commented: "We will offer the opportunity first to our existing branded suppliers. We have good working relationships with them which we can build on." One home furnishings retailer played an active role in the development of new small suppliers because of the long-term benefits of working with suppliers who, as a consequence, developed business thinking closely aligned with that of the retailer.

In some cases, the commitment of the retailer to the relationship is considerable. Examples were given, in the survey, of retailers providing loan finance for investment programmes by suppliers and of retailers educating suppliers in new production technologies. There are also examples of quasi-vertical integration similar to those described as present in some industrial markets[24] where suppliers are effectively totally dependent on, and controlled by, the retailer.

Results from the formal questionnaire survey are shown in Table 2. Advantages are seen by both retailer and manufacturer in the development of such ongoing relationships. This is consistent with the work of Baligh[25] who was able to show theoretically that firms which co-operate most closely with other firms in a vertical relationship obtain the best returns on investments, but incur high implementation costs. This has clear parallels with a retailer strategy of investing in vertical relationship to enhance horizontal competitive power.

The retailer's needs for specific quality, consistent offering and timely delivery are most likely to be met by partners familiar with the trading methods and requirements of the retailer. Retailer market share is thereby increased because consumer needs are being met.

Once a reliable supplier has been found, there is a reluctance to switch to unknown suppliers because of the attendant risks to competitive position. Such relationships rarely take contractual forms but are based on an understanding that continuing business will normally be done between the two partners. If other suppliers, not part of this offer, supply at lower prices, switching is unlikely

Table 2 Results from the formal questionnaire survey

Question:

To what extent do you agree or disagree with this statement: "We prefer to remain with the same suppliers from year to year wherever possible"?

Replies of multiple retail buyers

	Meat retailers	Home furnishings	Sports and leisure clothing	Fish retailing	Total
Agree strongly	5	7	3	3	18
Agree slightly	4	2	6	4	16
Neither	1	1	1	1	3
Disagree slightly	1	0	1	2	4
Disagree strongly	1	0	0	0	1
	12	10	11	10	42

Question:

To what extent do you agree or disagree with this statement: "We prefer to remain with the same retail customers from year to year wherever possible"?

Replies of manufacturers

	Meat processing	Home furnishings	Sports and leisure clothing	Fish retailing	Total
Agree strongly	14	12	14	15	55
Agree slightly	1	2	1	—	4
Neither	—	—	—	—	—
Disagree slightly	—	1	—	—	1
Disagree strongly	—	—	—	—	—
	15	15	15	15	60

to occur, unless the differential is considered substantial and the retailer is assured the new supplier could replicate all the supply conditions of the existing supplier, which may in itself be a lengthy process. Price is not the sole variable affecting decisions to change supplier; rather, it is part of a particular total trade marketing package which the supplier puts together, often with input from the retailer, to address an individual retailer's wants. The retailer incurs extra costs in this joint work but appears to prefer this approach to a more market-oriented one.

The emphasis so far has been on retailer manipulation of the marketing channels, but, equally, manufacturers benefit from, and have always sought, stable relationships. It is a *sine qua non* in marketing that a dominant objective is to gain and then to keep customers. Prior to the development of strong multiple retailers, manufacturers ensured stability through their dominance of marketing channels via strong manufacturer brands and predetermined marketing mixes. Two factors, however, have now changed. First, retailers and manufacturers are cooperating in the development of marketing mixes. Secondly, the manufacturer now works with a smaller number of relationships, each of them of great importance. As a consequence, the manufacturer also gains through benefits of smooth working relationships, despite their considerable initial investment cost.

Co-operation with the retailer does carry costs for the manufacturer. These may be summarised as increased risk through dependence on fewer customers, costs in meeting any additional quality or service requirements, system optimisation resulting possibly in some sub-system sub-optimisations and dependency possibly generating psychological costs, for example, a loss in confidence to innovate. Manufacturers who find these costs unacceptable can move away by product diversification into markets where co-operation is not expected. There is some evidence that this has happened in the food sector, with some manufacturers moving towards supply of the more traditionally structured catering sector rather than meet the conditions required by food retailers.

Factors Making for Stability in Vertical Relationships

The degree of stability is one component of the trade marketing mix and its relative importance depends on the different elements in the retailer's purchasing requirement. Factors acting to increase the extent of stability in relationships are listed in Table 3. The more demanding the quality requirements, the more flexible is the response required of suppliers, and the greater is the potential benefit of stability. The more specific the delivery and ordering patterns, the more important the product to the retailer and the greater the need for joint product development work, the more stable the relationship is likely to be because of the costs and risks of change. This situation characterises many areas of grocery retailing but most notably those involving short-life products in the chilled food sector. There is also increasing evidence of this in clothing and furnishings sectors.

A further factor of significance is the choice of suppliers available to retailers. As retailers' order sizes have risen, and their quality requirements have become more demanding, so the number of suppliers capable of supplying their needs has also fallen. Just as there is a dualism in retailing, with the contrast between the large mass merchandiser and the small specialist in some sectors, so there is a growing dualism between the relatively larger (but not necessarily very large) suppliers who have geared up to meeting the needs of the multiples and those who are precluded from this by their size or lack of facilities. By contrast, in areas where price is the dominant element in purchasing and where purchasing is a discrete, discontinuous process, as characterised by some areas of clothing retailing, the degree of stability involved in relationships is much smaller. There are signs, however, even here, that the discrete discontinuous nature of these relationships is changing. The steady trend to shorter-length fashion cycles, the increasing reluctance of retailers to hold stock with the consequent emergence of "just-in-time" delivery systems has led to increasing needs for flexible responses and short lead times and hence to greater stability in relationships.

There are also aspects of the changes in retailing which reduce the need for stable relationships. Where retailer brands have replaced manufacturers' brands,

Table 3 Factors making for stability in relationships between multiple retailers and their suppliers in the UK

	Factor	Role	Directions of change
1.	High and consistent quality	Stability important where regular delivery of major range items required and with items difficult to manufacture/ or where high-quality hygiene standards mandatory	Becoming more important as is quality increasingly used as a horizontal competitiveness weapon by major multiple retailers
2.	Need for flexible response	More likely to be achieved when supplier well adapted to working with retailer, i.e. within context of long-term working relationship. More significant for delivery of goods in continuous demand (groceries) than for bi-annual seasonal ordering (clothing)	Becoming major factor as: (a) "just-in-time" delivery systems introduced and lower stockholding by retailers (all sectors) (b) fashion changes become more frequent so flexible quicker response by manufacturers (clothing)
3.	Joint product development work required	Most critical with retailers with proactive approaches towards new product development work. This is a function of (a) size of retailer (b) market niche sought. The more precisely targeted the retailer's marketing concept, the larger the retailer, and the greater the degree of product differentiation, the more significant this factor becomes	Large retailers have buying teams and expect considerable interaction between themselves and their suppliers: set-up costs are high encouraging stability. However, some retailers seeking less interaction to encourage more proactive approaches by manufacturers
4.	Specific delivery systems required	Most critical with products requiring specialist distribution into stores, e.g. meats, fresh fish and some chilled foods	Probably becoming less important as third-party distribution systems have grown, particularly in specialist areas
5.	Frequent contact through frequent ordering	Most critical for goods ordered continuously	The future development of computerised systems which link retailers and manufacturers with different technologies may make switching between supply sources easier
6.	Wide product ranges required from a limited number of suppliers	This increases the costs of changing suppliers because of the greater complexity of business	Becoming less important for distribution reasons in some sectors with increased availability of third-party distribution. Still significant in sectors where manufacturer performs a product assembly role for retailers

7.	High physical degrees of product differentiation	When the product is difficult to replicate, the retailer is more likely to stay with same supplier	Important for products with special effects and designs (some areas of fabrics and furnishings)
8.	Strong manufacturer brands	Retailer will wish to stock these lines	Own-label developments have affected non-promotion supported manufacturer brands but will not significantly erode the market shares of major manufacturer brand leaders
9.	Number of suppliers	When there are few alternative sources of supply, the degree of stability is higher, but this will depend on the intensity of competition among the suppliers	International sourcing of higher-value products, such as clothing, increases the number of sources of supply and reduces the need for stability as long as point (2) is not relevant. Overall, very variable depending on manufacturing sector involved.

this has increased the ability of retailers to switch suppliers because the manufacturer is not identifiable at consumer level. For standardised products widely available, this has encouraged the entry of new suppliers and has broken down some existing relationships with branded manufacturers. Even here, however, there are some signs of a reversal of this process where switching between suppliers for price reasons has led to variability in offerings to consumers. Consistent quality is an important aspect for retailer brands as quality is a consciously designed component of the product and is designed to be an integral part of the total retailer offering. Variations in quality can have a negative effect on horizontal competitiveness for the retailer.

Stability may alternatively be imposed on the retailers by manufacturers. Where sources of supply are limited, the supply options available to retailers are similarly limited. This occurs most noticeably in the use of the strongly supported manufacturer brands. The retailer continues to stock these products as part of the required product assortment by customers. Such products are essential to the product range if market share is to be maintained. Increasing support for key brands has been one strategy adopted by major manufacturers, as a means of retaining their stable relationships with retailers, so ensuring both retailer and manufacturer market share. In these cases, the control over major, if not all, elements of the marketing mix is likely to be in the hands of the manufacturer. Another example revealed by the survey was of manufacturers initiating interacting ordering and scheduling systems between individual manufacturers and retailers, so raising the cost to the retailer of switching to other sources of supply.

Competition Within a Framework of Stable Relationships

Stability, however, should not be confused with lack of competition at the retail–manufacturing interface. Stable relationships are of value to retailers as long as the costs do not outweigh the benefits. Thus retailers, and manufacturers, use mechanisms to ensure that the terms of the relationship do not become significantly out of line with those which might obtain through other suppliers or customers. Both sides also take measures to ensure that risk is not increased by close relationships with a limited number of suppliers or customers. The main mechanisms for this which were identified from interviews were:

> *Dual sourcing of supplies* – This is used both as a method of risk reduction and as a means of ensuring competition amongst suppliers. Equally, suppliers will seek to ensure where possible that the number of their customers, albeit few, is split so that they would not be threatened by the loss of any single account.
>
> *Limited use of contracts* – For both sides, it provides a means of responding to changes in market conditions outside the relationship by adjusting terms of dealing as necessary, but without necessarily putting the relationship at risk.
>
> *Searches of the market* – Both suppliers and retailers will continue to search the market for guidelines as to how the relationships should change in the light of changing market conditions.
>
> *Support for suppliers* – Where capable suppliers are very few in number, smaller suppliers may be maintained through difficult periods by the retailers to preserve choice of supply sources over the longer term.
>
> *Use of interactive communications and ordering systems* – The development of common interactive systems such as "TRADANET" reduces the administrative costs of switching suppliers, as well as improving the information available to retailers. This will not necessarily reduce the stability of relationships particularly where other variables such as product quality are also relevant.

At the extreme, complete control of suppliers could be sought by retailers by a process of backward vertical integration within a corporate framework[8]. There are examples where this has occurred. The clothing and home furnishings retailer, Laura Ashley, obtains a high proportion of its supplies from its own manufacturing facilities. A number of clothing retailers have manufacturing capabilities (or manufacturers have retail facilities), for example Ellis and Goldstein with their DASH range sold through DASH in-store concessions. In general, however, most retailers are unenthusiastic about full vertical integration.

Manufacturers, particularly those with strong brands and notably in the clothing sector, have considered operating their own stores, but there is considerable potential risk in tying retailing to manufacturing facilities which might prove to be of the wrong sort should demand conditions change. The danger that in a fully integrated organisation facilities would become product led rather than market led was stressed by several of the retailers who were interviewed. In the case of two food retailers who are part of groups with food manufacturing units, the manufacturing and retailing arms of each company are run autonomously to avoid this danger. The alternative of stable but non-permanent relationships with suppliers is preferred because this offers the benefits of stability without the lack of flexibility implicit in full management integration.

Trade Marketing

The changes described in this article have considerable implications for the nature of marketing by manufacturers to retailers. First, Viros[26] has suggested that manufacturers are moving towards an "individual customer focus", which views product, selling, promotion, logistics and pricing as an integrated whole to be decided in the light of the position of the individual retailer. This view is supported by the interview survey reported in this article. Second, it is likely to be appropriate to place more emphasis on the process of development of relationships which go through various stages from initial contact to the development of stable longterm patterns. This has already been suggested in the industrial marketing area by Hakannson[7], Blois[15] and others. Third, the marketing mix in part emerges not solely as a discreet entity from the strategies of the manufacturers, but through interactions within the relationship with retailers. With fewer larger customers, segmentation strategies may be based on individual retailers, but, additionally, a relevant factor in selecting target retail customers is likely to include the ease of access to individual retailers by new suppliers, measured by the strength of existing relationships. Finally, channel managers are faced with difficult requirements to operate old and new channel structures alongside each other. The implications of such changes are far reaching for the academic study of marketing channels and for the practice of channel management.

References

1. Dawson, J.A. and Sparks, L., *Issues in Retailing*, Scottish Development Department, Edinburgh, 1985.
2. Douglas, E., *The Economics of Marketing*, Harper and Row, New York, 1975.
3. Baumol, W.J., Panzar, J.C. and Willig, R.D., *Contestable Markets and the Theory of Industrial Structure*, Harcourt Brace Jovanovich, New York, 1982.
4. Grant, R.M., "Manufacturer–Retailer Relations: The Shifting Balance of Power", in Johnson, G. (Ed.), *Business Strategy and Retailing*, Wiley, Chichester, pp. 150–79.
5. Dawson, J.A. and Shaw, S.A., "Horizontal Competition in Retailing and the Structure of Manufacturer–retailer Relationships", *Fourth International Conference on Distribution*, Milan, 1987.
6. Arrow, K.J., *The Limits of Organisation*, W.W. Norton, New York, 1974.
7. Hakansson, H., *International Marketing and Purchasing of Industrial Goods*, Wiley, New York, 1982.
8. Anderson, E. and Weitz, B.A., "Make or Buy Decision: Vertical Intergration and Marketing Productivity", *Sloan Management Review*, Vol. 27 No. 3, 1986, pp. 3–19.

9.   Brown, W.B., "Firm Like Behaviour in Markets: The Administered Channel", *International Journal of Industrial Organisation*, Vol. 2 No. 3, 1984, pp. 263–76.

10. Williamson, O.E., *Markets and Hierarchies*, Free Press, New York, 1975.

11. Arndt, J., "The Domestication of Markets: From Competitive Markets to Administered Interorganisational Marketing Systems", in Lusch, R.F. and Zinszar, P.H. (Eds.), *Contemporary Issues in Marketing Channels*, University of Oklahoma, Norman, 1979, pp. 55–61.

12. Mattesson, L-F., "An Application of a Network Approach to Marketing: Defending and Changing Market Positions", *Research in Marketing, Supplement*, No. 2, p. 265.

13. Dixon, D.F. and Wilkinson, I.F., "Toward a Theory of Channel Structure", *Research in Marketing*, Vol. 8, 1986, pp. 27–70.

14. Macmillan, K. and Farmer, D., "Redefining the Boundaries of the Firm", *Journal of Industrial Economics*, Vol. 27, 1979, pp. 277–85.

15. Blois, K.J., "Supply Contracts in the Galbrathian Planning System", *Journal of Industrial Economics*, Vol. 24 No. 1, 1979, pp. 29–39.

16. Steiner, R.L., "Basic Relationships in Consumer Goods Industries", *Research in Marketing*, Vol. 7, 1984, pp. 165–208.

17. Jeuland, A.P. and Shugan, S.M., "Co-ordination in Marketing Channels", in Gautschi, D.A. (Ed.), *Productivity and Efficiency in Distribution Systems*, North Holland, New York, 1983. pp. 17–34.

18. Reve, T. and Stern, L.W., "Inter-organisational Relations in Marketing Channels", *Academy of Management Review*, Vol. 4, 1979, pp. 405–16.

19. McCammon, B.C., "Perspectives for Distribution Programming", in Bucklin, L.P. (Eds.), *Vertical Marketing Systems*, Scott Foresman, 1970.

20. Gaski, J.F., "The Theory of Power and Conflict in Channels of Distribution", *Journal of Marketing*, Vol. 48, 1984, pp. 9–29.

21. Porter, M.E., *Competitive Strategy*, Free Press, New York, 1980.

22. Robinson, T.M., "Why UK Retail Multiples Purchase Clothing Overseas", *Journal of Sales Management*, Vol. 3 No. 1, 1986, pp. 7–13.

23. Wright, J., "Trade Marketing: An Australian Survey", in Gattorna, J. (Ed.), *Insights in Strategic Retail Management*, MCB University Press, Bradford, 1985, pp. 117–49.

24. Blois, K.J., "Vertical Quasi-integration", *Journal of Industrial Economics*, Vol. 20 No. 3, 1972, pp. 253–72.

25. Baligh, H.H., "Co-operating and Competing in Shared and Unshared Marketing Decision Variables", *Research in Marketing*, Vol. 8, 1986, pp. 131–80.

26. Viros, C.R., "Gaining Competitive Advantage through Distribution – The Changing Balance between Suppliers and Customers – Opportunities and Exposures", *Strategies for Retail Profit and Growth*, ESOMAR, Amsterdam, 1986, pp. 263–78.

Chapter 4

Retail Strategy and Power

RETAILERS DO NOT OPERATE in a vacuum; they are in a competitive struggle for survival and growth. There is an extremely large range of business scale in retailing and an enormous number of births and deaths in the stock of outlets and businesses. In most cases the casualties are smaller independent retailers, but occasionally high-profile, large multiple retailers can go out of business. In an attempt to ensure survival and growth, retailers develop strategies and plans to obtain products, handle store-based resources and gain the capital to expand. Some are more successful than others.

Retailers increase in scale through a range of strategies and actions including organic growth, mergers and acquisitions, internationalization and diversification into new fields. Improved operations, use of technologies, financial management, marketing and branding and the ability to raise capital for development are all critical to business success and growth. In most countries, retailing has been transformed by such activities from a predominantly independent-based sector to one where multinational chains and strong national retailers are economically dominant. These firms generally are innovative, creative and ambitious to expand further.

Only a couple of decades ago, it would have been inconceivable that the world's largest company would have been a retailer and that considerable controversy would have been generated by their actions. But that is the case with Wal-Mart (Brunn 2006). In the UK, Tesco, once a by-word for 'pile it high, sell it cheap' market-barrow-style trading to lower-income groups, has been transformed into the 'darling' of the stock market (Seth and Randall 1999) and the demon of one section of the socially concerned population (www.tescopoly.org). With over 30 per cent of the UK grocery market and seemingly continuously extending into new products, services and countries (Seth and Randall 2005), Tesco is one of the top twenty firms in the UK on many counts and for some is arguably the most important British institution. Similar claims of increased firm scale of key retailers can be made in many countries. The growth of these large retail enterprises has increased concentration in retailing.

That some retailers have grown so large is no accident. Their strategies utilize understanding of the consumer to put the 'right' products and services in front of them in the 'right' locations. The largest retailers do this day-in and day-out, across the world in a variety of retail formats. The retailer's product (the store formula) has been cleverly created, amended, developed, altered and occasionally abandoned as consumer and other circumstances dictate.

It might seem that understanding consumers and giving them what they want from a portfolio of stores is a straightforward way to success. But, there is no given right to be successful or to continue in business. Arraigned against the retailer are a range of factors. Chief amongst these are, of course, competitors, which may have similar targets and ideas. These competitors fight not only for the same consumers but also often for the same products to sell and the best sites to sell from. They can easily 'copy' many of the best ideas. Various governmental bodies are also involved, both in a general intervention in markets, as for example in regulating the rules of advertising, sale prices or competition, and more specifically in retail terms through permitting land-use development in the form of new stores, such as out-of-town hypermarkets.

The rising scale of retail companies has meant that the retailer–manufacturer relationship has changed, as discussed in the previous chapter of this book. For a long time, manufacturers controlled the supply and price of goods to consumers. Retailers were essentially passive recipients of manufacturers' products and strategies. However, as retailers have grown in size, they have realized that their distinctive position and knowledge gives them power. Large retailers have power both horizontally (over other retailers) and vertically (over suppliers, producers and distributors). How they use this power is a significant issue. Should we be concerned about this scale increase and concentration? Should we care, provided that Asda/Wal-Mart can supply jeans at £3 a pair?

As shown at the end of Chapter 3, in many countries retailers now dictate the terms and conditions of supply. This has brought them into conflict with previously powerful lobbies, such as farmers, who have seen their significance, power and profits erode. Government regulators have seen the continuing increase in concentration, scale and market shares in the retail sector and asked whether this trend is in the consumer interest? As retailers get ever larger, and concentration increases, so fewer large firms dominate the market (individual corporate strategies become ever more successful). One regulatory concern is that the level of competition decreases and prices for consumers rise as retailers extract oligopolistic profits. Second, government regulators have also been keen to ensure that no collusion exists, in the form of vertical restraints, between retailer, producer and distributor which would act against the consumer interest, for example in restricting supply and/or raising prices. How can and should we measure and understand retail power in these various contexts? Is this rise of retail power good or bad for consumers? If it is perceived as bad, then what should be done about it? At what point should retail mergers and retail company growth be permitted or stopped? Given that retail company success is due (at least in part) to consumer behaviour, why should bureaucrats intervene in a natural consumer market process? How do these issues develop internationally given the global scale and ambitions of some retailers? These are the questions that this chapter confronts.

This chapter is, however, not focused directly on the development and management of retail strategy. Instead it considers the implications of the outcomes of successful retail strategies. It is concerned with strategy as it results in the growth and use of power and in the ways in which government and others react to and attempt to constrain the effects of this changing retail structure and practice, and so in turn the ways in which retailers 'work around' the restrictions placed on them and devise new approaches and strategies. There are two areas brought together in this chapter:

1   *Becoming a Dominant Retailer.* The rise of retailer power and associated increases in concentration is a relatively new phenomenon. It can be seen through the strategies and growth of particular retailers. As some retailers become ever more successful so they dominate and make and remake the market to suit their operational and strategic preferences. Burt and Sparks (2003) present the concept of the dominant chain in food retailing and focus on Tesco in the UK. They demonstrate how retail power can be used to structure the market and to produce a spiral of growth that can have adverse consequences for competitors and potentially in some eyes, consumers.

2   *The Rise of Retail Power.* While one firm may dominate a sector, the cumulative rise in retailer power and scale has brought high levels of market and sector concentration. This has been identified across many countries and raises a number of issues, including those of consumer benefit and welfare. The Dobson and Waterson (1999) paper included here considers the issues involved in the rise of retailer power in the food retail sector. Issues of how power is identified by economists and others, used by retailers and reined in by regulators and governments have become ever more significant, investigated and debated.

This chapter tends to focus on food retailing and the UK. This is not to say that some of the issues are not relevant to non-food sectors or to other countries. In international terms concentration in the UK is relatively high and has attracted considerable research. Power has more resonance in the food sector, as food is always an emotive topic, farmers tend to be vocal lobbyists, food prices are key political indicators and spending on food is the highest proportion of consumer retail spending. As sector boundaries blur, however, these issues are also blurring and the power of leading retailers *per se* is becoming a significant issue at local, national and international levels.

It should also be noted that there are some who believe that retailers have not increased their power over the last few decades (Ailawadi 2001 provides this viewpoint and a review of supporting evidence). We would argue that this view stems from a narrow conceptualization of both retailing and power, an over-concern with manufacturing, producers and promotions, and an insularity due to focusing on the US national market alone. As will be shown, the European literature (and much of the US literature) is convinced about the rise of retail power, even if they are divided over its implications and the need for, and form of, any remedies.

Becoming a Dominant Retailer

The ways in which the largest retailers in the world are perceived tends to be somewhat bi-polar. For many consumers and indeed industry commentators and retail professionals these are excellent businesses which are expertly run, have clear strategies and goals and provide consumers with what they want, time and time again. For others, these retailers represent the unacceptable face of capitalism with their rapacious behaviours, adverse social and competitive effects, general bland lack of sense of place and ubiquity, their exploitation of labour, land, producers and consumers and their reduction in general quality of life. Wal-Mart is the current 'lightning rod' for almost all the ills of the USA (see Brunn 2006 for some of these positions) and in the UK, Tesco is fast approaching an equivalent status (see www.tescopoly.org). Some of these concerns are undoubtedly genuine and reflect deeply held views of how society and economy should be organized. Others tend, however, to be somewhat self-serving and reflect the competitive position in which other businesses find themselves. How else can one explain Wal-Mart's call for Tesco in the UK to be controlled and cut down to size as it is 'too difficult a competitor' (Burt and Sparks 2006).

Retailers such as Tesco, Wal-Mart, Carrefour, IKEA and Metro have achieved their positions through the execution of appropriate strategies over several decades. The position they occupy reflects their success in this planning and implementation, and the continuing use of the power that they have accumulated to further their aims. To some extent these retailers have become dominant players in their distribution and retailing sectors. It is this fact of dominance that alienates those who are excluded, but of course is used to give millions of consumers precisely what they want from their retail stores.

The idea of large retailers dominating markets raises a number of questions. What do we mean by dominance? How do some retailers achieve and use this dominant position? Does this power and dominance have adverse consequences that demand regulation? If so, what form might this take? It is only relatively recently that such questions have taken on such significance, as for many, retailing and retailers were a minor part of the economy, made up of small, passive operations running local shops. The new, modern, retail reality is far removed from this.

There are numerous studies of power in the distribution channel, going back many years (e.g. French and Raven 1959; Emerson 1962; El-Ansary and Stern 1972; Hunt and Nevin 1974). However, many of these have developed in the economists' production orientation tradition (Tucker 1975). As such they do not reflect the realities of modern retailing. From within the subject Steiner (1991) identifies many of the problems with this approach. Dawson (2000), pointing out that retailing is 'different', identifies a wide range of issues in modern retailing that affect power conceptualizations. Smith (2006) notes that even now 'standard economic tools do not always translate easily . . . into a theory of distribution' (p. 34). Round (2006) asks if we really understand retail power and its use. Whilst recent years have seen something of a change in approach by economists to the subject (e.g. Clarke *et al.* 2002; Betancourt 2004), we start here with a management conceptualization of retail growth and dominance.

The Burt and Sparks (2003) paper considers the UK food grocery sector and the use of power to create and maintain a position of dominance. Their paper focuses on Tesco as the dominant chain in the UK and explores how Tesco uses its position of power to further its strategies. At the core of their paper are two key points that have been separately considered by others. First, they note that the overwhelming focus of many economists on price competition tends to miss the point about how retailers operate, compete and satisfy consumers (Clarke 2000; Dawson 2000). Second, they note the derivation and use of power in both the vertical and horizontal channel dimensions. This combination in a 'spiral of growth' provides a mechanism for considering what it is that retailers actually combine in the creation of their business and in achieving success.

In a *vertical* dimension channel power is used to reorganize and to manage the supply chain. This takes a number of forms but includes the active search for better supply terms and product range enhancement (e.g. Ogbonna and Wilkinson 1996, 1998; Bloom and Perry 2001). Typically the development of supply chain management in firms such as Tesco has seen a greater control of activities, a larger scale of operation, a reduction in the number of suppliers and partners and a broadening of the products handled (Sparks 1986; Smith and Sparks 1993, 2004; Smith 1998). Significant in both vertical and horizontal dimensions is the use of the retailer brand to enhance vertical control and to develop new products with producers (Burt 2000; Burt and Sparks 2002). This retailer brand development in the food sector is far more sophisticated and extended in Europe (particularly the UK) than in the USA (Hughes 1996; Steenkamp and Dekimpe 1997, Bergès-Sennou *et al.* 2004; Ailawadi and Keller 2004). There are clear links here to the research discussed in Chapters 2 and 3.

In the *horizontal* dimension, power is used to invest in operational activities that grow sales and sales density through enhancing consumer attractions which in turn contribute to corporate retail brand development (Burt and Sparks 2002). In the case of Tesco this has included investment in an above-average capital investment programme (Wrigley 1991, 1992a, b, 1994, 1996, 1998), service additions in-store and in new areas such as financial services (Alexander and Pollard 2000), staff training and development, enhanced promotional spending and brand-building (Burt and Sparks 2002), customer retention and loyalty card initiatives such as Clubcard (Humby *et al.* 2003) and distinctive local market trading responses to competitors (Competition Commission 2000).

These activities provide a number of benefits to the retailer concerned. Lower costs can be achieved in some aspects of the operation, which allows enhanced investment in customer-facing activities and in the information and supply systems of the business. The retailer becomes both more efficient and more effective in customer terms (provided they meet the 'right' customer needs). Many of these activities may also drive up costs for rivals, which may be less able to afford such spending. So, for example, in the UK, Tesco is seen to have higher pay rates to achieve better labour, spend more on obtaining the best sites for store development, tie in producers and distributors to the company, including by retail brand development, spend more on brand building and advertising, and on learning about consumers and using that learning both nationally and locally. Other retailers often have to settle for 'second best', particularly in store development sites. The consequence has been the extension of Tesco's reach and market share lead over its rivals, some of whom have struggled, gone out of business, been taken over or sought to merge.

One of the important 'assists' that dominant chains get in this process comes from restrictions on new store development (particularly if the locations sought are out-of-town). If store sites are restricted then new stores can not simply emerge to compete with the existing locations. A store chain is thus very hard to develop from the 'ground-up' as the hard discounters have found in the UK since the early 1990s. Even Wal-Mart, which had high hopes for the expansion of Asda when it took over in the late 1990s, has found it difficult to accelerate the growth of the chain and thus to compete with Tesco (Burt and Sparks 2006). It is inconceivable that a large-store mainstream food chain could enter the UK from abroad and build a competitive operation one store at a time. This suggests the presence of barriers to entry. These issues are similar, though not as dramatic, where the non-food retail format is located on out-of-town locations. They do not arise to the same extent in for example fashion retailing, where stores are in the high street, town centres and shopping centres.

If one chain pulls away from the others and becomes market dominant, then in an economy where new store development is restricted, how can its lead be eroded? Two main avenues would appear to be important. First, there is no right for any retailer to assume that it will continue to be successful (see the retailer listings in Hall *et al.* 2001). The retailer itself may grow complacent. Consumers may get bored with the 'same old thing'. Competitors may judge the changing consumer market more accurately. Retail market share can be lost very quickly if consumers decide not to use the stores. For example, in the UK grocery market Tesco was a 'laughing stock' to some extent less than thirty years ago (Akehurst 1984) and trailed the market leader Sainsbury and others considerably. Second, the government regulatory authorities may step in, arguing that market dominance is not in the public interest and needs to be rectified in some way. Choices include removing barriers to entry or store development, reducing the power of the market leader by a forced break-up/store sell-off or the strengthening of competitors, possibly by the permission of mergers amongst the leading 'second tier' operators. These are big and dramatic steps with many possible unintended social and economic consequences. The arguments over many of these are forming the basis of the 2006–07 UK Competition Commission investigation of the food sector (see below).

The rise of a dominant chain as the extreme version of a large retailer raises many issues. It suggests that conceptualizations of retailing based on perfect competition and consumers and retailers driven solely by price are misguided. So how should we think about modern retailing with its high levels of concentration and large firms? Can market dominance power work in the consumers' interests? Should success in retail operations over a sustained period of time be 'rewarded' by the non-market (artificial) weakening/strengthening of competitors and competition? At what point do consumers get bored? How should social and economic costs and benefits of market dominance and its possible rectification be identified, costed and managed?

The Rise of Retailer Power

Despite the rise of major retailers such as Tesco, retailing is dominated numerically by independent single-shop businesses. The increasing size of individual retail businesses is neither a new phenomenon, nor is it only present in a few countries. The rise of multiple retailers has been well documented, for example in Europe (Baden-Fuller 1985; Scott 1994; Colla 2004; Morelli 2004), the USA (Wrigley 2002) and Asia (Dawson and Larke 2004, 2005; Larke and Causton 2005).

This increasing size of retailers was for many years pretty much ignored by economists, who clung to a narrow definition of retailing and views that included aspects of perfect competition amongst myriads of small retailers and supply dominance by manufacturers (Dawson 2000). Management scholars on the other hand had become well aware of both the size and the significance of the rise of retailer power (Burt and Sparks 2003). This awareness took a number of forms, but focused not only on the size of the individual firm, but also on the macro-tendency towards polarization and concentration within the retail sector. As more multiple retailers continued to grow in scale and scope, so the *cumulative* balance of power swung towards retailers and away from manufacturers and others in the supply chain. At the same time as this concentration of vertical power (Dawson and Shaw 1989), so too the multiple retailers concentrated power in a horizontal dimension (Wrigley 1987), with competitive effects on other forms of retailing, most notably the independent sector and cooperative societies.

There are a number of inter-related issues raised by the increasing size of firms and concentration levels in retailing (Moir 1990; London Economics 1997). One is over the possible presence of vertical restraints (Dobson and Waterson 1996). A second concern is that as concentration rises so the differences between the prices paid to producers (in food, notably farmers) and the prices paid by consumers reflect retailers extracting excess profits from their power and position in the supply of products (Dobson *et al.* 1998). Or, put another way, they buy cheap and sell dear, thus disadvantaging both producers and consumers (Clarke *et al.* 2002). Third, if concentration is high then collusion amongst retailers might be found, leading to higher prices for consumers (Cotterill 1986; Smith 2004). Fourth, if barriers to entry exist then the system could be seen to be working against the consumer interest (Chevalier 1995; Marsden *et al.* 1998).

The paper by Dobson and Waterson (1999) represents the emerging engagement of some economists with this real world retail reality. Through an examination of the concentration of food retailing in a number of countries (but focused on the UK in the context of UK and EU regulators), they investigate the benefits and problems of such changes in power balance. They consider how regulators should respond to greater concentration in retailing by answering 'the important but difficult question (of) how much retail concentration is desirable?' (p. 155).

The relationship between concentration and prices is critical, but controversial. Dobson and Waterson (1999) point to the UK as being the most concentrated major country in Europe in terms of food retailing, and also as having the highest prices and the most profitable retailers. This starting point is, however, not accepted by all commentators, depending as it does on a far-from-perfect definition of the key measures within a rapidly changing sector. Wrigley (1993) on this basis had previously pointed to 'abuses of market power' in the UK food retailing sector. But, this relationship is subject to considerable problems of measurement, particularly when international comparisons are attempted (Burt and Sparks 1997). In retailing as a whole there are many measurement problems both nationally and internationally (see Reynolds *et al.* 2005 for a recent example in the context of productivity measurement). It is unclear, for example, that any comparison of prices and retail operations in supermarkets/superstores/hypermarkets in say France, the UK, the USA and China would be really comparing standardized and similar retailer propositions and consumer requirements. Nonetheless, there is a widely held view that the more competitive (less concentrated) USA market model provides cheaper prices for consumers (Cotterill 1986, 1997, 2006). Such a view discounts not only the larger size of the US market, but also the destruction of many town and city centres in the USA by the unfettered 'slash and burn' approach to urban sprawl, which drives the efficiency and productivity levels. Other countries may not wish, or be able, to go down this road.

In the USA there has always been great concern about the possibility of adverse consequences from power (Cotterill 1997). Legislation such as the Robinson-Patman Act has been used successfully to constrain retail concentration and power (Wrigley 1999, 2001). Major retailers, such as A&P, have been broken up by order of the government regulators (Tedlow 1990). Potential mergers have been blocked by regulators in a number of retail sectors (Wrigley 1997, 1999, 2001, 2002; Dobson and Waterson 1999). In the UK, there were two investigations of retail power in the food sector in the 1980s (i.e. MMC 1981; OFT 1985), but essentially multiple retailers were seen to be acting broadly in the consumer interest. In Australia there has been great concern over food retail concentration and the 'power of two' (Round 2006), but views on whether the position represents consumer disadvantage vary, as does the applicability of lessons from the UK/USA situations (Cotterill 2006; Round 2006; Smith 2006). As Round (2006) comments, the issue may be market conduct rather than structure.

Dobson and Waterson (1999) outline a framework to consider retail power and policy regulation (p. 137):

- Have retailers enough seller (horizontal) market power to affect prices and quantities traded, or to threaten viability of traders at other distribution stages, without attracting entry as a result?
- Do existing retail firms exercise buyer power against weaker firms, enhancing market failures?
- Does the exercise of buyer power actually benefit consumers?

- Do restrictions (imposed or agreed) on retailers and suppliers reduce the variety enjoyed by consumers?
- Alternatively, are there significant productive efficiency gains from market practices that restrict the number of dealers or their product range?

These questions have proved fundamental in ongoing debates over the nature of food retailing and concentration in the UK. The election of the Blair Labour government in 1997 was accompanied by a government inspired campaign against retailers and perceived high food prices. This was based fundamentally on flawed international price comparisons (Sparks 2002), but set the scene for a Competition Commission investigation of the grocery sector (Competition Commission 2000).

The conclusions of the Competition Commission report have been hotly debated (Wrigley 2001). The reaction amongst the media and smaller retail operators was almost one of disbelief. Several years of food price deflation, a reversal of the strength of Sterling and the entry of Wal-Mart (Burt and Sparks 2001) had, however, changed the situation somewhat from the time of the 1997 election. One leading retailer commented that they were charged with having too high prices and found guilty of having too low prices. Far from finding that food retailers were colluding to make excess profits and keep prices to consumers high, the report concluded that food retailers were driving down prices to producers and passing these lower prices on to consumers. Retailers were found guilty of not always treating their suppliers as well as they could, but as this translated into lower prices for consumers, this was again seen to be in the public interest. No policy recommendations could be identified which would improve the position for consumers.

For those outside the 'big three' food superstore operators, the conclusion was obvious: in order to remain competitive they had to gain scale. Thus, Morrisons launched a takeover of/merger with Safeway in 2003. This announcement, which given its scale implications had to be referred to the regulatory authorities, set off a bidding war for Safeway. All the major retailers wanted to gain their store assets to add to their own scale. The Competition Commission had to rule on each possible takeover, eventually allowing only Morrisons to acquire Safeway (Competition Commission 2003) but even then forcing them to divest some stores in areas of too much overlap (Competition Commission 2005).

The decisions of the Competition Commission (2000, 2003, 2005) essentially argued for a position whereby there would be four main competitors in the food market at the national level and at least three at the local level. By allowing Morrisons and Safeway to merge, they combined two smaller chains to provide a stronger fourth competitor. By forcing some sell-offs of stores, they sought to make sure that local market dominance was minimized.

To some extent, this makes sense provided the balance amongst the 'big four' is roughly equal. But, when one chain is dominant (Burt and Sparks 2003) and the second and third are some way behind the leader, strengthening the fourth chain may simply postpone the inevitable. This essentially is what happened in the UK in the middle part of the 2000s. Tesco continued to strengthen. The competition authorities controversially decided that as the main food shop and the convenience store (top-up) shop were separate markets, there was no basis for denying Tesco permission to takeover T&S Stores and other smaller convenience store chains. Asda and Sainsbury 'trod water', and Morrisons and Safeway took several years to make the merger operationally fit, let alone succeed.

The question of the appropriate market for investigation (raised by Dobson and Waterson 1999) has continued to be important and controversial. Retailers operate in national and global contexts, but the effects of their actions are felt by consumers at the local level. These effects have changed as retailing has changed (Clarke *et al.* 2006; de Kervenoael *et al.* 2006; Guy 1996; Jackson *et al.* 2006). The Competition Commission (2000, 2003, 2005) has become increasingly active and interested in local rather than regional or national market shares and is even looking closely at single-town situations. This interest is also reflected in Dobson and Waterson's (2005) concern over price-setting at the local level and the plea by Cotterill (2006) for more detailed and varied approaches to local market definition.

In the UK the definition issue remains alive. The Association of Convenience Stores persuaded the House of Commons All-Party Parliamentary Small Shops Group (APPSSG) to look at the issues involved, particularly with respect to Tesco's purchase of convenience stores. Legal action was also started against the regulators. The APPSSG (2006) report, with all its inherent partiality, set the tone for another referral of the grocery market to the Competition Commission in May 2006 (with the report now due in 2008). In addition to issues previously covered (e.g. suppliers), the referral this time is concerned with barriers to entry including (Competition Commission 2006):

- whether the planning regime constrains a grocery retailer seeking to enter or expand in an area, including possible barriers resulting from the 'needs' test, the 'sequential' test, land availability, and the planning process itself;
- whether any barriers to entry disadvantage particular retailers or types of retailer;
- whether there are significant differences in how the planning system is implemented in different parts of the UK that could impact on barriers to entry;
- whether any retailers or groups of retailers are using the planning system or land ownership in such a way as to restrict entry of others, e.g. land banks, restricting use of land on sale, paying excessive prices to prevent other operators from obtaining land;
- whether there are any other barriers related to scale or form of entry.

The importance of land-use planning for retailing is notable, reflecting the importance of location in retail activities (see Guy 2006 and Competition Commission 2007). It is hard, however, not to see the sector as having operated at least in part in recent decades in the public interest. But, the 'Dobson and Waterson' question has to be posed: how much retail concentration is desirable? After all, perhaps there is no simple answer to this question. The Competition Commission, though, has to come to some conclusions at national and local levels (Competition Commission 2007 provides some early thinking).

Despite (or perhaps because of) no real conclusion in the literature as to the issues arising from dominant chains and retailer power, the debate continues. Within this, Dobson and Waterson have played an important part. The themes they pursued in their 1999 paper have been subsequently developed in their book (Clarke *et al.* 2002) and in papers (Dobson *et al.* 2003; Dobson and Waterson 2005; Dobson 2005). The latter paper emphasizes the dangers that Paul Dobson sees in continued retail power growth and the economic dependency of manufacturers and producers on retailers. He sees this as detrimental to product quality, variety and innovation and thus eventually to consumers. But, this is still really unproven and overly relies on a view of retailers as passive and unconcerned over such topics. Is this right?

One point of departure with Dobson is perhaps summed up in his definition of retailer buyer power (Dobson 2005, p. 532): 'Retailer buyer power is essentially the ability of leading retail firms to obtain from suppliers more favourable terms than those available to others buyers or which would otherwise be expected under *normal* conditions' (emphasis added). We would question what 'normal' means in this context. We would certainly deny that it should mean a return to a producer-led distribution system, which failed economies in the past. Why is it not 'normal' for retailers to construct and manage the distribution channel, in their, and consumers' interests?

Summary

Retailers develop strategies and seek to implement these. Some are more successful than others at achieving their goals for development and growth. Over time there is an imbalance created among retail businesses. Some become larger and more powerful than others. At the most extreme, some retailers are truly dominant in their market and use this dominance and power to structure the vertical and horizontal dimensions of competition for their benefit.

This creation and use of power raises in some minds questions of public policy. Are there disadvantages to the concentration of retail markets and power? If there are disadvantages, then what 'remedies' need to be imposed to control these organizations? Such concerns underpin the retail developments in countries as diverse as the USA, the UK, Japan, India, Thailand, Turkey and Singapore. All have differing legislation on retailing planning and development, reflecting their particular current circumstances. The issue has become a significant global one as retailing internationalizes. Developing countries, in particular, are concerned about comparatively unconstrained developments by large, often foreign, retailers which are perceived to be undermining traditional retail operations and behaviours. Whilst foreign incomers point to innovation and modernization, established small retailers claim a cultural, social and indeed economic mission for the country. How can such conflicting points of view and beliefs about the role of retailing in economic and social development and the 'right' balance of power be reconciled?

References

Ailawadi KL (2001) The retail power-performance conundrum: what have we learned? *Journal of Retailing*, 77, 299–318.

Ailawadi KL and Keller KL (2004) Understanding retail branding: conceptual insights and research priorities. *Journal of Retailing*, 80, 331–342.

Akehurst G (1984) 'Checkout': the analysis of oligopolistic behaviour in the UK retail grocery market. *Service Industries Journal*, 4, 189–242.

Alexander A and Pollard J (2000) Banks, grocers and the changing retailing of financial services in Britain. *Journal of Retailing and Consumer Services*, 7, 137–147.

All-Party Parliamentary Small Shops Group (2006) *High Street Britain: 2015*. London: APPSSG.

Baden-Fuller C (1985) Rising concentration: the UK grocery trade 1970–1980. In K Tucker and C Baden-Fuller (eds) *Firms and Markets*. London: Croom Helm.

Bergès-Sennou F, Bontems P and Réquillart V (2004) Economics of private labels: a survey of literature. *Journal of Agricultural and Food Industrial Organization*, 2, Article 3, 23. Retrieved from http://www.bepress.com/jafio on 23 October 2006.

Betancourt R (2004) *The Economics of Retailing and Distribution*. Cheltenham: Edward Elgar.

Bloom PN and Perry VG (2001) Retail power and supplier welfare: the case of Wal-Mart. *Journal of Retailing*, 77, 379–396.

Brunn S (ed.) (2006) *Wal*Mart World: The World's Biggest Corporation in the Global Economy*. New York: Routledge.

Burt SL (2000) The strategic role of retail brands in British grocery retailing. *European Journal of Marketing*, 34(8), 875–890.

Burt SL and Sparks L (1997) Performance in food retailing: a cross-national consideration and comparison of retail margins. *British Journal of Management*, 8, 133–150.

Burt SL and Sparks L (2001) The implications of Wal-Mart's takeover of ASDA. *Environment and Planning A*, 33, 1463–1487.

Burt SL and Sparks L (2002) Corporate branding, retailing and retail internationalisation. *Corporate Reputation Review*, 5, 194–212.

Burt SL and Sparks L (2003) Power and competition in the UK retail grocery market. *British Journal of Management*, 14, 237–254.

Burt SL and Sparks L (2006) Asda: Wal-Mart in the United Kingdom. In S Brunn (ed.) *Wal*Mart World: The World's Biggest Corporation in the Global Economy*. New York: Routledge, 27–43.

Chevalier JA (1995) Capital structure and product market competition: empirical evidence from the supermarket industry. *American Economic Review*, 86, 703–725.

Clarke I (2000) Retail power, competition and local consumer choice in the UK grocery sector. *European Journal of Marketing*, 34, 975–1002.

Clarke I, Hallsworth A, Jackson P, de Kervenoael R, Perez del Aguila R and Kirkup M

(2006) Retail restructuring and consumer choice. 1. Long term changes in consumer behaviour: Portsmouth 1980–2002. *Environment and Planning A,* 38, 25–46.

Clarke R, Davies S, Dobson P and Waterson M (2002) *Buyer Power and Competition in European Food Retailing.* Cheltenham: Edward Elgar.

Colla E (2004) The outlook for European grocery retailing: competition and format development. *International Review of Retail, Distribution and Consumer Research,* 14, 47–69.

Competition Commission (2000) *Supermarkets: a Report on the Supply of Groceries from Multiple Stores in the United Kingdom.* Norwich: The Stationery Office.

Competition Commission (2003) *Safeway plc and Asda Group Limited (owned by Wal-Mart Stores Inc); Wm Morrison Supermarkets PLC; J Sainsbury plc; and Tesco plc: a Report on the Mergers in Contemplation.* Norwich: The Stationery Office.

Competition Commission (2005) *Somerfield plc/Wm Morrison Supermarkets plc. A Report on the Acquisition by Somerfield plc of 115 stores from Wm Morrison.* Norwich: The Stationery Office. Available online from www.competition-commission.org.uk/inquiries/ref2005/Somerfield/index.htm

Competition Commission (2006) *Groceries Market Investigation: Issues Statement.* London: TSO. Available at http://www.competition-commission.org.uk/inquiries/ref2006/grocery/index.htm

Competition Commission (2007) *Groceries Market Investigation: Emerging Thinking.* London: TSO. Available at http://www.competition-commission.org.uk/inquiries/ref2006/grocery/index.htm

Cotterill RW (1986) Market power in the retail food industry: evidence from Vermont. *Review of Economics and Statistics,* 68, 379–386.

Cotterill RW (1997) The food distribution system of the future. Convergence towards the US or UK model? *Agribusiness,* 13, 123–35.

Cotterill RW (2006) Antitrust analysis of supermarkets: global concerns playing out in local markets. *Australian Journal of Agricultural and Resource Economics,* 50, 17–32.

Dawson JA (2000) Viewpoint: retailer power, manufacturer power, competition and some questions of economic analysis. *International Journal of Retail and Distribution Management,* 28, 1, 1–4.

Dawson JA and Larke R (2004) Japanese retailing through the 1990s: retailer performance in a decade of slow growth. *British Journal of Management,* 15, 73–94.

Dawson JA and Larke R (2005) The role of medium-sized firms in retail change in Japan. *International Review of Retail, Distribution and Consumer Research,* 15, 401–422.

Dawson JA and Shaw SA (1989) The move to administered vertical marketing systems by British retailers. *European Journal of Marketing,* 23(7), 42–51.

de Kervenoael R, Hallsworth A and Clarke I (2006) Macro-level change and micro-level effects: a twenty-year perspective on changing grocery shopping behavior in Britain. *Journal of Retailing and Consumer Sciences,* 13, 381–392.

Dobson P (2005) Exploiting buyer power: lessons from the British grocery trade. *Antitrust Law Journal,* 72, 529–562.

Dobson P and Waterson M (1996) *Vertical Restraints and Competition Policy,* Research Paper 12. London: Office of Fair Trading.

Dobson P and Waterson M (1999) Retailer power: how regulators should respond to greater concentration in retailing. *Economic Policy,* 28, 134–156.

Dobson P and Waterson M (2005) Chain-store pricing across local markets. *Journal of Economics and Management Strategy,* 14, 93–119.

Dobson P, Waterson M and Chu A (1998) *The Welfare Consequences of the Exercise of Buyer Power,* Research Paper 18. London: Office of Fair Trading.

Dobson P, Waterson M and Davies SW (2003) The patterns and implications of increasing concentration in European food retailing. *Journal of Agricultural Economics,* 54, 111–125.

El-Ansary A and Stern LW (1972) Power and measurement in the distribution channel. *Journal of Marketing Research,* 9, 47–52.

Emerson RE (1962) Power-dependence relations. *American Sociological Review,* 27, 31–41.

French RP and Raven B (1959) The basis of social power. In D Cartwright (ed.) *Studies in Social Power.* Ann Arbor, MI: University of Michigan Press.

Guy CM (1996) Corporate strategies in food retailing and their local impacts – a case study of Cardiff. *Environment and Planning A,* 28, 575–602.

Guy CM (2006) *Planning for Retail Development.* London: Routledge.

Hall P, Marshall S and Lowe M (2001) The changing urban hierarchy in England and Wales, 1913–1998. *Regional Studies,* 35, 775–807.

Hughes A (1996) Retail restructuring and the strategic significance of food retailers' own labels: a UK–USA comparison. *Environment and Planning A,* 28, 2201–2226.

Humby C, Hunt T and Phillips T (2003) *Scoring Points: How Tesco Is Winning Customer Loyalty.* Kogan Page: London.

Hunt S and Nevin J (1974) Power in a channel of distribution: sources and consequences. *Journal of Marketing Research,* 11, 186–193.

Jackson P, Perez del Aguila R, Clarke I, Hallsworth A, de Kervenoael R and Kirkup M (2006) Retail restructuring and consumer choice. 2. Understanding consumer choice at the household level. *Environment and Planning A,* 38, 47–68.

Larke R and Causton M (2005) *Japan – a Modern Retail Superpower.* Basingstoke: Palgrave Macmillan.

London Economics (1997) *Competition in Retailing,* Research Paper 13, London: Office of Fair Trading.

Marsden T, Harrison M and Flynn A (1998) Creating competitive space: exploring the social and political maintenance of retail power. *Environment and Planning A,* 30, 481–498.

Moir C (1990) Competition in the UK grocery trades. In C Moir and JA Dawson (eds) (1990) *Competition and Markets.* Basingstoke: Macmillan, 91–118.

Monopolies and Mergers Commission (1981) *Discounts to Retailers*. London: HMSO.

Morelli C (2004) Explaining the growth of British multiple retailing during the golden age: 1976–94. *Environment and Planning A*, 36, 667–684.

Office of Fair Trading (1985) *Competition and Retailing*. London: HMSO.

Ogbonna E and Wilkinson B (1996) Inter-organizational power relations in the UK grocery industry: contradictions and developments. *International Review of Retail Distribution and Consumer Research*, 6, 395–414.

Ogbonna E and Wilkinson B (1998) Power relations in the UK grocery supply chain. *Journal of Retailing and Consumer Services*, 5(2), 77–86.

Reynolds J, Howard E, Dragun D, Rosewell B and Ormerod P (2005) Assessing the productivity of the UK retail sector. *International Review of Retail, Distribution and Consumer Research*, 15, 237–280.

Round DK (2006) The power of two: squaring off with Australia's large supermarket chains. *Australian Journal of Agricultural and Resource Economics*, 50, 51–64.

Scott P (1994) Learning to multiply – the property market and the growth of multiple retailing in Britain 1919–39. *Business History*, 36, 1–28.

Seth A and Randall G (1999) *The Grocers: the Rise and Rise of the Supermarket Chains*. London: Kogan Page.

Seth A and Randall G (2005) *Supermarket Wars: Global Strategies for Food Retailers*. Basingstoke: Palgrave Macmillan.

Smith DLG (1998) Logistics in Tesco. In J Fernie and L Sparks (eds) *Logistics and Retail Management*. London: Kogan Page, 154–183.

Smith DLG and Sparks L (1993) The transformation of physical distribution in food retailing. *International Review of Retail Distribution and Consumer Research*, 3, 35–64.

Smith DLG and Sparks L (2004) Logistics in Tesco: past, present and future. In J Fernie and L Sparks (eds) *Logistics and Retail Management*, 2nd edn. London: Kogan Page, 101–120.

Smith H (2004) Supermarket choice and supermarket competition in market equilibrium. *Review of Economic Studies*, 71, 235–263.

Smith RL (2006) The Australian grocery industry: a competition perspective. *Australian Journal of Agricultural and Resource Economics*, 50, 33–50.

Sparks L (1986) The changing structure of distribution in retail companies. *Transactions of the Institute of British Geographers*, 11, 147–154.

Sparks L (2002) The findings have surprised some shoppers. *International Journal of Retail and Distribution Management*, 30, 126–133.

Steenkamp J-B and Dekimpe M (1997) The increasing power of private labels: building loyalty and market share. *Long Range Planning*, 30, 917–930.

Steiner RL (1991) Intrabrand competition – stepchild of antitrust. *Antitrust Law Bulletin*, 36, 155–200.

Tedlow RS (1990) *New and Improved: The Story of Mass Marketing in America*. London: Butterworth-Heinemann.

Tucker KA (1975) *Economies of Scale in Retailing*. London: Saxon-House.

Wrigley N (1987) The concentration of capital in UK grocery retailing. *Environment and Planning A*, 19, 1283–1288.

Wrigley N (1991) Is the 'Golden Age' of British grocery retailing at a watershed? *Environment and Planning A*, 23, 1537–1544.

Wrigley N (1992a) Sunk capital, the property crisis, and the restructuring of British food retailing. *Environment and Planning A*, 24, 1521–1530.

Wrigley N (1992b) Antitrust regulation and the restructuring of grocery retailing in Britain. *Environment and Planning A*, 24, 727–749.

Wrigley N (1993) Commentary: abuses of market power? Further reflections on UK food retailing and the regulatory state. *Environment and Planning A*, 25, 1545–1557.

Wrigley N (1994) After the store wars: towards a new era of competition in food retailing? *Journal of Retailing and Consumer Services*, 1, 5–20.

Wrigley N (1996) Sunk costs and corporate restructuring: British food retailing and the property crisis. In N Wrigley and M Lowe (eds) *Retailing, Consumption and Capital*. Harlow: Addison Wesley Longman, 116–136.

Wrigley N (1997) Foreign retail capital on the battlefields of Connecticut: competition regulation at the local scale and its implications. *Environment and Planning A*, 29, 1141–1152.

Wrigley N (1998) Understanding store development programmes in post-property-crisis UK food retailing. *Environment and Planning A*, 30, 15–35.

Wrigley N (1999) Market rules and spatial outcomes: insights from the corporate restructuring of US food retailing. *Geographical Analysis*, 31, 288–309.

Wrigley N (2001) Local spatial monopoly and competition regulation: reflections on recent US and UK rulings. *Environment and Planning A*, 33, 189–194.

Wrigley N (2002) Transforming the corporate landscape of US food retailing: market power, financial re-engineering and regulation. *Tijdschrift voor Economische en Sociale Geografie*, 93, 62–82.

Editors' Commentary

THIS ARTICLE IS CO-AUTHORED by Steve Burt and Leigh Sparks. Details of Steve Burt have been provided in association with his other article in this volume (pp. 161–162). Leigh Sparks is Professor of Retail Studies at the Institute for Retail Studies at the University of Stirling. After a first degree in geography from the University of Cambridge, Leigh joined John Dawson in the University of Wales at Lampeter to complete his PhD on Employment Characteristics of Superstore Retailing. Whilst there, Steve Burt also moved to Wales to begin his PhD. Leigh joined John Dawson in Stirling on an ESRC project in 1983 and has remained there ever since, becoming Professor in 1992. In between spells as Dean of the Faculty of Management and Head of the Department of Marketing, he has been a Visiting Professor at Florida State University and the University of Tennessee. Leigh is co-editor of *The International Review of Retail, Distribution and Consumer Research* and is on the editorial board of a number of marketing journals.

Leigh Sparks has carried out research on a wide range of retail topics, broadly organized under the heading of structural and spatial change in retailing. Within this catch-all, he has explored in detail a number of retail companies, including Kwik Save, William Low, Shoprite, Wal-Mart, Marks & Spencer and 7-Eleven and a number of retail operations (logistics, supply chains, employment) and implications (food deserts, loyalty schemes). He has maintained a long-standing interest in retail planning, collaborating with the National Retail Planning Forum and other organizations including the Scottish Office. His research has been funded by many organizations including the ESRC, Scottish Executive, the Department of Health and the Department of Trade and Industry. Leigh was the only academic on the high-level UK Government Retail Strategy Group which emerged from the work he and Steve Burt carried out for the DTI into the competitive structure of UK retailing.

Steve Burt and Leigh Sparks have been colleagues throughout their academic life. This is only one of many papers that they have co-authored. They bring together their expertise on structural changes and spatial change at a time when the spatial changes taking place in UK grocery retailing have called into question the nature of competition on a spatial basis. 'Power and Competition in the UK Retail Grocery Market' identifies trends in the UK grocery market which have created an oligopolistic market. The degree of concentration in the UK grocery market has been a matter of considerable concern for the UK competition authorities and this paper arose from work for one of the major grocery retailers during one of the seemingly never-ending competition inquiries into the sector.

Key Publications

Sparks L (1986) The changing structure of distribution in retail companies. *Transactions of the Institute of British Geographers*, 11, 147–154.

Lord JD, Moran W, Parker AJ and Sparks L (1988) Retailing on three continents: the discount food store operations of Albert Gubay. *International Journal of Retailing*, 3(3), 1–54.

Sparks L (1990) Spatial-structural relationships in retail corporate growth: a case study of Kwik Save Group plc. *Service Industries Journal*, 10(1), 25–83.

Smith DLG and Sparks L (1993) The transformation of physical distribution in food retailing. *International Review of Retail Distribution and Consumer Research*, 3, 35–64.

Burt SL and Sparks L (1994) Structural change in grocery retailing in Great Britain: a discount re-orientation? *International Review of Retail, Distribution and Consumer Research*, 4, 195–217.

Sparks L (1995) Reciprocal retail internationalisation: the Southland Corporation. Ito-Yokado and 7-Eleven convenience stores. *Service Industries Journal*, 15(4), 57–96.

Sparks L (1996) Space wars: Wm Low and the 'auld enemy'. *Environment and Planning A*, 28, 1464–1484.

Burt SL and Sparks L (1997) Performance in food retailing: a cross-national consideration and comparison of retail margins. *British Journal of Management*, 8, 133–150.

Fernie J and Sparks L (1998 and 2nd edn 2004) *Logistics and Retail Management*. London: Kogan Page.

Findlay A and Sparks L (1998-2007) *A Bibliography of Retail Planning*. London: National Retail Planning Forum (annual updates and rewrites and planner briefing papers).

Sparks L (2000) Seven-Eleven Japan and the Southland Corporation: a marriage of convenience? *International Marketing Review*, 17(4/5), 401–415.

Burt S and Sparks L (2001) The implications of Wal-Mart's takeover of Asda. *Environment and Planning A*, 33, 1463–1487.

Mellahi K, Jackson TP and Sparks L (2002) An exploratory study into failure in successful organisations: the case of Marks and Spencer. *British Journal of Management*, 13, 15–29.

Smith DLG and Sparks L (2004) Logistics in Tesco: past, present and future. In J Fernie and L Sparks (eds) *Logistics and Retail Management*, 2nd edn. London: Kogan Page.

Burt SL and Sparks L (2006) Asda: Wal-Mart in the UK. In S Brunn (ed.) *Wal-Mart World*. New York: Routledge, 27–43.

Cummins S, Findlay A, Higgins C, Petticrew M, Sparks L and Thomson H (2007) Reducing inequalities in health and diet: findings from a study on the impact of a food retail development. *Environment & Planning A,* 40(2), 402–422.

Website

http://www.marketing.stir.ac.uk/STFPAGES/sparks/page.htm

POWER AND COMPETITION IN THE UK RETAIL GROCERY MARKET

Steve L. Burt and Leigh Sparks

The UK retail grocery market is widely recognized as being oligopolistic. This has raised concerns over the level and use of power by the leading retailers. This paper considers the changes in the UK retail grocery market in the context of a discussion of power. This discussion focuses on the possibility of a dominant chain arising in the market. Vertical and horizontal relationships and price and non-price competition form the organizing principles of the analysis. Policy implications are suggested and other conclusions are drawn.

British Journal of Management, Vol. 14 (2003), pp. 237–254. © 2003 British Academy of Management.

Introduction

AFTER THE MONOPOLIES AND Mergers Commission (MMC) (1981) and Office of Fair Trading (OFT) (1985) studies into competition in the UK retail grocery market, concentration continued to increase. In the UK, the locus of 'power' in the distribution channel shifted away from branded goods manufacturers towards retailers. In many product markets (including grocery) retailers have assumed channel leadership, utilizing improved demand and customer information to develop their brand position and overall retail offer (Burt, 2000; Wileman and Jary, 1997). As fewer retailers have taken a larger share of the grocery market, the 'gatekeeping' role traditionally assigned to retailers because of their location in the channel has assumed greater significance, raising concerns over the extent and use of retail power (Clarke *et al.*, 2002). This has been seen most recently in the 'battle' for Safeway.

As grocery retailers became stronger relative to other channel members, the fear was that the power balance had tipped too far in the retailers' favour. Press reports based upon often crude international price comparisons (see London Economics (2000) and AC Nielsen (2000) for more balanced considerations), together with the crisis in the farming industry, fuelled concerns that British grocery retailers were exploiting their market power to the detriment of suppliers and consumers. Such concerns had been raised before (e.g. Wrigley, 1987, 1991) but with little impact. In the mid-to-late 1990s, amid widespread press concerns and other reports (e.g. Dobson, Waterson and Chu, 1998), the government ordered a Competition Commission investigation of the sector. Whilst the Commission found little evidence of abuse of market power in terms of pricing and profits, it did express concerns over treatment of suppliers (Competition Commission, 2000). The media and other commentators remain wary about retailer power.

Underlying much of the public and academic discussion of retail power is an assumption that price is the sole motivator for consumer grocery-buying behaviour. Whilst price is a key competitive element in retailing, numerous studies argue that other factors contribute to or determine purchase (see for example Buttle, 1985; Darden and Lusch, 1983; Donovan and Rossiter, 1982; Mitchell and Kiral, 1999). Product range and quality, convenience via store location and access, store ambience and additional service facilities all feature amongst the motives for store choice. This mix of influencing factors is reflected regularly in market research surveys (e.g. Table 1). It could be argued that British grocery retailers have utilized their channel power to develop a total (i.e. not solely price-based) retail offer which satisfies these emerging consumers' needs and values.

Power has always existed within distribution channels. Channel power is understood to derive from the interaction of three factors:

- the levels of dependency which exist between channel members (e.g. Brown, Lusch and Muehling, 1983; Dickson, 1983; Emerson, 1962; Hunt and Nevin, 1974);
- the form and location of power amongst channel members (e.g. El-Ansary

Table 1 Considering where to shop: the most important factors

All Households (%)	1994	1997	2000
Good quality fresh produce	3.5	3.5	14.3
High quality products	3.8	2.7	7.7
Good value for money	19.9	13.5	33.1
Ease of parking	20.6	21.0	5.4
Special in-store promotions	2.3	3.4	3.5
Good range of products	15.1	14.0	10.7
Good quality own labels	6.9	5.1	2.7
Convenient location	13.4	16.0	13.8
Low prices	9.6	14.4	6.7
Other reasons	0.4	0.4	2.1
Helpful staff	0.5	0.8	—
Store is clean and tidy	3.8	5.2	—

Source: Niesen Homescan Household Survey in AC Nielsen, *The Retail Pocket Book*, various years.

and Stern, 1972; French and Raven, 1959; Gaski, 1984; Lusch and Brown, 1982);

- the level of conflict and co-operation within a channel, and the means by which conflict is resolved (e.g. Anderson and Narus, 1990; Etgar, 1979; Gaski and Nevin, 1985; Reve and Stern, 1979; Rosenberg and Stern, 1971).

The core issues from a policy perspective are not the existence of market power but the *ownership* and *use* of power, and the *effect* of this use.

The way in which many economists view retailing however, with an overwhelming emphasis on price, a lack of consideration of retail branding and some misunderstanding of the activities undertaken by retailers, constrains the relevance of some of their work. Dawson (2000) for example has argued that economists have rarely understood retailing, preferring a production orientation. He argues that they do not understand the functions retailers undertake, mis-specify the nature of inter-firm relationships, focus on price rather than non-price competition and have few accurate measures of performance and consumer benefits. Recently however, some economists have begun to re-evaluate the complex competitive issues the sector raises. We identify five areas where this recent work is perhaps applicable to the retail sector and to our understanding of it.

First, a focus on a direct relationship between concentration and prices remains of interest (Cotterill, 1986, 2000). Marion (1998), Dobson and Waterson (1997), Cotterill and Haller (1992) and Bresnahan and Reiss (1991) however emphasize the impacts of market position and entry in concentrated markets. Bresnahan and Reiss (1991) suggest that three competitors are required for a competitive market: fewer than three sees excess prices and more than three has little effect on prices. Cotterill (1999) however rejects any notion that higher prices are due to more service provision in food retailing, arguing that concentration alone is the fundamental variable defining market prices. It is questionable however whether this model really incorporates service delivery in modern superstores and whether it fully applies in all markets (e.g. the UK).

Second, and arising from the analysis above, many have begun to recognize that retailers are not passive players in a simplistic production to consumption channel. Dobson and Waterson (1997) emphasize the increase in power that retailers have gained, but stress that this power is both buying and selling power (see also Clarke *et al.*, 2002). Retailers focus on both horizontal and vertical (upstream and downstream) considerations. Dawson (2000) comments that consumers purchase a service from retailers, but that retailers 'manufacture' that service using products (including some manufacturer brands) and services (which include operational attributes of stores such as queues, as well as formally recognized services such as pharmacy, insurance etc).

Third, the competitive structure of retail markets has been reconsidered and consumer choice has been recognized as important to their operation (Waller, 2001). This emphasis on choice has lead to a more detailed examination of non-price issues. Armstrong and Vickers (2001) rethink what it is that people buy from retailers. Marion (1998) examines non-price competition and differentiation, including the use of non-price issues to enhance strategic distance amongst companies. This source of differentiation has also been the focus of the work of Tang, Bell and Ho (2001).

These more complex views of competition and power come together in considerations of dominant firms and chains. Balto (2001) points to the ability of a single retail chain to exercise real market power. Riordan (1998) has focused on the earlier work of Salop and Scheffman (1983) and demonstrated how raising rivals' costs is a viable competitive approach in retailing. Salop and Scheffman (1983) suggested that disadvantaging competitors provides a benefit that allows a dominant firm to increase market share or prices. A number of possible ways of raising costs can be identified, including supply agreements and exclusive dealing, wage rises, compliance costs, advertising and development races, service enhancements and vertical integration. Smith (2002), Waller (2001) and Clarke *et al.* (2002) have explored some of these.

Finally, these fundamental considerations of power and markets have an impact on policy research and development. The clearest UK statements of this are by Clarke *et al.* (2002), but these issues also fundamentally underpin the Competition Commission enquiry and report (2000). Riordan (1998), Scherer (1999) and NERA (1999) have examined similar policy issues and Chen (2001), Bresnahan and Reiss (1991) and Smith (2002) have discussed the implications of developments in retailing on vertical and horizontal integration, and merger and demerger policy.

This paper aims to raise and discuss these issues about how power and competition may be understood and may develop in an oligopolistic market, such as the UK retail grocery market. The paper first introduces briefly the growth of an oligopolistic market in the UK retail grocery sector, suggesting that a dominant chain is an important concept arising from such a market. It then considers the conditions under which a dominant retail chain emerges and the competitive behaviours that may characterize such a chain. Sector-wide implications are then considered. Finally some conclusions are drawn.

The Growth of an Oligopolistic Market in Grocery Retailing in the UK

In virtually every retail sector there has been increasing market concentration in recent decades. A larger proportion of retail sales is accounted for by a reduced number of retail organizations. In the grocery sector there has been reference to a 'big four' or 'big five' since the mid-1980s. The addition of new stores, the acquisition of competing floor space, and the rigorous implementation of customer-focused operating strategies have increased market share and concentration ratios. New store formats and locations, an emphasis on competitive pricing, the widening of product and service ranges, and improvements in store ambience and service levels are visible outcomes of these strategies (Seth and Randall, 1999).

Market concentration is commonly equated to market power. Market-share statistics are seen as a proxy measure of this power. However, when assessing market concentration on the basis of market share it is important to acknowledge a number of issues relating to the measures employed (see for example, Clarke *et al.*, 2002; London Economics, 1997). The definition of 'food' or 'grocery' varies amongst data sources. In particular the inclusion or exclusion of everyday healthcare and other non-food household product ranges and organizations serving certain segments of the market (e.g. limited line discounters, the co-operative societies, and Marks & Spencer) can significantly influence the baseline figures (see Table 2). Further caveats with respect to national market-share figures arise, as a result of definitional changes over time and issues of regionality. The historical evolution of the sector, with different companies expanding from different regional heartlands, means that market share figures for individual companies vary significantly from region to region (Table 3). Local market shares may be more important than regional or national figures (a point emphasized in Competition Commission, 2000), reflecting the local nature of consumer purchasing of groceries and the local nature of grocery retailing competition. The definition here is also problematic however, a point well illustrated by the surprise over the Office of Fair Trading's referral of Morrison in the Safeway takeover battle.

Nonetheless, we can state that the market share taken by the largest grocery chains has risen. The sector is now commonly regarded as exhibiting an oligopolistic structure. Time series data show a consistent pattern of growth at a national level (see Table 4). Since 1991, the CR4 ratio (Tesco, J Sainsbury, Asda and Safeway) has grown by almost 30%. The data also illustrate the relative growth experienced by individual companies. Boosted by the 1994 acquisition of Wm Low (Sparks, 1996), Tesco saw its market share rise by over 50% during the 1990s, as it overtook Sainsbury to become the largest grocery chain. Whilst Asda, particularly since the Wal-Mart takeover (Burt and Sparks, 2001) has seen a similar growth in market share (albeit from a much lower base), both Sainsbury

Table 2 National market share (%) 1998/1999, by source

Company	Taylor Nelson Sofres (1999)	IGD (1999)	Competition Commission (1998/9)
Tesco	21.1	15.6	23.0
Sainsbury	17.6	11.8	18.7
Asda	12.7	9.1	12.2
Safeway	9.3	7.4	11.5
Somerfield	4.1	6.2	9.8
Marks & Spencer	—	2.9	4.9
Morrison	4.1	3.0	3.9
Waitrose	—	1.9	3.0
Iceland	—	1.9	3.0
Others	31.1	40.2	1.0
Total	100	100	100
Concentration ratios			
CR1	21.1	15.6	23.0
CR2	38.7	27.4	41.7
CR3	51.4	36.5	53.9
CR4	60.7	43.9	65.4
CR5	64.8	50.1	75.2/69.3*

Notes: Market definition: Taylor Nelson Sofres – retailer share track (179 markets: pack-
    aged grocery, fresh foods & toiletries/healthcare);
IGD – Total market size includes M&S food sales, retailers where food sales exceed 50%,
    CTNs where food-related items exceed 35%, chemists and VAT;
Competition Commission – groceries defined as food, alcoholic and non-alcoholic drinks,
    cleaning products, toiletries, household goods. 'All grocery stores' category.
* 75.2% taking largest five company shares; 69.3% presented by Competition Commis-
    sion (Morrison replacing Somerfield as C5 company).

and Safeway have experienced relatively small gains. Despite references to the
'big 4', by 1999, the ex-VAT domestic food sales of Tesco were 30% larger than
Sainsbury's UK grocery operation and approximately twice the size of either
Asda or Safeway. It could be argued that a dominant chain was emerging in the
market.

Whilst scale is clearly a key driver in determining power, it is important in
understanding the changes in British grocery retailing that the role of centralized
management systems, standardization and information control are recognized
(Burt, 1989). These three complementary factors are crucial in leveraging scale
at the organizational level. Although scale may be most visible at a local level
(through the size and availability of stores in a given catchment area) it is the
harnessing of this local scale at national level which ultimately provides the basis
for channel control and changes in existing power relationships. A feature of
British grocery retailing during the 1980s and early 1990s was a managerial
approach that saw the reduction of storelevel decision-making in favour of
corporate control at the centre. This managerial trend found favour not only
with the multiple chains but also with collaborative groups and even belatedly

Table 3 Regional market shares (%), 1991, 1995, 1999

a) 1991

Region	Asda	Sainsbury	Tesco	Safeway	Somerfield	Morrisons
GB	8.2	16.4	14.7	7.9	4.8	1.7
London	6.4	29.4	16.2	8.4	3.5	0.0
Midlands	8.0	16.9	10.8	7.1	5.1	1.7
N. East	11.4	8.8	4.9	15.1	3.7	6.6
Yorkshire	10.1	9.9	9.2	4.1	3.5	7.4
Lancs	12.4	7.3	10.0	3.6	2.6	3.4
South	4.7	21.4	24.1	8.7	5.8	0.0
Scotland	12.8	2.2	14.4	17.4	5.6	0.0
E.England	3.2	26.7	18.8	3.4	5.2	0.2
Wales & W	8.5	13.1	19.9	6.8	6.5	0.0
S.West	4.2	3.3	24.5	5.4	16.3	0.0

b) 1995

Region	Asda	Sainsbury	Tesco	Safeway	Somerfield	Morrisons
GB	9.5	17.7	17.4	8.2	5.0	3.2
London	5.9	31.1	21.1	8.5	3.4	0.0
Midlands	9.9	15.2	13.5	7.7	6.4	4.9
N. East	13.8	7.3	6.3	14.0	3.9	10.2
Yorkshire	10.9	10.8	10.1	6.5	3.1	11.8
Lancs	14.8	10.3	11.8	3.9	3.5	6.5
South	5.9	25.4	27.9	7.8	4.5	0.0
Scotland	13.9	4.2	13.7	17.4	6.2	0.1
E.England	4.3	25.0	27.0	3.5	4.5	0.2
Wales & W	11.1	14.4	21.1	6.9	7.2	0.0
S.West	5.2	13.6	18.9	8.8	14.7	0.0

c)1999

Region	Asda	Sainsbury	Tesco	Safeway	Somerfield	Morrisons
GB	12.7	17.6	21.1	9.3	4.1	4.1
London	8.1	29.5	26.9	7.9	3.0	0.4
Midlands	12.4	18.2	17.2	9.8	3.9	6.1
N. East	18.8	7.8	5.2	13.9	1.5	12.0
Yorkshire	15.2	9.7	14.1	6.4	2.6	15.5
Lancs	19.9	11.0	15.2	4.6	2.2	8.0
South	8.7	22.9	30.1	10.0	4.5	0.0
Scotland	18.8	4.9	16.9	19.2	6.2	0.5
E.England	8.0	22.6	29.2	5.9	5.4	1.1
Wales & W	13.1	14.3	26.1	8.2	6.3	0.0
S.West	6.9	15.0	22.1	11.6	13.0	0.0

Source: Taylor Nelson Sofres Superpanel – month 08.

Table 4 Changes in national market share (%) over time

a) Taylor Nelson Sofres data

Company	1991	1992	1993	1994	1995	1996	1997	1998	1999	% Change 1991–1999
Tesco	14.0	14.3	14.9	15.7	18.1	19.0	20.0	20.9	21.1	+50.7
Sainsbury	16.5	16.9	17.3	17.0	17.5	17.4	17.0	18.0	17.6	+6.7
Asda	8.4	8.2	8.4	8.9	9.7	10.8	11.5	12.2	12.7	+51.2
Safeway	8.0	8.1	8.6	8.5	8.4	9.0	9.4	9.5	9.3	+16.3
CR4	46.9	47.5	49.2	50.1	53.7	56.2	57.9	60.6	60.7	+29.4
Somerfield	4.6	4.4	4.8	5.2	4.9	4.5	4.5	4.3	4.1	−98.0*
Kwik Save	4.3	5.3	5.8	5.6	5.5	5.5	4.9	4.5	–	–
Morrisons	1.8	2.2	2.7	2.9	3.3	3.5	3.4	3.7	4.1	+127.8

b) IGD data

Company	1991	1992	1993	1994	1995	1996	1997	1998	1999	2000	% Change 1991–2000
Tesco	9.9	10.1	10.4	11.4	13.4	14.2	14.8	15.2	15.6	16.2	+63.6
Sainsbury	11.3	11.9	12.1	12.3	12.2	12.2	12.4	12.2	11.8	11.5	+1.7
Asda	6.5	6.3	6.5	6.7	7.2	7.8	8.3	8.4	9.1	9.5	+46.2
Safeway	7.2	7.3	7.5	7.6	7.3	7.6	7.6	7.6	7.4	7.5	+4.2
CR4	34.9	35.6	36.5	38.0	40.1	41.8	43.1	43.8	43.9	44.7	+28.1
Somerfield	4.7	4.3	4.3	4.4	4.2	4.0	3.8	6.9	6.1	5.0	−36.7*
Kwik Save	3.2	3.8	4.1	4.0	4.2	4.1	3.5	–	–	–	–
M&S	3.2	3.0	3.1	3.1	3.0	3.1	3.0	2.9	2.9	2.8	−12.5
Morrisons	1.7	1.7	1.9	2.2	2.4	2.5	2.5	2.6	3.0	3.3	+94.1
Waitrose	1.7	1.7	1.6	1.6	1.7	1.8	1.8	1.8	1.9	2.0	+15.0
Iceland	1.3	1.5	1.6	1.7	1.7	1.7	1.6	1.7	1.7	1.7	+30.8

Note: * Somerfield percentage changes based on Somerfield and Kwik Save share in 1991.

the Co-operative movement. The centralization of decision-making, availability via EPOS systems of data at the product item level, and the implementation of standardized store formats (Burt and Sparks, 1997), allowed retailers to change the existing balance of power in the distribution channel, and to take on the channel leadership role traditionally held by manufacturers. Retailers began to compete as brands, rather than simply as traders (Burt, 2000; Wileman and Jary, 1997). Operational efficiencies derived from centralized distribution and logistics and improved workforce scheduling provided both customer service and cost management benefits. Customer-focused marketing strategies, high-quality store environments, innovative rather than commodity retail brand ranges, and various customer service initiatives followed (Burt and Sparks, 2002).

Over this period the UK grocery channel is widely regarded as also having taken on the behavioural characteristics of an administered vertical marketing system (Dawson and Shaw, 1989). Retailers used their increased power and influence in the distribution channel to move away from conventional relationships, in which channel members (e.g. suppliers, wholesalers, retailers, consumers) are loosely focused on each other with efforts concentrated on dyadic relationships with the next member of the channel. This system allows for inefficiencies (and costs) in the channel as functions and activities (e.g. stock holding) are replicated by different channel members, and relationships between members are characterized by short-term deals, conflict and rivalry with bargaining over price to the fore (Doel, 1996; Hughes, 1996). In contrast, the administered vertical-marketing system requires channel members to view the total distribution channel as a managed network of aligned members. Relationships in this type of channel are based upon information sharing and tend to be more collaborative and long term in nature. Numerous authors comment on the development of such an approach in the UK (see for example, Doel, 1999; Duke, 1998; Hogarth-Scott and Parkinson, 1993; Hughes, 1999; Ogbonna and Wilkinson, 1996, 1998). Administered systems still contain power relationships however, although the nature and implications of the use of this power is altered.

The Rise and Implications of a Dominant Retail Chain

Conceptually, the observed growth in the power of the retail sector can be related to the countervailing power thesis (Galbraith, 1952). The rise of retail chains and the growth of retail brands counteract the power held traditionally by manufacturers. This was believed by Galbraith to be in the consumers' interest, owing to high levels of competition amongst retailers. Opponents of this argument, such as Reisman (1980), believe that the basic premise – that the large confront the large – is not always the case. In reality, large retailers may confront smaller suppliers, and 'original' rather than 'countervailing' power arises. In this case, what Adams (1987) terms 'coalescing' power develops. Whether it is countervailing or original power that develops, it is the *use* of this power which is the key to understanding the workings of the market and future market developments.

The direction of development of the UK grocery market raises questions for future market structures and, in particular, market behaviour. If continued, the forces of market concentration, which contributed to the construction of an oligopolistic market in the first place, could ultimately lead to further strengthening of one or possibly two organizations. The market may begin to take on more monopolistic or duopolistic features. Out of a retail oligopoly may rise one or two chains, which have the potential to use their market power to maintain their position at the expense of others. As opportunities to grow to national scale either organically or through the acquisition of minor players (the definition of these alters over time as shown by Safeway) in the market decline, so the barriers to growth faced by the 'fringe' or non-dominant retailers rise. This is true at the national level, but as the Competition Commission (2000) identified, may be prevalent at the regional and local level.

Increasing scale allied to efficient and appropriate operation and investment which meets customer demand allows an organization to increase its share of sales faster than can others. This enables cost to fall across the organization and provides further investment for operational activities which, if correctly targeted, will in turn continue to attract customers, increase sales and market share. In effect a 'circle of growth' driven by scale, investment and efficient asset utilization develops at both outlet and organizational level. As some companies experience faster rates of sales growth than others, the 'circle' becomes a 'spiral of growth' (Figure 1). As the spiral turns faster, barriers to entry (and competition costs) are raised and it becomes difficult for some organizations to stay on the spiral.

At the unit level, the growth of large out-of-town or edge-of-town stores has been explained by continued investment in scale and facilities (NatWest Securities, 1995). Large stores built on non-central sites benefit from lower unit costs (e.g. lower occupancy costs, lower operating and distribution costs and support overheads which are spread across more sales) whilst at the same time providing attractive customer facilities (wider product ranges, easier access and

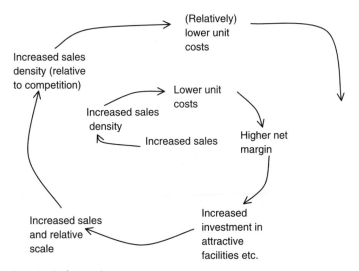

Figure 1 The spiral of growth

parking, longer trading hours etc). Sales rise, sales density (sales per square foot) increase and unit costs are consequently lowered, allowing further investment in existing and new sites and facilities. As the sector or geographical area approaches high penetration or saturation such a process slows or reverses, with falls in superstore sales density encouraging new retail formats to be utilized.

To date, empirical studies of scale effects at the outlet level in retailing are limited. As Tucker (1975, 1980) notes (though not in grocery) methodologies and measures of scale and costs vary, as do the types of store and sample sizes used. Shaw, Nisbet and Dawson (1989) reviewed previous work produced mainly on 1970s data which shows limited evidence of operating cost economies with scale (with the exception of some labour costs economies), a view confirmed in their own study, based on a major UK grocery chain. However, they emphasized the crucial link between outlet scale and organizational scale: 'it should be recognised that a complete view of retail cost functions should involve an analysis of interaction between firm level and store level economies'. A similar point is made by Clarke et al.'s (2002) emphasis on retailers' possession of both buying and selling power.

Shaw, Nisbet and Dawson (1989) also emphasized the significance of sales density: 'The appropriate measurement of scale in a store is a combination of sales area and sales density. Sales area is not sufficient on its own as differing sales densities reflect differing degrees of capacity utilization and will alter levels of costs'. The sales density/capacity utilization relationship is important for future market structures given the relative sales densities achieved by different organizations (Table 5). The importance of sales density was acknowledged by the Competition Commission (2000) as a more important influence on cost structures at store level than economies of scale: 'a given increase in sales density will lead to a proportionately lower increase in staff costs . . . This effect has a much more significant impact on staff costs than economies of scale'.

Even assuming that there are no economies of scale at outlet level in store operating costs – i.e. the operating costs for each company can be apportioned at the same rate (%) – then the operator with the highest sales density can accrue a higher net margin. This may be taken as profit or, if margins are held at an industry level, may be re-invested, which in turn further increases sales density. If, however, some scale economies are available at the outlet level – such as in labour, distribution and general support costs – then utilization is even more efficient in the stores with the highest sales densities, and yet greater returns are achieved. The 'spiral of growth' becomes self-perpetuating. Subordinate retailers either fail to compete or are ejected from the spiral. The surplus may be re-invested by the taking of lower net margin through the introduction of additional facilities (Figure 1). It can also be taken by lower net margins through price reductions (Figure 2). Both approaches seek to drive volume up, stimulate the rate of sales growth, enhance sales density and lead to lower unit costs and better asset utilization (Figure 2). The price discount/cost reduction approach may perhaps be best exemplified by Wal-Mart (Burt and Sparks, 2001), and the facilities provision by Tesco (Burt and Sparks, 2002), though it is recognized that such approaches are not entirely mutually exclusive and retailers may have elements of both.

Table 5 Space utilization – sales density and sales area

	£ Sales per square foot per week*				Sales area** (000 sq ft)	
	1995/96	2000/01	Change (£) 1995–2000	Change (%) 1995–2000	Net change (000 sq ft) 1995–2000	As at 1.1.2001
Tesco	16.59	20.11	+3.52	+21.2	+4923	17563.9
Sainsbury	20.09	18.54	−1.55	−7.7	+2948	13413.0
Asda	13.77	19.08	+5.31	+38.6	+1943	10152.5
Safeway	12.60	15.21	+2.61	+20.7	+988	10304.4
Somerfield	9.29	8.00	−1.26	−13.9	−2100	11087.3
Morrisons	13.91	17.19	+3.28	+23.6	+1391	3917.0
Waitrose	14.11	15.86	+1.75	+12.4	+690	2364.2
Iceland	6.95	10.35	+3.40	+48.9	+119	3700.4

Notes: * Based on total UK grocery retail turnover (excluding VAT) and net sales area on IGD stores database.
** Net changes in sales area including new stores and extensions.

Source: Calculated from IGD, various years.

Dobson, Waterson and Chu (1998) observe essentially the same pattern. Growth and market concentration at a national level increases organizational scale, which provides lower unit costs through greater buying power. As a consequence sales and profits increase, providing the capital and scope to invest in attractive customer facilities (branding/quality/range extension/service etc) or in price reductions which in turn lead to a further sales increase and relatively lower costs. In these circumstances the *absolute* costs of competing in such a way increase. The potential arises for what Dobson, Waterson and Chu (1998) term a 'virtuous circle' of growth dominated by one or two organizations, whose lower *unit* costs enable them to assume market leadership providing that they continue to offer an attractive customer package. As this situation develops, it provides the theoretical ability for the dominant organization(s) to exploit their position of 'power' to maintain this 'spiral of growth' and, potentially, to accelerate it. This scenario could result in reduced or at best 'managed' competition:

> Exploiting (that) access helps to build scale and yields larger margins, which can in turn be invested, among other things, in branding and product development expertise. Holding down expenses and capital requirements while exploiting arbitrage opportunities also creates efficiencies of scale, freeing capital that can be used to expand access and build expertise. Ultimately, retailers exploiting the virtuous circle of access, scale, and expertise will lock in strong competitive advantages that will help them drive their own strategic destinies and shape the industry all over the world.
>
> (Incandela, McLaughlin and Smith, 1999)

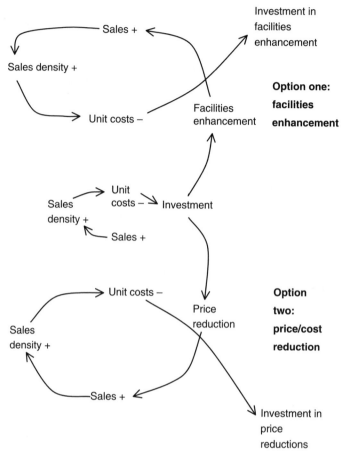

Figure 2 Alternative growth spirals

Competitors are, in effect, reduced to a subordinate position. The demands of the consumer market require them to match the initiatives of the dominant chain(s) to remain attractive to customers. However their cost base is dictated by the dominant chain(s). Without the same advantages of scale and lower unit costs, the subordinate chains are unable to fully compete on the same terms. They become followers, with competitive terms dictated by the market leader. We would argue that it is precisely this position that confronted Asda in the early 1990s and in essence they had to withdraw from expansion (Seth and Randall, 1999; Wrigley, 1992, 1994). Similar considerations underpinned the initial Morrisons/Safeway takeover bid. In order to exploit this position, the levels of return achieved by the dominant chain(s) may fall in the short term, as sales enhancing investments are made, but the scope exists in the longer term for profit and market manipulation. This competitive scenario is at the heart of the price/concentration issue identified earlier (e.g. Cotterill, 1999, 2000; Dobson and Waterson, 1997; Marion, 1998). The policy question behind this (do higher market shares lead to enhanced consumer welfare or higher prices?) is clearly fundamental to any view of the future of food retailing and to legislation and regulation of the sector (Balto, 2001; Clarke *et al.*, 2002; Competition Commission, 2000; Dobson and Waterson, 1999; Moir, 1990).

Characteristic Behaviours of Dominant Retail Chains

The ability of a dominant chain to 'manage' competition arises from the use of power to manage competition in two directions, vertical competition (achieved by supply chain management) and horizontal competition (achieved by raising rivals' costs and creating barriers to entry). Dobson, Waterson and Chu (1998) focus primarily on the use of power arising from their 'virtuous circle' of growth, in a vertical context. They imply that all retailers in the sector benefit from greater power in supplier relationships and that increased average gross and net margins suggest that 'retailers are increasingly able to retain the benefits of their increased bargaining power rather than passing them on to consumers' (see also Moir, 1990). This perspective focuses attention on one aspect of retail competition, price, and on the issue of excess profits. The discussion has focused on margin, which Dawson (2000) describes as an ill-suited measurement of performance given the changed activities of retailers. Less attention has been paid to the London Economics (1997) report, which suggests that retailing differs from other sectors of the economy and which highlights the importance of considering horizontal competition in retailing. Any assessment of market structure and power in retailing can not divorce the vertical use of power from the horizontal use of power.

If a dominant retail chain were to evolve, one way for it to maintain and strengthen its position would be to use its market power to increase the attractiveness of its offer to consumers whilst driving up the cost base for competitors, i.e. the facilities enhancement option on the growth spiral. This approach of raising rivals' costs has been identified before (Salop and Scheffman, 1983; Riordan, 1998). The dominant chain would be willing and, by virtue of scale, better able to incur extra operating costs and take a reduced return in the short run in the hope of long-term gains through market dominance. Such a situation would be evidenced by characteristic behaviour patterns in both vertical and horizontal relationships (Harvey (2000) considers some of these behaviours). To some extent these behaviour patterns then become the norm within the market place. The issue then is whether one (or two) organizations become powerful enough to dictate the market behaviours of others, setting both the competitive agenda and cost structures in the sector. This section considers the forms in which this might occur.

Dominant chain behaviour in vertical relationships

Characteristic behaviours of a dominant chain in respect of vertical relationships would see the use of channel power at a central level to manage the supply chain. This would take the form of seeking better supply terms (i.e. control of supply/distribution costs) and product range enhancement (i.e. unique product/service offers). Both of these approaches deliver the improved margins and sales increases required to drive the growth spiral. Typical behaviours might include:

Supply/distribution cost management. The cost of goods sold (i.e. product costs and distribution costs) is the single largest expense item on a retail company's profit and loss account. In broad terms in the grocery market this item accounts for around 75–80% of sales. Since the abolition of RPM the ability of retailers to negotiate supplier deals and manage prices and margins across a full product offer has grown, and improvements in logistics systems have allowed retailers to source from further afield – in effect increasing supply side capacity. As retailers control the traditional access routes to the consumer, through the ownership of floor- and shelf-space, market share exploited through centralized buying processes provides greater scope to negotiate volume and other discounts. In addition to volume discounts other allowances may be requested – e.g. slotting allowances; exclusivity contracts; promotional support etc – all of which contribute to profit generation and/or add to the attractiveness of a particular chain through the provision of a set of offers throughout the store product range. Some of these activities could be seen as anti-competitive (Competition Commission, 2000).

Central to supply/distribution cost management is information management. Continued investment in IT systems providing product item data allows improved monitoring of product movement throughout the supply chain. This, alongside the industry-wide move towards centralized distribution facilities and the contracting-out of distribution activities (Smith and Sparks, 1993), and more recent applications such as sales-based ordering and the implementation of ECR initiatives, allow further efficiency gains through the management of stock levels and product movement, and the development of more coordinated retailer–supplier relationships. The industry now operates a (customer-determined) demand chain, rather than a (producer-oriented) supply chain, reflecting this new emphasis. The ability of the largest chains to participate in and fund these initiatives, whilst maintaining acceptable levels of return for shareholders may be greater than others. The centralized logistics systems of Tesco, for example, have been identified as world class (McKinsey, 1998), whilst Wal-Mart's investment in technology for its supply chain has been enormous.

Management of the supplier base. As noted earlier, the sector has moved towards managing the grocery channel as an administered system. This has involved the transfer of responsibility and performance of various activities (and associated costs) amongst the members of the channel. By viewing the channel as a single system, costs may be removed from the supply chain (e.g. more efficient stock management through store-based ordering systems), sub-contracted to lower cost providers (e.g. third-party distribution) or transferred to others in the channel (e.g. ready-for-shelf packaging which reduces store handling costs). In addition to such rent-seeking behaviour, from which the retailer is likely to gain the most, this approach to channel management has seen a structural adjustment of the supplier base. Larger chains have reduced the number of suppliers through the delisting of products (Davies, 1994), and identification of preferential suppliers, particularly for unique products such as retail brand ranges. This behaviour influences the structure of the supply side of the market through increased supplier dependency and an increase in costs for other suppliers, who lose economies of scale (Bloom and Perry, 2001). To a considerable extent the gains from such activities are similar to those proposed for vertical integration and the effects may be the same (Riordan, 1998). In an administered system however, retailers can change the supply base when new suppliers become available (possibly globally).

Product range enhancement. Whilst the above behaviour provides direct cost benefits to the retailer, allowing for improved margin contributions, a further dimension arising from administered vertical marketing channels is the ability of retailers to collaborate with manufacturers to enhance product ranges. This is most evident in the development of retail brand ranges within the UK. The emphasis upon a retail brand product range characterized by high quality, innovative products is a feature of British grocery retailing which retailers in many other countries are attempting to follow. Many new product ranges (e.g. ready-made meals) have been introduced to the market under the retailer's brand rather than any manufacturer brand. Whilst changes in consumer tastes may have altered the basic product component of the market, the development of new ranges and the speed of response/introduction derives from retailer/manufacturer linkages. By definition, retail brands are unique to the company concerned and provide a source of differentiation from competitors. In the UK, the common strategy has been to enhance product ranges not just through the re-labelling of commodity products but by using the retail brand range to emphasize continued product development and innovation (Burt, 2000; de Chernatony, 1989; Laaksonen and Reynolds, 1994). Retailer brand image and position thus becomes a critical competitive and differentiating factor and one that retailers have extended enormously, including into distinct added-value consumer segments of the market (e.g. children, diabetics) and non-food product and service areas (Burt, 2000; Burt and Sparks, 2002).

We have argued here that large retailers can undertake and resource these activities to a greater extent than smaller retailers and that from this process a dominant chain could emerge. In essence, the large retailers are organizing the vertical channel to enhance their horizontal competitive positions (see below). Clarke *et al.* (2002) point out that buying associations are far stronger in continental European grocery retailing and that as a consequence small-scale individual retailers have been able to obtain at least some of the benefits outlined above. In the UK, such buying associations are not as well developed.

Dominant chain behaviour in horizontal relationships

In respect of horizontal relationships (i.e. competitive actions versus other retailers), the logic of the growth spiral would see the dominant chain use its market power to invest in operational activities which grew sales and sales density through enhancing consumer attraction (e.g. price/quality/service initiatives), which in turn contribute to brand building. This requires capital investment and increases costs, although organizational scale would mean that the relative unit costs to the organization would be maintained whilst increasing the overall sector and competitor operating costs. This might involve:

Above average capital investment programmes. Relative to many other countries, land costs in the UK are expensive (Competition Commission, 2000; London Economics, 2000). The development of an oligopolistic market with the major retailers following a similar operating strategy (i.e. out-of-town superstores) has further increased costs. Store fitting costs – décor, equipment, technology etc – have increased and refurbishment cycles have shortened. The sunk capital involved in property sites is a recognized feature of the sector (e.g. Wrigley, 1992, 1994) and retailers responded with accounting techniques which maximize the positive balance sheet implications of these investments (Shiret, 1991, 1992). A dominant chain may be in the position to bid and pay more for development sites, build up land banks, increase representation of its trading fascia in a specific market through more expensive format variations, or employ spoiling tactics at the planning application stage. As a consequence they could increase the average store costs for the sector as a whole, whilst being more able to finance those costs themselves. In the United States, Chevalier (1995) has shown how markets with a high LBO debt-laden retail presence become 'less tough' due to reduced price competition and reduced investments on existing stores. This then attracted increased market entry. If store refurbishment is ongoing and expensive, entrants or existing retailers may become less attractive to consumers if they fail to invest.

Service additions. A further way of influencing the cost structure of the sector is through the addition of services and related activities. The incorporation within stores of service counters (bakery/fish/delicatessen/hot meals), pharmacies, post offices, dry cleaning, creches, cash dispensers, coffee shops and cafeterias can increase the attractiveness of a store to consumers. The costs of these activities may be higher and the floorspace productivity sometimes lower than other traditional retail activities. The retailer benefits from the service and the additional core sales as well as 'locking-in' the customer. The extension of opening hours, in some cases to a 24-hour period, is a further service addition which raises the absolute costs of operation. A chain with the ability to spread the cost of these activities over the whole organization would be able to add such services at lower unit cost than competitors. The competition may feel obliged to 'follow the leader' but may in fact be less able to afford to do so.

Service additions are a form of product range extension. To this end the reputation of the retailer brand name is crucial to the ability of an operator to make or match such moves. Recent brand extensions into financial services (Alexander and Pollard, 2000) have only been possible, from a marketing perspective, because retailers have invested heavily in the quality and service-assurance elements of the retail offer. In short, consumers trust the brand (Burt and Sparks, 2002). The differential ability of chains to invest in brand-building activity impacts the success of the brand with consumers.

Premium labour costs. Changes in the structure of the retail labour market, allowing greater flexibility in workforce scheduling are an extensively recorded feature of the British grocery sector (e.g. Freathy and Sparks, 1994). Traditionally grocery retailing has been regarded as a low-skill occupation characterized by low wages and high levels of labour turnover. Ultimately however, retailing requires people to operate stores. The purchase transaction takes place at a checkout and involves interaction between store staff and customers. As retailers increasingly compete on the basis of customer service, improved training and staff incentives to reduce labour turnover and build commitment to the company become important. This may be reflected in higher labour costs, whether via wage rates, share incentive schemes and other bonus payments, or improved staffing levels at times of peak customer traffic to allow service developments such as bag packing and trolley assistance. Again the scale economies of a dominant chain would allow the relative costs of these initiatives to be borne whilst increasing the overall market labour costs (Table 6). A clear example of this is the ability of larger retailers to absorb the introduction and subsequent rate increases in the national minimum wage.

Increased promotional spend/brand-building activities. Increasing attractiveness to consumers has involved considerable investment in building brands. Attractive (but expensive) store environments, the addition of service facilities, retail-brand led product innovation and customer service practices have contributed to the perception of the leading retailers as high quality brands. In brand recall surveys, retailers are now amongst the most easily recalled brand names. This perception is fuelled by increased retail advertising expenditures, albeit from a much lower base than brand manufacturers (Davies, 1991; Fulop, 1983). Whilst the costs of above-the-line promotional spend may be funded either directly or indirectly by suppliers, the ability of a dominant organization to support a higher relative promotional spend than competitors and to maintain investment to enhance brand image is increased. The relative advertising and promotional spend of Tesco's 'Finest' range and Marks & Spencer food range may have helped alter perceptions of each retailer's offer.

Customer retention/loyalty card initiatives. The net worth of loyal customers is recognized by many studies to be higher than that of promiscuous customers (e.g. Pearson, 1994). In addition, loyal customers are regarded as being cheaper to retain than attracting new customers. Customer retention is ultimately

Table 6 Wage rates and recent pay settlements

| | Recent pay settlements (%) | | | |
	1999	2000	2001	£ per hour*
Tesco	2.70	3.10	3.60	5.20
Sainsbury	2.50	2.00	2.80	4.40–5.71
Asda	2.60	3.00	3.00	4.51
Safeway	2.65	2.85	3.00	4.49
Somerfield	2.50	3.00	2.50	4.12
Morrisons				4.44
Iceland				4.32
Minimum wage				4.10

Note: * Current rates of pay for point of sale staff, aged 18 or over, exclusive of premium or bonus payments, allowances, zonal pay, profit share or induction period rates.

Source: Incomes Data Services Report 841, September 2001, pp. 12–17.

achieved through customer satisfaction and is reinforced, in a highly visible way, through specific loyalty related initiatives. The high-profile introduction of various forms of loyalty cards provides retailers, at a cost, with further information on their consumer markets which can in turn be used to reinforce their power relative to suppliers. These initiatives incur substantial costs in terms of the scheme set up, running costs and information management. Less sophisticated schemes to engender loyalty and consumer retention may include voucher-based schemes to be redeemed by schools or other 'good causes'. The costs of rewards or incentives are often funded by supplier promotions, which can be leveraged more effectively when scale is larger. Again the dominant retailer, by virtue of scale, is better placed to offset these costs than subordinate chains. The withdrawal from loyalty schemes by Asda (only a trial started) and Safeway, were driven by the high cost of such operations, the investment needed to obtain meaningful information and a desire to invest savings in store deals and prices, thus providing more differentiation from the competitive paradigm (Tang, Bell and Ho, 2001).

Local market trading responses. In addition to the scope for a dominant chain to bring scale to bear on factors at the national or organizational level, its market position allows the chain to manipulate competition at *local*, i.e. outlet level, to keep pressure upon competitors' cost structures. This could occur in a local market as a competitive operation or could be targeted at times of possible local market destabilization, such as new store entry or refurbishment. The regional and local market dimensions to market structure and behaviour were central themes in the Competition Commission (2000) study and are critical concerns in the current Safeway considerations. As noted earlier, owing to the implications of sales density for capacity utilization at the store level, any local competitive actions which limit sales densities within competitors' stores will have implications for cost structures and more specifically the rate of return achieved at local level. In short, power derived and leveraged at a national level may allow a differential, store-level market response depending on local circumstances. Such responses would entail localized activities that raise competitors' costs and reduce returns. Such activities may make competitors' stores marginal in terms of their rate of return. These activities could include:

- trading-hour extension in specific locations, which whilst providing a service to a segment of the local community increases local-level costs if competitors elect to match this service;
- payment of premium labour rates, influencing the local labour market and competitors' employment costs either through requiring them to match rates or by stimulating labour turnover rates;
- introduction of selective service extensions, to increase the attractiveness of the store offer such as Post Offices and pharmacies or bag-packing and other labour-based service activities;
- local market pricing strategies, involving price leading or price matching on selected items of the product range, whilst national scale and vertical power reduces the relative cost of lower prices and other service items are retained.

Implications

The discussion above has outlined a number of factors that could be exploited by leading or dominant retailers to dictate behaviour in the market, enhance their own position and to 'force' competitors to undertake particular activities. These factors are clearly interrelated. With company specific data it would be possible to prioritize and quantify the relative importance and impact of these activities and factors. This however is beyond the scope of this current paper.

We would argue that the British grocery retail sector has seen many of these activities. A number are documented in the Competition Commission (2000) report. The effects of a corporately differentiated 'spiral of growth', and the differential ability (and possibly desire) to use power, are seen in the market. A dominant chain has emerged (Tesco), driving the growth spiral. A number of other retailers have found it increasingly hard to invest in their position (Sainsbury, Safeway) and some have struggled to stay on the spiral (Somerfield, Iceland). Asda has undergone an enormous transformation both before and after the takeover by Wal-Mart (Burt and Sparks, 2001) in an effort to regain competitiveness after it was manoeuvred into a subordinate position in the early 1990s. Similar but less dramatic steps have had to be taken by Sainsbury and Safeway to attempt to protect their positions. Regional businesses (Morrisons, Waitrose) have been able to compete in their core regions, but these retailers are to some degree protected by institutional ownership factors. We would argue that many of these changes and behaviours derive from the long-term vision and activities of a business seeking dominance of its market. This raises a number of implications.

The evolving structure of the British retail grocery market raises concerns for competition (Clarke *et al.*, 2002; Competition Commission, 2000). The market is oligopolistic. Little attention has been given to how current behaviour in the market may affect market structure in the future. This paper suggests that the current use of both vertical and horizontal power has led to a situation where one (or two) dominant chains develop. This may see a situation where the average industry costs rise and returns could fall in the short run (though see below), but at the same time the service and quality levels of the retail offer remain high or are increased. By virtue of their ability to leverage scale at an organizational level, the lower unit costs of the dominant chain allows them to absorb lower returns in the short-run to a much greater extent than others in the sector, who assume a subordinate role.

The future question for the structure of the sector is the inevitability of the current growth spiral and the ability of all the current players to remain on this spiral. The potential for this growth spiral to be broken by organic entry from outside seems limited. New entrants are faced with significant barriers and impediments to entry (Burt and Sparks, 1995; Dobson, Waterson and Chu, 1998; London Economics, 1997). The oligopolistic market, the problems of site acquisition and the nature of horizontal competition currently makes entry into the British retail grocery market by means other than corporate acquisition virtually impossible.

Of equal significance to the future of the spiral and the competitive structure of the market, is the ability of existing retailers to continue to grow and develop. As the spiral continues to revolve, the ability of the dominant organization to reinvest profit (derived from scale economies and efficiencies in increasing the attractiveness of their offer to consumers) and to determine market 'norms', grows. As sales growth is a driver of the spiral, competitors are often 'forced' to comply with these norms or risk a fall in sales. Such a decline in sales and sales density, at the same time as the dominant chain dictates cost structures can prove traumatic.

Wal-Mart's entry into the British grocery market via Asda has added to the pressure upon the subordinate chains, as the growth spiral takes another turn (Webb, 2002). While in terms of size Asda remains substantially smaller than the dominant chain, Tesco, the international scale and resources of Wal-Mart provide further real and perceived leverage and vertical power. The 'virtuous spiral' of growth is fundamental to the Wal-Mart approach to retailing. In their case, however, the profits derived from scale are used to present an unbeatable price offer. This raises sales and in turn drives up sales density. Subordinate chains are faced with cost structures based on the industry norm but are unable to match the attractiveness of the price offer – sales and sales densities fall or remain static with the consequent implications for long-term survival. Pressure may thus be exerted from both price (Asda) and facilities/services (Tesco) approaches.

Conclusions

This discussion has focused on the UK retail grocery market, which is widely recognized as oligopolistic. We have examined the derivation of retail power and focused on the changing use of retail power in both vertical and horizontal dimensions. Underlying our discussion has been the potential for development and use of power by individual chains. In passing, the discussion has implicitly underscored a view that economists' treatment of retailing and retail power has often found it difficult to get to grips with the activities undertaken by retailers. From this discussion we draw two main areas of conclusions.

First, there is clearly the potential for a dominant chain or possibly a duopoly to emerge, through the activities outlined here. We discuss this mainly at the national level, but the Competition Commission (2000) clearly recognizes such a position currently at various local market and regional levels. This dominant position has been, and will be achieved, by the various activities outlined earlier and by harnessing the 'spiral of growth'. This seems to be continuing to function, through currently perhaps with more focus on raising consumer expectation, rather than on outright cost-based competition amongst competitors.

From this, we identify two sets of implications, First, there are clear policy implications for the UK. Whilst, the Competition Commission (2000) recognized the situation, no action was possible under current land-use planning legislation, to challenge local monopolies or regional duopolies over sites. This needs to be addressed. More critically perhaps, some consideration needs to be given to the position of 'marginal' retailers in the oligopoly. Would it be preferable perhaps to have three large chains all competing in each region, rather than to have the current 'big two plus small two' arrangement (although we recognize the 'big two' does vary)? Should competition authorities actively signal that one more merger amongst the largest chains would be permissible? Such questions are at the heart of the current considerations of the various offers for Safeway.

A second implication of the dominant chain/spiral of growth thesis is the location or geography of the spiral and thus of policy concerns. Here, the paper has focused on the UK, but it is clear that many of the activities outlined no longer exist within national boundaries. The activities of retailers are increasingly global, so perhaps our frame of reference for policy needs to switch accordingly. In this case, perhaps our national policy decision should be to create a 'national champion' (as encouraged in France by the merger of Promodès and Carrefour under perceived threat of Wal-Mart's entry). This would enable potentially stronger competition globally. If as many believe, there will only be 4–6 global food retailers in a few years time, then to what extent is it important to ensure that at least one of these is British? It will be readily appreciated that these two policy implications identified above, may pull in opposite directions. This does perhaps suggest that a wide-ranging policy debate is overdue.

Our second area of conclusions is about the nature of power. We argue that in retailing (perhaps differentially to other sectors, but this needs more research), the nature of power has changed. We have emphasized the links between vertical and horizontal competition and outlet and organizational scale. Sales density has been identified as a fundamental component of power in retailing as it reflects asset utilization. The basis of competition is not price-fixated in the UK and non-price competition has been an important component of retailers' design of their offer. This focuses attention on the activities of retailers. It is apparent that the components in-store have been altered and extended, but equally elements of the supply systems are also as likely to be undertaken by retailers as by manufacturers or others. As Dawson (2000) points out, the measurement of retailer activities is more complex than perhaps ever before. The issues we have identified in this paper should ask us to question whether we are measuring and comparing appropriate metrics when we consider retailer power.

Again, we would wish to draw two different sets of implications from this conclusion. First, we need new tools and analyses to consider the components of retail power. Standard approaches and measures e.g. margin, may be less appropriate. Economists and others need to rethink what it is that consumers purchase from retailers, and what it is that retailers 'manufacture'. This is not necessarily a straightforward task. Second, we might question whether our observations on this point are country-specific. If they are (see Ailawadi, 2002) then international comparisons are being undertaken perhaps erroneously and certainly without due contextual analyses of retailers' and others' activities. However, the increasing internationalization of grocery retailing raises questions about the use of retail power in pan-national markets. Perhaps we will see a more standardized retail activity which will make international comparisons of retailer power more credible and accurate. Until then however, we should probably tread carefully.

This paper has raised issues about the dimensions, development and use of power in the UK retail grocery market. By so doing, we believe we have developed a discussion that has resonance for wider considerations of retailing, retail power, policy and internationalization. In this context, it would be of value to see similar discussions of other countries and case analyses of specific retailers.

References

Adams, W. A. (1987). 'Countervailing Power'. In: J. Eatwell, M. Milgate and P. Newman (eds), *The New Palgrave: A Dictionary of Economics*, pp. 704–706. Macmillan, London.

Ailawadi, K. L. (2002). 'The Retail Power-performance Conundrum: What Have We Learned?', *Journal of Retailing*, **77**, pp. 299–318.

Alexander, A. and J. Pollard (2000). 'Banks, Grocers and the Changing Retailing of Financial Services in Britain', *Journal of Retailing and Consumer Services*, **7**(3), pp. 137–147.

Anderson, J. C. and J. A. Narus (1990). 'A Model of Distributor Firm and Manufacturing Firm Working Partnerships', *Journal of Marketing*, **54**(January), pp. 42–58.

Armstrong, M. and J. Vickers (2001). 'Competitive Price Discrimination', *RAND Journal of Economics*, **32**, pp. 579–605.

Balto, D. A. (2001). 'Supermarket Merger Enforcement', *Journal of Public Policy and Marketing*, **20**(1), pp. 38–50.

Bloom, P. N. and V. G. Perry (2001). 'Retailer Power and Supplier Welfare: The Case of Wal-Mart?', *Journal of Retailing*, **77**, pp. 379–396.

Bresnahan, T. F. and P. C. Reiss (1991). 'Entry and Competition in Concentrated Markets', *Journal of Political Economy*, **99**(5), pp. 977–1009.

Brown, J. R., R. F. Lusch and D. D. Muehling (1983). 'Conflict and Power-dependence Relations in Retailer–Supplier Channels', *Journal of Retailing*, **59**(Winter), pp. 53–80.

Burt, S. L. (1989). 'Trends and Management Issues in European Retailing', *International Journal of Retailing*, **4**(4), pp. 1–97.

Burt, S. L. (2000). 'The Strategic Role of Retail Brands in British Grocery Retailing', *European Journal of Marketing*, **34**, pp. 875–890.

Burt, S. L. and L. Sparks (1995). 'Understanding the Arrival of Limited Line Discount Stores in Britain', *European Management Journal*, **13**, pp. 110–119.

Burt, S. L. and L. Sparks (1997). 'Performance in Food Retailing: A Cross-national Consideration and Comparison of Retail Margins', *British Journal of Management*, **8**, pp. 133–150.

Burt, S. L. and L. Sparks (2001). 'The Implications of Wal-Mart's Takeover of Asda', *Environment and Planning A*, **33**, pp. 1463–1487.

Burt, S. L. and L. Sparks (2002). 'Corporate Branding, Retailing and Retail Internationalisation', *Corporate Reputation Review*, **5**, pp. 194–212.

Buttle, F. (1985). 'Measuring Food Store Image Using Kelly's Repertory Grid', *Service Industries Journal*, **5**, pp. 79–89.

Chen, Y. (2001). 'On Vertical Mergers and their Competitive Effects', *RAND Journal of Economics*, **32**, pp. 667–685.

Chevalier, J. A. (1995). 'Capital Structure and Product-market Competition: Empirical Evidence from the Supermarket Industry', *American Economic Review*, **85**, pp. 415–435.

Clarke, R., S. Davies, P. Dobson and M. Waterson (2002). *Buyer Power and Competition in European Food Retailing*. Edward Elgar, Cheltenham.

Competition Commission (2000). *Supermarkets: A Report on the Supply of Groceries from Multiple Stores in the United Kingdom*. The Stationery Office, Norwich.

Cotterill, R. W. (1986). 'Market Power in the Retail Food Industry: Evidence from Vermont', *The Review of Economics and Statistics*, **68**, pp. 379–386.

Cotterill, R. W. (1999). 'Market Power and the Demsetz Quality Critique: An Evaluation of Food Retailing', *Agribusiness*, **15**(1), pp. 101–118.

Cotterill, R. W. (2000). 'Dynamic Explanations of Industry Structure and Performance'. *Food Marketing Policy Center Research Report 53*, University of Connecticut (http://www.are.uconn.edu/FMKTC.html – accessed 18 July 2002).

Cotterill, R. W. and L. E. Haller (1992). 'Barrier and Queue Effects: A Study of Leading US Supermarket Chain Entry Patterns', *The Journal of Industrial Economics*, **XL**, pp. 427–440.

Darden, W. R. and R. F. Lusch (eds) (1983). *Patronage Behaviour and Retail Management*. Elsevier Science, Amsterdam.

Davies, G. (1991). 'Retailer Advertising Strategies', *International Journal of Advertising*, **10**, pp. 189–203.

Davies, G. (1994). 'The Delisting of Products by Retail Buyers', *Journal of Marketing Management*, **10**, pp. 473–493.

Dawson, J. A. (2000). 'Viewpoint: Retailer Power, Manufacturer Power, Competition and Some Questions of Economic Analysis', *International Journal of Retail and Distribution Management*, **28**(1), pp. 1–4.

Dawson, J. A. and S. A. Shaw (1989). 'The Move to Administered Vertical Marketing Systems by British Retailers', *European Journal of Marketing*, **23**(7), pp. 42–51.

De Chernatony, L. (1989). 'Branding in an Era of Retailer Dominance', *International Journal of Advertising*, **8**, pp. 245–260.

Dickson, P. R. (1983). 'Distributor Portfolio Analysis and the Channel Dependence Matrix: New Techniques for Understanding and Managing the Channel', *Journal of Marketing*, **47**(Summer), pp. 35–44.

Dobson, P. and M. Waterson (1997). 'Countervailing Power and Consumer Prices', *The Economic Journal*, **107**(March), pp. 418–430.

Dobson, P. and M. Waterson (1999). 'Retailer Power: Recent Developments and Policy Implications', *Economic Policy*, **28**(April), pp. 135–164.

Dobson, P., M. Waterson and A. Chu (1998). *The Welfare Consequences of the Exercise of Buyer Power*. Research Paper 18. Office of Fair Trading, London.

Doel, C. (1999). 'Market Development and Organisational Change: The Case of the Food Industry'. In: N. Wrigley and M. Lowe (eds), *Retailing, Consumption and Capital*. Chapter 3, pp. 48–67. Longman, London.

Doel, C. (1999). 'Towards a Supply Chain Community? Insights from Governance Processes in the Food Industry', *Environment and Planning A*, **31**, pp. 69–85.

Donovan, R. J. and J. R. Rossiter (1982). 'Store Atmosphere: An Environmental Psychology Approach', *Journal of Retailing*, **58**(Spring), pp. 34–57.

Duke, R. (1998). 'A Model of Buyer-Supplier Interaction in UK Grocery Retailing', *Journal of Retailing and Consumer Services*, **5**(2), pp. 93–104.

El-Ansary, A. and L. W. Stern (1972). 'Power and Measurement in the Distribution Channel', *Journal of Marketing Research*, **9**(February), pp. 47–52.

Emerson, R. E. (1962). 'Power-dependence Relations', *American Sociological Review*, **27**(February), pp. 31–41.

Etgar, M. (1979). 'Sources and Types of Intrachannel Conflict', *Journal of Retailing*, **55**(Spring), pp. 61–78.

Freathy, P. and L. Sparks (1994). 'Contemporary Developments in Employment in UK Food Retailing', *Service Industries Journal*, **14**, pp. 499–514.

French, R. P. and B. Raven (1959). 'The Basis of Social Power'. In: D. Cartwright (ed.), *Studies in Social Power*. University of Michigan Press, Ann Arbor.

Fulop, C. (1983). 'Retailer Advertising and Retail Competition in the UK', *International Journal of Advertising*, **2**, pp. 365–376.

Galbraith, J. K. (1952). *American Capitalism: The Concept of Countervailing Power*. Houghton Mifflin, Boston.

Gaski, J. F. (1984). 'The Theory of Power and Conflict in Channels of Distribution', *Journal of Marketing*, **3**(Summer), pp. 9–29.

Gaski, J. F. and J. R. Nevin (1985). 'The Differential Effects of Exercised and Unexercised Power Sources in a Marketing Channel', *Journal of Marketing Research*, **22**(May), pp. 130–142.

Harvey, M. (2000). 'Innovation and Competition in UK Supermarkets', *Supply Chain Management*, **5**(1), pp. 15–21.

Hogarth-Scott, S. and S. T. Parkinson (1993). 'Retailer–Supplier Relationships in the Food Channel: A Supplier Perspective', *International Journal of Retail and Distribution Management*, **21**(8), pp. 11–18.

Hughes, A. (1999). 'Retail Restructuring and the Strategic Significance of Food Retailers' Own Labels: A UK–USA Comparison', *Environment & Planning A*, **28**, pp. 2201–2226.

Hughes, A. (1999). 'Constructing Competitive Spaces: The Corporate Practice of British Retailer–Supplier Relationships', *Environment and Planning A*, **31**, pp. 819–839.

Hunt, S. and J. Nevin (1974). 'Power in a Channel of Distribution: Sources and Consequences', *Journal of Marketing Research*, **11**(May), pp. 186–193.

Incandela, D., K. L. McLaughlin and C. Smith (1999). 'Retailers to the World', *The McKinsey Quarterly*, **3**, pp. 84–97.

Institute of Grocery Distribution (1999). *Grocery Retailing 1999: The Market Review*. IGD Business Publications, Letchmore Heath.

Laaksonen, H. and J. Reynolds (1994). 'Own Brands in Food Retailing Across Europe', *Journal of Brand Management*, **2**(1), pp. 37–46.

London Economics (1997). *Competition in Retailing*. Research Report 13. Office of Fair Trading, London.

London Economics (2000). *Rip-off Britain: Myths and Realities*. A report prepared for the British Retail Consortium. London Economics, London.

Lusch, R. F. and J. R. Brown (1982). 'A Modified Model in the Marketing Channel', *Journal of Marketing Research*, **18**(August), pp. 312–323.

Marion, B. W. (1998). 'Competition in Grocery Retailing: The Impact of a New Strategic Group on BLS Price Increases', *Review of Industrial Organization*, **13**, pp. 381–399.

McKinsey (1998). *Driving Productivity and Growth in the UK Economy*. McKinsey Global Institute, London.

Mitchell, V.-W. and H. R. Kiral (1999). 'Risk Positioning of UK Grocery Multiple Retailers', *International Review of Retail Distribution and Consumer Research*, **9**, pp. 17–39.

Moir, C. (1990). 'Competition in the UK Grocery Trades'. In: C. Moir and J. A. Dawson (eds), *Competition and Markets*, pp. 91–118. Macmillan, Basingstoke.

Monopolies and Mergers Commission (1981). *Discounts to Retailers*. HC311. HMSO, London.

National Economic Research Associates (1999). *Merger Appraisal in Oligopolistic Markets.* Research Paper 19. Office of Fair Trading, London.

NatWest Securities (1995). *Out of Town Expansion, R.I.P.?* NatWest Securities, London.

Nielsen, A. C. (2000). *A Report into International Price Comparisons.* A report prepared for the Department of Trade and Industry. AC Neilsen, London.

Office of Fair Trading (1985). *Competition in Retailing.* HMSO, London.

Ogbonna, E. and B. Wilkinson (1996). 'Inter-organizational Power Relations in the UK Grocery Industry: Contradictions and Developments', *International Review of Retail Distribution and Consumer Research*, **6**, pp. 395–414.

Ogbonna, E. and B. Wilkinson (1998). 'Power Relations in the UK Grocery Supply Chain', *Journal of Retailing and Consumer Services*, **5**(2), pp. 77–86.

Pearson, S. (1994). 'How to Achieve Return on Investment from Customer Loyalty – Part II', *Journal of Targetting, Measurement and Analysis for Marketing*, **3**, pp. 124–132.

Reisman, D. (1980). *Galbraith and Market Capitalism.* Macmillan, London.

Reve, T. and L. W. Stern (1979). 'Interorganizational Relations in Marketing Channels', *Academy of Marketing Review*, **4**, pp. 405–416.

Riordan, M. H. (1998). 'Anticompetitive Vertical Integration by a Dominant Firm', *American Economic Review*, **88**, pp. 1232–1248.

Rosenberg, L. J. and L. W. Stern (1971). 'Conflict Measurement in the Distribution Channel', *Journal of Marketing Research*, **8**, pp. 437–442.

Salop, S. C. and D. T. Scheffman (1983). ' "Raising Rivals" Costs', *American Economic Review*, **73**, pp. 267–271.

Scherer, F. M. (1999). 'Retail Distribution Channel Barriers to International Trade', *Antitrust Law Journal*, **67**, pp. 77–112.

Seth, A. and G. Randall (1999). *The Grocers: The Rise and Rise of the Supermarket Chains.* Kogan Page, London.

Shaw, S. A., D. J. Nisbet and J. A. Dawson (1989). 'Economies of Scale in UK Supermarkets: Some Preliminary Findings', *International Journal of Retailing*, **4**(5), pp. 12–26.

Shiret, T. (1991). *Tesco Plc: A Company Capitalising Too Much Interest.* Credit Lyonnais Laing, London.

Shiret, T. (1992). *How Much Hot Air Do You Like With Your Accounts?* Credit Lyonnais Laing, London.

Smith, H. (2002). 'Supermarket Choice and Supermarket Competition in Market Equilibrium', *Review of Economic Studies (forthcoming)*, Paper available for download at http://www.econ.ox.ac.uk/Members/howard.smith/homepage.htm.

Smith, D. G. and L. Sparks (1993). 'The Transformation of Physical Distribution in Food Retailing', *International Review of Retail Distribution and Consumer Research*, **3**, pp. 35–64.

Sparks, L. (1996). 'Space Wars: Wm Low and the Auld Enemy', *Environment and Planning A*, **28**, pp. 1465–1484.

Tang, C. S., D. R. Bell and T. -H. Ho (2001). 'Store Choice and Shopping Behaviour: How Price Format Works', *California Management Review*, **43**(2), pp. 56–74.

Tucker, K. A. (1975). *Economies of Scale in Retailing.* Saxon-House, London.

Tucker, K. A. (1980). 'A Survey of Cost and Size Relationships in Retailing'. Paper presented at the first CESCOM Conference on the Economics of the Distributive Trades, Rome, September.

Waller, S. W. (2001). 'Antitrust as Consumer Choice', *University of Pittsburgh Law Review*, **62**, pp. 535–544.

Webb, S. (2002). 'Global Retailing – A Beginning', *Oxford Retail Digest*, **34**, pp. 62–64.

Wileman, A. and M. Jary (1997). *Retail Power Plays: From Trading to Brand Leadership*. Macmillan, Basingstoke.

Wrigley, N. (1987). 'The Concentration of Capital in UK Grocery Retailing', *Environment and Planning A*, **19**, pp. 1283–1288.

Wrigley, N. (1991). 'Is the "Golden Age" of British Grocery Retailing at a Watershed?', *Environment and Planning A*, **23**, pp. 1537–1544.

Wrigley, N. (1992). 'Sunk Capital, the Property Crisis, and the Restructuring of British Food Retailing', *Environment and Planning A*, **24**, pp. 1521–1527.

Wrigley, N. (1994). 'After the Store Wars: Towards a New Era of Competition in Food Retailing?', *Journal of Retailing and Consumer Services*, **1**, pp. 5–20.

Editors' Commentary

PAUL DOBSON HAS BEEN Professor of Competition Economics in the Business School at Loughborough University since 1999. He previously held posts at the universities of Nottingham and St Andrews. His background is in economics and his particular interest is in strategy. He holds a PhD from the University of London. Paul has authored books on strategic management and researched a wide range of company strategy issues. His current research interests focus on industrial economics and competition policy with particular regard to the economics of vertical restraints and the economics of buyer power and retail competition. He has published widely on these latter topics in books and articles and has extensive consultancy and advisory experience. He has produced a number of commissioned reports and acted as an adviser to competition authorities.

Michael Waterson is Professor of Economics at Warwick University. He is also an industrial economist and his research focuses on competition and regulation. His interests include the economics of retailing, covering locational and vertical restraint issues, competition in regulated industries, regulation, access pricing and the comparative analysis of regulatory regimes.

As retailers have increased in power, and retailing has become increasingly concentrated, the competition authorities within individual countries and the European Union have become concerned about how best to regulate the sector in order to ensure consumer welfare and yet maintain a competitive and dynamic retail sector. Paul Dobson and Michael Waterson have collaborated on a number of research projects, particularly on food retail topics and the implications of increasing concentration in the UK in food retailing. Much of this research has been carried out for the Office of Fair Trading. It is this research that forms the basis of 'Retailer Power: Recent Developments and Policy Implications'.

In 'Retailer Power: Recent Developments and Policy Implications' Paul Dobson and Michael Waterson apply their views of strategic management and competition policy and governance to understand how retailer strategy can be meaningfully regulated. Retailers have been successful in developing strategies which increase their power and the size of their businesses. This has changed the sector in terms of supplier–retailer relations, the bases of competition and the ease of entry into the sector. The article discusses the various types of restraints and how they impact on competition, the dynamism of the sector and consumer welfare. Policy considerations, including vertical relations and mergers and acquisitions policy, are discussed and evaluated. These issues have become even more important since the time of publication of this paper, due to continuing increases in the scale and power of retail firms and continued debate by competition authorities and others of the appropriate form and level of regulation of retailing.

Key Publications

Dobson P and Starkey K (1993) *The Strategic Management Blueprint.* Oxford: Blackwell.

Dobson P and Waterson M (1996) *Vertical Restraints and Competition Policy,* Research Paper 12. London: Office of Fair Trading.

Dobson P and Waterson M (1997) Countervailing power and consumer prices. *Economic Journal,* 107, 418–430.

Dobson P, Waterson M and Chu A (1998) *The Welfare Consequences of the Exercise of Buyer Power,* Research Paper 18. London: Office of Fair Trading.

Dobson P, Clarke R, Davies S and Waterson M (2001) Buyer power and its impact on competition in the food retail distribution sector of the European Union. *Journal of Industry, Competition and Trade,* 13, 247–281.

Coppi L and Dobson P (2002) The importance of market conduct in the economic analysis of mergers – the Interbrew saga. *European Competition Law Review,* 23, 386–391.

Clarke R, Davies S, Dobson P and Waterson M (2002) *Buyer Power and Competition in Food Retailing.* Cheltenham: Elgar.

Waterson M (ed.) (2003) *Competition, Monopoly and Corporate Governance: Essays in Honour of Keith Cowling.* Cheltenham: Elgar.

Dobson P, Waterson M and Davies SW (2003) The patterns and implications of increasing concentration in European food retailing. *Journal of Agricultural Economics,* 54, 111–125.

Dobson P (2005) Retail performance indicators in the nation of shopkeepers. *International Review of Retail, Distribution and Consumer Research,* 15, 319–327.

Dobson P (2005) Exploiting buyer power: lessons from the British grocery trade. *Antitrust Law Journal,* 72, 529–562.

Dobson P and Waterson M (2005) Chain-store pricing across local markets. *Journal of Economics and Management Strategy,* 14, 93–119.

Websites

http://www.lboro.ac.uk/departments/bs/staff/bspwd.html
http://www2.warwick.ac.uk/fac/soc/economics/staff/faculty/waterson/

RETAILER POWER: RECENT DEVELOPMENTS
AND POLICY IMPLICATIONS

Paul Dobson and Michael Waterson

It is common, but incorrect, to view retailing as a highly competitive activity. Unlike manufacturing, retailing has displayed a trend towards much higher concentration, reinforced by actions of retailers themselves, such as emphasis on own-label brands. This may introduce distortions arising from exercise of market power or may create countervailing power to that already enjoyed by manufacturers. Acknowledging increased market power within retailing raises new issues for competition authorities. We develop a consistent framework of analysis and use it to examine two issues: attitudes to retail mergers and exclusivity arrangements between retailers and their suppliers.

Introduction

RETAILING IS BIG BUSINESS. Ranking firms by revenue, retailing includes Belgium's largest company, Delhaize 'Le Lion'; Tesco and J. Sainsbury from the UK top ten; the giant Metro group in Germany; and Wal-Mart Stores, number four in the USA and the eighth largest company in the world, with $119 billion turnover and 825 000 employees (*Fortune*, 3/8/98). Retailing is getting more concentrated over time: the top ten grocers in Europe were 28% of the market in 1992, but 36% by 1997.[1] The behaviour of retailers matters for consumers. Cross-country studies of pricing for near-identical products (e.g., cars, televisions, compact discs, branded sportswear, groceries) find big differences between prices across European countries and between Europe and the USA.[2] The European Commission is to start examining why Europeans pay substantially more on average than US consumers.

These price discrepancies are hard to explain by variation in the cost of producing or transporting the goods that retailers sell; nor are they likely to arise simply from different costs within the retail business itself. Despite some national and regional variation in the cost of labour in retailing and the rental for retail premises (Treadgold, 1990), neither is large enough to explain the observed price dispersion.[3] An alternative explanation is cross-country differences in the market power of retailers. For world revenue from food retailing, the top three in *Fortune*'s list are European: Metro of Germany, Carrefour of France, and Tesco of the UK. Of the world's major food retailers, the UK Asda group is number one for profit as a proportion of revenue.[4] Retailer power is an

Economic Policy, Vol. 28 (1999), pp. 134–156, 162–164. © CEPR, CES, MSH.
We would like to thank David Begg, an anonymous referee, our discussants, Kai Konrad and Carmen Matutes, and the Economic Policy Panel for helpful comments. The views expressed in this paper are ours alone. We take full responsibility for any errors or omissions.

issue in Europe, now the subject of an investigation by the UK Office of Fair Trading (1998), and closely related to the EU Green Paper on Vertical Restraints (January 1997), from which policy proposals are now being drawn. The European Commission is also concerned with the buyer power of retailers and its impact on producers; recently, it commissioned a study of food retail distribution. A common concern is how to maintain competition.

Retailer power is on the increase, as Table 1 illustrates for the grocery market. However, there is an interesting divergence of experience. In the UK, where retailing is most concentrated, the buyer group share is equal to the retailer share. Retailers are the largest purchasers of groceries from producers. In other countries, the buyer share is significantly more concentrated than the retailer share, reflecting the considerable importance to the industry of buying groups such as Germany's Markant Handels, the country's largest food buyer; Spain's large purchasing groups Euromadi and IFA Española, its numbers one and two; and France's Intermarché, again the largest in the country in terms of turnover.

The final column of Table 1 shows quite remarkable differences in prices for a standard food 'basket' across European countries. In the USA a basket cost 69% of what the same basket cost in the UK. Retailing is much less concentrated in the USA than in European countries. Although the UK is most concentrated, others are not far behind. Hence, the fact that UK retailers simultaneously enjoy selling power and buying power may largely explain why UK supermarket chains are so highly priced and profitable relative to the European average. In particular, the powerful buyer groups that are present in other countries may restrain otherwise powerful sellers. This evidence, selective as it is, has implications for our framework of analysis.

Table 1 Rising concentration in retail grocery, 1988–96 (market shares and cross-country price dispersion)

| | Top 5 grocers (national market share, %) | | | | | Price of a basket of goods (UK = 100) |
| | Retailers | | | Buyer groups | | |
	1988	1992	1996	1992	1996	August 1998
UK	53	60	64	60	64	100
Netherlands	59	59	61	69	72	61
Belgium	52	53	56	79	82	62
France	42	49	52	60	63	74
Germany	27	37	41	79	83	65
Spain	19	23	25	40	44	n.a.

Sources: Retailer and buying group shares from Nielsen; price of a basket of goods from *Sunday Times* articles of 23/8/98 and 30/8/98. UK is average of J. Sainsbury and Tesco basket prices, Netherlands is Albert Heijn, Belgium is Delhaize, France is Leclerc, Germany is Globus, and USA is Safeway. Locations of stores within country not disclosed.

According to standard analysis, based on a single-stage model of market power, powerful retailers buy their goods from manufacturers (such as Nestlé and Unilever) that are at least as powerful. However, this analysis is inappropriate. We need to examine power relations within the supply and distribution chain to understand behaviour and assess its impact on welfare. There are at least two broad areas of concern: one relating to retail power *per se*; the other associated with the practices engaged in between buyers and sellers in distribution. Table 2 sets out the key issues. We need to think about not merely whether retailers have market power as sellers, but also whether they have market power

Table 2 A framework for analysis

Question	Relevant evidence
1. Have retailers enough seller (horizontal) market power to affect prices and quantities traded, or to threaten viability of traders at other distribution stages, without attracting entry as a result?	● Substantial mark-ups by retailers. ● High profits. ● Stable and substantial market shares. ● High and stable concentration. ● Limited availability of suitable sites. ● Restrictive licensing, for new entrants or new formats.
2. Do existing retail firms exercise buyer power against weaker firms, enhancing market failures? *When retailers have both buyer and seller power, there must be concern about further mergers.*	● Substantial proportion of suppliers' outputs purchased by one firm or a small number of firms. ● Significant arrangement of terms of purchase by this firm or firms.
3. Does the exercise of buyer power actually benefit consumers? *If so, countervailing benefits mitigate other adverse effects of seller power.*	● Pecuniary economies of scale, average costs lowered, benefits passed on. ● For example, generic private-label goods at significantly lower prices than branded products.
4. Do restrictions (imposed or agreed) on retailers and suppliers reduce the variety enjoyed by consumers?	● Evidence of exclusive supply arrangements or pricing restraints, territorial restrictions, specific custom designs, idiosyncratic specification.
5. Alternatively, are there significant productive efficiency gains from market practices that restrict the number of dealers or their product range? *If so, efficiency gains can justify exclusive or selective distribution, or exclusive dealing. If not, these actions may consolidate seller power, perhaps with the connivance of manufacturers.*	● Search costs: is a substantial service element required (to allow consumers to make an informed choice), which is feasible only when there are restrictions on suppliers? ● Type of good: is the good low value, frequently bought? ● Economies of scope in supplying a range – are they extensive? If so, there is little cost in a retailer adding a line and little case for restricting the number of lines. ● Mutual agreement in restrictions rather than evidence of imposition?

as buyers; in the latter case, we need to examine how this interacts with the selling power of their suppliers. Direct policy applications include attitudes to further consolidation of power through merger, and the restrictive practices prevalent in distributing goods and services to consumers.

In the remaining sections, we first examine the retailing industry in more detail, arguing against the traditional view that retailing behaviour approximates a competitive industry. We then develop the 'two-stage' analysis required when market power exists at more than one stage of the supply and distribution chain. This analysis makes predictions that can be used to evaluate emerging trends and to formulate policy proposals. Table 2 provides a road map of where we want to go.

Oligopoly and Consolidation in European Retailing

Economic analysis has traditionally viewed retailers as lacking in market power. Their suppliers, powerful producers that are few in number, are thought to have sufficient market power to impose contractual obligations on powerless retailers. A particularly strong form of this argument has been adopted by the Chicago approach to vertical relations (Telser, 1960; Posner, 1976; Bork, 1978), which views retailing as perfectly competitive, with the standard characteristics of easy entry, numerous firms and a high degree of buyer and seller mobility in response to small price differences.

In contrast, we contend that most areas of retailing display market power in some form. In some circumstances, retailing may be approximated by monopolistic competition, where firms are slightly differentiated and entry, although not free, is relatively easy. However, in an increasing number of markets, retailing is better viewed as competition between a small number of strategic players. Large retail chains now have substantial market shares, can dictate trading relations with manufacturers, and earn large profits. Even in retail sectors highly fragmented on a national scale, the localized nature of retailing competition for some goods, due to consumers' search costs, means that the number of retailers operating in a given outlet class is usually small. Several studies have confirmed that retail prices are correlated with local retailing concentration levels (Marion et al., 1979; Cotterill, 1986; Marvel, 1989; and Bresnahan and Reiss, 1991).

Effective entry into retailing is not as easy as traditionally claimed. Licensing and planning restrictions impede new entry not just for building on greenfield sites, but for setting up in industries such as the retailing of petrol, pharmacy products and alcohol. Even where entry is possible, incumbents have advantages from the best location, from experience and from reputation. Entrants also face the prospect of incurring sunk costs in entering markets that need investments in highly specific assets, such as distribution and marketing systems.

A second reason for market power in retailing, which reinforces incumbency advantages, is economies of size and scope, which give large retailers a cost advantage over smaller rivals. Increasing returns arise for two reasons: fixed costs (for demonstration and storage facilities) that can be spread over high output levels, and variable costs that also fall with scale, particularly when economies are present from buying in bulk. Economies of scope in retailing arise from using common display, storage and sales-recording facilities for a variety of products, allowing fixed costs to be shared across different product lines. Hence, economies can be found at a number of levels. Individual shops give way to large superstores; businesses take the form of chain stores, now dominating most areas of retailing activity; and at the corporate level, diversification and internationalization have led to retailing conglomerates and multinational operators.

Exploiting these economies has led to considerable changes in retailing in the industrialized nations in the last two decades: heavy investment in retailing, rapid growth in superstores and hypermarkets, the expansion of out-of-town and edge-of-town retail parks, and the proliferation of retail chains groups, sharply increasing business concentration in retailing.

Yet experiences have varied considerably across countries. Levels of development differ. Table 3 documents variation within European retailing. In large part, this reflects differences in economic, cultural and political backgrounds. Northern Europe has larger retail enterprises, a high proportion of multiple chains and a lower density of enterprises, and higher concentration levels. Southern Europe has high densities of enterprises and outlets where small independent retailers predominate; concentration is lower. Within this simple division, there is marked variation by country; Belgium is a particularly interesting mixture.

The snapshot in Table 3 conceals the considerable consolidation that took place in the last decade, especially in the grocery market. In the UK, the share of sales of fast-moving consumer goods (FMCG) by supermarkets was 20% in 1960, but 85% by 1997, with the top 2% of stores controlling 47% of grocery sales (Nielsen, 1998). The number of grocery retail outlets fell from over 140 000 to below 40 000 in the UK during 1960–97, from 152 000 to 41 700 during 1968–94 in France, and from 212 700 to 69 000 in the former West Germany during 1955–89. Even in southern Europe, the trend is visible. In Portugal, during 1989–93 the number of grocery stores fell from 40 700 to 37 000; in Italy, food stores declined from 339 400 to 287 000 during 1983–93. As indicated by Table 1, the decline in the total number of retail grocers and the development of chain store groups, at the expense of independent retailers, caused a sharp rise in national concentration levels.

Concentration also increased in other areas of retailing: for example, in furniture, electrical goods, clothing, toys, books and DIY. Much of this increase reflected organic growth of larger retailers opening new superstores and expanding their smaller stores. However, mergers and acquisitions also played a role.[5] Moreover, the number of cross-border mergers and alliances is increasing, with the likely effect of increasing concentration at the aggregate European level (Dawson, 1993).

These developments have had a big economic impact. Firstly, heavy investments by retailers, particularly in larger store formats and improved logistics, have raised productivity. For the UK during 1980–94, Dobson et al. (1998) find that retail sales (in real terms) per outlet increased by 53% and per employee by 23%. These efficiency improvements have gone hand in hand with a considerable increase in the market share of the leading retailers. Over the same period, the combined share of the top five retailers in the UK increased by 63% to the point

Table 3 Differences in the structure of retailing in Europe

	Retail sales (% of GDP)	Number of firms (000s)	Number of firms per 10 000 people	Workers per firm	Sales share of top 5 firms (%)
Austria	18	40	50	7.3	35
Belgium	17	120	118	2.0	43
Denmark	20	48	91	4.2	37
Finland	22	33	65	4.0	72
France	24	452	79	4.5	31
Germany	20	436	53	6.6	31
Greece	31	175	168	1.9	11
Ireland	20	29	90	4.5	39
Italy	31	888	155	2.7	11
Luxembourg	26	4	87	5.6	31
Netherlands	20	103	67	6.2	34
Norway	20	38	88	3.2	53
Portugal	32	132	133	2.8	23
Spain	19	511	130	3.0	35
Sweden	15	55	62	5.3	66
Switzerland	20	42	59	5.1	51
UK	20	300	51	8.7	30

Sources: Authors' calculations based on Eurostat (1997, table 1a), and data from
Corporate Intelligence on Retailing (1998).

where they controlled around a quarter of all retail goods sales. At the same time, the average gross margin on goods (the difference between total sales and purchases of goods, as a percentage of sales) rose by 16% across the whole sector. In food retailing, the increase in gross margins is more marked, rising by a fifth during 1984–92; for the very large chains, with 100 or more outlets, the average gross margin increased by a third.

A number of factors may account for these increases, including cutting out the wholesalers to buy direct from manufacturers, and improved store amenities. However, higher margins may simply reflect the exercise of increased market power, either in squeezing suppliers or in raising prices to customers.

Some support for the market power view, at least for the UK, is offered by the rise in net margins, particularly for large retailers, which coincided with higher market concentration. The average net margin for the leading 50 retailers in the UK rose from 4.6% in 1984 to 5.1% in 1992 (Azoulay, 1995). Dobson *et al.* (1998) find that, during 1984–94, the average net margin (profit to sales ratio) across the top five retailers increased by 35%, while their market share increased by 50%. The rise in net margin for food retailers was even higher, from 4% in the early 1980s to 6.5% by the mid-1990s.

The significance of these figures is apparent from international comparisons. Tordjman (1994) finds that, although French and German companies dominate in terms of size and turnover, British retailers are the most profitable in Europe: the top six profit-earners in Europe are all UK-based firms. Similarly, profit margins are considerably higher in the UK than in other European countries. For the grocery trade, Tordjman shows that average net margins among large retailers in the UK are three times higher than in France, Germany, Italy or Spain; France has the highest productivity per square metre and the lowest gross margins.

Retailer power is not specifically a British concern, even if the UK is in the vanguard. The prospects of increased profitability for major store groups across Europe are strong: the largest retailers are increasingly in a position to exert buying power to their advantage; and increased retail branding (see Table 4 below) will increase consumer loyalty and enhance firms' market power.

Large retail chains can negotiate favourable terms with their suppliers, providing a further competitive advantage over smaller rivals. Increasingly, it is retailers that dictate terms and conditions of trade as manufacturers compete for access to selling space in the more concentrated retail markets (Dawson and Shaw, 1990; Foord et al., 1996). Large retailers not only negotiate volume discounts from suppliers, but obtain other benefits from them: examples include charging suppliers 'slotting allowances' for access to prime shelf-space, and 'market development funds' to pay for local 'co-operative advertising' and in-store displays (Brookes, 1995; Shaffer, 1991a). Competitive pressure on suppliers is further enhanced by retailers' own-label brands that are vigorously promoted within the store.

Many arm's-length buyer–supplier relationships (often with agents as intermediaries) have given way to the use by powerful retailers of closely controlled 'preferred' suppliers, which can in turn subcontract production, creating a supplier hierarchy. For the retailer, risk is shifted on to the preferred suppliers, which are responsible for delivery and quality, but receive very narrow margins. Consequently, these retailer–supplier relationships are highly asymmetric. The retailer can exercise detailed control over the production process (usually dictating the technology required and providing exact product specifications), without carrying the burden of ownership. But for the manufacturers concerned there may be a reluctance to undertake investments, given the uncertainty over whether the relationship will be continued.

Besides squeezing manufacturer margins, dominant retailers may oblige producers to supply on an exclusive (or selective) basis, denying supplies to known discounters to undermine their position. Toys'R'Us, the largest toy retailer in the USA with a quarter of the market, was found to have induced toy-makers in the USA to cut off supplies to discounters (warehouse clubs), thereby keeping prices high and reducing consumer choice (FTC, 1997).

Concerning retail branding, consumers usually view retailers as imperfect substitutes. Reasons for preferring one particular store to another, apart from price, include location, accessibility, layout, ambience, product range, sales personnel and service. Differentiation among retailers dampens competition. Note that differentiation exists for large and small stores alike. A small specialist store, successfully differentiating itself from rivals, may have greater market power than a large retailer in direct competition with neighbouring retailers.

Retailers therefore put great effort into distinguishing their service from that of competitors. Large multiproduct chain stores have developed own brands to attract customers to their stores to buy, and continue to buy, goods from them

Table 4 Own-label penetration in European packaged grocery (% of market)

	1980	1990	1995
France	7	14	17
West Germany	5	14	20
Italy	5	6	8
Spain	2	6	7
UK	23	31	38

Source: A.C. Nielsen.

rather than from rivals. Large retailers have thus been heavy users of advertising to promote their brands.

Retail branding has become especially important for retailers with similar product ranges to rivals, notably in grocery and clothes retailing. It has the double benefit of differentiating services on the selling side and providing bargaining power on the buying side to counter the selling power of brand manufacturers. The manufacturer's position is especially weak if retailers develop own-label products, which break the manufacturer's link with consumers that has been built up through direct appeal, typically through advertising (Corstjens and Corstjens, 1995). The service reputation of retailers means that their own brands commonly command a significant premium over 'no brands' (*Marketing*, 29/7/93), yet by free-riding on manufacturers' advertising and reputation for the leading brands, own-label products can undercut leading brands. Selling own-label products is an important form of brand extension for retailers, reinforcing a store's image and building customer loyalty.

Furthermore, by using buying power to obtain own-label goods at the lowest possible price, retail margins on these goods can be substantially greater than margins on manufacturer branded goods, thereby enhancing retailer profitability (Mills, 1995). Table 4 illustrates the increased penetration of own labels for packaged grocery items. As these levels rise, the power of the largest grocers rises, increasing their prospects of higher profits.

Analysis

The foregoing discussion has important implications for economic analysis of retailing. It is wrong to view retailers as powerless agents that merely distribute the products of their powerful principals, the manufacturers. This approach is associated with the Chicago School tradition, advocating a *laissez-faire* approach to vertical restraints. Instead, as argued by Steiner (1991), one should recognize two distinct stages of retailing, dealing with suppliers and with customers, each of which may involve the exercise of market power by retailers. This also allows for a clear distinction between interbrand and intrabrand competition and the linkage between them: consumers make two choices – what to buy and where to buy it.

Figure 1 Two-stage analysis of distribution

We now use this approach to examine the competition effects of a range of market practices, from vertical restraints (exclusive dealing, resale price maintenance, other contractual terms) to the effects of increased concentration on retail buying and selling power. Our major concern is whether this gives rise to socially beneficial countervailing power (against manufacturer power) or simply results in further market power detrimental to the social interest.

There are generally two opposing sets of effects: productive efficiency benefits, but reduced competition. Consider a market with several manufacturers, M_1 to M_n, and several retailers, R_1 to R_n as in Figure 1. Consumers may benefit from efficient trading arrangements. Contractual restraints between M_i and R_j may internalize externalities that otherwise arise from the independent actions of the trading parties, perhaps by removing pricing distortions (such as successive mark-ups), by allowing precommitments that facilitate optimal investment levels, or by eliminating avoidable transaction costs such as search costs. Such contracts allow lower prices of final goods. But vertical restraints and higher retailer concentration also dampen competition between retailers, leading to higher prices and less choice for consumers. The policy dilemma is to identify the market conditions in which detrimental effects are likely to outweigh beneficial effects on social welfare.

We divide the analysis of retail competition and supplier arrangements into two broad considerations. First, we examine vertical relations and retailer–supplier contracts, then we discuss general effects of higher concentration in retailing. We assume that standard results of competition analysis are well known, and focus instead on issues illuminated by this new emphasis on the mediation of relations between powerful retailers and powerful suppliers.[6]

Features of contracts

Exclusivity arrangements. Recent economic analysis of exclusivity restraints – whether for purchasing, supply or territory – shows that such practices can increase efficiency but reduce competition. A blanket policy, outlawing or allowing all such arrangements, is inappropriate. A case-by-case approach to competition policy is needed. However, economics is helpful in revealing market conditions under which one set of factors may dominate the other.

The potential benefits from vertical restraints have been shown by extensions to the traditional Chicago School analysis (Marvel, 1982; Ornstein, 1989). Intricate agreements may be needed to allow manufacturers and retailers to invest in the optimal level of selling and promotion activities. These arguments will be important when the retail service affects the perceived quality of a good, or is a key source of information to consumers about product quality. However, manufacturers also wish to establish exclusive arrangements with reliable dealers to make it harder for rivals to set up a competing distribution system. Exclusivity agreements may then form a powerful barrier to entry (Comanor and Frech, 1985).

Exclusivity agreements can also diminish competition between existing firms. Two-stage analysis of distribution has been used to show how this can be achieved by exclusive territory agreements (Rey and Stiglitz, 1988, 1995) or by exclusive dealing agreements (Lin, 1990; O'Brien and Shaffer, 1993; Besanko and Perry, 1994).

Dobson and Waterson (1994) consider the market conditions under which exclusive dealing may be expected to operate against the public interest by reducing interbrand and intrabrand competition. Suppose oligopolistic manu-facturers, each producing a differentiated brand, supply monopolistically com-petitive retailers that are differentiated by the services they offer consumers. By employing exclusive dealing contracts, manufacturers obtain higher margins, both by precluding in-store interbrand competition and by reducing intrabrand and between-stores interbrand competition, since fewer retailers of each brand can be supported in the market if there are fixed costs associated with retailing. The higher intermediate prices set by manufacturers under exclusive dealing induce retailers to set higher final prices. By dampening competition, manu-facturers' profits can be higher but social welfare lower than in the case where exclusive dealing contracts are outlawed. This is particularly so if there are significant unrealized economies of scope in retailing (additional retailing costs of expanding the product range are low) as a consequence of exclusive dealing being imposed.

Analogously, oligopolistic retailers imposing exclusive supply contracts on (powerless) suppliers may profitably dampen competition between retailers when this allows them to specialize in selling a different brand or product from their rivals, thus avoiding intense head-to-head competition. Again, this may be privately profitable, particularly when intrabrand competition would otherwise be intense and economies of scope in retailing are low (Dobson and Waterson, 1996a). However, this may be against the public interest because it reduces consumer choice and can raise final prices. Accordingly, a move from multiple-brand retailing to a situation where retailers specialize in offering an exclusive but limited range – for example, by selling own-label products that are distinct from those of rivals, since contracted suppliers cannot sell the same product to rivals – may adversely affect social welfare.

Exclusivity restraints may not be unilaterally imposed by one side of the market, but instead arise from the joint interest of trading parties who bargain over terms and conditions. Dobson and Waterson (1996b) examine the mutual incentive for firms to adopt exclusive trading relationships that restrict both manufacturer and retailer to deal only with the other. Potential advantages from such a contract may include using side payments between the two parties to internalize externalities that adversely affect joint profits due to independent successive price setting, as well as limiting direct interbrand and intrabrand competition when retailers specialize in selling different products, hence avoiding head-to-head competition and cannibalization of sales.

However, by limiting the options of both retailer and manufacturer, such contracts may also imply lost sales opportunities. Exclusive trading is attractive to firms when differentiation is weak across either manufacturers' products or retailers' service. Private and social interests diverge in these circumstances because consumers face less variety. In contrast, social and private interests may coincide when differentiation is moderate; then the inefficiency associated with successive pricing distortions from non-exclusive trading becomes important. Internalizing such externalities can lead to net gains for firms and consumers alike.

Pricing restraints. Despite a general ban on resale price maintenance (RPM) throughout the EU and North America (OECD, 1994), the social welfare implications of RPM are still controversial, not least because exemptions remain (such as medicaments in the UK). Moreover, the threat of refusal to supply may induce maintenance of higher prices whether or not RPM officially exists.

Much of the debate has centred on the use of RPM by manufacturers to control freeriding by dealers; Telser (1960) discusses pre-sales service levels, Marvel and McCafferty (1984) discuss quality certification. Discount retailers may offer a reduced level of service and gain custom by undercutting high-service retailers that have made investments in providing information and demonstration facilities to consumers, and built a reputation for service provision and the stocking of quality products. Manufacturers wish to eliminate free-riding when it has an adverse effect on demand, using RPM to prevent intrabrand price competition directly, and thus encouraging retailers to compete through service provision.

However, in contrast to the Chicago School assertion that any activity that boosts demand must benefit society (for example, Bork, 1978), it is unclear that more service investment, particularly related to pre-sales service, is socially desirable. Sales promotion is not costless. If most people are well aware of the product already, the extra effort to capture marginal consumers adds little consumer benefit, but may add substantially to costs and thus prices. Control devices, such as RPM or other contract terms that induce this effort and are privately profitable, *may* make consumers as a whole worse off (White, 1985).[7] Nevertheless, where consumers do gain from the additional level of service, RPM can be welfare enhancing and thus socially desirable.

This analysis of manufacturer-induced RPM, to combat service underprovision and underinvestment by dealers, assumes that retailers have no market power. In contrast, an argument with a long tradition is that RPM may be collectively sponsored by retailers in a dealer cartel to limit downstream competition (Pickering, 1966). Here the restraint coordinates price fixing by retailers. Thus, a horizontal price-fixing agreement, which might otherwise be difficult to sustain, is disguised and enforced by a vertical restriction. The restriction also protects the dealer cartel against new entry by retail chains with lower cost structures. In both cases, downstream competition is limited, raising retail prices and reducing welfare.

Retailer pressure may work even in the absence of a formal dealer cartel. Sharp (1985) claims that manufacturers are susceptible to the pressure of key retailers with a significant degree of market control. Shaffer (1991b) analyses how retailers individually seek to contract with powerless manufacturers. Slotting allowances and RPM serve a strategic role in dampening downstream competition, generating higher retail prices and profits. Slotting allowances offer retailers a direct up-front payment, but provide an indirect benefit by committing retailers to accept a wholesale price above a manufacturer's production marginal cost, which raises retail prices.[8] In a similar way, commitment to a high retail price by one retailer through an RPM contract induces a rival to raise its own price, increasing profits for all retailers. Shaffer shows that when individual supplier–retailer contracts, including wholesale price terms, are observable, retailers will individually and jointly induce manufacturers to pay slotting allowances rather than use RPM. If, however, contracts are unobservable by rivals, who therefore cannot signal their mutual intention to dampen competition by accepting high wholesale prices, RPM may be used by a retailer to encourage rivals to raise retail prices.

As with analysis of exclusivity arrangements, we can extend the view that pricing restraints are unilaterally imposed by one side of the market to consider arrangements bargained by mutual consent. Dobson and Waterson (1997a) analyse bilateral duopoly, including negotiation over intermediate prices when different degrees of differentiation exist between both manufacturer products and retailer services. We consider the competition effect of eliminating price competition at the retail level when RPM is adopted.[9] There are two opposing effects on social welfare. Double margins, where manufacturers and retailers make successive price mark-ups, may be avoided, but RPM may dampen interbrand competition: without RPM, dealers press manufacturers to cut margins and keep prices low.

RPM can be socially beneficial when retailers' bargaining strength is relatively weak but their services are significantly differentiated; it is then that the double-margins problem is most severe. When the reverse conditions apply, in the absence of RPM retailers would use their greater bargaining strength to negotiate low transfer prices, but be forced by intense retail competition to set low mark-ups and pass on the benefits of their reduced costs to consumers. However, it is precisely in these circumstances that the firms will collectively wish to employ RPM to avoid intense competition, as unrestricted pricing has a detrimental effect on profits at both levels. Here, the firms' collective interests conflict with the public interest. The only exception is where interfirm and interproduct connections are slight, and when RPM is both privately and socially desirable (to avoid the intense double mark-up problem). In general, RPM is adopted by firms to protect profits by denying consumers low prices.

Consolidation in retailing: benefits from countervailing power?

Greater concentration in markets is generally of concern to policy-makers. Unless there are large cost savings from economies of scale and scope, the reduction in competition is likely to raise prices and be against the public interest. Double margins are of particular concern because the output-level distortion is exacerbated. Yet, competition authorities, particularly in Europe, have been largely unmoved by higher retailer concentration, expecting economies of scale and scope to deliver lower costs and prices. In particular, it has been suggested (MMC, 1981; OFT, 1985) that consolidation enables retailers to extract discounts from manufacturers, which can be passed on to the consumers as lower prices – a version of Galbraith's (1952) controversial countervailing power hypothesis.[10]

This argument is contentious, since greater concentration at the retail level may afford firms a simultaneous increase in both their buying and selling power. The former improves their relative bargaining position, exerting downward pressure on intermediate prices and reducing problems of double margins; the latter allows higher price–cost margins, increasing the total surplus available to firms. If the second effect is large enough, higher concentration leads to higher consumer prices.

Dobson and Waterson (1997b) consider these issues in a market setting where a single supplier bargains with differentiated oligopolistic retailers. The producer individually negotiates intermediate prices with each retailer, then retailers independently set retail prices. What is the effect of higher retail concentration? As the number of retailers declines, the manufacturer has fewer alternatives available, reducing its bargaining power. But remaining retailers have higher profit margins. Despite lower bargaining power, suppliers may be able to raise prices, getting a reduced share of a larger cake. If so, prices to consumers rise with retailer concentration: retailers pay more for supplies and also have higher profit margins.

Conversely, if higher retailer concentration leads to little rise in selling power (retailer differentiation is small), the fall in the supplier's relative bargaining power may be sufficient to lower supplier prices enough to make consumer prices fall, despite slightly higher profit margins in retailing. Within the framework of Dobson and Waterson (1997b), this is a rare occurrence. Broadly, the services of competing retailers must be very close substitutes for each other, and the number of competing retailers very limited. Furthermore, if the retailers have an alternative, even if less desirable, supply source, this further reduces the likelihood of lower prices, the outcome implied by the countervailing power view.

Moreover, in situations where retail consolidation is likely to yield countervailing power benefits, intense downstream competition in a highly concentrated market can have a destructive effect on the supplier's profit. It may then be profitable for the supplier to avoid these problems by trading with only one of the retailers, refusing to supply the rest, even if this allows the retailer to derive monopoly profits. This further damages consumer welfare through higher prices and lost retail service variety.

In conclusion, there is little to suggest that countervailing power is a reliable self-regulatory mechanism to protect consumers. Consolidation at the retailing level is in the public interest only if the services of competing retailers are very close substitutes and refusal to supply is ruled out. Yet, one feature of the retail market is the major firms' attempts to distinguish themselves from each other in terms of their image and retail offer: for example, by retail branding. In such circumstances, we cannot guarantee that the effects of retail concentration are beneficial.

In terms of retail grocery, the countervailing power view is unsupported by the evidence. Connor *et al.* (1996) conclude unequivocally: 'Nothing in our empirical work can be construed as support for the idea that retailer competition kept the US food manufacturing from becoming more concentrated in the 1980s.' Moreover, studies finding evidence that buyer power has any countervailing effect, such as Schumacher (1991), are necessarily based only on indirect estimates of buyer concentration, whose reliability is hard to assess.

As regards merger or co-operation between buyers to form a buyer group, pooling purchasing resources may yield efficiency benefits from reduced costs; again these must be set against anti-competitive effects. For a clear welfare benefit, costs must fall sufficiently to outweigh higher profit margins, so that lower prices are passed on downstream. This may be the case for cross-border retailer buying alliances in the EU, if they consist of one alliance member per member state; these retailers are then not direct competitors in selling to final consumers.

The Policy Dimension

The preceding analysis indicates a clear need for a case-by-case approach to competition policy, but also offers insights into the circumstances in which the public interest is likely to require intervention by the competition authorities. In this section, we focus on implications for vertical relations policy and for merger policy. We analyse these in turn, and illustrate each with a case study using the framework of Table 2.

Vertical relations policy

The existing policy framework governing retailer linkages within the EU is largely provided by EC Article 85.[11] Article 85(1) prohibits agreements in fairly broad terms, but many vertical agreements can obtain either 'block exemption' or individual exemption under 85(3). There are currently block exemptions for exclusive distribution, exclusive purchasing (including special provisions for beer and petrol), motor vehicle distribution arrangements, franchise agreements and intellectual property. The present arrangements regularize most of the major trading activities that are potentially exclusive.

Article 86 may also be relevant where a dominant firm in the industry imposes restraints (tie-ins or full-line forcing) on those it supplies. But in general, the legislation in this area is framed in terms of agreements. Service franchising, for example, entails substantial restrictions on distributors' activities, but such agreements are considered benign because they have been entered voluntarily. Similar restrictions on tying or full-line forcing might attract opprobrium if they were unilaterally imposed on unwilling retailers.

A fundamental review of the EC Commission's approach to vertical restraints began in 1996, so far resulting in an EU Green Paper on Vertical Restraints (January 1997), outlining policy options for comment and a subsequent statement of its preferred choice. The present intention is to adopt broader block exemptions and abandon industry-specific rules, but to use market-share thresholds as a basis for offering exemptions, the threshold varying according to the type of restraint (or combination of restraints) and taking account of whether the practice is specific or market-wide. RPM and restraints preventing inter-member-state parallel trade remain prohibited.

Market-share thresholds aim to provide a structural measure of market power. Our framework (see again Table 2) suggests that, unless significant market power exists at manufacturer or retailer level, vertical restraints are unlikely to be socially harmful. However, when firms have market power, vertical restraints act against the public interest if competition-dampening effects outweigh any efficiency advantages. When restraints reduce variety for consumers or impede price competition, anti-competitive effects are important: for example, in limiting head-to-head intrabrand or in-store interbrand competition. Conversely, efficiency gains may be significant where retail service is important (the product is a complicated, high-value, infrequently purchased item needing considerable sales service), where the restraint is mutually agreed between the parties (not imposed by one side), and when economies of scope are limited (Dobson and Waterson, 1996c).

The case of the British beer industry. The British beer industry offers an interesting study of the power of both retailers and manufacturers, and the difficulty of designing an appropriate policy.[12] Our analysis draws on Dobson and Waterson (1996c) and Slade (1998). The industry was investigated in a famous report by the Monopolies and Mergers Commission (MMC, 1989). Brewers were highly vertically integrated. Significant power resided in retail–wholesale links. The brewers together owned 75% of the 60 000 public houses in the UK, with 29% being directly managed and 71% tenanted (where the publican pays a rent, but accepts significant restrictions on products, sources and activities allowed). Six national brewers provided 75% of UK beer production, 74% of the brewer-owned estate and 86% of additional ties through loans to publicans. Regional brewers, though much smaller, operated similar practices. Entry into retailing was considerably restricted by planning and licensing regulations – a significant barrier to new retail developments – reinforced by the high level of exclusivity in the industry, making wholesaling a marginal activity. Market shares of the major brewers were quite stable and prices were rising in real terms, particularly for lager, then seen as a premium product.

Existing retail firms had little market power to exercise against brewers. Even retail and wholesale chains that existed independently of brewers were unable to influence much their terms of purchase in the 'on' trade (sale to public houses for consumption on the premises). Powerful purchasers in the 'off' trade (take away) did extract concessions from brewers. But 'on' and 'off' consumption are poor substitutes for final consumers.

The MMC report concluded, among other more far-reaching findings discussed below, that the restrictions on retailers reduced variety to the detriment of consumers; specifically, that restricting the range of ales to one brewer's products should be eased, allowing the retailer to incorporate a 'guest ale' among the offerings.

Brewers argued that the system of tied estates offered efficiency benefits, such as encouraging investment in amenities, although these were probably modest given the nature of beer and its consumption: a simple, inexpensive, repeat purchase, branded product, sold through a convenience outlet. Given economies of scope in retailing different brewers' beers side by side, limitations on variety also seem to entail substantial inefficiency. Thus, the efficiency justifications for exclusivity arrangements are dubious from consumers' viewpoint. Exclusivity arrangements probably reflected an effort by brewers to consolidate their power.

The other major change instituted by the MMC (the subsequent 'beer orders') was the forced divestment, by each major brewer, of half the number of its pubs in excess of 2000; thus, a brewer with 3600 pubs had to give up 800. Reducing vertical integration was intended to reduce protection for upstream market power. The brewers reacted with a variety of strategies. Grand Metropolitan quit the brewing business; Courage quit the pub trade.

A number of long-term exclusive supply arrangements between brewers and newly created pub chains were nevertheless allowed by the Office of Fair Trading, which administered the divestment programme. Alongside the remains of the vertically integrated network was created a new set of powerful retail chains facing a number of powerful brewers, with the retail chains often contracted to sell their former owner's products. There was also subsequent consolidation by merger (e.g., Courage and Scottish & Newcastle breweries) and other realignments in the brewing industry. By 1994 the largest three brewers had 68% of the market, up from around 47% at the time of the MMC inquiry. The position of the free wholesale trade remains marginal.

Slade (1998) finds that during 1988–94, holding constant demand and costs, beer prices rose in tied houses (associated with a particular brewer's products), but not in free houses, which were unaffected by the structural changes in the industry. This evidence suggests that the substitution of exclusive arrangements for vertical integration resulted in the creation of double mark-ups, powerful brewers and powerful retailers each taking a cut. Yet brewers' profits did not rise as a result of the higher prices. In fact, the wholesale price received by brewers fell on average. The new chains used their bargaining power to negotiate volume discounts, which were not then passed on to their pub tenants. In terms of Table 2, retail firms now had buying power, which was not exercised to the benefit of consumers.

More recently, some of the initial exclusive agreements have expired or been reduced by subsequent developments, and new pub chains have developed, buying beer from several sources. In addition, the rigid licensing structure appears to have been eased. The longer-term outlook may be rosier for consumers. Nevertheless, the case shows clearly the importance of considering the likely competitive moves by the major players when implementing policies to remedy a perceived market failure.

Mergers policy

While organic development has driven concentration in most retail sectors, mergers have still been important, and are on the increase. Traditionally, mergers have been examined by competition authorities at national level, since mergers generally involved retailers from the same country. However, cross-border mergers between retail groups have become more common (610 recorded by Corporate Intelligence Research during 1990–4 alone). The European Commission has taken on investigations of merger proposals, not just because of increased cross-border proposals (e.g., the recent *Metro/Makro* concentration),[13] but also because national concentrations can affect foreign producers and so require Commission investigation. The European Commission can also refer cases to member states, following a request under Article 9, when it considers examination by national authorities more appropriate.[14] Reviewing Commission investigations, Morgan (1994, 1997) shows that it has generally taken a favourable view of mergers. A recent exception, the case of *Kesko/Tuko*,[15] which we discuss below, may indicate a tightening of policy.

To assess the welfare effects of a merger, the first problem confronting a competition authority is determining how broadly or narrowly to define the market. As emphasized by NERA (1993), two key dimensions need consideration: the geographic extent of the market and the substitutability between products offering similar services. There may be large differences between the selling side and the buying side of the market, requiring separate consideration of each (as indicated by separate questions in Table 2). As an example, consider the market for retail grocers. On the selling side, competition may be localized – consumers face a limited number of stores within easy travel distance – and is also segmented by retail service (superstore versus small convenience store), but with a wide product choice and many near substitutes for a particular food brand or item. In contrast, on the buying side, except perhaps for locally grown fresh produce, the market for purchasing grocery items will be national or international, but because of the specific nature of supply for particular brands/items, the product dimension might be defined quite narrowly. Moreover, individual suppliers may be economically dependent on particular distributors (especially when long contracts are prevalent).

The US authorities have traditionally taken a much more stringent line on proposed mergers involving retailers than European authorities, choosing narrow market definitions despite the fact that less stringent planning controls in the USA make entry easier. This is most notable in the Supreme Court's stance in enforcing Section 7 of the Clayton Act in *Von's*,[16] where the merger of two grocery retailers operating in Los Angeles was prevented even though they accounted for only 7.5% of sales in Los Angeles, based on concerns of the trend towards increasing concentration in this local market.

The sophistication with which competition authorities apply economic analysis was illustrated recently by the case of *Staples/Office Depot*[17] in the USA. The Federal Trade Commission (FTC) argued that the relevant product market was the sale of office supplies through office supply superstores; superstores were thus significantly different from small independent stationery stores or large diverse general retailers. The FTC produced econometric evidence to show substantial cross-elasticity of demand among consumers of the various superstores, but little cross-elasticity between the superstores and other sources of consumable office supplies. Given this very narrow definition of the market, concentration was found to be very high, Office Depot and Staples being the two largest chains. Moreover, the evidence showed that prices were on average substantially lower in cities where two office supply superstore chains competed than where only one superstore was located, and were even lower in cities where three chains faced each other: the difference in prices between one-chain cities and three-chain cities was around 13%. This econometric analysis provided strong evidence that the proposed merger between Staples and Office Depot would have a significant anti-competitive effect in raising prices.

In addition to retailer selling power, competition authorities may also consider the nature of supplying industries and whether the retailers command buying power over these. As expressed by questions 2 and 3 in Table 2, if buyer power is against relatively powerless suppliers, there are concerns about abuse of monopsony power, which might include a detrimental impact on producer (suppliers') surplus and the long-term viability of suppliers. On the other hand, if buyer power is linked with significant seller power at the upstream level, then, as argued in the Analysis section, it is more likely that the existence or enhancement of buyer power is beneficial: buyer power may have a socially beneficial countervailing effect by negating the detrimental effects of upstream seller power.

The Kesko/Tuko *decision.*[18] All the above issues are present in the recent proposed merger of two leading Finnish supermarket chains, Kesko and Tuko, considered by the European Commission.[19] The Commission analysed the market in three ways: the retail market for daily consumer goods;[20] the cash-and-carry market for daily goods; and the market for procurement of daily consumer goods. The Commission distinguished, at the retail level, between 'supermarkets and other stores able to provide the wide selection that enables the consumer to purchase most of the household necessities in a "one-stop shop", with attendant convenience such as parking facilities, trolleys etc.'; and other shops (kiosks, petrol stations, etc.). The relevant market is then defined quite narrowly as 'the provision of a basket of fresh and dry food-stuffs, and non-food household consumables, sold in a supermarket environment'. The geographical market was defined by the Commission as a store's catchment area within twenty minutes by car.

The Commission observed that the average market share of the largest retailer in each member state of the EU is 18%. Kesko had 40% before the merger; the Finnish retail market was accordingly highly concentrated. With Tuko, its share increased to 60%. Even excluding purchases made through Kesko/Tuko by independent retailers such as Stockman, Kesko's share was still 55% (and indeed 80% of the cash-and-carry market). In different local areas, Kesko's share varied between 40% and 90%. This led to a presumption of dominance by Kesko, reinforced by its control over large retail outlets, customer loyalty schemes, use of private-label products, its distribution system, and the position of Kesko's central organs as buyers of daily consumer goods. All these factors were viewed as raising barriers to entry.

In terms of buyer power, Kesko was perceived as an essential 'gate keeper': no major supplier could manage without Kesko. Suppliers were found to be dependent on Kesko for 50–75% of their sales in Finland. Conversely, Kesko was found not to be dependent on any individual supplier to the same extent, with own label (20–30% of its sales) a key element in its buyer power.

The merger was prevented on the grounds that it would create a dominant position and significantly impede effective competition. The Commission rejected Kesko's offers to divest certain wholesaling and cash-and-carry outlets, together with the creation of a new block. Since the prohibition decision, Kesko has been asked to sell the assets it acquired from Tuko to restore competition on the retail and cash-and-carry markets (Reuters, 19/2/97).

The Commission's analysis and coverage of the issues was broad, taking account of seller power, buyer power and productive efficiency concerns. We view this as desirable given the nature of the market. However, the decision ultimately rested on a structural interpretation of the market, not detailed economic analysis.

Concluding Remarks

Retailing across Europe comprises a fascinating mixture of common themes and considerable diversity; even the 'common' format of McDonald's restaurants differs from country to country! A number of important elements come together in retailing. First, considerable changes in retail formats and offers have taken place over the last half-century – much more significant, we would argue, than changes in production – in particular, the development of supermarkets and the spread of chain stores. Many of these may be desirable. Further significant changes are on the way as a result of Internet retailing. Indeed, some would claim that this obviates any policy concern about retail power. We do not take this sanguine view, because it is hard to see why producers would willingly submit to ultra-competitive means of doing business. In any case, retailing involves service, which is difficult to charge for separately, and shop-based retailers will not provide service if purchases are subsequently made elsewhere. Service might shrink to sub-optimal levels. Yet emerging formats are difficult to curtail: one-stop shops, 'category killers' and the like are all part of the competitive process and need policy consideration.

Retailing is an area where the political-economy aspects of regulation loom large. Consumers are individually inconsequential, but all voters are consumers; collectively they have a powerful voice. Small businesses, in the shape of existing 'family' retailers, have a voice too, and do not want to see chain stores and shopping centres take their trade. But big is not necessarily bad. Supermarkets in turn, given their sites, wish to lobby to discourage further developments to trading practices. Unions ally with the (Protestant) Church to 'keep Sunday special'. Farmers wish supermarket buying power to be leavened by the existence of producer co-operatives. Of all these pressure groups, only consumers are pressing for a workably competitive retail environment.

One of the most positive features of retailing, where it exists, is the presence of buying groups – very much a European phenomenon. Not only do these offset manufacturer power – a much better counterweight than retailer buying power – but they also facilitate the continued survival of the small local retailer amidst a sea of chain stores. Comparisons are difficult, but what evidence we have suggests that they provide a powerful brake on the pricing freedom of large retailers without ossifying existing structures: for example, they can participate in own-brand activities as easily as retailers. We need more research on how they can be encouraged to develop.

Where strong exclusivity arrangements have existed for many years, retailing formats seem to lack the dynamism seen elsewhere and have outlived much of their usefulness. One example is car retailing, which still maintains arrangements appropriate for an industry selling small numbers of cars from each of many producers, for which substantial service attention was required. Consumers in search of a good price find the task irksome and the search process complex. Another example is books, where special treatment with respect to resale price maintenance has led to numerous inefficient sellers. Retail pharmacy in many European countries provides a third example. None of these examples implies that all vertical restraints are inappropriate, but they all need active review. Exclusivity should be seen as desirable only when it delivers clear benefits: for example, in service. In designing policy remedies, a particular difficulty is gauging how the industry will react, as the beer case study shows. Banning particular restraints is likely to lead to structural changes in the industry.

Similarly, left to themselves, retailers in many areas show a powerful tendency to combine. Consolidation proceeds apace, although the number of successful pan-European retailers is significantly lower than the number of successful brands. Current structure also differs from country to country. Consolidation is not necessarily undesirable. Empirical research shows power moving into fewer hands; analysis and policy prescription has to recognize the market power enjoyed by retailers, manufacturers and often both. Economies of scale and scope, gains from precommitment to service and investment levels, and internalization of spillovers all imply that efficiency in retailing may involve considerable scale accompanied by considerable market power. In many European countries, retailing may still be undesirably fragmented.

However, retailer power cannot be understood in isolation: retailers are supplied by powerful suppliers, themselves in many cases pan-European. The important but difficult question concerns how much retail concentration is desirable. Since the answer depends on the organization of suppliers as well as the nature of consumers, there is as yet no reason why the optimal degree of retail concentration should be the same across countries; it may be appropriate for the UK to have higher concentration than Greece.

It is only very recently that analysis of retailing has developed an appropriate framework, and we are still working out the answers in particular cases. It can be argued that the EU views mergers very much too sympathetically. The Commission has a long way to go before it engages in the type of analysis (both theoretical and empirical) commonplace in, say, a merger investigation by the US Federal Trade Commission (as in the *Staples/Office Depot* case). But this is a route that Europe needs to take. Retailer power is a feature of commercial life in Europe, retailing is big business, and potential effects on consumers and welfare are substantial. Europe's existing diversity, paradoxically, may also offer the best hope of a better understanding of the issues involved: as citizens travel around the EU, they will surely be struck by differences in retailing arrangements and may be prompted to press for better analysis and a more informed discussion of the appropriate competition policy.

Notes

1   Press release (8/8/98) by retail analysts M+M Eurodata (http://www.mm-eurodata.de/english).

2   Compared with the USA, compact disc prices were higher by 16% in Germany, 24% in Denmark, 27% in Italy, 37% in France and 40% in the UK (*Guardian*, 28/3/98). Even larger differences were noted for electrical goods such as televisions and radio cassette recorders.

3   Retail rental data in *Main Streets Across the World 1997/98* (Healey and Baker, 1998) show the top areas of New York commanding higher rents than Munich's Kaufingerstrasse or London's Oxford Street. Rental rates for major US locations vary between $807 and $4844 per square metre; those for Germany vary less, between $1050 and $2625, while for the UK they are between $1534 and $4025. Such snapshots do not suggest that rentals in Europe vastly exceed those in the USA.

4   Wal-Mart Stores, much of whose sales come from food retailing, is classified as a general merchandiser; in that category Marks & Spencer has a profit margin nearly twice that of any other major general merchandiser.

5   For example, in the UK, from 1980 to 1996 there were 51 recorded merger and acquisition transactions valued in excess of £100 million, and the recorded total for the retail sector over this period was £24 950 million from some 939 UK purchases.

6   In particular, we do not discuss vertical restraints determined largely by the manufacturer, such as tying, full-line forcing, aggregated rebate schemes and selective distribution (Dobson and Waterson, 1996c). Tying is a controversial area, given recent US decisions about Kodak and Microsoft.

7   A similar argument applies to store density. By raising retail prices through RPM, the manufacturer induces entry by retailers, and previously unserviced demand is supplied. Some people are better off (those previously poorly served), but others, already well served, are worse off. It is unclear that overall welfare increases.

8   Retailers may argue that a fee for shelf space rations scarce space among competing goods; making producers pay up-front attracts only those goods in which producers are confident enough to offer 'insurance' against poor performance. Shaffer's point is that this practice can represent a market co-ordinating device when contracts are relatively transparent, serving to dampen competition.

9   Implicit in this analysis is the assumption that products and retail service provision are not affected by the form of price competition.

10   An arm's-length relationship would suggest that prices rise with retail concentration. For a critical view, see Adams (1987). The hypothesis has several variants (Connor *et al.*, 1996).

11   National-level policy is also important. Many countries have policy significantly different from the EU framework. OECD (1994) summarizes the position for several OECD member countries.

12   There is a European dimension, as the *Delimitis* brewery case shows (*Delimitis, Stergios* v. *Henningerbrau AG*, 1992, 5 CMLR 210).

13   Case no. IV/M.1063, 28/11/1997.

14   The proposed acquisition of Casino by Promodès (both French supermarket chains) was recently referred to the French authorities for investigation (31/10/1997).

15   Case no. IV/M.784 (OJEC L110, 26/4/1997).

16   *United States* v. *Von's Grocery Company*, 384 US 270 (1966).

17   *Federal Trade Commission* v. *Staples, Inc. and Office Depot, Inc.*, Civ. no. 97–701 (TFH) (1997) – see Pitofsky (1997).

18   All references are to Case no. IV/M.784 (OJEC L110, 26/4/1997).
19   The necessary 'Community dimension' was found on the basis that 30% of Kesko's purchases were imported.
20   Daily goods are described as the 'basket of daily consumer goods that consumers expect to find in a supermarket environment'.

References

Adams, W. (1987). 'Countervailing power', in J. Eatwell, M. Milgate and P. Newman (eds.), *The New Palgrave: A Dictionary of Economics*, Macmillan, London.

Azoulay, R.A. (1995). 'The changing face of UK retailing, 1982–1992', unpublished MA dissertation, University of Nottingham.

Besanko, D. and M.K. Perry (1994). 'Exclusive dealing in a spatial model of retail competition', *International Journal of Industrial Organization*.

Bork, R.H. (1978). *The Antitrust Paradox: A Policy at War With Itself*, Basic Books, New York.

Bresnahan, T.F. and P.C. Reiss (1991). 'Entry and competition in concentrated markets', *Journal of Political Economy*.

Brookes, R. (1995). 'Strategic implications for fresh produce suppliers', *Journal of Business Research*.

Comanor, W.S. and H.E. Frech III (1985). 'The competitive effects of vertical agreements', *American Economic Review*.

Connor, J.M., R. Rogers and V. Bhagavan (1996). 'Concentration and countervailing power in the US food manufacturing industries', *Review of Industrial Organization*.

Corporate Intelligence on Retailing (1998). *The European Retail Handbook*, London.

Corstjens, J. and M. Corstjens (1995). *Store Wars*, Wiley, Chichester.

Cotterill, R. (1986). 'Market power in the retail food industry: evidence from Vermont', *Review of Economics and Statistics*.

Dawson, J. (1993). 'The internationalization of retailing', in R.D.F. Bromley and C.J. Thomas (eds.), *Retail Change: Contemporary Issues*, UGL Press, London.

Dawson, J. and S. Shaw (1990). 'The changing character of retailer–supplier relationships', in J. Fernie (ed.), *Retail Distribution Management*, Kogan Page, London.

Dobson, P.W. and M. Waterson (1994). 'The effects of exclusive purchasing on interbrand and intrabrand rivalry', Warwick Economics Working Paper no. 94–15, University of Warwick.

Dobson, P.W. and M. Waterson (1996a). 'Product range and interfirm competition', *Journal of Economics and Management Strategy*.

Dobson, P.W. and M. Waterson (1996b). 'Exclusive trading contracts in successive differentiated duopoly', *Southern Economic Journal*.

Dobson, P.W. and M. Waterson (1996c). 'Vertical restraints and competition policy', Research Paper no. 12, Office of Fair Trading, London.

Dobson, P.W. and M. Waterson (1997a). 'The competition effects of resale price maintenance', mimeo, University of Nottingham.

Dobson, P.W. and M. Waterson (1997b). 'Countervailing power and consumer prices', *Southern Economic Journal*.

Dobson, P.W., M. Waterson and A. Chu (1998). 'The welfare consequences of the exercise of buyer power', Research Paper no. 16, Office of Fair Trading, London.

Eurostat (1997). *Retailing in the European Economic Area 1996*, European Commission, Brussels.

Foord, J., S. Bowlby and C. Tillsley (1996). 'The changing place of retailer–supplier relations in British retailing', in N. Wrigley and M. Lowe (eds.), *Retailing, Consumption and Capital*, Longman, Harlow.

FTC (1997). 'FTC judge upholds charges against Toys'R'Us', FTC press release (FTC file no. 941 0040; docket no. 9278).

Galbraith, J.K. (1952). *American Capitalism: The Concept of Countervailing Power*, Houghton-Mifflin, Boston, MA.

Healey and Baker (1998). *Main Streets Across the World: A Guide to International Retail Rents*, London.

Kuhn, K.-U. (1997). 'Nonlinear pricing in vertically related duopolies', *Rand Journal of Economics*.

Kuhn, K.-U. and X. Vives (1995). 'Excess entry, vertical integration and welfare', CEPR Discussion Paper no. 1293.

Lin, Y.J. (1990). 'The dampening-of-competition effect of exclusive dealing', *Journal of Industrial Economics*.

Marion, B.W., W.F. Mueller, R.W. Cotterill, F.E. Geithman and J.R. Schmelzer (1979). *The Food Retailing Industry: Market Structure, Profits and Prices*, Praeger, New York.

Marvel, H.P. (1982). 'Exclusive dealing', *Journal of Law and Economics*.

Marvel, H.P. (1989). 'Concentration and price in gasoline retailing', in L.W. Weiss (ed.), *Concentration and Price*, MIT Press, Cambridge, MA.

Marvel, H.P. and S. McCafferty (1984). 'Resale price maintenance and quality certification', *Rand Journal of Economics*.

Mills, D.E. (1995). 'Why retailers sell private labels', *Journal of Economics and Management Strategy*.

Monopolies and Mergers Commission (1981). *Discounts to Retailers*, HMSO, London.

Monopolies and Mergers Commission (1989). *The Supply of Beer*, HMSO, London.

Morgan, E.J. (1994). 'European community merger control in the service industries', *Service Industries Journal*.

Morgan, E.J. (1997). 'European community merger policy in the service industries: the second phase', *Service Industries Journal*.

NERA (1993). 'Market definition in UK competition policy', Research Paper no. 1, Office of Fair Trading, London.

Newmark, C. (1990). 'A new test of the price–concentration relationship in grocery retailing', *Economics Letters*.

Nielsen (1998). *The Retail Pocket Book 1998*, NTC Publications, Oxford.

O'Brien, D.P. and G. Shaffer (1993). 'On the dampening-of-competition effect of exclusive dealing', *Journal of Industrial Economics*.

OECD (1994). *Competition Policy and Vertical Restraints: Franchising Agreements*, Paris.

Office of Fair Trading (1985). *Competition and Retailing*, London.

Office of Fair Trading (1998). 'OFT announces enquiry into supermarkets', Press Release no. 33/98 (30/7/1998), London.

Ornstein, S.I. (1989). 'Exclusive dealing and antitrust', *Antitrust Bulletin*.

Pickering, J.F. (1966). *Resale Price Maintenance in Practice*, George Allen and Unwin, Hemel Hempstead.

Pitofsky, R. (1997). 'Staples and Boeing: what they say about merger enforcement at the FTC', paper presented to Business Development Associates, Washington, DC (23/9/1997).

Posner, R.A. (1976). *Antitrust Law: An Economic Perspective*, University of Chicago Press, Chicago, IL.

Rey, P. and J. Stiglitz (1988). 'Vertical restraints and producers' competition', *European Economic Review*.

Rey, P. and J. Stiglitz (1995). 'The role of exclusive territories in producers' competition', *Rand Journal of Economics*.

Schumacher, U. (1991). 'Buyer structure and seller performance in US manufacturing industries', *Review of Economics and Statistics*.

Shaffer, G. (1991a). 'Capturing strategic rent: full line forcing, brand discounts, aggregate rebates, and maximum resale price maintenance', *Journal of Industrial Economics*.

Shaffer, G. (1991b). 'Slotting allowances and resale price maintenance: a comparison of facilitating practices', *Rand Journal of Economics*.

Shaffer, G. (1995). 'Rendering alternative offerings less profitable with resale price maintenance', *Journal of Economics and Management Strategy*.

Sharp, B.S. (1985). 'Comments on Marvel: how fair is fair trade?', *Contemporary Policy Issues*.

Slade, M.E. (1998). 'Beer and the tie: did divestiture of brewer-owned public houses lead to higher beer prices?', *Economic Journal*.

Steiner, R.L. (1991). 'Intrabrand competition: stepchild of antitrust', *Antitrust Bulletin*.

Telser, L. (1960). 'Why should manufacturers want fair trade?', *Journal of Law and Economics*.

Tordjman, A. (1994). 'European retailing: convergence, differences and perspectives', *International Journal of Retail and Distribution Management*.

Treadgold, A. (1990). *The Costs of Retailing in Continental Europe*, report for the Oxford Institute of Retail Management.

White, L.J. (1985). 'Resale price maintenance and the problem of marginal and inframarginal consumers', *Contemporary Policy Issues*.

Chapter 5

International Retailing

RETAILING IS GENERALLY VIEWED as a domestic activity. Because the market is local, retailing often is referred to as 'internal trade' in statistics and reports. As such, it takes place in all countries. Whilst some authors view 'international retailing' as the study of retailing in countries other than their own, we consider 'international retailing' to be an activity in which a retailer undertakes retail functions in more than one country. It is this latter view that forms the basis of this chapter.

Until the advent of the Internet and retailers such as Dell and Amazon, the market, from a retail viewpoint, was generally local, often very local. Even for mail order firms it was usually, at best, national. The local nature of the market, however, belies the fact that a retail firm may operate internationally. International activity by the retail firm occurs not only in the sourcing of goods for resale and in the sourcing of the means of distribution, but also in the operation of sales systems whether by hypermarkets, convenience stores, catalogues, direct selling or some other retail format.

Over the history of retailing there are examples of a few retailers realizing the opportunities of this international perspective, but as a major aspect of strategy international retailing is relatively recent. Historically, there are examples seen with the international origin of items on sale in nineteenth-century department stores and modest multi-store operation by high-fashion stores targeting the wealthy in London, Paris and other major cities (Crossick and Jaumain 1999). Through the first half of the twentieth century there were some valiant attempts by retailers to open stores in other countries. Hollander's (1970) seminal book recounts many of these activities both in Europe and by American retailers exploring Central and South America. Fletcher and Godley (2000a, b; Godley and Fletcher 2001) provide examples of the early international retailers in the UK. Whysall (1997) has provided an insightful study of the American ownership of Boots in the UK during the 1930s. Shaw and Alexander (2006) provide a detailed case of the role played by individuals in these early examples of international activity. It is, however, in the last quarter of the twentieth century that major changes in the ways retailers viewed the scope of their activity began to be apparent through a more international perspective. The large retailers greatly expanded their direct purchasing activities from foreign sources. Additionally, these firms have extended their retail operations to move into multiple national markets, sometimes on different continents. The extent of this widening of strategic and operational horizons is a significant feature of the development of the retail sector from the late twentieth century.

The magnitude of the change can be readily illustrated. The 100 largest retailers in the world in 2005 collectively accounted for 26 per cent of global retail sales. Whilst in 1986 over half the largest 100 firms were in a single domestic market, by 2005 it was barely a quarter. The number of these very large firms operating in ten or more countries has increased over the twenty years from five to thirty-four. Operating internationally for the major retailers had become, by early in the twenty-first century, the standard situation and is now not so much a key success factor as a key non-failure factor for large retailers.

Outside the 100 largest retailers, the increased international activity is evident across all sizes of firm, although it manifests itself in different ways. Large firms outside the top 100 and medium-sized firms copy the pattern of the largest firms with entry into new markets and increased foreign sourcing. But even for the small firms there is now a greater presence of foreign sourced goods as wholesalers and buying groups have provided the importing know-how. For the smallest micro-firms, of which there are still very many in retailing, internationalization occurs in a different guise. Although there is increased international sourcing through wholesalers, we also see many owner-managers coming from migrant communities, thus internationalizing the sector through its management cadre. This is seen in many markets. There are numerous examples. Chinese owners of micro-firms operating clothing stores in the Milan, Pakistani owners of convenience stores in the UK, Turkish owners of micro-firms in retailing in Germany and Chinese owners of stores in Thailand, are examples.

Given the size and speed of this shift of retailing from being domestic to being international, in many ways it is not surprising that the sectoral shift has been paralleled from the late 1980s with an expanding academic interest in retailer internationalization. As with the retailers' efforts at internationalization, there were sporadic but important academic studies before a surge in activity in the late twentieth century. Significant broad-based contributions prior to the mid-1980s were made by Hollander (1970), Waldman (1978) and Martenson (1981), who reviewed earlier studies and made prescient forecasts of the growth of the activity. Martenson's review of IKEA provided a rich foundation for many other studies of this firm as it has expanded into a leading international retailer. In addition to the reviews, two other streams of study can be seen at this time. One is related to the steady development of European integration as a 'Common Market'. Typical of this stream are studies by Knee (1966), Jefferys (1973) and Jackson (1973) on the pitfalls and planning required for moves within Europe and by Distributive Trades EDC (1973) and Commission of European Communities (1981) on the institutional framework a retailer might expect when they move. The second stream concerns the export of retail 'know-how', often in the guise of the transfer of 'modern' retail methods to 'underdeveloped' economies (Kaynak 1980, 1985; Goldman 1981; Truitt 1984). From these precursors there was a substantial increase in academic research from the mid-1980s which provides the substantive content of this chapter.

This academic interest has not been confined to papers in journals of business disciplines as important contributions have been made from across the social science spectrum. There are many ways of considering the managerial and academic development of international retailing. In this chapter we have chosen one way: to focus on the period since the mid-1980s and to view the development of the topic in the four phases of:

- describing patterns and borrowing from existing foundations of knowledge;
- searching for explanations through mechanisms and typologies;
- understanding specific processes and operations in foreign markets;
- broadening the intellectual bases with analyses in wider contexts.

The four papers selected for inclusion illustrate aspects of each of the four phases. Inevitably the academic literature does not all fall comfortably into these four phases with leaders and laggards evident when we look in detail at the material. Nonetheless, by considering the phases we can see the richness of the work that has been produced and also highlight where gaps still exist in our understanding of such a complex and dynamic process as retailer internationalization.

The papers show the development of managerial and academic ideas since the mid-1980s as both the activity of international retailing and its study have increased in importance. The papers have been selected to be typical of particular discourses since the mid-1980s and to reflect the different academic traditions that have been brought to bear on the study of retail internationalization.

1   *Describing Patterns and Borrowing from Existing Foundations of Knowledge.* As the surge in international activity was starting so it was described and its study drew on the existing academic base in international business. A substantial body of research had been undertaken on the internationalization of manufacturing firms and the growth of multinational business. Theory and case studies had been developed. The theory was translated to be used to address the internationalization of retailing, particularly the balance between standardization and adaptation. Case studies focused on descriptions of the moves of retailers to different countries. The first article (Salmon and Tordjman 1989) draws on the ideas of international business to explore the standardization–adaption debate. The paper has been widely cited and some twenty years after its genesis it is arguably regarded as seminal.

2   *Searching for Explanations through Mechanisms and Typologies.* As the extent of internationalization increased, so academic researchers began to look for

reasons for the variety seen in international activity. The attraction of borrowing concepts from established literature in manufacturing remained strong, but questions were also being asked of how relevant the existing theory was to explain the variety and complexity of international retailing. The second paper (Dawson 1994) draws attention to this debate and emphasizes the variety of activities and mechanisms of entry apparent in the international moves by retailers. Papers of this time were starting to look for typologies in the patterns of retailers' moves in order to try to understand and explain the patterns being described. Dawson's paper reviews the then current state of discourse from a European perspective.

3   *Understanding Specific Processes and Operations in Foreign Markets.* The increase in variety of retailers that were becoming international through the 1990s resulted in more detailed study of the nature of the processes involved in the generation of international activity. The processes of adaption to the foreign market are one group of such processes. The article from this genre by Goldman (2001) considers how 'formats' are adapted as they are transferred, in this case into the emergent economy of China. The managerial activity of retailers had become more sophisticated by the late 1990s as retailers realized the nature of the new markets being entered. All markets are essentially local. Academic studies looked at the nature of adaption and how operations were adjusted in detail to entry and subsequent network growth.

4   *Broadening the Intellectual Bases with Analyses in Wider Contexts.* By the early twenty-first century international retailing had become widespread. European- and American-based retailers had moved out of their own culture realm and into both each others and to East Asia and Latin America. Until this time the academic literature had focused on successes and expansion but some high-profile failures, one of which is considered in the fourth article (Wrigley and Currah 2003), alerted academics to the need to consider both sides of performance of the firm: success and failure. The scale of international activity and its consequences were also being linked to the broader process of globalization. In the early years of this century the bases of retailer internationalization were widened considerably in their spatial, managerial and disciplinary contexts. The paper is based on results from a research project undertaken by geographers (Wrigley *et al.* 2005), that linked retail internationalization with the wider discourse on globalization of spatial economic systems.

Describing Patterns and Borrowing from Existing Foundations of Knowledge

Although there were isolated and important studies of international retailing prior to the mid-1980s (Goldman 1974, 1981), we have chosen to focus this chapter on post-1985 material. It was at about this time that major retailers had come to terms with the need to use marketing methods, rather than sales techniques, in order to compete effectively for consumers. Thus the more successful retailers, particularly in Europe and North America, were involved in creating new formats and formulae to target more accurately defined consumer segments. Expansion of store networks was often rapid as new ideas were implemented. A consequence was that traditional domestic market competition became more intense and as a result new markets were sought not only within the domestic arena with new formats and formulae but also by moving outside the domestic market with successful concepts. Whilst domestic growth was important it was insufficient in many cases to satisfy the aspirations of the new marketing-driven retailers. Salmon and Tordjman (1989) illustrate this argument with their examples of Vendex (see also Burt 1989) with its multi-format approach, French hypermarket firms who attempted to take their strong domestic concept to USA, and Benetton, who expanded internationally the store network of their clearly targeted knitwear concept.

A second facilitating factor of the time was the continuing integration of markets in Europe that led to the Single European Market agenda of 1992 (Pellegrini 1991). Thus through the second half of the 1980s, awareness of the conditions in non-domestic markets, particularly with Western Europe, was being raised by national governmental and EU propaganda (Treadgold 1988; European Commission 1991; Tordjman and Dionisio 1991).

A third factor to encourage increased international operation was also starting to become apparent, although initially it is doubtful if retailers realized its significance for multi-market operation. This was the start of a convergence of information and communication technologies. In the late 1980s these technologies were largely separate, but experimental applications were being tested that brought the two technologies together in domestic operations. The significance of these experiments in convergence was such that they would allow, in the 1990s, the control and coordination of extended networks of procurement, logistics and retail establishments. National boundaries were therefore no longer a barrier to effective managerial control of a network firm.

It was against this background that the academic work focused on describing which firms were exploring the different international markets. With a few notable exceptions (Laulajainen 1987), the body of research was quite fragmented. Some of the studies concentrated on describing then current activities, whilst others placed the contemporary pattern into a historical context. These studies included descriptions of foreign retailers operating in a country and from a specific country (Seigle and Handy 1981; Mitton 1987; Hamill and Crosbie 1990; Exstein and Weitzman 1991; Davies 1994; Sternquist 1997; Muniz-Martinez 1998), accounts of moves into 'less developed countries' (Connors *et al.* 1985; Kaufmann and Leibenstein 1988; Malayang 1988; Trappey and Kuan 1996) as well as descriptions of the transatlantic flows of expertise (Kacker 1985, 1988) that resulted in stores in foreign ownership, either side of the Atlantic. They included studies of specific formats (Dawson 1984; Ho and Sin 1987), studies of the activity of individual firms (Bunce 1989; Treadgold 1991; Laulajainen 1991a, b, 1992), studies of individual entrepreneurs (Lord *et al.* 1988) and descriptions of activity in particular sectors (Burt 1991). In general, these papers sought to describe which firms were moving to which countries with what types of operation. As such, they provided a number of building blocks for the development of subsequent studies. The range and differences in approach of the studies, resulted in a rich variety, but one in which it was difficult to make comparisons and develop generalities.

In order to provide a framework, academics turned to established ideas drawn from research literature in International Business. A substantial body of studies exist on the nature and degree of adaption of management when they enter foreign markets and the aspects of management that may be transferred in a standardized way. Salmon and Tordjman (1989) drew on key ideas from this body of literature, notably those coming from Harvard Business School at the time (Levitt 1983; Quelch and Hoff 1986) to elaborate the spectrum between standardization and localization in retailing and relate it to different patterns of retail activity. They identified two main patterns of 'global retailers' and 'international retailers'. Global retailers were considered as being at the standardization end of the spectrum: 'The global retailers, because they re-use an already proven formula, with a centralised organisation of their operations, are capable of very rapid expansion' (p. 7). Along the spectrum are the multinational retailers who 'consider their subsidiaries to be a portfolio of geographically dispersed businesses for each of which they adapt their standard formula to fit the local conditions' (p. 8). This contrast has been widely used in subsequent studies. The key concepts that Salmon and Tordjman highlighted were that it is management that is centralized in global retailers and marketing that is adapted in multinational retailers, and that the internationalization strategy will polarize between the two extremes. They argued that multinational activity will grow when bulk, weight and perishability inhibit international procurement, but that in the future the homogenization of consumer demand will means that the global strategy will be the more successful. The paper's importance rests on its foundation and widely quoted nature.

The paper provided a foundation for several studies, most notable being those of Treadgold and Davies (1988) and Treadgold (1990). These studies extended the basic idea of a dichotomy of strategies as used by Salmon and Tordjman to place them in a cost–control framework from high cost–high control to low cost–low control and then to relate these to the geographical scope of firms. Through an application of this approach to the empirical studies that had been undertaken, Treadgold categorized the approaches to internationalization to provide for the late 1980s a typology of international retailer activity.

These studies were bounded by their time. They did not foresee the change taking place in management as a result of the convergence of information and communication technologies (ICT). The imperative of standardization associated with central control implicit in the global model was able to be relaxed, with control still being possible but with a more adapted model. Thus the convergence of ICT allowed network firms to evolve with local adaptions controlled centrally and different degrees of adaption being possible in different parts of the store, for example with more standardization for back-of-store processes and more adaptability for front-of-store (customer-interacting) processes.

Searching for Explanations through Mechanisms and Typologies

The range and variety that characterized international activity in the 1980s and which was reflected in academic descriptions into the early 1990s, generated a wish from managers for a more strategic approach and a search by academics for explanations of the descriptions of activities of firms.

Alexander developed, in a series of papers (1990, 1995; Akehurst and Alexander 1995) and a book (1997), studies of the motives of retailers in pursuing an international approach. He classified the motives into those emanating in the domestic market that were called push factors and those in the target foreign market that were called pull factors. Survey evidence, supported by other workers (Williams 1992a, b; Kawabata 1999; Quinn 1999) showed that there was a complex mix of push-and-pull factors at work with varying strength apparent in the various component factors. The surveys revealed that international activity was gaining in importance as a growth strategy but the motives behind the markets entered, the mechanisms used and the environmental constraints in host markets (Davies 1993; Letosk *et al.* 1997) were still far from being fully understood (Wrigley 1989).

Dawson (1994), in the paper included in this chapter, makes this point strongly by pointing to a substantial range of strategic and tactical reasons that were either reported by individual firms as their reasons for moves or that could be interpreted from their actions. The paper also attempted, in trying to bring together a wide range of studies, to open discussion on the extent to which retailer internationalization has different characteristics from the internationalization of manufacturing, a theme taken up again in later work (Dawson and Mukoyama, 2006a). The paper also sought to look at mechanisms for internationalization as linked to the form of retailing, in an attempt to understanding the generic strategies of firms moving internationally. Burt (1993, 1995) followed this theme with empirical studies that recorded the timing of international activity, the countries selected and the mechanisms used for initial entry. Pellegrini (1994) also explored the entry mechanisms. The conclusions to these studies was that at a macro-scale there was some structure in the patterns of the directions and methods used by international retailers, but that when disaggregated by sector or by format, the patterns became much more difficult to interpret. The specificities of the firm have to be considered in order to understand the process at work. The call, in many of these papers, was that more detailed study within a consistent framework was needed.

The search for some common terminology and the disentangling of sectoral and firm specific factors was the central contribution of Helfferich *et al.* (1997). Their view was that the nature of international retailing could be encapsulated in five parameters:

- geographic scope
- cultural spread
- cultural orientation
- marketing
- management

They also argue that these factors are mediated by cultural factors of the foreign markets. Even then, however, they conclude by stating, 'in order to understand events in the fluid world of international retailing fully, there is a great need for case studies featuring famous as well as less well-known retailers across a broad international spectrum' (p. 304).

Studies of individual firms were acknowledged as being important. They were often detailed but addressed very different aspects of the international experience. The volumes *International Retailing: Trends and Strategies*, edited by McGoldrick and Davies (1995), and *European Cases in Retailing*, edited by Dupuis and Dawson (1999), contained several such studies, each exploring different aspects of the process in different firms: Toys 'R' Us, Marks & Spencer, Promodès, IKEA, Kookai, Body Shop, and Carrefour. These and other cases studies (e.g. Treadgold 1991; Takahashi 1994; Sparks 1995; Welsh *et al.*) addressed different issues in different ways and whilst providing valuable insights individually, it proved difficult to use established general concepts (Simpson and Thorpe 1995; Vida and Fairhurst 1998; Alexander and Myers 2000) or develop new ones, to explain the process at the firm level.

A significant factor to understanding the academic study of international retailing is the changes that take place in the market environments of retailers. Comment has already been made on the increasing economic, political and social integration within Western Europe that encouraged retailers, particularly European-based firms but also some North American retailers, to look for markets across Europe. By the mid-1990s major opportunities for new markets were appearing in central Europe and to a lesser extent in East Asia. For retailers in Western Europe where competition was intense in all countries, moves within Western Europe simply meant moving from one crowded market to another. The opening of Central European markets, initially from 1989 in an unstable way, but from around 1993 with more stable economies, provided the basis for a wave of international retail activity through the second half of the 1990s, such that within a little over ten years the major retailers across most of central Europe were from Western Europe. The academic study of this flood of investment into central Europe monitored and classified the moves of the retailers from Germany, France and UK and considered how these retailers affected economic structures and, in effect, created a consumption culture (Drtina 1995; Mueller and Broderick 1995; Savitt 1996; Pütz 1997a, b, 1998; Dawson and Henley 1999a, b; Drtina and Krásny 1999; Michalak 1999, 2001; Haendle 2002). Because the environment was different, new insights were gained on strategies of retailers in emergent markets and the nature of sectoral responses to rapid developments in competition. Much of the research was empirical and tended to draw on the concepts established in earlier studies.

What Dawson's paper and many others missed in the mid-1990s, was the realization that the need was not for studies of individual firms, but to consider the processes in much more detail at the level of the firm and on a comparative basis across firms. The study of form and structure, even at the firm level, needed to be supplemented by studies of process. This was necessary not only to differentiate the study of international retailing from manufacturing, but to understand the adaption process and the flows of knowledge in the firm. The studies of individual firms, even when considering a temporal perspective neither addressed the detail of the process nor really explored the nature of the knowledge that underpinned the international operations, allowing Burt (1995) to argue that the only generalization about internationalization possible at the firm level is the uniqueness of activity at this level. These process-related studies were to come later.

Understanding Specific Processes and Operations in Foreign Markets

The internationalization of retailing is a process that affects all the activities of the retail firm, irrespective of whether these activities are primarily strategic or operational. The ability to adapt these processes to conditions in the environment is central to the success, or otherwise, of the retailer in the foreign environment. As retailers have gained more experience in their international operations, so they have become more successful in adapting across a larger number of diverse countries and into countries with a culture substantially different from that of their home market. The concept of psychic distance was developed (Dupuis and Prime 1996; Evans *et al.* 2000; Evans and Mavondo 2002) as a way of exploring the degree of difference between operating environments and so the extent of adaption that is likely to be necessary. In addition to consideration of the extent of adaption, the combination of areas of retailing in which adaptation takes places is also important. A number of studies deconstructed adaption in order to consider the individual aspects of retail activity in which adaption takes place. Studies explored adaption of format (Goldman 2001), product range (Mukoyama 2000) and brand (Burt and Carralero-Encinas 2000; Moore *et al.* 2000).

The third paper (Goldman 2001) in this chapter explores one deconstructed aspect of adaption, namely the format. The paper considers adaption in the supermarket format in an environment, China, which, for some of the retailers in his survey, is very different from the home environment of the retailers concerned. One of the important aspects of the paper is the inclusion of both European and Asian retailers in his study of how they have adapted their operations to the Chinese market. Goldman distinguishes between the adaptions that were made on an *ad hoc* reactionary basis and those that were planned with adaption being a continuing process. He continues to attempt to categorize different approaches by identifying six format transfer strategies (Table 3, p. 413). The paper is important in the way that it focuses on the format as the creation of the retailer and the need to adjust this in response to factors both external and internal to the firm. Goldman's conclusion was that 'Format transfers turned out to be much more complex and varied than previously described' (p. 416) and that 'We found the transfer process to be long, detailed and systematic in about half the cases and short, superficial and non-systematic in the other group' (p. 418). The study has provided an important sign-post for future studies of format adaption.

A significant area where attempts have been made to deconstruct the adaption of retailers is in the nature of the mode of entry to the foreign market. The major modes of acquisition, internal expansion, franchising, and joint ventures have been extensively described (Alexander 1997). More detailed work has been undertaken to explore the adaptions undertaken in each of these modes together with the mechanisms of trading alliances (Bayley *et al.* 1995). Sparks (2000) explored a specific acquisition as an example of a class of entry modes. Doherty (2000) shows the important role of the individual executive in shaping the nature of the international retailer offering and as such its adaption to local markets (see also Dawson 2001). This approach has also sought to place the franchise approach within a theoretical framework that emphasizes the role of the individual both in an agency framework (Quinn 1998; Doherty 1999; Doherty and Quinn 1999), in a power framework (Quinn and Doherty 2000) and also in a more general relationship framework (Doherty and Alexander 2004).

Alongside the work on franchising there have been limited studies of other entry modes. Wong (1998) explored the nature of joint ventures involving Japanese and Hong Kong-based firms and Palmer and Owens (2006), more recently, undertook a study that considered the broader nature of joint ventures in international retailing.

Research on entry and adaption by Wrigley (1997a, b, 2002a, b) explored a different processual issue, namely the role of capital and the financial sector in influencing the nature of the internationalization and associated adaption process (see also Palmer and Quinn 2003). Wrigley's detailed study of the experience of Sainsbury in the USA (Wrigley 2000) considered the adaption of strategy that takes place following entry. As with the work of Palmer on joint ventures, the issues associated with the level of the knowledge base of the participant managers begin to appear as a factor to be considered in the nature of adaption to the foreign market, not least in its regulatory conditions (Wrigley 1997c).

That adaption is widespread after market entry was well established in a range of studies undertaken in the late 1990s and early 2000s. This adaption issue was widely perceived and led Gielens and DeKimpe (2001) to question whether international entry decisions of retail chains matter in the long run if adaption is so great?

The difficulty inherent in many of the studies of adaption is disentangling the adaption that has taken place due to the internationalization process and the changes that take place in a retail operation as it evolves competitively irrespective of the domestic or international dimensions. Thus, in purely domestic firms there is adaption over time, to changes in management, consumers and environment, across many aspects of the retail firm's activity. Sales outlets change, organizational structures change, sourcing systems change, marketing and merchandising policies change, and so on in the domestic firm. For the international firm, a different set of changes may be apparent but the nature of the relationship between change in domestic and international operations is often not clear, with all the change in the international operation being laid at the door of the internationalization process. This does not invalidate the considerable amount of research on adaption but indicates that not all the adaption patterns identified in an operation in a non-domestic market are due to internationalization.

Broadening the Intellectual Bases with Analyses in Wider Contexts

The surge in international activity by retailers in the twenty-first century not only generated academic research exploring this growth of activity (Larke 2005; Dawson and Mukoyama 2006b) and research that built on earlier themes (Vida 2000; Dawson 2003; Dries et al. 2004; Evans and Bridson 2005; Jackson and Sparks 2005; Roberts 2005; Burt and Mavrommatis 2006; Picot-Coupey 2006), but also resulted in a wider base of academic ideas being applied to the study of the process. This wider base is apparent in three areas particularly:

- a growing interest in the issues surrounding the failure and retrenchment of international activity;
- the application of concepts and theories on the transfer of knowledge within and between retail firms in the internationalization process;
- the relationship of retailer internationalization to the wider discourse on globalization.

The final paper selected for this chapter considers issues of retrenchment in international retailing. Wrigley and Currah (2003) consider the experience of Royal Ahold in Latin America. The paper focuses on the organizational stresses caused by international activity and the factors that militate for 'success' or 'failure'. The paper explores the nature of the relationship between the firm and the economy and society in which it is embedded. The nature of this socio-economic-political society has influences on the success, or otherwise, of the firm. From the extended case study they conclude that five conditions exist that are important to the study of retail internationalization, and which provide a guide to future research:

- Retail internationalization includes processes of growth and retrenchment. These processes are different and not simply mirror images of each other.
- There is need for more clarity of terms and a consistent framework for case study analysis. Concept development is difficult with the current plethora of approaches.
- The interaction between host and home country and the changes within home and host country are all relevant to an understanding on the retail internationalization process.
- International retailers are involved in competitive relationships with many different groups (Da Rocha and Dib 2002; Fernie and Arnold 2002). These include competitive relationships with other retailers for many different resource inputs, with suppliers of goods for control of supply chain processes and with the suppliers of finance.
- Retail investment in a market involves the creation of consumer values and involvement in the development of the retail sector generally. This theme is akin to the McDonaldization effect of Ritzer (1993).

Wrigley and Currah (2003) rightly stress the importance of the environment on the performance of the firm, but it is important not to underestimate the differences in perception of this environment that can be assumed by different firms.

The growing number of studies of international divestment and failure, in various guises (Alexander and Quinn 2002; Burt *et al.* 2002; Burt *et al.* 2003, 2004; Alexander *et al.* 2005; Jackson *et al.* 2005; Bianchi and Ostale 2006), explore the influential factors associated with the external environment of the firm and those within the firm and under the control of its managers. These considerations of various forms of divestment are in line with the five points of Wrigley and Currah which broaden the debate on the nature of the internationalization process in retailing.

The knowledge and perception of managers is central to the success or otherwise of international activity. Goldman makes passing reference to 'experience and learning advantages generated through operation in diverse environments' (2001, p. 225) but the importance of knowledge and its transfer into and throughout the firm has become a significant research theme in the early 2000s. Palmer (2006) has explored this in respect of his work on joint ventures. Jonsson and Elg (2006) focus on internal transfers of knowledge inside the firm and Wang (2005) studied the role of the knowledge broker in these internal transfers. Palmer (2005) explored the process in Tesco's international moves and, with Quinn, developed a framework (Palmer and Quinn 2005) in which research on knowledge acquisition and transfer could be studied. Hurt and Hurt (2005) explored how knowledge transfer was constrained by a lack of understanding between French managers as instituting knowledge and Polish employees using knowledge. This theme of knowledge transfer is in an early stage of development. What makes it particularly interesting and differentiates it from work in a non-retail context is the network structure, often very substantial in size, of retail operations (Currah and Wrigley 2004).

The third area where the discourse on retail internationalization has widened is placing the internationalization of retailing within the broader context of the globalization of economies. This broader interest results not only from the growth of sourcing of retail products from Africa and East Asia (Dolan and Humphrey 2000, 2004) but also from the increased activity of European, North American and Japanese retailers in emergent markets, particularly in East Asia. The East Asian countries, and particularly China and South Korea have become consumer markets in which Japanese, European and American retail management styles are in direct competition with each other for the first time. The nature of globalization as a competition between different managerial cultures and philosophies has become well illustrated by the actions of retailers in the emergent markets (Gamble 2003, 2006). A potential framework for considering the impacts of internationalization has been provided by Dawson (2003) and this has been extended and amplified by Coe (2004) and Coe and Hess (2005). Coe and Hess (2005), building on the work of Henderson *et al.* (2002) focus particularly on supply chain dynamics and the relationships with suppliers in East Asia. They suggest that international retailers have been important agents in:

- creating systems of centralized procurement and sourcing of products for resale;
- upgrading logistics infrastructure;

- changing contractual and behavioural relationships in supply chains;
- changing the physical and organizational structure of the supply chain;
- generating and implementing standards in supply chain systems.

This broadening of the intellectual bases of internationalization is apparent in such studies that explore the interdisciplinary dimensions of the processes involved (Dicken *et al.* 2001).

Summary

Over more than twenty years the research on retailer internationalization has progressed through a sequence from description of firms' activities through attempts to categorize these activities and into an analytical stage of focusing on the processes in internationalization. Most recently the research has broadened its base to encompass more concepts in attempts to gain understanding of the impacts and effect of the process. The four papers in this chapter typify the research at each of these stages of research evolution. Over this period also, the amount of international activity by retailers has increased steadily. This increase in activity seems likely to continue for the foreseeable future. The research issues are perhaps less clear but it seems likely that the research base will continue to widen as the complexity of the internationalization becomes apparent, more firms become involved and the spatial spread of activity widens. As international retailing becomes more mature so it might be expected that research will develop that considers the nature of competition involving international retailers and explores whether and how this is different from competition when firms operate only nationally.

References

Akehurst G and Alexander N (1995) The internationalisation process in retailing. *Service Industries Journal*, 15(4), 1–15.

Alexander N (1990) Retailers and international markets: motives for expansion. *International Marketing Review*, 7(4), 75–85.

Alexander N (1995) UK retail expansion in North America and Europe: a strategic dilemma. *Journal of Retailing and Consumer Services*, 2(2), 75–82.

Alexander N (1997) *International Retailing*. Oxford: Blackwell.

Alexander N and Myers H (2000) The retail internationalisation process. *International Marketing Review*, 17(4/5), 334–353.

Alexander N and Quinn B (2002) International retail divestment. *International Journal of Retail and Distribution Management*, 30, 112–125.

Alexander N, Quinn B and Cairns P (2005) International retail divestment activity. *International Journal of Retail and Distribution Management,* 33(1), 5–22.

Bayley J, Clarke-Hill CM and Robinson TM (1995) Towards a taxonomy of international retail alliances. *Service Industries Journal*, 15(4), 25–41.

Bianchi CC and Ostale E (2006) Lessons learned from unsuccessful internationalisation attempts: examples of multi-national retailers in Chile. *Journal of Business Research*, 59, 149–157.

Bunce ML (1989) The international approach of Laura Ashley. In *Adding Value to Retail Offerings*, ESOMAR Proceedings, 101–106.

Burt L (1989) Trends and management issues in European retailing. *International Journal of Retailing*, 4(4), 3–97.

Burt SL (1991) Trends in the internationalisation of grocery retailing: the European experience. *International Review of Retail, Distribution and Consumer Research*, 1(4), 487–515.

Burt SL (1993) Temporal trends in the internationalisation of British retailing. *International Review of Retail, Distribution and Consumer Research*, 3(4), 391–410.

Burt SL (1995) Retail internationalisation: evolution of theory and practice. In PJ McGoldrick and G Davies (eds) *International Retailing: Trends and Strategies*. London: Pitman, 51–73.

Burt SL and Carralero-Encinas J (2000) The role of store image in retail internationalisation. *International Marketing Review*, 17(4/5), 433–453.

Burt SL and Mavrommatis A (2006) The international transfer of store brand image. *International Review of Retail Distribution and Consumer Research*, 16(4), 395–413.

Burt SL, Dawson JA and Sparks L (2003) Failure in international markets: research propositions. *International Review of Retail Distribution and Consumer Research*, 13(4), 355–373.

Burt SL, Dawson JA and Sparks L (2004) The international divestment activities of European grocery retailers. *European Management Journal*, 22(5), 483–492.

Burt SL, Mellahi K, Jackson TP and Sparks L (2002) Retail internationalization and retail failure: issues for the case of Marks and Spencer. *International Review of Retail, Distribution and Consumer Research*, 12, 191–219.

Coe NM (2004) The internationalisation/globalisation of retailing: towards an economic-geographical research agenda. *Environment and Planning*, A36, 1571–1594.

Coe NM and Hess M (2005) The internationalization of retailing: implications for supply network restructuring in East Asia and Eastern Europe. *Journal of Economic Geography*, 5, 449–473.

Commission of European Communities (1981) Measures taken in the field of commerce by member states of the European Communities. *Commission of European Communities Commerce and Distribution Series 10*.

Connors S, Samli AC and Kaynak E (1985) Transfer of food retail technology into less developed countries. In AC Samli (ed.) *Technology Transfer*. Westport, CT: Quorum, 27–44.

Crossick G and Jaumain S (1999) *Cathedrals of Consumption: The European Department Store, 1850–1939*. London: Ashgate.

Currah A and Wrigley N (2004) Networks of organizational learning and adaptation in retail TNCs. *Global Networks*, 4(1), 1–23.

Da Rocha A and Dib LA (2002) The entry of Wal-Mart in Brazil and the competitive responses of multinational and domestic firms. *International Journal of Retail and Distribution Management,* 30, 61–73.

Davies BK (1993) Trade barriers in East and South East Asia: the implications for retailers. *International Review of Retail, Distribution and Consumer Research,* 3(4), 345–366.

Davies BK (1994) Foreign investment in the retail sector of the People's Republic of China. *Columbia Journal of World Business,* 29(3), 56–69.

Dawson JA (1984) Structural-spatial relationships in the spread of hypermarket retailing. In E Kaynak and R Savitt (eds) *Comparative Marketing Systems.* New York: Praeger, 156–182.

Dawson JA (1994) The internationalization of retailing operations. *Journal of Marketing Management,* 10, 267–282.

Dawson JA (2001) Strategy and opportunism in European retail internationalization. *British Journal of Management,* 12, 253–266.

Dawson JA (2003) Towards a model of the impacts on retail internationalisation. In JA Dawson, M Mukoyama, S Chul Choi and R Larke (eds) *The Internationalisation of Retailing in Asia.* London: Routledge-Curzon, 189–209.

Dawson JA and Henley JS (1999a) Internationalisation of hypermarket retailing in Poland: West European investment and its implications. *Journal of East-West Business,* 5(4), 37–52.

Dawson JA and Henley JS (1999b) Internationalisation of retailing in Poland: foreign hypermarket development and its implications. In K Jones (ed.) The *Internationalisation of Retailing in Europe.* Toronto: Centre for Study of Commercial Activity, 22–27.

Dawson JA and Mukoyama M (2006a) Retail internationalisation as a process. In JA Dawson, R Larke and M Mukoyama (eds) *Strategic Issues in International Retailing.* London: Routledge, 31–50.

Dawson JA and Mukoyama M (2006b) The increase in international activity by retailers. In JA Dawson, R Larke and M Mukoyama (eds) *Strategic Issues in International Retailing.* London: Routledge, 1–30.

Dicken P, Kelly PF, Olds K and Yeung HW-C (2001) Chain and networks, territories and scales: towards a relational framework for analysing the global economy. *Global Networks,* 1(2), 89–112.

Distributive Trades EDC (1973) *The Distributive Trades in the Common Market.* London: HMSO.

Doherty AM (1999) Explaining international retailers' market entry mode strategy: internalization theory, agency theory and the importance of information asymmetry. *International Review of Retail, Distribution and Consumer Research,* 9(4), 379–402.

Doherty AM (2000) Factors influencing international retailers' entry mode strategy: qualitative evidence from the UK fashion sector. *Journal of Marketing Management,* 16, 223–245.

Doherty AM and Alexander N (2004) Relationship development in international retail franchising: case study evidence from the UK fashion sector. *European Journal of Marketing,* 38, 1215–1235.

Doherty AM and Quinn B (1999) International retail franchising: an agency theory perspective. *International Journal of Retail and Distribution Management,* 27(6), 224–236.

Dolan C and Humphrey J (2000) Governance and trade in fresh vegetables: the impact of UK supermarkets on the African horticulture industry. *Journal of Development Studies,* 37, 147–176.

Dolan C and Humphrey J (2004) Changing governance patterns in the trade in fresh vegetables between Africa and the United Kingdom. *Environment and Planning,* A36: 491–509.

Dries L, Reardon T and Swinnen JFM (2004) The rapid rise of supermarkets in central and eastern Europe: implications for the agrifood sector and rural development. *Development Policy Review,* 22(5), 525–556.

Drtina T (1995) The internationalisation of retailing in the Czech and Slovak republics. *Service Industries Journal,* 15(4), 191–203.

Dritina T and Krásny T (1999) Czech retailers face a heavy attack of international chains. In M Dupuis and JA Dawson (eds) *European Cases in Retailing.* Oxford: Blackwell, 110–122.

Dupuis M and Dawson JA (eds) (1999) *European Cases in Retailing.* Oxford: Blackwell.

Dupuis M and Prime N (1996) Business distance and global retailing: a model of analysis of key success/failure factors. *International Journal of Retail and Distribution Management,* 24(1), 30–38.

European Commission (1991) Towards a single market in distribution. *Communication of European Commission,* 41 (COM91–41).

Evans J and Bridson K (2005) Explaining retail offer adaptation through psychic distance. *International Journal of Retail and Distribution Management,* 33(1), 69–78.

Evans J and Mavondo FT (2002) Psychic distance and organisational: an empirical examination of international retailing operations. *Journal of International Business Studies,* 33(3), 515–532.

Evans J, Treadgold A and Mavondo FT (2000) Psychic distance and the performance of international retailers: a suggested theoretical framework. *International Marketing Review,* 17(4/5), 373–391.

Exstein M and Weitzman F (1991) Foreign investment in US retailing: an optimistic overview. *Retail Control,* (January), 9–14.

Fernie J and Arnold SJ (2002) Wal-Mart in Europe: prospects for Germany, the UK and France. *International Journal of Retail and Distribution Management,* 30, 92–102.

Fletcher SR and Godley AC (2000a) Foreign direct investment in British retailing 1850–1962. *Business History,* 42(2), 43–62.

Fletcher SR and Godley AC (2000b) Foreign entry into British retailing 1850–1994. *International Marketing Review,* 17(4/5), 392–400.

Gamble J (2003) Transferring business practices from United Kingdom to China: the limits and potential for convergence. *International Journal of Human Resource Management,* 14(3), 369–387.

Gamble J (2006) Multinational retailers in China: proliferating 'McJobs' or developing skills? *Journal of Management Studies*, 43(7), 1463–1490.

Gielens K and DeKimpe MG (2001) Do international entry decisions of retail chains matter in the long run? *International Journal of Research in Marketing*, 18, 235–259.

Godley A and Fletcher SR (2001) International retailing in Britain 1850–1994. *Services Industries Journal*, 21(2), 31–46.

Goldman A (1974) Outreach of consumers and the modernization of urban food retailing in developing countries. *Journal of Marketing*, 39, 8–16.

Goldman A (1981) Transfer of retailing technology into lesser developed countries: the supermarket case. *Journal of Retailing*, 57(2), 5–29.

Goldman A (2001) The transfer of retail formats into developing economies: the example of China. *Journal of Retailing*, 77(2), 221–242.

Haendle M (2002) The process of hypermarket retail internationalisation from Germany to Poland. PhD thesis, Bradford University Management Centre.

Hamill J and Crosbie J (1990) British retail acquisitions in the US. *International Journal of Retail and Distribution Management*, 18(5), 15–20.

Helfferich E, Hinfelaar M and Kasper H (1997) Towards a clear terminology on international retailing. *International Review of Retail, Distribution and Consumer Research*, 7(3), 288–307.

Henderson J, Dicken P, Hess M, Coe NM and Yeung HW-C (2002) Global production networks and the analysis of economic development. *Review of International Political Economy*, 9: 436–464.

Ho S and Sin Y (1987) International transfer of retail technology: the successful case of convenience stores in Hong Kong. *International Journal of Retailing*, 2(3), 36–48.

Hollander S (1970) *Multinational Retailing*. East Lansing, MI: Michigan State University.

Hurt M and Hurt S (2005) Transfer of managerial practices by French food retailers to operations in Poland. *Academy of Management Executive*, 19(2), 36–49.

Jackson G (1973) Planning the move to the continent: questions that must be asked. *Retail and Distribution Management*, 1(6), 14–16.

Jackson P and Sparks L (2005) Retailer internationalisation: Marks and Spencer in Hong Kong. *International Journal of Retail and Distribution Management*, 33(10), 766–783.

Jackson P, Mellahi K and Sparks L (2005) Shutting up shop: understanding the international exit process in retailing. *Services Industries Journal*, 25(3), 355–371.

Jefferys J (1973) Multinational retailing: are the food chains different? *CIES Quarterly Review*, 8(3).

Jonsson A and Elg U (2006) Knowledge and knowledge sharing in retail internationalization: Ikea's entry into Russia. *International Review of Retail, Distribution and Consumer Research*, 16(2), 239–256.

Kacker MP (1985) *Transatlantic Trends in Retailing: Takeovers and the Flow of Know-how*. Westport CT: Quorum Books.

Kacker MP (1988) International flow of retailing know-how: bridging the technology gap in distribution. *Journal of Retailing*, 64(1), 41–67.

Kaufmann PJ and Leibenstein H (1988) International business format franchising and retail entrepreneurship: a possible source of know-how for developing countries. *Journal of Development Planning*, 18, 165–179.

Kawabata M (1999) Why have Japanese retailers crossed borders? Reconsideration of motive studies. *Journals of Business Studies Ryukoku University*, 39(2).

Kaynak E (1980) Transfer of supermarketing technology from developed to less developed countries: the case of Migros-Turk. *Finnish Journal of Business Economics*, 29(1).

Kaynak E (1985) Global spread of supermarkets: some experiences form Turkey. In E Kaynak (ed.) *Global Perspectives in Marketing*. New York: Praeger.

Knee D (1966) Trends towards international operations among large-scale retailing enterprises. *Rivista Italiana di Amministrazione*, 2, 107–111.

Larke R (2005) The expansion of Japanese retailers overseas. *Journal of Global Marketing*, 18(1/2), 99–120.

Laulajainen R (1987) *Spatial Strategies in Retailing*. Dordrecht: D Reidel.

Laulajainen R (1991a) International expansion of an apparel retailer: Hennes and Mauritz of Sweden. *Zeitschrift fur Wirtschaftsgeographie*, 35(1), 1–15.

Laulajainen R (1991b) Two retailers go global: the geographical dimension. *International Review of Retail, Distribution and Consumer Research*, 1(5), 607–626.

Laulajainen R (1992) Louis Vuitton Malletier: a truly global retailer. *Annals of the Japan Association of Economic Geography*, 38(2), 55–77.

Letosk R, Murphy D and Kenny R (1997) Entry opportunities and environmental constraints for foreign retailers in China's secondary cities. *Multinational Business Review*, Fall, 28–40.

Levitt T (1983) The globalization of markets. *Harvard Business Review*, 61(3) 92–102.

Lord JD, Moran W, Parker AJ and Sparks L (1988) Retailing on three continents: the discount food store operations of Albert Gubay. *International Journal of Retailing*, 3(3), 1–54.

McGoldrick PJ and Davies G (eds) (1995) *International Retailing: Trends and Strategies*. London: Pitman.

Martenson R (1981) *Innovations in Multinational Retailing: IKEA on the Swedish, Swiss, German and Austrian Furniture Markets*. Göteborg: University of Göteborg.

Malayang RV (1988) The distribution industry in Asian NIES and ASEAN countries and the effects of the entry of Japanese retailers. *Management Japan*, 21(2), 15–20.

Michalak WZ (1999) Foreign direct investment and Polish retail. In K Jones (ed.) *The Internationalisation of Retailing in Europe*. Toronto: Centre for Study of Commercial Activity, 14–21.

Michalak WZ (2001) Retail in Poland: an assessment of changing market and foreign investment conditions. *Canadian Journal of Regional Science*, 24(3), 485–504.

Mitton A (1987) Foreign retail companies operating in the UK: strategy and performance. *Retail and Distribution Management*, 15(1), 29–31.

Moore CM, Fernie J and Burt S (2000) Brands without boundaries: the internationalisation of the designer retailer's brand. *European Journal of Marketing*, 34(8),
919–937.

Mukoyama M (2000) The standardization–adaptation problem of product assortment in the internationalization of retailers. In MR Czinkota and M Kotabe
(eds) *Japanese Distribution Strategy*. London: Business Press.

Mueller RD and Broderick AJ (1995) East European retailing: a consumer perspective. *International Journal of Retail and Distribution Management*, 23(1),
32–40.

Muniz-Martinez N (1998) The internationalisation of European retailing in America:
the US experience. *International Journal of Retail and Distribution Management*, 26(1), 29–37.

Palmer M (2005) Retail multinational learning: a case study of Tesco. *International
Journal of Retail and Distribution Management*, 33(1), 23–48.

Palmer M (2006) International retail joint venture learning. *Service Industries Journal*, 26(2), 165–187.

Palmer M and Owens M (2006) New directions for international retail joint venture
research. *International Review of Retail, Distribution and Consumer Research*,
16(2), 159–179.

Palmer M and Quinn B (2003) The strategic role of investment banks in the retailer
internationalisation process: is this venture marketing? *European Journal of
Marketing*, 37(10), 1391–1408.

Palmer M and Quinn B (2005) An exploratory framework for analysing international
retail learning. *International Review of Retail Distribution and Consumer
Research*, 15(1), 27–52.

Pellegrini L (1991) The internationalisation of retailing and 1992 Europe. *Journal of
Marketing Channels*, 1(2), 3–27.

Pellegrini L (1994) Alternatives for growth and internationalization in retailing.
International Review of Retail, Distribution and Consumer Research, 4(2),
121–148.

Picot-Coupey K (2006) Determinants of international retail operation mode choice:
towards a conceptual framework based on evidence from French specialised
retail chains. *International Review of Retail Distribution and Consumer
Research*, 16(2), 215–237.

Pütz R (1997a) New business formation, privatisation and internationalisation:
aspects of the transformation of Polish retail trade. *Die Erde*, 128, 235–249.

Pütz R (1997b) Einzelhandel in Polen. Interne Restrukturierung und Internationalis-
ierung am Beispiel Wroclaw. *Geographische Rundschau*, 49(9), 516–522.

Pütz R (1998) *Einkelhandel im Transformationsprozess* am Beispiel Polen. Passau:
L.I.S.

Quelch JA and Hoff EJ (1986) Customizing global marketing. *Harvard Business
Review*, 64(3), 59–68.

Quinn B (1998) Towards a framework for the study of franchising as an operating mode for international retail companies. *International Review of Retail, Distribution and Consumer Research*, 8(4), 445–467.

Quinn B (1999) The temporal context of UK retailers' motives for international expansion. *Service Industries Journal*, 19(2), 101–116.

Quinn B and Doherty AM (2000) Power and control in international retail franchising. *International Marketing Review*, 17(4/5), 354–372.

Ritzer G (1993) *The McDonaldization of Society*, Thousand Oaks, CA: Pine Forge Press.

Roberts GH (2005) Auchan's entry into Russia: prospects and research implications. *International Journal of Retail and Distribution Management*, 33(1), 49–68.

Salmon W and Tordjman A (1989) The internationalisation of retailing. *International Journal of Retailing*, 4(2), 3–16.

Savitt R (1996) Transformation and marketing developments in Skala of Hungary. In AA Ullmann and A Lewis (eds) *Privatisation and Entrepreneurship: the Managerial Challenge in Central and Eastern Europe*. London: Haworth Press, 141–152.

Seigle N and Handy C (1981) Foreign ownership of food retailing. *National Food Review*, Winter, 14–16.

Shaw G and Alexander A (2006) Interlocking directorates and knowledge transfer of supermarket techniques from North America to Britain. *International Review of Retail, Distribution and Consumer Research*, 16(3), 375–394.

Simpson EM and Thorpe DI (1995) A conceptual model of strategic considerations for international retail expansion. *Service Industries Journal*, 15(4), 16–24.

Sparks L (1995) Reciprocal retail internationalisation: the Southland Corporation, Ito Yokado and 7-Eleven convenience stores. *Service Industries Journal*, 15(4), 57–96.

Sparks L (2000) Seven-Eleven Japan and the Southland Corporation: a marriage of convenience? *International Marketing Review*, 17(4/5), 401–415.

Sternquist B (1997) International expansion of US retailers. *International Journal of Retail and Distribution Management*, 25(8), 262–268.

Takahashi Y (1994) Toys R Us fuels changes in Japan's toy distribution system. *Journal of Marketing Channels*, 3(3), 91–112.

Tordjman A and Dionisio J (1991) Internationalisation strategies in retail business. *Commission of the European Communities, DGxxiii, Series Studies Commerce and Distribution*, 15.

Trappey C and Kuan L (1996) Retailing in Taiwan: modernisation and the emergence of new formats. *International Journal of Retail and Distribution Management*, 24(8), 31–37.

Treadgold A (1988) Retailing without frontiers. *Retail and Distribution Management*, 16(6), 8–12.

Treadgold A (1990) The developing internationalisation of retailing. *International Journal of Retail and Distribution Management*, 18(2), 4–11.

Treadgold A (1991) Dixons and Laura Ashley: different routes to international growth. *International Journal of Retail and Distribution Management*, 19(4), 13–19.

Treadgold A and Davies R (1988) *The Internationalisation of Retailing.* Harlow: Longman.

Truitt N (1984) Mass merchandising and economic development: Sears Roebuck & Co in Mexico and Peru. In S Shelp *et al.* (eds) *Service Industries and Economic Development.* New York: Praeger.

Vida I (2000) An empirical inquiry into international expansion of US retailers. *International Marketing Review,* 17(4/5), 454–475.

Vida I and Fairhurst A (1998) International expansion of retail firms: a theoretical approach for future investigations. *Journal of Retail and Consumer Services,* 5(3), 143–151.

Waldman C (1978) *Strategies of International Mass Retailers.* New York: Praeger.

Wang F (2005) Cross-border knowledge management: strategic dilemmas in a global firm. PhD thesis, University of Cambridge.

Welsh DHB, Raven P and Al-Mutair N (1998) Starbucks international enters Kuwait. *Journal of Consumer Marketing,* 15(2), 191–197.

Whysall P (1997) Interwar retail internationalisation: Boots under American ownership. *International Review of Retail, Distribution and Consumer Research,* 7, 157–169.

Williams DE (1992a) Motives for retailer internationalisation: their impact, structure and implications. *Journal of Marketing Management,* 8, 269–285.

Williams DE (1992b) Retailer internationalization: an empirical inquiry. *European Journal of Marketing,* 26(8/9), 269–285.

Wong MML (1998) Motives of Hong Kong–Japanese international joint ventures in retailing. *International Journal of Retail and Distribution Management,* 26(1), 4–13.

Wrigley N (1989) The lure of the USA: further reflections on the internationalisation of British grocery retailing capital. *Environment and Planning,* A21, 283–288.

Wrigley N (1997a) British food retail capital in the USA – part 1: Sainsbury and the Shaw's experience. *International Journal of Retail and Distribution Management,* 25(1), 7–21.

Wrigley N (1997b) British food retail capital in the USA – part 2: giant prospects. *International Journal of Retail and Distribution Management,* 25(2), 48–58.

Wrigley N (1997c) Foreign retail capital on the battlefields of Connecticut: competition regulation at the local scale and its implications. *Environment and Planning,* A29, 1142–1152.

Wrigley N (2000) Strategic market behaviour in the internationalization of food retailing: interpreting the third wave of Sainsbury's US diversification. *European Journal of Marketing,* 34(8), 891–918.

Wrigley N (2002a) The globalization of retail capital: themes for economic geography. In GL Clark, M Feldman and MS Gertler (eds) *The Oxford Handbook of Economic Geography.* Oxford: Oxford University Press, 292–313.

Wrigley N (2002b) Transforming the corporate landscape of US food retailing: market power, financial re-engineering and regulation. *Tijdschrift voor Economishe en Sociale Geografie,* 93, 62–82.

Wrigley N and Currah A (2003) The stresses of retail internationalization: lessons from Royal Ahold's experience in Latin America. *International Review of Retail, Distribution and Consumer Research*, 13(3), 221–243.

Wrigley N, Coe N M and Currah A (2005) Globalizing retail: conceptualizing the distribution-based transnational corporation (T N C). *Progress in Human Geography*, 29(4), 437–457.

Editors' Commentary

WALTER SALMON IS THE Stanley Roth, Sr., Emeritus Professor of Retailing, at the Harvard University Graduate School of Business Administration. He joined Harvard Business School in 1956. His key interests are consumer marketing and retailing, including aspects of organization, logistics and information in retailing and how retailers can balance consumer demands for choice with demand for low prices. Walter Salmon has served on the boards of a number of major corporations including Cumberland Farms, Harrah's, Neiman Marcus, Cole National Corporation, PetsMart and Hannaford Brothers. The case method of teaching at Harvard has meant that much of his writing has been focused on the development of cases. His two books *Introduction to Retailing: Text and Cases* and *Strategic Retail Management: Text and Cases* provide significant teaching materials. He has been an inspiration to many students and is often cited as the academic who inspired the founder of Staples.

The article selected here was co-authored with André Tordjman, during the time when Tordjman was a Visiting Scholar at Harvard Business School (HBS) with Walter Salmon. André graduated with a doctorate in Business Administration from La Sorbonne University in Paris. At that time of writing this paper, Tordjman was working at HEC Graduate School of Management in Paris. Subsequently however he moved into industry and became the Marketing Director of the French retailer, Auchan from 1998 to 2005, having previously had various other senior jobs with the company. He is now the Director of New Concepts at Auchan and General Manager of Little Extra, a concept he developed for the group. Tordjman has described his work at Auchan as changing the position from a situation where the suppliers define the Auchan's strategy to one where Auchan defines the strategy with input from them.

Salmon and Tordjman, in this paper, drew on key ideas to elaborate a spectrum between standardization and localization in retailing and relate it to different patterns of retail activity. They identified two main patterns of 'global retailers' and 'international retailers'. Global retailers were considered as being at the standardization end of the spectrum. Along the spectrum are the multinational retailers who adapt their standard formula to fit the local conditions. This contrast has been widely used in subsequent studies. The key concepts that Salmon and Tordjman highlighted were that it is management that is centralized in global retailers and marketing that is adapted in multinational retailers, and that the internationalization strategy will polarize between the two extremes. The paper's importance rests on its foundation and widely quoted nature.

Key Publications

Salmon WJ and Cmar KA (1987) Private labels are back in fashion. *Harvard Business Review,* 65, 3, 99–106.

Tordjman A (1988) The French hypermarket – could it be developed in the States? *Retail and Distribution Management,* 16(4), 14–16.

Salmon WJ (1989) Retailing in the age of execution. *Journal of Retailing,* 65, 368–378.

Buzzell RD, Quelch JA and Salmon WJ (1990) The costly bargain of trade promotion. *Harvard Business Review,* 68(2), 141–149.

Ortmeyer GK, Quelch JA and Salmon WJ (1991) Restoring credibility to retail pricing. *Sloan Management Review,* 33, 55–66.

Tordjman A and Dionisio J (1991) Internationalisation strategies in retail business. *Commission of the European Communities, DGxxiii, Series Studies Commerce and Distribution,* 15.

Salmon WJ (1993) Crisis prevention: how to gear up your board. *Harvard Business Review,* 71(1), 68–75.

Bell DE and Salmon WJ (1996) *Strategic Retail Management.* Cincinnati, OH: Southwestern Publishing.

Bell DE and Salmon WJ (1996) *An Introduction to Retailing.* Cincinnati, OH: Southwestern Publishing.

Bell R (2003) Uniquely Auchan: retailing as invention. Interview with André Tordjman, Marketing Director of Auchan. In C Cuthbertson and J Reynolds (eds) *Retail Strategy: The View from the Bridge.* London: Butterworth Heinemann, 202–208.

Lal R, Bell D and Salmon WJ (2004) Globalization of retailing. In J Quelch and R Deshpande (eds) *The Global Market: Developing a Strategy to Manage across Borders.* San Francisco, CA: Jossey-Bass, 288–312.

Website

http://pine.hbs.edu/external/facPersonalShow.do?pid=12312

THE INTERNATIONALISATION OF RETAILING

Walter J. Salmon and André Tordjman

MANUFACTURERS HAVE ALREADY DEVELOPED an international view of their markets, and the largest among them have prepared

---

International Journal of Retailing, Vol. 4, No. 2 (1989), pp. 3–16.

themselves for worldwide marketing of their products: this is the concept of a global market, which has evolved because the consumer cultures of the western nations are becoming increasingly interlinked.

Paradoxically, retailing retains a strong national character. The internationalisation of retailing is not a new phenomenon, but it remains partial and marginal. However, during the past three decades, retailers have increasingly concerned themselves with the international market, which has broadened its scope. The retailers' interest extends across both food and non-food sectors, and involves a wide range of business formats. For some companies, international operations already represent a significant proportion of their activities and income.

Many obstacles have restrained the internationalisation of retail:

- the size of the firms, often small-scale and independent, and without either the financial capacity or the managerial culture necessary for international expansion;
- the high priority given to national expansion through geographical diversification and through a wider range of activities;
- insufficient knowledge of foreign conditions and markets;
- the drive for productivity, particularly by concentrating purchases on a national scale.

Today these obstacles have been reduced. Large retail firms have the financial and human resources available. They have saturated their national markets, and have attained the limit of the benefits of mass production. They are better informed about their foreign customers, whose behaviour and expectations are becoming more closely aligned with those of their own domestic market.

Apart from the homogenisation of the groups of consumers, there are other reasons which explain the rapid internationalisation of retail, and which favour the export of the business formats, as well as the products themselves. The development of international commerce and the opening up of national frontiers encourage the export of capital and of business acumen. Technological progress in the fields of transport and communication enable merchandise and information to be circulated at very low cost.

An evolution of the strategies used has accompanied this acceleration in the internationalisation of retailing. Retailers first developed the investment strategy. This involves obtaining a financial stake in retail abroad, and thus consists of a transfer of money from the country of origin to the host country, with the intention of buying all or part of a working retail chain.

Among the reasons for this international investment strategy, one should note: the search for a rate of growth and viability superior to that obtainable in the country of origin, the diversification of financial and political risks, the rapid acquisition of part of the existing market in those countries where the creation of shops would be costly and risky, and the learning of business know-how for those types of retail not mastered by the foreign investor.

The retailers which employ such an investment strategy are generally large-scale companies, nationally diversified, which are looking for new growth opportunities abroad. Vendex International, a Dutch group with a turnover of more than 15 billion Florins in 1986, illustrates well this approach. With interests in more than ten national sectors, involving 80 different enterprises, it added interests in the USA, Brazil, Japan and the UK, all effected by buying a stake in an existing retail chain. Certain French hypermarket groups have also obtained stakes in American firms. For example, Promodès bought Red Food Stores supermarket chain; Docks de France, which controls 183 (Lil'Champ Food) convenience stores; Rallye has diversified its portfolio of businesses with a stake in Athlete's Foot; and Carrefour now owns 20 per cent of the capital of Costco.

More recently, retailers have made use of two other strategies for their international development. They are, on the one hand, the multinational strategy, which involves the implantation of autonomous affiliates operating comparably to the parent company, but adapted to the local market; and, on the other hand, the global strategy, which corresponds to a reproduction outside their national frontiers of a formula which is known to be successful in the country of origin.

This article concentrates on the analysis of multinational and global strategies in order to study the marketing and managerial implications of each one.

The Global Strategy

The global strategy is defined as the faithful replication of a concept abroad. Those who have decided to use a global strategy operate beyond national borders, as if their targeted market was homogeneous, thereby ignoring all national or regional differences. Global retailers address those groups of consumers who, independent of the country in which they live, have similar lifestyles and expectations.

The chains of specialised stores, such as Benetton, Laura Ashley, Conran, IKEA, and Marks & Spencer have in particular developed a global strategy. Others, within the franchise sector, are joining in strongly with global strategies of their own (Yves Rocher, Speedy, McDonalds).

A Standardised Marketing Strategem

Global retailers are faced with two potentially conflicting forces (Waldman, 1978). The first is the need to adapt to the local market conditions in order to better satisfy consumer expectations. The second is the desire to utilise their corporate resources in order to benefit from economies of scale. Buzzell (1968) and Quelch and Hoff (1986) suggested that rather than taking an extreme position, the marketer should balance between the advantages of standardisation and the necessity of responding to the heterogeneous nature of national markets. In contrast, Levitt (1983) advanced the idea that, because the needs and expectations of consumers around the world are becoming irrevocably more homogeneous, the multinational strategies will become obsolete and will be replaced by global strategies.

The global retailers have mainly followed Levitt's approach. Even if they have occasionally adapted to local market conditions at a very superficial level, they have a global definition of their segmentation of customers, and a single market posture for all their shops. The standardisation of their marketing techniques is a consequence of choosing a global strategy. The range of products, the store decor, the advertising, the prices, and the level of service are all comparable (Table 1).

Vertical integration

The global retailers possess another distinctive characteristic: their vertical integration is accentuated. For some of them this extends from the conception of the products, through production and quality control, to retailing.

The original concept, together with good business sense, is often at the root of the success of the global retailers. Terence Conran, Giuliana Benetton, Laura Ashley, and Ingar Kamprad (IKEA) have personally marked their companies with a particular style, and Marks & Spencer is working in collaboration with its suppliers on a more elaborate range of exclusive products. This interaction between the products and the shops which sell them confers a significant advantage, based on a unique and distinctive product line. Under a brand name or a private name, global retailers are developing a choice of merchandise

Table 1 Standardisation of the marketing mix of global retailers

	Benetton/Laura Ashley	IKEA/Conran	Marks & Spencer
Assortment	The stores have the same assortment sold under a brand name	The products are the same, but the size of assortment varies according to the country	The products are much the same. Only the size of the store influences the range of choice
Service	Identical standard of service and sales method	Identical standard of service and sales method	Identical standard of service and sales method
Price	Pricing policy decided by the head office in each country	Pricing policy decided by head office and local representatives in each country	Standard pricing policy throughout Europe, but discounts decided nationally
Promotion	Same "united colors of Benetton" theme, and same advertising and catalogue	Same slogans but adapted to the local market – IKEA uses four separate catalogues in the world	Determined by country, based essentially on the stores themselves
Decor	Identical presentation and display	Identical presentation and display	Comparable presentation and display

which matches the particular expectations of the consumers whom they wish to attract. They are concentrating on products with a long life-cycle, thereby limiting the uncertainty attached to fashion forward products.

Certain global retailers are also mastering the techniques of production. They guarantee the manufacture and design as well as the quality of the merchandise. Because they work with a longer lead time than the retailers who are supplied by industry, the global retailers take more inventory risk than the less well-integrated retailers. In order to reduce this risk, and to gain greater flexibility in their production management, they subcontract a part of their manufacturing. Benetton makes use of a network of 220 subcontractors, who contribute 40 per cent of the weaving of the wool, 60 per cent of the garment fabrication, and ten per cent of the finishing. Each of these subcontractors uses the same know-how, standards, and technology as Benetton. In contrast, Marks & Spencer does not integrate the production, but all its goods carry its brand name, St Michael.

Finally, logistics play an important role in the global strategy. Shops around the world are supplied from several centralised warehouses, which are fully automated and integrated. The success of the specialised international chains depends upon the combination of a global marketing strategy supported by a modern, flexible production system, and by an effective supply network.

There are, however, other retailers, who have integrated neither the conception of their products, nor their manufacture, but are developing global strategies. Toys "Я" Us, the leading toy retailer in the United States, has recently set up stores in Europe (Britain, Germany, and soon France) using its successful toy-supermarket concept. The shops offer a wide range of brand name products sold at a low price throughout the year. Toys "Я" Us has reproduced the global concept, and it seems that by acting as the retailer for many multinational toy manufacturers, Toys "Я" Us will benefit from negotiations at an international level.

Managerial implications

Putting a global strategy into effect has many managerial implications. First of all, the organisation of operations becomes strongly centralised. All decisions involving the company are made at the highest level. Little initiative is allowed of the representatives from the shops, whose role is reduced to following the regulations and procedures laid down by the head office. They have practically no influence on the tactical and strategic organisation of the retail outlets. All policies covering the product line, the merchandising, service and communication are defined in detail by the head office. Even for variables as sensitive as prices or discounts, the local representatives cannot act of their own accord, since these things are decided at a national level.

After that, an effective, permanent information system is required in order to control the activities of the network. This system, which is usually computerised, enables detailed data to be collected on sales and required restocking, so that special offers can be evaluated, and the product line can be adjusted if necessary (especially such things as style and colours).

The global retailers, because they re-use an already proven formula, with a centralised organisation of their operations, are capable of very rapid expansion. Benetton, Laura Ashley, IKEA, as well as Yves Rocher, McDonalds, and Speedy, have been able to develop their networks largely because their standard formula can be replicated cheaply and swiftly. The market studies carried out prior to the opening of a shop, the necessary financing, and the recruitment of management do not slow down the expansion of these chains abroad. Retail units can therefore be made operational and viable quickly. Benetton, which today controls nearly 5,000 shops around the world, doubled its network between 1983 and 1987 (see Table 2). Laura Ashley multiplied the number of its shops eight-fold between 1980 and 1987 (see Table 3). IKEA has opened more than 60 outlets since 1974, and now operates in 17 countries (Table 4). For other global retailers, such as Marks & Spencer, the expansion of their network is complicated by difficulties in finding appropriate large retail spaces in city centres. Finally, the standardisation of their activities enables retailers to benefit from economies of scale as much from the point of view of sales, as for production, distribution, shop management, advertising, and personnel training.

Table 2 Benetton's internationalisation (1987)

Countries	Stores %	Sales %
Italy	34.8	38.4
Germany	10.2	12.8
France	13.2	10.0
Great Britain	7.3	6.4
Austria	1.8	1.8
Switzerland	2.6	3.0
Spain	3.4	1.0
US	15.4	15.1
Other countries	11.3	11.5
Total	100.0	100.0

Source: Annual Reports.

Table 3 Laura Ashley's internationalisation (1987)

	Stores %	Sales %	Retail space %	Profit %
UK	37.7	42.9	44.0	37.0
North America	36.3	42.8	32.0	55.0
Europe	20.3	12.2	20.0	5.0
Others	5.7	2.1	4.0	3.0
Total	100.0	100.0	100.0	100.0

Source: Annual Reports.

Table 4 IKEA's internationalisation (1987)

	Sales %	Surface %
Scandinavia	30.7	30.0
West Germany	33.0	28.0
Rest of Europe	22.0	26.0
Rest of World	14.3	16.0
Total	100.0	100.0

Source: Annual Reports.

Many factors explain the successful expansion of the global retailers. These retailers concentrate their efforts in those sectors of the market with clearly defined expectations. They present a single front, linking the shop to its merchandise and they benefit from reduced costs in various parts of their network. Further expansion is likely to occur if these advantages are maintained. However, there are two principal dangers: first, their strong specialisation makes them vulnerable to changes in consumer attitudes and to attacks by their competitors; and second, their incapacity to take the nuances of local markets into account can prevent them from keeping up to date with market trends.

The Multinational Strategy

Contrary to the global retailers, the multinational retailers consider their subsidiaries to be a portfolio of geographically dispersed retail businesses, for each of which they adapt their standard formula to fit the local market conditions. The basic concept remains the same, but certain alternations are necessary to suit specific expectations in each national market. The internationalisation of the hypermarkets is definitely the best illustration of the multinational strategy. "One-stop shopping" (all types of products sold at a discount under one roof) has been reproduced in all sorts of countries, but the types of produce and the brands sold vary according to the expectations of the consumers in each country. This multinational approach is practised by C&A, but with a much higher degree of standardisation under the control of each country. While consumer homogenisation inspired the global strategy, other reasons are at the origin of the multinational strategy of the French hypermarket chains:

- the restrictions imposed by the Loi Royer have been the decisive factor which has led these firms to look abroad for growth opportunities, because their national markets have been restrained;
- the mastery of technical and commercial know-how, together with satisfying results from diversification in their home market, have encouraged French entrepreneurs to make their initial concepts more viable, and to spread out their financial risks;
- a search for new challenges, and an international image, has perhaps influenced the choice of country made by successful market leaders.

The internationalisation of the hypermarkets started in the countries bordering on France (Belgium, Switzerland, Germany and England). It then spread to those countries with a large potential for growth, but where modern retailing was almost non-existent (Spain, Portugal, Italy, Brazil, and Argentina). Today international hypermarkets exist in other countries as well, such as the US and Taiwan.

With the exception of the US, where their success has not yet been proven, the hypermarkets have basically developed in those countries where they have a competitive advantage over the local retailers. The mastery of business know-how in a favourable environment has enabled the French chains to realise increased profits and remarkable rates of expansion. Today group results show a significant contribution from abroad, which is likely to continue to increase (Tables 5 and 6).

Adapted marketing strategy

The multinational retailers have a global definition of their formula; but they adjust certain important aspects of it to suit local situations.

The hypermarkets have tried to preserve the causes of their success – a tight control over management costs, a limited provision of service to their customers, and the use of very small profit margins, which are offset by the large volume of sales. C&A has preserved the kernel of its strategy in all the countries in which it operates; namely a recognisable line of clothing for men, women and children, all at reasonable prices. In addition to the reproduction of these key

Table 5 Carrefour's internationalisation (1988)

	France	Brazil	Spain	Other
Stores (%)	64.0	10.0	20.0	2.0
Selling area (%)	66.0	12.0	20.0	2.0
Sales (%)	80.0	8.0	11.0	1.0
Profit (%)	66.0	13.0	19.0	1.0
Investments (%)	58.0	12.0	27.0	3.0
Profit (% sales)	1.24	2.3	2.6	2.6

Source: Annual Reports.

Table 6 Promodès internationalisation (1986)

	France	Abroad
Sales (%)	70.0	30.0
Profit (%)	23.0	77.0

Source: Annual Reports.

elements, each marketing variable is adapted to suit their clientele and to face up to the local competition.

The product range may vary from country to country, and even between different shops, depending on local market conditions and the exigencies of supply. The choice of products at C&A is determined at a national level, each shop being obliged to follow the national guidelines. This is in contrast to the hypermarkets, where the range of goods is decided by each individual outlet for two reasons: firstly, each outlet must adapt itself to the micro-market conditions of the zone in which it operates; secondly, for goods which are perishable, bulky or require rapid turnover, the services offered by national or local suppliers become of prime importance.

Pricing policy varies according to the country (at C&A), and according to each outlet (for the hypermarkets). C&A devises its policy and profit margin at a national level, and requires all outlets within each country to follow the national guidelines. The hypermarkets (which essentially sell basic and brand name products for which prices must be adjusted carefully to attract customers and to face up to local competition) allow their shop managers more autonomy in deciding price levels.

Advertising policy is specific to each country. The amount of advertising varies, as does the choice of media, depending on cost, availability and relative effectiveness. Advertising for C&A is national; it is regional for the hypermarkets. The level of service offered does not vary between countries, but evolves with consumer habits.

The managerial implications of a multinational strategy

The multinational retailers manage decentrally much more than their global counterparts. While the parent company approves major strategic options, such as localisation of the sales outlets, or recruitment of executives from abroad, it allows a considerable degree of autonomy to the local national teams, who decide upon the marketing mix at the sales outlets. This decentralisation of responsibility is very marked in the case of the hypermarket managers, who choose the product line and the suppliers, fix the profit margins according to the local competition, determine the level of service offered, decide upon the advertising themes, and select the advertising media. Such a delegation of power requires those concerned with the definition and operation of the marketing policy of their department to be competent, well trained and capable of acting swiftly. Such delegation is very limited for the managers of C&A, who have little independence within the guidelines set by the national executive (Table 7).

In order to remain true to their original concept, while taking local nuances into account, the multinational retailers use mixed management teams, composed of both native and expatriate executives. The corporate culture of each company, which is crucial if the original formula is to be adhered to, is transmitted by the home country executives to the local management during training programmes.

Table 7 Marketing and management of international retailers

Marketing	Management	
	Decentralised	Centralised
Standard	C&A*	Benetton
		Laura Ashley
Adjusted	Carrefour	IKEA
	Auchan	Conran
		Marks & Spencer

* The management of C&A is decentralised at the international level but strongly centralised inside each country.

The choice of a multinational strategy has three principal strategic consequences. First, the multinational retailers have a weaker development capacity than their global counterparts. The scale of investment required for each shop, and the difficulty of recruiting high-level managers to run each sales outlet limits the replication of their formula. During the past 20 years, Carrefour has opened fewer than 40 sales outlets abroad, compared to over 1,000 for Benetton between 1984 and 1986.

Secondly, the multinational retailers do not benefit much from economies of scale. They profit from their acquired experience, but, in contrast to the global retailers, the international expansion of their network does not invoke a reduction in the costs of retailing, supplying and advertising. The multinational retailers concentrate their activities in a few countries in order to achieve a large presence at a local level, sufficient to significantly reduce supply and management costs. However, C&A benefits from a concentration of its purchases from certain international suppliers.

The diversity of experience encourages a transfer of techniques and an enrichment of the global know-how of the organisation. The French hypermarket chains have exported their formulae, but have learned in return new techniques from the countries in which they have set up operation (fish retailing from Spain and the handling of funds from Brazil). The head offices of the countries in which C&A operates exchange information about local markets and suppliers. Finally, the development of an international image has stimulated executive recruitment, and opened up new career prospects for those ready to take on new challenges.

In the future, multinational retailers, in contrast to global retailers, will gain market share in businesses in which the bulk, weight, or perishability of the merchandise inhibits international procurement. In addition they will become more important in the retailing of product categories less subject to abrupt changes in lifestyles and fashion. Food and related lines of merchandise are, therefore, sectors of distribution in which multinational retailing will grow.

The multinational retailers will expand in those countries where they possess a competitive advantage over the local competition, and where they can find good retail space for their shops, which limits the number of suitable development sites.

Conclusion

The internationalisation of retail should continue to accelerate. The homogenisation of consumer groups around the world, the reduction in costs of transportation, improved circulation of information and especially the retailers' international vision of their marketplace should favour this trend. With a unified European market, which reaffirms the wish of those countries to effect a single large market as envisaged by the Treaty of Rome (1957), it is to be expected that the internationalisation of retail firms will be strengthened, and that retailing will thus experience the same evolution as production did in the 1970s.

All three strategies outlined previously and summarised in Table 8 will be used, but the global strategy will realise the strongest growth rate. In effect, the global retailers will benefit more than the others from consumer homogenisation around the world, and from the harmonisation of standards, which will facilitate the distribution of products between countries.

Several consequences should follow from retail internationalisation. For the retailers themselves, opportunities and threats from outside national frontiers will have to be studied. Retailing on the European scale began in the 1970s, with the export of certain successful marketing formulae. However, in comparison with the exchange of products, this development remains limited. Will it be spurred on by the unified European market? If not, will the Europeanisation of retailing come about thanks to American retailers, motivated by a new market without trade barriers? Those American retailers who began the internationalisation of retail after the war by setting up operations in Europe have had difficulty in penetrating certain countries. These difficulties have been linked to the cost of suitable premises, over-restrictive legislation concerning the opening of shops, local management problems and the need for capital to finance the national expansion of the parent company. Firms such as Jewel Company, J.C. Penney, Sears Roebuck, Safeway and Woolworth have progressively reduced, and in some cases totally stopped their investments on the other side of the Atlantic. With the opening of a single unified market in Europe, American firms are expected to retain their interest there. Toys "Я" Us, The Limited, and The Gap are some examples of chains which will affect the European competition.

The European retailers, as well as defending their home markets, are aiming to move into other markets in Europe, as well as in the rest of the world. Their international expansion will make use of alliances between traders of different expertise in different countries, and by grouping companies together to achieve greater concentrations.

Even though the European retailers are actively concerned with the European market, many of them will continue to invest in the USA, for the following reasons:

Table 8 International retail strategies

	Global	*Multinational*	*Investment*
Definition	Replicate the same formula worldwide	Adapt the formula to local conditions	Transfer of money for buying partially or totally an existing retail company in a foreign country
Business formats	Speciality chains	Hypermarkets, department stores, variety stores	Retailers/non-retailers operators
Marketing	Global segmentation and global positioning	Reproduction of the concept but adaptation of the content	
	Standardisation of marketing mix	Adaptation of marketing mix	
	Uniform assortment, price, store design, service, advertising	Similar worldwide definition of store decor, price strategy, service strategy	No real marketing implications
		Adjustment of assortment and advertising strategies	
Organisational implications	Vertical integration of design function, production process, distribution system	Multidomestic approach	Portfolio of foreign operations
Management implications	Centralised management	Decentralised management	Partially controlled management
	Excellent information system	Frequent communications with HQ	
	Rapid capacity to growth	Average capacity to growth	Fast international expansion
	Large economies of scale	No economies of scale	Lower risk
	Very little transfer of know-how	Important transfer of know-how	Transfer of skills

- the size of the market and the level of disposable income far exceeds that in any single European country;
- the comparatively low cost of land and of leases enables rapid expansion;
- the stable political climate and the relative absence of restrictive legislation reassures all foreign investors;
- the observation of new techniques and concepts which can then be used in the European market.

In 1985, Europeans invested $5.55 billion in American retailing, in contrast to the $2.5 billion invested by Americans in European retailing. Just three

Table 9 Foreign investments in US retailing

	Belgium	France	Germany	Netherlands	UK	Switzerland	Others	Total
Million dollars	112	136	610	1099	2989	73	36	5055
%	2.7	2.7	12	21.7	59	1.4	1	100

Source: *Foreign Direct Investment Position in the United States,* US Department of Commerce, Bureau of Economic Analysis (1985).

countries, the UK, the Netherlands and Germany accounted for 90 per cent of this investment (Table 9).

The globalisation of retailing will have other consequences. It will probably encourage independent traders to form associations with each other in order to pool their expertise and resist the multinational retailers. It will speed up the replacement of backward equipment in southern Europe, often at a large social cost.

The manufacturers will be equally affected by this internationalisation. In certain sectors, well-integrated retailers will be able to compete with them. In others, manufacturers will have to negotiate with multinational retailers whose economic size will force them to make extra concessions. There will be a large demand for high level executives who can interpret changes in consumer expectations, manage operations abroad, and negotiate at an international level both for the retailers and the manufacturers.

Finally, more intense competition together with the transfer of techniques between various markets should provide the consumer with better quality service and an improved range of available goods.

References

Buzzell, R. D. (1968), "Can You Standardise Multinational Marketing?", *Harvard Business Review*, November–December.
Levitt, T. (1983), "The Globalisation of the Markets", *Harvard Business Review*, May–June.
Quelch, J.A. and Hoff, E.J. (1986), "Customising Global Marketing", *Harvard Business Review*, May–June.
Waldman, C. (1987). *Strategies of International Mass Retailers*, Praeger Publishing.

Sources

"Actualités mondiales", *LSA*, No. 985, 7 June 1985, p. 134.
"Actualités mondiales", *LSA*, No. 831, 5 February 1982, p. 85.
"Actualités mondiales", *LSA*, No. 993, 20 September 1985, p. 172.
"Actualités mondiales", *LSA*, No. 1008, 10 January 1986, p. 80.
"American Retreat", *Dun's Business Month*, August 1984, p. 69.
"L'Andalousie de Continente", *Points de vente*, 15 March 1986, p. 48.

Benetton, *Annual Report 1985*.

Benetton, "Retail Basic Study", *Morgan & Stanley*, Walter F. Loeb, 29 October 1986.

"BHS to Harness the Habitat Image", *Investors Chronicle*, 27 November 1985, p. 74.

"Bilan de Santé de 29 Entreprises de Distribution", *LSA*, No. 957, p. 90.

"Brésil, Argentine, Terre de Croissance Pour les Hyper", *LSA*, 19 June 1981, p. 76.

Carrefour, *Annual Report 1986*.

"Carrefour Hypermarkets Slated for 2 US Locales", *Supermarket News*, 17 November 1986.

"Companies On The Move – February", *Investors Chronicle*, 11 March 1983, p. 59.

Conran Stores Inc., Retail Research, *Capel-Cure Myers*, 5 November 1981.

"Conran's Grand Design", *Market Place*, Spring, 1984.

"Conran's Recipe for Mothercare", *Advertising Age*, November 1983, p. 7.

"Continent Madrid, du Meilleur cru", *Points de vente*, 15 September 1984.

"Continent Porto", *LSA*, 4 January 1986, p. 19.

"Destination L'Espagne", *Hyper*, July 1984.

"La Distribution Française a l'étranger", *LSA*, No. 957, p. 90.

Euromarché, *Annual Report 1985*.

"The Europeanization of American Retailing", *Standard and Poor's Industry Surveys*, 7 November 1985.

"Europe's US Shopping Speed", *Fortune*, 1 December 1980, p. 83.

"European Target Specialty Chains", *Chain Store Age Executive*, January 1982.

"Fnac", *Market Place*, Summer 1986.

"Foreign Retail Companies Operating in the UK", *Retail & Distribution Management*, January–February 1987.

"France-Etats Unis, Promodès arbitre le match de la productivité", *Points de vente*, March 1985.

French, Nigel, *A Global Perspective of Consumer Changes*, NRMA conference, New York, 13 January 1987.

"French-based Carrefour Tests US Hypermarket", *Discount Store News*, 10 November 1986.

"French Trend to Hypermarkets Gains Momentum", *Supermarket News*, 13 February 1987, p. 13.

Galeries Lafayette, *Annual Report 1985*.

"Habitat Acquires Stake in French Leisure Group", *Financial Times*, 29 June 1985, p. 10.

"Habitat France prend le contróle de la Maison de la Redoute", *LSA*, No. 859, 1 October 1982.

"Habitat/Heal", *Investors Chronicle*, 25 February 1983, p. 41.

"Habitat Mothercare", *Investors Chronicle*, 8 June 1984, p. 68.

"Habitat Mothercare", *Investors Chronicle*, 15 July 1986, p. 48.

"Habitat Mothercare", *Investors Chronicle*, 9 December 1983, p. 61.

"Habitat Mothercare", *Investors Chronicle*, 10 June 1983, p. 66.

"Habitat Mothercare – Globe Trotting", *Investors Chronicle*, 6 July 1984, p. 44.

"Habitat Mothercare – Widely Spread", *Investors Chronicle*, 12 July 1985, p. 52.

"Habitat Posts 19% Profit Gain From Fiscal 1985", *Wall Street Journal* (Europe), 7 June 1985, p. 5.

"Habitat Steps in on Richard Shops Deal", *Financial Times*, 1 October 1983, p. 1.

"Habitat to Buy 34% of FNAC, GMF Boosts Stake to 50.1%", *Wall Street Journal* (Europe), 1 July 1985, p. 4.

"Habitat to Open Two Stores in Netherlands", *Financial Times*, 22 May 1985, p. 8.

Harvard Business Case, Benetton case (A) & (B).

Hollander, Stanley C., *Multinational Retailing*, MSU International Business and Economic Studies, Michigan State University, East Lansing, 1970.

"How A Major Swedish Retailer Chose a Beachhead in the US", *Wall Street Journal*, 17 April 1987, p. 37.

"IKEA, le choc des prix", *LSA, December*, 1981, p. 48.

"IKEA, Premier magasin en France", *LSA*, No. 811, p. 11.

"IKEA et coopcréent un magasin en commun", *LSA*, No. 987, pp. 79.

"IKEA, développement et Strategie", *LSA*, No. 866, p. 10.

Kacker, Madmar P., *Transatlantic Trends in Retailing*, Quorum Books, 1985.

Kuin, Pieter, "The Magic of Multinational Management," *Harvard Business Review*, November–December 1972.

Laura Ashley, *Annual Report 1986*.

"Laura Ashley", *Investor's Choice*, 29 November 1985, p. 22.

"Laura Ashley Inc.", *Market Place*, Autumn 1986.

"Laura Ashley, Retail Research", *Capel-Cure Myers*, April 1986, October 1986.

"Laura Ashley Aims for Retail Rating for its Rag Trade Hybrid", *Investors Chronicle*, 29 November 1985, p. 22.

"Laura Ashley, Welsh Lessons from Business", *The Economist*, 15 December 1985, p. 88.

"Laura Ashley to Seek Full Listing on London Exchange", *Wall Street Journal* (Europe), 11 July 1985, p.5.

"Laura Ashley Dies, Leaving Company's Plan in Limbo", *Wall Street Journal* (Europe), 18 September 1985, p. 5.

"Laura Ashley Plans Initial Public Share Offering of $91 Million", *Wall Street Journal*, 25 November 1985, p. 4

"Laura Ashley, Investors Scramble to Buy Shares in LA Group", *Wall Street Journal* (Europe), 29 November 1984, p. 9.

"Laura Ashley's Pattern", *Financial Times*, 18 October 1986, p. 9.

"Laura Ashley Opts for Welsh Expansion", *Financial Times*, 11 December 1984, p. 8.

"Laura Ashley to Open Clothes Factory in Wrexham", *Financial Times*, 24 November 1985, p. 6.

"Le Cas Promodès: de Caen a Chicago", *Sciences et vie economique*, 9 October 1985, p. 57.

Le Printemps, *Annual Report 1986*.

"Le Redeploiement International: une exigence pour le commerce Francais", *Institut du Commerce et de la Consommation*, Paris, September 1985.

"Made in Wales", *Market Place*. Winter 1985–1986.

Marks and Spencer, *Annual Report 1985*.

"Market Place", Laura Ashley Inc., Autumn 1986.

"Market Place", Laura Ashley Inc., Winter 1985/86.

Marketing Review, Spring 1986.

Martenson, Rita, *Innovation in Multinational Retailing*, University of Gothenburg, 1981.

"The New Immigrants: Europeans are Changing the Face of American Retailing", *Chain Store Age Executive*, February 1986, p. 16.

"Non Stop Meubles", *LSA*, No. 883, 1 April 1983, p. 79.

"Now Conran's Magic Misses its First Trick", *Financial Times*, 12 June 1986, p. 12.

"L'Offensif Orientale du Printemps", *LSA*, No. 943, p. 111.

Porter, Michael E., *Competition in Global Industries*, Harvard Business School, 1986.

"Promodès, Hors de I'Exagone", *CPA Management*, 1 Trimestre 1981.

"Promodès, Poursuite de la Restructuration", *LSA*, No. 1030, p. 22.

"Promodès sans Frontières", *Points de vente*, 1 June 1984, p. 48.

"Promodès, évolution très Positive des Activités Etrangères", *LSA*, 24 May 1985, p. 85.

Promodès, *Annual Report 1986*.

"Red Food Stores, le Succès d'une forte image de marque", *LSA*, 13 November 1987.

Salmon, Walter, J., *Is the Balance of Power between Manufacturers and Retailers in the United States Changing?*, World Conference of Retailers, 22 October 1986, Zurich, Switzerland.

"Sir Terence Calls His Customers to Heal's", *Financial Times*, 18 February 1987, p. 8.

"Storehouse View", *Market Place*, Summer 1986.

Survey of Current Business, *Direct Investments Abroad*, August 1985–86.

Tordjman, A., *A Comparative Study of Distribution in Six European Countries*, Esomar, June 1986.

Tordjman, A., *L'Appareil Commercial Francais. Structures, Evolutions, Tendances*, Cahier de Recherche du Centre, HEC/ISA, 1985.

"A Touch of Class, It's Paid Off for Habitat-Mothercare", *Barron's*, 3 December, 1984, p. 68.

"UK's Mothercare Gets US Operation on its Feet", *Advertising Age*, 6 February 1984, p. 32.

"Une Grande Aventure pour Promodès, son internationalisation," *LSA*, 7 June 1985, p. 20.

Editors' Commentary

THIS IS THE SECOND article by John Dawson in this volume. Readers are referred to the earlier commentary (pp. 259–261) for his main biographical details. The internationalization of retailing has been of long-standing interest to John Dawson. He has carried out research in a number of countries and published extensively on the topic. The selected paper is seminal. The paper tries to understand the scope of retail internationalization and to define the attributes of the activity that should be the focus of study. The article follows on from work on comparative and international retailing in the early stages of Dawson's career. Since its publication, internationalization has become a personal and an academic focus. The paper was the result of a research project on internationalization and was originally presented as a keynote paper at the EMAC conference hosted by ESADE, Barcelona.

The research Dawson has undertaken in other countries, and his network of colleagues and fellow researchers from many different countries, have furnished him with an unparalleled breadth of expertise on the topic. This has enabled him to appreciate the potentials and pitfalls, the changes in the market and new ways of engaging in retail internationalization. His PhD in the 1960s was on European retailing and he has throughout his research career maintained an interest in retail policies and developments within Europe (however this is defined at the time). Japan has been a special interest for almost twenty years and he has visited the country on numerous occasions, sparking a research interest in both Japan and Asian retailing generally.

Dawson's paper points to a substantial range of strategic and tactical reasons that were either reported by individual firms as their reasons for international moves or that could be interpreted from their actions. The paper also attempts, in trying to bring together a wide range of studies, to open discussion on the extent to which retailer internationalization has different characteristics from the internationalization of manufacturing, a theme taken up again in later work. The paper also sought to look at mechanisms for internationalization as linked to form of retailing, in an attempt to understanding the generic strategies of firms moving internationally. It has proved enormously influential in framing further studies in the area.

Key Publications

Dawson, JA (1982) *Commercial Distribution in Europe*. London: Croom Helm.

Dawson JA and Sato T (1983) Controls over the development of large stores in Japan. *Service Industries Journal*, 3(4): 136–145.

Dupuis M, Dawson JA and Salto L (1999) *European Cases in Retailing*. Oxford: Blackwell.

Dawson JA and Henley J (2000) Internationalisation of hypermarket retailing in Poland: Western European investments and its implications. *Journal of East–West Business*, 5(4): 37–52.

Dawson JA (2001) Strategy and opportunism in European retail internationalisation. *British Journal of Management*, 12: 253–266.

Dawson J, Mukoyama M, Choi SC and Larke R (eds) (2003) *The Internationalisation of Retailing in Asia*. London: RoutledgeCurzon.

Dawson JA, Burt SL and Sparks L (2003) Failure in international retailing. *International Review of Retail, Distribution and Consumer Research*, 13: 355–373.

Dawson JA and Larke R (2004) Japanese retailing through the 1990s: retailer performance in a decade of slow growth. *British Journal of Management*, 15(1): 73–94.

Burt SL, Dawson JA and Sparks L (2004) The international divestment activities of European grocery retailers. *European Management Journal*, 22(5): 483–492.

Dawson JA and Lee J-H (eds) (2005) *International Retailing Plans and Strategies in Asia*. Binghamton, NY: Haworth.

Dawson JA and Larke R (2005) The role of medium sized firms in retail change in Japan. *International Review of Retail, Distribution and Consumer Research*, 15: 401–422.

Dawson JA, Larke R and Mukoyama M (eds) (2006) *Strategic Issues in International Retailing: Concepts and Cases*. London: Routledge.

Dawson JA (2007) Scoping and conceptualising retailer internationalisation. *Journal of Economic Geography*, 7: 373–397.

Website

http://www.retaildawson.com/

INTERNATIONALIZATION OF RETAILING OPERATIONS

John A. Dawson

International retail operations may be defined as the operation, by a firm or alliance, of shops, or other forms of retail distribution, in more than one country. Such operations have an extensive history. Motives for retailers to operate internationally are considered. Theoretical explanations have not been well developed but a potentially useful framework exists with the transaction cost paradigm. International operations may be achieved within several different organizational structures with some firms adopting different approaches for different markets. The empirical evidence of international retail activity lacks a sound survey base but some tentative generalities are drawn.

Introduction

RETAILERS ARE INVOLVED IN a variety of international activities. The international sourcing of products is one of the key functions of retailers who bring together assortments from many sources. Retailers copy ideas and management systems from those in other countries, there generally being little secrecy about and no copyright on many aspects of the operation of a shop. Consumers may cross national borders in search of a better offer even to the extent that some retail systems, such as that of Andorra, are heavily dependent on foreign consumers. Retail managers are recruited from other countries, bringing with them new ideas and retailing methods. The funding of retailing is increasingly international as the large firms raise finance for developments, and call for funds, from the international financial institutions. Retailers also have international operations which sell products and operate shops in more than one country, sometimes undertaking direct foreign investment, at other times participating in licensing agreements, occasionally exporting products and sometimes becoming involved in joint ventures and operational alliances. Within this considerable variety of possible ways that retailers internationalize, this paper is concerned with one only, that of international retail operations, some of the other international activities having been considered elsewhere (Dawson 1993).

The amount and variety of forms of international retail operations have increased in recent decades, due to many factors not least the increase in size of retail firms and attempts to reduce trading barriers amongst countries. Such internationalization, however, is not an entirely new phenomenon. There is a

Journal of Marketing Management, Vol. 10 (1994), pp. 267–282. © 1994 The Dryden Press.
The author acknowledges the useful comments made by Susan Shaw in the development of this paper.

substantial history of international retail operations. Already in the late nineteenth century Lipton stores operated in USA, Canada, Australia, Ceylon, South Africa and Germany although, for commercial reasons, several of these market entries were short lived (Mathias 1967). Other retailers who also began to develop internationally in the late nineteenth century subsequently retrenched for different reasons. Julius Meinl of Vienna was founded as a grocery retailer in 1862 and by 1939 had stores in Germany, Poland, Czechoslovakia, Hungary, Yugoslavia, Rumania, Bulgaria and Italy, but after the war the stores in the Soviet-bloc countries were nationalized and many others had been destroyed. Some stores in Austria were rebuilt in the 1950s and 1960s, and provided the basis for chain store expansion into Germany and Italy, and for the firm to re-enter Poland, Czechoslovakia and Hungary in the late 1980s in the wake of the privatization of the retail sector. In the first half of the twentieth century and in the immediate post-war era several American retailers moved into South American and European countries, most notably Sears, Roebuck, which had 53 stores in Latin America by 1957 (Wood and Keyser 1953; Fritsch 1962; Truitt 1984) and FW Woolworth who entered Canada in 1907, UK in 1909, Germany in 1926, Mexico in 1954 and Spain in 1965. Again, however, these developments were not always a great success and most of these foreign operations have been disposed of.

In the two decades immediately after the war many other smaller ventures occurred, some of which had influence far beyond their size. For example, the move into the UK of GEM International, which operated an early version of the warehouse club in the USA, provided prototypes in the UK, at Leeds and Nottingham, for the early superstores, with GEM eventually selling its UK operations to ASDA in 1966. Since the late 1960s however there has been a more substantial movement towards the international operation of stores and the remainder of this paper considers the extent and some of the reasons for this increase in international store operations.

Definitions

Retailers are required, if they are to be successful, to respond to the culture of their customers. Any move towards multi-store operations has to acknowledge that culture varies through space. This is particularly apparent when retailers choose to operate in diverse cultures whether within one country or across national borders (Martenson 1987, 1988). International retail operations may be defined as the operation, by a firm or alliance, of shops, or other forms of retail distribution, in more than one country. Such a definition encompasses the operations of companies such as GIB, Vendex, Aeon and Ahold which operate separate chains of stores in different countries, of companies such as IKEA, Sogo and Toys R Us which operate a single chain on an international basis, of organizations such as Body Shop and Bally which operate their own stores and franchise arrangements in several countries, and of alliances such as Intersport and Spar which have members drawn from several countries and an international central management for a range of business functions.

Many of the issues associated with operating in more than one country are the same as operating within culturally different, and sometimes autonomously governed, regions of the same country. For example, within Europe the issues and different requirements associated with operating stores in both the Autonomous Regions of Andalucia and Catalonia in Spain may be less onerous than operating stores across the national frontier between Belgium and Holland—the cultural differences of consumers, employees and business practices are less in the international context than in the national one in this example. More examples of this type may occur in Europe as the Single Market mechanisms become effective and currency convergence begins to be a wider reality but at the same time regional consciousness in social issues and cultural identities become more overt (Burt 1989; Dawson 1991). Nonetheless, it is useful to isolate international retail operations as a particular case of retail activity because national borders still have meaning for the political, governmental and judicial environment in which retailers operate.

The international operations of retailers, defined in the current way, have been subject to substantial study since the early reviews of European (Knee 1966) and American (Yoshino 1966) activity and the more substantial studies by Carson (1967) and Hollander (1970). Experimental moves, not all successful, by some larger European retailers were considered briefly by Dawson (1978) and more substantially by Waldman (1978). The attempts by American retailers to help in the modernization of retailing in developing countries was considered by Goldman (1974a; 1974b) and the European adventures of American retailers was considered by Kacker (1985). Although there were some international activities by European retailers in exploring new national markets in the first period of Euro-fervour in the early to mid 1970s (Jackson 1973; Distributive Trades EDC 1973; Burt 1993), the project to remove the physical, technical and fiscal barriers to trade in Europe by 1 January 1993 encouraged retailers to broaden their horizons (Filser 1990; European Commission 1991) and in turn has stimulated a body of empirical research considering the trans-border moves within Europe. It is with these more recent international moves that the remainder of this paper is concerned.

Reasons for Moves to International Operations

The research on international retail activity has been dominated by empirical studies and lacks an adequate conceptual and theoretical framework. It is tempting, as suggested by Whitehead (1992) to try to apply directly the substantial theoretical studies in the internationalization of manufacturing but there are grave dangers in such an approach. Not all this work is of relevance to retailing.

Dunning (1981, 1988) in a general consideration of direct foreign investment (DFI), irrespective of sector, suggests three factors which together are of importance in establishing whether a firm develops direct investment in international operations (i.e. establishes shops of their own). If present individually they generate different forms of indirect internationalization (Dunning and Norman 1985). The three factors are as follows:

- Ownership-specific advantages in which the firm has an innovatory product, process or business method which gives to the firm competitive advantage in the market; examples from retailing (with which Dunning does not deal explicitly and in his substantial study of 1993 in effect ignores) are retail brand products (Body Shop, Laura Ashley) or an individually refined sales method (Benetton, Aldi, McDonalds). These advantages may be obtained by licensing or franchising without DFI.

- Location-specific advantages in which the potential host country has particular cost advantages or market opportunities not present in the home country; for retailing, differentials in the cost of land and labour or differentials in market growth and existing market structure illustrate this factor with the differentials between France and Spain in both respects representing a specific example (Treadgold 1990). Again most of these benefits can be obtained through indirect investment methods.

- Internalization advantages in which the organization of the firm or some environmental factor results in ownership and locational advantages only being released through DFI; examples of the constraints might be legal impediments to franchising, an absence of firms suitable to be licensed, unfamiliarity with the business concept in the host country, the appearance of acquisition opportunities, etc.; Sears, Roebuck's direct investments in Latin America were apparently influenced by the lack of indigenous managerial expertise, Carrefour's hypermarket development in USA may well have been perceived in the same way, Ahold's American stores resulted from suitable acquisition opportunities being present (Kacker 1990; Hamill and Crosbie 1990).

Dunning's three factors approach, and subsequent work (Kojima 1982), provide a possible framework for considering the internationalization of retail operations but, perhaps more importantly, they serve to highlight the considerable differences between DFI decisions in retailing and manufacturing sectors and even between the organization and management of firms in the two sectors (Pellegrini 1992). Examples of these differences in organization and management are:

- the balance between centralized and decentralized decision making;
- the relative importance of organizational and establishment scale economies;
- the degree of spatial dispersion in the multi-establishment enterprise;
- the relative size of establishment to the size of the firm;
- the relative exit costs if decisions are reversed;
- the speed with which an income stream can be generated after an investment decision is made;
- different cash flow characteristics;
- the relative value of stock and hence importance of sourcing.

All these items, and others, serve to differentiate the manufacturing firm and the retail firm, and in many cases have relevance to the internationalization process.

These differences call into question suggestions for the direct application to retailing of the stages (Aharoni 1966; Wilkins 1974), approaches and theories of

DFI and internationalization (Buckley 1983) developed for manufacturing firms (Welch and Luostarinen 1988; Leontiades 1985). The network approach to the analysis of internationalization (Hakansson 1982; Johanson and Mattsson 1988, 1991) which is widely applied, may have relevance to the study of retail alliances, and in some cases of joint ventures, but in general the network approach is directed towards the understanding of vertical international relationships rather than the horizontal ones which occur in retailing. As such the approach is of more use in exploring the international sourcing activities of retailers rather than the internationalization of operations, with which this paper is concerned.

The approach to the study of internationalization using the transaction cost paradigm is of potential use in a retail context but again has to be used with care. There are many approaches through the analysis of transaction costs (Kay 1991). In many cases transaction costs are used to explain manufacturer's vertical relationships and although relevant to sourcing decisions of retailers in general, such an approach appears to have limited specific relevance to explicit international retail buying decisions. An approach using concepts of transaction costs has potential application, however, to explaining horizontal international activity but there appear to be gaps between the expectations generated by the paradigm and reality.

Hennart (1991) points out that most of the applications of the transaction cost paradigm in internationalization of horizontal activities have explored the knowledge factor (Casson 1987) and have developed this in the context of protected knowledge, for example through patents. When patents can be easily established and defended then licensing will be more prevalent and when knowledge is difficult to codify then direct investment is more likely. Within the retail context this would suggest that franchise type internationalization will be used when store formats can be well defined, and protected in some way, and this corresponds to the situation with Body Shop or Benetton. But, there are many examples of well defined formats which are internationalized by direct investment such as Aldi, Parfumerie Douglas or Gap. In these latter cases, however, although the format is well defined they are less easily protected from copying, exceptions perhaps being IKEA and Hennes and Mauritz, where control is effected through the strong retailer branding of products. Hennart (1991) also points to "the choice between franchising independent owners and establishing company owned outlets will depend on the comparison of two types of cost; that of monitoring the work effort of employees vs that of specifying and enforcing a minimum level of quality by contract" (p. 89). If quality standards are easily defined and outlets are dispersed, with consequential high costs of monitoring employees then franchising type approaches are more likely. Conversely if quality levels are difficult to stipulate and outlets are relatively concentrated then direct operation is more likely. Whilst the former is typified by Tie Rack and the latter by Carrefour hypermarkets or Sogo department stores, nonetheless it is again easy to find examples of the direct operation of store types in which quality standards are easily defined (Netto, Toys R Us, Yves Rocher) and of franchise type arrangements in which quality definition is difficult (Promodès, Printemps).

Given the characteristics of retailing, not least the wide spatial distribution of stores in retailing it is possible that the relative levels of market transaction costs and internal organization costs vary within the firm. In such a case different markets might be addressed in different ways. For example, Marks and Spencer operate franchise type arrangements in Portugal, Greece and Hungary where internal organization costs might be expected to be high and operate their own shops in larger markets such as France and the compact markets of Belgium and Holland, whilst in some other markets they undertake export sales. But again such distinctions do not explain the complete pattern with franchising used in the compact Austrian market. Bally, with 424 shops and 82 per cent of its sales in 1991 outside its home country, operates through wholly owned subsidiaries, joint ventures, shop in shop alliances, franchising and product licensing. What is unclear, however, is whether these different approaches relate to differences in transaction costs and in operational costs in different markets. Analysis of the balance, within the firm, between costs of market transactions and internalized transactions is a potentially interesting area of research in retail internationalization.

There would seem to be a range of interesting areas in the application of the transaction cost paradigm to the explanation of the reasons for and the mechanisms of international retail operation. Research on this theme will need to take the issues raised in the studies of international production (Kay 1991), but to build on and adapt these ideas to make them applicable in the retail context.

Empirical studies (Alexander 1990; Treadgold 1991; Treadgold and Davies 1988; Salmon and Tordjman 1989; Tordjman and Dionisio 1991; Burt 1991; Laulajainen 1987, 1991a) provide many reasons for the establishment of foreign retail operations. These include:

- perceived current or imminent market saturation in the home market; this factor is suggested as particularly important when the home country has a relatively small market, such as Holland or Belgium, and so is relevant to the international moves of Ahold, GIB and Vendex;
- limits placed on domestic growth in the home country by public policy controlling new store development or limiting further growth in market share of a firm; it is suggested that the Loi Royer in France, which was created to limit hypermarket development encouraged hypermarket operators to look for development opportunities in other countries;
- presence of an unexploited market or growth market in the host country; this factor has been suggested as important in moves during the 1980s into Spain particularly by French retailers and moves into Eastern Europe after 1989 and is seen clearly with Courts moves into the Caribbean and East Asian countries with young and rapidly increasing populations such that in 1992 44% of sales were outside the UK. This can also be seen as relevant to the expansion of other retailers including Toys R Us, The Gap, Aldi, IKEA, Disney Shop and Body Shop. Companies with a strong brand based on abstract attributes (Barwise 1993) may view new markets in this opportunistic way, for example Laura Ashley and Body Shop;
- higher profits (net margin or return on investment) obtained in the host country because of differences in competitive and/or cost structures (Treadgold 1990); this is the case with Marks and Spencer which had in

1992 a net trading margin of 12.4% on its UK stores and 16.0% for its stores in continental Europe;

- the spreading of risk across several, possibly unrelated, markets; the diversified holdings of Metro, Tengelmann, Kaufhof and Vendex and the moves by food retailers into DIY retailing are suggested as examples;
- use of surplus capital or the gaining of access to new capital sources at lower cost than in the home country; some moves by Japanese retailers in the second half of the 1980s suggest this factor;
- entrepreneurial vision; Marks and Spencer's moves into Canada appeared to owe much to the enterprise of then top management, the determination of Katsu Wada to internationalize Yaohan and moves by Ratners into USA or by C&A into several countries might be similarly categorized; this may also be called opportunism;
- an opportunity to get access to new management ideas or technology which will then be transferred to the home country; this may be important in areas such as use of information technology having been suggested as one reason for Sainsbury's move to USA and to a lesser extent, marketing. Edvardsson et al. (1992) suggest it can also affect concepts of customer service in the home country operations. It is often possible to get access to the management ideas through a subsidiary interest rather than full operational involvement as has been shown by Carrefour's investments in Costco, Carpetland and Office Depot;
- consolidation of buying power either within the firm or through joint-buying arrangements; this may be a countervailing reaction to the internationalization of manufacturers; this has been suggested as relevant to some of the moves within Europe of food retailers and in the DIY sector;
- encouragement, possibly inducement, by major manufacturer-suppliers wishing to enter new markets in which they currently have limited presence; suggestions have been made that major toy manufacturers have been supportive of moves by Toys R Us into Europe and Japan, and manufacturers of designer brand products may encourage the international expansion by retailers such as Louis Vuitton, Gucci and Dunhill;
- removal of barriers to entry, notably in the single market initiative in Europe, which may reduce the attraction of joint ventures in favour of international expansion;
- follow existing customers abroad; the establishment of small branches of major Japanese department stores in major European capital cities allows loyal customers to continue using the store when on holiday or working in the host country;
- the opportunity to realize monopolistic profits and to gain access to the most profitable segments by being the pioneer in a new market; this may have influenced some entrants into Eastern European countries, such as K Mart in Czechoslovakia.

This list is of reasons for international moves, not necessarily reasons for successful moves. Success or failure in international expeditions by retailers can be ascribed to many more factors than are listed here. Although there are many failures in international retail operations, for example the withdrawal from Spain in 1993 of the Dutch group Macintosh, there is surprisingly little research on the reasons for failure or on the empirical study of withdrawals from international operation.

Dimensions to International Operations

The two key dimensions for a typology of international retail operations are the mechanism by which internationalization is achieved and where in the overall organization decision making resides for the retail business in the host country. It has been suggested earlier that there are aspects of transaction costs theory which might be used to explore which of the different mechanisms are used in specific cases of international retail operations.

The actual mechanisms to achieve internationalization of operations may be summarized as:

- internal expansion in which a company opens individual shops using incompany resources;
- merger or takeover with the acquisition of control over a firm in the host country;
- franchise type agreements in which the franchisee in the host country use the ideas of the franchisor based in the home country (Eroglu 1992);
- joint-ventures which may take a variety of forms for the joint operation of retailing, including in-store concessions, between a firm in the host country and one in the home country and joint development activity between two entrant firms into the host country; often such joint ventures result in one partner buying out the others in order to maintain the position in the market;
- non-controlling, but operationally influential, interest in a firm in the host country being taken by a firm in the home country (Clarke-Hill and Robinson 1992); an example is the 28% of Kwik Save (UK) owned by Dairy Farms (Hong Kong), itself 47% owned by a subsidiary of Jardine Matheson, which gives Dairy Farms considerable influence over the appointment of senior executive positions in Kwik Save.

Some of the advantages and disadvantages of the different mechanisms are summarized in Table 1. In addition to these mechanisms is the very specialist one of purchase at auction of previously state owned stores. This method is one favoured in Eastern Europe, for example in Hungary in 1992 there was an auction of 150 shops formerly the property of state chain Kozert with German company Tengelmann purchasing 24 and the Belgium food retailer Louis Delhaize purchasing 10. This type of activity may be considered as a special case of the takeover mechanism.

A retailer may use more than one method as they develop the scale and variety of international operations. "The internationalization process varies from company to company, but even within one company there can be great

Table 1 Advantages and disadvantages of alternative mechanisms to establish retail international operations

Mechanism	Advantages	Disadvantages
Internal expansion	Can be undertaken by any size of firm Experimental openings are possible with modest risk and often modest cost Ability to adapt operation with each subsequent opening Exit is easy (at least in early stages) Allows rapid prototyping	Takes a long time to establish a substantial presence May be seen by top management as a minor diversion Requirement to undertake full locational assessment More difficult if host market is distant from home market Requires firm to become familiar with host country property market Lack of suitable sites in host country
Merger or takeover	Substantial market presence quickly achieved Management already in place Cash flow is immediate Possibility of technology transfer to home firm May be used as a way to obtain locations quickly for conversion to the chosen format	Difficult to exit if mistake is made Evaluation of takeover target is difficult and takes time Suitable firms may not be available Substantial top management commitment necessary Management of acquired firm may be unsuited to new operation
Franchise type agreements	Rapid expansion of presence possible Low cost to franchisor Marginal markets can be addressed Local management may be used Wide range of forms of agreement available Use locally competitive marketing policy	Possibly complex legal requirements Necessary to recruit suitable franchisees Difficult to control foreign franchisees May become locked into an unsatisfactory relationship
Joint-ventures	Possible to link with firm already in market Help available to climb learning curve and to overcome non-tariff barriers Possible to move later to either exit or make full entry into the market Share entry costs with other entrant	Necessary to share benefits Difficulties in finding a suitable partner
Non-controlling interest	Find out about market with minimal risk Allows those who know the market to manage the operation	Passive position Investment made over which little influence

differences" (Edvardsson *et al.* 1992, p. 81). Marks and Spencer, for example, acquired existing companies in Canada and USA, have developed through internal expansion in France and Belgium, undertook initially a joint venture in Spain, have used franchise type arrangements in Greece and initially in Hong Kong, entered Hungary with a joint venture before moving to a franchise type arrangement, and had a noncontrolling interest in the company which sold, for several years, St Michael products in Japan. The international expansion of Aldi (Table 2) illustrates a very different pattern with a dominant mode of internationalization, that of internal expansion. The pattern of expansion is, first one of internal expansion or small scale takeover into nearby and culturally similar countries, then with a major acquisition in a non-European market and finally, expansion across a broad front involving small acquisitions and single store openings. Forsgren (1989) suggests that in the early stages of internationalization a firm will use foreign acquisition as a preferred method and then will move towards foreign DFI so that there is "a negative correlation between a firm's degree of internationalization and its propensity to use foreign acquisition as a foreign direct investment" (p. 147). This would seem at odds with the experience of Aldi and of several other retailers who have crossed national borders in Europe, but may well fit with the record of transatlantic internationalization.

The second key dimension to classifying international operations is the extent to which managerial decision making is centralized at a head office in the home country or is delegated to host country operations. Rugman (1981) has argued, mainly in respect to vertical relationships, that the theory of internationalization, i.e. international retail operations in our present context, is also a theory of centralization in decision making. Such a view has to be questioned in the horizontal retail context. This centralization aspect of management is related partly to whether the retail operations are virtually the same from country to country (for example McDonalds, Toys R Us, Aldi, Virgin) or whether the shops reflect the regional and national society in which they operate (for example Dixons' operation of Silo in the USA, Carrefour's individual hypermarket operations in Spain, Argentina, Brazil, Portugal, Taiwan and USA). Salmon and Tordjman (1989) make this distinction, terming the retailer "global" if there is great similarity in operation from country to country and "multi-national" if there are

Table 2 International expansion of Aldi

Country	Year of first opening	Stores at end 1991	Sales bill. DM	Market share %
Germany	1948*	2400	22.5	12
Austria	1960	180	1.9	8.5
Holland	1975	265	1.4	5
USA	1975	225		
Belgium	1976	255	1.8	9
Denmark	1977	144	0.7	3
France	1988	35		
UK	1989	37		
Spain	Aldi logo used by IFA – Espanol			
Italy		15		
Poland		1		

*First store in former East Germany opened in September 1990.

explicit national differences. There exists in reality a continuum between the extremes of one global identity and a locally tailored identity, but any of the five mechanisms of establishment shown in Table 1 may be applied at the global or the multinational sections of this continuum. The Virgin operation within mainland Europe, for example, is controlled by three offices, one in Paris for French speaking Europe, one in Frankfurt, and a third in Madrid. Each has its own marketing and finance directors and have considerable influence over local marketing policy. There is, however, central control over the concepts of Virgin Megastore and satellite store formats and importantly over marketing strategy.

There is a third form to the organization of international retail operations which is typified by organizations such as Jardine Matheson, Aeon, Ahold, GIB, Vendex and Delhaize le Lion. In these cases there is a corporate structure comprising several operational divisions each of which has considerable autonomy but which in some cases are themselves operating internationally. The group becomes a holding company in these cases, and may, as with Jardine Matheson, have a range of non-retail interests in a conglomerate style organization. The activities of this type of organization fits uncomfortably in the global-multinational continuum concept.

There are an additional two variables which usually are important in classifying retail operations. These are the market position of the retail offer, for example whether a discount store, premium brand store, mass mail order, etc. and the format of retailing, for example whether hypermarket, brand concession in a store, convenience store, lifestyle boutique, mail order, etc. It might be hypothesized that these two variables will affect both the mechanism of international establishment and the position on the global-multinational axis. Perhaps a strong premium brand might lead to a global approach through internal expansion or tightly controlled franchising, possibly exemplified by Louis Vuitton (Laulajainen 1992), Body Shop or Dunhill (Gapps 1987); the large floorspace mass merchandise hypermarket might lead to a multinational approach with joint-ventures and possibly takeover as a favoured way to become established, exemplified by Promodès. But such hypotheses can be questioned by examples which run counter to the suggested relationships and, as pointed out above, a single firm may use several approaches to gaining an international presence. There is still need for substantial research to relate market position and format type to the different forms of international presence (Robinson and Clarke-Hill 1990). The relationships, if they exist at all, are far from clear.

The Extent and Directions of International Operations

Comprehensive information on the extent of the international operation of retailers is not available but data collected by Corporate Intelligence Group (1990, 1992) and a data base for food retailing in Europe compiled by Burt (1991) provide an indication, and conclusions on recent trends, at least for European retailers, can be drawn.

The data from Corporate Intelligence Group are concentrated on international activities of retailers who are headquartered in an EEC country and of retailers from outside EEC which have established an activity in the EEC. Partial information is provided on the non-European international activity of these two groups of firms. The data include activities made from before 1970 until 1991. The database is not complete and excludes many activities made within this 20-year period but which proved unsuccessful and the firm exited the foreign market. Nonetheless, despite problems with completeness, the data allow interesting conclusions to be drawn.

- A total of 2057 activities were recorded and ascribed to 459 firms. Of the 2057 activities, 1321 were within EEC countries and of these 1090 were undertaken by firms headquartered with the EEC.
- There was a notable increase during the second half of the 1980s in the number of international actions by the 459 retailers. This trend continued into the 1990s with 450 actions recorded after 1990 compared with 371 between 1985 and 1989. Difficulties of tracing the early moves may account in part for these figures but this is only a partial explanation.
- Retailers from France, Germany and UK account for almost 70% of the EEC based firms involved in international actions. These firms account for almost three quarters of the international actions recorded within the EEC.
- Internationalization is more common amongst non-food retailers than food retailers. Of the 1321 activities recorded with the EEC countries, 869 were in non-foods and 286 in foods. The relative low level of international activity of food retailers was also noted by Waldman (1978).

The difference between food and non-food sectors is partly but not wholly accounted for by there being more non-food retailers. Another reason may be that food, more than fashion, has a strong local cultural aspect to consumer choice which limits opportunities for scale economies in buying to be achieved through international operations. Jefferys (1973), also noting the difference, points to the priority of food retailers, particularly in the 1960s, being the development and exploitation of the new methods and techniques in food retailing associated with supermarkets and this gave them little time to consider international expansion. Reasons for the relative success of non-food retailers in internationalizing in Europe are:

- many of the non-food formats are small and require limited capital and managerial cost for their establishment;
- entry and exit are easier with small formats;
- formats often target small consumer segments which limits expansion in domestic markets;
- single brand stores give a unique competitive advantage to the format (Williams 1992) which is suitable for international transfer;
- non-food formats are more suited to franchising;
- there are strong economies of replication which can be transferred to the host country;
- the cachet of a foreign retailer is easier to stimulate in non-food than in food retailing.

Burt (1991) confirms several of the general trends more specifically for food retailing indicating a similar increase in activity from the late 1980s and the proportional dominance of retailers based in France, Germany and the UK. He also indicates that whilst British retailers have favoured moves to other English speaking countries, notably Ireland and USA (Burt and Dawson 1989), French retailers have favoured Spain and USA whilst German retailers have concentrated on Austria and USA. A quarter of the 230 actions studied, irrespective of home country within Europe, involved moves to USA. Wrigley (1989) and Hallsworth (1990) consider some of the attractions of the USA from a European viewpoint whilst Siegle and Handy (1981) viewed the early moves from an American perspective. The attraction of cultural closeness at least for the initial international moves of a retailer, are also indicated as important for Swedish retailers (Martenson 1981; Laulajainen 1991b) and can be seen also in the substantial number of moves, in both directions, between Canada and USA, of firms such as Dylex, Silcorp, Battery One-Stop, TJX Companies, Sherwin-Williams, Pier 1 Imports and many others.

Burt, using the data on European food retailers, suggests differences in preferred mechanisms with French food retailers tending to favour joint-ventures, minority interests and more co-operative approaches whilst British firms have favoured acquisition. Within the food sector most retailers (64% of the 67 companies considered) have been involved in only one or two international actions. Decisions to open stores in another country are not taken lightly (Jackson 1973) and a gradualist approach to international expansion is usually taken.

Conclusion

There is an inexorability about the increase in international activity apparent in retailing. Of the largest 25 retailers in Europe ranked by sales (Management Horizons 1992) only four are not involved in operating stores in more than one country either directly or with joint ventures. Even these four are involved in other forms of international marketing alliance. The internationalization process having been set in motion seems to quicken its pace of operation. In 1989 nine of the largest 25 retailers in Europe were operating exclusively nationally. International operations whilst still only undertaken by a small minority of all retail firms are increasingly common activities within the large firms. There are, however, a large number of small firms which are now part of large international alliance-based networks of retailers.

A substantial amount of empirical descriptive research already exists on the internationalization process in retailing but it is still not clearly understood. The process, for many reasons, is substantially different from the internationalization process in manufacturing firms. Whilst some concepts may be borrowed from the literature on industrial internationalization, for example the four component framework developed by Gannon (1993) may be of use, it is unlikely to be directly applicable to the retail sector. The structures of the sectors are different, the processes of evolution differ, and there are differences in the behaviours of the various participants in the process. Internationalization of retail operations is at a relatively early stage compared with other aspects of internationalization, such as international sourcing and also in comparison with the manufacturing sector.

Within the retail sector key features of the internationalization process are the need for the adaption of management practices and processes in response to the cultural character of the host country. For some retailers this adaptation has proved to be particularly difficult even in moves to apparently culturally similar environments. A second key aspect of retail internationalization is the important role played by individual entrepreneurs who are able to take an international perspective. A third conclusion to be drawn from the research base is that retailers are often unaware of the impact on and value for the firm of the process of internationalization. As an area of research in marketing the internationalization of retail operations holds great promise for theoretical advance and for explanatory empirical study, with opportunities to link studies of retail internationalization with broader study of the internationalization of the firm. The dynamism of the European environment for retailers makes Europe a particularly suitable laboratory for such studies in the 1990s.

References

Aharoni, Y. (1966), *The Foreign Investment Decision Process*, Boston, Harvard University Press.

Alexander, N. (1990), "Retailers and International Markets: Motives for Expansion", *International Marketing Review*, **7**, No. 4, pp. 75–85.

Barwise, P. (1993), "Brand Equity: Snark or Boojum?", *International Journal of Research in Marketing*, **10**, No. 1, pp, 93–104.

Buckley, P. J. (1983), "New Theories of International Business". In: *The Growth of International Business*, (Ed.) Casson, M. (London), Allen and Unwin.

Burt, S. L. (1989), "Trends and Management Issues in European Retailing", *International Journal of Retailing*, **4**, No. 4, pp. 3–97.

Burt, S. L. (1991), "Trends in the Internationalization of Grocery Retailing: The European Experience", *International Review of Retail Distribution and Consumer Research*, **1**, No. 4, pp. 487–515.

Burt, S. L. (1993), "Temporal Trends in the Internationalization of British Retailing". Paper to ESRC Seminar: International Issues in Retailing. Manchester.

Burt, S. L. and Dawson, J. A. (1989), "L'internazionalizzazione del commercio al dettaglio Inglese, *Commercio*, **35**, pp. 137–157.

Carson, D. (1967), *International Marketing*, New York, Wiley.

Casson, M. (1987), *The Firm and the Market*, Oxford, Blackwell.

Clarke-Hill, C. M. and Robinson, T. M. (1992) "Co-operation as a Competitive Strategy in European Retailing", *European Business and Economic Development*, **1**, No. 2, pp. 1–6.

Corporate Intelligence Group (1990), *International Retailers in Europe*, Oxford, Oxford Institute of Retail Management.

Corporate Intelligence Group (1992), *Cross-border Retailing in Europe*, London, Corporate Intelligence Group.

Dawson, J. A. (1978), "International Retailers", *Geographical Magazine*, **51**, No. 3, pp. 248–249.

Dawson, J. A. (1991), *Le Commerce de Détail Europeen*, Paris, Presses du Management.

Dawson, J. A. (1993), "The Internationalization of Retailing". In: *Retail Change: Contemporary Issues*, (Eds) Bromley, R. D. F. and Thomas, C. J. (London), UCL Press.

Distributive Trades EDC (1973), *The Distributive Trades in the Common Market*, London, HMSO.

Dunning, J. H. (1981), *International Production and the Multinational Enterprise*, London, Allen and Unwin.

Dunning, J. H. (1988), "The Eclectic Paradigm of International Production: A Re-statement and Some Possible Extensions", *Journal of International Business Studies*, **19**, pp. 1–31.

Dunning, J. H. (1993), *Multinational Enterprises and the Global Economy*, Wokingham, Addison-Wesley.

Dunning, J. H. and Norman, G. (1985), "Intra-industry Production as a Form of International Economic Involvement: An Exploratory Analysis. In: *Multinationals as Mutual Invaders: Intra-industry Direct Foreign Investment*, (Ed.) Erdilek, A. (London), Croom Helm.

Edvardsson, B., Edvinsson, L. and Nystrom, H. (1992), "Internationalization in Service Companies", *Service Industries Journal*, **13**, No. 1, pp. 80–97.

Eroglu, S. (1992), "The Internationalization Process of Franchise Systems: A Conceptual Model", *International Marketing Review*, **9**, No. 5, pp. 19–30.

European Commission (1991), "Towards a Single Market in Distribution", *Communication of European Commission*, COM91 41.

Filser, M. (1990), "L'enjeu Strategique du Marche Unique pour less Firmes de Distribution", Universite de Bourgogne, CREGO, Working Paper, 9005.

Forsgren, M. (1989), "Foreign Acquisitions: Internalization or Network Interdependency", *Advances in International Marketing*, **3**, pp. 141–159.

Fritsch, W. R. (1962), *Progress and Profits: The Sears, Roebuck story in Peru*, Washington DC, Action Committee for International Development.

Gannon, M. (1993), "Towards a Composite Theory of Foreign Market Entry Mode Choice: The Role of Marketing Strategy Variables", *Journal of Strategic Marketing*, **1**, No. 1, pp. 41–54.

Gapps, S. (1987), "Global Marketing. Management Horizons", *Retail Focus*, Summer, pp. 3–78.

Goldman, A. (1974a), "Growth of Large Food Stores in Developing Countries", *Journal of Retailing*, **50**, No. 2, pp. 139–189.

Goldman, A. (1974b), "Outreach of Consumers and the Modernization of Urban Food Retailing in Developing Countries", *Journal of Marketing*, **38**, No. 4, pp. 8–16.

Hakansson, H. (Ed.) (1982), *International Marketing and the Purchasing of Industrial Goods*, Winchester, Wiley.

Hallsworth, A. G. (1990), "The Lure of the USA: Some Further Reflections", *Environment and Planning*, A22, pp. 551–8.

Hamill, J. and Crosbie, J. (1990), "British Retail Acquisitions in the US", *International Journal of Retail and Distribution Management*, **18**, No. 2, pp. 15–20.

Hennart, J-F. (1991), "The Transaction Cost Theory of the Multinational Enterprise". In: *The Nature of the Transnational Firm*, (Eds) Pitelis, C. N. and Sugden, R. (London), Routledge.

Hollander, S. C. (1970), *Multinational Retailing*, East Lansing, Michigan State University Press.

Jackson, G. I. (1973), "Planning the Move to the Continent: Questions that must be Asked", *Retail and Distribution Management*, **1**, No. 6, pp. 14–16.

Jefferys, J. (1973), "Multinational Retailing: Are the Food Chains Different", *CIES Quarterly Review*, **8**, No. 3.

Johanson, J. and Mattsson, L.-G. (1988), "Internationalization in Industrial Systems: A Network Approach. In: *Strategies in Global Competition*, (Eds) Hood, N. and Vahine, J.-E. (London), Routledge.

Johanson, J. and Mattsson, L.-G. (1991), "Strategic Adaption of Firms to the European Single Market. In: *Corporate and Industry Strategies for Europe*, (Eds) Mattsson, L.-G. and Stymne, B. (Amsterdam), North Holland.

Kacker, M. P. (1985), *Transatlantic Trends in Retailing*, Westport, Greenwood.

Kacker, M. P. (1990), "The lure of US retailing to the foreign acquirer". *Mergers and Acquisitions*, **25**, No. 1, pp. 63–68.

Kay, N. M. (1991), "Multinational Enterprise as Strategic Choice: Some Transaction Cost Perspectives". In: *The Nature of the Transnational Firm*, (Eds) Pitelis, C. N. and Sugden, R. (London), Routledge.

Knee, D. (1966), "Trends Towards International Operations Among Large-scale Retailing Enterprises", *Rivista Italiana di Amministrazione*, **2**, pp. 107–11.

Kojima, K. (1982), "Macroeconomic Versus International Business Approaches to Foreign Direct Investment", *Hitotsubashi Journal of Economics*, **23**, pp. 1–19.

Laulajainen, R. (1987), *Spatial Strategies in Retailing*, Dordecht, Reidel.

Laulajainen, R. (1991a), "International expansion of an apparel retailer: Hennes and Mauritz of Sweden", *Zeitschrift fur Wirtschaftsgeographie*, **35**, No. 1, pp. 1–15.

Laulajainen, R. (1991b), "Two retailers go global: The geographical dimension", *International Review of Retail Distribution and Consumer Research*, **1**, No. 5, pp. 607–626.

Laulajainen, R. (1992), "Louis Vuitton Malletier: A truly global retailer". *Annals of the Japan Association of Economic Geographers*, **38**, No. 2, pp. 55–70.

Leontiades, J. C. (1985), *Multinational Corporate Strategy*, Lexington, Lexington Books.

Management Horizons (1992), *Europe's Leading Retailers*, London, Management Horizons.

Martenson, R. (1981), *Innovation in Multinational Retailing*, Gothenburg, University of Gothenburg.

Martenson, R. (1987), "Culture Bound Industries? A European Case Study", *International Marketing Review*, **4**, No. 3, pp. 7–17.

Martenson, R. (1988), "Cross-cultural Similarities and Differences in Multinational Retailing. In: *Transnational Retailing*, (Ed.) Kaynak, E. (Berlin), Walter de Gruyter.

Mathias, P. (1967), *Retailing Revolution*, London, Longman.

Pellegrini, L. (1992), "The Internationalization of Retailing and 1992 Europe", *Journal of Marketing Channels*, **1**, No. 2, pp. 3–27.

Robinson, T. M. and Clarke-Hill, C. M. (1990), "Directional Growth by European Retailers", *International Journal of Retail and Distribution Management*, **18**, No. 5, pp. 3–14.

Rugman, A. M. (1981), *Inside the Multinational: The Economics of Internal Markets*, London, Croom Helm.

Salmon, W. J. and Tordjman, A. (1989), "The internationalisation of retailing". *International Journal of Retailing*, **4**, No. 2, pp. 3–16.

Siegle, N. and Handy, C. R. (1981), "Foreign Ownership in Food Retailing", *National Food Review*, Winter, pp. 14–16.

Tordjman, A. and Dionisio, J. (1991), "Internationalization Strategies of Retail Business",

Commission of the European Communities, DG XXIII, Series Studies, Commerce and Distribution, 15.

Treadgold, A. (1990), *The Costs of Retailing in Continental Europe*, London and Oxford, Longman/Oxford Institute of Retail Management.

Treadgold, A. (1991), "The Emerging Internationalization of Retailing: Present Status and Future Challenges", *Irish Marketing Review*, **5**, No. 2, pp. 11–27.

Treadgold, A. and Davies, R. L. (1988), *The Internationalization of Retailing*, London and Oxford, Longman/Oxford Institute of Retail Management.

Truitt, N. S. (1984), "Mass Merchandising and Economic Development: Sears Roebuck & Co. in Mexico and Peru". In: *Service Industries and Economic Development*, (Eds) Shelp, S. *et al.* (New York), Praeger.

Waldman, C. (1978), *Strategies of International Mass Retailers*, New York, Praeger.

Welch, L. S. and Luostarinen, R. (1988), "Internationalization: Evolution of a Concept", *Journal of General Management*, **14**, No. 2, pp. 35–55.

Whitehead, M. (1992), "Internationalization of Retailing: Developing New Perspectives", *European Journal of Marketing*, **26**, Nos 8/9, pp. 74–79.

Wilkins, M. (1974), *The Maturing of Multinational Enterprise*, Boston, Harvard University Press.

Williams, D. E. (1992), "Retailer Internationalization: An Empirical Inquiry", *European Journal of Marketing*, **26**, Nos 8/9, pp. 8–24.

Wood, R. and Keyser, V. (1953), *United States Business Performance Abroad: The Case Study of Sears, Roebuck de Mexico, S.A.*, Washington DC, National Planning Association.

Wrigley, N. (1989), "The Lure of the USA: Further Reflections on the Internationalization of British Grocery Retailing Capital", *Environment and Planning*, **A21**, pp. 283–288.

Yoshino, M. Y. (1966), "International Opportunities for American Retailers", *Journal of Retailing*, Fall, pp. 1–10.

Editors' Commentary

ARIEH GOLDMAN HAS BEEN the Chairman of the Marketing Department in the Hebrew University in Jerusalem and Director of the Jerusalem School of Business Administration, where he holds the Kmart Chair in Retailing and International Marketing. Most recently he has been on sabbatical leave at the University of Surrey, following previous visiting positions at several US universities and also in Hong Kong and Shanghai (CEIBS). His PhD (entitled 'Dramatic Changes in Retail Systems') is from the University of Berkeley in California and stimulated an early interest in the development of large food stores in developing countries. This has been a life-long focus of his research, although Arieh Goldman has also pursued other interests in his research career, including pricing, income and behaviour, consumer tastes and consumer outreach. From broad studies of change in retailing systems, by the 1990s his interests in Asian countries directed his research towards more detailed and systematic studies of retail format development in China and Japan.

As well as being a significant author in his own right, Arieh Goldman is also on the editorial boards of several leading retail and marketing journals, including the

International Review of Retail, Distribution and Consumer Research and the *Journal of Retailing.*

Arieh Goldman has published several papers on Chinese retailing, of which the selected paper is just one. Strategic positioning of emerging and transferred formats is a topic on which he has a wealth of research expertise. 'The Transfer of Retail Formats into Developing Economies: The Example of China' is concerned specifically with the transfer of formats as part of the internationalization process and the development of retailers' global strategies. As retailers seek to expand their operations internationally, not only to countries with similar development levels and similar economic and political systems but also to developing countries, they face new challenges in deciding on appropriate formats. The paper resulted from an in-depth research project over several years, based in CEIBS, Shanghai, that involved a substantial programme of extended interviews with managers in twenty-seven firms.

The paper considers adaption in the supermarket format in an environment, China, which, for some of the retailers in his survey, is very different from the home environment of the retailers concerned. One of the important aspects of the paper is the inclusion of both European and Asian retailers in his study of how they have adapted their operations to the Chinese market. Arieh Goldman distinguishes between the adaptions that were made on an ad hoc reactionary basis and those that were planned with adaption being a continuing process. The paper is important in the way it focuses on the format as the creation of the retailer and the need to adjust this in response to factors both external and internal to the firm.

Key Publications

Goldman A (1974) Outreach of consumers and the modernization of urban food retailing in developing countries. *Journal of Marketing,* 39, 8–16.

Goldman A (1974) Growth of large food stores in developing countries. *Journal of Retailing,* 50(2), 50–60.

Goldman A (1981) The transfer of retailing technology into the less developed countries: the case of the supermarket. *Journal of Retailing,* 57(2) 5–29.

Goldman A (1982) Adoption of supermarket shopping in a developing country: a selective adoption phenomenon. *European Journal of Marketing,* 16, 17–26.

Goldman A (1991) Japan's distribution system: institutional structure, internal political economy and modernization. *Journal of Retailing,* 67, 154–181.

Goldman A (1992) Evaluating the performance of the Japanese distribution system. *Journal of Retailing,* 68, 11–39.

Goldman A and Qin Zaho (1998) Intermediate supermarkets in China: origins, evolution and prospects. *Journal of Marketing Channels,* 6(3/4), 87–108.

Goldman A, Krider R and Ramaswami S (1999) The persistent competitive advantage of traditional food retailers in Asia: wet markets' continued dominance in Hong Kong. *Journal of Macromarketing,* 19(2), 126–140.

Goldman A (2000) Supermarkets in China: the case of Shanghai. *International Review of Retail Distribution and Consumer Research,* 10, 1–23

Goldman A, Ramaswami S and Krider R (2002) Barriers to the advancement of modern food retail formats: theory and measurement. *Journal of Retailing*, 78, 281–295.

Website

http://bschool.huji.ac.il/facultye/goldman/academic.html

THE TRANSFER OF RETAIL FORMATS INTO DEVELOPING ECONOMIES: THE EXAMPLE OF CHINA

Arieh Goldman

The focus of this research is the strategy of international format transfer by retailers into developing countries. Transfer strategies are defined in terms of a format change pattern and the factors motivating the format change decision. Earlier studies and anecdotal evidence have indicated that retailers have pursued different format transfer policies. Some retailers transfer their total format unchanged while others introduce extensive changes. The research intent is to ascertain the set of determinants that control the extent of change to be employed. As basis for this evaluation, I interviewed executives from twenty-seven different foreign retailers with respect to their entrance into Chinese home market. These retailers emanated from a variety of other countries and operated a range different retail formats such as supermarkets, hypermarkets, specialty stores, department stores, wholesale-clubs and shopping centers in China. The analysis of these data revealed the existence of six distinct transfer strategies. Basic conditions affecting the extent of transfer change were found to relate to differences in economic conditions between China and the home countries and the market segments that were targeted in China.

Introduction

WITH THE PROCESS OF retail internationalization gaining momentum, retailing is fast becoming a global industry. Indeed, many of the world's prominent retailers already derive a significant proportion of their sales from

---

Journal of Retailing, Vol. 77 (2001) pp. 221–242.
The research was supported by the Kmart Center for International Retailing and Marketing, by the Davidson Agribusiness Center (Hebrew University) and by CEIBS (Shanghai). The author thanks the editor, L. P. Bucklin, for his commitment and many helpful comments.

international operations (Kuipers, 1999). Early internationalization activities largely involved moves among developed economies. As of the new millennium, however, this pattern is changing as a growing number of international retailers shift their attention to developing economies (Barth *et al.*, 1996; Hentzepeter, 1999; Reuling, 1998; Stores, 1998). They are driven by the opportunities in these countries, such as high growth rates, growing middle-class, weakness of local retailers, and the maturation of retailing in the developed economies.

Central to the success of these international transfers is the retailer's capabilities and format transfer strategy. Retail formats identify the central elements defining a retailer's strategy. Thus, format strategy is often the key to an international retailer's ability to gain a strong competitive position in host countries.

The number of format transfer possibilities is large. The retailer must determine whether to transfer its format unchanged or modify it and whether any change should be extensive or limited. The wrong choice may lead to serious negative consequences. The failure to adapt when the host and home countries are highly dissimilar, for example, may lead to a waste of resources, the squandering of opportunities and an increased potential for failure. Yet, format modifications may entail significant costs, operating risks and difficulties, and the loss of key strengths embedded in the original home format.

The failure of international expansion plans is often format related. Examples at the time of this research include Kmart's withdrawal from the Czech Republic, Slovakia and Singapore. This was largely caused by its failure to adapt its North American discount department store format to the conditions in these countries. Ahold and Park and Shop left China and Park and Shop left Taiwan upon concluding that their conventional supermarket format was not viable there. Carrefour recently announced that it was leaving Hong Kong because the territory could support only few of its large hypermarkets.

Despite the importance of the format decision, we still lack a systematic analysis of the format transfer question. The literature has identified only two format transfer patterns: *as is* transfers and an *adaptation* option. The latter lumps together all other transfer possibilities. Furthermore, format transfers have been identified as driven by only two forces, the motivation to leverage advantages from global operations and the need to adapt to local conditions.

In this study of twenty-seven foreign retail companies operating in China, executives involved in the entry decisions were interviewed in depth about their format transfers to this country. My goal was to gain an understanding sufficient to improve transfer decisions and reduce risks and costs. Hopefully, this research may also serve as a base for future research into questions such as the role formats play in a retailer's global strategy and the impact of format transfers on a retailer's operations in host countries.

I first review the main issues associated with the transfer of retail formats into developing countries. This review served as the basis for developing the list of issues discussed with the interviewees. I then employ an inductive (grounded) study. Instead of formulating hypotheses for testing, this approach emphasizes the derivation of concepts and theory from qualitative, case based, research. Findings are then discussed and I conclude with a discussion of the results and point to directions for future research.

Issues Underlying Retail Format Transfers

The concept of a retail format

The retail format, the entity being transferred, is discussed in the retailing literature in a variety of contexts: the history of retailing and the evolution of retail formats (Bucklin, 1972; Betancourt & Gautschi, 1990; Messinger & Narasimhan, 1997), retail management (Ghosh, 1990; Mason & Mayer, 1987), and the transfer of retail technologies and formats (Hollander, 1970; Goldman, 1981; Kacker, 1985, 1988).

A distinction is often drawn between the *offering* and the *know-how* parts of the format. The first includes the *external* elements (e.g., assortment, shopping-environment, service, location and price) delivering the functional, social, psychological, esthetic and entertainment benefits attracting consumers to stores. The second, the *internal* part, determines a retailer's operational strength and strategic direction. It consists of the *retail technology* dimension containing the systems, methods, procedures and techniques the retail company uses and of the *retail culture,* that includes the repertoire of concepts, norms, rules, practices and experiences. This dimension enhances retailer's ability to evaluate situations, identify trends and opportunities, and deal with problems. Whereas the external elements are visible to consumers, many of the know-how ones are tacit (Inkpen & Dinur, 1998; Nonaka, 1994).

The role of retail formats

The retail format identifies a retailer's capabilities and serves as the unifying component of the competitive plan. The specification of retail service-output levels, operational efficiencies embodied in the retail technology, and the learning and experiences contained in the retail culture, determine the position the retailer secures in the market place.

This view of the format is grounded in the retail internationalization literature (Akerhurst & Alexander, 1996; Dawson, 1994; Kacker, 1988; Pellegrini, 1991; Sternquist, 1998). For example, the *ownership* factor (Dunning, 1988), a key advantage a retail company moving internationally might enjoy (Dawson, 1994; Pellegrini, 1991) is based on innovative outputs, price, business concepts, methods, technologies and experiences embedded in both parts of the format.

The literature assumes transfers are driven only by the goal of gaining a competitive advantage in the targeted host country. This ignores the possibility of transfer decisions being guided by additional, more global, goals going beyond the retailer's position in the targeted host country.

Format transfer options

The number of format transfer possibilities is large. Retailers must decide whether to transfer each format element unchanged or alter it in some way. If change is to occur, the executives need to decide which elements will be affected and the magnitudes.

The literature (Akerhurst & Alexander, 1996; Hollander, 1970; Kacker, 1985, 1988; Rosenblum et al. 1997; Salmon & Tordjman 1989; Segal-Horn & Davidson, 1992), however, paints a simplified picture of format transfers. It discusses only two format transfer possibilities: *as is* and *adaptation*. The first is viewed as a largely special case limited to retailers catering to global segments. All other transfer options are bundled into the *adaptation* transfer pattern. While no explicit discussion of various adaptation possibilities is provided, the tendency is to view transfers, especially into developing countries, as involving a large degree of adaptation.

Format change determinants

Changing a format involves costs, difficulties and risks. It often requires the expenditure of resources and may be associated with diminished effectiveness, damage to the retailer's global standing and the forfeit of scale and standardization advantages. On the other hand, benefits may be too gained from adapting the format to the new environment.

As is transfers carry with them costs, difficulties and risks. Format elements may be costly to transfer, not relevant or lose effectiveness in the new environment. These negative consequences need to be evaluated against the potential benefits to the retailer from keeping the format intact. These considerations are influenced by the conditions in the host country, compatibility between host and home countries, the retailer's global strategy, and the type of the retail firm.

This cost-benefit framework was developed by retail modernization researchers who viewed the transfer of modern retail formats into developing countries as a major tool for economic modernization (Food and Agricultural Organization, 1973a, 1973b; Findlay et al. 1990; Goldman, 1981; Harrison, 1974; Slater & Riley, 1969; Samiee, 1993; Savitt, 1988). It also underlies more recent studies of retail internationalization (Dawson, 1994; Kacker, 1988; McGoldrick & Davies, 1995).

Host country conditions. These may constrain retailers' ability to realize the capabilities embedded in the format. They may also create opportunities for retailers to leverage format advantages.

Studies of the transfer of retail formats into developing countries emphasize the difficulties modern retail formats face there. These studies identified consumers, supply and distribution conditions, government policies, and the domestic retail system as limiting "as is" transfers of elements such as assortment, service, location and price. In addition, technologies and methods geared to the developed home market conditions were found to be inappropriate in developing countries.

Home country's level of development. This factor affects the level of compatibility between host and home countries. Retailers transferring formats into developing economies from developed countries positioned lower on the development ladder can be expected to face fewer transfer difficulties than retailers transferring retail formats from highly developed home markets.

Retailer's global position. The advantages generated from global operations, and the limitations on their utilization in host countries were extensively discussed in the internationalization literature (Craig & Douglas, 2000; Douglas & Craig, 1995; Prahalad & Doz, 1987).

These include (1) *Scale Economies and Standardization* advantages derived through global sourcing of products and equipment, standardization of operations, elimination of duplications and the global use of specialized skills. (2) *Experience and Learning* advantages generated through operation in diverse environments and dealing with a large variety of problems, challenges and opportunities. (3) *Global flexibility* advantages enabling retailers to move resources, expertise, innovative concepts and methods across markets. (4) *Specialization* advantages enjoyed by retailers serving global segments or particular need-sets.

The international retailing literature tends to emphasize the importance of the more tangible, economic advantages (scale and standardization) largely ignoring the others.

Study Methods

Research approach

A qualitative study focusing on foreign retailers' entrance into China was conducted during 1996, and 1997. The research, based on the Grounded Theory principles, studied a sample of foreign retailers operating in China.

The Grounded Theory (Glaser & Strauss, 1967; Glaser, 1978; Strauss & Corbin, 1990) emphasizes the process of theory development through continued interaction between data collection and concepts. Analysis of data from case studies leads to the formulation of tentative concepts and variables. The process continues throughout the study. As new cases were added, the data were reanalyzed and concepts refined. Recent examples of the use of this approach in marketing include Manning *et al.* (1998) and Reid (1999).

Sample

No reliable list of foreign retailers in China exists nor is there agreement among experts regarding their numbers. The myriad entry arrangements contribute to the confusion; only few foreign retailers received a central government license (Asia Pulse, 1998, 2000), most acquire a city or a district license. Consequently, a retailer often operates with different joint-venture partners, using different licenses and names in each city or even in the same city. In addition, some retailers avoid the need for a foreign retail permit by using local retailers', manufacturers', or real-estate companies' licenses. Similarly, many luxury retailers operate counters in department stores. The large number of little-known retailers from other parts of Asia adds to the difficulties.[1]

Given this situation, the following sampling method was used. A systematic review of published data in Chinese and English about the operation of foreign retailers in China was conducted. It included newspapers, business publications, research and consulting reports and official publications. The list was augmented with the help of informants: foreign and Chinese retail executives, consultants and government officials. We continued to update the list as the study proceeded (Waldorf & Biernacki, 1981).

These sources yielded ninety-eight names of international retailers. These retailers were contacted and, after explaining the study's goals and procedures, twenty-seven agreed to cooperate.

The sample included retailers from home countries at different levels of development, operating a variety of formats. The retailers also differed in their size, resources and their international experience. Table 1 profiles the retail

Table 1 Profile of the retailers studied (N = 27)

Retail category	Retail company's original home country	Time since entry (years)	International operations	
			Countries	Regions
Luxury specialist	Italy	3	Many	Many
Luxury specialist	Italy	3	Many	Many
Luxury specialist	UK	2	Many	Many
Supermarket	Japan	2	None	—
Shopping center	Japan	1	Few	Only Asia
Clothing specialist	Hong Kong	2	Few	Only Asia
Department store	Hong Kong	2	None	—
Shopping center	Taiwan	2	None	—
Shopping center	Hong Kong	2	None	—
Supermarket	Hong Kong	4	Many	Only Asia
Department store	France	1	Many	Asia, Europe
Clothing specialist	Hong Kong	3	Few	Only Asia
Clothing specialist	Hong Kong	3	Few	Only Asia
Clothing specialist	Hong Kong	3	Few	Only Asia
Supermarket	Holland	1	Many	Many
Hypermarket	France	1	Many	Many
Wholesale club	Singapore	3	None	—
Department store	Japan	2	Many	Many
Department store	Japan	3	Many	Many
Department store	Japan	2	Many	Many
G.M.S.	Japan	2	Many	Many
Wholesale club	U.S.	1	Many	Many
Department store—GMS	Thailand	1	None	—
Department store	Malaysia	4	None	—
Supermarket	Hong Kong	2	Few	Only Asia
Department store	Hong Kong	3	Few	Only Asia
Department store	Hong Kong	3	Few	Only Asia

companies studied in terms of their category classification, home country, time since entry, and international operations outside China.

Interviewing

Face-to-face interviews were conducted with senior executives of these companies. In fifteen of the cases, a number of executives (2–4) were interviewed and in twelve, one. In all twenty-seven cases at least one of the interviewees was directly involved with the entry into China and the format transfer decisions. Out of a total of fifty-seven executives interviewed, forty-nine had taken an active part in the planning and/or implementation of the transfer.

The author conducted all interviews. Translators were used in cases of executives who preferred to be interviewed in their own language of either Japanese or Chinese.

The executives were asked to reconstruct the transfer decision process (chronology, key decisions, background studies, etc.), describe how the transferred format differed from the home format, identify the considerations underlying the format transfer and discuss their influence on the transfer decisions. They also provided information about the actual entry, postentry format changes and the reasons.

Information was also collected about the profile of the retail firms: the firm's size, sales, history, product lines, strategies, positioning in China and in other countries, and how it organized its global operations. The interviews were guided by the literature-based list of issues.

The interviews were nondirective (McCracken, 1988). The executives were encouraged to freely discuss their experiences and evaluations. This method, inherent to the Grounded Theory, has been found appropriate in China (Adler et al., 1989). Interviews lasted three to four hours and all were taped.

Examples of format transfers into other countries were frequently used to illustrate various aspects of the transfer process. It was strongly emphasized, however, that the examples were indicative and that the executives should focus on what happened in their own case.

Also, respondents were often asked to summarize discussions of an issue by making formal, overall judgments. For example, in the case of the number of format elements changed (modified or dropped), executives were presented with a benchmark list of typical elements included in the offering and know-how components. They discussed the changes made in detail and then summarized the discussion using a five-point scale (none, very few, few, many, very many). Similarly, compatibility levels were evaluated using a three-point scale.

Follow-up interviews were undertaken in twenty-two of the cases after an initial analysis of data. Their aim was to clarify issues, collect supplementary information and receive feedback regarding tentative conclusions. In six of these companies executives identified as intimately connected with the transfer decisions, but residing outside China were contacted, and interviewed by telephone.

Finally, background information about the relevant environmental conditions in China was also collected. To learn about the supply and distribution arrangements, executives from manufacturing companies (Chinese and joint ventures) and wholesalers were interviewed. To learn about the regulatory environment, government's influence and infrastructure conditions, government officials supervising the retailing and distribution areas and research officers in distribution research institutes were interviewed. Trained Chinese research assistants were used as translators in these interviews.

Analysis

The interview tapes were transcribed and analyzed. The analysis was based on detailed instructions and definitions. These were continuously refined as the process of identifying the format change patterns, the factors driving the transfer and classifying the retail companies continued. The data were reanalyzed a number of times. Tentative conclusions were derived, discussed by interview team members, and, when possible, also with executives of the retail companies.

The analysis consisted of a number of steps. The interview team first classified the retailers into groups based on the number of format elements changed. We then identified the forces driving the format change decisions and classified them based on insights gained during the literature review and during the interviews. We then sorted the retailers in each format change group on the basis of these drivers. We continued sorting until homogeneous subgroups emerged, that is retailers in each subgroup were motivated by the same specific decision driver. Cases of disagreement were resolved by further discussion and the collection of additional data.

Findings

Format change patterns

Four format change patterns were identified: cases where all format elements were transferred *unchanged,* cases involving changes in *very few* elements, in a *few* elements, and lastly, where *very many* were changed. We found no cases where *many* elements were changed. This may be a sampling issue or a perceptual one as the executives seemed to have difficulties differentiating between *many* and *very many* format changes.[2]

Executive summary judgments were used to classify a retailer into one of these four categories. These determinations were made after a detailed discussion of the specific format changes made. The number of changes identified by the executives ranged between thirty-four in the most extreme case to zero.

The profile of the retailers classified into each of the four format change groups is shown in Table 2. With the exception of the no-change group, all others included retailers that differed on major characteristics such as formats, home countries and international experience.

Table 2 Format change pattern groups

Format change pattern[1]	Number of companies	Number of format changes (range)	Company examples	Formats	Number of countries outside China	Home country
No format change	3	0	Gucci Dunhill Escada	Luxury specialists	Many	Europe
Very limited ("very few")	10	3–5	Goldlion Crocodile Wings Ahold Carrefour	Clothing specialty, supermarket, hypermarket, department store, wholesale club	None, few, many	Asia Europe USA
Limited ("few")	6	4–9	Sogo Seibu Isetan Parkson	Department store, GMS	Few, many	Asia
Extensive "very many")	8	22–34	Pacific Orient Wellcome Printemps	Clothing specialty, Shopping center, Supermarket, Department store	None, few	Asia Europe

[1] The basis for classification is executive summary judgments.

Next I identify and discuss the drivers motivating format change decision of the retailers classified into each of the four format change pattern groups. I then characterize the nature of the transfer decision process followed.

Factors driving format transfers

The interviewees identified a variety of factors as influencing their format change decisions. We classified these factors into three general groups.

Host country conditions. These motivated retailers to avoid transferring *as is* elements that were expected to encounter difficulties, costs and problems as a result of incompatibilities between the home and host countries. On the other hand, they also motivated retailers to exploit opportunities. Expected *limitations* included consumer-side difficulties (purchasing power, preferences, mobility), supply-side problems (supplier reliability, product quality and availability), restrictive laws and regulations, undeveloped distribution, technological and legal infrastructures, government intervention, and lack of adequate retail sites. Expected *opportunities* included Chinese retailers' weakness, opportunities for new formats, pent-up demand, Chinese retailers eager to enter into joint venture agreements, suppliers' willingness to cooperate, government's support, political, economic and personal connections, and the potential for gaining pioneering advantages.

Retailers' global position. These considerations included opportunities to leverage global advantages, limitations on their use in China and the potential damage to global standing. The *opportunities* included economic advantages (global sourcing, use of advanced technologies, standardization), use of specialized knowledge and expertise, unique skills, financial resources, image, brands, and reputation, and experience in handling problems. The *limitations* included legal, political and economic barriers to importation, restrictive regulations, under-developed legal system and lack of infrastructures. Retailers were also motivated by concerns with potential *damages* to their global position as a result of pressures to lower standards in China.

Global strategy. Some retailers viewed the move into China in the context of the company's long-term global strategy. In these cases a company's behavior in China was influenced by the role the operation in China was expected to play in the implementation of the global strategy. These considerations, in turn, influenced the format change decisions.

Format transfer drivers: the four format change groups

Using the above classification of format change drivers, the interview team inspected the twenty-seven companies identifying the key motivations driving each company's transfer decisions. In many cases a single factor was found to totally dominate other considerations. Others were motivated by a combination of factors.

We then looked at the companies classified into each of the four format change groups, checking whether they were driven by the same factors. In two groups the same general driver motivated the retailers introducing the same format changes. In the other two variations existed justifying further divisions into subgroups.

Transfer drivers characterizing the "no-change" format group. The transfer decisions of the retailers making "as is" format transfers were driven by the motivation to ensure the operation in China would not damage their global standing. The members of this group were luxury specialists who targeted a well-defined "global" segment (Craig & Douglas, 2000; Salmon & Tordjman, 1989; Segal-Horn & Davidson, 1992) consisting of foreigners and upward mobile and affluent Chinese. Management realized the incompatibilities between the conditions in China and in their home markets, but resisted adaptation in the belief that even minor format changes could damage their brand, global image and unique offering.

To function in the sometimes-inhospitable Chinese environment, management developed an *enclave* policy, minimizing their dependence on Chinese resources and inputs. For example, retailers like Gucci, Escada and Dunhill imported *all* products and store features from abroad. Tariffs and import barriers increased costs and prevented exploiting advantages from global sourcing and standardization. Consequently, this policy limited these retailers' appeal to a small, consumer group.

Transfer drivers characterizing the extensive format change group. The retailers in this group were influenced by the opportunities in China, completely ignoring other considerations. They were driven by the motivation to exploit these opportunities quickly and gain pioneering advantages (Lieberman & Montgomery, 1998; Nakata & Sivakumar, 1995).

We identified two subgroups that differed in their specific motivations. The retailers in the first were motivated by the goal of becoming important players in China. The retailers in the second were driven by regional ambitions with China serving as a testing ground for a prototype format to be used in similar Asian countries later.

Three of the five retailers included in the first group (Pacific, Orient, New World) were property developers from Hong Kong[3] and Taiwan. Political, economic and personal connections with local officials and Chinese conglomerates were expected to lead to favorable joint-venture deals, exemptions from regulations, subsidized loans, and access to prime retail resources (sites, brands, suppliers, personnel). They operated in their home markets large shopping-office complexes, leasing out most retail activities. In China, they built similar projects but managed the retail components themselves, totally adapting them to Chinese conditions.

The two other retailers in this group aimed to exploit pent-up demand. One, Wellcome, a large, mass market oriented, Hong Kong supermarket chain, was the first supermarket company to enter China. Unsure of mass-market demand for its Western supermarket concept, it opened an up-market store, targeting what it perceived to be an unsatisfied demand for higher quality supermarkets. In the process, it introduced major changes in assortment, service and price levels. The other, Printemps, a French department store, saw an opportunity to capture the same consumers by establishing a luxurious Western department store in China. It opened an up-market version of its international, department store format. Adapting to local supply conditions, it deviated from its practice outside China and relied on licensees operating their own areas in the stores.

The three retailers in the second subgroup were driven by goals beyond China and viewed the format transfer into China in the context of their overall Asian strategy. The first, a supermarket chain (Bai-Lo), belonged to Yaohan, a diversified Asian retailer. Before entering China, Yaohan had only limited supermarket experience. Licensees operated the supermarket sections inside its General Merchandise Stores (GMS) in Japan, Hong Kong and Singapore. In China, it opened its first stand-alone supermarket chain. It also reshaped its assortment, dropping many categories and adding new ones. Whereas its supermarkets outside China emphasized high quality perishables, they offered no perishables in China. In addition, it drastically downgraded the store environment and service, and, in contrast to the situation outside China, emphasized low prices. Yaohan planned to expand in China and also use this format as the vehicle for moving into other Asian countries[4].

Another Yaohan-owned company, Nextstage, opened in China a huge shopping center complex that differed markedly from the small shopping centers Yaohan operated around its department stores in other countries. In this case too, it planned to use this format as a base for its Asian expansion.

The third retailer, Giordano, operated a large chain of small apparel stores in Hong Kong. In China it developed a new clothing store concept. Its stores were much larger, offering more varied assortment. In addition, whereas it owned its Hong Kong stores, its Chinese stores were operated by franchisees. The new format was to become the base for its Asian expansion.[5]

Transfer drivers characterizing the very limited format change group. The transfer decisions of the ten retailers introducing *very few* format changes were driven by the belief that home formats performing well would be equally successful in China since many home-host country conditions were similar. Management anticipated few transfer difficulties and felt only minor format changes were necessary.

Three of the home countries (Hong Kong, Singapore and Taiwan) were considerably more developed than China, with higher per-capita incomes and developed infrastructures. However, management believed the similarities in relevant conditions outweighed the differences. Specifically, these countries were evaluated as being compatible to China in conditions such as consumers (small homes, frequent shopping trips, similar preferences, same values), retail environment (coexistence of traditional and modern formats, domination of traditional formats), supply and distributions systems (small suppliers, fragmented channels), high-density, urban centers and strong government involvement in retail and distribution.

Clothing retailers in this group (GoldLion, Crocodile, Apple) transferred unchanged most of their offering elements, opening stores carrying the same assortments and brands, similar store atmosphere, service and prices. No supply problems were expected because they had worked for years with Chinese suppliers. Similarly, few changes were made in retail methods since these companies already used relatively simple technologies.

The supermarket and department store retailers in this group (Sincere, Wings, Park and Shop) behaved somewhat differently. While they also transferred *as is* many offering elements, all expected supply problems in key product areas. Consequently, they introduced more assortment and price changes. In addition, they transferred simplified versions of their retail technologies. However, the overall format changes were also judged as being quite limited involving "very few" format elements.

Transfer drivers characterizing the limited format change group. The retailers in this group operated Japanese style department store and GMS formats. Four originated from Japan (Jusco, Sogo, Isetan, Seibu), one from Malaysia (Parkson), and one from Thailand (Lotus). All operated in other Asian countries. All faced the same problem: The department store format in China was developed and highly popular. Scores of state-owned Chinese department stores existed in every city and the format has served for decades as the backbone of the Chinese retail system. Consequently, the transfer decisions of these retailers were driven by the goal of gaining a competitive advantage over the established Chinese department stores.

These retailers believed in the superiority of their Japanese department store and GMS formats, and, consequently, aimed to transfer, unchanged, as many as possible of the external offering elements. They were concerned, however, with the ability of Chinese manufacturers to supply them. These considerations led them to rely more heavily than in other Asian countries on imports and to emphasize departments supported by strong local suppliers. To counter the higher prices resulting from the heavy emphasis on imports, they downgraded store environment and service levels.

Home country retail technologies and methods were also judged as too complex. Consequently, they used simplified technologies transferred from their operations in other Asian countries.

Global considerations also influenced the transfer. An important caveat was the maintenance of the *Japanese* image of these stores. This consideration enhanced the tendency towards an *as is* transfer countervailing the pressures to downgrade service and shopping environment.

To help instill their Japanese retail culture and methods, a large number of Japanese managers were brought over. Their experience in other developing Asian markets was expected to help the Chinese stores overcome the anticipated supply problems.

Transfer decision process

In twelve of the cases studied the transfer decision process was surprisingly short, seemingly superficial and nonsystematic. Hardly any studies were conducted and no hard data used. Decisions were mostly based on anecdotal evidence and executives' impressions from visits to China.

A number of reasons explain this pattern. First, the companies were mostly small with limited international experience. They followed in China the same practices used in opening new stores in their home markets. Given a perceived weakness and an underdeveloped state of Chinese retailing, they also believed in the superiority of their formats and expected no demand-side problems. Lastly, they expected their joint-venture partners to help them overcome anticipated supply and operational problems.

In the other fifteen cases the decision process was long, detailed and systematic. It was based on expert analyses and on consumer studies. Few of these companies even opened representative offices years before their retail entry into China to coordinate the transfer process. Not surprisingly, these were mostly large, experienced retailers with extensive international operations.

Transfer dynamics: preplanned, postentry format changes

Seven of the retailers studied made major postentry format changes. Some were unplanned, made in response to problems or opportunities; others were preplanned. Our interest here is in the second group.

The retailers preplanning postentry modifications were highly experienced international companies. They viewed the transfer as an ongoing process. Format changes made at time of entry were regarded as tentative and subject to amendment in the future, contingent on expected developments.

For example, based on their experience in other developing countries, the supermarket retailers in this group (Carrefour, Park and Shop) anticipated major supply problems in fresh food categories. Consequently, at the entry these retailers offered only a token selection. Plans were in place, however, to develop a supply base for these categories by forging close ties with selected suppliers. They also planned to enlist local officials to modernize state-owned fresh food processing and distribution facilities. When, a year or two after entry, the planned reshaping of the supply system was achieved, these retailers modified the assortment again; this time they moved it closer to the home format configuration.

The positive payoffs from this behavior were clearly evident. These retailers reacted fast to entry problems, adapting original format elements to local conditions and losing in the process some key format strengths. However, when the right conditions materialized, they reverted, fast and effectively, to the original format situation, thereby regaining key format advantages.

Discussion

Format transfer strategies

The investigation of format transfer in prior years found them to be driven only by two forces: the motivation to leverage global advantages and the need to adapt to local conditions. Our findings suggest this view of transfer drivers to be limiting. First, transfers were often motivated by an additional factor, the retailer's global strategy. In these cases, format changes were determined by the role retailing in the host country was expected to play in the firm's global strategy. Second, some host country drivers operated to limit transfer change. For example, where local, host country retailers were weak; this factor may limit foreign adaptation to local conditions. Third, retailers introducing the same format changes were sometimes driven by different considerations.

On the basis of these findings, we draw two conclusions. First, it is useful to refer to the specific factors driving format changes rather than to general forces. Second, the understanding of format transfers should be based both upon format change patterns and the specific factors driving them.

The concept of a *transfer strategy* resolves these problems. It combines these two dimensions and recognizes the impact of specific drivers found to determine format change behavior of a subgroup of retailers. To identify the specific transfer strategies used by the foreign retailers entering China, we looked at the factors driving format transfers in each of the four format change groups. Each configuration of a format change pattern and a specific driver was designated as a transfer strategy. We identified six such strategies. Below, we discuss each and identify the conditions when each strategy is appropriate. The strategies, the factors driving them and the characteristics of the companies using each are summarized in Table 3. In addition, we identify the connection of each strategy to one of the four format change groups reflecting the number of format elements changed.

Table 3 Format transfer strategies: the case of China

Strategies	Number of companies	Drivers	Number of format elements changed	Orientation	Extent of the retailer's international involvement
(1) Global niche protection	3	Protecting global standing from lowering of standards	None	Global	Very high
(2) Opportunism	5	Exploiting opportunities (connections, pent-up demand)	Very many	Host country	None, limited
(3) Format pioneering opportunity	3	A "leading edge" country	Very many	Global	High
(4) Format extension: compatible countries of origins	7	High compatibility between home and host countries enables a simple format extension	Very few	Host country	None, limited
(5) Portfolio-based transfer	3	Using formats or format elements from most similar country.	Very few	Host country	High
(6) Competitive position oriented	6	Gaining competitive superiority over strong local retailers	Few	A mix of host country and global	High

Global niche protection strategy. This reflects an *as is* transfer driven by the motivation to protect and help retain the retailer's global niche position among the members of a targeted global segment. The importance of global segments for retail transfers has been recognized before (Salmon & Tordjman, 1989; Segal-Horn & Davidson, 1992), but these discussions emphasized only the opportunities these segments provide for global operation. In the Chinese case, the transfer was dominated by a different consideration. It was the protection of the format's integrity against the expected pressures for adaptation to Chinese conditions.

This transfer strategy is relevant in situations where a *specialist* retailer (Lambkin & Day, 1989) pursues a niche strategy targeting a small *global* segment. The retailer is likely to face pressures to increase sales by changing the format in order to appeal to other consumer groups or cater to additional needs of the targeted segment. This situation is typical in developing economies. It may occur also in developed countries when the global segment targeted by the retailer happens to be small.

Opportunism strategy. This is driven by the goal of exploiting opportunities in the host country. Retailers pursuing it are willing to change a large number of format elements in order to exploit opportunities fully. In extreme cases, retailers may even establish a largely new format that keeps only few of the original home format's elements.

Two types of opportunities may drive this strategy: political, economic and personal connections and demand and supply side opportunities. While both are highly relevant in developing countries, they may also be important in developed ones.

The study identified two types of retailers likely to pursue this strategy. The first were entrepreneurs who lacked a commitment to any retail format or a retail strategy. They were highly flexible and reacted fast to business opportunities. The second group included retailers which, upon judging that a limited potential for their original formats existed in China, decided to develop new format versions better geared to the needs of untapped and promising segments.

Format pioneering opportunity strategy. This is driven by retailers' global strategic vision. The specific transfer is viewed in the context of that global strategy and regarded as a step in its implementation. The format pioneering strategy is relevant when the host is a *leading edge* country (Yip, 1992). The importance and centrality of these countries means that formats succeeding there can later be successfully used in similar countries. Thus, the overriding consideration is to develop a format that will completely fit host country conditions.

Large, experienced retailers with extensive international operations, guided by a global vision, are more likely to use this strategy. It is interesting to note that the retailers pursuing a portfolio based transfer strategy (discussed later), actually used in China formats developed as a result of an earlier implementation of this strategy. All had the above profile. As formats may be pioneered to fit a variety of targets this strategy is equally relevant in developing and developed countries.

Format extension: compatible countries of origin. This strategy is relevant when formats are transferred from highly compatible home countries. In this situation, very few format adaptations are needed. These transfers require few resources, limited amount of effort and minimal risks. Consequently, as was the case in China, smaller retailers with limited international experience are more likely to use it. These retailers expect quick consumer acceptance because of their format's superior outputs. On the other hand, the compatibility is expected to minimize supply-side difficulties.

This strategy, too, is equally relevant in cases of format transfers among developed countries and from developed into developing countries.

Portfolio-based Format Extension strategy involves the transfer of formats from compatible countries that are not the format's original home. These formats may have been developed through an earlier implementation of a format pioneering strategy or as a result of a series of successive adaptations of the original format to conditions in different countries.

Large, diversified, retail companies operating a variety of formats in many countries are more likely to pursue this strategy. These companies often possess a portfolio of formats from which they can choose an appropriate one. This strategy may involve the transfer of whole formats or of format elements culled from different countries.

Competitive positioning oriented. This is found when the foreign retailer's main concern is the expected competition from strong local retailers operating similar formats. To gain competitive superiority, the foreign retailer needs to maximize the strengths of the transferred format and minimize transfer costs and difficulties. Consequently, the retailer will transfer "as is" format elements contributing most towards this goal and change or drop elements if they make limited contributions and/or are costly to transfer. The retailer is likely to be indifferent towards elements that are easy to transfer but make no contributions towards the superiority goal.

The retailer's global position may impact these calculations as follows: (1) advantages from global operation may strengthen some format elements, enhancing their potential to make contributions and thus increasing the likelihood of their "as is" transfer. (2) The retailer's global position may prevent it from introducing needed adaptations in elements that are central to the retailer's global standing.

Given the weakness of the retail system in developing economies, this scenario is more relevant in developed countries. Since many local retailers in these countries operate the same formats as the foreign entrants, only foreign retailers possessing especially strong formats with unique features can hope to achieve superiority. Others will try to enter by leveraging nonformat global advantages such as superior resources, financial strengths and political connections. These advantages increase the importance of finding strong joint venture partners or acquiring strong local companies.

Format change patterns

Most format transfers into China involved limited format adaptations. Sixteen of the twenty-four retailers that made format changes modified few or very few format elements. The other eight introduced extensive format changes.

These findings contradict the conclusions of earlier studies. The retail modernization literature, emphasizing the incompatibilities between developed and developing countries and the limitations on the transfer of modern retail formats, recommends major format adaptation (Slater & Riley, 1969; Goldman, 1981). Similarly, the retail internationalization literature draws the same conclusions but for different reasons. Recognizing the widely divergent demand, supply and competitive conditions in different countries and retailers' inability to generate meaningful global advantages, this literature recommends major adaptations to host country conditions (Barth *et al.*, 1996; Rosenblum *et al.*, 1997).

Two factors explain our study's findings of limited format changes. First, many retailers transferred formats from compatible Asian countries. Second, retailers facing Chinese retailers operating the same formats felt adaptation to Chinese conditions would dilute the competitive strength of their formats.

Effects of global and host country factors on the transfers

Considerations relating to the global operation might typically be expected to minimize format change while host country unique characteristics might shift decisions towards adaptations (Jain, 1989; Rosenblum *et al.*, 1994). The study reveals a more complex picture. First, a global orientation may influence transfers beyond the benefits of standardization. We found that retailers influenced by global considerations were also interested in protecting their global position, not strengthening their operation in China. Second, in contrast to the literature, we found cases where a global orientation was associated with a high degree of format adaptation. Specifically, the retailers pursuing the format pioneering strategy were motivated by global considerations, but emphasized adaptation to Chinese conditions. Third, we found situations where limited format changes were associated with a host country orientation, not a global one as found in the literature.

In agreement with the literature's predictions, we found that none of the retailers studied was able to leverage economic advantages from their international operations. Many enjoyed, however, major, noneconomic, softer global advantages such as experience, learning and flexibility.

Conclusions

Transfer complexities

Format transfers turned out to be much more complex and varied than previously described. First, contrary to expectations, transfers frequently involved limited format modifications. Many retailers entering China were small and based in neighboring Asian countries with similar cultures. These smaller retailers introduced limited format changes. In addition, some of the large global retailers circumvented the adaptation problem by using in China a format selected from their format portfolio. We also found some retailers to be reluctant to adapt their formats to Chinese conditions for fear of becoming too similar to local competitors operating the same format. The only retailers making drastic format adaptations were the retailers driven solely by the aim of exploiting opportunities in China.[6]

Second, transfer decisions are assumed to be guided by one goal, how to strengthen retailers' competitive position in the host country. We found, however, cases where considerations beyond the host country, relating to the role formats play in the implementation of global strategies, took precedent. This means that format transfers should be studied in the context of retailers' overall strategies, not in isolation.

Third, transfers are viewed by the literature as being driven by two opposing forces: leveraging global advantages versus the need to adapt. We found these factors' influence to be more complex. A global orientation may also lead to format adaptation while a host country one may be associated with limited format changes.

Fourth, the literature emphasizes global economic advantages generated through standardization and scale economies. We found noneconomic global advantages such as experience, learning and flexibility in resource allocation to be much more important.

Fifth, we found retail transfers into China to be dominated by relatively small Asian retailers located close to China or in Asian countries with similar cultures and economic environments. This possibility has been largely missed by the international retailing literature. By focusing on transfers from highly developed countries into less developed ones, Western research may have over-emphasized the role of large and famous global retailers, ignoring the format transfers by many relatively unknown retailers moving across countries with highly compatible environments.

Sixth, transfers are an activity that takes place over time. Some retailers planned to continue and modify the transferred formats, contingent on the appearance of expected changes in economic conditions. This finding highlights the importance of flexibility and reversibility in a transfer strategy and preserving the ability to restore elements modified at entry.

Finally, we found that in some cases the transfer decision process was short, nonsystematic and superficial. These firms displayed an attitude of *let's try and see what happens*. These were smaller, less experienced retailers. They were not aware of the many potential difficulties and lacked the resources needed to engage in a systematic transfer decision process.

Generalizing the findings

Although the six format transfer strategies identified above were derived from factors and situations typical to China, they may have application elsewhere. They may be equally relevant for retail transfers to other developing countries and possibly for developed ones. The strategies' relative importance, however, is likely to vary in different countries. The number of retailers following each strategy in the present study reflects the peculiarities of the sample and of the Chinese situation.

Study Limitations and Future Research Directions

Format transfers should not be studied in isolation. The role formats play in the retailers' overall strategy and the relationships between the overall strategy and the behavior of retailers in host countries should be jointly studied. Such joint evaluation may also help understand the relationship between format transfers and retailer's success in different host countries. This approach may further lead to the use of additional format change measures; the significance of the change upon the retailers' strategies is an example.

The concept of a format needs to be developed further. A differentiation between *core* and *peripheral* elements seems appropriate. The core represents key elements that are always present, whereas the peripheral ones are more likely to be changed as a function of the transfer circumstances.

Similarly, the relationships between transfer strategies and format elements should be studied. There were indications in the present study that an elements' importance varied across different types of strategies. For example, the *external* (offering) elements played a highly important role in the case of the retailers following the competitive position oriented and the format extension strategies. They were essential in securing consumers' acceptance of the transferred formats. In contrast, the know-how format component was much more important in the case of the portfolio-based transfers.

We found the transfer process to be long, detailed and systematic in about half the cases and short, superficial and nonsystematic in the other group. In addition, some of the retailers studied made preplanned, postentry format changes. Future studies should look at the influence of these differences on the success of the transfer process.

The study of format transfers should be expanded to other countries. A systematic research plan involving home and host countries at different levels of development should help validate the transfer strategies identified here. Also, the six transfer strategies identified in this research are not exhaustive. Additional transfer strategies are likely to be identified in future studies. For example, a strategy driven by the hope of leveraging global economic advantages should be mostly relevant in developed countries. Similarly, a new version of the competitive position oriented strategy involving more substantial format changes is also feasible.

The present study is exploratory, qualitative and it is based on a convenience sample. Future studies should involve representative samples and could proceed in two directions. Studies exploring further the relationships of the format to overall strategies should use the same inductive, case study based, approach. At the same time formal, quantitative, studies testing the generalizations developed in this study and validating the transfer strategies identified should be conducted.

Notes

1   Based on available sources, I estimate there were 500–600 retail Joint Ventures in 1997. The number of international retailers operating in China through Joint Ventures (most) and licensing arrangements, was estimated at 200–300. (Some operated few joint ventures). See also Asia Pulse (1998; 2000).

2   As can be seen in Fig. 2, the range of actual changes in the "very many" category was large compared to the other change categories.

3   Since 1997 Hong Kong is part of China. It is treated here as a separate home country, for two reasons. Its economy and polity are more developed and, even after unification, Hong Kong remained a separate economic and political entity. Second, all the retail transfers studied here took place when Hong Kong was under British rule.

4   Financial and managerial difficulties forced Yaohan into bankruptcy in 1998.

5   This company closed operations in China in 1998 due largely to political feud between its founder (a Hong Kong newspaper magnate) and Chinese officials.

6   The validity of this assertion depends on the whether the sample included a disproportionate number of small retailers from neighboring countries. We feel this conclusion is not biased by the convenience nature of the sample for two reasons. First, some sixty percent of our list of international retailers operating in China, a list that served as a

basis for contacting the companies eventually studied, were small firms from neighboring Asian countries. Second, many of these retailers refused to cooperate. Thus, if a bias exists in the sample, it is against these small retailers.

References

Adler, N.J., N. Campbell and A. Laurent (1989). In Search of Appropriate Methodology: From Outside the People's Republic of China Looking In, *Journal of International Business Studies, 20*(1), 61–74.

Akerhurst, G. and N. Alexander, eds. (1996). *The Internationalization of Retailing.* London, England: Frank Cass.

Asia Pulse. (1998). A Profile of China's Retail Industry, November 8.

Asia Pulse. (2000). Retail Giants Increasing Investments in China, June 30.

Barth, Karen, Nancy J. Karch, Kathleen McLaughlin and Christiana Smith Shi. (1996). Global Retailing, *The McKinsey Quarterly, 1*, 116–125.

Betancourt, Roger and David Gautschi. (1990). Demand Complementarities, Household Production, and Retail Assortments, *Marketing Science, 9*(Spring), 146–161.

Bucklin, L. P. (1972). *Competition and Evolution in the Distribution Trades.* Englewood Cliffs, N.J.: Prentice Hall.

Craig, Samuel, C. and Susan P. Douglas. (2000). Configural advantages in global markets, *Journal of International Marketing, 8*(1), 6–26.

Dawson, John. (1994). Internationalization of Retail Operations, *Journal of Marketing Management, 10*, 267–82.

Douglas, Susan P. and C. Samuel Craig. (1995). *Global Marketing Strategy.* NY: McGraw Hill.

Dunning, J.H. (1988). The Eclectic Paradigm of International Production: A Restatement and Some Possible Extensions, *Journal of International Business Studies, 19*(1) 1–31.

Food and Agricultural Organization. (1973A). *Development of Food Marketing Systems for Large Urban Areas, Latin America.* Rome, Italy: F.A.O Press.

Food and Agricultural Organization. (1973B). *Development of Food Marketing Systems for Large Urban Areas, Asia and Far East.* Rome, Italy: F.A.O Press.

Findlay, Allan M., R. Paddison and J. Dawson, eds. (1990). *Retailing Environments in Developing Countries.* London, England: Routledge.

Ghosh, Avigit. (1990). *Retail Management.* Orlando, FL: The Dryden Press.

Glaser, Barney G. and Anselem L. Strauss. (1967). *The Discovery of Grounded Theory: Strategies for Qualitative Research.* NY: Aldine Publishing Company.

Glaser, Barney G. (1978). *Theoretical Sensitivity. Advances in the Methodology of Grounded Theory.* Mill Valley, CA: The Sociology Press.

Goldman, Arieh. (1981). Transfer of a Retailing Technology into The Less Developed Countries: The Supermarket Case, *Journal of Retailing, 57*(Summer), 5–29.

Harrison, Kelly. (1974). *Improving Food Marketing Systems in Developing Countries: Experience From Latin America.* East Lansing, MI: Latin American Studies Center, Michigan State University.

Hentzepeter, Vincent. (1999). Central Europe: The Battlefield of Food Retail, *Elsevier Food International, 4*(October), 46–55.

Hollander, Stanley. (1970). *Multinational Retailing.* East Lansing, MI: Michigan State University Press.

Inkpen, Andrew C. and Adva Dinur. (1998). Knowledge Management and International Joint Ventures, *Organizational Science*, 9(July–August), 454–468.

Jain C. Subhash. (1989). Standardization of International Marketing Strategy: Some Research Hypotheses, *Journal of Marketing*, 53(January), 70–79.

Kacker, M. (1985). *Transatlantic Trends in Retailing*. Westport, CN: Quarum Books.

Kacker, M. (1988). International Flow of Retail Know-How: Bridging the Technology Gap in Distribution, *Journal of Retailing*, 64(Spring), 41–67.

Kuipers, Pascal. (1994). Top Retailers, *Elsevier Food International*, 4(October), 15–23.

Lambkin, Mary and George S. Day. (1989). Evolutionary Processes in Competitive Markets: Beyond the Product Life Cycle, *Journal of Marketing*, 53(Summer), 4–20.

Lieberman, B., Marvin and David B. Montgomery. (1988). First Mover Advantages, *Strategic Management Journal*, 9, 41–58.

Manning, Kenneth, C., William Bearden and Randall Rose. (1998). Development of a Theory of Retailer Response to Manufacturers' Everyday Low Cost Programs. *Journal of Retailing*, 74(Spring), 107–137.

Mason, J. Barry and Morris L. Mayer. (1987). *Modern Retailing: Theory and Practice*, fourth edition. Plano, Texas: Business Publications, Inc.

McCracken, Grant. (1988). *The Long Interview*. Newbury Park, CA: Sage Publications.

McGoldrick, P.J. and G. Davies, eds. (1995). *International Retailing: Trends and Strategies*. London, UK: Pitman.

Messinger, Paul R. and Chakravarthi Narasimhan. (1997). A Model of Retail Formats Based on Consumers' Economizing on Shopping Time, *Marketing Science*, 16(1), 1–23.

Nakata, Cheryl and K. Sivakumar. (1995). Factors in Emerging Markets and Their Impact on First Mover Advantages, *Marketing Science Institute*, Working Paper, Report 95–110, September.

Nonaka, Ikujiro. (1994). A Dynamic Theory of Organizational Knowledge, *Organizational Science*, 5, 14–37.

Pellegrini, Luca. (1991). The Internationalization of Retailing and 1992 Europe, *Journal of Marketing Channels*, 1(2), 3–27.

Prahalad, C.K. and Y.L. Doz. (1987). *The Multinational Mission: Balancing Local Demands and Global Vision*. NY: The Free Press.

Reid, David McHardy. (1999). Changes in Japan's Post-Bubble Business Environment: Implication for Foreign-Affiliated Companies, *Journal of International Marketing*, 7(3), 38–63.

Reuling, Eddy. (1998). Global Retailers Conquer Emerging Markets, *Elsevier Food International*, 3 (May): 21–24.

Rosenbloom, Bert, Trina Larsen and Rajiv Mehta. (1997). Global Marketing Channels and the Standardization Controversy, *Journal of Global Marketing*, 11(1), 49–64.

Salmon, Walter J. and Andre Tordjman. (1989). The Internationalization of Retailing, *International Journal of Retailing*, 4(2), 3–16.

Samiee, Saeed. (1993). Retailing and Channel Considerations in Developing Countries: a Review and Research Propositions, *Journal of Business Research*, 27, 103–130.

Savitt, Ronald. (1988). The State of the Art in Marketing and Economic Development, in *Research in Marketing, Supplement 4, Marketing and Development*, 12–32.

Segal-Horn, Susan and Heather Davidson. (1992). Global Markets, The Global Consumer and International Retailing, *Journal of Global Marketing*, 5(3), 31–61.

Slater, Charles C. and Riley, Harold. (1969). *Market Processes in the Recife Area of Northeast Brazil*. East Lansing, MI: Michigan State University, Latin American Studies Center.

Sternquist, Brenda. (1998). *International Retailing.* New York, NY: Fairchild Publications.

Stores. (1998). Global Powers of Retailing, Section 3, January.

Waldorf, D. and P. Biernacki. (1981). Snowball Sampling: Problems and Techniques in Chain Referral Sampling, *Sociological Methods and Research*, *10*, 141–163.

Yip, George, S. (1992). *Total Global Strategy: Managing for Worldwide Competitive Advantage.* Englewood Cliffs, NJ: Prentice Hall.

Editors' Commentary

RETAIL RESEARCH IN THE UK has for a number of decades had a strong geographical disciplinary background. Many of those working in the area were once, or still are, geographers. Whilst some geographers interested in retailing moved to Business Schools from the early 1980s, a number remained in geography departments. Pre-eminent amongst these would be Neil Wrigley who almost single-handedly had maintained a retail research interest within geography, both through his personal efforts and through the stream of PhD students he has supervised. This research has both a geographical flavour and at the same time attempts to incorporate some of the business and marketing strands of research. It is symptomatic that Neil Wrigley is the founding co-editor of *The Journal of Economic Geography*. The paper selected here, part of a wider project funded by the ESRC, represents this matching of economic geography and business and follows logically on from the research interests of Neil Wrigley since the late 1980s.

Neil Wrigley is currently Professor of Geography at the University of Southampton, where he has been since 1991. He has long worked on retail topics and has authored and edited books on geographical aspects of retailing contributing to both geographical and retail literatures. He has a BA from the University of Wales, a PhD from the University of Cambridge and a D.Sc. from the University of Bristol. Early in his career Neil Wrigley made significant contributions to quantitative studies in particular on categorical data analysis, discrete choice modelling, longitudinal/panel data analysis, modifiable areal unit and census data analysis. However, even in the 1980s he had developed an interest in retail topics with articles on the use of panel data and store loyalty when he was based in Cardiff as Professor of City and Regional Planning.

He has held ESRC and Leverhulme Research Fellowships, an Erskine Fellowship (New Zealand), and was Senior Research Fellow, St Peter's College, Oxford (1996–97). He has held visiting positions at many overseas universities including the University of Boston, University of California Los Angeles, University of California Santa Barbara, University of Toronto, George Mason University, Karlsruhe University (Germany), Macquarie University (Australia) and the University of Canterbury (New Zealand).

Neil Wrigley's research focuses on economic geography – in particular, issues relating to the firm, corporate finance, corporate strategy and the economic landscape, with specific reference to the restructuring, regulation and globalization of the retail industry. He has written many widely cited papers on changing conditions of competition and regulation in the US and UK retail industries, US and pan-European retail consolidation, issues of retail development and finance, e-commerce, the globalization of retail capital and rise of transnational retail corporations. Most recently his retail research has focused around ESRC-funded projects on *Food Deserts in British Cities* and *Transnational Retail and Buyer Driven Supply Chains in the Global Economy*.

The co-author of this article is Andrew Currah who is currently a Career Development Fellow at the School of Geography at the University of Oxford. Andrew Currah joined the School of Geography in May 2006, having studied geography at the University of Cambridge, before moving to the University of Southampton to complete a Master's degree, and then back to Cambridge to complete his Doctorate. His broad interest is in the economic and geographical relationships between technological innovation, competition and industry structure, that is, how products, firms, regions and industries are created, destroyed and reconfigured over time. In addition to his work with Neil Wrigley on these aspects in a retail context, Andrew Currah focuses on the changing structure of the media and entertainment industries in a digital and networked economy, with particular reference to California.

This paper considers issues of retrenchment in international retailing. The authors consider the experience of Royal Ahold in Latin America. The paper focuses on the organizational stresses caused by international activity and the factors that militate for 'success' or 'failure'. The paper explores the nature of the relationship between the firm and the economy and society in which it is embedded. The nature of this socio-economic–political society has influences on the success, or otherwise, of the firm.

Key Publications

Wrigley N (1985) *Categorical Data Analysis for Geographies and Environmental Scientists*. Harlow: Longman.

Wrigley N, Guy C, Dunn R and O'Brien L (1985) The Cardiff consumer panel – methodological aspects of the conduct of a long-term panel survey. *Transactions of the Institute of British Geographers*, 10(1): 63–76.

Wrigley N (ed.) (1988) *Store Choice, Store Location and Market Analysis*. London: Routledge.

Wrigley N (1987) The concentration of capital in UK grocery retailing. *Environment and Planning A*, 19, 1283–1288.

Wrigley N (1989) The lure of the USA: further reflections on the internationalisation of British retailing capital. *Environment and Planning A*, 21, 283–288.

Wrigley N (1991) Is the 'Golden Age' of British grocery retailing at a watershed? *Environment and Planning A*, 23, 1537–1544.

Wrigley N (1992) Sunk capital, the property crisis, and the restructuring of British food retailing. *Environment and Planning A*, 24, 1521–1530.

Wrigley N (1992) Antitrust regulation and the restructuring of grocery retailing in Britain and the USA. *Environment and Planning A*, 24, 727–749.

Wrigley N (1993) Abuses of market power – further reflections on UK food retailing and the regulatory state. *Environment and Planning A*, 25, 1545–1552.

Wrigley N and Lowe M (1996) *Retailing, Consumption and Capital*. Harlow: Longman.

Wrigley N (1998) Understanding store development programmes in post-property-crisis UK food retailing. *Environment and Planning A*, 30, 15–35.

Wrigley N (1998) PPG6 and the contemporary UK food store development dynamic. *British Food Journal*, 100, 154–161.

Wrigley N (2001) Local spatial monopoly and competition regulation: reflections on recent UK and US rulings. *Environment and Planning A*, 33, 189–94.

Wrigley N and Lowe M (2002) *Reading Retail: A Geographical Perspective on Retailing and Consumption Spaces*. London: Arnold.

Wrigley N (2002) Food deserts in British cities: policy context and research priorities. *Urban Studies*, 39, 2029–40.

Wrigley N, Guy C and Lowe M (2002) Urban regeneration, social inclusion and large store development: The Seacroft development in context. *Urban Studies*, 39(11), 2101–2114.

Wrigley N, Warm DL and Margetts BM (2003) Deprivation, diet and food retail access: findings from the Leeds 'food deserts' study. *Environment and Planning A*, 35, 151–88.

Wrigley N and Currah A (2005) Globalizing retail: conceptualizing the distribution based transnational cooperation. *Progress in Human Geography*, 29(4), 437–457.

Wood S, Lowe M and Wrigley N (2006) Life after PPG6 – recent UK food retailer responses to planning regulation tightening. *International Review of Retail, Distribution and Consumer Research*, 16, 23–41.

Coe NM and Wrigley N (2007) Host economy impacts of transnational retail: the research agenda. *Journal of Economic Geography*, 7, 341–371.

Websites

http://www.geog.soton.ac.uk/public/about/staff/
     asprofile.asp?init=NW&smclass=about&cfile=about

http://www.geog.ox.ac.uk/staff/acurrah.php and www.andrewcurrah.com

THE STRESSES OF RETAIL INTERNATIONALIZATION: LESSONS FROM ROYAL AHOLD'S EXPERIENCE IN LATIN AMERICA

Neil Wrigley and Andrew Currah

Written prior to the financial crisis of the world's third largest retailer following its announcement of accounting irregularities on 24 February 2003, this paper uses a case study of Ahold's struggles to manage significant investment in the unpredictable business environments of Latin America to focus attention on the stresses internationalization poses for the retail firm. It offers a picture of retail multinationals facing distinctive organizational challenges as they seek to transpose internal and inter-firm practices to markedly different institutional environments, and of a highly contested retail internationalization process – not least by the suppliers of finance. It concludes by drawing out five lessons for retail internationalization theory from Ahold's experiences.

A postscript then summarizes the events following Ahold's revelation of significant accounting irregularities through to the announcement of its decision on 3 April 2003 to withdraw from South America. That postscript assesses what further insights the corporate scandal has revealed about Ahold's management of its significant investment in the region.

Introduction

AFTER A LONG PERIOD in which research on the retail internationalization process focused heavily on the *implementation* of international expansion, there has recently been an important refocusing of attention on strategic aspects of *sustaining* expansion in the face of the inevitable stresses internationalization poses for the firm. In turn, this has led to a valuable switching of concern from establishing the motives for internationalization and assessing modes of market entry (e.g. Williams 1992; Doherty 1999; Alexander and Myers 2000), to a focus on issues of divestment and market exit (Alexander and Quinn 2002; Burt *et al.* 2002; Meyer-Ohle 2002) and on periods of retrenchment and strategic reappraisal in the internationalization process (Wrigley 2000a). In this paper, we make a further contribution to that reorientation via a case study of Royal Ahold's struggles following its expansion in the late 1990s into the emerging markets of Latin America. Moreover, we seek to do that by positioning our case

The International Review of Retail, Distribution and Consumer Research, Vol. 13, No. 3 (2003), pp. 221–243.
©2003 Taylor & Francis Ltd.
This paper forms part of a wider research project on 'Globalizing retail' supported by the ESRC under award RO22 25 0204. The authors are grateful for ongoing discussions with leading food retail analysts at ABN-AMRO, Credit Suisse First Boston, Deutsche Bank and Merrill Lynch, and for the opportunity to participate in industry conferences organized by those investment banks. They are also grateful to Royal Ahold for allowing them to clarify facets of the Latin American operations during interviews held with Ahold in the Netherlands in late 2002.

study within a conceptual framework with origins in the comparative study of forms of industrial capitalism (Berger and Dore 1996; Boyer and Hollingsworth 1999; Whitley 1999, 2002) – one which focuses on how firms are likely to manage their international investment in contrasting business systems associated with distinctive varieties of market economy (Whitley 2001).

Within that framework, we concentrate upon what have been termed 'particularistic' economies which combine a 'weak and/or predatory state . . . with weak collective intermediaries and norms governing economic transactions' (Whitley 2001: 38) and which typically produce adversarial, unpredictable business environments. Our focus is on the challenges Ahold has faced in managing significant investment in the unpredictable, weakly institutionalized business environments of Latin America, particularly as those economies have lurched, during 2001/2002, into a period of renewed economic crisis. We examine the mechanisms used by Ahold to attenuate the risk of entering those markets and show how those mechanisms, in the context of 'particularistic' business environments and economic crisis, rather than attenuating risk have sometimes compounded it. We pose questions about the problems of *sustaining* international retail investment when capital markets are concerned about the destruction of firm value in that investment, and 'the stresses in the relationship between management and suppliers of finance which can quickly develop if the internationalization process is perceived to threaten the strategic credibility of the firm' (Wrigley 2000a: 914). Our picture is of emerging retail multinationals facing distinctive organizational challenges as they seek to transpose and adapt their internal and inter-firm practices to markedly different institutional environments, and of a highly contested retail internationalization process. Our broader aim is to contribute to an important rebalancing of approaches to the retail internationalization process which, until recently, have seemed 'to be covering only one part of the internationalization story' (Burt *et al.* 2002: 214).

'Particularistic' Business Environments and 'Merchant Economy' Firms

Emerging from comparative study of forms of industrial capitalism, a rich vein of research has focused during the past decade on the extent to which the organizational forms and practices of transnational corporations (TNCs) are influenced by national macro-regulatory institutions, and by 'market rules' governing such things as capital markets, labour market practices, competition policy and corporate governance (in economic geography, for example, see the work of Christopherson (1993; 1999; 2002) and Gertler (1997; 1999; 2001). Debate has focused on how firms from contrasting business systems associated with distinctive varieties of industrial capitalism are likely to manage their international investment. In particular, research has explored the extent to which TNCs can transpose their internal and inter-firm practices (their 'home' way of doing things) to their foreign subsidiaries. To what extent, it has asked, can distinctive organizational competencies learned via the operation of those subsidiaries be transferred back into the domestic operations of the TNCs to provide new competitive capabilities?

Building on that tradition, Whitley (2001) explores the management of international investment by TNCs using a three-dimensional typology. That framework essentially cross-relates particular types of firm to the distinctive types of business/institutional environment in which those firms are seen to develop. It then explores via a series of questions (relating to likely levels of FDI, characteristic risk management strategies, extent and mode of control of subsidiaries, likely levels of integration of subsidiaries into the local economy, and extent of organizational learning from subsidiaries) how firms from those contrasting business systems are likely to manage their international investment.

Three distinct and idealized business environments are recognized, each 'dominated by different institutional arrangements controlling access to capital and skills' which, in turn, encourage 'different ways of coordinating and controlling economic activities' allowing quite different sorts of firms to emerge (Whitley 2001: 38). The three environments are termed:

1   *particularistic* – 'combining a weak and/or predatory state . . . with weak collective intermediaries and norms governing economic transactions, and predominantly paternalistic authority relationships';
2   *collaborative* – in which the 'state plays an important coordinating and development role' or encourages private associations to do that, and which have 'a number of important institutions that together lock key actors into each others destinies';
3   *arm's length* – in which 'the state acts more as a regulator than coordinator, finance flows through competitive capital markets rather than banks, and training is more a matter for individual investment than for coordinated collaboration between state agencies, employers and unions' (Whitley 2001: 39).

The latter two environments are often referred to elsewhere in the 'varieties of capitalism' literature as '*coordinated*' and '*merchant economies*' respectively, with two variants of the co-ordinated/collaborative model being recognized – a German 'stakeholder capitalism' form and a Japanese variant (Dore 2000; O'Sullivan 2000).[1]

Associated with these business environments, Whitley recognizes three idealized types of firms, which he terms 'opportunistic', 'cooperative hierarchies', and 'isolated hierarchies' respectively. The terminology matters less than the fact that the former are seen to be products of environments where the state is 'poorly integrated and controlled by private rent-seeking elites', and are characterized by corporate decision making which often involves 'gaining political or related forms of support . . . subject to radical change at short notice', and whose control is frequently direct and personal by owners whose dominant objective is often family wealth creation (Whitley 2001: 39–41). The latter, in contrast, are characterized by separation of ownership and control or, as Shleifer and Vishny (1997) would put it, the separation of management and the suppliers of finance typical of merchant economies (or Anglo-American market capitalism) where 'capital is typically managed in investment portfolios with financial claims traded on highly liquid capital markets' (Whitley 2001: 42).

In this paper we focus on this latter type of firm, a retail TNC which, because of its dominant orientation to the US market, can be viewed as essentially the product of a 'merchant economy' institutional environment, albeit one whose continental European base ensures some important characteristics of the 'stakeholder capitalism' model – not least in terms of corporate governance and accounting standards. It is a firm seeking to manage, subject to capital market scrutiny, international investment in unpredictable, weakly institutionalized 'particularistic' business environments liable to rapid politically-induced change and economic instability. To succeed in its expansion into these environments and their local cultures of consumption, it must, as we have argued elsewhere (Wrigley and Currah 2003), of necessity seek to become 'close to market' and to 'invest in embeddedness'. However, fixing of capital in place (via store/ distribution networks but also via partnerships and joint ventures) brings with it intense vulnerability to the vagaries and exigencies of those 'particularistic' business environments. Moreover, seeking to expand in such environments via a process of merger and acquisition rather than organic expansion inevitably implies dealing with what Whitley terms 'opportunistic' firms and organizations. That is to say, firms and organizations whose control is frequently direct and personal, that are often vitally dependent on political and related forms of support, and in which the objective of protection of family wealth is frequently pronounced.

Before we can explore these issues, however, we first need some essential background on the retail TNC in question, and the history of its investment in the 'particularistic' economies of Latin America.

Royal Ahold – Growth and Debt

Despite being the world's third largest retailer in terms of sales, behind Wal-Mart and Carrefour, Royal Ahold remains a remarkably under-discussed firm in the retail internationalization literature. Its 10-year sales and operating profit history (1991–2001), shown in Figure 1, reveals a remarkable period of aggressive growth, largely through acquisition, with sales forecast to rise to around EUR 75 billion by 2003. Moreover, it is unusual in terms of the emerging retail TNCs in that its home market does not dominate its sales and profits profile. Rather, its operations in the USA do, accounting for 59% of its sales and 62% of its operating profit in 2001. As detailed in Wrigley (2002), by the end of 2001, Ahold was firmly established among the 'top five' group of US food

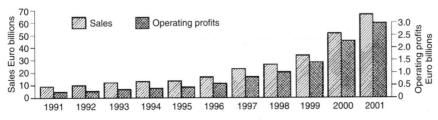

Figure 1 Ahold's global sales and operating profits 1991–2001

retailers with 1,609 stores spread along the east coast, including regionally dominant chains (Stop & Shop, Giant, etc.) in the densely populated Boston–Washington, DC corridor. In addition, it had entered the US food service sector and, very rapidly by acquisition, become the second largest operator in the USA.

During this decade of explosive growth, Ahold had enjoyed unstinting support from the financial community and had funded its growth through the capital markets via cross-listing in the USA and access to low cost capital. In the four-year period 1998 to 2001, Ahold spent a total of EUR 16.4 billion on acquisitions and raised EUR 9.7 billion of new equity. The consequence was that it became highly leveraged. Its reported net debt at the end of 2001 was EUR 12.4 billion. However, taking account of capitalization of operating leases, that figure was EUR 22.4 billion. As world equity markets began to spiral downwards from their tech-stock/dot.com mania highs, and the accountancy scandals of Enron and WorldCom cast a shadow over firms such as Ahold that had grown by aggressive merger and acquisition supported by high levels of debt, Ahold's market valuation collapsed. By early 2003, it was barely one-third what it had been a year earlier. During that intervening year, Ahold's earnings visibility had come under sustained critical investor scrutiny, reconciliation of its earnings under differing Dutch and US accounting standards had caused problems, and its recent acquisitions in Europe and Latin America were seen to expose it to significant potential liabilities. It had been forced to issue successive profits warnings and to announce a dramatic retreat from its previous corporate strategy of acquisition-driven growth to one of consolidation and organic, 'capital-efficient' growth. The equity market had effectively become closed to Ahold for funding purposes, and downgrading of its credit rating ensured that it had strictly limited access to the debt markets. Announcing a lowering of Ahold's credit rating from 'stable' to 'negative' in July 2002, Moody's (cited in ABN–AMRO, 2002a, 3) stated:

> Ahold's Baal rating reflects its geographical diversity, its scale in the consolidating food retail industry, the quality of its retail operations, and management's talent in locating and integrating high quality acquisitions, *mitigated by an aggressive growth strategy, a high tolerance for financial leverage, and a reliance on joint venture partners which may limit its strategic flexibility*.

Ahold in Latin America

It is against this background that Ahold's management of its significant investment in the 'particularistic' economies of Latin America must be assessed. What lessons can be drawn from its risk management strategies, the nature and mode of control of its subsidiaries, and the extent of Ahold's organizational learning from its experiences? And how do these match up in the case of a dominantly merchant economy retail TNC (albeit with some critically important 'stakeholder capitalism' characteristics) with the hypotheses about the management of investment by such firms in 'particularistic' business environments that can be generated from Whitley's largely, though not exclusively, production-TNC oriented framework? More generally, what insights does Ahold's experience in Latin America offer for study of the retail internationalization process? Before we can make these assessments, however, a brief summary of Ahold's expansion into, and operations in, Latin America is necessary.

The attractions of emerging markets

Like a group of its European food retail peers, Ahold was attracted towards investment in emerging markets from the mid-1990s onwards by two inter-related factors. The first factor related to the visibility of the super-normal 'first mover' returns on investment which firms like Carrefour, which had led the push into those markets, had been able to make. Carrefour had demonstrated in countries such as Brazil, Argentina and Taiwan that very rapid rates of revenue growth, market share gains, and returns on invested capital were possible, from operations with relatively low levels of capital intensity, in markets in which competition to Western-style large-store corporate retailing with its accompanying distribution/logistics and systems–operation know-how was minimal. Licences to open new stores were easy to obtain, capital requirements for site acquisition and store construction were low, variable costs represented by labour were very attractive, and the existing retailers operating in those markets typically had little purchasing scale and operated in an inefficient manner. The second factor involved a combination of increasing pressure on traditional components of sales growth (new retail space, 'like for like' growth, and inflation) in their home markets, and the free cash flow generated from dominant, or at the very least, secure and defensible core domestic markets. In a context in which the contribution to growth that European food retailers were able to obtain from newly opened retail space had become increasingly problematic due to a significant tightening of the regulatory environment (e.g. *Loi Rafferin* in France, *PPG6* in England, etc.), and faced by modest 'like for like' growth rates in their core markets and labour cost pressures in a low and declining inflation environment, expansion into emerging markets was increasingly viewed as offering a 'growth vehicle'. In turn, that was seen as helping sustain earnings growth in the medium to longer term, and as helping to provide an enhanced 'growth company' type equity valuation with the increased financial flexibility bestowed by that. Essentially, free cash flows were redirected by embryonic European retail TNCs into a strategy of international diversification into less mature, potential growth markets, and the process was facilitated by access to low-cost capital. Debt financing for expansionary growth could be raised very cheaply in Europe and North America in the low-inflation environment of the late 1990s, and equity financing could also be secured with relative ease by firms whose international ambitions had frequently been translated into enhanced equity valuations (Wrigley 2000b).

Entry and expansion

Ahold's entry into Latin America – first into Brazil in December 1996 and sub-sequently, in January 1998, into Argentina, Chile, Peru, Paraguay and Ecuador – must be viewed in the context of that broader story of potential growth markets, free cash flow redirected from mature core markets, and ready access to low cost capital. However, as the credit rating agencies' views of Ahold make clear, Ahold brought to that story a reputation of managerial skill in identifying high quality acquisitions and integrating those acquisition smoothly and effectively into an evolving model of global retail operation which stressed an 'intelligently federal' model with a focus on local partnerships, format adaptation, best practice knowledge transfer, and backend systems integration.

Table 1 outlines Ahold's successive acquisitions and joint ventures in Latin America 1996–2002 – a period of considerable corporate activity involving 11 acquisitions, several ownership-stake increases, and four joint ventures. As Figure 2 shows, by mid 2002, Ahold operated or had a major stake in 776 stores across 10 countries. Those in Central America (282 stores in Guatemala, Costa Rica, Nicaragua, El Salvador and Honduras) are controlled by CARHCO, a joint venture between Paiz-Ahold (a partnership in which Ahold has a 50% share and which controls La Fragua, the leading food retailer in Guatemala) and CSU, the leading food retailer in Costa Rica and Nicaragua. Paiz-Ahold holds a two-thirds stake in CARHCO and, in consequence, Ahold effectively controls one-third of the joint venture. As a result, and potentially confusing in terms of any rapid inspection of Ahold's figures in Latin America, the sales of the 150 La Fragua stores which had previously been included in Ahold's results for Latin America are 'deconsolidated' from 2002 onwards.[2]

In simple terms, as Figure 2 shows, sales in the region rose from EUR 1.19 billion in 1997 to a peak of EUR 5.08 billion in 2000, representing almost 10% of Ahold's global sales. Operating profits in the region in the same year rose to 9% of Ahold's global total. By the end of 2001, as economic crisis began to take hold in Argentina, sales and profits increases in Latin America began to stall, with the region's contribution to Ahold's global totals falling back to around 7.5% in both cases. During 2002, as economic crisis deepened in Argentina, became more widespread in Latin America, and was accompanied by devaluation of several currencies including the Argentinian Peso and Brazilian Real, that trend accelerated. (Although it is important to note that the 'headline' declines in the region's sales and profits appear, at first sight, greater than they actually are as a result of the deconsolidation of La Fragua following the inauguration of the three-party Central America joint venture.)

Destruction of firm value?

Throughout Ahold's expansion in Latin America during the late 1990s, debate had raged in the financial analysis community about the returns on invested capital Ahold was likely to be able to achieve, and the extent to which investment in those potential 'growth' markets was, in fact, likely to be destructive of firm

Table 1 Ahold's acquisitions and joint ventures in Latin America 1996–2002

Date	Country	Acquisition/joint venture	Description	Cost
Dec. 1996	Brazil	Bompreço	50% voting share (35% total equity) in 3rd largest Brazilian food retailer – market leader in northeast region operating 50 stores	$285 mill.
June 1997	Brazil	SuperMar	Operator of 50 stores in state of Bahia – acquired by Bompreço (50% Ahold). 42 stores retained – renamed Bompreço Bahia	R$65 mill.
Jan. 1998	Argentina, Chile, Peru, Paraguay, Ecuador	Disco, Santa Isabel	Establishment of DAIH, 50% partnership with Velox Retail Holdings. DAIH controlled a 50.4% stake in Disco, largest food retailer in Argentina (110 stores) and a 37% stake in Santa Isabel, 2nd largest food retailer in Chile and Peru with operations in Paraguay and Ecuador (90 stores)	$538 mill.
Feb. 1998	Chile	Santa Isabel	Stake raised to 65%	
Dec. 1998	Argentina	Disco	Stake raised to 90.3%	
May 1999	Argentina	Supamer	71-store chain in province of Cordoba, integrated into Disco	Not disclosed
May 1999	Argentina	Gonzalez	11-store chain in province of San Juan, integrated into Disco	Not disclosed
May 1999	Brazil	Petipreço	6 stores in Bahia, integrated in Bompreço	Not disclosed
Oct. 1999	Argentina	Pinocho	8 stores in city of La Plata, integrated into Disco	Not disclosed
Dec. 1999	Guatemala, El Salvador, Honduras	La Fragua	Establishment of 50/50 partnership Paiz-Ahold which controlled 80% stake in 119-store chain La Fragua (leading food retailer in Guatemala with presence in El Salvador, Honduras)	Not disclosed
Jan. 2000	Argentina	Ekono	Chain of 10 large stores in Buenos Aires, integrated into Disco	EUR 145 mill.

Continued overleaf

Table 1 Continued

Date	Country	Acquisition/joint venture	Description	Cost
July 2000	Brazil	Bompreço	Acquisition of remaining 50% of voting shares and additional 10.9% of non-voting shares	Not disclosed
Jan. 2001	Chile	Agas	14-store chain in Santiago, integrated into Santa Isabel	Not disclosed
July 2001	Brazil	–	5 hypermarkets from Carrefour, integrated into Bompreço	Not disclosed
Oct. 2001	Brazil	Bompreço	Remaining non-voting shares acquired	Not disclosed
Nov. 2001	Costa Rica, Nicaragua, Guatemala, El Salvador, Honduras	CARHCO	Establishment of 3-party joint venture bringing together retail activities of Paiz-Ahold and CSU in Central America (253 stores). CARHCO now holds 80% stake in La Fragua previously held by Paiz-Ahold.	Not disclosed
Dec. 2001	Brazil	G Barbosa	9th ranked Brazilian food retailer operating 32 large stores in states of Sergipe and Bahia. No change in fascia.	Not disclosed
July 2002	Argentina, Chile, Peru, Paraguay	Velox Retail Holdings	Former partner in DAIH defaults on loans. Ahold required to buy out Velox and assume full ownership of DAIH	$452 mill.
Oct. 2002	Chile	Santa Isabel	Acquisition of approximately 27% of shares to raise holding to 97%	$50 mill.

value. Unlike Carrefour's 'first mover' advantages a decade earlier, Ahold faced a position in those markets where competition from new entrants, and emulation of best practices by incumbents (Goldman 2001; Da Rocha and Dib 2002), was driving up the capital intensity of their food retail industries and eroding the competitive advantages and returns of the retail TNCs. It also faced a position where appropriate pricing of assets available for acquisition, in the context of endemic economic and monetary instability, posed extremely difficult problems for market entrants seeking a merger and acquisition expansion route. Merrill Lynch (2003: 3) refers to that as the tendency 'to pay what might be termed "second world" prices for stores/sites that yield "third world" sales/profit'.

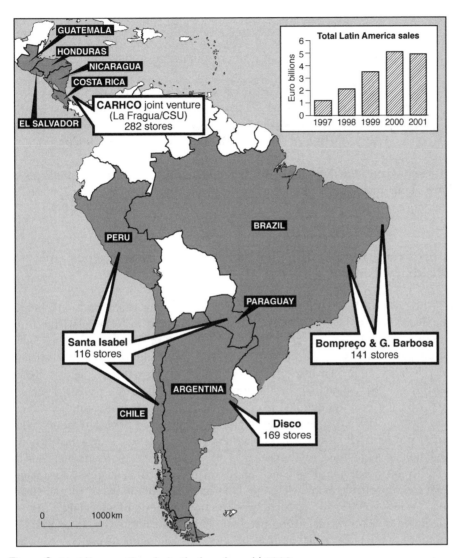

Figure 2 Ahold's operations in Latin America mid 2002

In a report issued in late 1999, Deutsche Bank's well-known food retail analyst, Didier Rabattu, concluded that, despite Ahold's acknowledged financial skills:

> every dollar Ahold has invested in Latin America over the last three years (group equity and assumed debt combined) is now worth less than half its original value.
>
> (Deutsche Bank 1999: 38)

By late 2002, and despite continued acquisition activity by Ahold in the region in the intervening years (Table 1), that 'destruction' of firm value was clearly accelerating. Asked, therefore, in September 2002 during a rather unusual question and answer session for major investors hosted by ABN-AMRO, whether Ahold should have operations in emerging markets, Ahold CEO, Cees van der Hoeven, with recent events in Latin America uppermost in his mind, replied:

> Yes, we think so. But we've learned a lot over the years. We've learned a lot in terms of what formats, what markets, in what part-nerships, and at what risk premium.
>
> (ABN-AMRO, Ahold Q&A Roundtable Transcript 2002b: 35)

Let us now consider these issues in the broader context of the questions posed above about managing and sustaining retail investment in the 'particularistic' economies of Latin America.

Appropriate Partnerships – Risk Management Strategies and Subsidiary Control

In Whitley's (2001: 51) framework, firms from both 'merchant' and 'stakeholder capitalism' oriented economies considering investment in 'particularistic' busi-ness environments are seen as unlikely to be willing to commit 'a large propor-tion of their key resource to countries where uncertainty over property rights and reliability of formal institutions remains high'. However he acknowledges that this may be overridden by the imperatives of 'the large potential market and/or major cost reductions associated with these environments'. In these cases, he sees risk management strategies as being based primarily on exerting market power over local business partners and the state – 'since institutional regulation of economic relationships is weak in these environments, relying primarily on economic dominance and straightforward short-term advantages seems more probable than developing long-term collaborations or formal struc-tures' (Whitley 2001: 53). In turn, he views the high level of uncertainty in such economies as encouraging strong parental control of subsidiaries. In contrast, it is in more predictable 'collaborative' business environments whose co-ordinated social systems make gaining access to the established networks and alliances that dominate those economies difficult, at least initially, that Whitley sees these firms proceeding via the development of alliances and partnerships.

In contrast to Whitley's hypotheses, Ahold's characteristic risk management strategy in the 'particularistic' economies of Latin America (like some of its European peers, specifically Casino, and Promodès prior to its merger with Carrefour) has relied strongly on partnerships and incremental stake raising. However, as Whitley does suggest, in proceeding via this route firms like Ahold are likely, 'to rely on market power to short circuit the process of building alliances as well as on their firm-specific competitive advantages to attract local business partners' (Whitley 2001: 54). In practice, as Table 1 documents, Ahold participated in four joint ventures in Latin America between 1996–2002. Its initial joint venture with Bompreço and its subsequent Paiz-Ahold (La Fragua chain) joint venture in Central America, involved family-controlled, closely-held firms with strong retail operation credentials. In exchange for the capital and retail-systems based competitive advantages which it was able to inject into these firms, Ahold secured the local/national political and business-environment influence offered by the Paes Mendonça and Paiz families. As a result, it was rapidly able to achieve the 'embeddedness' in real-estate and labour markets, supply systems, and local cultures of consumption which retailers such as Wal-Mart seeking organic expansion in markets such as Brazil and Argentina without joint venture partners and with significantly less cultural adaptation were struggling to achieve.

The subsequent development of these partnerships appears to have been largely successful. In the case of Bompreço it followed the classic pattern of an incrementally increasing stake by Ahold and tighter control of the subsidiary, but with continuing inputs in terms of managing the local political/business arena from the original partner. Within four years, the Paes Mendonça family had exited the partnership (with family wealth preservation clearly prominent in that decision to cash in) and Ahold had smoothly transitioned to having total operational/financial control with its own CEO and management team in place without loss of the vital local political influence in northeast Brazil wielded by João Carlos Paes Mendonça.

In contrast, in the case of the DAIH (Disco Ahold International Holdings) joint venture with Velox Retail Holdings (VRH), Ahold partnered with a financial sector organization that, by default, had acquired control of a key retail asset – the leading food retail chain in Argentina. In entering that partnership, Ahold became contingently liable in respect of outstanding indebtedness owed by VRH to certain banks – VRH being part of the wider Velox group, which held interests in various banks in Argentina, Paraguay and Uruguay. In that way, Ahold became exposed, in a classic sense, to the unpredictabilities of partnering, in Whitley's terms, with an 'opportunistic' organization deeply embedded in the (frequently murky) financial-political nexus at the heart of the 'particularistic' business systems of Latin America. During the period of linkage of the Argentinian Peso to the US dollar in the late 1990s and relatively strong economic growth, those contingent liabilities remained only potential. However, as the Argentinian financial crisis began to unfold and spread to other parts of Latin America, accompanied by devaluation of the Peso and Real, the banking system slipped into turmoil. The controlling family of the Velox group came under intense pressure to safeguard their own interests.[3] Despite assurances from VRH that it intended to be a long-term partner in DAIH (reported by Ahold in its December 2001 20-F filing with the US Securities and Exchange Commission), by July 2002 VRH had defaulted on its debts. As a result, under the terms of its joint venture agreement, Ahold became exposed to a 'put' option given to various banks by VRH as collateral for its investment in DAIH. In effect, Ahold could be required by those banks to purchase all of VRH's shares in DAIH at a fixed price which considerably exceeded their current market valuation. VRH's default triggered that option, and Ahold was forced to announce an exceptional charge of EURO 490 million to assume full ownership of DAIH and to cover the 'goodwill impairment' on its Argentinian assets as a result of the devaluation of the Peso.

In that way, what had been viewed by Ahold at the time of its market entry into Argentina as an important risk attenuation mechanism, had been transmuted via the vagaries of the 'particularistic' business environment and the 'opportunistic' nature of its joint venture partner, into a mechanism for compounding that risk. What remained, as Clarke and Rimmer (1997) have argued more generally about the retail internationalization process, was merely the extent of organizational learning within the firm likely from that unanticipated outcome of its investment in the joint venture.

Appropriate Markets, Formats and Risk Premiums – Transferring Organizational Competencies

In Whitley's (2001: 53) framework, investment by firms from both 'merchant' and 'stakeholder capitalism' oriented economies in 'particularistic' business systems is seen as being accompanied by the transfer of firm-specific competitive advantages to those subsidiaries, but a limited likelihood that those subsidiaries will develop distinctive organizational competencies or become highly integrated into local economies. Clearly, however, important elements of these hypotheses are unlikely to hold in the case of the retail TNC. As we have noted above, the retail TNC must of necessity seek to become 'close to market' and must, by default, 'invest in embeddedness'. But it must do that, as Dawson (1994: 267) highlighted in a context in which protection of knowledge is difficult and in which there is extensive copying of ideas – that is to say, with key parts of the competitive advantages which it seeks to transfer to its subsidiaries open to scrutiny and constantly at risk of imitation and appropriation by competitors. In this context, it is useful as Goldman (2001: 223) has suggested to draw a distinction between:

> the *offering* and *know-how* parts of the [retail] format. The first includes the *external* elements (e.g. assortment, shopping-environment, service, location and price) delivering the functional, social, psychological, aesthetic and entertainment benefits attracting customers to stores. The second, the *internal* part, determines a retailer's operational strength and strategic direction. It consists of the *retail technology* dimension containing the systems, methods, procedures and techniques the retail company uses and of the *retail culture*, that includes the repertoire of concepts, norms, rules, practices and experiences.

Due to the inherently open nature of the store and the retail offering, it is the former elements which are particularly at risk of imitation and appropriation by competitors. Consequently, it is the process-based knowledge assets deployed behind the scene in the 'back region' which are of critical significance – the intangible assets of management systems, and know-how in the form of expertise on logistics, supplier negotiations, merchandising, financial management and so on highlighted by Doherty (1999).

Unlike its major retail-TNC rivals (particularly Wal-Mart, Carrefour and Tesco) who were globalizing using a dominantly large hypermarket format, Ahold adopted a model of global retail operation that was multi-format and which stressed local adaptation. The firm-specific competitive advantages which it sought to transfer to its subsidiaries were, in that sense, even more tightly located than its peers in the 'back region' intangible assets of IT systems and best-practice knowledge transfer regarding financial management, logistics, supplier negotiations, private label development, real estate strategy and so on. The question must be, therefore, how successful has that model proved in Latin America, and what did Cees van der Hoeven imply with his statement about Ahold learning from its experiences in Latin America about appropriate formats, markets and risk premiums?

Ahold's back-end integration/front-end adaptation approach to global retail operation has been operationalized in Latin America, as elsewhere, in two ways. First via support teams. These take two forms: those that are drafted in at the time of an acquisition (20 or 30 people strong) to very rapidly transfer best practice from elsewhere in the Ahold group and establish performance targets; and those located in the Latin America Competence Centre in Argentina, whose task (with support from Ahold's head office in the Netherlands) is to sustain and improve performance in the medium term and gradually to assume a region-wide role in co-ordinated purchasing, common IT platforms, private-label development, format differentiation, real estate strategy, and so on. Second, via the operation of Ahold's 'virtual network' launched in 2000. This is a knowledge and benchmarking network which divides the firm's global operations into 14 'knowledge areas' and then subdivides each into specialized networking groups which might be termed, following Kozinets (1999), 'virtual communities' of practice. Within these networking groups, benchmarks can be established, performance measured and monitored, and opportunities for improvement rapidly identified. In that way, local tacit knowledge can be leveraged (Stenmark 2001) and fused with more codified expertise, and fragmented organizational competencies can be integrated.

However, what is clear is that Ahold has learned in Latin America, but also from its operations in Southeast Asia and in parts of Europe, the limits to what can be achieved with this approach to global retail operation. Although Ahold's debt-encumbered position and its sudden inability to raise funding for new acquisitions has, by default, prompted a focus on rationalizing its portfolio, the lessons of Latin America have also been that market position (in the sense of market share/leadership and format mix) is paramount. Ahold had clearly entered markets (notably Chile, Peru and Paraguay) where the scale and store-base (network and format mix) of the operation it had acquired and then attempted to improve, and the nature of its partnerships, were fundamentally flawed in a competitive sense and were unlikely to be other than underperforming. Announcing its change of strategy in mid 2002, Ahold indicated that it would seek to divest such underperforming assets. It came as no surprise then, in February 2003, that Ahold announced it was in talks regarding a possible sale of its Santa Isabel Chilean chain (77 stores) to Chilean retailer Cencosud S.A., whose wholly-owned subsidiary Hipermercados Jumbo operates hypermarkets and DIY stores in Chile and Argentina.

In the context of risk premiums, Ahold had clearly calculated those during its Latin American acquisition phase in accordance with standard financial practice. Moreover, it had actively managed its foreign currency exposure across its global operations using what it refers to as a 'material hedging' technique – whereby it finances its operations in local currency borrowings to the extent possible, or via intercompany loans. However, in Argentina that had not proved possible and Disco was financed substantially with third-party US dollar loans. As a result, devaluation of the Peso in late 2001 substantially increased the costs of Disco's debts and required Ahold to take an exceptional charge of Euro 214 million to earnings and Euro 148 million to shareholders' equity. Moreover, despite the 'Pesofication' decree issued by the Argentinian government in early 2002, which allowed conversion of certain third party US dollar debt into Pesos at a rate of 1 to 1, Ahold still had significant exposed US dollar debt and was forced to take further charges reflecting the devaluation of the Peso in 2002.

Despite the higher 'hurdle rates' which Ahold clearly demanded in terms of returns on invested capital from its Latin American operations, with the benefit of hindsight, the risk premiums which Ahold, in common with many other TNCs, attached to investments in the unpredictable economies of Latin American in the late 1990s proved to be unduly optimistic. The unravelling of the weakly institutionalized business systems of Latin America in the wake of the Argentinian crisis in one sense simply confirms Whitley's (2001: 40) characterization of 'particularistic' economies as comprised of formal institutions 'too weak to provide the basis for predictable outcomes from strategic investment'. However, in the context of the continued attraction of the growth potential of these markets to the retail TNCs, it also highlights the need for more 'robust' investment. That is to say, investment structured financially to be robust to the probability of host-economy financial crisis, bouts of hyper-inflation, etc., and structured operationally to produce sufficient scale and market dominance to provide a sustainable platform for longer-term profitable growth.

Five Lessons for Retail Internationalization Theory

1. Retail internationalization is inevitably accompanied by periods of retrenchment and strategic readjustment

Cases of firms in which retail internationalization has unfolded in the sequential manner once described by Johanson and Vahlne (1977) are extremely rare. Even with the financial resources of the world's largest industrial corporation at its disposal, Wal-Mart's path to internationalization for example, has hardly been smooth, and has involved exit from Indonesia, struggles in China, and the accumulation of considerable start-up losses on Germany (Fernie and Arnold 2002). Achieving 'global reach' by a retail TNC will, in Whatmore and Thornes' (1997: 302) terms, inevitably be a 'laboured, uncertain and, above all, contested process of "acting at a distance" ', and constant strategic renewal is necessary for long-term sustainability. In that context, it is remarkable that studies of the retail internationalization process have taken so long to focus on the stresses internationalization inevitably poses for the firm and the periods of retrenchment and strategic readjustment which accompany those stresses.

Case studies of retrenchment or 'failure' by international retailers are still extremely rare. As Schoenberger (1997) so clearly demonstrates, firms flinch in the face of high sunk costs, and corporate lock-in and the social asset structures of managers can significantly delay essential strategic reconfiguration even though firms realize its need and may even understand the structure of the transformation required. Not surprisingly, firms have a vested interest in 'wip[ing] failed activities from their record books or public memory' (Burt *et al.* 2002: 193).

2. We need a vocabulary to conceptualize and case studies to describe that process

In an interview conducted with Ahold's Director of Investor Relations (Huib Wurfbain) by one of the authors in November 2002, Wurfbain advanced the view that, in terms of the corporate structures of it food retail industries,

> Latin America is ready for a *dealing of cards* in terms of assets . . . there are too many bits and pieces which will need to get together or asset swap.

Given the relatively small size of total retail sales available in some Latin American countries, Wurfbain suggested that an international food retailer needed either a major market share (perhaps 30–40% or so) for success, or else should not be present in those markets. In consequence, he outlined a view of a period of strategic divestment and readjustment in international investment in Latin American retailing in which there was likely to be complex and interlocking dimensions to the possible corporate activity of Ahold and its peers. As Burt *et al.* (2002: 214) have suggested, this 'raises the issue of what is meant by failure in internationalisation . . . there are [likely to be] elements of closure, failure, exit and divestment, as well as complicated activity switching. Our lexicon to describe, understand and conceptualize this is insufficiently developed'.

We agree. To shift from a focus in studies of retail internationalization which for too long has concentrated on the implementation of internationalization to one which concentrates simply on 'deinternationalization', defined as divestment and market exit, lacks sufficient subtlety and misses that 'complicated activity switching'. In this context it is worth nothing that Michael Jensen (1993: 848) once reminded financial economists how:

> even when managers do acknowledge the requirement for exit, it is often difficult for them to accept and initiate the shut down decision. For the managers who must implement those decisions . . . (it) causes personal pain, creates uncertainty and interrupts or side-tracks careers. Rather than confronting this pain, managers generally resist such actions.

As a result, we need, at the very least, to examine divestment and exit in the broadest possible fashion 'based on a view of the firm as an accumulated portfolio of tangible and intangible assets, differentiated in their specificity, maintained and depreciating at varying rates and offering varying options in terms of competitive strategy' (Clark and Wrigley 1997: 345). We also need case studies of the many other features characteristic of periods of retrenchment and strategic reappraisal – asset swapping to produce local dominance (see Wood 2001), selective/strategic divestment, regional operational alliances, transformations of the organizational form and capital structure of subsidiaries, and so on.

3. The dialectic nature of the retail internationalization process must be appreciated – the institutional characteristics of both 'host' and 'home' economies are vital

Our paper has concentrated to a large extent on the challenges Ahold has faced in managing significant investment in the 'particularistic' economies of Latin America. However, those challenges have clearly been compounded by the institutional characteristics of the business systems (in Ahold's case the 'merchant' economy of the USA as much as the more 'stakeholder capitalism' oriented system of the Netherlands) in which the firm is based. Whilst embeddedness in the institutional matrix of economies in which 'financial claims [are] traded on highly liquid capital markets' (Whitley 2001: 42) provided significant competitive advantage to Ahold during its long period of acquisition-driven growth – allowing those acquisitions to be financed by successive equity placements and high levels of debt – a rapid and major shift in financial sentiment in those economies had a fundamental impact upon Ahold's ability to manage its investments. What had once been an important competitive advantage in a rapidly globalizing and consolidating industry – namely Ahold's high tolerance for financial leverage – suddenly became an important competitive disadvantage as it was forced to 'tear up the script' of its previous corporate strategy and adopt a new strategy of organic 'capital-efficient' growth.

We submit that this reciprocal relationship of the institutional matrix of the 'host' and 'home' economies is vital to any understanding of the internationalization of retailing. More generally, we would also argue that the dialectical relationship of:

> the complexity of the embeddedness process in which both the place of origin and the other places in which TNCs operate influence the ways in which such firms behave and how they, in turn, impact upon such places
> (Dicken 2000: 282)

is also vital. This relationship which Schoenberger (1999) once characterized in terms of 'the firm in the region and the region in the firm', is something we have considered in more detail elsewhere (Wrigley and Currah 2003). However, given the stress traditionally laid in the retail internationalization literature on 'the need for the adaptation of management practices and processes in response to the cultural character of the host country' (Dawson 1994: 278) and the need reciprocally to understand the impact on, and potential value of, such adaptation for the firm, it would seem to us to have particular pertinence in the case of the retail TNC. Moreover it would appear to be intimately connected to issues emerging from the reciprocal relationship of the institutional matrix of 'host' and 'home' economies.

4. Retail internationalization is a highly contested process – not only in terms of market competition but also in terms of the relationship between the firm and suppliers of finance

It follows from what has been discussed that the laboured and uncertain process of achieving 'global reach' by a retail TNC is a highly contested one – not only in terms of the competition which must be faced in the markets entered but in addition, and often more decisively, in terms of the struggle between the firm (or more precisely its management) and the suppliers of its finance. Whilst it is important to understand that the increasing capital intensity of the food retail industries of emerging markets, and the emulation of best practices by incumbents, have eroded the 'first mover' returns once enjoyed by the initial entrants to those markets, it is equally vital to understand 'the stresses in the relationship between management and suppliers of finance which can quickly develop if the internationalization process is perceived to threaten the strategic credibility of the firm' (Wrigley 2000a: 914). We submit that these vitally important relationships between firms and the suppliers of finance, often mediated through investment bank monitors (analysts) of financial performance (Sparks 1996; Wrigley *et al.* 2003), are inappropriately under-discussed issues in retail internationalization theory.

5. Retail investment in emerging markets involves development of an industry and shaping of a consumer society – by default it implies long-term, embedded and sustained investment

Finally, it bears repeating that retail investment in emerging markets of the type considered in this paper has, since the mid 1990s, fundamentally shaped both the characteristics of the food retail industries of Latin America, East Asia and Central/Eastern Europe, and the nature of consumer society in those economies. The inflow of investment has had significant impacts on the organizational and logistical structure of the wider distribution sector in those economies. In addition to transforming the corporate landscape of organized retailing and introducing new retail formats, what might broadly be termed 'lean retail' distribution skills have been transferred by the retail TNCs to their subsidiaries. However, even the most centrally-controlled and technology-dependent of those subsidiaries have, by necessity, been obliged to integrate themselves into local economies and consumption practices to ensure competitiveness (Davies 2000;

Da Rocha and Dib 2002). In turn, emulation of the 'back region' practices and retail formats of the TNCs by indigenous players has occurred (Goldman 2000; Lo *et al.* 2001) – although the importance of those indigenous players differs significantly between regions. In this context, as our corporate interviewees in Ahold and the other retail TNCs have frequently suggested to us, the argument about short-term 'destruction of firm value' needs, at the very least, to be set in the context of potential longer-term creation of value, as the growth potential of markets being transformed by that industrial and societal change is captured. Once a retail TNC has made a substantial 'investment in embeddedness' in an emerging market, the time-lag experienced between set-up and generation of significant revenue streams (Dawson 1994: 270) and the 'exit sunk costs' (Clark and Wrigley 1997) involved in withdrawal from embedded networks, by default, implies a vested interest in sustaining that investment.

The critical issue then is what type of investment lends itself best to long-term sustainability. Clearly there is a profound difference between international investment driven largely on the basis of retained earnings without undue recourse to shareholder equity or debt financing (Wal-Mart, Tesco, Carrefour in its pre-Promodès era, etc.) on the one hand, and international investment driven in exactly that manner with the acceptance of high leverage (Ahold, Delhaize, Casino, etc.) on the other – see Hutchinson and Hunter (1995), McCafferty *et al.* (1997) and Wrigley (1999) for discussion of these issues of debt, leverage and financing in the retail firm. Nevertheless the mixture in the case of Ahold of: high levels of firm debt; investment in unpredictable 'particularistic' economies; suppliers of finance who perceive internationalization to be threatening the strategic credibility of the firm and who operate in economic systems in which financial claims are traded on highly liquid capital markets where sentiment has turned negative; together with facets of corporate goverance (from the 'stakeholder capitalism' elements of Ahold's makeup) which to a certain extent encourage less primacy to be assigned to shareholders than in pure Anglo-American 'merchant economy' firms, appears to us to be a potentially explosive one.

Postscript – the Ahold Crisis and Its Latin American Dimensions

On 24 February 2003 Ahold stunned financial markets by disclosing significant accounting irregularities involving a $900 million overstatement of its reported and expected earnings in 2001 and 2002. Although the majority of this over-statement related to its US Foodservice operation, Ahold also announced that it was investigating the legality of certain transactions and their accounting treat-ment at Disco in Argentina. In addition it reported that, as a result of informa-tion not previously available to the company's auditors, it would be restating its historical financial statements so as to proportionally consolidate under Dutch and US accounting rules DAIH (Disco Ahold International Holdings), and also Bompreço and Paiz-Ahold for the periods during which they were 50% owned by the company. The accounting scandal, which the press rapidly christened 'Europe's Enron', resulted in the immediate resignations of Ahold's CEO (Cees van der Hoeven) and CFO (Michael Meurs) and a fall of two-thirds in Ahold's market capitalization to just 10% of the level it had stood at a year before. In the USA the Securities and Exchange Commission launched an investigation into the affair, and with Ahold teetering on the edge of liquidity problems a rescue loan of Euro 3.1 billion from a group of five banks and financial institutions had rapidly to be put into place to stabilize its financial position.

The corporate scandal at Ahold has vitally important implications for the nature of financial regulation and corporate governance – not only in the Netherlands, but also more widely across the 'stakeholder capitalism' economies of continental Europe. We will deal with those issues in detail in subsequent papers. Here it is appropriate to concentrate simply upon what the scandal has revealed about Ahold's management of significant investment in the weakly insti-tutionalized business environments of Latin America, and what the implications are likely to be in terms of its future position in those markets.

In our discussion, above, of Ahold's joint venture with Velox Retail Holdings (VRH) we drew attention to 'the unpredictabilities of partnering with an "oppor-tunistic" organization deeply embedded in the (frequently murky) financial–political nexus at the heart of the particularistic business systems of Latin America', and we showed how Ahold's contingent liability in respect of VRH's indebtedness to certain banks had resulted in it being forced, in July 2002, to take an exceptional charge of $452 million to assume full ownership of DAIH. We also noted how a substantial part of the Ahold's investment in Disco had not been hedged in the company's usual fashion but instead had been financed with third-party US dollar loans. As a result, we showed how devaluation of the Peso had substantially increased the costs of Disco's debts and required Ahold to take significant exceptional changes to earnings and shareholders' equity.

What the Ahold corporate scandal has so far revealed is something of the extent of the murkiness of the waters into which Ahold was actually drawn in its dealings with its DAIH partner, and the 'opportunistic' nature of that partner. VRH, as we noted above, was a subsidiary of Velox Group which owned (or had controlling stakes) in banks in Paraguay, Argentina and Uruguay. In turn Velox Group was controlled by the Peirano family. What is now clear (*Financial Times*, 27 February 2003: 26) is that, following the turmoil in the banking system which accompanied the financial crisis as it spread outwards from Argentina, and which led to the Velox owned banks being placed under central bank control, three members of the Peirano family were arrested on fraud charges relating to attempts to transfer funds out of South America to a Velox affiliate bank regis-tered in the Cayman Islands. Most significantly, it also appears that a fourth member of the family, who at that time was Chairman of DAIH, was also served with an arrest warrant in June 2002, some weeks before standing down in July 2002 from the management board of Disco-Ahold and the supervisory board of Ahold (*Financial Times*, 28 February 2003: 26). Although it is as yet 'unclear whether the transactions [at Disco] being probed by the forensic accountants are in any way related to the wider issues of alleged fraud perpetrated by members of the Peirano family' (*Financial Times*, 27 February 2003: 26), the independent Dutch corporate watchdog, Sobi, has suggested that they may be and has accused the former Ahold CEO of, at the very least, mismanagement in relation to the

DAIH joint venture. One immediate result of the initial investigation of transactions irregularities at Disco, however, has been the resignation of Disco's CEO, CFO and two other directors, and the installation into Disco of an Ahold team from the Netherlands 'to offer active support for the company, enforce controls, and ensure compliance with Ahold's business principles' (Ahold press release 27 February 2003). In addition, a further investigation into Disco's books and records has now been announced (26 March 2003) by Ahold.

Coming on top of the fundamental shift in corporate strategy which had already been forced on Ahold during 2002 as it had gradually lost the confidence of, and access to, capital markets, the accounting irregularities announced in February 2003 looked certain to see the demise of Ahold as a proto-global retail corporation. The aggressive growth strategy and high tolerance for financial leverage which had served the company so well in the context of the rapidly consolidating and globalizing industry of the late 1990s had, in radically changed financial markets, became a liability. Moreover, the strengths of the Ahold 'intelligently federal' model of global retail operation with its focus on local partnerships, format adaptation, best practice knowledge transfer, and back-end systems integration was seen to be undermined by poor judgement and insufficient managerial control of joint venture partners. Not only were capital markets 'reliving the spectacle of a highly acquisitive company playing fast and loose with its accounts' (*Financial Times*, 3 March 2003) but also Ahold's reputation for managerial skill in identifying high quality acquisitions and integrating those acquisitions smoothly and effectively into on evolving model of global retail operation had been exposed as a myth.

Within the evolving Ahold crisis, although the focus will inevitably be on the huge overstatement of earnings in its US foodservice business and on the widening investigations of US federal regulators into the role of suppliers such as ConAgra and Sara Lee, it is the Latin American irregularities which are arguably particularly damaging to Ahold's future as an international retailer and to its former CEO. Viewed in Whitley's terms, those Latin American irregularities concern an essentially merchant economy firm – albeit one whose 'stakeholder capitalism' characteristics allowed 'no proper checks on [its] powers to print new equity' (*Sunday Times* 2 March 2003) – which, at the very least, had been sucked into and lost control of a joint venture in an unpredictable, weakly institutionalized business environment. In retrospect, it can be seen to have partnered with a classic example of Whitley's 'opportunistic' organization whose control was direct and personal by owners with a dominant objective of family wealth preservation. In the process, and more generally in Latin America, Ahold had clearly struggled to appropriately price the assets available to it for acquisition and had arguably over-capitalized its international operations in the region. Indeed the announcement by Ahold on 3 April 2003 that it was intending to divest its entire operations in South America was accompanied by speculation by financial analysts that, so devalued were those assets, that perhaps only Euro 600 million might be raised from the sale of over 500 stores generating approximately Euro 3 billion per annum in sales.

Ahold's decision to sell off its South American operations has been rationalized in terms of its need to concentrate on its more mature and stable markets and to generate funds to pay down its debt. For those reasons, the South American withdrawal is likely to be accompanied by divestment of its operations in Southeast Asia, Spain and Central Europe. Clearly the 'fire sale' nature of the divestments will ensure that maximizing the value received for these assets is likely to prove extremely difficult. Moreover, there is no certainty that these divestments will stave off the need to relinquish control of some of Ahold's 'crown jewels' – notable its market leading Northeast US chains (particularly Stop & Shop) and its domestic market core business (Albert Heijn). The lessons of the collapse of Ahold's international ambitions, and the model of global retail operation which it promoted so fervently during the late 1990s, will clearly be learned by the remaining retail TNCs even as they mobilize to absorb the most strategically valuable of Ahold's assets. And within that emerging story, we submit that the lessons which can be drawn from Ahold's experience in attempting to manage significant investment in the volatile, weakly institutionalized 'particularistic' business environments of Latin America are likely to prove particularly germane.

Notes

1   Note, however, that commentators have increasingly argued that whilst there may at one point have been a distinctive 'German model' of corporate governance and financial structure of the type outlined by Dore (2000) and O'Sullivan (2000), enormous pressures were brought to bear on that model in the late 1990s by global economic forces. In particular, there was a rapid adoption of international accounting rules and firms were increasingly obliged to adopt corporate governance practices consistent with their listing on Anglo-American securities markets. As a result, Clark and Wojcik (2003a; 2003b) argue that there are now a number of German models each more or less tuned to global financial imperatives, and that the so-called 'German model' is best understood as a rhetorical device rather than a persistent set of institutions.

2   From January 2002 earnings from La Fragua are reported by Ahold in its quarterly and annual reports under the 'income from unconsolidated subsidiaries' heading – specifically that deriving from the CARCHO joint venture.

3   See 'Postscript' for further details of what this 'safeguarding of their own interests' meant in practice.

References

ABN-AMRO (2002a) *Ahold. A-holding on to BBB+?* ABN-AMRO Bank NV, London, 24 October.

ABN-AMRO (2002b) 'Ahold Q&A Roundtable Transcript', ABN-AMRO Equities (UK) Ltd, London, 2 September.

Alexander, N. and Myers, H. (2000) 'The retail internationalization process', *International Marketing Review*, 17: 334–53.

Alexander, N. and Quinn, B. (2002) 'International retail divestment', *International Journal of Retail and Distribution Management*, 30: 112–25.

Berger, S. and Dore, R. (eds) (1996) *National Diversity and Global Capitalism*, Ithaca: Cornell University Press.

Boyer, R. and Hollingsworth, J.R. (1999) *Contemporary Capitalism: The Embeddedness of Institutions*, Cambridge: Cambridge University Press.

Burt, S.L., Mellahi, K., Jackson, T.P. and Sparks, L. (2002) 'Retail internationalization and retail failure: issues from the case of Marks and Spencer', *International Review of Retail, Distribution and Consumer Research*, 12: 191–219.

Christopherson, S. (1993) 'Market rules and territorial outcomes: the case of the United States', *International Journal of Urban and Regional Research*, 17: 274–88.

Christopherson, S. (1999) 'Rules as resources: how market governance regimes influence firm networks'. In Barnes, T.J. and Gertler, M.S. (eds) *The New Industrial Geography: Regions, Regulation and Institutions*, London: Routledge, pp. 155–75.

Christopherson, S. (2002) 'Why do national labour market practices continue to diverge in the global economy? The 'missing link' of investment rules', *Economic Geography*, 78: 1–21.

Clark, G.L. and Wrigley, N. (1997) 'Exit, the firm and sunk costs: reconceptualizing the corporate geography of divestment and plant closure', *Progress in Human Geography*, 21: 338–58.

Clark, G.L. and Wojcik, D. (2003a) 'An economic geography of global finance: ownership concentration and stock price volatility in German firms and regions', *Annals of the Association of American Geographers* (forthcoming).

Clark, G.L. and Wojcik, D. (2003b) 'Financial valuation of the German (regional) model'. Paper presented at Association of American Geographers Annual Conference, New Orleans, March.

Clarke, I. and Rimmer, P. (1997) 'The anatomy of retail internationalization: Daimaru's decision to invest in Melbourne, Australia', *Service Industries Journal*, 17: 361–82.

Da Rocha, A. and Dib, L.A. (2002) 'The entry of Wal-Mart in Brazil and the competitive responses of multinational and domestic firms', *International Journal of Retail and Distribution Management*, 30: 61–73.

Davies, K. (2000) 'The Asian economic recession and retail change: the implications for retailer strategies in Asia', *International Review of Retail, Distribution and Consumer Research*, 10: 335–53.

Dawson, J.A. (1994) 'Internationalization of retailing operations', *Journal of Marketing Management*, 10: 267–82.

Deutsche Bank (1999) *Global Food Retailing: Part 2*, Deutsche Bank AG, London, 29 October.

Dicken, P. (2000) 'Places and flows: situating international investment'. In Clark, G.L., Feldman, M. and Gertler, M.S. (eds) *The Oxford Handbook of Economic Geography*, Oxford: Oxford University Press, pp. 275–91.

Doherty, A.M. (1999) 'Explaining international retailers' market entry mode strategy: internalisation theory, agency theory and the importance of information asymmetry', *International Review of Retail, Distribution and Consumer Research*, 9: 379–402.

Dore, R. (2000) *Stock Market Capitalism: Welfare Capitalism – Japan and Germany Versus the Anglo-Saxons*, Oxford: Oxford University Press.

Fernie, J. and Arnold, S.J. (2002) 'Wal-Mart in Europe: prospects for Germany, the UK and France', *International Journal of Retail and Distribution Management*, 30: 92–102.

Gertler, M.S. (1997) 'The invention of regional culture'. In Lee, R. and Wills, J. (eds) *Geographies of Economies*, London: Arnold, pp. 47–58.

Gertler, M.S. (1999) 'The production of industrial processes'. In Barnes, T.J. and

Gertler, M.S. (eds) *The New Industrial Geography: Regions, Regulation and Institutions*, London: Routledge, pp. 225–37.

Gertler, M.S. (2001) 'Best practice? Geography, learning and the institutional limits to strong convergence', *Journal of Economic Geography*, 1: 5–26.

Goldman, A. (2000) 'Supermarkets in China: the case of Shanghai', *International Review of Retail, Distribution and Consumer Research*, 10: 1–21.

Goldman, A. (2001) 'The transfer of retail formats into developing economies: the example of China', *Journal of Retailing*, 77: 221–42.

Hutchinson, R.W. and Hunter, R.L. (1995) 'Determinants of capital structure in the retailing sector in the UK', *International Review of Retail, Distribution and Consumer Research*, 5: 63–78.

Jensen, M.C. (1993) 'The modern industrial revolution, exit and the failure of internal control systems', *Journal of Finance*, 48: 831–80.

Johanson, J. and Vahlne, J.E. (1977) 'The internationalization of the firm – a model of knowledge development and increasing foreign market commitments', *Journal of International Business Studies*, 8: 23–32.

Kozinets, R.V. (1999) 'E-tribalised marketing? The strategic implications of virtual communities of consumption', *European Management Journal*, 17: 252–64.

Lo, T.W.C., Lau, H.F. and Lin, G.S. (2001) 'Problems and prospects of supermarket development in China', *International Journal of Retail and Distribution Management*, 29: 66–76.

Merrill Lynch (2003) *Carrefour: The Harsh Reality of Returns*, Merrill Lynch & Co., London, 7 February.

Meyer-Ohle, H. (2002) 'The crisis of Japanese retailing at the turn of the millennium', *International Review of Retail, Distribution and Consumer Research*, 12: 13–28.

McCafferty, K., Huchinson, R.W. and Jackson, R. (1997) 'Aspects of the finance function: a review and survey of the UK retailing sector', *International Review of Retail, Distribution and Consumer Research*, 7: 125–44.

O'Sullivan, M. (2000) *Contests for Corporate Control: Corporate Governance in the United States and Germany*, Oxford: Oxford University Press.

Schoenberger, E. (1997) *The Cultural Crisis of the Firm*, Oxford: Blackwell.

Schoenberger, E. (1999) 'The firm in the region and the region in the firm'. In Barnes, T.J. and Gertler, M.S. (eds) *The New Industrial Geography: Regions, Regulation and Institutions*, London: Routledge, pp. 205–24.

Shleifer, A. and Vishny, R.W. (1997) 'A survey of corporate governance', *Journal of Finance*, 52: 737–83.

Sparks, L. (1996) 'Investment recommendations and commercial reality in Scottish grocery retailing', *Service Industries Journal*, 16: 165–90.

Stenmark, D. (2001) 'Leveraging tacit organizational knowledge', *Journal of Management Information Systems*, 17: 9–24.

Whatmore, S. and Thorne, L. (1997) 'Nourishing networks: alternative geographies of food'. In Goodman, D.J. and Watts, M.J. (eds), *Globalizing Food: Agrarian Questions and Global Restructuring*, London: Routledge, pp. 287–304.

Whitley, R. (1999) *Divergent Capitalisms: The Social Structuring and Change of Business Systems*, Oxford: Oxford University Press.

Whitley, R. (2001) 'How and why are international firms different? The consequences of cross-border managerial coordination for firm characteristics and behaviour'. In Morgan, G., Kristensen, P.H. and Whitley, R. (eds) *The Multinational Firm:*

Organizing Across Institutional and National Divides, Oxford: Oxford University Press, pp. 27–68.

Whitley, R. (ed.) (2002) *Competing Capitalisms: Institutions and Economies*, Cheltenham: Edward Elgar.

Williams, D. (1992) 'Motives for retailer internationalization: their impact, structure and implications', *Journal of Marketing Management*, 8: 269–85.

Wood, S. (2001) 'Regulatory constrained portfolio restructuring: the US department store industry in the 1990s', *Environment and Planning A*, 33: 1279–304.

Wrigley, N. (1999) 'Corporate finance, leveraged restructuring and the economic landscape: the LBO wave in US food retailing'. In Martin, R.L. (ed.) *Money and the Space Economy*, Chichester: Wiley, pp. 185–205.

Wrigley, N. (2002a) 'Strategic market behaviour in the internationalization of food retailing: interpreting the third wave of Sainsbury's US diversification', *European Journal of Marketing*, 891–918.

Wrigley, N. (2002b) 'The globalization of retail capital: themes for economic geography'. In Clark, G.L., Feldman, M. and Gertler, M.S. (eds), *The Oxford Handbook of Economic Geography*, Oxford: Oxford University Press, pp. 292–313.

Wrigley, N. (2002) 'Transforming the corporate landscape of US food retailing: market power, financial re-engineering and regulation', *Tijdschrift voor Economische en Sociale Geografie*, 93: 62–82.

Wrigley, N. and Currah, A. (2003) 'Globalizing retail: scoping the distribution-based TNC', *Progress in Human Geography*. (forthcoming).

Wrigley, N., Currah, A.D. and Wood, S.M. (2003) 'Investment bank analysts and knowledge in economic geography', *Environment and Planning A*, 35: 381–7.

Conclusion

IN THE TWENTY YEARS to 2006, Wal-Mart increased its annual sales from $12 billion to $367 billion; Carrefour moved from opening five hypermarkets per year to opening two per week; Polish retailing changed from state control to all but one of the 10 largest firms being foreign owned; and retail floor space in Great Britain increased by 33 per cent. With these sorts of changes over the last two decades, what might we expect over the next twenty years? Can we even contemplate the type of changes that may take place? Certainly, simple extrapolation will not help very much. What is evident from the last twenty years is that the processes of retailing themselves have changed, rather than simply operating at a faster pace. In this concluding chapter, we suggest a few of the issues that will challenge retail management and retail research over the next twenty years. In doing so we pose some questions that we believe are important for debates on the future of retailing and its academic study.

The Growth of Large Retailers

It is evident that the role of retailing within economic systems has changed and is likely to continue to change. The power of retailers to generate change in national economies will increase even above present levels – if left unchecked. Public policy at national levels, as a generality, has been benign in the past. Attempts to intervene in any fundamental way have rarely been evident. Policy makers have been slow to understand the nature of the changes in retailing that have been taking place. It seems likely that this will not continue, as consumer spending as a proportion of GDP increases and alongside this there is a steady increase in market concentration. Policy concerns, however, are likely to move rapidly from a national level to become multinational issues as retailers source products and operate stores globally. Attempts, during 2007, by the military government in Thailand, state governments in India, and various policy agencies in Poland to limit foreign retail investment, together with competition agency activity in respect of large food retailers in the UK and large retailers in China, are all symptomatic of an increasing realization by governments of the substantive changes taking place in retailing and the power of retailing to generate widespread economic change. We believe that such interventions at a national level are likely to become more frequent and that coordinated inter-national interventions will start to be attempted. The retailers' responses are likely to be ones of seeking to engage in and contribute to wider social and economic issues by emphasizing their potential to act in quasi-governmental ways by delivering local social and economic change, for example in health, education and catalysing efficien-cies in small firms, and by active involvement in broader campaigns, for example poverty alleviation, environmental protection and sustainability, and improved work-ing conditions for workers in production sectors. As a consequence, retailer strategies will change in fundamental ways as the balance of power amongst the various stake-holders shifts.

One possible consequence of this type of change may be that *retailer*, as a term to describe a type of firm, may become increasingly obsolete. Firms, or at least large firms, are taking on a much broader remit of customer interaction and service provi-sion than has been the case for retail firms in the past. At the same time firms not formerly involved in selling directly to final consumers are likely to attempt to move into the retail market. Whilst the strength of the retailer's brand may be extended into a variety of other activities, such as housing provision, education and health care, at the same time non-retailer brands may become the basis of new retail operations by these brand owners.

In considering the management of these very large firms in retailing, strategic challenges increase as the firms grow in size. For the large multinational retailer it is increasingly necessary to have, in effect, multiple strategies related to global regions or to format networks. Already for example, we see within Carrefour that Carrefour hypermarkets and Dia discount supermarkets are in several ways different organiza-tions with different strategies within the overall Carrefour firm. This divisionalization of large firms may become more widespread with autonomous divisions responsible for a global region, a format and even a function, for example with property being moved into a separate division from retail operations. Such changes in organizational structures are also likely to be necessary as the large retailers achieve sizes that introduce diseconomies of scale in operational information and communication costs but still seek to retain the strategic flexibility to introduce new formats and to learn from strategically relevant knowledge gained across the whole firm.

The strategic use of inter-firm alliances is also likely to change as firms get larger. This will pose a new set of issues for competition agencies and for the stra-tegic management of retail firms. The extent of cross-shareholding in the retail sector is only one example of the more complex pattern of alliance-type relationships. The portfolio of investments by Iceland-based Bauger is an example of what may become more widespread. Alliances and cooperations in buying are also likely to increase, in part as a response to concerns about 'food miles' and the extension of such concepts to other products. The calculation of the carbon footprint of products, albeit fraught with considerable difficulties and grounds for widespread disagreement over methods of calculation, may well encourage inter-firm alliances and cooperation in supply-chain activities. A further area where alliances may develop more strongly is in inter-firm trading of retail brand items. As retailer brands increase in strength so they become tradeable assets similar to the brands of manufacturers. There is already some trade in retail brand items; for example Waitrose food brands are available in 23 countries although they only have stores in the UK. Such brand alliances, and ones that use the overall brand strength of the retailer, may become a more common way for large retailers to enter markets, such as India, from which they are excluded by public policy activity.

Some examples of the type of question really being posed by the discussion in the last few paragraphs are as follows.

- Are there limits to growth for the retailer?
- What mechanisms, if any, will curtail the continued expansion of large retailers?
- Will consumer activism and/or government regulation halt, or even reverse, the growth of larger firms in retailing?
- What type of organizational structure will emerge for the multinational, multi-format, multi-sector firm in retailing?
- What are the social consequences of retail gigantism?

Theory in Retail Research

Whilst there are likely to be developments in the strategies of retailers over the next twenty years, we also expect there to be developments in the ways that retail research is undertaken and in the theorization of the dynamics of the sector. The various chapters of this reader show the large amount of research on retailing, but theoretical contributions are relatively small in number compared to empirically based studies. There is now a substantial body of empirical knowledge, from an academic perspective, and opportunities exist for theory development.

There are many potential areas where theory would help the academic understanding of retailing. What has become clear from the empirical work is that positivistic philosophies are unlikely to generate meaningful theoretical developments in retailing. Cause-and-effect processes in retailing are not positivistic with the same result occurring from the same set of causes on each occasion. Many of the processes that are subject to theorization are fuzzy by nature. Situational factors are particularly important as it becomes even more apparent that retailing is a response to cultural phenomena. Research philosophies of critical realism appear more relevant to understanding retailing.

Within such a philosophical base there are several likely areas for development in the coming decades. For example, theories of interaction within the sector that encompass competitive and non-competitive relationships are important. Specifically, for example, there is a need for a clearer theoretical understanding of events consequent on the entry of a new large store or a new firm into an existing market. The theorization and modelling of the competitive impact of new investment would give us a greater understanding of a variety of events that, in effect, are generic aspects of network dynamics. The conceptualization is in reality the same if the new store is a Wal-Mart superstore entering a town in the USA, a Tesco superstore in a town in the UK, an IKEA store entering a city in Japan, or a Zara store entering a high street in the Netherlands. The concept of the impact of investment in a new or remodelled store, or a new firm entering into an existing competitive system is a generic topic. Theorization of what is happening in such situations would help us understand much better the dynamic nature of retail systems.

A second example of an area that would benefit from advances in theory is in customer interactions with merchandising in-store. Chapter 1 of this reader has illustrated the research on consumer behaviour and has indicated the presence of some key models. There has been extensive work on modelling store choice. The models in effect are complex descriptions of the processes involved. These models are essentially inductive models that move from description to attempted explanation but do not move into theory. In terms of the in-store behaviour of the retailer and the consumer/customer, there are fewer inductive models and theory is notable by its absence. Again, there are generic topics involved considering the way that behaviour is modified by managerial activity and vice versa within a designed environment. And, again, we are in areas where positivistic and linear models are of limited value. Consumer behaviour is not a set of automatic responses to stimuli designed by managers. To develop theory we will need to explore relativist and constructionist philosophies to underpin the theory.

A third example of the many areas where advances in theory are needed is the nature of knowledge flows within the networked management structures that are evident in retailers. An approach through structuration theory could be one way of exploring a framework that would allow empirical studies of knowledge flows in retailers to have a firmer theoretical base. By considering practices within the knowledge flows, it could be possible to consider not only the individuals, and their roles as broker, generator and so on, but also the nature of the firm itself, in terms of networked organization, culture and so forth.

These three examples illustrate the areas where theory development could take place. They are only illustrations and there are many other possible areas for theorization. Development of theory is neither easy nor quick. The ethos of retailing is to get quick results. Increasingly the pressure on academic research is also for quick results. Theorization is seldom quick; nonetheless it is a fundamental aspect of the advancement of knowledge, in this case about retailing. The questions for the future that are posed by considerations of the need for more theory are as follows.

- What philosophical approach(es) should be used to explore theory in retailing?
- What are the generic processes in retailing that might be susceptible to theorization?

●   Given the universality of retailing across space, are a-cultural, theoretical concepts realistic?

The Nature of Managerial Aspects of Retail Change

Although in an academic context theory is important, from a managerial context in retailing the activities and processes are of more practical concern. Over the next two decades, through the ways that retailing is developing as shown in this reader, major challenges will emerge for the practice of retailing. It would be possible to identify many aspects of management that are likely to change throughout the retail firm. In the space available here, it is possible to pick only a few that we believe will be important in the coming years.

Retailers compete most effectively by being different. To compete in this way retail management has to innovate consistently with new ways of communicating with consumers, of creating new store formulae, of developing new relationships with suppliers and, in general, generating new ways to improve the productivity of all the assets and resources of the retailer. For large retailers, an aspect of their competitive advantage will be that the innovation comes from within the firm and is, in effect, proprietary to the firm. The innovation sources may involve consumers, suppliers, their own managers and other sources, but by internalizing, the innovation processes the resulting benefits will become competitively advantageous. Competition therefore is likely to be defined in new ways, not simply in terms of the more traditional marketing mix, although remaining competitive in these respects will be essential and a 'non-failure' factor.

The nature of retailing requires the application of various technologies in order to make the retail processes operate efficiently. Retailers therefore are substantial users of technology that they draw from many different sources. For retail operations management, the concept of technology is broadly drawn. Technology is applied across a range of activities – material handling technologies, building and construction technologies, food, textile, and other materials technologies, in addition to the information and communication technologies. The nature of technological change will mean that, in retailing, all these technologies will generate new applications in the next few years. What these applications will facilitate will depend on the missions and cultures of particular firms. For some firms that wish to pursue environmental sustainability as a major objective the applications will be towards this end. For other firms that wish to pursue global expansion as a major objective, then some other applications may be more relevant. Whatever the objective, however, we believe that the management of technology, and its risks, will make retail operations for consumers and retailers alike very different in the future.

In contrast to the developments in technological applications, with their inevitable base in 'engineering' of some form, there will be major developments in the next decade or more, in branding by retailers. One of the factors behind the success of many retailers in recent years has been their decision to take control of branding away from manufacturers and to control brands as a retailer activity. This has enabled retailers to invest in their brands, to build brand loyalty and to undertake brand extension. Undoubtedly, this will continue. Brands will increase in importance, both strategically and operationally, within the overall management of the retail firm. Over the next decade, we believe that new ways to manage the retail brands will emerge – corporate brands, sales formula brands, and item brands. Some firms will seek to integrate brand values across the whole firm; others will seek to operate a portfolio of brands. In Chapter 2 of this reader, we asked, but did not answer, what the next generation, the fifth generation, of retail brand items might look like. In a similar vein, we can ask how branding of sales formulae will develop. Brand concepts will not stagnate, but will certainly evolve in the next decade. The retail operations and management issues around branding are considerable, as firms become more international in sourcing and operations. We believe that branding and brand management will become the major differentiating factors amongst competing retailers.

Attempting to look at the future of retail operations and their management poses a wealth of questions suitable for debate. We have raised only three topics here. There are many more. Possible questions are as follows

- How extendable into other sectors and transferable to other markets is retailer branding?
- How will operational cost structures in the sector change if society demands more environmental sustainability from the retail sector?
- As retail operations use technologies to seek to personalize retailer–consumer relationships, do issues of personal privacy protection make the exercise counterproductive?
- To what extent can technologies be integrated to optimize, on a continuing basis, the total operation of a store – can the store be modelled in its totality?

Techniques of Retail Research

Finally, given that academic research in retailing is increasing in many countries, it is useful to consider how the undertaking of this research might change over the next twenty years. It is only a little over twenty years ago that the first Chair in the area in the UK was established at Stirling University. Now there are fortunately many more. In the future we hope for even more. Retail research is somewhat eclectic. Nonetheless, a body of knowledge has developed about the ways that retailers operate and the implications of their activity for a wider society. The papers reviewed in the chapters of this book show the diversity of research that has been undertaken. Into the future, the scope of topics in retail research is likely to be even more diverse.

In developing the body of knowledge, it can be argued that after the basic studies of recent decades, we should now be attempting to address more directly actual situations in retailing. This case is particularly strong in respect of studies of consumer–retailer interactions, where research in the past has often drawn on rather contrived student samples in order to test hypotheses. Having tested the hypotheses in this way, they are seldom taken into the real world to be tested with real consumers in real shopping situations. There is a dearth of sound replicative studies. Over the next twenty years we would expect that empirical research increasingly will be designed in ways that take account of actual situations in retail activity. There is, after all, not only a plethora of real shoppers to sample but also a considerable number of retail environments into which studies can be framed.

Research increasingly is a group effort. The lone researcher studying their own particular problem is less and less the model for academic research. In the physical sciences, teams of several hundred work on projects scheduled over decades. Retail research has certainly not reached this level but it seems likely that in the future the case will become stronger for significant groups of researchers, each focusing on a particular issue in an integrated, but maybe spatially dispersed, team.

Retail research has used a variety of techniques both quantitative and qualitative in order to gain understanding of the processes at work. From much of the quantitative work what is increasingly apparent is that processes are non-linear in nature and interactions amongst variables, including feedback effects, are significant. Many of the techniques used in analysis are not fully suited to this non-linearity. This issue, coupled with statistical techniques that expect normal distributions to the variables being analysed, causes difficulties in assessing the significance of results from analyses. Maybe the time has come for a rigorous consideration of the techniques of analysis being used and the development or application of new techniques more suited to modelling non-linear processes and to non-normal distributions. Simple distributional transformations that, in effect, allow a firm the size of Wal-Mart to be considered in the same distribution as an independent single-shop convenience store firm is not an answer to the non-normality of the distribution of firm size.

Any serious area of academic study considers both the history of its subject matter and the history of the study of its subject matter. With some notable exceptions, the history of retailing and of the study of retailing has been poorly served in the past. This is a surprising omission given the remarkable transformation of retailing whether over the last 200 years in China, over the last fifty years in UK, or over the last twenty years in Thailand. It is hoped that over the next two decades there will be more research activity looking at how retail processes operated before the recent transformational period, and also research on how retailing has been researched over the past 200 or more years.

The types of question that are raised when we begin to consider how the study of retailing may change into the future are as follows.

- How can we generate research teams that focus on key research issues?
- Is there a research requirement for shared creation and availability of substantive databases on specific topics?
- Is there a case for more replication of projects in a search for generality?
- Is there a way that academic research and commercial research on retailing can find common ground?
- How can we ensure that historical research has accurate sources available to it?

Endnote

In this conclusion we have raised a few of the many issues for debate that could frame discussions on the future directions of the study of retailing. We hope that within this reader we have indicated the scope of retailing as an area of study and have raised questions in the minds of readers. That we are all involved directly in retailing, on a frequent basis, means that we often have strong views of what firms in retailing do – and do not do. From the studies reproduced here and the references to published material we hope we have given a lie to the view that retailing is only a passive agent that responds to consumers and to suppliers. We view retailing as a very active force that is both shaping consumer society and directing suppliers. And, we believe it is a force that is increasing both in its directive strength and the subtlety of its response.

Index

Note: *italic* page numbers denote references to Figures/Tables.